Terrorism, Intelligence and Homeland Security

To the one person in this world that greets me every morning with a smile, is my constant and steady companion during the day, and keeps me warm at night ... my wife, Mary. With love and affection always.

Bob

In a sentence, this book is for my family. More specifically it's for my patient, wise, and beloved wife, Paige, who I admire for many reasons, including her passion for leading a free medical clinic for indigent and low-income individuals and families. Also it's for our much-loved children, Traci, husband Brian, and Olivia, Kellie, husband Steve, and Keira, Colin, and sweet Maggie who left us too early, Randy, the best brother anyone could have and his wife, Debbie, a devoted nurse, their children, John Matthew and Erin, my sister Pat and her Michael and Annie, my devout sister Chris, and my brother-in-law, another Steve. Finally, I am grateful to our parents, all of whom have gone ahead, Dr. Joseph and Kathryn Mercer and Lt. Colonel Rudolph and Julia Swanson.

Mike

Terrorism, Intelligence and Homeland Security

Robert W. Taylor
The University of Texas at Dallas

Charles R. Swanson
The University of Georgia

PEARSON

Boston   Columbus   Indianapolis   New York   San Francisco   Hoboken
Amsterdam   Cape Town   Dubai   London   Madrid   Milan   Munich   Paris   Montréal   Toronto
Delhi   Mexico City   São Paulo   Sydney   Hong Kong   Seoul   Singapore   Taipei   Tokyo

Editorial Director: Andrew Gilfillan
Senior Acquisitions Editor: Gary Bauer
Editorial Assistant: Lynda Cramer
Director of Marketing: Dave Gesell
Marketing Manager: Thomas Hayward
Marketing Assistant: Les Roberts
Senior Managing Editor: JoEllen Gohr
Program Manager: Tara Horton
Project Manager: Susan Hannahs
Senior Operations Supervisor: Vince Scelta

Operations Specialist: Deidra Skahill
Senior Art Director: Diane Ernsberger
Cover Designer: Carie Keller, Cenveo
Cover Art: Stocktrek Images/Getty Images
Full-Service Project Management: George Jacob,
    Integra Software Services, Inc.
Composition: Integra Software Services, Inc.
Printer/Binder: Courier/Kendallville
Cover Printer: Courier/Kendallville
Text Font: ITC Century Std, 9.5/12

Acknowledgements of third party content appear on page with the text, which constitutes an extension of this copyright page.

Many of the designations by manufacturers and sellers to distinguish their products are claimed as trademarks. Where those designations appear in this book, and the publisher was aware of a trademark claim, the designations have been printed in initial caps or all caps.

Library of Congress Cataloging-in-Publication Data

Taylor, Robert W.
    Terrorism, intelligence, and homeland security/Robert W. Taylor, Charles R. Swanson.—First Edition.
        pages cm
    ISBN 978-0-13-351712-5—ISBN 0-13-351712-8
    1. United States. Department of Homeland Security.   2. Terrorism—United States—Prevention.
3. National security—United States.   4. Intelligence service—United States.   I. Swanson, Charles R., 1942-   II. Title.
    HV6432.4.T39 2016
    363.325'1630973—dc23

                                                                                2014038789

10 9 8 7 6 5 4 3 2 1
V011

                                                                Paper Bound:
                                                                ISBN 10:   0-13-351712-8
                                                                ISBN 13: 978-0-13-351712-5

                                                                Loose Leaf:
                                                                ISBN 10:   0-13-410541-9
                                                                ISBN 13: 978-0-13-410541-3

Brief Contents

Contents

PART II   *Typologies, Organizational Structures, Tactics and Critical Processes of Terrorism*

PART III *Responding to the Challenges of Terrorism*

PART IV *Combatting Terrorism and The Future*

CHAPTER 14 **Combatting Terrorism** 334

Preface

Terrorism – Intelligence – Homeland Security are three subjects that often dominate today's news events. No other issues are so prominent, so compelling, or so critically important to our communities and our nation than these three separate but interconnected topics. Nothing is more contemporary!

Some argue that as a nation, we are still suffering from the lingering effects of the attacks on September 11, 2001, an event that clearly changed our world forever. On that day, our security weaknesses were exploited, our vulnerability was exposed, and our fear became real. For the last decade and half we have struggled to dramatically improve the security of our homeland from attack, whether these attacks are from aircraft hijackings, the use of biological agents, or more sophisticated cyber attempts to infiltrate crucial infrastructures. In this effort, we have sent troops to the Middle East to quell international threats in Iraq, Afghanistan, and now Syria; we have expanded our intelligence gathering and analysis capabilities to filter even our largest social media technologies; and we have developed entirely new departments of government to protect us, and to respond to emergencies whether they be caused by man-made terrorist events or natural disasters. Billions of dollars have been spent in this effort to make us safer. More importantly, our zeal to be safer and more secure has tested the limits of our government and the basic democratic values of "life, liberty and the pursuit of happiness" that underscores our country. Nothing is more important!

Hence, the decision to write this book was an easy one, inasmuch as we had previously collaborated for years on other co-authored books (*Criminal Investigation* and *Police Administration: Structures: Processes, and Behavior*). It was also an opportunity to contribute to the discussion of some of the most important issues of our times. More importantly, we thought there was room for a new book. In looking at the existing works, it seemed some disproportionately concentrated on historical aspects of terrorism without discussing it sufficiently in a modern context. Other volumes focused on terrorism without addressing homeland security or didn't give enough attention to the basics, such as "How did we get here?" Although interesting, edited volumes were typically too narrow in scope.

We have written a book that is historical, contemporary, and exciting while also interrelating terrorism, intelligence and homeland security. Our goal was to write a book that focused on students—one that serves as an introductory textbook to this complex set of topics. In doing that we also produced a book that instructors will find easy to use.

This book has four elements that are of the utmost importance:

1. *The book is written in a clear and concise manner, aimed at piquing student interest and learning.* We stay focused on our readers, providing them with both interesting content and thought-provoking features. Embedded in the content are *Information Links* to Internet sites that contain extended insights on important topics. We wrote many case studies to illustrate chapter content and make it come alive; and we filled each chapter with interesting pieces of information that were directly aimed at sparking discussion. For instance, each *Box* ends with a compelling question, and forces students to think about and discuss critical issues presented in each chapter while *Quick Facts* provide short doses of information that spark interest in the subject under discussion.

2. *The book is compelling.* This book is carefully researched and presents content from the latest findings in the literature. As important, interviews with key leaders in the intelligence field, heads of departments, agents within the FBI and members of local task forces, as well as friends returning from battle fields in Iraq and Afghanistan provided keen insight into issues addressing the reality of combatting terrorism. Hence, the book represents not only a strong scholarly approach to

the study of terrorism, but also incorporates the real-world experience of federal agents, police officers, and soldiers tasked with preventing the next terrorist attack on our country. In addition, the photographs in each chapter were personally selected by the authors after careful attention to detailed research. To the best of our knowledge, none of these images have previously been used in a college textbook. The pictures command attention and are accompanied by carefully written captions that tell a story, adding value to each image.

3. *The book is simultaneously historical and contemporary.* We believed it was essential for readers to understand the background of people, ideas, and organizations. At the same time, readers are provided with current information about new issues in the field. This approach provides readers with a unified and cutting-edge understanding of terrorism, intelligence, and homeland security and their interrelationship. For instance, readers will learn not only about the Islamic State, a newly emerged terrorist organization in the Middle East, but also about the historical factors that led to its development and how the international community is responding to this new and emerging international threat.

4. *The book is well-organized and has unique chapters.* The book is divided into four separate parts. Part One provides a solid framework in which to understand terrorism. Because some significant threats originate in the Middle East, we provide strong chapters that explain the geography, history, culture and religion of this complex area. We give significant time to understanding the complexities of Islam and the rise of radicalization in chapters that are well written and easy to read. Part Two focuses on terrorist groups, their organization, and their critical processes. These are important foundational chapters that provide unique interdisciplinary discussions on terrorist structures and strategies such as recruitment and retention of members, lone wolf strategies, and suicide bombing attacks. We provide strong chapters that differentiate between state-involved terrorism, single-issue terrorism, separatist or nationalist movements, and terrorism from the left and right wings. In Part Three, we discuss America's vulnerabilities to terrorism and present the governmental agencies that are tasked with preventing terrorism. We discuss the intelligence community and the myriad Constitutional issues that have sparked controversy in our country through the USA PATRIOT Act (e.g., clandestine spying on U.S. citizens, the use of drones, "enhanced" interrogation techniques and the abuse or torture of prisoners, and use of the military in preventing terrorism domestically). In every case, we tried to provide a *balanced* approach to understanding the issues that we face as a nation, providing security from real threats while still safeguarding civil and personal liberties. And finally, in Part Four, we define the forces that combat terrorism on a daily basis. In a one-of-a-kind chapter, we focus on those agencies that have anti-terrorism or counterterrorism as part of their primary missions. Again, the emphasis here is in on clarity, and the provision of pin-point information in an easy to read format.

Organization

This section is not a table of contents, but rather an informative dialogue highlighting each chapter of the book.

We did not write a comprehensive history of terrorism chapter, although the first and second chapters have an overview of some of its milestones. It seemed more useful to write shorter history sections in the context of the content of chapters, linking the past and the present together in order to bring meaning to contemporary issues.

Chapter 1: Defining, Conceptualizing and Understanding Terrorism

This chapter introduces the subject of terrorism and some of the topics and issues that are explored in more detail in later chapters. In the introduction section, reasons why it is important or perhaps essential to understand terrorism are identified, for example, challenges such as the emerging tactic of system disruption and Black Swan events that are so different they will be difficult to predict, but will impact on us nonetheless.

There was terrorism before we had a name for it. To this day scholars, governments, and international organizations, such as the United Nations, struggle to find a common definition of terrorism. One barrier to understanding terrorism is the surplus of competing and conflicting definitions. The chapter also addresses how our individual and cultural perspectives affect how we think about terrorism and create barriers to understanding it. The chapter concludes by contrasting war and war crimes, irregular war, and terrorism.

Chapter 2: Political Ideology and the Historical Roots of Terrorism

Chapter 2 is a foundational chapter for the entire book. It represents a significant work on the historical development of terrorist ideology. The chapter begins with a discussion of political ideology as the general belief system on which society is based and the mechanisms in which people undertake to achieve this perspective. Terrorism has a direct effect on the social structure of society. People depend on a framework of informal and formal rules that foster mutual respect and trust. Terrorism substitutes this trust with insecurity and fear. Essentially, terrorism attacks the very bases of social order, culture, and government. Chapter 2 explores the political and social theory that motivates certain groups—from the genesis of revolutionary ideology and terror to contemporary hate crime and radical Islamic movements. We start with the historic left-wing ideologies of socialism and communism as expressed by Karl Marx, Fredrick Engels, Pierre-Joseph Proudhon, and Vladimir Lenin in Europe and Russia at the end of the 19th century and trace ideological ties to more contemporary perspectives of revolution in South America and the Middle East as expressed by Che Guevara, Carlos Marighella, and Sayyid Qutb. A focus on the development of Latin American leftist groups like FARC and ELN in Colombia, the Tupamaros in Uruguay, and Sendero Luminoso (Shining Path) in Peru brings our discussion to the concept of a "guerrilla war" as part of a revolutionary strategy in some cases, and as terrorism in others. We also explore the development of the "new left" in Europe during the 1960s, including the Red Brigades, the Red Army Faction (also known as the Baader-Meinhof Gang), the Revolutionary Cells, and its feminist leaning auxiliary group, the Red Zora, bringing us full circle from the inception of left-wing, political revolutionary thought to more contemporary anti-imperialist and anti-colonial ideology.

The final part of this chapter focuses on the historical roots of terrorism in the Middle East, from early anti-colonial ideology and the mandate system developed at the end of World War I to the establishment of Israel and the beginning of the Palestinian Resistance movement. The chapter sets up Chapter 3, by exploring the early tenets of oil, politics, and radical Islam in the modern era.

Chapter 3: Understanding the Middle East and Islam

This book has five sets of chapters that are so closely intertwined we think of them as "twin chapters." Chapters 3 and 4 are the first set of the "twins." In Chapter 3, we start with the assertion that knowing some history of the Middle East, a few laws, and a handful of definitions is not sufficient grounding to assert one has a grasp on the Middle East and Islam. The chapter provides a basic understanding of Islam, but there is more to be learned. To fully understand the Middle East you must also fully understand Islam. Illustratively, some critics maintain that the "problem" with Islam is that it has never undergone a reformation, as has Christianity. The Muslim view is there has never been a need for it. In their view, the Archangel Gabriel revealed the Word of God to Muhammad and he, in turn, faithfully recorded it.

The vast majority of Muslims in America are good and decent people who practice their religion peacefully. Some Islamic religious leaders have twisted the meanings of Islamic concepts. For instance, "jihad" actually refers to a Muslim's struggle to overcome adversity and submit to the will of God. Jihad addresses an inner, spiritual struggle against sin, not a war against others. The twisted definition of jihad fuels hatred, violence, and grisly actions, such as the recent beheadings of American journalists, English aid workers, and others by members of the Islamic State.

The concluding section of the chapter ends with an explanation of Islam's five pillars of faith: (1) Shahada (Testimony of faith); (2) Salat (Prayer); (3) Zakat (Giving a portion of your annual income to those in need and to support Islam). (4) Sawm (Fasting); and (5) Hajj (Pilgrimage to Mecca).

Chapter 4: The Rise of Radical Islam

Islam is one of the world's great religions. Like Judaism and Christianity, it is one of the three primary monotheistic religions, meaning it is a religion that believes in one all-loving and powerful God. The histories of these three great religions are inseparably intertwined. So what events took place within Islam that led to such a vast radicalization of basic principles within the religion? This chapter explores that change and focuses on the political dimension of Islamic fundamentalism. It analyzes the radicalization of Islam in both traditions, Sunni and Shia (Shiite). Much of the discussion is centered on the Arab Revolution beginning after World War I and culminating in the Arab Spring of 2010, the ideologies that form major radical movements in today's Sunni tradition—the Wahhabi movement, the Muslim Brotherhood, the Salafi movement, and the Jihadist-Salafi movement. Each is discussed in terms of their primary philosophical leader and the contemporary evolution of the movement today as visible throughout the Middle East.

The radicalization of Sunni Islam has been an historic process, led by a number of key individuals. The chapter is laced with boxed items and commentary that provide a basic understanding of the historical complexities associated with radical Islam as proscribed by philosophical leaders such as Muhammad ibn Abd al-Wahhab, Hassan al-Banna, Sayyid Qutb, Ahmed Yassin, Abdul Rahman, Ahman al-Zawahiri, and Usama bin Laden as well as active Sunni groups, such as the Palestinian Islamic Resistance Movement (Hamas), al-Qaeda, al-Qaeda in the Arabian Peninsula (AQIP), Abu Sayaaf, and the Islamic State.

The final part of the chapter addresses the radicalization of the Shia (or Shiite) tradition within Islam, concentrating on the ideologies expressed by Ayatollah Ruhollah Khomeini during the Iranian Revolution of 1979. His thoughts provide the ideological foundation for today's Islamic Republic of Iran. The other primary Shia group discussed in this chapter is that of Hezbollah, under the leadership of Hassan Nasrallah, a group active throughout the world but centered in Lebanon.

Chapter 5: Terrorist Organizations and Structures

Chapters 5 and 6 are the second set of "twin chapters" in that they are interrelated: Both focus on terrorist organizations. Chapter 5 largely deals with how these groups are arranged and Chapter 6 scrutinizes the processes with which terrorist organizations operate. Organizational theory is a tool that explains how formal organizations are structured and relate to their environment. It can be applied to such disparate entities as General Motors, *The New York Times*, Girl Scouts, concentration camps, Red Cross, Hamas, and the Department of Defense. In Chapter 5, organizational theory is the lens by which we examine and explain the structure of terrorist organizations. We do so without requiring readers to learn, or be conversant with, organizational theory because this book is on a different subject.

The application of organizational theory to terrorist structures can provide important information about them. It reveals how authority is distributed, how work will be accomplished, and some indication of their relative importance of leaders. While it is important to understand what terrorist organizations do, Chapters 5 and 6 reveal some things about what they are.

Other topics in Chapter 5 include dilemmas of terrorist organizations, types of terrorist cells, organizational structures used by terrorists (such as hierarchical, umbrella, and virtual), the selection of targets, suicide bombing attacks, and how terrorist organizations end. The literature on how terrorist organizations end does not contemplate a movement that ends in a caliphate, but which we indeed have as an ending, in light of the geographic control the Islamic State has achieved with startling speed.

Chapter 6: Critical Processes of Terrorist Organizations

In this chapter we shift our analysis from how terrorist organizations are organized to essentially asking the question, "What does it take for a terrorist organization to be successful administratively and operationally?"

Like many other types of organizations, terrorists need administrative or organizational tools, which are the things they must accomplish to foster the organization's viability. To be operationally successful terrorists must also have command of these operational tools. Chapter 6 covers these topics with examples and case studies. One of the organizational tools discussed is the financing of the group, with special attention given to funding via hawalas, narcotics trafficking, and other criminal activities, sponsorships and donations, charities, and even the trading of bitcoins.

Chapter 7: Typologies of Terrorism: State-Involved and Single or Special Issue Movements

Chapters 7 and 8 are another set of "twin chapters," both dealing with typologies of terrorism. To avoid having one very long chapter we wrote two shorter chapters. We logically grouped movements in those chapters not by geography, but by their ideologies. Typologies logically group things, such as terrorist movements. In contrast, taxonomies create groups based on statistical analysis. We used typologies because there is insufficient data to create full taxonomies of terrorism. The history of each identified terrorist group is covered and Chapters 7 and 8 are replete with examples and case studies to provide concrete meaning.

Chapter 7 scrutinizes four types of terrorism in which the political state is involved: state terrorism, state-enabled terrorism, state-sponsored terrorism, and state-perpetrated/international terrorism. By and large, single/special-issue terrorism are still concerns, but towards the lower end of the threat scale. "Fading" may be a reasonable description of these movements, which includes the Animal Liberation Front (ALF), Earth Liberation Front (ALF), and Anti-Genetically Modified Organisms (GMO) groups, which oppose "frankenfood."

Chapter 8: Typologies of Terrorism: The Right and Left Wings and Separatist or Nationalist Movements

A large portion of this chapter covers right-wing groups, which envision having a homogenous "racially pure" country. All right-wing groups have in common "enemies" such as the "Zionist Occupied Government" (ZOG); illegal immigrants; people of color; and Lesbians, gay, bi-sexual, and transgender people (LGBT). Having a group to oppose promotes in-group solidarity, which helps to perpetuate the existence of right-wing movements (e.g., Hitler used the Jews for this purpose and the English Defence League targets Muslims). Right-wing movements in America include the Ku Klux Klan, neo-Nazis, and the anti-federalist/Christian Patriot groups.

Left-wing groups identified globally in the chapter include Sendero Luminoso (Shining Path) in Peru; the Red Army Faction (RAF) that operated mainly in Germany, but also in France, Switzerland, and the Netherlands; the Red Brigades in Italy; Revolutionary Armed Forces of Columbia (FARC), the Seung Fein in China, and the Weather Underground in the United States. The left wing historically has been unsuccessful in achieving its goal: replacing existing governments with ones that are based on Marxist-Leninist principles.

Separatist/nationalist movements are typically subnational groups who want a homeland. The groups often share a common culture, language, and history. Examples include the Kurdistan Workers Party, the Tamil Tigers, the Eritrean Liberation Front, and the Second Vermont Republic. Ireland's drive to become an independent country is discussed, as are the similarities between the Anglo-Irish War and the American Revolution

Chapter 9: Intelligence and Terrorism

Chapters 9 and 10 represent yet another set of "twins." In Chapter 9 , we define intelligence and counterintelligence and, more importantly, define plaguing questions that continue to impede our ability to prevent terrorism. For instance, the final report of a Congressional Advisory Panel after 9/11, commonly known as the Gilmore Commission, identified several issues relating to the failure of the intelligence community to prevent terrorism. These included a failure to provide timely, accurate, and specific intelligence information to law enforcement, security, and military agencies, as well as an overly bureaucratic and decentralized structure (particularly within the FBI) that hindered a unified and coordinated effort between federal and local agencies to address the terrorist threat. While some of these issues continue, the intelligence community has worked hard to overcome many of these obstacles.

We address the complexity of the intelligence community in Chapter 9, defining the agencies involved in the intelligence community, including the Federal Bureau of Investigation (FBI), the Central Intelligence Agency (CIA), the National Security Agency (NSA), and the relatively new roles of the Office of National Intelligence and the National Counterterrorism Center. We also present an overview of other agencies within the intelligence community and explore "fusion centers," which have become common entities at the state and local level aimed at better coordinating the intelligence efforts between all divisions of government—federal, state, tribal, county, and city.

Chapter 10: Intelligence, Terrorism and the U.S. Constitution

In Chapter 10, we address head-on the issues that surround the use of intelligence and intelligence gathering as a tool to prevent terrorism that seem to dot our newspapers on a near weekly basis. We closely examine the USA PATRIOT Act and discuss specific incidents that question and, in some cases, answer how far our government should go to protect our citizens. Specifically, we discuss the conflicts between the PATRIOT Act and the First, Fourth, and Fifth Amendments to the U.S. Constitution as related to the practice of extraordinary rendition, "enhanced" interview techniques and torture of suspected terrorist prisoners, the use of the military to supplement civilian police in conflict to the Posse Comitatus Act, police agencies that infiltrate political and religious groups that clearly blurs the line between policing and intelligence gathering, and the use of drones as both an offensive weapon in the Middle East and as a spying tool domestically. These issues and others are discussed in light of current events and the highlighted cases involving Bradley/Chelsea Manning, Wikileaks, and Edward Snowden.

Chapter 11: Homeland Security

Eleven days after the 9/11 attacks, Pennsylvania Governor Tom Ridge was appointed as the first director of the Office of Homeland Security by President George W. Bush. His job was to develop, oversee, and coordinate a new, comprehensive national strategy to safeguard the country against terrorism and respond to any future attacks. Over a year later, on November 25, 2002, the U.S. Department of Homeland Security (DHS) was created as a stand-alone agency, composed of 22 different pre-existing federal agencies. It was the largest reorganization of the federal bureaucracy since the National Security Act of 1947. Chapter 11 provides an overview of the key agencies assigned to DHS, such as the U.S. Coast Guard (USCG), U.S. Citizenship and Immigration Services (USCIS), Immigration and Customs Enforcement (ICE), Customs and Border Protection (CBP), Transportation Security Administration (TSA), U.S. Secret Service, and the Federal Emergency Management Agency (FEMA). The chapter explores each agency's role in fulfilling the core homeland security mission of preventing terrorism and enhancing the security of the United States.

Chapter 12: America's Vulnerability to Terrorism

Chapters 12 and 13 represent our final set of "twin" chapters. They are slightly different than the other sets as they are not extensions of the same subject matter, but rather complements to each other. In Chapter 12, we discuss openly America's vulnerability to terrorism. We define "critical infrastructure" and focus our work around the National Infrastructure Protection Plan (NIPP) that provides a framework in which to discuss potential target sites and give a reasonable risk assessment for each of the 16 sectors identified in NIPP. The discussion in Chapter 12 is all about "prevention" *now*, before an event, and providing an "all-hazard" plan that protects critical resources from any kind of catastrophe or disaster regardless of causation, natural (e.g., flood, fire, hurricane, tornado, or earthquake) or man-made (e.g., terrorist strike; large cyber-attack; mass shooting at a school, mall, or sporting event; or surprise attack from a foreign government). In Chapter 13, our discussion moves from prevention to response and mitigation—the effort to reduce loss of life and property by lessening the impact of such an event

Chapter 13: Emergency Management

While FEMA is the key federal agency for the emergency management of a terrorist attack or natural disaster *after* the event, a myriad of other agencies have specific roles in responding to and recovering from a disaster. For instance, the coordination of local relief agencies, food banks, shelters, and the like fall within the FEMA management guidelines, while specific responses to public health issues from open sewage lines, biological agents, or even radiation may be more appropriately handled by another agency such as the Center for Disease Control (CDC), the Environmental Protection Agency (EPA), or the Nuclear Regulatory Commission (NRC)—all discussed in Chapter 13.

The chapter provides a strong historical piece on the evolution of emergency management culminating in an in-depth discussion on our current National Preparedness System. We address the possibilities of significant attack from weapons of mass destruction and CBRNE-borne weapons, and more importantly, the formal mechanisms of the Incident Command System that are currently in place to address such an unspeakable event—from local and state perspectives to specific federal roles. Chapters 12 and 13 discuss America's defensive posture (i.e., planning, preventing, mitigating, and responding to a critical terrorist strike or disaster), setting up Chapter 14: Combatting Terrorism.

Chapter 14: Combatting Terrorism

There is an important distinction between anti-terrorism (AT) and counterterrorism (CT). At the risk of oversimplification, the former is largely comprised of defensive actions, while the latter centers on offensive operations. Chapter 14 addresses AT and CT on the basis of a cross-section of the organizations that are executing those respective kinds of missions, although it must be noted that some of them perform both AT and CT activities. With respect to these activities, the military, federal agencies, state and local governments, and law enforcement agencies are covered. The role of the military is given substantial attention because of the array of units involved and their important contributions to America's national security. The chapter also examines types of action that can be taken against terrorists, including raids and direct action.

Chapter 15: Terrorism, Intelligence and Homeland Security: The Future

This concluding chapter of the book ties the subject matters of terrorism, intelligence, and homeland security together, and identifies various trends in terrorist activities. Many of the past attacks in the United States have been carried out by homegrown terrorists using lone wolf terrorist tactics. These events have been mostly bombings using very crude and non-sophisticated weapons. Internationally, al-Qaeda appears to be weakening and fractionalizing as a single group; however, their radical Islamic ideology appears to be increasing throughout the Middle East and the rest of the world. While America has been victimized repeatedly by attacks on our transportation sector (particularly the airline industry), future attacks that are cyber in nature pose a much more significant threat in the future. Much of our critical infrastructure—including water systems, power grids, gas pipelines, nuclear power functions, and financial and communication networks—were built long before the specter of terrorism was a consideration, and contain weak defenses against potential attacks by terrorists, rogue nations, or even sophisticated criminals. Indeed, rather than focusing on attacks that raise the public hysteria, such as attacks from weapons of mass destruction (WMD), it might be more prudent to assume that the next major terrorist attack may be cyber in nature.

The final chapter also includes an important segment on the role of the media during terrorist events and the impact of such events on the mind of the general public. Our concluding remarks in Chapter 15 focus not on the significant dangers and potential threats that lurk in an unstable world, but rather on the richness, strength, diversity, and resilience of America as we confront the future together, no different than generations before us.

Pedagogical Features

Each chapter includes the following pedagogical features to aid students and instructors:

Learning Objectives at the beginning of each chapter identify the core elements students need to learn.

Learning Objectives

After completing this chapter you should be able to:

1. State six reasons why we should understand terrorism.

2. Identify eight attacks in America that were racial, labor, or anarchist related from 1856 to 1920.

3. Trace the history of key events in terrorism from 1959 to 9/11/2001.

4. Explain Robespierre's concept of terrorism.

5. Distinguish between the federal definitions for international and domestic terrorism.

Key Terms in the margins define each term where it is first used in the text. At the back of the text is a comprehensive glossary of all the key terms.

Introduction

Typologies and taxonomies are both methods of classification. Sometimes they are used synonymously. However, there is a crucial difference. **Typologies** rationally group related concepts and other things into categories. In contrast, **taxonomies** have categories that are formed by empirically studying observable and measurable characteristics.

Typologies bring clarity and patterns out of what otherwise would be a chaotic mass of information.[1] They allow us to quickly see the differences and similarities in concepts by using carefully reasoned categories. The use of typologies allows us to have shared understandings and a common language about the categories.[2] Despite such advantages, typologies have shortcomings. Their categories are artificial creations. They are ideal or pure descriptions that cannot fully account for the rich diversity of reality. Some concepts may fit equally well into more than one category. Cases that cannot be comfortably slipped into any category are forced into the best fitting category despite the fact they have some features of other categories as well. Finally, typologies can lead to stereotyping.

Typologies
Rationally group related concepts and other things into categories.

Taxonomies
Categories that are formed by empirically studying observable and measureable characteristics.

Boxes throughout the chapters highlight interesting topics that are relevant to the chapter subject matter. Each box concludes with challenging questions aimed at sparking class discussion.

Box 15–1
Predicting Terror Attacks

Policies, laws, intelligence, and our fear level are all related to terrorism and can be based on a single attack. However, a specific attack by a specific group or individual is largely unpredictable in nature. While certain clues were overlooked in the months before 9/11, it's still difficult (if not impossible) to say with any certainty that the events of that day could have been predicted. Furthermore, the current trends in terrorism mean smaller-scale attacks perpetrated by individuals that are rarely the subject of previous law enforcement scrutiny, hence there is no historical data on these individuals.

Surprisingly, however, terror attacks may not occur as randomly as we once thought they did. That's the conclusion reached by Aaron Clauset, a 35-year-old data scientist in Denver, Colorado, who examined complex information related to terrorist attacks and identified statistical patterns behind the frequency and severity of terrorist attacks across the globe. What Clauset noticed about terror attacks is that they seemed to mirror earthquakes in some ways, following a power-law distribution. Earthquakes tend to occur in groups of really small quakes, followed by a handful of stronger medium-sized quakes, and then one or two really massive, devastating quakes. Clauset found that terror attacks followed the same pattern; for example, there had been scores of small terror attacks, a couple of medium-intensity attacks (like the Oklahoma City Bombing and the Lockerbie airline explosions), and then the massive 9/11 attack that killed 3,000 people. This is useful for law enforcement, security, and policy makers because the frequency and severity of "small" terrorist attacks may help to determine the likelihood of another "big one"; events like the attacks on Oklahoma City or Lockerbie should have suggested the potential for something much worse in the future.

Despite its seeming applicability to homeland security, Clauset's conclusions have not been utilized by the U.S. government. The methodology is complex, and perhaps beyond the capabilities of many of the agencies that would need to be involved in its use. Interestingly, Clauset points out the following implications for his findings:

If we believe the power-law is a fundamental property of terrorism— and it appears to be so in a very robust way—it's reasonable to conclude that there may be a really big terrorist attack coming … involving chemical, biological or radiological attacks. And almost surely, the probability of these kinds of events is much higher than people might expect. If we don't have some people thinking about this in the long term, we are going to be very surprised. We are going to be unprepared.[9]

Source: Excerpt from How Aaron Clauset Discovered a Pattern Behind Terrorist Attacks...And What It Told Him by Joel Warner. Published by Denver Westword, LLC, © 2013.

How effective and accurate do you think these types of prediction models are to police and security agencies?

Information Links direct readers to Internet sites that provide more information on chapter topics.

Information Link
For more information on Cambodia under the Khmer Rouge, visit the webpage for Tuol Sleng Genocide Museum in Phnom Penh, Cambodia at www.tuolsleng.com/history.php and The Killing Fields Museum at www.killingfieldsmuseum.com/s21-victims.html. Tuol Sleng Prison was a high school used as the notorious Security Prison 21 during the Khmer Rouge regime from 1975 to 1979. An estimated 20,000 prisoners were tortured and killed at the prison.

Macoute as "the central nervous system of Haiti's reign of terror."[51] Its violence continued for years even after Baby Doc lost power. Notably, in 1988, the Tonton Macoute invaded a mass at St. Jean Bosco Catholic Church in Port-au-Prince, killing 12 parishioners and wounding another 77 using spears, machetes, and guns.[52] Eventually, Haitians turned on the Macoute, occasionally killing them.

Cambodia—The Khmer Rouge: The communist **Khmer Rouge** (Red Cambodians) ruled during 1975–1979, having come to power by overthrowing the existing government. Its leader, Pol Pot, wanted to turn the clock back to "**Zero Year**," empty the cities, and return to an agrarian society. He set in motion a massacre of Buddhists, Catholics, Muslims, intellectuals, businessmen, foreigners, and other classes, such as people who wore glasses (which suggested they were literate), spoke a foreign language (possibly tainted by outside ideas), or lacked any agricultural or mechanical skills (not useful in the future).[53] Approximately 1.7 million Cambodians died from

---

Quick Facts boxes provide unique tidbits of information related to the chapter topics.

Quick Facts
Center of Gravity, System Disruption, and Terrorist Selection of Targets

Center of gravity refers to the *primary* sources of strength, power, and resistance for a nation or organization and that of an adversary.[61] These sources are identified through an analytical process. Ideally, when the vulnerabilities of a center of gravity are identified and successfully attacked, decisive results are produced.[62] This concept is similar to Robb's system disruption.

During World War II, Americans sent badly needed war goods and troops across the Atlantic Ocean to England by convoys, which usually consisted of 45 or more ships. To prevent this, Germans deployed U-boats (submarines). In 1942, 1,664 ships were lost in the Atlantic to U-boats.[63] America was losing ships faster than they could be replaced.

Although warships and planes protected the convoys, losses remained high. The heart of the problem was that there was an area in the North Atlantic, the air-gap, which was beyond the range of the Allied Powers' aircraft.

The Germans' center of gravity in the Battle of the Atlantic was that area that could not be patrolled by the Allied Powers' aircraft. America's development of the very long-range B-24 bomber (The Liberator) contributed substantially to a decisive reduction of ships lost to the German submarines. The B-24s provided a decisive victory that destroyed the Germans' center of gravity. By 1944, German submarines sank only 67 ships.[64] The result was that much-needed weapons, munitions, food, petroleum, and other essentials would reach England and be used in the war against the Axis Powers.

The major terrorist groups are sophisticated, and their recent announcements about attacking infrastructures reveal a well-developed targeting capability. These groups are developing and recruiting cyber experts, possibly to develop the tools needed for infrastructure attacks. The absence of infrastructure attacks against the United States (The "Great Satan") may reflect an absence of opportunity due to our vigilance. Alternatively, terrorists may not have a real intent to attack the infrastructure because just their announcements may cause us to spend perhaps billions to harden infrastructure targets. The lack of infrastructure attacks could also indicate that terrorists do not yet have the capability to do so. If such attacks do come they are likely to cause Robb's system disruption or weaken our centers of gravity. If their future attacks do strike infrastructures, people might be illuminating their lives with candles for an unknown period of time. Note that netwar and system disruption essentially refer to the same actions.

Summaries are organized around Learning Objectives that highlight the main points of each chapter.

Chapter Summary

SUMMARY BY LEARNING OBJECTIVE

1. **Describe broad trends in terrorism, including general statistics about frequency, location, and targets of attacks.**

   The number of terrorist attacks in the United States has declined since 2001, though fatal attacks have increased slightly since 2008; explosive devices remained the main types of weapons used, and over half of attacks were aimed at damaging property. Attacks perpetrated by individuals are also on the rise.

2. **Elaborate on the rise of homegrown and lone wolf terrorists and their weapons usage.**

   Homegrown terrorists are American citizens or legal residents who have become radicalized either on their own or through some form of recruitment by al-Qaeda. Increasingly, they act as "lone wolves," allowing them to operate under the radar. Such terrorists are more likely to use crude or easily obtained weaponry, and may communicate with terrorist organizations online or simply view materials of interest that have been posted by terrorist cells.

Review Questions at the end of each chapter pose a series of questions to test students' recall of the chapter information.

REVIEW QUESTIONS

1. What do the trends in terrorist activities tell us?
2. What is so dangerous about lone wolf operatives?
3. Describe how fractionalization of al-Qaeda will impact counterterror activities in the future.
4. How has Middle East unrest energized jihadist groups in the past several years?
5. What type of terrorist targets do you think will be most prevalent in the future?
6. Explain the thin line that media organizations must walk when reporting on terrorism.
7. What additional counterterrorism policies or strategies should be adopted to address new issues and paradigms in terrorism?

Critical Thinking Exercises at the end of each chapter require students to go further and think on the analytical level. Most of the exercises involve web research.

CRITICAL THINKING EXERCISES

1. **Interactive Terrorism Map.** Visit the website at www.globalincidentmap.com and view the global incident map. Click on one of the flashing items in the Middle East. How many of the incidents represent threats to critical infrastructure (oil and gas wells or pipelines) in the area? How many involve threats from radical Islamic groups? Now click on one of the flashing points in the United States or Europe. Discuss the above questions for the new area. Finally, notice that the entire map is delivered in real-time for subscribers. As a free user, the map is time-delayed 24 to 48 hours. Notice how many of the incidents are "hoaxes," or threats that never materialized. As a class, discuss the value of having real-time access to such a map for response measures, deployment of personnel, identifying trend activity, analytic examination of specific threats, research, and the like.

In addition to these pedagogical features, we devoted careful attention to the maps, tables, figures, and photographs, researching and selecting them ourselves, striving for a blend of informative historical images and also more current ones, many of which are compelling and tell a story by themselves.

Instructor Supplements

Instructor's Manual with Test Bank

Includes content outlines for classroom discussion, teaching suggestions, and answers to selected end-of-Review Questionsfrom the text. This also contains a Word document version of the test bank.

TestGen

This computerized test generation system gives you maximum flexibility in creating and administering tests on paper, electronically, or online. It provides state-of-the-art features for viewing and editing test bank questions, dragging a selected question into a test you are creating, and printing sleek, formatted tests in a variety of layouts. Select test items from test banks included with TestGen for quick test creation, or write your own questions from scratch. TestGen's random generator provides the option to display different text or calculated number values each time questions are used.

PowerPoint Presentations

Our presentations offer clear, straightforward outlines and notes to use for class lectures or study materials. Photos, illustrations, charts, and tables from the book are included in the presentations when applicable.

To access supplementary materials online, instructors need to request an instructor access code. Go to **www.pearsonhighered.com/irc**, where you can register for an instructor access code. Within 48 hours after registering, you will receive a confirming email, including an instructor access code. Once you have received your code, go to the site and log on for full instructions on downloading the materials you wish to use.

Alternate Versions

eBooks

This text is also available in multiple eBook formats including Adobe Reader and CourseSmart. *CourseSmart* is an exciting new choice for students looking to save money. As an alternative to purchasing the printed textbook, students can purchase an electronic version of the same content. With a *CourseSmart* eTextbook, students can search the text, make notes online, print out reading assignments that incorporate lecture notes, and bookmark important passages for later review. For more information, or to purchase access to the *CourseSmart* eTextbook, visit **www.coursesmart.com**.

Acknowledgments

Although it is insufficient compensation for their gracious assistance, we would like to recognize here the individuals who helped make this book a reality. Many good friends at "three letter agencies" and the military, all of whom wish to remain unnamed, read several chapters and made cogent comments, for which we are grateful. Several provided up-to-date information on issues relating to the Middle East as the chapters were being written.

Ms. Jennifer Davis-Lamm provided ongoing research and contribution to several chapters. We are forever indebted for her services. Mr. Jason Lane greatly assisted with research on Chapter 12: America's Vulnerability to Terrorism and Chapter 13: Emergency Management. Dr. Kelley Stone contributed to Chapter 13 as well, and allowed us to draw upon his excellent knowledge of fusion centers in Chapter 9: Intelligence and Terrorism. A special "thank you" to graduate students from the Turkish National Police, Dr. Suleyman Ozeren, Dr. Ahmet Yayla, Dr. Samih Teymur, and Dr. Mustafa Ozgular for their assistance in writing and developing Chapters 3 and 4. Their knowledge and patience greatly helped us understand the foundations as well as the historical evolution of Islam as presented in Chapters 3: Understanding the Middle East and Islam, and Chapter 4: The Rise of Radical Islam. Mr. Zeeshan Syed proofread Chapters 3 and 4 for accuracy, and Ms. Amy Kryzak proofed the entire manuscript through Grammarly.

Paige Cummings, Traci Swanson, and Kellie Pless also read and commented on the chapters, improving them. Our long-standing friend, Leonard Territo, went through materials very carefully, catching lapses. The Federal Bureau of Investigation provided photos and we are appreciative of the speed with which they responded to our requests.

We would like to thank the following reviewers for their comments and suggestions: Salih Hakan Can, Penn State University – Schuylkill Campus; Brian LeBlanc, Rivier University; Deborah Louis, Eastern Kentucky University; Pamela Mertens, Northeastern State University; James O'Sullivan, Pace University; John Padgett, Capella University; Carlos Parker, Cumberland County College; Jennifer Estis-Sumerel, Itawamba Community College; Lisa Ann Zanglin, Auburn University – Montgomery.

Lastly, we would like to thank our editors. Ms. Elisa Rogers, our developmental editor has just been wonderful during this entire project. Thank you, Elisa, for your time, energy and patience. And, to our managing editor, Mr. Gary Bauer, for his continued guidance and support. He was willing to "go to bat" for us on numerous occasions. We truly hope this book realizes his expectations. It has been a pleasure working with him, as well as the entire Pearson team.

Robert W. Taylor is currently a tenured full Professor and Director of the Executive Master of Science Program in Justice Administration and Leadership within the Department of Criminology at The University of Texas at Dallas. The Department of Criminology was recently ranked 5th in the world in academic excellence and strength of its Ph.D. program. Previous to this position, he was the Program Head for the Public Affairs Program—an academic program integrating the traditions of management, governmental affairs, policy analysis, and decision science in the public sector. The program hosted one of the largest graduate degree programs on campus including Doctoral (Ph.D.) and Master's Degrees in Public Affairs and Public Administration.

From January 2008 through 2010, Dr. Taylor was the Executive Director of the W.W. Caruth Jr. Police Institute at Dallas (CPI). The Institute was established through a $9.5 million grant from the Communities Foundation of Texas. Dr. Taylor was a principle party to the development of the Institute and was appointed the founding director by the University of North Texas System. The primary mission of the Institute is to provide direction and coordination of major training and research projects for the Dallas Police Department. The Institute represents a national "think tank" on policing strategies focused on major urban cities in the United States. Dr. Taylor remains a "Scholar-in-Residence" at the Institute. From 1996 to 2008, Dr. Taylor was professor and chair of the Department of Criminal Justice at the University of North Texas. He served in this capacity for thirteen years, and under his direction the Department gained national prominence, especially with the establishment of the Caruth Police Institute.

In 1995, Dr. Taylor took a leave of absence from university administration and teaching to join Emergency Resources International, Inc., the parent company of the famed "Red Adair" firefighters. His duties as Senior Vice-President, Crisis Management Division, included liaison with foreign governments and authorities, extensive contract negotiations, and the strategic development of a worldwide communication and information system. Dr. Taylor's major project was acting as team leader on the largest oil spill in history (3 million bbls), located in the remote Nenets District of Russia, over 200 miles north of the Arctic Circle.

For the past thirty years, Dr. Taylor has studied criminal justice administration and specifically police responses to crime and terrorism, focusing on issues in the Middle East. He has traveled extensively throughout the Middle East, meeting several heads of state in that region. He has acted as a consultant to numerous federal, state, and local agencies, and since September 11, 2001, Dr. Taylor has been a consultant to the U.S. Department of Justice working with the Institute for Intergovernmental Research (IIR) as a lead instructor in the State and Local Anti-Terrorism Training Program (SLATT). Dr. Taylor has also worked extensively throughout the Middle East, especially in the country of Turkey. He has been an instructor for the U.S. Department of State, Anti-Terrorism Assistance (ATA) Program (2001-2006) and taught internationally in the Executive Seminar on Cyber Terrorism presented to executives of foreign governments. Dr. Taylor holds appropriate top secret national security clearances through the JPASS system (archived).

Dr. Taylor has authored or co-authored over 200 articles, books, and manuscripts. Most of his publications focus on police administration and management, police procedures, international and domestic terrorism, drug trafficking, and criminal justice policy. His articles appear in numerous journals including *Defense Analysis* (University of Oxford, England Press), the *ANNALS* (American Academy of Political and Social Sciences), *Police Quarterly, Crime and Delinquency*, and the *Police Chief* (International Association of Chiefs of Police). Dr. Taylor is co-author of two leading textbooks, *Police Administration:*

Structures, Processes, and Behavior (Upper Saddle River, NJ: Pearson Publishing, 2012), currently in its 8th edition, and *Criminal Investigation* (New York: McGraw-Hill, 2012), currently in its 11th edition. These texts are used in over 500 universities, colleges, and police departments throughout the United States. He is also the senior author of *Juvenile Justice: Policies, Practices and Programs* (McGraw-Hill, 2014) in its 4th edition, *Digital Crime and Digital Terrorism* (Pearson, 2014) in its 3rd edition, and *Police Patrol Allocation and Deployment* (Pearson, 2011).

Dr. Taylor has an extensive background in academic and professional criminal justice, having taught at four major universities and serving as a sworn police officer and major crimes detective (lateral rank of sergeant) in Portland, Oregon, for over six years.

In 1984, Dr. Taylor was appointed as a Research Fellow at the International Center for the Study of Violence at the University of South Florida, Tampa, Florida, conducting various studies involving international and domestic terrorism, police training and management, public violence and homicide, computerized mapping, and international drug trafficking. He continues to conduct research in these areas and is the recipient of numerous grants and contracts (over $15 million in funded projects). His latest work is concentrated in four areas: (1) quality improvement in police agencies through advanced leadership and management practices; (2) international terrorism, especially Middle-Eastern groups, and the spread of radical Islam; (3) evaluation of community policing, Compstat, and intelligence-led policing strategies in the United States; and (4) intelligence analysis, fusion centers, and decision making, particularly during protracted conflict or crisis situations.

In 2004, Dr. Taylor was asked by the International Justice Mission in Washington, D.C., to assist in the training of the Cambodian National Police on child sex slavery and human trafficking as part of a large project funded through the U.S. Department of State ($1 million). His interest and research in this area has led to a leadership role in designing and developing training efforts in the United States aimed at raising awareness of the human trafficking tragedy for American law enforcement officers, funded in part through the U.S. Department of Justice. Dr. Taylor focuses on the nexus between human trafficking, drug trafficking, and the financing of terrorist incidents internationally and domestically. He continues this important work as a guest lecturer, speaking at conferences internationally on these subjects.

In 2003, Dr. Taylor was awarded the *University of North Texas, Regent's Lecture Award* for his work in the Middle East. In March 2008, the Academy of Criminal Justice Sciences presented Dr. Taylor with the prestigious *O.W. Wilson Award* 'in recognition of his outstanding contribution to police education, research and practice.'

Dr. Taylor has been a consultant to the U.S. Army, the U.S. Marine Corps, the U.S. Department of Homeland Security, the U.S. Department of Treasury, Federal Law Enforcement Training Center, the U.S. Secret Service, the Bureau of Alcohol, Tobacco, and Firearms, the U.S. Department of Justice, the Federal Bureau of Investigation, the Drug Enforcement Administration, the Police Foundation, the Police Executive Research Forum (PERF), the International Association of Chiefs of Police (IACP), and numerous state and local municipalities and private corporations. He has also conducted significant training in the United States protectorates of the U.S. Virgin Islands, Guam, and Saipan, and the countries of Canada, England, France, Switzerland, Thailand, Cambodia, Barbados, Northern Cyprus, Bahrain, Venezuela, Russia, Finland, United Arab Emirates, Kenya, Singapore, and Turkey. He is an active member of the Academy of Criminal Justice Sciences (elected National Chair of the ACJS Police Section – 2002), the American Society for Public Administration, and the American Society of Criminology.

Dr. Taylor is a graduate of Michigan State University (Master of Science, 1973) and Portland State University (Doctor of Philosophy, 1981).

Charles R. "Mike" Swanson enlisted in the Marine Corps when he was 17 years old, subsequently working as Patrol Officer and Detective with the Tampa Police Department. He joined Florida Governor Claude Kirk's staff as a Senior Police Planner and later as Deputy Director of the Governor's Council on Law Enforcement and Criminal Justice. Mike taught criminal justice courses at East Carolina University before accepting a faculty member in the Institute of Government (IOG) at the University of Georgia. Faculty members in the IOG are charged with carrying out programs of research, training, and technical assistance for Georgia units of state and local government. Mike specialized in reorganization of police departments to achieve enhanced performance.

For much of his 29 years in the IOG, Mike focused on three efforts:

1. *Designing promotional systems for police and fire departments.* Notably, he led a large city police department and a state patrol agency out of federal court, creating promotional systems that are still used and have not been successfully challenged. Mike has designed hundreds of valid and reliable written promotional tests and assessment center exercises. He has trained hundreds of assessors and directed more than 50 assessment centers.

2. *Training.* As Director of the IOG's Southeastern Law Enforcement Programs, he created and led advance training programs for more than 10,000 officers from 46 states and 4 foreign countries.

3. *Partnering with police departments to foster improvements.* Virtually on a daily basis for 29 years, Mike worked with police departments to resolve smaller to large-scale problems, often acting as a change agent. On a larger scale, he conducted analyses that were the basis of his reorganization of units or entire police agencies, as well as the consolidation of a large city police department with a county police agency. Many of Mike's more than 100 technical reports were written to support his work in this area.

Mike advanced through the administrative ranks of the IOG, Program Director, Division Director, Deputy Director, and retired as the Acting Director. His home in Athens, Georgia, is a musical hot spot with several internationally known bands residing there. One of his more unusual consulting jobs was advising a major touring band on how to recover a member's stolen guitar.

In addition to conference papers, refereed articles, and chapters in books, Mike has co-authored several books, including *The Police Personnel Selection Process, Introduction to Criminal Justice, Court Administration, Police Administration: Structures, Processes, and Behavior* (8th edition in progress), and *Criminal Investigation* (12th edition in progress).

Mike has received an array of recognitions, including a Distinguished Service Award and the Walter Bernard Hill Award from the University of Georgia, commendations from the Governors' of three states for contributions to public service, the O.W. Wilson Award for Distinguished Scholarship, a Service Award from the Georgia Association of Chiefs of Police, as well as becoming their First Honorary Chief of Police Award for service to that organization. As a consultant, Mike has worked with police agencies as far apart as the Elizabeth, New Jersey Police Department, the Dallas Police Department, and the Multnomah County (Oregon) Department of Public Safety. He has also taught abroad in the Shanghai Municipal Institute.

He received a Bachelor's and Master's degree from Florida State University and a Ph.D, in Political Science, with a concentration in public administration, from the University of Georgia.

Defining, Conceptualizing and Understanding Terrorism

CHAPTER

1

Members of the American National Socialist Movement (NSM) march against illegal immigration in Lansing, Michigan. Founded in 1974, it is a right-wing, Neo-Nazi, racist, and anti-immigration organization.

(© Zuma Press, Inc/Alamy)

Learning Objectives

After completing this chapter you should be able to:

1. State six reasons why we should understand terrorism.

2. Identify eight attacks in America that were racial, labor, or anarchist related from 1856 to 1920.

3. Trace the history of key events in terrorism from 1959 to 9/11/2001.

4. Explain Robespierre's concept of terrorism.

5. Distinguish between the federal definitions for international and domestic terrorism.

6. Contrast individual and cultural perspectives of terrorism.

7. Describe selective terrorism.

8. Explain why there are so many definitions of terrorism.

9. State why there is no terrorism definition acceptable to all United Nations members.

10. Explain why the database for terrorism is insufficient.

11. Using Hezbollah as an example, discuss the notion that terrorism is a contested concept.

12. Describe how Russia benefited from labeling the Chechnya insurgents as terrorists.

13. Explain why the criminal charges placed against Abdulhakim Muhammad confuse us.

14. Identify six acts punishable as war crimes.

Muslim
One who adheres to the Islamic faith. See Islamic.

Homegrown terrorists
Although there may be an exchange of electronic messages with a terrorist organization sending encouraging messages, homegrown terrorists have no formal connection to, or material support from, a terrorist movement, but may have some psychological affinity with one, or have their own particular cause, such as calling attention to deforestation in Brazil.

Taliban
Pashto, "student." The Taliban largely consists of members of the Pashtun tribes occupying parts of the border between Afghanistan and Pakistan. It is a fundamentalist Islamic movement that insists on strict enforcement of Sharia law. The Taliban came to power in Afghanistan in 1996 and was overthrown by Americans in 2001 for continuing to shelter Usama bin Laden, the leader of the 9/11 attacks.

Islam
The religion of Muslims, referred to earlier in history as Moslems, who believe there is no God but Allah and Muhammad is his prophet. It is Allah that founded Islam through Muhammad. Islam's religious book is the Qur'an (Anglicized as the "Koran").

Drone
Unmanned aircraft flown remotely. Unarmed drones are used for reconnaissance and armed drones can strike against enemy targets.

al Shabaab
A regional terrorist group affiliated with al-Qaeda.

Regional terrorist movements
RTMs may be independent and some of the larger ones may be affiliated with larger transnational terrorist organizations such as al Qaeda or the Islamic State.

al-Qaeda
Arabic, "The Base." Foreign terrorist organization (FTO) led by Usama bin Laden until his death in 2011; currently led by Ayman al-Zawahiri.

Introduction

It is important, perhaps essential, to understand terrorism. There are a number of reasons why.

First, for most of its long history, terrorism's impact was subnational or regional. While these threats still exist, in more recent decades a few terrorist groups have developed the capability to launch attacks transnationally, across the globe. This capability leaves many people wary and changes how some people live. The American experience following 9/11 illustrates this point: 33 percent of respondents in a national survey reduced their air travel and 25 percent reported avoiding certain cities and crowded places that might be targets of a terrorist attack.[1] In prudent anticipation of future attacks, some businesses now provide their employees with emergency kits,* an unknown number of families have created emergency plans; and confidence in the ability of governments to protect people has been shaken.[2]

Second, terrorism can be adapted with frightening speed to the needs of many causes. It is the violent equivalent of a Swiss Army knife. Some attacks can be thought of and carried out fairly quickly by a lone person or a handful of people with few resources. Although a great deal of attention is focused on radicalized **Muslims** from abroad, "homegrown terrorists" may live next door to you. In 2011, Janet Napolitano, then-Secretary of the Department of Homeland Security (DHS), noted "homegrown terrorism is central to the merging threat picture."[3] **Homegrown terrorists** have no formal connection to, or receive material support from, a terrorist movement, but may have some psychological affinity with one, or have their own particular cause, such as calling attention to deforestation in Brazil. We all have a responsibility to be aware of possible terrorist threats and should, as suggested by DHS, "report something if we see something."†

Third, the American preoccupation with protecting the homeland, as well as citizens, interests, and facilities abroad, can lead us into thinking that terrorism is a uniquely American problem. The data reveals a very different picture: In 2013, there were 9,707 terrorist attacks with 17,800 deaths around the world.[4] Three attacks in 2013 illustrate this point: (1) In Peshawar, Pakistan, 81 Christians worshipping in church were killed when two suicide bombers affiliated with the **Taliban**, a radical **Islamic** group that straddles the border region between Pakistan and Afghanistan, blew themselves up.[5] The attack was in protest to the U.S. use of **drones** against the Taliban; (2) gunmen from **al Shabaab**, a **regional terrorist movement** affiliated with **al-Qaeda**, seized the Westgate Mall in Nairobi, Kenya. Over the course of 12 hours they killed 67 people (see Figure 1–1). The attack was in reaction to Kenya sending troops to fight al Shabaab terrorists in Somalia; and (3) at the main train station in Volgograd, Russia, a suicide bomber, 26-year old Oksana Aslanova, killed 18 people.[6] She was twice widowed, her militant husbands killed in clashes with Russian forces. Such bombers are called "Black Widows" in Russia. It is believed the bombing was carried out at the order of an anti-Russian Chechen leader. The objective may have been to disrupt the Olympics, which started in Sochi, Russia, some 40 days later. Terrorism is demonstrably a worldwide issue and not simply an American phenomenon.

Fourth, it is said that those who make their living reading crystal balls are doomed to eat broken glass. Nonetheless, we accept the risk and assert it is more likely than not that there will be no quick and easy resolution to terrorism. The continuous possibility of an attack is akin to learning to live with an incurable disease.

Fifth, families are stressed by the deployment of its members to combat zones, struggle to adjust if they return with injuries, and grieve over their deaths. Service members that are deployed face dangers, often over multiple deployments. Their collective sacrifices give

---

*The content of kits vary, but may include water, light sticks, orange vests, energy/protein bars, basic first aid/trauma items, whistles, toilet paper, dust masks, and 24" pry bars. Some manufacturers provide kits for offices, home, cars, and "bugging out." These kits may also be for one person, a family of four, a group of ten people or other such configurations, including the type of emergency such as a pan epidemic or a biological/chemical agent attack.

†This slogan was developed by DHS in cooperation with New York's Metropolitan Transportation Authority (MTA) and has been prominently displayed in transportation facilities.

FIGURE 1–1
A women caught in the carnage at the Westgate Mall appears to be crying for help. The multiple small wounds on her face and left hand may have been caused by broken glass, but the blood seen partially underneath her suggests the possibility of one or more other wounds. The gunmen screened their victims. Those who claimed to be Muslims and could answer questions about Islam were freed and the others shot.

(Noor Khamic/Reuters/Corbis)

us a measure of security and deserve our respect. To demonstrate that respect many people are joining the Wounded Warrior Project and other efforts to help returning veterans adjust to their homecoming.

Sixth, terrorism evolves and adapts, presenting a continuous series of new challenges. Robb makes a compelling argument that terrorists are now waging a "New War" that has the potential to have a major impact on America's homeland without **weapons of mass destruction** (WMDs).[7] If this New War directed at infrastructures is successfully waged, our lives will be rendered much more difficult. Even more alarming, the New War can be waged indefinitely by both small conventional and cyber attacks. The latter can be effectively executed covertly from remote sites anyplace in the world.

Terrorists have not forsaken using improvised explosive devices (IEDs), suicide bombers, or attacks on specific targets, such as the U.S. Consulate in Benghazi, Libya, during 2012, which killed Ambassador Stevens and others. However, the larger New War goal of sophisticated terrorist movements opposed to the United States is to render it economically impotent and unable to "throw its weight around in the Middle East."[8] Fallows thinks that while we have seemingly blunted al-Qaeda's huge, spectacular attacks, the shift to New War attacks may prove to be more threatening.[9] Robb asserts the New War will feature **Black Swan events**, which are so different from what we know that they will be difficult to predict.[10]

How would the New War be potentially able to make America economically impotent? It relies on the new strategic weapon of "**system disruption**,"[11] attacking elements of the infrastructure, including oil pipelines and refineries, and communication, transportation, electrical, and water systems. The 9/11 attacks illustrate this type of warfare because the towers were filled with banking, finance, insurance, and other important infrastructure enterprises. Al-Qaeda spent perhaps $250,000 on it and in response America has expended $500 billion[‡] in the decades that followed.[12] In 2001, anthrax-tainted mail killed five people in the United States, cases that remain unsolved. In response, the U.S. Postal Service developed countermeasures costing $5 billion or $1 billion per fatality.[13] Attacks on Iraq's infrastructure have disrupted its economy: Electricity is only available 8–12 hours daily, corporations are leaving the country, new investment money is scarce, and unemployment is 50 percent.[14] A single attack on an Iraqi oil pipeline cost $2,000 and none of the attackers were caught, but it produced an income loss of $500 million, creating a return of 25,000 times the cost of the attack.[15] In mid-2014, intelligence sources indicated that the Kingdom of Saudi Arabia

Information Link
For a detailed analysis of terrorist attacks see Erin Miller and Travis Rudd, "START Provides 2013 Statistical Annex for Country Reports on Terrorism."

Weapons of mass destruction
There are at least 50 official definitions of WMDs in the United States and other national governments, as well as international organizations such as the United Nations.[16] A common thread in these definitions approximates: WMDs are nuclear, biological, chemical, radiological, and high explosive weapons capable of producing major destruction, mass casualties, and/or significant infrastructure damage.[17]

Black Swan Events
Future terrorist attacks that are so different from past experience and what analysts can reasonable foresee that they are unpredictable.

System disruption
System disruption attacks have been called the "new war." Instead of concentrating on attacks that produce mass casualties, system disruption attacks focus on the systems that are essential to our daily lives, such as mass transit, electrical grids, and water.

[‡] Other estimates are higher, including one of $3 trillion.

To the public, IS seemingly came out of nowhere in 2014, but intelligence services were previously aware of it. However, some services may have been mistaken about its capabilities. Unlike other terrorist organizations that simply want to inflict violence, IS is conquering and controlling land in Syria and Iraq with the goal of establishing a caliphate, which is an Islamic State. The concept of an Islamic State is discussed in detail in Chapter 3.

IS is so violent that it was "disowned" by al-Qaeda. IS grisly tactics include mass executions of captured Iraqi soldiers and beheading of Western captives, including aid workers and journalists. As IS gains control of areas, people are given the choice of converting to Islam or being killed.

Under American leadership an international coalition, including Arab countries, is waging an air war against IS, although some knowledgeable observers believe that eventually there must be "boots on the ground." When IS attacks, it is in close proximity to those opposing it. Without ground controllers on the ground to direct air attacks with great precision, air attacks cannot be conducted, reducing their value at a crucial point.

Although lacking air power IS is not impotent in terms of reacting to coalition air strikes. Using social media, it has recruited Westerners and trained some number of them in Syria with the intention that they will return to their home country and conduct a small attack by themselves or recruit people to make larger attacks.

Islamic State
A terrorist organization that became an international threat in 2014. Previously known as the Islamic State in Syria (ISIS) and the Islamic State in the Levant (ISIL). Known for its grisly beheadings for Westerners and mass executions of captured Iraqi soldiers.

Islamic: Of, or pertaining to Islam.
Practices or persons which adhere to the beliefs of Islam. See Islam.

was being targeted by the terrorist group **Islamic State** (IS).[18] Targets identified include desalinization plants, petroleum facilities, and government buildings,[19] all fitting within the strategy of system disruption.

America has many vulnerabilities, including oil platforms in the Gulf of Mexico, concentrated oil pipeline systems, lengthy railroad routes, numerous unprotected bridges and tunnels, and other sites. If systematically attacked by New War tactics, life as we know it would be considerably altered. In the New War, protecting the infrastructure is at least as important as fighting terrorists "over there."

Finally, terrorism compels local, state, tribal, and national governments to have significant policy and diplomatic discussions about how to combat it. The National Security Agency's (NSAs) massive anti-terrorism data collection programs were much in the news the last several years, illustrating how dealing with terrorism has implications for all of us. A 2013 Pew Research Center survey discovered that 56 percent of respondents believed that American courts do not go far enough setting limits on what NSA collects and 70 percent thought the government used the data for purposes other than fighting terrorism.[20]

Data such as this provokes serious national conversations about the balance between national security and Constitutional rights. We need to be able to follow such conversations knowledgably because they are at the very heart of the relationship between a government and its citizens. This issue is discussed in Chapter 10. Benjamin Franklin captured the essence of this discussion in 1759, when he observed "They that give up essential liberty to obtain a little temporary safety deserve neither liberty nor safety." Although the U.S. government is charged with preventing new attacks, it must simultaneously preserve those constitutional liberties and rights that define it. Every citizen is affected by how well that balance is struck.

The Concept Of Terrorism

There was terrorism before there was a word for it. The Romans conquered portions of the Middle East in the 1st century B.C. In Palestine for decades afterwards, the Jewish Sicarii (dagger men) concealed knives under their robes and used them to murder Romans and their supporters in crowds. For example, in the market and on festival days the Sicarii would strike, and then quickly disappear into the crowd. The Sicarii believed that Jews were the chosen people and being subordinated to the Roman Emperor was antithetical to their religious beliefs, making them stanchly anti-Roman.[21] In Iran during the 11th–12th centuries, a branch of Islam, the Nizari Ismailis, killed opposing leaders in the Middle East and became known as the "assassins."[22] There were nine European Crusades to the Holy Land, lasting from roughly end of the 11th to the end of the 13th century. During their travel to Palestine, some Crusaders slaughtered entire Jewish communities because they were not Christians.[23]

HARPER'S FERRY INSURRECTION—INTERIOR OF THE ENGINE-HOUSE, JUST BEFORE THE GATE IS BROKEN DOWN BY THE STORMING PARTY—COL. WASHINGTON AND HIS ASSOCIATES AS CAPTIVES, HELD BY BROWN AS HOSTAGES.

FIGURE 1–2
John Brown (1800–1859) stands alone in front of the left set of doors inside the federal armory at Harpers Ferry, Virginia. Brown and his followers seized the facility in the belief their action would provoke an uprising against slavery that they could arm. Robert E. Lee, then a colonel in the Union Army, led a force that killed some and captured others in this rebellious group. Brown was charged with treason and hung less than 90 days afterwards. A song about the incident was popular among Union troops during the Civil War (1861–1865). Lee later commanded the Confederate Army.
(Courtesy Library of Congress)

"Terrorism" only emerged as a term during the late 18th century in France. Early terrorism in the United States was typically racial, labor, or **anarchist** related. Examples include the following: (1) In 1856, John Brown, a vicious opponent of slavery, and his five sons went to Pottawatomie Country, Kansas, where they murdered and mutilated five pro-slavery settlers.[24] Three years later, he seized a federal armory, thinking he could provoke and arm an uprising against slavery (see Figure 1–2). (2) Founded in 1867, the Knights of the White Camellia were a secret racist Southern society akin to the Ku Klux Klan (KKK), which was established two years before.[25] In order to get their candidate elected in 1868, the Knights terrorized Louisiana voters for two weeks before the election with secret murders and raids that left 2,000 voters dead or injured.[26] The Knights' candidate handily won the election. (3) Throughout the 1880s Asians, especially the Chinese, were targeted for murder, assaults, and forced evacuation across all parts of the State of Washington.[27] (4) In 1886, a person believed to be an anarchist threw a bomb in Chicago's Haymarket Square that killed seven policemen present at a demonstration by striking workers.[28] (5) In 1892, Alexander Berkman, a Russian-born anarchist, shot and stabbed industrialist Henry Clay Frick in his Pittsburgh, Pennsylvania, office, wounding him.[29] Frick was chairman of the Carnegie Steel Company where nine steel workers were killed during a labor dispute. (6) Radical union leaders planted a bomb in the offices of the *Los Angeles Times* in 1910 that killed 21 people.[30] The bombing was in retaliation for the paper's anti-union stance. (7) In 1915, Eric Muenter planted a bomb with a timing device that detonated in the Reception Room of the U.S. Senate to dissuade the United States from entering World War I on the side of Great Britain and France. When arrested, he committed suicide by beating his head against the wall of his jail cell.[31] (8) A man driving a horse-drawn cart stopped at Wall Street in New York City in 1920 and disappeared into a crowd. Minutes later a bomb exploded, killing at least 30 people and injuring 300 others.[32] The attack was attributed to anarchists and never solved (see Figure 1–3). During the 1880s–1920s, anarchists were also active in Europe, the most important example of which is the assassination in 1914 of Austria's Archduke Ferdinand and his wife Duchess Sophie, which led to World War I.

Despite such terrorist events, America's level of concern regarding terrorism has historically been quite low. As recently as 60 years ago it got little attention. It was something that happened oceans away, "over there," in Europe and in the Middle East as several cases illustrate. In Spain, the Euskadi Ta Askatasuna (ETA, Basque Homeland and Freedom) was formed in 1959 with a goal to create a separate homeland in Northern Spain for ethnic

Anarchist
An anarchist believes in the political theory of anarchy. Pure anarchy is characterized by the absence of a central government and strong cooperation between members of a society. Anarchists seek to overthrow rulers and governments. Practical anarchists recognize the impossibility of actually achieving pure anarchy. Consequentially, they are willing to settle for a weak government that is minimally intrusive in the lives of its citizens.

FIGURE 1–3
One of the early anarchist bombings in the United States occurred in New York's Union Square during 1900. The anarchist only succeeded in killing two people, himself and one other man. This photograph of their bodies is believed to have been taken 20 seconds after the bomb exploded.

(George Grantham Bain Collection, Library of Congress)

Black September Organization
The Palestinian nationalist group that massacred members of the Israeli delegation at the 1972 Summer Olympics in Munich, Germany.

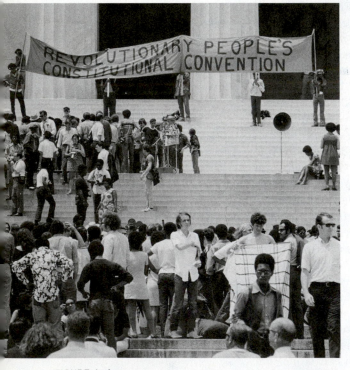

FIGURE 1–4
In 1970, the Black Panther Party called for a constitutional convention, which would unite women, gays, blacks, and independence for Puerto Rico into a comprehensive revolutionary movement. They met on the steps of the Lincoln Memorial in Washington D.C., to no great effect.

(Courtesy O'Halloran Thomas J/Leffler, Warren K/Library of Congress Prints and Photographs Divisio)

Basques.[33] ETA quickly adopted terror tactics, such as assassinations. The Baader-Meinhof Group (BMG) wanted to create more socialist states in Europe and between 1968–1977 and carried out deadly bombings.[34] Its successor was the Red Army Faction (RAF), which decided in 1998 that its goals could not be achieved and ceased operations. The Palestinian nationalist group **Black September Organization** massacred members of the Israeli delegation to the 1972 Summer Olympics in Munich, Germany.[35] The 1970s saw a handful of aircraft hijackings or "skyjackings." Despite these variations in attack modes, the country of Israel and its citizens have been the most consistent target of terrorists. Arguably, it has been under siege since its formation in 1948.

Despite theses events, terrorism has until relatively recently been at the margin of U.S. policy. A variety of events account for this position. It was a distant event that was not directed at the United States. The National Aeronautics and Space Administration (NASA) had people focused on manned orbits of the earth and a landing on the moon. The American Civil Rights Movement was also prominent in news media reports. Finally, the Vietnam War consumed our resources and energy, particularly from 1965 through 1975.

From the 1960s to 9/11, several important radical movements, such as Students for a Democratic Society, existed in the U.S. and some terrorist attacks were launched on Americans abroad. The Black Panther Party (See Figure 1–4), founded in 1966 was militant and violent from its beginnings, although it also provided some social assistance programs. It generally viewed governments as racist and repressive. Beginning in 1969, the Weather Underground, the "Weathermen," sought to overthrow the federal government, bombing the Capitol Building and the Pentagon in 1970 and 1971, respectively.

In 1979, Iranian Muslim extremists seized the U.S. Embassy in Tehran and held Americans hostage for over a year. In 1988, two Libyan men planted a bomb on Pan Am Flight 103 that was flying from London to New York City. It exploded over Lockerbie, Scotland, killing all 259 passengers and 11 Scots on the ground.[36] From 31,000 feet the explosion rained debris over 845 square miles,[37] creating what may be the largest crime scene ever processed. The motive for the bombing is believed to have been the reaction of Libya's leader, the late Muammar

Quick Facts
The Assassination of Rabbi Meir Kahane

Rabbi Kahane formed the Jewish Defense League, a right-wing group, to protect elderly and poor Jews living in unstable neighborhoods in New York City.[38] El Sayyid Nosair, a naturalized U.S. citizen born in Egypt, was acquitted of murdering Kahane in 1990, but received a prison sentence for possessing a pistol.[39] Nosair did so in the belief that Kahane declared war on Muslims, openly advocating genocide and ethnic cleansing.[40] Nosair later received a life sentence for being a co-plotter of the 1993 bombing attack on the World Trade Center.

Gaddafi, to several sharp, but brief, military actions in which his country lost aircraft and a naval vessel to the United States. In 1983, truck bombs exploded in the U.S. Marine Corps compound in Beirut, Lebanon, killing 241 Marines and 21 members of other services.

In 1998, the U.S. Embassies in Kenya and Tanzania were simultaneously hit by truck-driving suicide bombers. Thousands of people were injured and 224 died from those attacks. President Clinton responded by authorizing cruise missile attacks on terrorist facilities in Afghanistan and the Sudan.[41] A U.S. missile strike was made on a pharmaceutical factory in the Sudan on the grounds it was making chemical weapons, but the accuracy of that assessment has been debated within the American government.

In 1993, radical Muslims made their first attack on the North Tower of the World Trade Center in New York City. A Ryder truck with 1,200 pounds of explosives was parked in the underground garage of one of the towers.[42] When the explosives detonated, a hole 100 feet wide and several stories deep was created. Six people were killed, more than 1,000 injured, and 50,000 people were evacuated.[43] Only one of the seven perpetrators has escaped capture and conviction. In custody, one of the perpetrators said the plan was to have the North Tower knock down the other tower.[44] Eight years later the 9/11 attacks did cause both towers to collapse. In Yemen during 2000, two suicide terrorists detonated a boat filled with explosives alongside the USS *Cole*. This attack produced casualties and major damage, but more importantly it also seized the attention of the American government. However, the event that would transform our national agenda was yet to occur.

The attacks on September 11, 2001, were devastating, frightening, and compelled a national response. The attacks focused the United States on preventing terrorism from reaching our shores. Terrorism is currently the most important word in our political vocabulary and America annually spends billions of dollars combat it.[45] Despite America's relatively short history of dealing with terrorism, knowledgeable observers have distinguished between the "old" and "new" terrorism. One of the early voices in calling attention to the new terrorism was Laqueur, who in 1999 foresaw that "A new age of terrorism is dawning, but the old terrorism is far from dead"[46] (See Box 1–1). Other historical accounts of terrorism appear in connection with other topics in subsequent chapters.

There is a growing body of literature on terrorism, but there is still much to learn. However, two case studies demonstrate that we have come a long way from our earliest understandings of terrorism:

1) The word "terror" gained currency in the modern era during the French Revolution (1789–1799), which was caused by political, economic, and social upheaval. **Robespierre** bears substantial responsibility for the period within the revolution called the **Reign of Terror** (September 1793–July 1794).[47] It would have been better for France if Robespierre had remained an unimportant lawyer in Northern France.[48] Instead, he joined the revolutionary government in 1793. Robespierre quickly developed an appetite for using the guillotine to instill fear, and during the reign of terror over 16,000 people lost their heads to the guillotine,[49] including the King and his wife.

Robespierre lost the support of the people when he allowed a law to be passed that permitted the execution of those who were merely *suspected* of not supporting the revolution. Finally, the guillotine claimed Robespierre himself before the regime of terror ran its course. He attempted suicide to avoid public execution, but the gunshot merely shattered his jaw. In a 1794 speech, Robespierre claimed "Terror is nothing but prompt, severe, and inflexible justice. It is thus the emanation of virtue."[50] Ultimately for him, it seems that terror and virtue became synonymous.

Robespierre
A Frenchman and key architect of the reign of terror. He believed terror was the speedy, severe, and inflexible administration of justice from which virtue flowed. Seemingly, terror and virtue became synonymous to him.

Reign of Terror
Particularly violent period during the French Revolution France (1793-1794) when the guillotine was used to behead over 16,000 people including Robespierre. See Robespierre.

Box 1–1
The Old and New Terrorism

These descriptions of the "old" and "new" terrorism are broad. As a consequence there are exceptions to the way they are profiled here. Moreover, the "old" never really disappeared. Instead, the amount of terrorism fitting its description simply declined. Simultaneously, the "new" had its roots in the old, yet produced its own identity. To some extent, the new terrorism arose as the motives changed from predominately secular, non-religious reasons to a high frequency of religion-based reasons. As a result, the news media, governments, and scholars substantially shifted their attention to the new forms of terrorism. The descriptions of "old" and "new" terrorism provide some understanding of where terrorism has been and how it has changed.

The "**old terrorism**" generally is described as having specific political, social, and economic goals.[51] Because many, if not most, old terrorism goals were subnational they had some potential of being achieved by negotiation between the terrorists and the national government. As an illustration, ETA was ultimately able to obtain a Basque "homeland" with substantial autonomy within Spain. The old terrorism movements had a clearly defined organizational structure[52] and they targeted symbols of the government or social order being opposed.[53] Illustrations include embassies, national airlines, banks, and kidnappings and assassinations of business, military, and diplomatic personnel.[54] A communiqué in the name of the movement was issued after an attack that claimed responsibility for the attack and explained why it was carried out. In short, the old terrorism was comprehensible, albeit reprehensible.[55]

It is often difficult to specify with precision when a new trend begins. Some authorities point to 1979, when radicalized Muslims in Tehran, Iran, took U.S. Embassy staff hostages in 1979, as the onset of the "**new terrorism**." Others point to attacks in 1993 and 1995 as its starting period. In 1993 radicalized Muslims exploded a truck bomb in the parking garage under the North Tower of the World Trade Center.[56] In addition to the deaths and injuries, some $500 million in damages were caused.[57] In 1995 Sarin, a nerve agent, was released in the Tokyo subway system by Aum Shinrikyo. The Sarin killed six and 6,000 others received medical treatment. Aum is a religious cult that teaches that the end of the world is near and only its believers will survive the apocalypse.[58]

The new terrorism deliberately targets unarmed civilians with the desire to inflict mass casualties. The number killed is of vital importance because mass casualties create greater fear in the general population. A radical religious interpretation undergirds many terrorist attacks around the globe. Believing they are carrying out the will of God, some terrorists willingly become suicide bombers because they believe immediate entry into Paradise will be their reward.

The new terrorist organizational structures are often difficult to discern because many of the new terrorism groups are autonomous or only loosely affiliated.[59] Unlike the prior generation of terrorism, the new terrorism is more international.[60] Such movements also inspire the "amateur" **lone wolf attacks**.[61] The new terror organizations are nimble, quick to learn, and increasingly technologically savvy and operationally competent.[62] Terrorist movements based on radical religious interpretations may not claim responsibility for their attacks. They are uninterested in negotiating settlements and some groups seem eager to acquire weapons of mass destruction (WMDs).[63]

It is important to note that as terrorism continues to evolve, there are new "new terrorisms." Illustratively, system disruption attacks are a "new war" and IS's conquering lands in which to establish a caliphate is also a new iteration. However, IS still resembles other acts of terrorism in that it targets non-combatants.

How are the old terrorism and the lone wolf attacks contrasted?

Terrorism (General/Working definition)
The deliberate and unlawful use of threats or actual violence to inculcate fear, intended to intimidate or coerce individuals, groups, or governments to change their political, social or religious basis.

Old terrorism
Generally, it had specific political, social, and economic goals. Because the goals were limited some could ultimately be resolved by negotiation.

New terrorism
Most commonly, a religious belief undergirds the violence. New terrorism is more transnational than the old and unlike the old, it deliberately targets civilians/non-combatants to create fear. Many groups are autonomous or loosely affiliated with another group. Inspires lone wolf attacks. The new terrorism is nimble, quick to learn, technologically savvy, and operationally competent.

Lone wolf attack
A violent attack by a single perpetrator, acting alone, without any direction or assistance from an organization or another person.

2) In 1877, Colonel Trepov was the Governor of St. Petersburg, Russia, and had a man flogged for not removing his hat as Trepov approached.[64] Outraged at this injustice, Vera Zasulich shot and severely wounded Trepov the next year. At trial she was successfully defended by two claims by the defense. First, she was described as "a girl," although she was 29 years old. Second, she was acting to right a wrong as a terrorist, and therefore could not be a criminal.[65]

A **general working definition of terrorism** is the deliberate, unlawful use of threats, force, or actual violence to inculcate fear, intended to intimidate or coerce individuals, groups, or governments to change their political, social, religious, or ideological basis. Although noted in Box 1–1, it bears repeating that presently the main victims of terrorist violence are usually unarmed civilians unable to defend themselves. Table 1–1 summarizes the United States' legal definitions for international and domestic terrorism.

Because the United States is just one political state and suffered significant terrorist attacks, it was easier to enact and amend terrorist legislation. In contrast, the United Nations has not been able to draft a definition of terrorism acceptable to all member nations because they reserve the political right to themselves to determine what acts constitute terrorism. In 2002, the **European Union** offered a framework for terrorism legislation that was adopted by all of its members. In 2008, that framework was amended by prohibiting certain activities associated with terrorism, for example, teaching others how to make bombs and use firearms for terroristic purposes.[66] Members of the European Union are free to add their own legislative concerns to the European Union's supplied framework.

Quick Facts
The French Revolution, Royalty, and the Guillotine

In 1793, both King Louis XVI and his wife Marie Antoinette (1755–1793) were executed by the guillotine. It is alleged that when she heard that peasants were complaining they had no bread to eat, she said "Let them eat cake." While this "indictment" of her has been repeated often, there is no evidence that she actually uttered this phrase.

Ethnic Arabs have historically suffered from acts of terrorism, often from neighboring nations. Arab states were an early adopter of a definition of terrorism and terrorism offenses. In 1998, the Council of Arab Ministers of the Interior and the Council of Arab Ministers of Justice adopted a definition of terrorism: "Any act or threat of violence, whatever its motives or purposes, that occurs for the advancement of an individual or collective criminal agenda causing terror among people, causing fear by harming them, or placing their lives, liberty or security in danger, or aiming to cause damage to the environment or to public or private installations or property or to occupy or to seize them, or aiming to jeopardize a national resource." Mainline Muslims have been invested in seeing that their religion not be caught up in definitions of terrorism, which is both predictable and appropriate.

While the "new terrorism" targets non-combatants this practice is in sharp contrast to **selective terrorism**. The Irish attempted to gain their country's independence from the British Commonwealth during the Anglo-Irish war of 1919–1921. Lacking a "real" military, their ragtag **Irish Republican Army** (IRA) fought a guerilla war. The IRA picked the places to attack and then quickly faded away. The IRA's commander, **Michael Collins** (see Figure 1–5), used selective terrorism, targeting supporters, key members, and the institutions of the British Commonwealth. This is sharp contrast to the practice associated with the new terrorism of using indiscriminate violence to cause mass casualties among defenseless civilians.

■ TABLE 1–1
United States' Definitions of International and Domestic Terrorism

International terrorism means activities that:

(A) Involve violent acts or acts dangerous to human life that are a violation of the criminal laws of the United States or of any State, or that would be a criminal violation if committed within the jurisdiction of the United States or of any State;

(B) Appear to be intended to:
 (i) intimidate or coerce a civilian population;
 (ii) influence the policy of a government by intimidation or coercion; or
 (iii) affect the conduct of a government by mass destruction, assassination, or kidnapping; and

(C) Occur primarily outside the territorial jurisdiction of the United States, or transcend national boundaries in terms of the means by which they are accomplished, the persons they appear intended to intimidate or coerce, or the locale in which their perpetrators operate or seek asylum.

Domestic terrorism means activities that:

(A) Involve acts dangerous to human life that are a violation of the criminal laws of the United States or of any State;

(B) Appear to be intended to:
 (i) intimidate or coerce a civilian population;
 (ii) influence the policy of a government by intimidation or coercion; or
 (iii) affect the conduct of a government by mass destruction, assassination, or kidnapping; and

(C) occur primarily within the territorial jurisdiction of the United States.

Source: 18 United States Code, Chapter 113B, January 1, 2012.

Information Link
On the Internet visit the Google "1998 Arab Convention on the Suppression of Terrorism" to read the entire text of this seminal document.

European Union
The EU is a political and economic union founded in 1993 with 28 member nations that are primarily located in Europe.

Selective terrorism
Tactic advocated by Michael Collins, Commander of the Irish Republic Army (IRA). Instead of using unfocused, indiscriminate violence that killed many people, Collins used selective violence to focus on the people and institutions that supported continued British subjugation of Ireland. See Michael Collins and Irish Republican Army.

Irish Republican Army
Ireland's military arm during the Anglo-Irish War of 1919–1921.

Michael Collins
Commander of the Irish Republican Army (IRA) and advocate of selective terrorism.

International terrorism
As provided for by federal law, international terrorism involves violent acts or acts dangerous to human life that violate federal or state laws if committed within the jurisdiction of the United States or any state, which appear to be intended to intimidate or coerce a civilian population, influence the policy of government by mass destruction, assassination, or kidnapping, and occur primarily outside of the territorial jurisdiction of the United States or transcend national boundaries by the means by which they are accomplished, the persons they appear to intimidate or coerce, or the locale in which the perpetrators operate or seek asylum. See the federal definition in Table 1-1.

Domestic terrorism
As provided by federal law, domestic terrorism involves violations of federal or state law that appear to intimidate or coerce a civilian population or affect the policy of a government by intimidation or coercion, or affect the conduct of a government by mass destruction, assassination, or kidnapping and occur primarily with the territorial jurisdiction of the United States. See the federal legal definition in Table 1-1.

The EU's terrorism framework consists of:

(1) An objective element, as it refers to a list of instances of serious criminal conduct (murder, bodily injuries, hostage taking, extortion, fabrication of weapons, committing attacks, threatening to commit any of the above, etc.) and

(2) A subjective element, as these acts are deemed to be terrorist offences when committed with the aim of seriously

intimidating a population, unduly compelling a government or international organisation to perform or abstain from performing any act, or seriously destabilising or destroying the fundamental political, constitutional, economic or social structures of a country or an international organization.[67]

Individual perspective
A particular way of thinking about something, reduced to a simple image: on which side of the street do you stand?

Boston Tea Party
December 16, 1773, tax protest when colonists, disguised as Indians, threw tea from ships into Boston harbor.

Terrorism: Individual Perspective and Culture

Our views of terrorism are principally shaped by our individual perspectives and culture, a thread that runs throughout this book. A person's perspectives come from a process that incorporates multiple sources of data and at least some analysis of it. In contrast, culture is a pervasive collective experience that tends to produce people who share many values and ideas.

Individual Perspective

Individual perspective results from the process of evaluating issues, events, other people, groups, and nations and the underlying beliefs, intentions, and actions in order to assign meaning to them.[68] Individual perspective is produced out of a thoughtful and deliberate process that is to some degree analytical. In contrast, opinion is formed internally and may not rest on external observations or any degree of analysis. Opinion may be favorable, neutral, or malignant, such as racial hatred.

Reduced to a simple image, individual perspective is "what side of the street you stand on" for any given issue. Different people can see or know about the same event, but assign different meanings to it. The **Boston Tea Party** illustrates this point. In 1773, a group of 116 colonial men, some poorly disguised as Indians, boarded three ships at Boston's Griffin's Wharf, forced the crews below decks, and threw 90,000 pounds of the British East India Company's tea into the harbor (see Figure 1–6). Some colonists saw this is a bold act protesting English tax policy, whereas others were appalled by the act. Many colonists wanted no part of the subsequent revolution against England and moved to Canada, the Caribbean, and back to England. People in England saw the Boston Tea Party as defiance of the authority of Parliament and King George III. It is likely that everyone roughly had the same information. However, they formed radically different conclusions based on their perspectives. The Boston Tea Party happened before the idea of America becoming an independent nation took root in the colonies. However, it was an early event on the road to the American Revolution (1775–1783) and some theorists think it falls into the separatist/nationalism category of terrorism discussed in Chapter 8.

A more contemporary example of individual perspective comes from the terrorist attacks on September 11, 2001. The most common individual perspective is that al-Qaeda was responsible. However, conspiracy theorists have offered "competing" explanations, such as the government knew about the plot but didn't stop it because they wanted a reason to invade Iraq and Afghanistan. That reasoning is reminiscent of the allegation that President Roosevelt had prior knowledge of the Japanese plan to attack Pearl Harbor, but allowed it to happen to overcome Congress's sentiment to remain neutral in the war that was already being waged in Europe and Asia.

FIGURE 1–5
Michael Collins (1890–1922), often referred to as the "Big Fella," commanded the IRA and made effective use of selective terrorism. In 1922, he was the lone person killed in an ambush, suggesting he may have been the only target. Although a number of accounts have been written about the event, none has been widely accepted as authoritative.
(Courtesy Library of Congress)

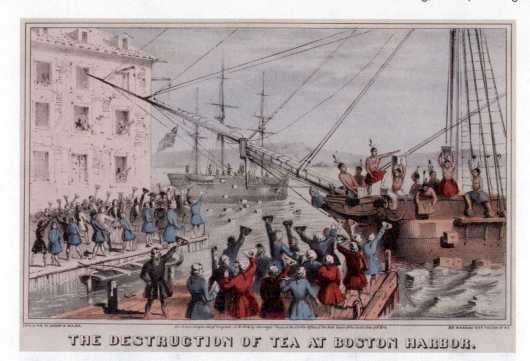

THE DESTRUCTION OF TEA AT BOSTON HARBOR.

FIGURE 1–6
Thousands of jubilant colonists greet those involved in the Boston Tea Party. Two-thirds of the raiders were 20 years old or younger.
(Nathaniel Currier, 1846. Library of Congress)

Al-Qaeda views the United States and other Western powers through a radicalized, extremist Muslim prism. The former head of al-Qaeda, **Usama bin Laden**[§] (1957–2011), helped plot the 9/11 attacks that turned four hijacked airliners into guided missiles. There were no survivors on any of the hijacked aircraft. American Airlines Flight 11 and United Airlines Flight 175 brought down the World Trade Center's Twin Towers in New York City, killing 3,000 civilians (see Figure 1–7). Trapped on burning floors, some people leapt to their death to avoid being burned alive.

Also on September 11, 2001, American Airlines Flight 77 struck the Pentagon (see Figure 1–8). Passengers aboard United Airlines Flight 93 courageously fought to retake

Usama bin Laden
Saudi Arabian-born American ally who supported Afghanistan mujahedeen's resistance against the Soviets. When the Soviets left, he turned against the Americans and masterminded the 9/11 attacks. Head of al-Qaeda until his death in a 2011 raid on his compound in Pakistan by U.S. troops (Seal Team 6).

FIGURE 1–7
Two days after the 9/11 attacks, a rescue specialist searches for survivors in the smoldering wreckage of the World Trade Center.

(Courtesy of the Federal Emergency Management Agency, photograph by Andrea Booher)

[§] Although "Osama" bin Laden is often used, his proper name is Usama bin Laden.

FIGURE 1–8
A portion of the damage caused at the Pentagon by the 9/11 attack that effectively used American Airlines Flight 77 as a guided missile.

(Courtesy Department of Defense)

control of their aircraft. Although it crashed in a field and near Shanksville, Pennsylvania, the passengers denied the terrorists use of it against their intended target. Most likely, that target was either the White House or the U.S. Capitol.[69] The attacks sent shock waves through city, state, and federal governments. Leaders debated whether more waves of attacks with deadlier weapons were coming. There was also a great deal of misinformation, such as the report that the U.S. Capitol had been bombed. The Federal Aviation Administration (FAA) ordered the immediate landing ("pancaking") of nearly 4,500 flights in America's airspace. Some 350,000 passengers found themselves grounded miles from their destination.[70] All arriving international flights were immediately diverted to Canada. Both of these actions were taken because the United States was unsure of how many other planes might be used as weapons. Other measures implemented included the evacuation of some elements of the federal government from Washington, D.C., and closing the U.S.-Mexican border.

Cultural Perspective

President George W. Bush characterized the September 11, 2001, attacks as "evil, despicable acts"[71] and Palestinian leader Yasser Arafat also condemned the attacks.[72] However, others in Middle Eastern countries crowded into the streets and celebrated joyously, praising **Allah** and chanting "**Allah u Akbar**."

Culture is defined as the shared beliefs, experiences, and behaviors that cause its members to substantially view things in a similar manner. In contrast to individual perspective, culture is a collective, accumulated experience. This shared experience often distinguishes one culture from another, including language, values, customs, history, law, and religion. Of course, sharing a common culture is not a guarantee that all members will have the same perspectives.

Anwar al-Awlaki (1971–2011) represents someone who was born in one culture, but changed his cultural identity (see Figure 1–9 and Box 1–2). He was born in New Mexico to Yemeni parents and earned degrees from Colorado State and San Diego State universities. After becoming a Muslim cleric, al-Awlaki was linked to over 19 terrorist operations.[73] He was adept at using social media to spread his propaganda messages of hatred and violence against the West and to attract and radicalize recruits. **Radicalization** describes the process

---

Information Link
Visit the 9/11 Memorial at www.911memorial.org. Explore the website and listen to the oral histories of first responders, recovery workers, and survivors of the attack.

Allah
Arabic, literally "The God;" the Islamic God.

Allah u Akbar
Arabic, Allah (God) is great or Allah is the greatest.

Culture
the shared beliefs, experiences, and behaviors, such as language, values, customs, history, law, and religion, that causes its members to substantially interpret things in a similar manner and distinguishes then from other cultures.

Anwar al-Awlaki
Born in New Mexico to Yemeni parents. Became radicalized Islamic cleric linked to 19 terrorist operations. Killed in Yemen by drone in 2011.

Radicalization
the processing of acquiring and holding extremist beliefs. See violent extremism.

of acquiring and holding extremist views. **Violent extremism** describes violent action taken on the basis of those extreme beliefs.[77]

The present radical Muslim culture views Western nations in general, and the United States in particular, very negatively. The people of Western nations are seen as the new or neo-crusaders making war on Islam, occupying its countries, misleading some of its leaders, plundering its riches, and defiling its women and holy sites. These issues are discussed in more detail in Chapter 4.

Violent extremism
Violent action taken on the basis of extremist beliefs.

Issues in Conceptualizing, Defining, and Understanding Terrorism

A number of factors contribute to the difficulties we have in understanding terrorism, including (1) multiple and complex definitions have proliferated; (2) the evidence base for terrorism is insufficient; (3) terrorism is a contested concept; (4) terrorism is evocative—it appeals to emotion and not intellect; (5) political power often determines those who are labeled "terrorists"; and (6) past prosecutorial decisions within the United States have confused people.

Bermuda Triangle of Terrorism
The hundreds of competing definitions of terrorism.

Definitions Have Proliferated

The existence of many definitions of terrorism was mentioned earlier in this chapter and needs further comment. There is a natural, physical world that exists and can be scientifically analyzed, for example, the composition of soil. To make sense of other things we intellectually construct meanings. The Fujita Scale (F-Scale) was created in 1971 to measure the intensity of tornadoes. The F-Scale and other constructs are artifacts or products of our intellect.

What we call reality largely consists of the world we create in our heads, which are filled with social constructs. They help us understand and organize our lives by virtue of the meaning we attach to them. Examples include marriage, loyalty, social status, happiness, and "bad neighborhoods." Some things such as gender have inherent qualities, but we create stereotypes about them, for example, "Women aren't good at science" and "Men are sloppy."

Terrorism is a non-natural world event and cannot be measured and characterized with scientific accuracy. Terrorism requires constructs to explain it. Figure 1–10 depicts how we construct our understanding of terrorism. It is a process that can be endlessly repeated, which accounts for numerous and complex definitions. Scholars and governmental agencies often develop definitions of terrorism that meet their needs. The combined efforts to define terrorism have created what Jenkins describes as the **"Bermuda Triangle of Terrorism."**[78] Definitions are intended to allow people to accurately distinguish one construct from another so that when we apply a label, such as terrorism, it is done with clear meaning. However, the surplus of terrorism definitions prevents us from doing so.

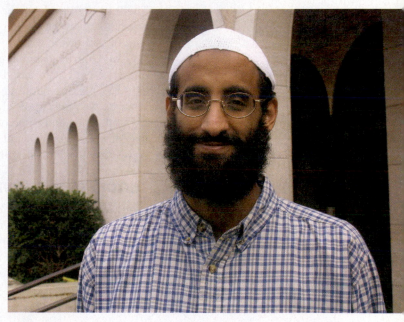

FIGURE 1–9
Anwar al-Awlaki in Falls Church, Virginia, about five weeks after 9/11, looking benign or perhaps smug. Several of the 9/11 hijackers attended the mosque where al-Awlaki was an imam. Because of his involvement in terrorist operations against the United States he was killed in Yemen from a missile fired from an American drone. That action ignited a debate over whether the President can authorize the death of a U.S. citizen without a trial and based on secret intelligence findings.
(© Dennis Brack/Newscom)

Box 1-2
Anwar al-Awlaki

Born in Las Cruces, New Mexico, Anwar al-Awlaki became a leading member of al-Qaeda's affiliate in Yemen. He was a senior recruiter as well as a spiritual motivator for al-Qaeda. He met with Umar Farouk Abdulmutallab (the Christmas Day bomber), who in late 2009 attempted to blow up a Northwest Airlines plane with a bomb concealed in his underwear. Major Nidal Malik Hassan, who killed 13 people and wounded many others at Fort Hood, Texas, exchanged emails in 2009 with al-Awlaki. Faisal Shahzad, who tried in 2010 to set off a car bomb in New York City's Times Square, called al-Awlaki an "inspiration."

Because al-Awlaki was involved in many operations, the federal government took the unprecedented action of placing him on a 2010 "capture or kill list" approved by President Barak Obama. After several attempts to capture him failed, al-Awlaki was killed in Yemen (September 30, 2011) by a Hellfire missile fired from a remotely flown drone.[79] Al-Awlaki's death caused significant controversy. The "targeted killing" of an American citizen was unprecedented in the United States. He was never charged nor convicted of a crime yet was killed by a CIA-led drone attack. The same attack killed three other individuals linked to al-Qaeda. The U.S. response to critics was swift and certain as President Obama announced:

> "The death of al-Awlaki is a major blow to al-Qaeda's most active operational affiliate. He took the lead in planning and directing efforts to murder innocent Americans ... and he repeatedly called on individuals in the United States and around the globe to kill innocent men, women and children to advance a murderous agenda. [The strike] is further proof that al-Qaeda and its affiliates will find no safe haven anywhere in the world.[80]

Source: Expert from "Two U.S.-Born Terrorists Killed in CIA-Led Drone Strike" by Jennifer Griffin. Published by Foxnew.com, © Sep 30, 2011.

Are there legal and moral issues surrounding the use of drones by U.S. intelligence and military forces to kill terrorist suspects, including American citizens, in foreign countries? If so, what importance should be attached to them?

The Evidence Base for Terrorism Is Insufficient

The terrorism evidence base supporting planning, strategic thinking, and policy-making is weak. A review of 14,006 terrorism articles over a 32-year period revealed that 54 percent of them were written in 2001 and 2002,[81] immediately following 9/11. Articles in peer-reviewed journals numbered only 4,458.[82] Ninety-six percent of those were "think" pieces, only 3 percent were based on empirical analysis, and case studies accounted for just 1 percent.[83] Without a publically accessible empirical database the question can be fairly raised: What do we really know about terrorism? Undoubtedly, such data exists within the control of intelligence and some other agencies and much of it should not be revealed because it may disclose methods and agents. Still, the lack of publically accessible empirical data may contribute to some misunderstandings about terrorism.

Terrorism Is a Contested Concept

Hezbollah (Arabic for the "Party of God") is a Muslim group that is simultaneously viewed as a political organization, terrorist group, and militia. It is primarily located in the Middle Eastern country of Lebanon and is headed by the radical cleric Sheik Hassan Nasrallah. Hezbollah was formed in response to the Israeli invasion of Lebanon in 1982. Hezbollah receives substantial arms, training, money, and intelligence from Syria and Iran.[84] This support is a **force multiplier**, which increases Hezbollah's operational capabilities and lethality. In late 2012, Hezbollah obtained a drone from Iran and assembled it. Hezbollah flew the unmanned aircraft into Israel where it was shot down.[85] The addition of many strike-capable drones to Hezbollah's inventory would be a significant escalation of its operational capabilities. Syria describes Hezbollah as a militia resisting Israeli aggression.

Hezbollah has operatives worldwide—in Europe, South and North America, and Africa. It is not presently viewed as a security threat by Latin American nations. They see it as a legitimate political organization.[86] However, some host nations have concerns that Hezbollah's presence could complicate their relationship with the United States.

Latin America's view of Hezbollah as a legitimate political organization hampers America's counterterrorism efforts. Hezbollah's presence in Latin America gives it a closer geographic location to the United States than its Middle East home. From this

Hezbollah
Arabic, "Party of Allahu." Fundamentalist Islamic FTO, supported by Iran and Syria, originally Lebanon-based, now present in many other locations.

Force multiplier
A military term that means a capability that when added to, and employed by, a combat unit significantly enhances its combat potential and increases the likelihood of a successful mission.

Terrorism Label Applied

Violent Event

Definition of Terrorism Written

FIGURE 1–10
The Definition Triangle
(Drawn with modification from Alex Schmid, "The Definitional Problem,"[87] *Case Western Reserve Journal of International Law*, Vol. 36, No. 2/3, Spring 2004, Table 1–18, p. 400)

Quick Facts
"Paper Terrorism"

Related to the proliferation of terrorism definitions is that "terrorism" is an elastic term that can be used in many contexts. "Paper Terrorism" refers to bogus suits, baseless liens, and other measures that are filed to clog the courts, harm the credit of public officials, hold up the sale or refinancing of property, and consume public resources to deal with them. A "sovereign citizen," angered by getting a traffic citation, filled false liens totaling $800,000 against the Chief of the Police Department employing the officer who issued the citation.[88]

To bolster their frivolous actions "sovereigns" create fictitious or misuse genuine documents, their own license plates and driver's licenses. Right-wing anarchists at heart, sovereigns believe all existing governments are illegitimate.[89] Sovereigns tend not to be violent, but the potential of dealing with sovereigns does pose a threat. During 2000–2012, sovereigns killed six police officers.[90]

Perhaps most paper terrorism is initiated by members of the Sovereign Citizen anti-government movement and sympathizers. There may be 300,000 sovereigns in a loose collection of groups.[91] The FBI considers sovereign-citizen extremists as a domestic terrorism movement.[92] At least 15 states have made it a crime to file "paper terrorism"–type actions. The Sovereign Citizen movement is further discussed in Chapter 8.

---

forward position Hezbollah could more easily launch attacks on the United States at the urging of its state sponsors of terrorism, Syria and Iran. Hezbollah is based on the minority Shi'a tradition of Islam and opposes the primary tradition of Sunni Islam, more commonly found throughout the Middle East and the world. Hence, on religion Hezbollah is at odds with most Islamic nations. The principles of Shi'a and Sunni Islam are discussed in Chapter 3; the radical perspectives of Hezbollah are elaborated upon in Chapter 4.

Hamas (The Palestinian Islamic Resistance Movement) is another radical fundamentalist Muslim Middle East organization designated as a FTO (foreign terrorist organization) by the U.S. government. Hamas is opposed to the existence of Israel and maintains a well-armed militia or paramilitary arm. It also provides substantial social services in Gaza, the West Bank, and Israel. Hamas funds have traditionally come from private donors in Saudi Arabia, oil-rich Persian Gulf nations, and charities operated for its benefit. Syria and Iran also provide support to Hamas.

Since the legislative elections of 2007, Hamas has been consolidating its control in the **Gaza Strip** (see Figure 1–11). Under the 1947 United Nations plan that partitioned Palestine, Israel was created. The Gaza Strip was to be an independent Arab country. However, Arab leaders rejected the plan because it created a Jewish homeland from territory formerly occupied by Arabs and religious sites sacred to Islam were located in Israel. The Gaza Strip is now claimed and governed by the Palestinian Authority under the 1993 Oslo Peace Accords between Israel and the Palestinian Liberation Organization (PLO). The Gaza Strip's long border with Israel has been problematic and the historical development of this conflict is further explored in Chapter 2. Attacks by terrorists on Israel and retaliation raids can easily be launched because of their geographical proximity.

In 2012, Hamas was actively fighting against terrorist groups affiliated with al-Qaeda because their presence and activities threatened an unofficial cease-fire between Hamas and Israel.[93] Israel killed the Hamas military commander Ahmed al-Jabari in 2012. As a consequence, a wider exchange of rockets took place between the two countries. This violence threatened to spiral out of control, but fortunately did not, begging the hotly contested question of "who is the terrorist?" To make matters even more confusing, Hamas won a majority of seats in the Palestinian Parliament in the January 2006 election, making it the legitimate ruling power in the Gaza Strip and the West Bank and forcing the United States and Israel to now negotiate with "former terrorists." In 2014, Hamas fired hundreds of rockets into Israel, which responded with hundreds of air strikes on launch sites, munitions storage locations, and Hamas command and control centers. This threatened to engulf the region in a wider conflict until an uneasy peace was restored.

Hamas

Arabic, "zeal," fundamentalist foreign terrorist organization (FTO) that provides extensive social service. It also has a well-armed militia/paramilitary arm. Opposed to the existence of Israel, Hamas has a strong presence in Palestine and Israel.

Gaza Strip

Administered by the Palestinian Authority, 25 miles long and from 3.5 to 7 miles wide. Situated on Eastern Mediterranean, bounded by Egypt to the South and Israel to its East and North.

FIGURE 1–11
The Gaza Strip is 25 miles long and has a width of 3.5 to 7 miles with a population of 1.5 million Palestinians.
(Courtesy of the U.S. Department of State)

Box 1-3
The United States' View of Hezbollah

The U.S. Department of State lists Hezbollah as a **foreign terrorist organization (FTO)**. An organization is listed as such if it engages in terrorist activity or has retained the capacity or intention to do so and it threatens U.S. nationals or America's national security.

Hezbollah's portfolio includes (1) two suicide truck bombings in 1983 in Beirut, Lebanon—the first was at the U.S. Embassy and the second at a Peacekeeping Compound largely staffed by American Marines; 2) the suicide bombings in Argentina of the Israeli Embassy (1992) and a Jewish Center (1994); and (3) the 1996 suicide bombing of Khobar Towers in Saudi Arabia

that killed 19 Americans, one Saudi, and 372 members of other nationalities.

There are several actual terrorist organizations that include "Islamic Jihad" in their full name. After Hezbollah's most notable attacks, a mysterious "Islamic Jihad" claimed credit for them. In some quarters it is believed this particular Islamic Jihad is a fictional group whose purpose is to confuse enemies and draw attention away from Hezbollah.[94]

Why is it difficult to accurately link a specific act of terrorism to particular terrorist groups? Are there drawbacks to labeling a group a FTO?

Foreign terrorist organization (FTO)
The U.S. Department of State lists an organization as a "foreign terrorist organization" if it engages in terrorist activity or has retained the capacity or intention to do so and it threatens United States nationals or America's national security.

Terrorism Is Evocative—It Appeals to Emotion and Not Intellect

Something that is evocative has the power to stir people. It produces strong feelings and causes them to recall potent images and revisit powerful memories. The mention of terrorism on the news rivets our attention and we are compelled to pay attention until we know the details. The public reaction to the 9/11 attacks was evocative and instructive. In the immediate wake of the attacks, a majority of Americans reported difficulty paying attention at school or work, felt depressed, and experienced sleep disruption or anger.[95] People with direct experience were six times more likely to experience post-traumatic stress disorder (PTSD) and they were nearly three times more prone to anxiety disorder.[96] They also had twice the probability of having some emotional difficulty.[97] Once a terrorist attack is experienced, the fear or anticipation of future attacks is intensified.[98] This intensification occurs because the attack becomes part of our frame of reference and lexicon. The attacks become embedded in our collective national conscious and some blame the government for failing to protect them. Some conspiracy-minded people believe the government committed the attacks or were complicit in it. A Pew Research Poll gathered data from persons who were at least eight years old on 9/11. Of them, 97 percent remembered where they were and what they were doing on that day.[99] By comparison, only 58 percent remembered where they were when the Berlin Wall fell.

Nations use the "terrorism" label to describe certain types of violent acts committed against them. However, they sometimes seem to lack the capability of critical introspection, which would require them to closely examine their own violent reprisals carried out in response to those acts.[100] Terrorism is a term that is so evocative and laden with meaning that many of us cannot entertain the thought that our allies or the United States would commit terroristic acts. Indeed, Americans generally believe that terrorism is "what the bad guys do."[101] What better way to distort the sovereign and legitimate interest of people than to associate them with illegitimate actions or sources? Such phrases as "guerrilla warfare," "revolutionary movement," and "radical extremist" only heighten ideological sentiment and play to emotion rather than intellect.[102]

The Ottoman Empire fought World War I as a German ally. At the end of the war, England and the allied powers occupied a large portion of the former Ottoman Empire. That area included what is now Syria, Palestine, Jordan, Lebanon, and Iraq. In 1923, one remnant of the Ottoman Empire became the Republic of Turkey. Britain ruled Palestine from 1923 to 1948.

Both before and after World War II, the Jewish people agitated for a homeland in Palestine and committed acts of terrorism. Illustratively, in 1944, Jewish operatives assassinated Lord Moyne (1880–1944), the British Minister of State, in Cairo to hasten the departure of the British from the Middle East. Two years later, they bombed the King David Hotel in Jerusalem, causing over 200 casualties. The hotel was headquarters for the British Army and the offices of the Civil Administration of Palestine. In 1948 Yitzak Shamir, who later served two terms as Israel's Prime Minister, was part of a team in Jerusalem that

FIGURE 1–12
An MQ-9 Reaper drone takes off from Kandahar Air Force Base, Afghanistan. The unmanned reaper is used for both operational and surveillance missions. Reapers have a 55' wingspan and a 27' length. They can be armed with Hellfire missiles and have a variety of optics/sensing capabilities.

(Courtesy James L. Harper/ U.S. Air Force)

assassinated Swedish Count Folke Bernadotte (1895–1948), a U.N. negotiator sent to the Middle East to mediate the Arab-Jewish violence that followed the partitioning of Palestine.

Many of the acts called terrorism by the British were committed by the Irgun Zvai Leumi, an underground Jewish defense organization. Its leader, Menachem Begin (1913–1992), later served his nation in different leadership positions, including that of Prime Minister. Begin was known to have a body double or look-alike at public functions to confuse would-be assassins.

In the war against terrorism, the United States uses armed drones to inflict casualties and destroy targets. America considers it an effective military use of technology (see Figure 1–12). However, those on the receiving end are likely to view it as terrorism because it, albeit unintentionally, causes the deaths of unarmed non-combatants. Although no country wants to be accused of terrorism, the military value of the drones is such that the United States defends their use and suffers the allegations. The potential use of drones for surveillance domestically has become quite controversial in the United States, an issue covered in Chapter 10.

Some people recall evocative events with great accuracy. In contrast, others disassociate with gruesome details to prevent being emotionally overwhelmed. They develop "cognitive blindspots" to preserve themselves. In one study subjects were asked to put five key events about 9/11 in order. Surprisingly, 63 percent could not do so even though they believed it was "the most unforgettable day" of their lives.[103] The greater the time lapse between an evocative event and an attempt to recall the details, the more likely distortions will occur for one reason or another.[104] Distortions occur when the mind unconsciously "fills in" blank spots in its memory. Another source of distortion comes from people receiving information after an event and unconsciously incorporating it into their memories, accepting it as their own genuine experience. People who are highly cooperative are particularly susceptible to "filling in" their memories.[105]

Political Power Determines Who Are Terrorists

It is well understood that governments have the political authority to apply labels; examples include "mentally ill," "poverty level," "child molester," and "disabled." These labels carry significant consequences, for example, they may determine eligibility for various types of assistance or preclude people from certain rights.

The difference between a group being labeled "insurgent" or "terrorist" may turn less on what they actually do and more on what the ruling government calls it in pursuit of national policy agendas. Chechnya is a rural, lightly populated land rich in oil, natural gas, and other

Box 1–4
Drone Use Attracts Sharp Criticism

Former President Jimmy Carter has criticized the use of drones to kill terrorist leaders as an abuse of human rights. A Pakistan official says drone strikes made in his country from Afghanistan bases are a violation of its sovereignty and he believes the attacks push people toward extremist groups. At the same time, he thinks, it pulls people away from democracy. Others have described the strikes as terroristic, arbitrary, and summary executions.

There have been civilian casualties, including children, in Iraq, Yemen, Afghanistan, and Pakistan. The exact number of civilian deaths is unknown or those reported are in dispute. Washington officials report a downward trend in civilian deaths. Some believe the reduction is caused by a "new method of scorekeeping." If a military-age male is killed during a drone strike, he is counted as enemy unless his innocence is proved posthumously. The United States has "downsized" drone munitions to reduce casualties and employs longer periods of surveillance to ensure target identification.

Do you think this use of drones constitutes an act of terrorism?

deposits.[106] Geographically, it is a combination of flatlands and the Caucasus Mountains. Chechens have been recognized as a distinctive people since the 17th century and are mostly Muslims. During 1818–1917, the Russians conquered and ruled Chechnya. Since that time, Russia has periodically been faced with Chechen independence movements. For instance, during World War II the Chechens' hatred of Russia resulted in their cooperation with the Nazis. In retaliation, at the end of the war Russian dictator Josef Stalin deported the Chechens to Siberia and Central Asia.[107]

During the late 1950s, surviving Chechens were allowed to return to their homeland. Since then several insurgencies, some using terrorists tactics, have been waged against Russia. Following 9/11, Russian President Vladimir Putin "relabeled" the insurgents as terrorists. Russia ostensibly seemed to join the global war on terror.[108] In 2004, Chechen terrorists seized control of a school in Beslan, Russia, and held 1,300 hostages, most of them school children and teachers. The Chechens threatened to kill their hostages if Chechen prisoners were not released. A three-day standoff ended when Russian security forces stormed the school. In the end, over seven hundred hostages were wounded and 186 children and 145 adults were killed![109]

Because Russia seemed to be "on board" with the fight against terrorism, the West substantially turned a blind eye to the "botched" Beslan siege. By relabeling Chechen insurgents as "terrorists," Russia's subsequent conduct averted a more immediate and higher level of international scrutiny and criticism.

Past Prosecutorial Decisions Confuse Us

The public does not have an expert knowledge of terrorism. We form our opinions on a basic and incomplete understanding of events and the laws that we think should be applied. It is not surprising that sometimes we agree and at other times disagree with how the government charges suspects. At the heart of our confusion is the expectation that certain perpetrators should be charged with terrorism and instead authorities charge them with a conventional criminal act.

Three cases are used to examine the points made above. The first reviews Abdulhakim Muhammad's murder and wounding of servicemen (2009) at a recruiting office. The second case analyzes Major Nidal Hasan's shooting rampage at Fort Hood (2009). The third case summarizes Wade Page's deadly rampage at a Sikh Temple (2012).

Case Study 1

Carlos Bledsoe
See Abdulhakim Muhammad.

Abdulhakim Muhammad
Born in America as Carlos Bledsoe. Bledsoe became a radicalized violent Muslim who murdered a soldier and wounded another in front of a Little Rock, Arkansas, military recruiting station because Americans were killing Muslims in Iraq and Afghanistan.

Carlos Bledsoe converted to Islam in Memphis, Tennessee, as a teenager and later took the name **Abdulhakim Muhammad**.[110] He spent 16 months in Yemen and received training in a terrorist camp.[111] He was deported from Yemen on several charges, including overstaying his visa, carrying falsified Somali identification papers, and possessing other forged documents.[112]

In 2009, 23-year old Muhammad shot a soldier to death and wounded another outside a Little Rock, Arkansas, recruiting office. Prior to the shooting, he was of interest to the FBI, but they lacked sufficient cause for a full investigation and no further action was taken. After the recruiting office shooting, the federal government deferred prosecution to the State of Arkansas, which charged Muhammad with capital murder, attempted capital murder, and ten counts of unlawful discharge of a firearm.[113] Muhammad pled guilty to the charges to avoid the death penalty. He is currently serving life in prison without the possibility of parole.

Although there was a connection with a foreign terrorist organization and several claims by Muhammad that he was on jihad or "holy war," to protest American attacks on his Muslim brothers, terrorism was not charged, raising questions. Some wonder if we are trying to classify as many events as possible as anything but terrorism to artificially keep the number of such attacks low and the public feeling safe. Others ponder whether Muhammad was charged with murder because a terrorism trial would have forced the disclosure of counterintelligence assets and capabilities. Some people believe if Muslims are involved in terrorist violence they are charged with something other than terrorism to avoid a backlash by **Islamaphobic** "loose cannons" against the vast majority of Muslims who are loyal citizens. In the final analysis, it may simply be that the evidence better suited a capital murder as opposed to a terrorism charge against Muhammad.

Case Study 2

Nidal Malik Hasan (see Figure 1–13) was born in Virginia to Palestinian parents and raised as a Muslim. As an adult, he became a physician and advanced to the rank of major in the Army. Hasan, a psychiatrist, was assigned to Fort Hood, Texas, while awaiting deployment to Afghanistan, which would have been his first assignment to a combat zone, an assignment he resented as a devout Muslim. He met and conversed with several well-known Muslim radicals, including Anwar al-Awlaki with whom he had a long relationship over the Internet. In 2009, Nidal Malik Hasan shot 13 people to death in a medical processing unit at Fort Hood and wounded 32 others while shouting "Allah u Akbar" as he fired.[114] All but one of his victims were soldiers.

Just before the shootings Hasan gave away all of his possessions,[115] something sometimes done in anticipation of one's own impending death. When moving we might have a yard sale or give some things away, but it is unlikely that we would dispose of everything. Speculatively, Hasan was prepared to die or perhaps wanted to die during his attack. However, he was unsuccessful in his attempt to become a martyr and was, instead, wounded and paralyzed from the waist down while on his shooting spree. Hassan was convicted in a military court of charges that included 13 counts of premeditated murder, but not any terrorism charges.[116] Sentenced to death, Hasan is currently imprisoned at Fort Leavenworth, Kansas. The Army has not executed a soldier since 1961.

The U.S. Department of Defense (DoD) characterized the Fort Hood shootings as "workplace violence." The federal government asserts that because there was no co-conspirator and no foreign direction, the Fort Hood shooting was not terrorism. Officially, Hasan simply snapped, "went postal," and started shooting—there was no violent radical religious underpinning.

Characterizing the attack as workplace violence seemingly ignores what we know about Hasan's Islamic radicalization, his advocacy for extremism, his series of communications with al-Alwaki, and his shouts of Allah u Akbar as he murdered people. In contrast to the DoD's position, a 2011 Senate report sharply concluded the Ft. Hood attack was "the worst terrorist attack on U.S. soil since 9/11."[117]

The decision not to charge Hasan with terrorism raises important issues. In some circles it is believed Hasan was charged with murder because federal agents and military officials mishandled identifying him as a terrorist threat and wanted to shift attention from themselves to Hasan. A murder charge is more immediately understood as compared to

Islamaphobic
An unfounded hostility toward Muslims resulting in a fear or dislike of all or most Muslims. Coined in 1991, the term was developed in the context of Muslims in the United Kingdom in particular and Europe in general.

Nidal Malik Hasan
Army psychiatrist who killed and wounded American troops at Ft. Hood, Texas. He was convicted by a military court and sentenced to death.

FIGURE 1–13
A photograph of a friendly appearing Major Nidal Malik Hasan prior to his military trial. His smile may have concealed an inner rage.

(Polaris/Newscom)

Box 1–5
Could the Fort Hood Shootings Have Been Prevented?

A case can be argued that Hasan's signs of religious radicalization were glossed over, ignored, or given insufficient weight by his superiors and federal agents. Nine different points support this position.

1) Hasan's supervisors at the Walter Reed National Military Medical Center expressed serious concern about his questionable behavior and judgment. Among their concerns were his strident views on Islam and worries about his competence. Despite these concerns they gave him positive performance evaluations that helped promote him.[118]

2) Hasan made three PowerPoint presentations titled "Why the War on Terror Is a War on Islam" when he was supposed to be presenting medical information.[119]

3) In a class presentation Hasan argued that U.S. military operations were not based on legitimate national security needs. He claimed that they were actually a war against Islam. The class was halted when the audience of military officers erupted in opposition. Some class members labeled him a "ticking time bomb."[120]

4) A questionnaire to be distributed to Muslim soldiers was prepared by Hasan. It included a question asking whether they should help enemies who were Muslims.[121] The question could also be understood to be encouraging the soldiers to be disloyal. The questionnaire was not approved for distribution.

5) Hasan told several contemporaries that he thought Sharia law takes precedence over the U.S. Constitution. This position is contrary to Hasan's military oath to defend the Constitution against all enemies foreign and domestic.[122]

6) Three 9/11 hijackers attended a Northern Virginian mosque at the same time Hasan did. His prayer leader was the radical cleric Anwar al-Awlaki, who also presided over the funeral of Hasan's mother.

7) In 2004, Anwar al-Awlaki went to Yemen. He was detained for allegedly plotting to kidnap a military attaché assigned to the U.S. Embassy.[123] Hasan ultimately exchanged some 20 emails with Anwar al-Awlaki, who federal agents knew was a radical extremist. Prior to Hasan's attack, federal agents were aware of only some of those emails. Federal agents concluded no threat or crime was involved and further investigation was not warranted because Hasan was thought to be conducting terrorism research using his actual name.[124]

8) The background check for a high-level security clearance for Hasan was seriously flawed. It did not include interviews with him, his co-workers, or supervisors.[125] Properly conducted, the issuance of the security clearance would have been at least problematic and Hasan would have been subject to a more thorough scrutiny.[126] Such an examination may have led to Hasan's separation from the military. A senior FBI official testified that in retrospect Major Hasan should have been interviewed after the emails with al-Awlaki were known.[127]

9) In the aftermath of the shooting, nine Army officers were disciplined for inaction, ranging from an oral reprimand to what is considered a career-ending letter of censure.[128] One officer explained some of the lapses: "People are afraid to come forward and challenge someone's ideology ... because there're afraid of getting an equal-opportunity complaint that will end their careers."[129]

Do you think the Fort Hood Shooting involving Nidal Malik Hassan could have been prevented? At what point do you think there was enough information to closely investigate him?

Uniform Code of Military Justice (UCMJ)
The UCMJ was established by the Congress and is the basis for military law in the United States.

Wade Michael Page
White supremacist who entered a Wisconsin Sikh Temple and murdered six and wounded three. After being wounded at the scene by police he died from a self-inflicted gunshot wound.

Skinhead
A white supremist group originally started in London, England, among working class, white youths in the 1960s; eventually becoming associated with a much larger subculture named for their close-cropped or shaven heads, military-style clothing including Nazi-type "jack boots," and hard rock, punk-style music.

Hammerskin Nation (HN)
a radical right-wing racist group.

the more complicated terrorism charge. Others assert the military wanted to appear politically correct and not anti-Muslim, and therefore used the murder rather than a capital terrorism charge. These possibilities notwithstanding, it may simply be that the **Uniform Code of Military Justice (UCMJ)** does not, in and of itself, contain a capital terrorism charge. Under the UCMJ's Article 134, the federal Assimilative Crimes Act (ACA) can be used to "incorporate" state and certain federal laws into the UCMJ for the state in which the military installation is located. However, no capital crimes can be incorporated.** Thus, to charge Hasan with capital terrorism the Army would have to waive jurisdiction to the federal courts, a choice that senior military commanders reasonably did not make when a workable murder charge was available.

Case Study 3

Wade Michael Page served in the Army (1992–1998) but was never in a combat zone. He was discharged and barred from re-enlisting for showing up drunk at formations and field exercises.[130] He lost a civilian truck-driving job for driving impaired and was also charged with driving under the influence in Colorado.[131] Along the way, he was in right-wing **Skinhead** bands specializing in the lyrics of hate.[132] Page described himself as a member of the **Hammerskin Nation** (HN). HN is a Dallas (Texas)-based group that advocates a "white power Skinhead" lifestyle and has a history of violence and hate crimes.[133] HN's 14-word goal is "We must secure the existence of our people and a future for white children."[134] In 2012, white supremacist Wade Page entered a Sikh Temple in Wisconsin. He shot six

---

** For example, see *United States v. French* (1959).

Box 1–6
Title 18, United States Code, Section 249, The Matthew Shepard and James Byrd, JR., Hate Crimes Prevention Act (HCPA, 2009)

State and federal hate crimes legislation has enhanced or "**accelerator sanctions**" for crimes rooted in hate or bias. Terrorism charges follow the same principle. It is the means by which society signals its revulsion about such offenses by specifying severe sentences for them. The HCPA was passed because of the realization that federal and state hate crimes legislation was inadequate. Two incidents provided the impetus for HCPA's passage.

In 1998, James Byrd, a 49-year-old African American, was seized by three white men in Jasper, Texas.[135] He was chained by his ankles to the back of a pickup truck and dragged down a road. The next morning police found 75 pieces of his body along a three-mile stretch of blood-stained road; his torso and an arm were located a mile from his head. Two of the three perpetrators were members of a white supremacist organization with racist tattoos. One man is serving a life sentence and the second is appealing his death sentence. The third perpetrator was executed in 2011 by lethal injection.

In 1998, two 21-year-old men saw Matthew Shepard drunk in a lounge. They offered him a ride with the intent to rob him.[136] The two perpetrators were disappointed they only got $30. Believing Shepard to be gay, the men savagely beat him. They tied him to a post where he was found 18 hours later. Shepard died after five days in the hospital. His assailants later pled guilty. Shepard's parents did a remarkable thing and asked the court to show mercy in sentencing their son's killers. Both men pleaded guilty to murder and were given life sentences.

The heart of HCPA makes it unlawful to willfully cause bodily injury—or attempting to do so with fire, firearm, or other dangerous weapon—when (1) the crime was committed because of the actual or perceived race, color, religion, national origin of any person; or (2) the crime was committed because of the actual or perceived religion, national origin, gender, sexual orientation, gender identity, or disability of any person and the crime affected interstate or foreign commerce or occurred within federal special maritime and territorial jurisdictions.

The law also provides funding and technical assistance to state, local, and tribal jurisdictions to help them to more effectively investigate, prosecute, and prevent hate crimes.

The law provides for a maximum 10-year prison term, unless death (or attempts to kill) results from the offense, or unless the offense includes kidnapping or attempted kidnapping, or aggravated sexual abuse or attempted aggravated sexual abuse. For offenses not resulting in death, there is a seven–year statute of limitations. For offenses resulting in death, there is no statute of limitations.

What do you think produces the kind and extent of hatred portrayed in the Byrd and Shepard cases? What, if any, potential connections do you see between the HCPA and terrorism?

---

people to death and wounded three others. Various news reports characterized the violence as a hate crime, murder, and a terrorist-like incident. It was initially reported that Page was killed by the police, but it was determined later that he committed suicide after being wounded.

We are left to wonder about Page's motive for the attack. Speculatively, Page may have mistaken the Sikhs for Muslims; he may have hated foreign-appearing people and his hatred toward foreigners could have been fueled by conversations with veterans returning from a combat zone. It may also be that Page was in a homicidal rage and wanted simply to kill people and the Sikhs were convenient targets.

The Sikh Temple violence was classified by the FBI as domestic terrorism and a "lone wolf attack."[137] Page apparently conceived of the idea for the shooting and carried it out alone. It is puzzling to understand why Page's murders were quickly labeled terrorism instead of murder or a hate crime (See Box 1–6). In both Hasan's and Page's cases there were officially no co-conspirators nor was a foreign terrorist organization involved, yet different charges were brought against them. Moreover, it is difficult to see Page's fact situation fitting into the legal definition of domestic terrorism as given in Table 1–1. Perhaps there was some organizational imperative to quickly produce successful terrorism investigations and classifying the Sikh Temple murders as domestic terrorism was easy with a dead perpetrator.

Some racist radical right message boards and forums commended their "brother" Page for what he did. Others scrambled to disassociate themselves with the murders.[138] Neo-Nazi Alex Linder wrote "Take your dead and go back to India and dump their ashes in the Ganges … this is not your country; it belongs to white men."[139]

These three case studies illustrate that the specific charges applied in terrifying and perhaps terroristic events are impacted not only by the fact situations, but also by a matrix of legal, operational, and political factors whose weight the public rarely learns. Moreover, we are not privy to the clash of views and needs among agencies in making such decisions. To some degree our confusion about what is terrorism is grounded in the reality that charging decisions are a "witch's brew" of factors. One alternative is to

Accelerator sanctions
For certain types of crimes, such as hate-based and terrorism, the law provides more severe sentences for persons convicted of them. It is how society demonstrates its revulsion about such crimes.

Information Link
Visit the official homepage of the Hammerskin Nation at www.hammerskins.net/index.html. The Hammerskin Nation declares itself as a leaderless group of men and women who have adopted the White Power Skinhead lifestyle. Note the global nature of the group; it is not only very active throughout the United States, but also has chapters in Australia, Canada, France, Germany, Hungary, Switzerland, Sweden, Portugal, Spain, Luxembourg, and New Zealand.

Qur'an
Often referred to as the "Holy Qur'an" or the "Noble Qur'an" is the central religious text of Islam, which Muslims believe to be a revelation from Allah (God) ... the Muslim equivalent of the Christian Bible.

Asymmetrical Warfare
In warfare it is the attempt to circumvent or undermine an opposing force's superior strengths while exploiting its weaknesses. Asymmetrical warfare often has a major psychological impact, such as shock or fear and often involves the use of non-traditional strategy, tactics, and weapons. Examples include the use of guerilla tactics against a powerful conventional army or flying hijacked planes into buildings.

Insurgency
A type of irregular warfare characterized by subversion, armed conflict, and occasional terrorism to overthrow the legally constituted government of a country.

conclude that the federal government invariably makes charging decisions solely on the legal merits of cases. The second and perhaps more likely alternative is that the United States is devolving itself from the "war on terrorism"—which means allowing captured terrorists to be tried in their own countries and charging as many terrorists as possible in America with specific criminal acts.

War, Irregular War, and Terrorism

War can be roughly divided into conventional and irregular war (IW). Conventional warfare occurs between nations and relies on direct military confrontation to defeat an adversary's armed forces, destroy its war-making capacity, or seize or retain territory in order to force a change in the adversary's government or policies.[140] IW, which encompasses "small wars," insurgencies, low-intensity warfare, and similar terms, is a messy and ambiguous term that does not lend itself to concise definitions.[141] Khalil characterizes this lack of concise definitions as being so messy that it is "futile" to try and distinguish between terrorists and insurgents.[142] IW usually involves a state and an opposing sub-state force, although sometimes it may include several sub-state forces. Because states are typically better organized and armed than the sub-state forces opposing them, the sub-state forces cannot engage them in conventional military engagements. They therefore use guerilla and often terror tactics, resulting in a style of warfare called **asymmetrical**. To illustrate, enemies of the United States would be pressed to defeat America in a conventional war because of our military strength. They would seek to fight us mixing modern technology and irregular warfare. They do not seek military victory on the field. Our enemies' goal is to exhaust our national will by undermining and outlasting our public support, as happened in Vietnam.

In Afghanistan, the United States and its allies are fighting the Taliban in a type of IW called an insurgency. An **insurgency** is an organized movement aimed at overthrowing a duly constituted government through the use of subversion and armed conflict.[143] It is a protracted political-military struggle designed to weaken the government's control and legitimacy and increase that of the insurgents.[144] In insurgencies, political power is the central issue.[145] As an aside, many countries, including the U.S., did not regard the Taliban government in Afghanistan to be duly constituted.

What "muddies the waters" when thinking about the Taliban as insurgents is the fact that it uses terror tactics in addition to more conventional armed conflict methods and receives both material and operational support from al-Qaeda and other Islamic radical groups, which attacked the U.S. Embassy and NATO Headquarters in Kabul, Pakistan, in 2011. Originally an anti-Soviet movement, the Taliban network became a mafia-like criminal enterprise that morphed into a terrorist organization and became officially identified as such by the U.S. Department of State.

Terrorism is not a type of irregular warfare; it is a tactic. International Humanitarian Law (IHL) prohibits, without exception, all acts during war that would constitute terrorism. Such acts are charged as war crimes; examples include executing civilians and prisoners of war (see Figure 1–14), taking hostages, bombing civilian population centers, reprisals against non-combatants, failing to provide medical care to captured prisoners, declaring that no quarter will be given, deliberately targeting religious and medical personnel, attacking non-defended locations, using prisoners for scientific experiments, and destroying property not required by military necessity.

FIGURE 1–14
Just before the end of World War II (1941–1945) a Japanese officer executes an Australian prisoner of war, which constituted a war crime.
(© Bettmann/Corbis)

Quick Facts
Nazi Reprisals Later Tried as War Crimes

In 1942, German General Reinhard Heydrich was assassinated in Prague by Czechoslovakian partisans. In reprisal, the Germans surrounded the villages of Lidice and Lezaky, which were believed to be the home of some partisans. All men and many boys were quickly executed. Women were sent to concentration camps. Some young children were adopted by German families, but others were gassed. Both villages were razed to the ground and their names removed from all German maps. After World War II ended, some Germans were charged with war crimes for their acts at Lidice and Lezaky. Lidice was rebuilt after the war, although Lezaky was not.

The United Nations (UN) International Criminal Court (ICC) is located in The Hague, Netherlands, and is the body that adjudicates war crimes. A more contemporary case was the trial of former Yugoslavia President Slobodan Milosevic (1941–2006), the so-called "Beast of the Balkans," on 66 counts of crimes against humanity, including genocide during the Balkans War of the 1990s. Tens of thousands of Bosnian Muslims were massacred during ethnic cleansing. Milosevic died in custody before his trial was concluded.

Chapter Summary

SUMMARY BY LEARNING OBJECTIVE

1. **State six reasons why we should understand terrorism.**

   (1) For most of its history terrorism was subnational or regional. In recent decades a few movements have shown the ability to launch attacks transnationally. This leaves people wary and changes how some people live. (2) Terrorism can be adapted with terrifying speed to the needs of many causes. It is the violent equivalent of a Swiss Army Knife. (3) Terrorism is not a uniquely American problem. (4) There will be no quick and easy resolution to terrorism. The continuous possibility of attacks is like learning to live with an incurable disease. (5) Families stress over their members being sent to a combat zone and dealing with some members who are injured or killed. These families deserve our respect. (6) Terrorism evolves and adapts, presenting a series of new challenges.

2. **Identify eight attacks in America that were racial, labor, or anarchist related from 1856 to 1920.**

   (1) John Brown's murder and mutilation of pro-slavery Kansas settlers in 1856. (2) Knights of the White Camellia terrorized voters in 1868 to get their candidate elected. (3) During the 1880s in the State of Washington Asians, and particularly the Chinese, were targeted for murder, assaults, and forced evacuations of that state. (4) In 1886, a bomb killed seven police officers at a demonstration of striking workers in Chicago's Haymarket Square. (5) In 1892, Henry Clay Frick, a Pittsburgh industrialist, was shot and stabbed in his office, but survived. (6) The *Los Angeles Times* was bombed in 1910 for its anti-union stand. (7) The Reception Room of the U.S. Senate was bombed in 1915 to prevent America from entering World War I in Europe. (8) The 1920 unsolved Wall Street bombing.

3. **Trace the history of key events in terrorism from 1959 to 9/11/2001.**

   (1) In 1959, ETA began a campaign for a homeland for Basques in Northern Spain, quickly turning to the use of terrorist tactics. (2) Formed in 1966, the Black Panther Party was quickly militant and violent. (3) During 1968–1977 the Baader-Meinhof Group used terrorist tactics to try and create socialist governments in Europe. (4) Beginning in 1969, the Weather Underground ("Weathermen") tried to overthrow America's national government. (5) The Palestinian nationalist group Black September massacred members of the Israeli delegation to the 1972 Munich Olympics to call attention to their cause. (6) During the 1970s terror groups hijacked a series of airplanes in an attempt to have authorities release imprisoned members of their group. (7) In Tehran, Iran militant Muslims took members of the U.S. Embassy hostage. (8) In 1983, suicide truck bombers attacked the U.S. Marine Corps Compound in Beriut, Lebanon killing 221 Marines and 21 other service members. (9) Two Libyan terrorists planted bombs during 1979, on Pan Am

Flight 103 which exploded over Scotland, killing the crew and all passengers, as well as people on the ground in 1988. (10) In 1988, the U.S. Embassies in Kenya and Tanzania were simultaneously attacked by terrorist Muslims driving suicide bomb vehicles. (11) In 1993, militant Muslims made their first attack on the North Tower of the World Trade Center by exploding a truck bomb in the parking garage. (12) In 2000, while in a Yemeni port, the USS *Cole* was attacked by Muslim terrorists who drove a boat alongside the *Cole* and detonated the cargo of explosives, causing substantial damage to the American ship. (13) The 9/11 attacks.

4. **Explain Robespierre's concept of terrorism.**

   To Robespierre, terrorism was nothing but prompt, severe, and inflexible justice.

5. **Distinguish between the federal definitions for international and domestic terrorism.**

   See Table 1–1 for complete definitions. At its simplest, domestic terrorism occurs, from the American perspective, primarily within the territorial jurisdiction of the United States. International terrorism occurs primarily outside of the territorial jurisdictional of the United States or transcends national boundaries in terms of the means by which the attacks are accomplished, the person(s) they appear intended to intimidate or coerce, or the locale(s) in which perpetrators operate or seek asylum. Both types of terrorism commit deadly attacks to create fear and influence government policy.

6. **Contrast individual and cultural perspectives.**

   Individual perspective results from the process of evaluating issues, events, other people, groups, and nations and the underlying beliefs, intentions, and actions in order to assign meaning to them. Individual perspective is produced out of a thoughtful and deliberate process that is to some degree analytical.

   Cultural perspective is the shared beliefs, experiences, and behaviors that cause its members to substantially view things in a similar manner. In contrast to individual perspective, culture is a collective, accumulated experience. This shared experience often distinguishes one culture from another, including language, values, customs, history, law, and religion.

7. **Describe selective terrorism.**

   Whereas present religious based terrorism targets defenseless civilians with the intent to inflict mass casualties and create fear, selective terrorism is carefully focused on supporters, key personnel, and institutions of the opposing force.

8. **Explain why there are so many definitions of terrorism.**

   There is a natural world filled with real, tangible things, such as weather and soil composition. Such things can be observed, measured, and analyzed. Our heads are also filled with what we call reality. In fact, these are social constructs that give us meanings about love, status, loyalty, and other non-natural world phenomenon. Terrorism is not a natural world phenomenon. It requires the development of social constructs to explain it. Individual observers and scholars of terrorism create social constructs to meet their needs, resulting in a staggering number of definitions of terrorism; additional definitions spring from other sources, such as the law and the definitions adopted by operating agencies. The result is a vast surplus of complex and varying definitions.

9. **State why there is no terrorism definition acceptable to all United Nations members.**

   Each member state reserves the right to define terrorism as they deem fit, often based on perspective and culture.

10. **Explain why the database for terrorism is insufficient.**

    A review of literature over a 32-year period discovered 14,006 articles on terrorism. Some 4,458 were in peer-reviewed journals, but of this number only 3 percent were based on empirical evidence. The scholarly database reflects a substantial amount of qualitative articles and "thinking" pieces about terrorism, but a significant shortage of empirical research.

11. **Using Hezbollah as an example, discuss the notion that terrorism is a contested concept.**

    Hezbollah is primarily located in Lebanon, where it was formed as a militia in opposition to the Israeli invasion of that country. In Latin America it is seen as a legitimate political organization, whereas the U.S. Department of State classifies it a foreign terrorist organization (FTO).

12. **Describe how Russia benefited from labeling the Chechnya insurgents as terrorists.**

    By designating the insurgents as terrorists, Russia seemed "on board" with the war on terrorism. Russia benefited because its subsequent attacks on the "terrorists" averted a more immediate and higher level of international scrutiny and criticism.

13. **Explain why the criminal charges placed against Abdulhakim Muhammad confuse us.**

    An American citizen born Charles Bledso changed his name to Abdulhakim Muhammad when he became a Muslim. He spent 16 months in Yemen and received terrorist training. On his return to America, he killed one soldier and wounded another by gunfire at a Little Rock military recruiting office. Although he spent time in a terrorist training camp and openly proclaimed several times he was on jihad to protest the U.S. war on his Muslim brothers, he was charged by the State of Arkansas with capital murder and other crimes. Was he charged with those crimes to keep the number of terrorist attacks low and the public feeling safer? Would a federal terrorist charge force the disclosure of counterintelligence assets and capabilities? Was the terrorist charge not employed to avoid a backlash by "Islamaphobics? Or, did the evidence simply better suit a capital murder charge?

14. **Identify any six of the ten acts punishable as war crimes.**

    (1) Executing civilians and prisoners of war, (2) taking hostages, (3) bombing civilian population centers, (4) reprisals against non-combatants, (5) failing to provide medical care to captured prisoners, (6) declaring that no quarter will be given, (7) deliberately targeting religious and medical personnel, (8) attacking non-defended locations, (9) using prisoners for scientific experiments, and (10) destroying property not required by military necessity.

REVIEW QUESTIONS

1. What four factors contributed to terrorism being at the margins of American policy going into the 1970s?
2. Following 9/11 a national survey revealed some Americans made two important changes to their lives. What were they?
3. What are homegrown terrorists?
4. Terrorism is not just an American problem. What data supports that assertion?
5. What does the "Bermuda Triangle of Terrorism" mean?
6. What is a "force multiplier? What is an example of it?
7. What is a "foreign terrorist organization?"
8. Under International Humanitarian Law (IHL) what are "war crimes?"
9. What is asymmetrical warfare?

CRITICAL THINKING EXERCISES

1. **Terrorism in History.** Think about some of the major historical events in history, from assassinations to revolutions to world wars. How many of these events could be perceived as acts of terrorism, or which specific acts within the events might be categorized as terrorist? For example, just considering World War II, think of all the incidents that occurred that could be "labeled" terrorist: The surprise attack on Pearl Harbor by Japan; the Bataan Death March; the treatment of Jews, Gypsies, the mentally ill, homosexuals, and other political prisoners in the Nazi concentration/death camps; the Nazi bombing of civilian population centers, such as London, England; the Allied fire-bombing of Dresden; and the dropping of nuclear bombs on Hiroshima and Nagasaki. Some of these events caused heavy civilian casualties. Looking at them, how do they fit into the framework of acts of terrorism, acts of war, and war crimes?

2. **The Wounded Warrior Project.** Visit the wounded warrior project as www.woundedwarriorporject.org. Why was the organization established and what is its mission? Review some of the programs that are offered through the project and consider how such activities assist others.

3. **The Charlie Hebdo Attack.** On January 7, 2015, a particularly grotesque terrorist attack occurred in Paris France. Three gunmen attacked the headquarters of Charlie Bebdo, a satirical magazine which had published controversial cartoons of the Prophet Muhammad. A total of 12 people were killed and 11 wounded. The attackers spoke fluent Arabic and French and were heard shouting, "The Prophet is avenged. A massive manhunt for the attackers was immediately underway.

What do we now know about this incident? Is it an example of ethnic Arabs who were French citizens radicalized in terrorist camps and who returned to carry out jihad? Why was the reaction to the cartoons so deadly? Is there an inherent conflict between freedom of expression and radicalized Muslims?

NOTES

1. "Americans and 9/11: The Personal Toll," Washington, D.C.: Pew Research Center, September 5, www.people-press.org/2002/09/05/i-americans-and-9/11-the-personal-toll.
2. Calvin Lawrence, Jr., "September 11th: 7 Ways 9/11 Has Changed Your Life," *ABC News*, pp. 4, 5, and 7, www.abcnews.go.com/us/september-11-ways-911-changed-life/story?id=14324226#7.
3. "'Napolitano' Domestic Terrorists Central to Threat Picture," *Fox News*, July 21, 2011, www.foxnews.com/politics/2011/07/21/Napolitano-domestic-terrorists-central-to-threat.
4. Erin Miller and Travis Rudd, "START Provides 2013 Statistical Annex for Country Reports on Terrorism," www.start.umd.edu/news/start-provides-2013-statistical-annex-country-reports-terrorism, April 30, 2014, p. 1.
5. Saima Mohsin and Emma Lacey-Bordeaux, "Suicide Bombers Kill 81 at Church on Peshawar, Pakistan," September 23, 2013, pp. 1–2, www.cnn.com/2013/09/22/world/asia/pakistan-attack.
6. Sounak Mukhopadhyay, "Who Is Oksana Aslanova—The Woman Suicide Bomber in Russia? *The International Business Times*, December 31, 2013, p. 1, http://au.ibtimes.com/articles/532270/20131231/russia-volgograd-bomb-blast-terror-attack-sochi.htm#.U73dfBavtol.
7. See John Robb, *Brave New War: The Next Stage of Terrorism and the End of Globalization* (Hoboken, New Jersey: John Wiley & Sons, 2008) for the extension of this and related arguments.
8. Ibid., from Forward by James Fallows, p. 9. The authors read the Kindle copy of Robb's book, which does not display page numbers. Thus, page numbers are by our own count and may differ from those in a "hard copy."
9. Ibid., p. 8.
10. Robb, *Brave New War*, p. 17.
11. Ibid., p. 28.
12. Ibid., p. 77.
13. Ibid., p. 119.
14. Ibid., p. 46.
15. Ibid., p. 13.
16. W. Seth Carus, *Defining "Weapons of Mass Destruction"* (Washington, D.C.: National Defense University Press, January 2012), p. 35.
17. Ibid., p. 34.
18. "Saudi Braces for a Renewed Jihadist Threat," *StratFor*, July 18, 2014, www.stratFor.com.
19. Loc. cit.
20. Text Yet to receive
21. There is literature that establishes the Scarii as part of the Jewish Zealots, while other works identify them as separate, but allied, movements. See "Zealots and Sicarii," *Jewish Virtual Library*, 2008, www.jewishvirtuallibrary.org/jsource/judaica/ejud_0002_0021_0_21428.html.
22. "Time Trip," *Current Events*, Vol. 101, Issue 6, October 12, 2001, p. 2.

23. Shmuel Shepkaru, "'Death Twice Over' Dualism of Metaphor and Realia in 12th Century Hebrew Crusading Accounts," *Jewish Quarterly Review*, Vol. 93, Issue ½, July–October 2002, p. 217, and "The Crusades," *PBS*, 2014, p. 1, www.pbs.org/wgbh/pages/frontline/shows/apocalypse/explanation/crusades.html.

24. Wayne C. Lee, *Deadly Days in Kansas* (Caldwell, Idaho: Caldwell Well Press, 1997), p. 4

25. Paul Leland Haworth, *The United States in Our Own Time* (New York, New York: C. Scribner' Sons, 1920), pp. 55–56.

26. Loc. cit.

27. "Anti-Chinese Riots in Washington State," Darthmouth College, undated, p. 1, www.dartmouth.edu/~hist32/History/S01%20-%20Wash%20State%20riots.htm.

28. "Eight Anarchists," PBS, 2008, p. 1, www.pbs.org/wgbh/amex/chicago/sfeature/sf_haymarket.html.

29. "People and Events," PBS, 2004, p. 1, www.pbs.org/wgbh/amex/goldman/peopleevents/p_frick.html.

30. Richard Brookhiser, "Domestic Terrorism: The Killers Next Door," *American History*, Vol. 48, Issue 4, October 2013, pp. 7–18.

31. Norman Rozeff, "Fugitive in Early San Benito," *The Sun Valley Times* (Harlingen, Texas), May 16, 2014.

32. "A Byte Out of History: Terror on Wall Street," Federal Bureau of Investigation, 2007, p. 1, www.fbi.gov/news/stories/2007/september/wallstreet_091307.

33. 1959 is the conventional date for the founding of ETA, but Shepard maintains it should be 1952. See William S. Shepard, "The ETA: Spain Fights Europe's Last Active Terrorist Group," *Mediterranean Quarterly*, Vol. 58, Issue 4, Winter 2002, p. 56.

34. For a detailed examination of the BMG see Jillian Becker, *Hitler's Children: The History of the Baader-Meinhof Terrorist Gang* (New York, NY: Harper Collins, 1979).

35. See Simon Reeve, *One Day in September: The Full Story of the 1972 Munich Olympics Massacre and the Israeli Revenge Operation "Wrath of God"* (New York, NY: Arcade Publishing, 2000).

36. "Byte Out of History: Solving A Complex Case of International Terrorism," Federal Bureau of Investigation, December 2003, p. 1, www.fbi.gov/news/stories/2003/december/panam121903.

37. Loc. cit.

38. Michael B. Mukasey, "The War on Terror: Where We Are and How We Got There," *New York Law School Law Review*, Vol. 56, Issue 1, 2012, p. 10.

39. Loc. cit.

40. Richard A. Serrano, "Early Terrorist in U.S. Condemns Today's Jihad," *The Los Angeles Times*, May 16, 2013.

41. "U.S. Missiles Pound Targets in Afghanistan, Sudan," *CNN News*, August 21, 1993, p. 1, /www.cnn.com/US/9808/20/us.strikes.02.

42. 1993 World Trade Center Bombing Fast Facts," updated to April 5, 2014, p. 1, www.cnn.com/2013/11/05/us/1993-world-trade-center-bombing-fast-facts/.

43. "1993 World Trade Center Bombing," 9/11 Memorial Organization, p. 1, www.911memorial.org/1993-world-trade-center-bombing.

44. "FBI 100: First Strike Global Terror in America," 2008, p. 1, www.fbi.gov/news/stories/2008/february/tradebom_022608.

45. Alex Schmid, "Terrorism—The Definitional Problem," *Case Western Reserve Journal of International Law*, Vol. 36, Issue 2/3, 2004, p. 376.

46. Walter Lequeur, *The New Terrorism* (New York: Oxford University Press, 1999), p. 32.

47. The information in this paragraph is drawn with restatement from Marisa Linton, "Robespierre and the Terror," History Today, Vol. 56, Issue 8, August 2006, pp. 23–29 and Marisa Linton, "Reign of Terror," *History Today*, Vol. 56, Issue 6, June 2006, p. 66.

48. Patrick L. Higonnet, "Robespierre's Rules for Radicals," *Foreign Affairs*, July/August 2012, p. 1, www.foreignaffairs.com/articles/137726/patrice-l-r-higonnet/robespierres-rules-for-radicals.

49. Tim McNeese, *The Age of Napoleon* (Boston, MA: Houghton, Mifflin, Harcourt, 2002), p. 11.

50. The speech, "The Republic of Virtue," appears in Richard C. Lyman and Lewis Spitz, editors, *Major Crises in Western Civilization*, Volume 2 (New York: Harcourt, Brace, and World, 1965), pp. 71–71.

51. Ian O. Lesser et al., *The New Terrorism*" (Santa Monica, CA: RAND Corporation, 1999), p. 8.

52. Loc. cit., with restatement.

53. Loc. cit., with restatement.

54. Loc. cit., with restatement.

55. The main points in this paragraph are drawn with restatement from Loc. cit.

56. Steven Simon and Daniel Benjamin, "America and the New Terrorism," *Survival: Global Politics and Strategy*, Vol. 42, Issue 1, p. 59 identifies 1993 as the "onset" of the new terrorism.

57. This account is drawn from Larry Neumeister, "WTC Bombing Ended Age of Innocence," *The Washington Post*, February 17, 2008; "The World Trade Center Bombing," (Washington, D.C.: Department of Homeland Security, February 1993). It is doubtful that the February 1993 date is for publication. The attack occurred on February 26, 1993 leaving only two days to complete the report; "FBI 100: First Strike: Global Terror in America," undated, www.fbi.gov/news/stories/2008/february/tradebom_022608; Thomas Copeland, "Is the 'New' Terrorism Really New? An Analysis of the New Paradigm for Terrorism," *The Journal of Conflict Studies*, Vol. 21, No. 2, Winter 2001, www.journals.hil.unb.ca/index.php/jcs/article/view/4265/4834; and "The World Trade Center Bombing," Anti-Defamation League, undated, www.archive.adl.org/learn/jttf/wtcb_jttf.asp.

58. See Dr. Yasuo Seto, "The Sarin Gas Attack in Japan and the Related Forensic Investigation," The Organisation for the Prohibition of Chemical Weapons," June 1, 2001, www.opcw.org.

59. "America and the New Terrorism," p. 8.

60. David Tucker, "What Is New About the New Terrorism and How Dangerous Is It?" *Terrorism and Political Violence*, Vol. 13, Issue 1, 2001, p. 1.

61. Loc. cit.

62. "America and the New Terrorism," p. 66.

63. Loc. cit.

64. See Ana Sijak, *Angel of Vengeance: The Girl Assassin* (New York: St. Martin's Press, 2008).

65. The verdict was later annulled and she quickly went to Switzerland. Some years later she was able to return to Russia, dying there in 1919.

66. Council of the European Union, "Council Framework Decision 2008/919/JHA of 28 November, amending Framework Decision 2002/475/JHA on Combating Terrorism," http://eur-lex.europa.eu/legal-content/EN/TXT/PDF/?uri=CELEX:32008F0919&from=EN.

67. "Europel TE-SAT 2013: EU Terrorism Situation and Trend Report," June 13, 2002, http://europa.eu/legislation_summaries/justice_freedom_security/fight_against_terrorism/l33168_en.htm.

68. Shali Wu and Boaz Keysar, "The Effective of Culture on Perspective on Perspective Taking," *Psychological Science*, Vol. 18. No. 7, July 2007, p. 600 with rephrasing and additions.

69. Thomas H. Kean, Chair, 9/11 Commission Report (Washington, D.C.: U.S. Government, 2004), p. 14.

70. Undated video, USAToday.com/Graphics/News/gra/gclearskies/Flash.htm.

71. Staff and Wire Reports, "Bush Vows Retaliation for Evil Acts," *USA Today*, September 12, 2001.

72. Fox News, September 12, 2001.

73. Brian Ross, "How Anwar-al-Awlaki Inspired Terror From Across the Globe," September 30, 2011, www.ABCNews.go.com/Blotter/Anwar-al-Awlaki-Inspired-Terrorism/Story?Id=14643383#UDA1KLGNFI.

74. "Not All Muslims Are Arab and Not All Arabs Are Muslims," Muslim Public Affairs Council, April 26, 2011, www.summits.mpac.org/blog/not-all-muslims-are-arab-and-not-all-arabs-are-muslims.

75. "Muslims," Pew Research, December 18, 2012, www.pewforum.org/2012/12/18/global-religious-landscape-muslims.

76. "Not All Muslims Are Arab and Not All Arabs Are Muslims," *Muslim Public Affairs Council*, April 26, 2011, www.summits.mpac.org/blog/not-all-muslims-are-arab-and-not-all-arabs-are-muslims.

77. Jerome P. Bjelopera, *American Jihadist Terrorism: Combating a Complex Threat* (Washington, D.C.: Congressional Research Service, November 15, 2011), p. 2.

78. Brian Jenkins, Statement Before the Subcommittee on Emerging Threats and Capabilities, Committee on Armed Services, U.S. Senate, 107th Congress, First Session, November 15, 2001. Retrieved electronically.

79. "Anwar al-Awlaki," *New York Times*, July 18, 2012, www.NYTimes.com/Topics/Reference/Timetopics/people/A/Anwar_al_Awlaki/Index.html.

80. Jennifer Griffin, "Two U.S.-Born Terrorists Killed in CIA-led Drone Strike," Fox News, April 7, 2010 and Kimberly Dozier, "Drones: Obama Administration's Weapon of Choice in the War on al-Qaeda," *The Washington Post*, October 30, 2011.

81. The data in this paragraph is drawn from Cynthia Lum, Leslie W. Kennedy, and Alison Sherley, "Is Counter Terrorism Policy Evidence Based? What Works, What Harms, and What Is Unknown? *Piscathema*, Vol. 20, No. 1, 2008, p. 36.

82. Loc. cit.

83. Loc. cit.

84. Much of this information is restated from "Hezbollah," *The New York Topics*, www.NYTimes.com/Top/Reference/Timestopics/Organizations/Hezbollah/Index.html, updated April 6, 2012.

85. Anne Barnard, "Hezbollah Says it Flew Iranian-Designed Drone into Israel," *The New York Times*, November 11, 2012.

86. The "contested concept" phrase is from William Constanza, "Hezbollah and Its Mission in Latin America," *Studies in Conflict and Terrorism*, Vol. 35, Issue 3, March 2012, pp. 193–210.

87. This point is made by Schmid, "Terrorism–The Definitional Problem," p. 395. The discussion of it by the present authors.

88. "Georgia Bill Attacks 'Paper Terrorism' as FBI Takes Aim at 'Sovereigns,'" *Southern Poverty Law Center, Intelligence Report*, Issue 146, Summer 2012, p. 1.

89. "Sovereign Citizen Movement," Anti-Defamation League, 2005, p. 1.

90. "Georgia Bill Attacks 'Paper Terrorism' as FBI Takes Aim at 'Sovereigns,'" p. 1.

91. David Zucchino, "Police Teach Tactics for Handling 'Sovereign Citizens,'" *Los Angeles Times*, April 5, 2013.

92. Counterterrorism Analysis Section, "Sovereign Citizens: A Growing Domestic Threat to Law Enforcement," *FBI Law Enforcement Bulletin*, Vol. 80, No. 9, September 2011, p. 20.

93. Fares Akram and Isabel Kershner, "Hamas Finds Itself Aligned with Israel on Extremist Groups," *The New York Times*, October 12, 2012.

94. Cyrus Miryekta, "Hezbollah in the Tri-Border Area of South America," U.S. Army, Combined Arms Center (CAC), Ft. Leavenworth, Kansas, Newsletter 11-15, February 2011, www.USACAC.Army.mil/CAC2/Call/Docs/11-15/Ch_11.asp.

95. Rachel Yehuda and Steven E. Hyman, "The Impact of Terrorism on Brain and Behavior: What We Know and What We Need to Know," *Neuropsychopharmacology*, Vol. 30, Issue 10, October 2005, p. 1774.

96. See Christine A. Henriksen, James M. Bolton, and Jitender Sareen, "The Psychological Impact of Terrorists Attacks: Examining A Dose-Response Relationship Between Exposures to 9/11 and Axis I Mental Disorders," *Depression and Anxiety*, Vol. 27, Issue 11, November 2010, pp. 993–1000.

97. Loc. cit.

98. Jackie Mardikian, "Mental Health Consequences of September 11: A Five-Year Review of the Behavioral Sciences Literature," *Behavior and Social Sciences Librarian*, Vol. 27, Issue 3/4, 2008, pp. 158–161.

99. "United in Remembrance, Divided in Policy," Pew Research Center, September 1, 2011, www.pewresearch.org/pubs/2095/911-september-11-attacks-terrorism-islamic-extremism-civil-liberties-iraq-afghanistan.

100. Kenneth J. Long, "Understanding and Teaching the Semantics of Terrorism: An Alternative Perspective," *Perspectives on Political Science*, Vol. 19, No. 4, Fall 1990, p. 203.

101. Brian Jenkins, *The Study of Terrorism: Definitional Problems* (Santa Monica, CA: The RAND Corporation, 1980), p. 1.

102. The concept that the word "terrorism" plays to emotion rather than intellect was first coined in 1982. See Robert W. Taylor and Harry E. Vanden, "Defining Terrorism in El Salvador: La Matanza," *The ANNALS of the American Academy of Political and Social Sciences*, 463, September 1982, pp. 106–118.

103. See Erik M. Altmann, "Reconstructing the Serial Order of Events: A Case Study of September 11, 2001," *Applied Cognitive Psychology*, Vol. 17, Issue 9, December 2003, pp. 1067–1080.

104. Elizabeth F. Loftus, "Intelligence Gathering Post-9/11," *American Psychologist*, Vol. 66, Issue 6, September 2011, p. 535.

105. Loc. cit.

106. Anup Shah, Crisis in Chechnya, Global Issues, accessed September 23, 2012, www. GlobalIssues.org/Article/100/Crisis-in-Chechnya#Background.

107. "Regions and Territories: Chechnya," November 22, 2011, www.News.BBC.Co.UK/2Hi/Europe/Country_Profiles/2565049.stm.

108. Dmitri V. Trenin, The Forgotten War: Chechnya and Russia's Future (Washington, D.C.: Carnegie Endowment for International Peace, November 2003), p. 1.

109. Nancy Ramsey, "The Horror of Belsan, Through the Eyes of the Youngest Survivors," *The New York Times*, September 1, 2005, www.NYTimes/2005/09/01/arts/television/01best.html.

110. James Dao and David Johnston, "Report of Motive in Recruiter Attack," *The New York Times*, June 6, 2009, www.NYTimes.com/2009/06/03/USRecruit.html.

111. Statement by Melvin Bledsoe, Father of Carlos Leon Bledsoe AKA Abdulhakim Mujahid Muhammad, Committee on Homeland Security, U.S. House of Representatives, Washington, D.C., March 10, 2011, p. 3.

112. James Dao, "Man Claims Terror Ties in Little Rock Shooting," *The New York Times*, January 21, 2010.

113. U.S. House of Representatives Tim Griffin, letter to President Barack Obama, June 1, 2012.

114. Steve Chapman, "Muslims and Mass Murder: Understanding the Fort Hood Attack," *Washington Report on Middle East Affairs*, Vol. 29, Issue 1, January/February, 2010, p. 30.

115. Maria Newman and Michael Brick, "Neighbor Says Hasan Gave Belongings Away Before Attack," *The New York Times*, November 6, 2009.

116. James C. McKinley, "Suspect in Ft. Hood Case Is Said to Be Paralyzed," *The New York Times*, November 14, 2009.

117. Joseph Lieberman, Chair, "A Ticking Time Bomb, A Special Report," U.S. Senate Committee on Homeland Security and Governmental Affairs," February 2011, p. 7.

118. "Army Reprimands 9 Officers in Fort Hood Shooting," *USAToday*, March 10, 2011, www.USAToday.com/News/Military/2011-03-10-Fort-Hood-Shooting_N.html.

119. Written Testimony of General Jack Keane, "A Ticking Time Bomb: Counterterrorism Lessons from the U.S. Government's Failure to Prevent the Fort Hood Attack," Hearing Before the Senate Committee on Homeland Security and Governmental Affairs, February 15, 2011, p. 2.

120. Loc. cit.

121. Ibid., p. 3.

122. Ibid., p. 2.

123. "Obituary: "Anwar al-Awlaki," September 20, 2011, www.BBC.Co.UK/News/World-Middle-East-11658920.

124. Elisabeth Bumiller and Scott Shane, "Pentagon Report on Fort Hood Details Failures," *The New York Times*, January 15, 2010.

125. Craig Whitlock, "Pentagon Inquiry: Supervisors Discounted Fort Hood Suspect's Worrisome Behavior," *The New York Times*, January 16, 2010, www.Washington Post.com/WP-Dyn/Content/Article/2010/01/15/AR2010011502010.html.

126. Craig Whitlock, "Pentagon Inquiry: Supervisors Discounted Fort Hood Suspect's Worrisome Behavior," *The Washington Post*, January 16, 2010, www.WashingtonPost. Com/WP-Dyn/Article/2010/01/15/AR2010011502010.html.

127. "FBI Official Testifies on Hasan Report," *Military.com*, August 2, 2012, www.Military.Com/ Daily-News/2012/08/02/FBI-Official-Testifies-on-Hasan-Report.html.

128. "Army Reprimands 9 Officers in Fort Hood Shooting."

129. Nancy Gibbs et al., "Terrified or Terrorist?" *Time*, Vol. 174, Issue 20, November 23, 2009.

130. Michael Laris, Carol D. Leonnig, and Sandhya Somashekhar, "Wade Michael Page: Excess Drinking Cost Sikh Temple Shooter His Military Career, Civilian Job," *The Washington Post*, August 7, 2012.

131. Loc. cit.

132. Erica Goode and Serg P. Kovalesker, "Wisconsin Kill Fed and Was Fueled by Hate Driven Music," *The New York Times*, August 6, 2012, www.NYTimes.Com/2012/08/07/US/ Army-Veteran-Identified-As-Suspect-inWisconsin-Shooting.Html?Pagewanted=All; and Ryan Lenz, "White Supremacists React to Sikh Massacre," Southern Poverty Law Center, August 7, 2012, www.SPLCenter.Org/Get-Informed/News/White-Supremacists- React-to- Sikh-Massacre.

133. Anti-Defamation League, "Alleged Sikh Temple Shooter Was a Member of Hammerskins; A Hard Core Racist Skinhead Group with a Hugh Presence in Florida," www.Regions.ADL. Org/Florida/News/Sikh-Temple-Shooter.html.

134. www.Hammerskins.net, accessed September 4, 2012.

135. The description of the Byrd murder is primarily drawn from Monica Rhor, "Texas Town Still Shadowed by Dragging Death," *USAToday*, June 6, 2008, www.USAToday.com/ News/Nation/2008-06-06-2161250099_x.html; and Carter. T. Coker, "Hope-Fulfilling or Effectively Chilling? Reconciling the Hate Crimes Prevention Act with the First Amendment," Vol. 64, No. 1, *Vanderbilt Law Review*, January 2011, p. 272.

136. "New Details Emerge in Matthew Shepard Murder," *ABC 20/20*, November 26, 2004, www.ABCNews.go.com/2020/Story?Id=277685&page=1#.UEexzOJgPFJ.

137. Aside from the FBI investigation, these factors are discussed by Jean Marc Flukiger, "The Radical Animal Rights Movement: Some Reflections for the Future," *Journal for the Study of Radicalism*, Vol. 2, No. 2, 2008, pp. 11–13. The Journal records the publication date as 2008, but in databases it is listed as 2009.

138. Lenz, "White Supremacists React to Sikh Massacre."

139. Loc. cit.

140. Special Forces Unconventional Warfare (Ft. Brag, N.C.: John F. Kennedy Special Warfare Center and School, September 2008), p. I–4.

141. Eric V. Larson et al., *Assessing Irregular Warfare* (Santa Monica: RAND Corporation, 2008), p. 8.

142. See James Khalil, "Know Your Enemy: On the Futility of Distinguishing Between Terrorists and Insurgents," *Studies in Conflict and Terrorism*, Vol. 36, Issue 5, May 2013, pp. 419–430.

143. Counterinsurgency Operations, FMI 3-07.22 (Ft. Leavenworth, Kansas: United States Army, October 2004), p. I–I.

144. Loc. cit.

145. Loc. cit.

Political Ideology and the Historical Roots of Terrorism

Learning Objectives

After completing this chapter, you should be able to:

1. Outline political ideology and explain how terrorism as part of a revolutionary strategy poses significant social consequences.

2. Describe the concept of political terrorism.

3. Discuss the evolution of leftist ideology, including how anarchism and Marxism contribute to leftist doctrine.

4. Define the concept of the vanguard and discuss how it contributes to modern terrorism.

5. Provide an overview of leftist terror cells, including Latin American and European groups.

6. Discuss how colonialism and the mandate system set the stage for future conflict in the Middle East.

7. Give an overview of how Israel was established and articulate its effects on the modern landscape of political terror.

8. Describe the secular "first wave" Palestinian terror groups.

9. Provide insight into how the United States and its policies have impacted terrorist ideology in the Middle East.

A member of the Black September Organization with a hood over his head on the balcony of a building holding Israeli athletes as hostages during the 1972 Summer Olympics in Munich, Germany. Probably no other picture in history is more symbolic of the beginning of terrorism in the modern age.

(Kurt Strumpf/AP Feature Photo Service/ Newscom)

Introduction

The subject of "politics" often provokes intense emotion, generates passionate discussion, and can frequently create extreme resistance to considering another person's point of view—this is obvious even during political discussions at the dinner table or seeing friends on Facebook tear into each other because of deeply held political convictions. Indeed, politics are sometimes so interwoven into people's psyches that it affects nearly every facet of their belief system.

And, as we learned in the previous chapter, the way that people think about or perceive their environment, government, and society—and the way they feel those entities should be structured—springs from a host of factors, including genetics,[1] family tradition, educational background, socio-economic status, religious affiliation, and geographical location (individual perspective and culture). These factors are not mutually exclusive, they are not simple, and they have wide-ranging effects on a person's belief system. **Political ideology**, then, is (on an individual level) "the set of beliefs about the proper order of society and how it can be achieved."[2] On a group level, political ideology is the "shared framework of mental models that groups of individuals possess that provide both an interpretation of the environment and a prescription as to how that environment should be structured."[3]

Political ideology
The set of beliefs about the proper order of society and how that order can be achieved.

Identifying with a particular political theory or ideology has also been shown as calming, as strange as that may seem when discussing terrorism. It can help reduce uncertainty, make a person feel more secure, and increase feelings of solidarity with others.[4] Unfortunately, one's ideology is often somewhat intransient and intractable, and at its most extreme it doesn't allow for any deviation nor is it particularly tolerant of criticism. As such, it's easy to understand "how" terrorists can add to and indoctrinate their ranks, particularly during times of perceived societal upheaval. Early historical writers[5] on the subject of terrorism suggested that terrorism must be part of a revolutionary strategy and that it poses significant social consequences as well:

- Terrorism has a direct effect on the social structure of a society.
- Terrorism upsets the framework of precepts, images, and symbols on which society is based and on which society depends and trusts.
- Terrorism destroys the solidarity, cooperation, and interdependence on which social functioning is based and substitutes insecurity, distrust, and fear.
- Terrorism attacks the very bases of social order, culture, and government.[6]

In this chapter, the political and social theories that motivate certain groups will be examined—from their genesis and historical significance to their influence on modern terrorist groups.[7]

Revolutionary Ideology and Terror

As will be discussed in the coming chapters, much of the collective "modern" experience with terrorism from the Middle East is based in radical Islam. Terrorism today is not seen as purely a political phenomenon, but rather as something that is mostly motivated by religious zealots that misinterpret the peaceful constructs of various world religious, whether Islamic, Judaic, or Christian. In contrast, however, many other groups have their historical roots imbedded in political theory and ideological grievance. Even the definition of **political terrorism** (see Chapter 1), according to most writers on the subject, rely on a definition from the early 1960s that defines it as "a symbolic act designed to influence political behavior based on extra-normal means, entailing the use or threat of violence."[8] Newer definitions of terrorism give religious ideology more emphasis or even equal footing with political motivations.

Political terrorism
A symbolic act designed to influence political behavior based on extranormal means, entailing the use or threat of violence.

Surprisingly, even those terrorist groups (like al-Qaeda) that spring primarily from religious ideology are deeply rooted in political and historical movements hailing from mid-19th century Europe. The ideologies that have had the greatest impact on modern terrorism are considered leftist, a term that has its roots in a French system of governmental

FIGURE 2–1

Although often associated with Russia because of his perspectives on socialism and communism, Karl Marx (1818–1883) lived much of his life in Western Europe and is buried in London. At the funeral, his close friend and collaborator Friedrich Engels uttered only one sentence: "On the 14th of March, 1883, a quarter to three in the afternoon, the greatest living thinker ceased to think."

(Courtesy AKG-Images/Newscom)

Left-wing
A political designation that encompasses ideologies more radical in nature, including anarchism and Marxism.

Marxism
The economic and sociological theories of Karl Marx and Friedrich Engels that encompassed a revolutionary view of social change.

Proletariat
A Marxist concept that describes the working class, peasants, or oppressed people.

Pierre-Joseph Proudhon
French philosopher who was the first person to declare himself an anarchist; instrumental in sparking French revolutionary activities in 1848.

Propaganda by the deed
An ideology that advocates acts of violence as a principal means of revolution.

continuum whereby more conservative politicians were physically seated on the right of an assembly and those considered more radical were seated on the left. This symbolism has informed political designations globally (such as current American culture wars between the "right" and the "left"), and the "leftist" label has certainly been applied to describe both liberal and anarchist ideologies.

Left-wing extremism is heavily rooted in the works of Karl Marx (see Figure 2–1) and Friedrich Engels in Russia during the 1800s.[9] Their theory (now called "**Marxism**"), seeks to change or eliminate a capitalist system that is perceived to be corrupt and oppressive in nature and restore power and autonomy to the working class. Although the goals are certainly laudable—to provide a better future for the working people (called the **proletariat** by Marx)—Marxism is heavily focused on the means to overthrowing government versus the maintenance of law and order. Left-wing theories are focused on revolution and anarchy, verses peaceful demonstration, to change governmental processes.

The ideology first gained traction after the political upheavals in 1848 Europe, known as the "Springtime of the People." The movement actually began in France, as a loose coalition of middle and working-class French people toppled the constitutional monarchy and advocated for self-rule. Within a few short years, similar movements were underway in Denmark—where their monarchy met a similar fate—as well as Poland, Germany, Austria, Hungary, and Italy.[10] Not all of the revolutionary uprisings were successful, but their violent nature left lasting impressions not only on the countries where they took place, but also on other revolutionaries around the world.

Anarchism

In Russia, some extremists identified with the most successful of the revolutionary theories express in France. As defined in Chapter 1, anarchism is a belief that there should be no centralized government and that society should be based upon voluntary cooperation and free association between individuals.[11] It was first expressed by a radical contributor to the ideology of the 1848 uprising in France, **Pierre-Joseph Proudhon**. He was the first person in history to declare himself an anarchist, and minted the phrase "property is theft," which spurred other anarchist groups in Russia and elsewhere (See Figure 2–2). Essentially, Proudhon posited that property ownership gives political power, and such power is all too often used to enslave those without it. The concept was convoluted and even Proudhon himself later refuted his catchphrase as being confusing.[12] However, his recantation was too late for Russia. Revolutionary actors like Petr Kropotkin, Mikhail Bakunin, and Sergei Nechayev took Proudhon's philosophies to heart, and began to violently advocate for the destruction of any centralized authority or government. The "people" of the middle and working class were to be the new "owners" of all property, and government would cease to exist.

For the most part, violent revolution and destruction was advocated via largely passive propaganda—accomplished by leaflets, parlor meetings full of intellectuals, and newspapers with pro-revolution language. Proudhon was much more the propagandist than the violent revolutionary that he often expressed in his writing. Violence in Russia began in 1869 when Necheyev and Bakunin published the groundwork for revolution and hence set the stage for the left-wing political theory:

> The revolutionary must have a single thought, a single goal: implacable destruction. Pursuing this goal coldly and relentlessly, he must be prepared to perish himself and to cause to perish, with his own hands, all those who would prevent him from achieving his goal.[13]

Source: Excerpt from Fanaticism: A Historical and Psychoanalyical Study by Andre Haynal, Miklos Molnar and Gerard de

Necheyev and his contemporaries promoted "**propaganda by the deed**," wherein acts of violence were advocated as a principal means of revolution—and proponents

Quick Facts
The Anarchist Cookbook

Anarchists believe that the world is in the epoch of capitalism and it is a historical necessity to advance socialism through violence and terrorism. As such, *The Anarchist Cookbook* by William Powell, first published in 1971, continues to be a popular manual for guerrilla and revolutionary tactics. It originally contained instructions for the manufacture of explosives, poisons, drugs, and rudimentary weapons. Later editions (available in pdf on the Internet) have added instructions on computer hacking and credit card fraud, basic electronic surveillance, sabotage, and GPS tracking. The familiar red Anarchist "Circle A" adorns newer editions of the book.

▲ The Anarchist "A" symbol.
(© miloje/Fotolia)

of revolution were encouraged to infiltrate among the people and to win their support, and organize themselves into small, clandestine cells that could easily strike at the very heart of their enemy without detection[14]—a tactic observed in more modern terrorist organizations. Ultimately, Necheyev's and Bakunin's philosophical tactics would be used against the very people who were supposed to revolt. The general populace suffered decades of agony under the totalitarian governments and dictatorships that would plague Russia and parts of Europe during the 20th century. However, the seed had been planted among revolutionaries worldwide, inspiring the use of dynamite among French anarchists and, in particular, the man known as one of the first advocates of mass terrorism, Emile Henry. Henry famously attempted to bomb the offices of a mining company in Carmeaus, France. He defended his use of explosives that harmed innocent women and children by stating that since the building was occupied by the **bourgeoisie** (or upper class), there could be no innocent victims.[15] A rash of political assassinations in the early 20th century can also be traced to the anarchist tactics espoused by Necheyev and Bakunin.

Information Link

For more information on anarchism, visit the Spunk Library at www.spunk.org. Search the site and notice the number of other anarchist websites globally.

Bourgeoisie

The wealthy upper class, those that were property owners.

THE STRUGGLE OF THE SLAV.

FIGURE 2–2

An anarchist wielding an axe fights the oppressive Russian government, symbolized as an octopus, trying to pull him down. The octopus wears a Tsar-like crown and royal robe. The powers the man fights are shown on the tentacles, such as graft, greed, oppression, and despotism.

(Courtesy J.Ottmann Lith/Library of Congress)

Quick Facts
The Invention of Dynamite

One technological advancement that changed the face of terrorism was the invention of dynamite in 1867 by Alfred Nobel. Initially invented to aid in the digging of mines and to aid in the construction of railroad tracks through difficult terrain, dynamite (made of the highly unstable nitroglycerin combined with the absorbent diatomaceous earth), was quickly adopted for more nefarious purposes by anarchist and populist movements in Russia and France and quickly spread to other movements around the globe.

▲ In 2014, an Arab fighter throws homemade dynamite toward forces loyal to Syrian President Bashar al-Assad. Dynamite has been an important weapon for revolutionaries and terrorists throughout time.

(Courtesy Khail Ashawi/Corbis)

Marxism

The Marxist movement sprang from the belief that power and wealth were too concentrated in the hands of just a few—it championed the industrial working class as the creators of society's wealth, and sought to share that wealth equally, rather than putting it all in the hands of the very elite (the bourgeoisie). Marx and his associate, Friedrich Engels, were commissioned by the Communist League (in 1847) to write down a complete theoretical and practical program for Russia. In their work, *The Communist Manifesto*,[16] Marx and Engel proscribe a political and social theory that directed the working class to violent revolution in an effort to overthrow the existing monarchies of Europe and Russia. Their target was **capitalism**, or governments with economies that focused on competition in a free market resulting in the ownership of private property. Capitalism was seen as exploitive, pitting one person against another for power; economic wealth was marked by the ownership of private property. Marx claimed that he had developed a scientific theory based on the laws of nature and the history of man.

According to Marx, man's history is that of a social class and class struggle (see Figure 2–3). Social class is based on wealth and the ownership of private property, and that all class struggle has been over attaining control of private property. Marx believed that man's history of existence was based on materialism, or the ownership of private property. He strongly believed that there was no god or divine creator, and that all earthly functions are explained in terms of economic and social class based, again, upon the ownership of private property. According to Marx, capitalism breeds corruption and decay as the free competitive marketplace leads to overproduction, which in turn reduces the value of property. Wealth becomes concentrated in a few hands, while the masses suffer the fate of exploitation and alienation.

Capitalism
Economies that focus on competition in a free market enterprise, valuing the ownership of private property to determine wealth.

The entire history of man and society was a drive toward a new, utopian state of government: **communism**. Communism is characterized by the total elimination of private property as well as government (see Figure 2–4). Under the communist state, all goods and services are owned in common and are available as needed. The most relevant to our discussion of terrorism is the transitional stage or social state from capitalism to communism, known as socialism. It was during this transitional state that violent revolution through terrorism occurred, as individuals resisted surrendering their private property to the government (or state). **Socialism** is the elimination of private ownership of property and the means to production. The government or state owns everything, and all people are equal in the social order. Revolution, then, is inevitable as the ruling classes are "purged" during the transition to socialism.[17]

Marx's entire theory is based on his perspective of history as a constant struggle between classes of society. He contended that his theory was economic, political, and social, as society evolved through epochs of time by violent revolution and struggle (Marxism), ever seeking to equalize society by overthrowing the capitalist system and creating a more equal social order where government owns all private property and eventually withers away. Marx believed that revolution was sparked by the **vanguard**, described as advanced and tenacious representatives of the working class, who would organize revolution and overthrow the bourgeois ruling class.[18]

The Vanguard

The concept of the vanguard was further developed by Vladimir Lenin in the early 20th century (see Figure 2–5). His Bolshevik Party was at the forefront of the Russian revolution, and hence Lenin believed that it was this party that would be the vanguard to arouse a level of political consciousness in all of society necessary for revolution. The vanguard exploits the differences in people existing in a heterogeneous population. They use differences among people to agitate and disrupt society, while at the same time attacking government through a variety of tactics. Terrorism is perceived as a legitimate military tactic designed to show

FROM THE DEPTHS

FIGURE 2–3
Class struggle is depicted by this lavish social event in a large ballroom attended by the well-to-do. The party is disrupted as a fist erupts through the floor, where the exploited underclass masses work and provide the foundation on which the wealthy rest.
(Courtesy Ker, William Balfour/Library of Congress)

Communism
The ideal utopian state as proposed by Karl Marx, characterized by the total elimination of privately held property and government.

Socialism
A Marxist perspective of a transitory and revolutionary period between capitalism and communism wherein the ruling class is "purged" from the land, all people are equal, and the government owns everything; the period is marked by violence and terrorism.

FIGURE 2–4
Historically, communists have tried to export their ideology. In Wisconsin, at a communist-sponsored summer camp in 1933, children are lectured on class struggle. Note the flag with hammer and sickle on it, the communist's symbol for the working people.
(Courtesy Underwood & Underwood/Corbis)

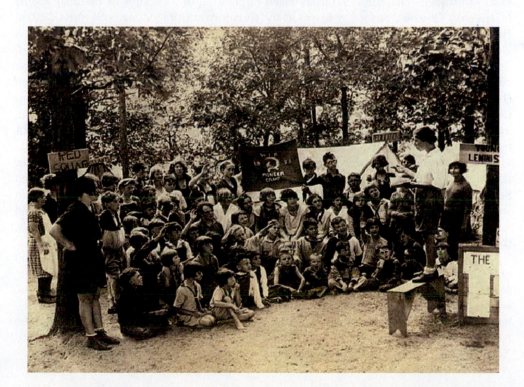

Quick Facts
Guerrilla Warfare in Vietnam

North Vietnamese Army (NVA) troops were well-trained regular Army soldiers who were sent to South Vietnam to fight. Main Force Viet Cong military units were recruited from South Vietnam and were uniformed and received training. They typically had advisors from North Vietnam attached to them. Local Viet Cong (VC) lacked uniforms, had little or no training, and were used to snipe at opposing forces or conduct small operations and then fade quickly away.

FIGURE 2–5
Vladimir Lenin was born to a solidly middle-class family; his interest turned to revolution after his older brother was executed for plotting to assassinate the Tsar. Lenin was a founder of the communist party, a major force in the Russian Revolution of 1917, and later Chairman of the Soviet government.

(Courtesy Library of Congress)

Vanguard
A concept that advocates a method of arousing a level of political consciousness among proletariats in order to foster the belief among them that revolution and any changes it brings are far preferable to the status quo.

Ernesto "Che" Guevara
An iconic, revolutionary figure in Latin America during the 1950s and 60s; he symbolized discontent with capitalism and colonization in the world, and believed that revolution was sparked by those most oppressed in a country—poor farmers living in rural areas.

the weaknesses and vulnerability of the existing government. As the government "cracks down" on individual civil liberties in an effort to stop terrorism, mass society further fractures with open antagonisms between groups of people and disruption of the existing way of life. Social order decays into rioting and eventual revolution.

According to Lenin, the vanguard was inherently a righteous calling to arms; as a result of this action, his Bolshevik Party used widespread violence and terrorism as a successful tactic throughout the Russian Revolution. And while the Bolshevik Party ultimately became the Communist Party of Russia, the concept of the vanguard not only represented those that "start the revolution," but also as a concept described how a relatively small group of revolutionaries can be groomed and teased into a cohesive political movement … and eventually a ruling government.

"Che" Guevara and the Promotion of World Revolution

The concept of the vanguard has evolved over time and been an instrumental force in revolutions throughout the world. **Ernesto "Che" Guevara** (1928–1967, see Figure 2–6) developed his ideas rooted in the establishment of a vanguard during the 1950s Cuban revolution.[19] Guevara believed that there needed to be an immediate impact on the political consciousness of the ruling party, and that immediate impact involved an armed revolution sparked by those most oppressed—the rural, agrarian-based population of a country. A medical doctor by training, Guevara was a key figure in the Cuban revolution, along with Fidel Castro. However, Guevara felt that only by taking Marxist principles outside Cuban borders to a global audience could he remedy the imperialism and capitalism that plagued the world. As such, he headed to Bolivia to rally a vanguard movement. Intellectual discourse was largely abandoned in favor of terrorism and guerrilla training; the tactic backfired when Guevara was unable to secure larger support from the local community. His "revolution in support of the people" of Bolivia was short-lived, and as a result a small group, including Guevara, were killed by members of the Bolivian military advised by U.S. CIA operatives in 1967.

Guevara was a Marxist revolutionary who became an iconic cultural hero throughout the world during a time when the tenets of capitalism were questioned and the United States was engaged in the controversial Vietnam War (1956–1975). The Vietnam War was a long and unpopular armed conflict that pitted the communist regime of North Vietnam and its southern allies, known as the "Viet Cong," against South Vietnam and its principal ally, the United States.

The divisive war ended with the withdrawal of U.S. forces in 1973 and the unification of Vietnam under Communist control two years later. More than 3 million people, including 58,000 Americans, were killed in the conflict.[20] In the United States and the Western world, a large anti-Vietnam War movement developed. This movement was both part of a much larger counterculture movement of the 1960s. Much of Che Guevara's writing formed the basis for Communist rhetoric during the Vietnam War and his picture symbolized the anti-American sentiment prevalent during this time period.[21]

Quick Facts
Che Guevara's Death and Legacy

Guevara went to Bolivia and led an unsuccessful communist insurgency. On October 8, 1967, he and a few remaining followers were attacked by a special Bolivian Ranger Unit supported by U.S. Special Forces "Green Berets" and Central Intelligence Agency (CIA) operatives. Guevara was lightly wounded and captured. The Bolivian government did not want Guevara to have a public platform at what would be a highly publicized trial, so the Bolivian Rangers were ordered to immediately execute Guevara and a cover story was issued that he was killed in combat.[22]

The emblematic and iconic photo of Che Guevara (see Figure 2–6) was very popular during the turbulent 1960s in the United States, especially after his death. It was often seen on posters, patches, hats, and T-shirts as both an expression of revolutionary Marxist thinking as well as contemporary style.

The concept of the vanguard did not die with Guevara. Today, elements of the process are seen in Islamic terror cells, and in many cases, terrorism remains the mark of the vanguard. Sayyid Qutb first wrote about that concept in his seminal work "Ma'alim fi al-Tariq" or "Milestones"—a book credited with informing much of Islamic jihad's ideology.[23] Qutb writes that the Islamic vanguard begins with preaching the movement, much like Marx and Lenin suggested, but then moves directly to violent means of terrorism as a means to spark wider revolution. Unlike Marx and Lenin, Qutb's movement had a strong religious overtone. He called it the duty of every Muslim to join in the "Holy Jihad" or "Holy War" against those who had "usurped the authority of God," Qutb knew that those in the ruling class would certainly not be inclined to surrender without a fight. This vanguard of violence and terrorism is the foundation for the modern concept of jihadism.[24] Refer to Chapter 4 for a more detailed discussion of Sayyid Qutb and his radical Islamic philosophies.

Leftist groups, then, with their roots in mid-19th century Europe, have demonstrably influenced modern terrorism philosophically and tactically. Elements of Marxism and Leninism—particularly the concept of the vanguard—have made their way into different factions of terrorism, from leftist to Islamic terror, as have anarchist principles of "propaganda by the deed." Historically, terrorism (widespread killing, assassinations, and bombings) was a major part of the violent cultural and social changes in Russia, France, Cuba, and elsewhere, and have always been part of an accepted strategy among the revolutionary left.

Information Link
Visit bio.truestory at www.biography.com. Search the site for the biography of Che Guevara. Listen to his biography, and watch the popular 2004 film entitled *The Motorcycle Diaries*, chronicling the written memoir of a 23-year-old Che Guevara as he rode his motorcycle throughout Latin America.

FIGURE 2–6
A 2010 hand-painted mural of Che Guevara superimposed on Cuba's flag in Old Town Havana, Cuba. It demonstrates the immense popularity that Guevara continues to enjoy, although he was killed nearly 50 years ago.

(Courtesy Carol M. Highsmith Archive, Library of Congress)

Latin American Leftist Groups

In Latin America, for example, several groups furthered Marxist ideology in action, engaging in guerrilla warfare just as "Che" Guevara advocated. Today, the most infamous of these is the *Revolutionary Armed Forces of Colombia (FARC)*, established in 1964 as the military wing of the Colombian Communist Party (see Figure 2–7). FARC purports to represent the rural, agrarian poor in Colombia by protecting their land interests against the wealthier classes of Colombia, the influence of the imperialist United States, the privatization of resources, and the influence of global corporations. FARC is a large operation with nearly 20,000 members. It operates in jungles and rural areas concentrated in southern and eastern Colombia. Its presence is established in roughly one-third of the country.[25] FARC is heavily armed, and is primarily funded by the drug trade, though its involvement in illegal drugs can vary regionally. FARC also secures money from ransom deals related to kidnappings, extortion, and illegal "taxes" levied on those it claims to defend. FARC is responsible for the majority of kidnappings in Colombia targeting foreign tourists, government officials both foreign and domestic, and wealthy landowners. It has also been responsible for assassinations of hostages, Colombian political figures, and, in 1999, the murder of three U.S. missionaries. Since 2007, when several key FARC leaders were killed, the group has experienced declining membership but remains a major force in Columbian politics; currently, FARC is engaged in peace talks with the Columbian government. However, attacks on oil and energy infrastructure have continued during this timeframe, as have strikes, protests, and roadblocks related to oil pipelines in areas where FARC has a presence. More troubling is the merger of FARC with the second-largest guerilla group in Colombia, ELN (the National Liberation Army). Leaders from both groups asserted in July 2013 that they were working in conjunction to "work for the unity of all political and social forces working to carry out profound changes in society" in Colombia.[26]

The *National Liberation Army (ELN)*, is also a Marxist group that operates in the Colombian countryside. Though much smaller than FARC, it too has profited heavily from the drug trade as it looks to replace the Colombian government with an **egalitarian democracy** that represents the rural peasant class. The ELN is mostly concerned with Colombia's policies toward mining and energy investment, and targets foreign businesses and oil pipelines for bombings, extortion, and kidnappings. ELN often targets multinational corporations that operate in the Colombian environment conducting lumber, mining, and drilling operations as well as the transportation of natural resources. Peace talks with ELN have not been fruitful—the Colombian government has asserted that it will not enter into any agreements or negotiations with the group until all hostages are released and reparations are made.

The *Tupac Amaru Revolutionary Movement (MRTA)* exists primarily in Peru and Argentina. However, the group, better known as the *Tupamaros*, was actually founded in neighboring Uruguay in the late 1960s. Named after the revolutionary Tupac Amaru who led a major indigenous revolt against the ruling Spanish monarchy in Peru during the 1780s, the Tupamaros are steeped in Marxist ideology. Their goal was and is to reform the governments of Peru and Uruguay, removing all imperialist elements, and create a society in which power, property, and prosperity were/are shared equally.[27] The Tupamaros in Uruguay were one of the most successful Marxist groups of the 1970s, robbing banks, kidnapping executives, and extorting money from various businesses. Unlike many of its other Marxist predecessors, the Tupamaros were true to their word and often distributed money to poor people living in urban slums around Montevideo. One of their more infamous actions was the killing of FBI Agent Dan Mitrione, a police advisor who was killed while training police officers in Uruguay in

Egalitarian democracy
The political concept that all humans are equal in fundamental political, economic, and social worth; hence social economic divisions or classes of people as well as centralized power should be diminished.

FIGURE 2–7
FARC—The Revolutionary Armed Forces of Colombia—was founded by the late Manuel Marulanda Velez in 1964. An estimated 50 percent of its nearly 20,000 members are under 19 years of age; more interesting, nearly 30 percent of the entire membership is female.

(Courtesy Tod Robberson/KRT/ Newscom)

1970.[28] Today the Tupamaros have been virtually wiped out by the Uruguayan government, and remnants of the group are active only in Peru.

Like FARC and ELN, today's MRTA operates in rural areas in Peru and uses kidnappings to further its objectives; it's a relatively small operation though, with membership estimated to be less than a thousand people. Although MRTA distinguished itself from other groups in the region by refraining from attacking innocent and unarmed resident populations, it has been responsible for several high-profile events. For example, in 1997, the group was responsible for various assassinations of Peruvian government leaders and for an infamous attack on the Japanese ambassador's residence in Lima. The kidnapping played out over four months and resulted in the death of one hostage and the injury of nearly 30 others. The resulting international publicity since the event has relegated the group to working in the remotest of areas in the country.

However, Peru's most notorious leftist group is *Sendero Luminoso* or *Shining Path*, which adopted core Marxist principles and added the teachings of their leader Abimeal Guzman, resulting in a mish-mash of mysticism, Marxism, teachings of Mao, and even racial bigotry. Shining Path claimed to be the "vanguard of the world communist movement" and was brutal in its methods—massacring peasants, government bureaucrats, police officers, and other local authorities, frequently hacking them with machetes and publicly displaying their body parts. Nearly 70,000 people—11,000 of them civilians—have been killed in skirmishes between Shining Path and the Peruvian government. Shining Path leader Abimeal Guzman was eventually captured in 1992 and called for his group to submit to a treaty with the government. The result of the capture caused Shining Path to splinter into factions, which today remain small and limited to the rural mountains of Perus. However, there is evidence of a resurgence of activity among the remaining factions, which have turned to narcotics trafficking to fund military-style attacks. The last five years have witnessed several small but deadly uprisings against police and military forces of Peru.[29]

In Argentina, complex political upheaval spawned several leftist groups. The *Montoneros* and the *People's Revolutionary Army* rose to infamy after a 1966 military coup in the country established an authoritarian-bureaucratic state. The Montoneros sprang from the Marxist left, viewing themselves as a vanguard for revolution, but also incorporating radical Catholic principles into their calls for justice and unity for all Argentinians. They formed urban guerilla cells, and carried out political kidnappings and assassinations to achieve their means. The People's Revolutionary Army, meanwhile, retreated to the country to build a revolutionary base that would root out the Argentine government in favor of proletarian rule. They, too, formed urban guerilla groups that orchestrated political kidnappings with large ransoms, and frequently attacked military and police interests in the country.

The concept of the urban guerrilla was proposed in contrast to Guevara's rural guerrilla. A Brazilian revolutionary, **Carlos Marighella**, led a series of successful guerrilla groups in Brazil from 1964 to 1973. His ideas of "liberating" Latin American countries from oppressive regimes through urban warfare were chronicled in his book *The Mini-Manual of the Urban Guerrilla*, and was a primer for the Tupamaros and the Montoneros.[30] Unlike their Peruvian, Uraguan, and Colombian counterparts, however, today little is left of either the Montoneros or the People's Revolutionary Army, or of any of the more "urban" guerrilla groups. A military takeover in 1976 resulted in a brutal backlash against these leftist groups and any other dissenting political cells were destroyed. Much of the activities aimed at destroying such movements were centered around the cities, or large urban areas, crushing the "urban guerrilla" concept.

Carlos Marighella
A Brazilian revolutionary who expressed the concept of guerrilla movements stemming from urban areas. His book, *The Mini-Manual of the Urban Guerrilla*, was very influential in Latin American leftist movements.

European Leftist Groups

While leftist groups in Latin America were fighting ostensibly a "guerrilla" war on behalf of the peasant and agrarian classes, European leftist terror groups of the same period identified more as "revolutionary thinkers." The "new left," which came about in the 1960s and lasted only a short time—until about 1974—was born of a period of Western prosperity, quite counter to the ideas proposed by Marx. However, student groups and human rights movements took advantage of this period of unprecedented freedom to embrace extreme

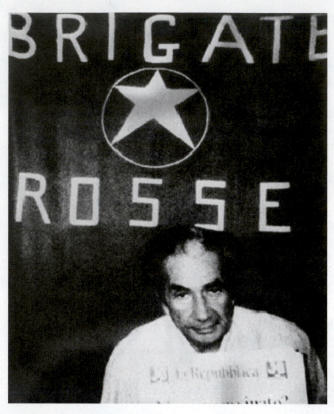

FIGURE 2–8
Aldo Moro was twice Italy's Prime Minister. In 1968, he was within sight of his home when the Red Brigades killed his bodyguards and took him prisoner. Moro was forced to pose for this picture under their banner. After 45 days he was put in the trunk of a car, covered with a blanket, and murdered by multiple gunshots.

(Courtesy EPA/Newscom)

Information Link
Visit the website www.baader-meinhof.com and learn about one of the most notorious terrorist gangs in history. Review the book by Richard Huffman cited on the website, *The Gun Speaks: The Baader-Meinhof Gang and the Invention of Modern Terror*.

left ideologies. Such movements looked at the Middle East and underdeveloped countries as being exploited by imperialist powers (Western powers such as the United States and European countries). According to the "new left," the citizens of those places became in essence the "working class," the groups that supported insurgency were looked at as the vanguard, and the leaders of European leftist groups embraced their roles as advocates for a global class struggle between capitalist nations and their victims. European philosopher Leszek Kołakowski succinctly identified the "new left" philosophy:

> The existing world order deserves destruction in all its aspects without exception. The revolution must be worldwide, total, absolute, unlimited, all-embracing [and] universal, and all partial reforms [are] a conspiracy of the establishment.... Capitalist society [is] an indivisible whole and [can] only be transformed or defeated as such.[31]

Source: Excerpt from Main Currents of Marxism. Vol. 3: The Breakdown by Leszek Kolakowski. Published by Oxford University Press, © 1978.

One of the most active of these new left groups was the *Red Brigades*, based in Italy. The group formed in 1969 and became one of the largest leftist groups in Europe, with thousands of members at its peak. Their blend of Marxist and Leninist ideology sought to overthrow the government in three phases, all involving campaigns of urban terror: first, a period of "armed propaganda," followed by an attack on the "heart of the state," and finalized by a state of "generalized civil war" which would be the death blow to the existing government. Initially, the group sought only to destroy property, targeting symbolic political sites, especially those related to the center-right Christian Democratic governments of Italy, Germany, and France. Police and factories were also targeted with bombings and arson.[32] However, kidnappings and assassinations soon followed, with the 1974 kidnapping of Genoa's Assistant Attorney General Mario Sossi, whose five bodyguards were murdered by the group, and the 1978 kidnapping and killing of Christian Democratic leader and former Italian Prime Minister Aldo Moro (see Figure 2–8). In 1981, American Brigadier General James Dozier was kidnapped by the group, though he was rescued. In its nearly 20 years of existence, the Red Brigades were extremely prolific; they were responsible for nearly 14,000 terrorist attacks.[33]

In Germany, the notorious *Red Army Faction (RAF)*—also known as the *Baader-Meinhof Gang*—was the most prominent leftist group of its era. Spurred by the killing of an activist in Berlin who was demonstrating against the Shah of Iran, a young radical named Andreas Baader mobilized a young group of German aristocrats against the government. Though many have suggested that the RAF had no real political goals, the group positioned itself as the vanguard of the oppressed third world and asserted that terrorism was the only reasonable strategy of their movement. In 1968, Baader detonated homemade bombs in two Frankfurt department stores, both of which caused fires but did not injure anyone. Baader was arrested and imprisoned in 1970, but later escaped with the help from a left-wing journalist named Ulrike Meinhof. The pair fled with several associates to Jordan, where they trained with members of the Popular Front for the Liberation of Palestine (PFLP) in guerilla warfare tactics, then returned to Germany where they robbed banks to subsidize their underground lifestyle. Baader was captured in 1972, followed by girlfriend and active member Gudrun Ensslin a week later, and then by Meinhof a few weeks later.

The trial for the members of the RAF started in 1975; in the meantime, a second generation of RAF had formed, composed of young German sympathizers. Soon the violence began anew. This new wave of violence diverged from any real political ideology, except to secure the release of the prisoners. The entire group disintegrated when Ulrike Meinhof committed suicide during a highly public trial (hanging herself in her cell). The remainder of the group, including Andreas Baader, was found guilty of murder and other crimes and sentenced to life in prison.

The RAF is one of the most notorious leftist groups in history. Three major incidents were carried out by its members, forever casting it in the lore of terrorist history. First, a public prosecutor in Berlin was killed by a hit squad in April. Second, in July 1977, a banking executive was murdered in his home. Third, in September 1977, Hanns Martin Schleyer—a powerful industrialist linked to the old German Nazi party—was forced out of his car and kidnapped. These actions by the RAF heralded a bleak period in terrorist lore commonly referred to as the "German Autumn."[34] During a five-week period, Schleyer's release was offered in exchange for the discharge of Baader, Ensslin, and several others from prison. As that was being negotiated, former friends and comrades from the Popular Front for the Liberation of Palestine (PFLP) hijacked a Lufthansa flight bound for Frankfurt on October 13, demanding the release of the RAF prisoners, two Palestinians held in Turkey, and $15 million in ransom. One pilot was executed as the plane hopped around the world for refueling. Finally, at a stop in Mogadishu, Somalia, on October 18, 1977, elite German federal police stormed the plane, killing all but one of the hijackers. Baader, Ensslin, and other members of the RAF committed suicide in their cells immediately following the failed attempt to garner their release from a German prison. Sadly, on October 19, 1977, at-large RAF kidnappers announced that they had also killed Hanns Martin Schleyer the day before.

The death of Baader and Meinhof signaled the beginning of the end for the RAF in Europe. Although splinter members perpetrated several assassinations and bombings well into the 1980s, it had weakened significantly. In 1998, members of the remnant group quietly dissolved into obscurity with a final statement: "The revolution says: I was, I am, I will be again."[35]

The *Revolutionary Cells*, and its feminist-leaning auxiliary group the *Red Zora*, were the least prominent of the three major European leftist groups. The group was Marxist in nature but eschewed the "underground" terrorist tactics of the RAF, preferring to integrate themselves into everyday life—holding jobs, raising families ... and waging bombing campaigns on the side. The anti-imperialist group (who viewed Israeli independence as an imperialist affront to Palestinians) was responsible for bombings at airports, military installations, and other symbolic government sites throughout the early to mid-1970s, and is probably best known for its role in the hijacking of Air France Flight 139 en route from Tel Aviv to Paris in 1976. Members of the Revolutionary Cell, in concert with members of the Popular Front for the Liberation of Palestine (PFLP), hijacked the Air France plane with 248 passengers. During the hijacking, Israeli and non-Israeli passengers were separated—the non-Israelis were allowed to depart the plane while Israeli passengers were held and eventually flown to Entebbe, Uganda.[36]

Acting on intelligence from various sources, the famous Operation Thunderbolt was planned for the raid on Entebbe. The operation was conducted at night on July 4, 1976. An Israeli Defense Force (IDF) special team of 100 commandos flew over 2,500 miles and landed on foreign soil in Uganda in an effort to rescue the Israeli passengers. The raid took only 90 minutes, during which 102 hostages were rescued, 5 Israeli commandos were wounded, and one, the unit commander, Lt. Col. Yonatan Netanyahu, was killed, as were all the hijackers. The "Raid on Entebbe" became a significant world event and marked the beginning of elite commando forces of countries around the world in an effort to counter terrorism with opposing tactical and military means. See Chapter 14 for more information on the development of counterterrorism units.

Historical Roots of Terrorism in the Middle East

As observed during the early 1900s, one particular political ideology—Marxism—formed the theoretical base of terrorism as part of a strategic or military tactic within a revolutionary movement. It is interesting to note that Marxism is considered an economic, social, and political theory, and that some groups used Marxist tenets to justify revolution in an attempt to end the plight of the working class and peasant people of a country (the proletariat), whereas others use a Marxist ideology as justification for participation in the illegal drug trade or as rationalization for the use of often indiscriminate force (bombings, assassinations, and kidnappings) against innocent individuals.

Box 2-1
Characteristics of the Left and the Right

On the ideological spectrum, leftist groups like the ones discussed here are at the very extreme—located far from moderate or centrist ideologies and even more distantly from fringe right-wing counterparts. What really sets leftist terror groups apart—and in fact, distinguishes all ideological groups from each other—is the types of groups that they "advocate," their techniques, and their endgame. For example, modern or centrist groups advocate for society in general, not focusing on one group or another but instead looking at the whole. Their process for advancing their cause is a group consensus—generally as part of a partisan democratic event such as voting—and the outcome is generally a balance between a gradual change with a nod to tradition or status quo. This is a good characterization of most modern American political groups, with labels from liberals to conservatives.

However, on the far right fringe of the spectrum, groups advocate for a specific race or ethnicity, religion, or nationality. Their endgame is a change based on a reaction to a perceived threat, that is, a changing values system or a new and pervasive culture that is upending a long-standing social order. Their methodology

for achieving their endgame involves a retreat or return to the "good old days"—a social movement that seeks to restore that cherished social order. These are characterized by the neo-fascist, neo-Nazi, and skinhead hate groups, such as the Ku Klux Klan, Aryan Nations, and the Christian Identity Church.

Far-left groups, by contrast, are much more future-oriented; they look to radical change, hoping to topple the social order of the past on behalf of certain societal classes (e.g., the working class or proletariats). Their movements are often based in a complex theoretical groundwork that describes those that have wealth and those that are oppressed (e.g., anti-colonialism, anti-capitalism, Marxism). The ultimate goal is liberation from a real or perceived oppressive government. This designation contains groups that often self-identify as communist, socialist, or anarchist, such as the Black Blocs, Earth Liberation Front, Weather Underground, and Popular Front for the Liberation of Palestine (PFLP).

Can you think of similarities or differences between the left and the right?

Marxist theory has also acted as the ideological foundation for groups interacting throughout the world—witness the collaboration between German leftist cells of the RAF and members of the Popular Front for the Liberation of Palestine (PFLP) during the 1970s. Groups like the Red Brigades and the Baader-Meinhof Gang viewed the Palestinian people as displaced working-class individuals without power being oppressed by the imperialist forces of the United States and Israel. This same ideological theme proved to be relatively dominant in the era of World War I and modern colonialism, an era that stretched through most of the 20th century and greatly impacted the Middle East. Marxism was often the ideological justification for groups that fought newly established colonial rule by European countries in the Middle East after World War I.

Colonialism and the Mandate System

Colonialism
A practice of domination, involving political and economic control of a territory.

The term **colonialism** refers to a practice of inhabiting a specific area outside the native country. Unfortunately, it often includes the social, political, and economic domination of the indigenous people of an area. Further, when a colonial power takes over a new territory, the natural resources and/or wealth of that territory is often transferred to the colonizing country.[37] For much of the early 20th century, most of the known world lived under the sovereignty of European colonial powers: British, French, German, Dutch, and the Ottoman empires ruled much of the Middle East, the Caribbean, India, and Africa. At the end of World War I, the fate of the colonies in the Middle East of the defeated "belligerents" (Germany and the Ottoman Empire) were divided between the triumphant countries of Great Britain and France. Though some of the allied forces tried to remain neutral (including the United States) and lobbied for the right to self-determination for many of these countries in the Middle East, it was clear that the Middle East would be subject to colonial annexation by the European victors of World War I.[38]

During World War I, both the British and the French realized the significant strategic importance of the Middle East, especially the potential wealth from oil that lie under its desert sands. Much of the Arabian Peninsula was open frontier ruled by individual tribes and no unifying government. At the end of the war, the Ottoman Empire was shattered and the British and French were eager to seize control of the area, particularly those areas that bordered the Mediterranean Sea (e.g., Egypt, Syria, Palestine), which could be used as easy shipping points to Western Europe. As a result, the **Sykes-Picot Agreement of 1916** was developed. The Sykes-Picot Agreement essentially carved up the Middle East into British

Sykes-Picot Agreement of 1916
An agreement between Great Britain and France as to the development of colonies resulting from the impending collapse of the Ottoman Empire after World War I.

and French "spheres of influence" upon the defeat of the Ottoman Empire. France would rule and colonize what is now the southeastern part of Turkey, plus territory in northern Iraq, Syria, and Lebanon; Great Britain would take possession of Transjordan, southern Iraq, and a few strategic ports in Palestine, allowing shipping access across the Mediterranean. Russia, the other victor of the World War I, lay claim to the northern Ottoman territories, now known as the Ukraine, Azerbaijan, Armenia, and Georgia.

To add insult to injury to the Arab Middle East, the **Balfour Declaration** emerged from Great Britain in 1917. It was essentially a diplomatic letter from British Foreign Secretary Alfred Balfour to a historically prominent Jewish family in Great Britain that formally signaled British support for the development of a new, sovereign Jewish state in the Middle East. The declaration was designed to win British Zionist support in England as well as provide a supportive ally in the Middle East. The Balfour Declaration was the first formal document from a European power to legitimize a "Jewish national homeland" in Arab-dominated Palestine.[39]

The end of World War I set forth the tenets of colonization in the Middle East and the potential for a Jewish state in the area. Arab interests were incensed—they had been promised by Allied forces during the war that the defeat of the Ottomans would begin the process of Arab sovereignty after the war. The Sykes-Picot Agreement and the Balfour Declaration sadly laid the early foundation of mistrust against Western countries that persists to this day.[40] The Paris Peace Conference in 1919 formally presided over by the "Big 4"—the United States, Great Britain, France, and Italy—formally created the League of Nations, a forerunner to the United Nations. Under Article 22 of the "Covenant of the League of Nations," the **mandate system** of dividing the Middle East into European colonies was established.[41] Syria, Lebanon, Tunisia, and Algeria were placed under French control, while Palestine, Transjordan (the area composed now of Israel and Jordan), and Egypt fell under Great Britain. The British also took, as part of their mandate, the three Ottoman provinces of Mesopotamia, Mosul, and Baghdad and Basra, defining what is now modern-day Iraq. The mandate system essentially charged Great Britain and France with administrative oversight of these territories, with responsibility for leading them toward eventual self-rule, but in reality, the two superpowers had no intention of ceding their newly acquired, wealthy territories (see Figure 2–9). Immediately following the implementation of the mandate, Arab nationalism rose throughout the Middle East and resistance against the new colonialism began.[42]

The fight against colonialism throughout the Middle East was informed by the same philosophical ideology: Marxism. Marx and Guevara identified colonialism as an outgrowth of a fully developed capitalist power. Colonialism was a natural extension of capitalism, according

Balfour Declaration
A formal letter from British Foreign Secretary Alfred Balfour in 1917 signaling British support for the development of a new, sovereign Jewish state in the Middle East.

Mandate system
the system of colonization after World War I dividing areas in Middle East, primarily between Great Britain, France, and Italy.

FIGURE 2–9
A map of the mandates or colonies established in the Middle East by the League of Nations after World War I. *Map:* Geoffrey Gaudreault, NPR; *Source:* A History of the Arab Peoples from The Middle East and the West: WWI and beyond by Mike Shuster. Copyright © 2004. Used by permission of NPR (National Public Radio).

Box 2–2
Frantz Fanon

A more specific—and forceful—ideology stemming from the mandate system in the Middle East was espoused by **Frantz Fanon**. Fanon was born in the French colony of Martinique, served in the French army, and was eventually assigned to Algeria, a part of the French mandate. He was a black man trained as a psychiatrist, and practiced in the French government, leading him to have direct contact with Arabs dominated by French colonization. He was horrified by stories of torture by the French, and eventually resigned his position in order to advocate for the native Algerian cause. Fanon's two masterpieces were "The Wretched of the Earth," published in 1961, and "Black Skins, White Masks," published in 1952.

Fanon was influenced by the writings of Jean-Paul Sarte as well as Karl Marx, and is credited with characterizing the action of colonization itself as a form of violence, stripping the indigenous population of power, history, culture, and identity, particularly when the colonizing power was predominately white over lands inhabited by people of color. Hence, Fanon insisted that decolonization would always be a violent act as well, "... *revolutionary violence is a cleansing force. It rids the colonized of their inferiority complex, of their passive and despairing attitude. It emboldens them and restores their self-confidence.*"[43]

Fanon's writings inspired not only a series of national liberation movements that signaled the end of the mandate system in the Middle East, but also sparked future revolutionary leaders globally, including Ali Shariati in Iran, Steve Biko in South Africa, Malcolm X in the United States, and Ernesto "Che" Guevara in Bolivia. He had a unique ability to write to the common man, indicating that each individual must be willing to sacrifice himself to strengthen the overall force of the revolution.[44] This is a concept that will be seen again and again in the evolution of terrorist ideology, from post-colonial Palestinian conflict to modern Islamic fundamentalism.

Can you think of other philosophers that influenced revolutionary writers in the future?

Frantz Fanon
A black revolutionary writer and medical doctor serving in the French army in Algeria. His writings sparked national liberation movements throughout the Middle East as well as the rest of the world.

to Marx, because expansion of capitalism was necessary to obtain more resources and create new marketplaces. It was simply another mode of production in the capitalist machine. [45]

Arab uprisings began immediately as a result of the mandate system. The first began in 1920, as a revolt against British control in Egypt, followed by another in Iraq the same year. A rural guerrilla war in Iraq was organized against the British with much success; however, British control of the air proved fateful to revolting forces, killing thousands of Iraqis. In 1925, a similar situation emerged against the French in Syria, and again the ruling country was able to use air power to reduce the revolt. Some scholars argue that these initial uprising against the colonial powers of Europe via the post–World War I mandate marked the beginning of a sustained Arab resistance against the West.[46]

Nominal independence was granted to Egypt in 1922 and to Iraq a decade later in 1932; however, Great Britain maintained sizable military forces in the region. It was not until after World War II that Egypt and Iraq completely escaped British control. Syria, Lebanon, Algeria, and Tunisia also remained under French rule until after World War II.

Palestinians
People of Arab descent tracing their cultural heritage to an area known as Palestine, now occupied by the country of Israel.

Arab resistance also increased in the British mandate area of Transjordan, containing what is now the Palestinian Territory, Israel, and Jordon. Since the Balfour declaration, Jewish emigration to the Zionist homeland of current-day Israel had numbered in the hundreds of thousands. In 1922, the Jewish population rose to about 11 percent of the populace—and another 300,000 arrived within the next decade.[47] This huge influx of foreign Jews further antagonized the Arab population of the area (known as **Palestinians**), and continued to fuel outbursts of violence aimed not only at the new Jewish settlers but also against British forces in the area. Tensions and violence culminated in 1935 to 1936, when the "Black Hand" organization, a militant Palestinian group organized by Sheikh Izz ad-Din al-Qassam, attacked, murdered, and publically maimed Jewish settlers in the Palestinian Territory. Al-Qassam was killed by British forces, sparking further outrage among the greater Arab population. Combined with another major spike in Jewish immigration that brought the Jewish population to more than 25 percent of the total Palestine territory, conditions were like a powder keg.[48] The result was a year-long Arab revolt marked by massacres on all sides; Jewish settlers were killed, British troops were killed, and Palestinians were killed. After an attempt to relocate Palestinians, British military forces continued to resort to military tactics to thwart revolting Arab Palestinians. By the end of the 1937, nearly 10 percent of the adult male Palestinian population had been killed, exiled, or maimed.[49] However, the events of World War II soon loomed large in the Palestinian Territory as well as throughout the Middle East, changing the course of Palestinian history and signaling the end of the mandate system of traditional colonialism in the Middle East.

The Impact of World War II and the Establishment of Israel

After World War II ended, areas subject to the mandate system in Syria, Lebanon, Iraq, and Egypt gained full independence from British and French rule. In the Palestinian Territory (referred to as just Palestine), however, control of the land was handed over to the newly formed United Nations (1947). Again, there was increasing unrest between Arabs and Jews in the area due to a continued and massive influx of Jewish immigrants during and immediately after World War II (see Figure 2–10). Hundreds of thousands had fled Nazi persecution and settled in their religious and cultural homeland.[50] **Zionists**, or those sympathetic to the creation of a Jewish state in Palestine, began to demand that Britain establish such a state by immediately issuing 100,000 immigration certificates to Jewish survivors of the Holocaust. Previously, Jewish immigration had been strictly curtailed by the mandate. Regardless, 70,000 immigrants flooded into Palestine illegally. The Zionists intensified diplomatic efforts directed at the United States, and President Harry S. Truman unsuccessfully asked Britain to reconsider their immigration policy.

Nearly 400 people were killed by Jewish and Arab militant groups in 1946 during violent uprisings of both Jews and Arabs against the British and each other. Anti-Semitic graffiti perpetrated by Arabs became a common sight in Jewish settlements throughout Palestine (see Figure 2–11). Political tension was again at an all-time high within the region, leading British officials to surrender the entire problem to the newly formed United Nations. The UN developed a Special Committee on Palestine, which set forth two proposals calling for the creation of separate Arab and Jewish states. The Arab nationalists rejected both suggestions, and reiterated their position that Palestine was a crucial part of the Arab-Muslim world and that the UN had no right to separate Palestine into a "National Jewish Homeland" and an "Arab Palestinian State."[51]

Zionists
People sympathetic to the creation of a Jewish state in the Middle Eastern area of Palestine.

FIGURE 2–10
Following World War II, Jews, many of them recently rescued from German concentration camps, flocked to Palestine. Jewish migration to Palestine was strictly limited so hundreds of thousands came illegally. The passengers swarmed off of the ships as quickly as possible, before the British could collect and return them to their place of origin.

(Courtesy AKG-Images/Newscom)

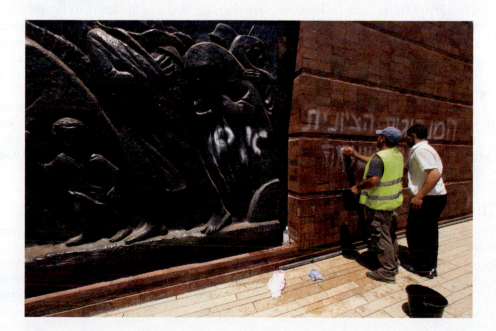

FIGURE 2–11
Anti-Semitic graffiti has been a continuous problem. At the Holocaust Memorial in Jerusalem in 2012, workers wash graffiti from the walls. Among the graffiti were slogans such as "Hitler, thank you for the Holocaust."

(© Jim Hollander/epa/Corbis)

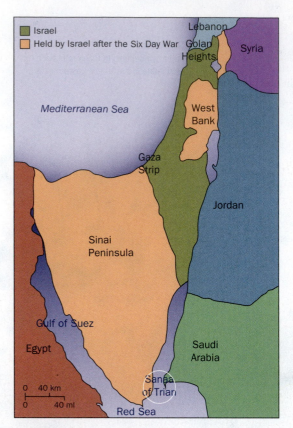

FIGURE 2–12

Israel was declared as a separate and independent country on May 14, 1948. It is a very small country, composed of only 8,500 square miles, located on the southeastern edge of the Mediterranean Sea, with a population of slightly over 8 million people (75% Jewish, 20% Arab, and 5% other). Its land mass and borders have significantly changed over the years as a result of wars and agreements with Palestinians and neighboring Arab states.

Information Link

Visit the Central Intelligence Agency Factbook on the Internet and learn about the histories of Israel, the Gaza Strip, and the West Bank at https://www.cia.gov/library/publications/the-world-factbook/docs/history.html.

Nonetheless, the United Nations adopted the partition plan on November 29, 1947. It gave just over 56 percent of Palestine to the Jewish state and about 43 percent to the Arab state, with the holy sites in Jerusalem remaining an international enclave. The approval prompted the withdrawal of British forces and immediately pitted Arabs against Jews living in the area. Zionist forces seized the moment to capitalize on British withdrawal and on May 14, 1948, declared an independent State of Israel to the United Nations, supported by only one vote, that of the United States. The action led to a full-scale war between the newly announced country of Israel and its neighboring Arab states of Jordan, Egypt, Lebanon, Syria, and Iraq. Arab military forces invaded Israel; most were unsuccessful, and hostilities ended in early 1949 with an armistice agreement that set the recognized boundaries of a new Israeli state and divided Jerusalem in half between the Jewish and Arab settlers. Israel retained a majority of the former Palestine, leaving only small areas along the Gaza Strip and the West Bank under Arab Palestinian control. These areas represented 25 percent of the former Palestinian territory.[52] (See Figure 2–12.)

Palestinians began to leave their homesteads "en masse" with the creation of the new state of Israel (1948–1949). The UN estimated that by 1949, almost a million Palestinian refugees fled to the smaller Arab-controlled areas of Palestine or to neighboring Arab countries like Jordan, Lebanon, and Syria. Destruction of the property of the fleeing Palestinians ensued, with many villages being leveled and subsequently rebuilt as new Jewish settlements.

The Arab position against Israel has not changed: The establishment of a Jewish state within Palestine was and is against all international law. The Zionist entity, according to the Palestinian Arabs, was never interested in sharing the lands as drawn in the original partition plan, but rather the development of a singular Zionist state (Israel) at the expense of the indigenous people of the land—the Arab Palestinians. Even today Israel is not formally recognized as a separate country by Palestinians and most Arab countries. On the other hand, Israel strongly argues that it has a right to exist as a separate nation, as a homeland for all Jews worldwide, and that the land is historically a Jewish homeland as well as an Arab location.

In addition to the dispute about whether Israel should even exist, other contentious factors are at work. Many of the sites located in Israel generally and in Jerusalem particularly have great meaning to all three of the monotheistic religions of Islam, Judaism, and Christianity, and often they are within just a few feet of each other.

The City of David, as Jerusalem is known, was the center of the first two Jewish commonwealths in Palestine. It was also the site of the first Temple built to worship God. The Wailing Wall, part of this first Temple, still exists in Jerusalem and is the holiest of Jewish sites.[53] However, Jerusalem is also the third holiest city in the Muslim faith. According to the Qur'an, Mohammed traveled to Jerusalem from Mecca and back in one night on a miraculous creature, accompanied by the angel Gabriel. While in Jerusalem, Mohammed visited the former site of the Hebrew Temple, ascending to heaven while standing on a rock in the Temple Mount. This rock was enshrouded and is now known as the Mosque of Omar. Another sacred mosque, known as al-Aqsa, was built for public prayer nearby. Jerusalem is also claimed by Christians as the area were Jesus died and was resurrected (see Figure 2–13).

The Palestinian Resistance Movement

The problem of Palestine quickly became the "lightening rod" for all Arab Muslims against Western influence in the region. In fact, Palestinians themselves became somewhat disenfranchised from the politics surrounding the issue. They were discouraged from using their own initiatives, and Egypt proclaimed that until the Arab states had a military superior to that of Israel and its allies, there should be no war. Syria claimed Egypt was ignoring

Quick Facts
Jewish and Arab Palestinians in Palestine

In 2013, the Jewish population in Israel exceeded 6 million; Palestinians within Israel numbered 1.4 million and 4.4 million resided in the West Bank, Gaza, and East Jerusalem. The birthrate among Palestinians lead census experts to predict that by 2016, the Palestinian population in the area will catch up to and then exceed the Jewish population.[54]

the Palestinian problem in favor of unifying the larger Arab-Muslim world.[55] Arab perspectives on a Palestinian homeland were seriously divided.

In early 1964, Egyptian President Jamal Abd al-Nasser convened the first Arab Summit Conference in Cairo regarding the plight of Palestine. As a result of this conference, a new entity was developed to represent the sole interests of Palestinian Arabs within the larger conflict with Israel. The conference, held in 1964, gave birth to a new organization known as the *Palestinian Liberation Organization (PLO)*, with a Palestinian Congress headed by **Ahmad Shuqayri**. The Palestinian Congress adopted a charter that affirmed a dedication to the liberation of Palestine and to the destruction of Israel. The Summit also established the Palestinian Liberation Army (PLA). However, neither entity (the PLO or the PLA) was independent of the greater Arab League, composed of Egypt, Saudi Arabia, Syria, Iraq, and other powerful Middle Eastern countries. Egypt retained effective control over the Palestinian Congress, emphasizing that broad military action was the most effective way to defeat the Israelis.[56] As a result, the PLA and the PLO were figureheads for the first three years of their existence. In fact, the creation of the PLO was more about restraining a growing Palestinian resistance movement and less about giving Palestinians a voice in a struggle that was co-opted by other Arab-Muslim nations. Consequently, those resistance groups began to criticize the passivity of the PLO and factions began to arise.[57]

Predictably, the PLO fractured into over a hundred different groups, each linked to the concept of a free and independent Palestinian state, but with a different ideology or methodology for achieving such a status. Many wealthy business entities within the PLO had links to more radical Palestinian organizations, some of them guerilla resistance groups, and began pushing for a more action-oriented position. Some of these groups had existed well before the PLO was even chartered. One such group was *al-Fatah*, which translates as "to open" from Arabic. The origin of this group was in the Union of Palestinian Students at Cairo University as early as 1952, under the leadership of an eloquent student named **Yassir Arafat**. The student group rallied Palestinians in support of direct assault against Israel, including clandestine commando raids against the general population of new Israeli settlers (terrorism as a tool of revolution). Al-Fatah was the largest of the PLO factions and was very successful in gaining support from other countries. Syria was an immediate ally; the Syrians had been waiting for a chance to challenge Egyptian president Jamal Abd al-Nasser for control over the broader PLO. Syria provided funds, training, and equipment to the new al-Fatah group that began conducting raids against Israel.[58]

Al-Fatah grew in strength and activity as Jordan and Saudi Arabia became strong supporters, both financially and militarily. By the end of the 1965, al-Fatah had become an accomplished guerrilla force, carrying out a variety of bombings and attacks against

FIGURE 2–13
The Temple Mount as seen from the Mount of Olives, where Christians believe that Judas betrayed Jesus. The Middle East and Jerusalem have for centuries been the location of fierce fighting, often between religions. The Crusades, which lasted nearly 200 years, are just one example.

(Courtesy Neil Farrin/Robert Harding/ Newscom)

Ahmad Shuqayri
The first head of the Palestinian Congress in 1964.

Yassir Arafat
The leader of the al-Fatah Palestinian group and later head of the Palestinian Liberation Organization (PLO).

Box 2–3
Yassir Arafat

Born in Cairo in 1929, Yassir Arafat became active in the struggle for a separate Palestinian state at an early age, rising to the leadership of al-Fatah, and then as head of the Palestinian Liberation Organization (PLO). In 1974, he became the first representative of a nongovernmental organization to address the United Nations. With a gun strapped to his hip, he compared himself to George Washington and Abraham Lincoln, and bluntly warned, "Today, I have come bearing an olive branch and a freedom fighter's gun. Do not let the olive branch fall from my hand."

In 1993, he was part of the U.S.-led Oslo Accords, meeting with Israeli Prime Minsters Shimon Perez and Yizhak Rabin. Based on an agreement from these meetings, the implementation of Palestinian self-rule was granted in the West Bank and the Gaza Strip. A year later, Arafat shared the Noble Peace Prize with his Israeli counterparts. On October 12, 2004, Yassir Arafat died after a relatively quick illness in Paris at the age of 75. Speculation abounded that he was poisoned with polonium, a radioactive metal, which led to the 2012 exhumation of his body. A Swiss team conducting the forensic investigation determined that he had 18 times the normal level of polonium in his bones and ribcage and stated they were 83% confident that polonium poisoning was the cause of his death. While controversy continues around his death, his life is remembered by fellow Palestinians as a constant struggle for his people, even amid accusations of widespread corruption and his continued support of terrorism and suicide bombing.

Do you think Arafat was a "thug" or a legitimate representative of his people?

FIGURE 2–14
Egyptian warplanes lie destroyed on an airport tarmac after a preemptive Israeli airstrike during the Six-Day War in 1967.

(© Getty Images)

Israeli military and citizen targets. As a result, the Israeli government became increasingly concerned that the stage was being set for a major invasion by combined forces of al-Fatah, Egypt, Syria, and Jordan. Israel retaliated by attacking al-Fatah strongholds in the West Bank, setting off back-and-forth violence that culminated in what is known as the Six-Day War (June 1967). (See Figure 2–14.) Israel further carried out a preemptive strike against Egypt and other Arab states, attacking airfields and destroying Egyptian as well as other Arab air forces. The Israeli military seized Gaza, the Sinai, and several other Arab-held strongholds throughout the region, nearly doubling the size of Israel and displacing an additional half-million Palestinians.

This defeat in 1967 led to the long-standing and dangerous belief by many Arabs that conventional warfare tactics would not work against the Israelis. With significant U.S. support, Israel maintained, and still boasts, one of the strongest and most modern military forces in world. As a result, more radical and vocal leaders within al-Fatah began to gain legitimacy within the ranks of the PLO. Palestinians began to call for the resignation of Ahmad Shuqayri in favor of leaders willing to use guerrilla and terroristic tactics against the Israelis, expressed by the revolutionary ideologies of Karl Marx, Che Guevara, and Frantz Fanon. By 1969, Yassir Arafat became chairman of the PLO, now an umbrella group of over a hundred loosely connected organizations focused on the establishment of an independent Palestine.[59] A change in approach was immediate and obvious in the adoption of the following amendments to the Palestinian National Charter, some of which echo Fanon's ideological writings:

- **Article IX:** Armed struggle is the only way to liberate Palestine and is therefore a strategy, not a tactic.

- **Article X:** Guerrilla, commando, and revolutionary actions form the nucleus of the popular Palestinian war of liberation. This requires its escalation, comprehensiveness, and the mobilization of all the Palestinian popular and educational efforts and their organization and involvement in the armed Palestinian revolution. It also requires the achieving of unity for the national struggle among the different groupings of the Palestinian people (within the PLO), and between the Palestinian people and the Arab masses, so as to secure the continuation of the revolution, its escalation, and victory.[60]

Al-Fatah recognized that differences between PLO factions could quickly detract from their primary mission. The sole aim of the group became the elimination of Israel and the establishment of an independent Palestinian state. Although al-Fatah continued to be the largest faction under the PLO umbrella, other, more radical groups also formed.[61]

The Popular Front for the Liberation of Palestine (PFLP) was the second largest group. The PFLP was a Christian-led Marxist organization founded by the late **George Habash** as a direct response to the Six-Day War of 1967. George Habash, code named "al-Hakim," or the doctor, was a Christian Palestinian doctor. He witnessed the mass expulsion of his people in 1948 and had previously led the Arab Nationalist Movement (ANM) as a medical student in Beirut. The PFLP established small cells throughout the West Bank and Gaza with support from Egypt and Syria. Habash's new group adopted a strong Christian Marxist ideology. It not only addressed the need to fight the Israelis, but also any imperialist nation (e.g., European nations or the United States) that was an active supporter of Israel or any Arab state that acted as a puppet government for perceived Western capitalist interests (e.g., Saudi Arabia and Jordan).[62] More interesting, Habash and the PFLP were Christian, strongly asserting that it was their Christian religious duty to assist the oppressed Palestinian people. Again, echoing the ideology of Che Guevara, the Palestinian struggle was seen by members of the PFLP as an integral part of a larger world revolution that included the Cubans, Vietnamese, North Koreans, and Chinese; the Palestinian struggle was but an extension of the world struggle against colonialism and capitalism sponsored by Western European countries and the United States.[63]

Leadership of the PFLP rested in the hands of two Christian Marxist physicians; George Habash became the political figurehead while his longtime friend, **Wadi Haddad**, directed military and guerrilla actions. In July 1968, the PFLP began a terrorist strategy aimed at bringing the Palestinian agenda to the attention of the entire world. The first modern hijacking of a commercial airlines (skyjacking) was conducted by Haddad and other members of the PFLP against an Israeli El-Al airliner. Known as "the Master," Haddad meticulously planned and orchestrated the entire skyjacking. The airliner was diverted from its original flight from Tel Aviv to Rome, and taken to Algeria. The PFLP gained world media attention from the event, and demanded that Palestinian prisoners be set free and that Israel retreat from all Palestinian lands. After nearly 40 days of negotiations all passengers and skyjackers walked free, as well as many demanded prisoners; however, no Palestinian territory was ever surrendered. The event marked one of the most successful terrorist events in history and set the stage for a flurry of skyjackings to come.[64]

The PFLP came to the forefront of Palestinian organizations as a result of successful skyjackings that hit the world stage, forcing one terrorism expert of the time (Brian M. Jenkins from the RAND Corporation) to coin the phrase that "terrorism was grand theater."[65]

Events were soon to change, and in September 1970, the grandest of all skyjackings performed by the PFLP backfired in the Jordanian desert. A great deal of tension had arisen between Jordanians and Palestinians as a result of mass immigration of Palestinians into Jordan.[66] King Hussein of Jordan further fanned the flames of tension by openly supporting a new Israeli-Arab peace proposal sponsored by the United States. The proposal called for an end to Israeli occupation of the lands taken during the Six-Day War in 1967, but did not satisfy the Palestinian demands for a complete withdrawal of the Israelis from all Palestinian lands. As a result, the PFLP began to launch small-scale attacks against Jordan throughout the summer of 1970. King Hussein was viewed as an American puppet and at least two different unsuccessful assassination attempts were made against him by the PFLP.[67]

On September 6, 1970, Wadi Haddad again planned and set into motion a series of skyjackings specifically designed to attract world attention and embarrass Jordan. Two airplanes (an American TWA airliner and a Swiss Air airliner) were simultaneously skyjacked and diverted to an abandoned airstrip in the Jordanian desert. Passengers and crew were forced to deplane their aircraft and were held hostage for four days. Another plane, an American Pan-Am jet, was flown to Cairo and blown up as soon as the passengers and crew exited. A fourth hijacking aboard an El-Al flight was thwarted that same day, but the PFLP managed to later hijack a fifth plane, a British Air jet, and land it next to the previously two skyjacked aircraft in Jordan.[68] As a result of these hijackings, the PFLP demanded and obtained the release of Palestinian prisoners in Britain, Switzerland, and West Germany in exchange for the skyjacked hostages.

George Habash
A Christian Marxist physician that led the Popular Front for the Liberation of Palestine (PFLP).

Wadi Haddad
A Christian Marxist physician that directed the military and guerrilla actions of the Popular Front for the Liberation of Palestine (PFLP); credited for developing the modern-day hijacking of airliners as a methodology and tactic of terrorism.

Box 2-4
The Seige at OPEC: A Collaboration of Terror

In late December 1975, a collaborative exercise in terror brought members of the European Red Army Faction, June 2nd Movement, and Red Cells together with a group of Palestinian terrorists as part of the largest hostage-taking event in history. The combined group attacked the Vienna headquarters of the Organization of Petroleum Exporting Countries (OPEC). OPEC is composed of oil-producing countries primarily in the Middle East. Organized by "Carlos the Jackal" (whose real name was Ilich Ramirez Sanchez), a Marxist-Leninist radical and now member of the Popular Front for the Liberation of Palestine (PFLP), the group stormed the embassy, killing three and taking nearly 100 hostages. The terror group demanded that a statement be made on Austrian radio and television every two hours or else a hostage would be killed every 15 minutes; Austrian officials complied with that demand—as well as a request for an airplane bound for Algeria.

Upon confirmation that the airplane had been procured, the terrorists released 50 Austrian nationals and boarded a bus for the airport. The plane flew to Algiers, where the remainder of the hostages (hailing from Saudi Arabia, Iran, Algeria, and the United Arab Emirates) were released and a $5 million ransom was obtained from Iran and Saudi Arabia. The PFLP retained $2 million of that sum; the rest funded various other Palestinian causes.

This siege was notable for several reasons. First, the level of partnership between the Palestinian PFLP and European leftist groups gave the Palestinians insight into Viennese and Austrian weaknesses, allowing them to exploit the hostage situation and leave the country successfully. Secondly, the sum paid in ransom was relatively huge, which likely set the stage for future ransom requests in a spate of hijackings throughout the late 1970s and into the early 1980s.

How do you think this incident impacted American policy? Do you think we should have a "no negotiation with terrorists" perspective or have things changed with more sophisticated terrorist groups?

However, the three empty jet airliners parked in the Jordanian desert were simultaneously blown up in front of onlooking TV cameras and a helpless Jordanian Army.[69] Skyjacking had again become "grand theater," and the PFLP was heralded as one of the most successful Marxist revolutionary groups of all time, spawning collaborations with similar groups throughout Europe (e.g., Red Army Faction, Baader-Meinhof Gang, Red Brigades).

Embarrassed on a global scale and in the midst of a civil war, Jordan reacted violently, sending troops to evacuate large settlements of Palestinians living along the Jordan River. Over the course of several days, up to 15,000 Palestinian men, women, and children were slaughtered and between 50,000 and 100,000 were left homeless.[70] The horrific event became known as Black September,[71] and pushed the PFLP to the edges of the Palestinian cause. Although the PFLP never regained its notoriety after September 1970, it continued to strike directly at Israel, often targeting innocent civilians. For the next several years, the PFLP conducted relatively small-scale car and bus bombings, assassinations, and killings of Jewish settlers primarily in the West Bank. The most spectacular of these attacks occurred in May 1972, in collaboration with members of the Red Army Faction and the Baader-Meinhof Gang that killed 24 people during an attack at Lod Airport in Israel.

The *Black September Organization (BSO)* is perhaps the most notorious, though short-lived, of the early Marxist Palestinian terrorist organizations. The BSO was primarily composed of former PFLP members and other smaller radical Palestinian factions expelled from Jordan during the events of Black September, 1970. The Black September Organization carried out a significant number of very violent attacks in Israel and left a lasting mark on the Israeli-Palestinian conflict of the time, as well as one of the most visible attacks associated with the concept of political terrorism as a whole. In November 1971, members of the BSO gunned down the Prime Minister of Jordan, Wasfi Tal, in broad daylight. One gunman knelt down and, in a gruesome display, appeared to lap up the blood of the slain Prime Minister.[72] A month later, the group tried to assassinate the Jordanian ambassador to England, Zeid al-Rifai, who had supported Jordan's crackdown on the Palestinians. Although severally wounded, al-Rifai survived the attack. In the same month, the group blew up a gasoline manufacturing plant in the Netherlands and oil tankers in Germany. In May 1972, the group hijacked a Belgian airliner, forcing it to land in Israeli territory. In July of that year, an Italian oil refinery was attacked and a bomb at a Tel Aviv bus terminal wounded eleven Israeli citizens.[73] Clearly, the BSO was actively at war using terrorism as its primary strategy.

No attack during this period was more shocking than the events at the Summer Olympic Games in Munich, Germany, in September 1972. Hooded and heavily armed Black September guerrillas jumped a fence and entered the Olympic Village in Munich. Two Israeli athletes were killed outright during the raid and another 11 were taken hostage. During an ensuing shootout with German police at the Munich Airport, nine of the eleven remaining hostages were killed, as were several of the BSO terrorists. Three of the gunmen were eventually captured but later released as part of the negotiations related to the hijacking of a Lufthansa aircraft just one month later. Their individual demise, as well as that of the mastermind of the attack, Abu Daoud, by members of the **Israeli Mossad** was chronicled in the 2005 movie *Munich*. Black September's actions at the 1972 Olympics in Munich were a direct affront to the entire world, as the Olympic Games have always been a symbol of global community and peace. The killings of the Israeli athletes alienated many who previously supported the Palestinian cause.

Outrage against the Palestinians was at an all-time high, and Yassir Arafat and his PLO were held responsible for the attacks, even though most Middle East experts seriously doubt that Arafat had prior knowledge of the earlier terrorist operations, much less power to actually control such activity within the highly radicalized BSO.[74] In any event, Arafat denounced all international terrorist attacks and mandated that further guerrilla actions be limited to the Israeli territories. As a result, BSO operations halted and the group faded into anonymity.[75]

The *Abu Nidal Organization (ANO)* was the last of the first-wave, primarily Marxist-oriented Palestinian groups to gain major international notoriety. Headed by a former PFLP member named **Sabri al-Banna**, the group was highly entrepreneurial, meaning that the group worked for a variety of countries, conducting "missions" that included paid assassinations and bombings throughout the Middle East. Code named Abu-Nidal (or "Father of the Holy Struggle"), al-Banna's group was highly radicalized and eschewed the moderate stance by senior PLO leadership like Yassir Arafat. Al-Banna believed that Israel must be destroyed at any cost, branding Arafat, the PLO, and the rest of the al-Fatah as traitors. The ANO launched international terrorist operations against Israeli government as well as PLO interests, assassinating ambassadors and leaders within each group. The Abu Nidal Organization has been financially backed by Syria, Libya, Iraq, and even Iran,[76] and claimed responsibility for more attacks on foreign and Arab interests than any other Palestinian terrorist organization to date. At one point the ANO was considered the most dangerous terrorist group in the world, seemingly conducting terrorist attacks for the highest bidder. Political ideology and cause gave way to financial benefit and mercenary action as Abu Nidal orchestrated attacks in the Middle East and Europe.

The Abu Nidal Organization was a very-well organized and technologically savvy operation that spanned the globe and reportedly had cells throughout the Middle East as well as in South America, Asia, and even the United States. From 1972 to 1994, the group conducted 90 attacks in 20 different countries, claiming the lives of over 900 people.[77] More interesting, Sabri al-Banna was never arrested and lived to the age of 65 in Iraq, under the protection of Saddam Hussein. In 2002, he was found dead in his flat as a result of three bullet wounds, two of which were in the back of his head. The official report reached the startling conclusion that he had committed suicide.[78]

Israeli Mossad
The intelligence and secret service unit of the country of Israel; responsible for carrying out extensive covert operations throughout the Middle East and the rest of the world.

Sabri al-Banna
A highly entrepreneurial revolutionary and mercenary who headed the Abu Nidal Organization (ANO).

Politics, Oil, and Terrorism in the Modern Era

The Palestinian groups discussed so far were the forerunners of modern Middle East terrorist organizations, but notably they were secular—meaning that their ideology was not based in religion, but more in the political theories of Karl Marx. These prominent Palestinian terrorist groups [al-Fatah, Popular Front for the Liberation of Palestine (PFLP), Black September Organization (BSO), and Abu-Nidal Organization (ANO)] clearly paved the way for more contemporary terrorist groups that eschewed political theory in favor of more radical Islamic (religious) ideology, as we discuss in Chapter 4.

Quick Facts
The Discovery of Oil in the Middle East

A British oil company (Burmah Oil) first discovered oil in Persia (now Iran) on March 26, 1908. However, large oil reserves were not fully developed until years later on the Arabian Peninsula (now Saudi Arabia) in 1938 by Standard Oil of California (SoCal) and the Texas Oil Company (Texaco); that same year, large oil finds were also discovered in the Kingdom of Kuwait by Gulf Oil Company. SoCal and Texaco were early partners in the development of Saudi Aramco, now boasting the largest proven crude oil reserves in the world, at more than 260 billion barrels.

▲ A 1932 view of an Iraq Petroleum Company oil well and camp near Kirkuk.

(Courtesy Library of Congress)

Since 1948, the Israeli-Palestinian conflict has been a central point of outrage by Arab radical groups in the Middle East. Bolstered by Marxist ideology and further inflamed by the perspectives of Fanon and other philosophers, these groups have also pointed to colonialism by European powers as the means of exploitation of the natural resources (particularly oil) in the Middle East. The United States has not been immune to this criticism, especially concerning relatively recent foreign policies and military interventions. Arab groups have long resented perceived "imperialist" actions by the United States in its quest for oil in the Middle East. Relying heavily on Marxist principles to inform their perceptions of and reactions to the unwelcome advances of a capitalist nation, bent on corralling resources and establishing new marketplaces full of Western commerce at the expense of Arab sovereignty, radical Middle East groups have pushed their cause and justified their use of terrorism.

The chief natural resource of the Middle East is, in fact, oil. This was brought to light in the late 1930s, as American and British oil companies made major discoveries in the area. As a result, the United States—which had largely tried to remain neutral when the League of Nations was first formed in 1919—was suddenly involved more and more in the foreign policy of the Middle East. American politicians proclaimed that the Middle East was "a stupendous source of strategic power, and one of the greatest material prizes in world history."[79] Middle East scholars have long argued that the dominant and driving force behind every U.S. action in the region has been the security of its access to oil.[80] Aid has been given to U.S.-friendly governments in the region, often at the expense of democratic rule. "Regional stability" has been much more about the ease of getting U.S. interests to an oil pipeline than about ensuring that the Arab population is entitled to live under governments that do not oppress their citizens. Former U.S. Senator John Foster Dulles said it best during a crisis involving Lebanon in 1958:

> "[We] must regard Arab nationalism as a flood which is running strongly. We cannot successfully oppose it, but we could put sandbags around positions we must protect: the first group being Israel and Lebanon, and the second group being the oil positions around the Persian Gulf."[81]

Many argue that this sentiment seemingly guided U.S. policies throughout much of the 20th century: from Israeli partition, to the support of the Shah in Iran in the 1950s—which landed the United States ownership of 40 percent of the oil fields in that country as a reward[82]—to involvement in the Iran-Iraq war in the 1980s, and to more recent military entanglements in Iraq and Afghanistan.[83]

Fundamentalist Arab groups argue that the presence of the U.S. military in the Middle East was used to "fan the flames" of neo-colonialism. Al-Qaeda, as well as other Arab groups, has always been violently opposed to the presence of American interests on Middle East soil, especially those on the Arabian Peninsula. Saudi Arabia is home to two of Islam's holiest sites (Mecca and Medina). The presence of half a million coalition soldiers near Mecca during the 1990s was seen as a defiling and defamation of Muslim holy land, and further represented America's desire for oil, backed up by a compelling military force in the region.[84] Radical Islamic groups led by Usama bin Laden rallied around his call to "purge" the United States from the Middle East (note the Marxian rhetoric), and sparked several international terrorist events against U.S. forces in the Middle East. Most notable was the attack on the USS *Cole* in 2000 while the ship refueled in the Yemen port of Aden. Bin Laden would justify his actions on 9/11 as an attack on the "Adulterous Nation" (United States) because of its support of Israel and the presence of military forces near the Islamic holy cities of Mecca and Medina in Saudi Arabia.[85]

On March 20, 2003, the United States launched ground attacks in Iraq to "disarm Iraq of weapons of mass destruction, to end Saddam Hussein's support for terrorism, and to free the Iraqi people."[86] The United States emphasized the links between Hussein and terrorism in a post-9/11 world, which was enough to sustain a presence in the country for more than a decade in what was deemed by some as a "creeping militarization of American foreign policy."[87] The invasion and the long-standing occupation of Iraq, which culminated in the capture of Saddam Hussein in 2003 and his execution in 2006, has resulted in a violent and unstable country. More importantly, most of the country's population is susceptible to the influence of a radicalized Iran. From March 2003 to February 20, 2014, 5,314 American soldiers died in Iraq military operations and another 51,895 were wounded.[88] Estimates for Iraqi deaths range from 120,000 to 200,000 people, and economic loss is in the billions of dollars.[89] American soldiers went to Iraq believing that they would secure their country from future terrorist attacks, and indeed, the financial and military strength of al-Qaeda has been significantly reduced because of U.S. military actions in Iraq, Afghanistan, and Pakistan (see Figure 2–15). However, Iraq has become the symbol of anti-American sentiment among terrorist groups, and again, a breeding ground for radical Islamic ideology; all aimed at further reinforcing Arab sentiments that the United States is not only an imperialist force, but an enemy to all of Islam.

Levant
A geographic and cultural area on the Eastern Mediterranean Sea, composed primarily of modern-day Syria, Lebanon, Jordan, and Israel.

The Islamic State

Many of the radical Sunni fighters loyal to al-Qaeda suffered dramatic losses to U.S. forces during the Iraq War. Coupled with the loss of political power and the establishment of a majority Shiite-led government in Iraq, many fled to neighboring countries, and in particular Syria, where violent revolution already in progress was pitting Sunnis against a Shiite-backed al-Assad government. The early name of this group became widely known as ISIS (or the Islamic State in Syria). Syrian rebel groups quickly welcomed these hardened fighters; however, they soon realized that the Iraqi group had a much larger goal than toppling the al-Assad regime—their goal was to establish a new "Islamic State in Iraq and the Levant." The **Levant** is a geographic and cultural area on the Eastern Mediterranean Sea, composed primarily of modern-day Syria, Lebanon, Jordan, and Israel.

FIGURE 2–15
A Bradley Fighting Vehicle is engulfed in flames from an improvised explosive device (IED) during the Iraqi War. A medic is profiled on top of the vehicle as he tries to enter the vehicle and rescue soldiers. He later received America's second highest award, the Distinguished Service Cross, for extraordinary heroism.
(Courtesy U.S. Army)

The new Islamic State of Iraq and the Levant (ISIL) was successful in carving out a portion of land in the heart of the Middle East in which to build an Islamic state and recruit other like-minded Sunnis worldwide. The rise of ISIL was quick and historical, occurring along the banks of the Tigris and Euphrates Rivers, a region commonly known as the cradle of civilization.

In July 2014, the leader of the ISIL, Abu Bakr al-Baghdadi, declared himself "caliph" over the area he controlled and announced the establishment of the new "caliphate." He then changed the name of the group to the Islamic State, and within a month (August 2014) he led attacks on Kurdish territories in northern Iraq, prompting an immediate response by the United States—retaliatory air strikes and bombing of IS-held areas. He called upon all Muslims around the world to pledge support and allegiance to him and his country. As we will learn in the next chapter, these are powerful words in the Muslim world, and ones which position al-Baghdadi and the Islamic State as significant challenges in the future.

The discussion of terrorism in this chapter has traced its evolution from Marxism and left-wing terror groups full circle to Islamic fundamentalism. The historical roots of terrorism in the Middle East lay in 19th century France, and weave their way through Eastern Europe to World War I's colonial legacy of the mandate system. The establishment of Israel after World War II, the frequent intervention of military forces in the Holy Lands of Islam, and the quest for oil by Western nations only helped to coalesce bitter Arab groups against one enemy.[90] The vestiges of those actions remain a threat to the stability of the entire Middle East, and to the safety and security of Western nations—especially the United States.

Chapter Summary

SUMMARY BY LEARNING OBJECTIVE

1. **Outline political ideology and explain how terrorism as part of a revolutionary strategy poses significant social consequences.**

   Political ideology (on an individual basis) can be defined as the set of beliefs about the proper order of society and how it can be achieved. On a group level, political ideology is the shared framework of mental models that groups of individuals possess that provide both an interpretation of the environment and a prescription as to how that environment should be structured. Identifying with a particular political theory or ideology has also been shown as calming, as strange as that may seem when discussing terrorism. It can help reduce uncertainty, make a person feel more secure, and increase feelings of solidarity with others. However, one's ideology may become extreme and may not allow for any deviation or tolerance of criticism. As such, extreme political ideology often uses terrorism as part of a revolutionary strategy. In that role, terrorism may have a direct impact on social structure and pose significant social consequences. Terrorism upsets the framework of precepts, images, and symbols on which society is based and on which society depends and trusts. Terrorism destroys the solidarity, cooperation, and interdependence on which social functioning is based and substitutes insecurity, distrust, and fear. And finally, terrorism attacks the very bases of social order, culture, and government.

2. **Describe the concept of political terrorism.**

   Political terrorism can be defined as "a symbolic act designed to influence political behavior based on extra-normal means, entailing the use or threat of violence." Recall that political terror is based on a set of ingrained beliefs that stem from the way people think about their environment, government, and society—and that those beliefs are often inflexible.

3. **Discuss the evolution of leftist ideology, including how anarchism and Marxism contribute to leftist doctrine.**

   Leftist ideology seeks to change or eliminate a system that is corrupt or oppressive in nature, and seeks to restore authority to those who have built the economy on their backs (i.e., the proletariat). Anarchism advocated violent revolution along with the rise of the working class and promoted "propaganda by the deed." Marxism gave leftism intellectual roots, championing the working class as the creators of society's wealth and encouraging them to overthrow the capitalist system and equalize wealth distribution.

4. **Define the concept of the vanguard and discuss how it contributes to modern terrorism.**

The vanguard conceptually posits that political consciousness among the working class should be stimulated and nurtured so that a cohesive and political movement can be developed. The vanguard is the primary group of talented and advanced individuals leading the cause. It is, in Marx words, the "catalyst for change." This concept has evolved so that, in modern terror groups, political consciousness is not enough for a vanguard—it must be paired with acts of violence to be effective, hence many terrorist groups perceive themselves as the vanguard in a revolutionary movement, whether regionally or globally.

5. **Provide an overview of leftist terror cells, including Latin American and European groups.**

Groups that espouse Marxist ideologies include the Revolutionary Armed Forces of Columbia, or FARC, which purports to represent the rural, agrarian poor in Columbia by protecting their land interests against the wealthier classes of Columbia, the influence of the imperialist United States, the privatization of resources, and the influence of global corporations. The National Liberation Army, or ELN, also a pro-Marxist group that operates in the Colombian countryside, seeks to replace the Columbian government with an egalitarian democracy that represents the rural peasant class. Tupac Amaru Revolutionary Movement (or MRTA) exists in Peru, and was founded in Marxist ideology to reform the Peruvian government, removing all imperialist elements, and create a society in which power, property, and prosperity were shared equally. Shining Path, or the Communist Party of Peru, claimed to be the vanguard of the world communist movement, and was brutal in its methods. Argentina's Montoneros sprang from the Marxist left, viewing itself as a vanguard for revolution and forming urban guerilla cells to carry out political kidnappings and assassinations to achieve their means. The People's Revolutionary Army, meanwhile, retreated to the country to build a revolutionary base that would root out the Argentine government in favor of proletarian rule.

In Europe, Italy's Red Brigades formed in 1969, and became one of the largest leftist groups in Europe with thousands of members at its peak. Their blend of Marxist and Leninist ideology sought to overthrow the government in three phases, all involving campaigns of urban terror. The Red Army Faction—also known as the Baader-Meinhof Gang—was the most prominent leftist group of the era. The leaders of the group trained in Jordan with the Popular Front for the Liberation of Palestine in guerilla warfare tactics, then returned to Germany where they robbed banks to subsidize their underground lifestyle. They are notorious for the German Autumn, a series of kidnappings and hijackings that culminated in the fall of 1977. Finally, the anti-imperialist Revolutionary Cells was responsible for bombings at airports, military installations, and other symbolic government sites throughout the early to mid-1970s, and is probably best known for their role in the hijacking of an Air France airliner in 1976 with the Popular Front for the Liberation of Palestine (PFLP).

6. **Discuss how colonialism and the mandate system set the stage for future conflict in the Middle East.**

At the end of World War I, a series of treaties divided the former Ottoman Empire into a series of British and French "spheres of influence." This encroachment into Arab lands engendered a series of uprisings throughout the Middle East, further inflamed by the mandate system—which gave Great Britain rule over Palestine, which had previously been legitimized as a Jewish homeland by the Balfour Declaration.

7. **Give an overview of how Israel was established and articulate its effects on the modern landscape of political terror.**

Control of Palestine was handed over to the newly formed United Nations in 1947 by Great Britain. At that time, there was increasing unrest between Arabs and Jews in the area due to the massive influx of Jewish immigrants during World War II. The United Nations adopted a partition plan on November 29, 1947, giving just over 56 percent of Palestine to the Jewish state and about 43 percent to the Arab state, with the holy sites in Jerusalem remaining an international enclave. This prompted the withdrawal of the British and an immediate escalation of force between the Arabs and Jews living in the area. On May 14, 1948, the Israeli Declaration of Independence was proclaimed, leading to a full-scale invasion of Israel by the Arab states of Jordan, Egypt, Lebanon, Syria, and Iraq. The invasions were largely unsuccessful, and hostilities were ended in early 1949 by an armistice agreement that set the recognized boundaries of a new Israeli state, dividing Jerusalem in half between the Jews and Arabs. Israel retained a majority of the former Palestinian state, leaving only small areas along the

Gaza Strip and the West Bank under Arab control. These areas made up only 25 percent of the former Palestinian territory. Tensions and mistrust against Western powers for their support of the establishment of Israel have persisted, leading to anti-colonial and anti-Western sentiment that has motivated generations of Middle East terror groups.

8. Describe the secular "first wave" Palestinian terror groups.

The Palestinian Liberation Organization, or PLO, is dedicated to the liberation of Palestine and to the destruction of Israel. The PLO, which has been linked to the more radical guerilla group al-Fatah, adopted principles of armed resistance in the late 1960s under the leadership of Yasser Arafat. The Popular Front for the Liberation of Palestine (PFLP) is a Christian-led Marxist-Leninist group founded in 1967 by the late George Habash. The group rose to infamy in the late 1960s and early 1970s with a series of terrorist attacks, including airline hijackings, assassination attempts, and guerilla tactics aimed first at Jordan, then directly at Israeli targets. The Black September Organization is perhaps the most notorious of these first-wave Palestinian terror organizations, likely formed from radical members of both al-Fatah and the PFLP. Black September is best known for a series of brutal and high-profile terror attacks in the 1970s, including the 1972 attacks against Israeli athletes during the Munich Olympics. Finally, the Abu Nidal Organization (ANO) split from the PLO in the early 1970s. The Abu Nidal organization has been financially backed by Syria, Libya, Iraq, and Iran. It's responsible for more attacks on foreign and Arab interests than any other Palestinian terrorist organization to date, and moved its headquarters to Iraq in the mid-1980s. Its organizational prowess has inspired many modern terror organizations.

9. Provide insight into how the United States and its policies have inflamed terrorist ideology in the Middle East.

United States oil interests—plus its long-standing support of the Israeli state—have long been a source of anger among Arab nationalists, who decry the imperialist actions of the United States and other Western countries. Nationalists and Islamic fundamentalists use Marxist-Leninist principles to inform their perceptions of and reactions to the unwelcome advances of the United States. Such sentiment has been further exacerbated due to U.S. actions in and around Iraq, most notably due to the U.S. presence in Arab holy lands as part of an offensive around Iraq and the long-standing occupation and destabilization of Iraq.

REVIEW QUESTIONS

1. Describe how political ideology can influence a person's entire world view.
2. What are the basic tenets of Marxism, and how do you see its effects in modern Middle Eastern terror?
3. How do you think Latin American and European terror organizations inspired present-day Arab terror organizations?
4. What was the mandate system and how do we see its lasting effects in Middle Eastern conflict?
5. How is the United States perceived by the Arab world, and why? How does this influence terrorist ideology?

CRITICAL THINKING EXERCISES

1. **The Impact of Oil in the Middle East.** Visit the homepage for Saudi Aramco at www.saudiaramco.com/en/home.html and Life-Time Magazine at http://life.time.com. Search these sites for stories on the discovery of oil in the Middle East. Learn about the history and culture of the Middle East in 1945 when the oil industry just began in that region. Notice the photos of the region and compare them to more modern times. How much has the landscaped really changed in half a century? Visit the home pages of some of the wealthiest Middle East countries like Saudi Arabia, Bahrain, Qatar, Kuwait, and the United Arab Emirates. Notice the significant improvements in health, education, and welfare of the individuals in those countries. Notice also that each of these countries is a royal monarchy. How do you think the form of government and the pervasive religion of Islam in the region has impacted the economic development of the Middle East—both negatively and positively?

2. **Terrorism as the Nexus of Politics and Violence.** In 1997, Bruce Hoffman, an international expert on terrorism and political violence at the RAND Corporation in Santa Monica, California, wrote a compelling article entitled "The Modern Terrorist Mindset: Tactics, Targets and Techniques" (New York: Columbia International Affairs Online Working Paper, October 1997). In that article, Hoffman explores the mindset of terrorists and the tactics they use in seeking political change. He contends that terrorism is where politics and violence intersect in the hopes of producing power … power to dominate and coerce, to intimidate and control, and ultimately to effect fundamental political change. Discuss this concept in history. Has any terrorist movement ever been successful in achieving not just political change through revolution, but also long-term international recognition as a ruling party or existing government? Can you give any examples? Interestingly, Hoffman indicates that in modern times, most terrorist groups do not reach the final steps of authority and governance of their homeland or country … but that was in 1997. Have things changed, particularly in the Middle East?

NOTES

1. Peter K. Hatemi and Rose McDermott, "The Genetics of Politics: Discovery, Challenges, and Progress," *Trends in Genetics*, Vol. 28, Issue 10, pp. 525–533.
2. R. S. Erikson and K. L. Tedin, *American Public Opinion* (New York: Longman, 2003).
3. A. D. Denzau and D. C. North, "Shared Mental Models: Ideologies and Institutions," *Elements of Reason: Cognition, Choice and the Bounds of Rationality*, Arthur Lupia, Mathew D. McCubbins, and Samuel L. Popkin (New York: Cambridge University Press, 1994).
4. J. T. Jost, C. M. Federico, and J. L. Napier, "Political Ideology: Its Structure, Functions, And Elective Affinities," *Annual Review of Psychology,* Vol. 60, pp. 307–337.
5. See the works of Ernesto Guevara, *Guerrilla Warfare* (New York: Vintage Books, 1961); Franz Fanon, *The Wretched of the Earth* (Paris: Maspero Press, 1961); Carlos Marighela, *Mini-Manuel of the Urban Guerrilla* (Baltimore, MD: Pelican Books, 1971), and Martha Crenshaw Hutchinson, "The Concept of Revolutionary Terrorism," *Journal of Conflict Resolution*, Vol. 16, No. 3, September 1972.
6. As an officer assigned to the Intelligence Division of the Portland Police Bureau in 1975–76, Dr. Robert W. Taylor was part of an inter-agency task force assigned to train officers on domestic terrorism. Their manual, from which these "social consequences" of terrorism was developed, was never published; however, it was used as a basis for training throughout California, Oregon, and Washington. See also Jennifer L. Merolla and Elizabeth J. Zechmeister, *Democracy at Risk: How Terrorist Threats Affect the Public.* Chicago Scholarship Online, DOI:10.7208/chicago/9780226520568.001.0001, March 2013.
7. See the works of Karl Marx and Friedrich Engels, including *The Communist Manifesto* (New York: Penguin Books, 1998) and *Das Kapital* (New York: Knopf Doubleday, 1977).
8. T. P. Thornton, "Terror as a Weapon of Political Agitation," *Internal War: Problems and Approaches*, Harry Eckstein (Westport, CT: Praeger Press, 1980) (New York: Free Press, 1964).
9. See the works of Karl Marx and Friedrich Engels, including *The Communist Manifesto* (New York: Penguin Books, 1998) and *Das Kapital* (New York: Knopf Doubleday, 1977).
10. R. J. W. Evans and Hartmut Pogge von Strandmann, eds., *The Revolutions in Europe 1848–1849* (New York: Oxford University Press, 2000), p. 4.
11. See *Anarchism and Anarcho-Syndicalism: Selected Writings by Marx, Engels and Lenin* (New York: International Publishers, 1972).
12. Pierre-Joseph Proudhon, *No Gods, No Masters: An Anthology of Anarchism* (Oakland, California: AK Press, 2005).
13. A. Haynal, M. Molnar, and G. de Ruymege, *Fanaticism: A Historical and Psychoanalytical Study* (New York: Schocken Books, 1983).
14. Yves Ternon, "Russian Terrorism, 1878-1908," *The History of Terrorism: From Antiquity to Al Qaeda.*, Gerard Chaliand and Arnaud Blin (Los Angeles, University of California Press, 2007).

15. Ibid.

16. Karl Marx and Friedrich Engels, *The Communist Manifesto* (New York: Penguin Books, 1998).

17. Ibid.

18. Laura Desfor Edles, *Sociological Theory in the Classical Era: Text and Readings* (Thousand Oaks, California: Pine Forge Press, 2005).

19. Jon Lee Anderson. *Che Guevara: A Revolutionary Life* (New York: Grove Press, 1997).

20. See www.history.com/topics/vietnam-war.

21. See N. Van Hieu, *"Special War"—An Outgrowth of Neo-Colonialism* (Forest Grove, OR: Normount Armament Co., 1966).

22. Peter Kornbluh, *The Death of Che Guevara: Declassified* (Washington, D.C.: George Washington University, The National Security Archive, undated), p. 1. The most recent citation in this source is 1997, so it was published then or more recently.

23. Marc Sageman, *Understanding Terror Networks* (Philadelphia: University of Pennsylvania Press, 2004).

24. Sayyid Qutb, *Social Justice in Islam* (North Haledon, NJ: Islamic Publications International, 2000.)

25. Stephanie Hanson, "FARC, ELN: Colombia's Left-Wing Guerillas," Council on Foreign Relations. August 19, 2009, http://www.cfr.org/colombia/farc-eln-colombias-left-wing-guerillas/p9272.

26. ColumbiaPeace.org."Columbia Peace Process Update," www.colombiapeace.org/2013/07/16/colombia-peace-process-update-july-15-2013/.

27. Carlos Nunez, *The Tupamaros: Urban Guerrillas of Uruguay* (New York: Times Change Press, 1970).

28. David Ronfeldt, *The Mitrione Kidnapping in Uruguay* (Santa Monica, CA: RAND Corporation, 1987).

29. Kathryn Gregory, "Shining Path, Tupac Amaru (Peru, Leftists)," Council on Foreign Relations, August 27, 2009, www.cfr.org/peru/shining-path-tupac-amaru-peru-leftists/p9276.

30. Carlos Marighella, *The Mini-Manual of the Urban Guerrilla*, available at www.marxists.org/archive/marighella-*carlos*/1969/06/minimanual-urban-guerrilla/.

31. Leszek Kolakowski, Main *Currents of Marxism, Vol. 3: The Breakdown* (Oxford: Oxford University Press, 1981).

32. Mervyn F. Bendle, "Terrorism and the New Left in the Sixties," *National Observer*, No. 71, Summer 2006–2007, pp. 8–28.

33. Clarence Martin, "Understanding Terrorism: Challenges, Perspectives and Issues" (Thousand Oaks, California: Sage Publications, 2013).

34. Clare Murphy, "Who Were the Baader-Meinhof Gang?" BBC News, February 12, 2007, http://news.bbc.co.uk/2/hi/6314559.stm.

35. Statement presented by the Red Army Faction, on its dissolution in Germany, March 1998.

36. Stanford University, "Mapping Militant Organizations: Revolutionary Cells," www.stanford.edu/group/mappingmilitants/cgi-bin/groups/view/353.

37. Stanford Encyclopedia of Philosophy, http://plato.stanford.edu/entries/colonialism/.

38. Nele Matz. "Civilization and the Mandate System under the League of Nations as Origin of Trusteeship," *Max Planck Yearbook of United Nations Law*, Vol. 9, 2005, pp. 47–95.

39. Gerard Chaliand and Arnaud Blin, "Terrorism in Time of War," *The History of Terrorism: From Antiquity to Al Qaeda* (Berkely, CA: University of California Press 2007).

40. David Fromkin, *A Peace to End All Peace, The Fall of the Ottoman Empire and the Creation of the Modern Middle East.* (New York: Holt 1989).

41. Rene Albrecht-Carrie, *Diplomatic History of Europe Since the Congress of Vienna* (New York: Harpercollins College Publishers, 1958).

42. Much of this discussion is taken from a discussion entitled "The Middle East and the West: World War I and Beyond" featured on National Public Radio's "All Things Considered" on August 20, 2004, available at www.npr.org/templates/transcript/transcript.php?storyId=3860950.

43. See Frantz Fanon, *The Wretched of the Earth* (Grove Press, New York: 2004).

44. Erin McCoy, "Franz Fanon's Call to Anti-Colonial Violence," ProQuest Discovery Guides, http://www.csa.com/discoveryguides/fanon/review.pdf.

45. Karl Marx, *Capital: A Critique of Political Economy, Vol. 1 (1867),* translated by Ben Fowkes (New York: Random House, Vintage Books, 1977).

46. See Bernard Lewis, *The Middle East: A Short History of the Last 2000 Years* (New York: Touchstone, 1995).

47. BBC News, "A History of Conflict: Arab Discontent," http://news.bbc.co.uk/2/shared/spl/hi/middle_east/03/v3_ip_timeline/html/1929_36.stm.

48. Weldon Matthews, *Confronting an Empire, Constructing a Nation: Arab Nationalists and Popular Politics in Mandate Palestine* (London: I.B. Tauris and Co, 2006).

49. Rashid Khaledi, *The Iron Cage: The Story of the Palestinian Struggle for Statehood* (Boston: Beacon Press, 2006).

50. Mark Tessler, *A History of the Israeli-Palestinian Conflict* (Indianapolis, IN: Indiana University Press, 1994).

51. Ibid.

52. British Broadcasting Company (BBC) News Online, "History of Conflict: Establishment of Israel," http://news.bbc.co.uk/2/shared/spl/hi/middle_east/03/v3_ip_timeline/html/1948.stm.

53. See Tessler, *A History of the Israeli-Palestinian Conflict.*

54. See www.washingtonpost.com/blogs/worldviews/files/2013/01/Screen-shot-2013-01-01-at-12.12.53-PM.png.

55. Aryeh Yodfat and Yuval Arnon-Ohanna, *PLO: Strategy and Tactics* (New York: St Martin's Press, 1981).

56. Shaul Mishal, *The PLO Under Arafat: Between Gun and Olive Branch* (London: Yale University Press, 1986)

57. John W. Amos II, *Palestinian Resistance: Organization of a Nationalist Movement* (New York: Elsevier Books, 1981).

58. See Tessler, *A History of the Israeli-Palestinian Conflict.*

59. See Mishal, *The PLO Under Arafat.*

60. Abridgement from the Palestinian National Charter: Resolutions of the Palestine National Council. 1967, affirmed in July 1–17, 1968, available at http://avalon.law.yale.edu/20th_century/plocov.asp.

61. See Amos II, *Palestinian Resistance*; and Helena Cobban, *The Palestinian Liberation Organisation: People, Power and Politics* (Cambridge: Cambridge University Press, 1984).

62. See Yodfat and Arnon-Ohanna, *PLO: Strategy and Tactics.*

63. See N. Van Hieu, *"Special War"—An Outgrowth of Neo-Colonialism* (Forest Grove, OR: Normount Armament Co., 1966).

64. International Policy Institute for Counter-Terrorism, "Terrorist Organizations: The Popular Front for the Liberation of Palestine," www.ict.org.il/.

65. Brian M. Jenkins, *International Terrorism: A New Kind of Warfare, 1974,* available at www.rand.org/pubs/papers/2008/P5261.pdf.

66. Ely Karmon, "Fatah and the Popular Front for the Liberation of Palestine: International Terror Strategies (1968–1990)," International Policy Institute for Counter-Terrorism, www.ict.org.il/.

67. See Tessler, *A History of the Israeli-Palestinian Conflict.*

68. Ibid.

69. See Karmon, "Fatah and the Popular Front for the Liberation of Palestine."

70. See "What was the 1970 Jordanian-Palestinian Conflict Known as Black September?" *Israeli-Palestinian Conflict*, available at http://israelipalestinian.procon.org/view.answers.php?questionID=000435.

71. See ICT, "Terrorist Organizations: The Popular Front for the Liberation of Palestine."

72. See Tessler, *A History of the Israeli-Palestinian Conflict.*

73. See Yodfat and Arnon-Ohanna, *PLO: Strategy and Tactics.*

74. See Amos II, *Palestinian Resistance*; and Thomas L. Friedman, *From Beirut to Jerusalem* (New York: Farrar Straus Giroux, 1989).

75. See Yodfat and Arnon-Ohanna, *PLO: Strategy and Tactics.*

76. International Policy Institute for Counter-Terrorism, "Terrorist Organizations: The Abu Nidal Organization," www.ict.org.il/.

77. Ibid.

78. Ewen MacAskill and Richard Nelsson, "Mystery Death of Abu Nidal, Once the World's Most Wanted Terrorist," *The Guardian*, August 19, 2002.

79. Foreign Relations of the United States, Vol. 8 (Washington: Government Printing Office, 1945).

80. See Noam Chomsky and Gilbert Achcar, *Perilous Power: The Middle East and U.S. Foreign Policy: Dialogues on Terror, Democracy, War and Justice.* (New York: Penguin Books, 2007); Bernard Lewis, *What Went Wrong? The Clash Between Islam and Modernity in the Middle East* (New York: Harper Perennial, 2003); and Daniel Yergin, *The Prize: The Epic Quest for Oil, Money and Power* (New York: Free Press, 1991).

81. Michael Bishku, "The 1958 American Intervention in Lebanon: A Historical Assessment," *American-Arab Affairs,* Vol. 31 (Winter 1989–1990).

82. See discussion entitled "Early US-Iran Relations" at www.strausscenter.org/hormuz/u-s-iran-relations.html.

83. Sheldon Richman, "Ancient History: US Conduct in the Middle East Since World War II and the Folly of Intervention," *Cato Instititute Policy Analysis No. 59,* 1991.

84. Philippe Migaux, "Al Qaeda," *The History of Terrorism: From Antiquity to Al Qaeda.* (Berkely, CA: University of California Press 2007).

85. The motives of Usama bin Laden relating to his actions on September 11, 2001, have been well documented in his fatwas (or messages) delivered in August 1996 and February 1998, as well as his "Letter to America" (November 24, 2002) and his taped broadcast on the attacks in 2004.

86. "Operation Iraqi Freedom: President Discusses Beginning of Operation Iraqi Freedom," http://georgewbush-whitehouse.archives.gov/news/releases/2003/03/20030322.html.

87. David Drezner, "Diplomacy is Dangerous Business, a Fact Washington Needs to Remember," Foreignpolicy.com, November 19, 2012, www.foreignpolicy.com/posts/2012/11/19/diplomacy_is_dangerous_business_a_fact_washington_needs_to_remember.

88. See U.S. Department of Defense, available at www.defense.gov/news/casualty.pdf.

89. Exact numbers are unavailable; however, estimates are provided by Iraq Body Count. See www.iraqbodycount.org/

90. See Barnard Lewis, *The Crisis of Islam: Holy War and Unholy Terror* (New York: Random House, 2004).

Understanding the Middle East and Islam

CHAPTER 3

Learning Objectives

After completing this chapter, you should be able to:

1. Describe the geographical, historical, and cultural aspects of the Middle East.

2. Explain the misconceptions of Westerners over Muslims and vice versa and the political instability in some of the Middle East countries.

3. Give a brief history of the development of Islam in the Middle East.

4. Describe the differences between the Sunni and Shi'a traditions within Islam.

5. Describe the concept of "jihad" from both an Islamic and Western perspective.

6. Name the five pillars of Islamic faith and briefly discuss them.

Mecca, Saudi Arabia is Islam's holiest city and the birthplace of the Prophet Muhammad. Nearly one million Muslims, many of them on a pilgrimage, gather for Laylat al-Qadr (Arabic for "The Night of Destiny"). It is the anniversary of Allah's Messenger revealing the first portion of the Qur'an to the Prophet Muhammad. Laylat al-Qadr falls on the 27th day of Ramadan, the month of fasting.

(© JTB Media Creation, Inc/Alamy)

Introduction

The world of the Middle East and Islam is very different in comparison to the United States. It is characterized by a unique history, culture, religion, and perspective not observed in the West. Most Westerners have a limited understanding of the Middle East and Islam, often diluted by stereotypes, misinformation, and inaccurate characterizations by the popular media. Movies such as *Lawrence of Arabia*, *the Sheik of Baghdad*, and *Raiders of the Lost Ark* all contribute to this dilution. In balance, people in the Middle East and other Islamic countries often have a corresponding misunderstanding of Westerners. Their understanding is often formed by information from religious zealots, old American television shows, MTV, and a local media that is simultaneously pro-Muslim and often anti-Western. People from the West and the Middle East have a great deal of room in which to increase their mutual understandings.

The Middle East: Strife, Misunderstandings, and Turmoil

Based both on real differences and misconceptions, terrorism often pits people and cultures against each other. Some Westerners leap to the conclusion that the radical Muslims they hear about on the news from faraway places like Afghanistan, Iraq, Lebanon, or Chechnya are representative of all Muslims from those countries. Conversely, drone strikes and news reports of crimes by Western troops confirm the worst notions that Muslims have about Westerners.

To genuinely understand terrorism requires something more than knowing a few definitions and laws. Comprehending terrorism in a deeper way requires a careful examination of the social, political, and/or religious positions taken by the parties involved in a conflict. After analysis, it may be possible to reach a conclusion about different ideologies. Illustratively, Usama bin Laden (UBL) urged Muslims to kill Americans wherever they found them because there were no "innocent" Americans. However, much of the world, including most Muslims, was repelled by the notion that even a radicalized view of a religion would urge the slaughter of non-combatant children and women.

Comprehending the "realities" involved in insurgencies, civil wars, insurrections, revolutions, or other labels of irregular warfare can also be difficult. Terrorism is a tactic commonly used in the irregular wars that seem so common in the Middle East. Is it the government or insurgents, both of which use terrorism, that really represent the best interests of the people? Could both or neither have those best interests in mind? Are these irregular wars really just over the form of government to be instituted or maintained and who is in power? Is it morally wrong for the majority to rise up against control by a minority that imposes their will, views, and practices upon them? When a democratically elected official suddenly institutes measures and practices that began to alter the form of government and there is no recall or impeachment provision, what should be done? These issues occupy center stage in the Middle East where the governments more than occasionally come face-to-face with groups in their population who violently pursue their visions of the future. The rise and fall of Egyptian President Mohamed Morsi illustrates some of these issues.

President Mohamed Morsi was democratically elected in 2012. He rapidly lost popular support because he seemed unable to govern, used excessive force to quell civic uprisings, and economic problems continued to increase. Even more troubling to a majority of citizens was that Morsi, a former leader and heavily supported by the **Muslim Brotherhood (MB)** was moving Egypt toward an Islamic state, which the military also opposed. Seventy percent of Egyptians were dissatisfied with Morsi and 74 percent lacked confidence in the MB to actually govern.[1]

In 2013, after just one year in office, the military removed Morsi from power and established an interim government. However, the minority Muslim Brotherhood strongly supported Morsi and demanded his release and reinstatement. The MB and other pro-Morsi factions held massive demonstrations in Cairo and other Egyptian cities (see Figure 3–1) that produced over 1,000 deaths among military, police, and pro and anti-Morsi factions. At

Muslim Brotherhood (MB)
An Islamic fundamental movement stemming from the writings of the radical Islamic scholars Hassan al-Banna and Sayyid Qubt in 20th century Egypt. See Chapter 4.

the same time, the MB and/or its supporters attacked, vandalized, and/or burned at least 60 Egyptian Christian churches and an unknown number of Christian businesses.[3] There were also pro-Morsi demonstrations in a number of other countries, although they were far less violent.

Initially, the military arrested some 35 Muslim Brotherhood members who died while in custody. There are two narratives for their deaths. The first is that while in a truck convoy the MB members suffocated from tear gas fired at them to prevent their escape. The second is that they were summarily executed (shot) while in the trucks.[4] No follow-up investigation was ever conducted to confirm the actual cause of death.

After the Muslim Brotherhood prisoners in the convoy were suffocated or executed, the MB canceled public demonstrations and rallies. The reason for the cancellations may be twofold. First, the convoy deaths, and second, the interim government continued arresting MB members on sight throughout the country, including most of its declared leaders. From among those arrested in the crackdown 1,000 or more were killed in mass shootings.[5] Additionally, a court issued an injunction dissolving the Muslim Brotherhood and seized its assets.[6] However, the MB did not buckle under to the forces arrayed against it. The MB announced it had been an important historical and cultural element of Egyptian and Islamic society for nearly a century and that an illegal judicial decision couldn't change that fact.[7] More about the historical relevance of the Muslim Brotherhood in Egypt is discussed in the next chapter. Unforeseeable events are yet to unfold in Egypt. Based on presently available information, it is seems likely that there will be more violence before the situation stabilizes.

> **Information Link**
> For more information on the Muslim Brotherhood, visit the official English homepage at www.ikhwanweb.com/.

FIGURE 3–1
Morsi supporters shout slogans in support of him during a demonstration in Cairo. Emotions ran high at these demonstrations and some spiraled out of control and into deadly violence.

(© epa European pressphoto agency b.v./Alamy)

Quick Facts
Decline of Support for Usama Bin Laden and al-Qaeda

Even before his death in 2011, support for both Usama bin Laden and al-Qaeda had substantially declined according to surveys of six predominately Muslim nations.[8] For example, between 2003 and 2011, confidence in UBL in the Palestinian Territories plummeted from 72 to 34 percent. Confidence in him to "do the right thing" was lowest in Jordan (13 percent), Turkey (3 percent), and Lebanon (1 percent).

In 2012, support for al-Qaeda was highest in Egypt (21 percent), but dropped quickly in Jordan (15 percent), Pakistan (13 percent), Turkey (6 percent) and Lebanon (1 percent).[9]

Support for al-Qaeda, whose ideology is a radicalized version of Islam, has plummeted and appears not to be sustainable over time across entire Islamic populations. Counterterrorism efforts must turn a lack of support for al-Qaeda into active assistance in combating it.

Coup d'état

The sudden and quick illegal seizure of a government by a small group of existing governmental people, usually a group from within the existing military.

The United States finally called the removal of President Mohamed Morsi by the Egyptian military a "**coup d'état**" and cut off much of its foreign assistance to one of its few friends in the region. The Egyptian military (under current leader and President of Egypt, Field Marshal Abdel Fattah el-Sisi), thinks of the United States favorably. Many of its leaders have been trained in America, and annually, Egypt and the United States conduct joint military exercises.

The Middle East: Geography, History, and Culture

The Middle East extends from the western Saharan plains of Africa (Morocco, Algeria, and Tunisia) across the vastness of Libya and Egypt and the deserts of Saudi Arabia to the eastern mountains of ancient Persia—Iran, Afghanistan, and Pakistan (see Figure 3–2). The area is bordered to the north by the remnants of the great Ottoman Empire—Turkey,

FIGURE 3–2

The modern Middle East is an enormous area extending from North Africa to Western Asia. The area is composed of multiple cultures, races, ethnicities, tribes, and nationalities.

Kazakhstan, and Kyrgyzstan—and to the south by the beginnings of the jungles of the Dark Continent in southern Chad, the Sudan, and Somalia. The Middle East is comprised of over a billion people representing almost every religion and a variety of cultures. It also has significant historical sites, some of which are referred to as "the cradles of civilization," in the Nile River Valley in Egypt and Mesopotamia on the plains between the Tigris and Euphrates Rivers in Iraq. The geographical vastness of the Middle East produces such diverse cultures that none of them can singlehandedly represent the region.

The Middle East is also a region of the world dotted with thriving modern metropolitan cities such as Istanbul, Cairo, Tehran, Dubai, and Riyadh, where billions of dollars in commerce are exchanged each day, yet in other areas people still live as they did centuries ago, herding a few sheep and making a marginal living out of the land. This contrast between the coexisting new and ancient ways is among the contradictions found in the Middle East. Another key contradiction is that the region hosts historical and implacable enemies of the West as well as friends and nations who stand shoulder-to-shoulder with it.

Americans Ask: "Why Attack Us?"

After 9/11, a question many Americans asked was "Why attack us?" Contained within that question is the notion that we see ourselves as "good people" living in a progressive, human-rights-oriented nation. There is data to support that view. A Pew Research Center survey concluded that 81 percent of Americans have a positive opinion about this country.[10] Moreover, the United States has a long history of helping others. Illustratively, following World War II (1941–1945), the United States gave its former foes Germany and Japan $29.3 and $15.2 billion, respectively, in foreign aid to help rebuild their economies.[11] Annually, America gives $4 billion for humanitarian and disaster relief in countries around the globe and advocates for human rights.[12] Other humanitarian aid is provided by private American organizations. In combination, these efforts deliver food to those suffering from malnutrition; produce safe drinking water; give refugee relief to those fleeing wars or droughts; provide training, seeds, implements, and farm animals to help people become self-sufficient; reduce deaths from common diseases by giving inoculations; build schools that reduce illiteracy; and lower infant mortality rates by 10 percent.[13] America leads the charge to end poverty and hunger throughout the world. Given such data, why was the United States attacked on 9/11? The answer to that question has nothing to do with what Americans think about their country and everything to do with what others think and how they experience the United States.

Surprisingly, a survey of countries whose population is predominately Muslim revealed substantially negative perceptions of the personal traits of Western people, particularly Americans. However, when the same survey queried non-Muslims in the United States, Russia, and Western Europe ("Westerners"), both negative and positive traits were associated with Muslims (see Table 3–1). Viewed as a country, America's reputation in countries with substantial Muslim populations is varied. There is no monolithic, global "Muslim view" of the United States (see Table 3–2). What is striking about the data is that Americans as individuals are seen negatively, but opinions of the United States as a country are more favorable.

Countries with populations that hold sharply negative opinions about Westerners and America may also have areas that terrorists can use as safe havens and a population from which they can recruit. However, those advantages are not sufficient to form a critical mass,[14] to move it from agitation to action.

There is an assumption that if the root causes of terrorism can be identified then they can be eradicated.[15] There is, however, as we learned in Chapters 1 and 2, no unified general theory that does so. As a behavior, terrorism is too complex and varied to be captured with the stroke of a single

TABLE 3–1

How Muslims and Westerners See Each Other: The Top Five Traits*

Muslims See Westerners as:	Westerners See Muslims as:
1. Selfish (68%)	1. Fanatical (58%)
2. Violent (66%)	2. Honest (51%)
3. Greedy (64%)	3. Violent (50%)
4. Immoral (61%)	4. Generous (41%)
5. Arrogant (57%)	5. Arrogant (39%)

* All "Westerners" were non-Muslims.

Source: "Muslim-Western Tensions Persist: Common Concerns about Islamic Extremism," *Pew Research Center (Washington, D.C.) July 21, 2011.* See: www.pewglobal. org/2011/07/21/muslim-western-tensions-persist/

Box 3–1
Who Was Usama Bin Laden?

The son of a wealthy construction magnate, Usama bin Laden (UBL) was born in 1957 in Saudi Arabia. He was raised as strict Sunni Muslim and rose to power within the fundamental Islamic movement as a student of Ayman al-Zawahiri in Egypt, who is the contemporary head of al-Qaeda. In 1979, he used his father's money and machinery to help the "mujahedeen" ("holy warrior") of Afghanistan to rid their country of the Soviets. It was during this time that UBL's notoriety and fame began to rise in the Arab world. For nearly 10 years (1979–1989), the United States provided financial aid to the mujahedeen through the Pakistani Army. Bin Laden became frustrated with Western influence in the Middle East, and particularly with U.S. support of then King Fahd in Saudi Arabia. He became closely associated with Islamic radicals in Egypt that became the core members of his new group, al-Qaeda (the Base), and in 1996 declared war against the "Great Satan" (the United States). He was obsessed with destroying what he believed was a foreign government aimed at "adulterating" his sacred homeland of Saudi Arabia.

FBI MOST WANTED FUGITIVE

MURDER OF U.S. NATIONALS INSIDE AND OUTSIDE THE UNITED STATES; CONSPIRACY TO MURDER U.S. NATIONALS OUTSIDE THE UNITED STATES; ATTACK ON A FEDERAL FACILITY RESULTING IN DEATH

USAMA BIN LADEN

Courtesy JJM Stock Photography/Alamy

The activities of al-Qaeda and bin Laden against the United States are significant:

1998: Suicide bombings of the U.S. embassies in Kenya and Tanzania killing 224 people

2000: Suicide bombing of the USS *Cole* in Yemen killing 17 American sailors

2001: Attacks on the World Trade Center and the Pentagon killing more than 3,000 people

As the mastermind and leader behind the September 11, 2001, attacks, Usama bin Laden became a major target of the War on Terror and was placed on the FBI's Ten Most Wanted Fugitives List with a $25 million bounty. On May 2, 2011, bin Laden was shot and killed inside a compound in Abbottabad, Pakistan, by members of the U.S. military (Navy Seal Team 6) in a covert operation authorized by President Barak Obama. The 2012 feature film, *Zero Dark Thirty*, chronicles the U.S. intelligence manhunt and neutralization of the "the world's most dangerous terrorist."

Did 9/11 impact you or your family? What impact did 9/11 have on the United States? Are there lingering effects? If so, what are they?

TABLE 3–2
Opinions of America by Countries with Predominately Muslim Populations*

Countries With Lowest Favorable Opinions	Countries With Most Favorable Opinions
1. Pakistan (11%)	1. Senegal (81%)
2. Jordan (14%)	2. Nigeria (69%)
3. Egypt (16%)	3. Malaysia (55%)
4. Palestine Authority (16%)	4. Lebanon (47%)
5. Turkey (21%)	5. Tunisia (42%)

*Surveys could not be conducted in some Muslim countries.

Source: "Muslim-Western Tensions Persist: Common Concerns about Islamic Extremism," Pew Research Center (Washington, D.C.) July 21, 2011. See: www.pewglobal.org/2011/07/21/muslim-western-tensions-persist/

theory, although there are some gross similarities across different types of terrorism, for example, there must be a guiding purpose or doctrine that is compelling enough that it attracts recruits, financial supporters, and eventually, the willingness of some to die for the cause.

As pointed out in Chapter 1, terrorism is evocative—"it plays to emotion not intellect."[16] It strikes at the very heart of who we are as Americans. On September 11, 2001, for the first time in our modern history, the United States was rocked by an attack on its own land. People were afraid as their daily lives were impacted and changed forever; the privileges and lifestyle that we so enjoyed in this country appeared to be jeopardized. The ability to move about and travel freely was restricted. It was a contemporary day "of infamy" and one that not only changed the lives of many Americans, but also left them asking "why?"

Part of the answer to "why us?" lies with Usama bin Laden (UBL) and al-Qaeda. UBL announced to the world that one of the primary reasons for the attack was our lack of knowledge about the true political and economic conditions of the Middle East. UBL justified the 9/11 attacks as a response to America and its allies which "disrespected" Islam by stationing their troops near Holy sites (see Figure 3–3), exploiting the riches of the region, and supporting puppet right-wing dictators, for example, Egypt under former President Hosni Mubarak, who helped to further subjugate Muslims. UBL made it very clear that he believed Western goals in the Middle East were much more motivated by its self-interest and quest for oil than in safeguarding the human rights of the people in that land.

Kingsley identifies four common "Whys" that explain terrorism: (1) Western scholars tend to blame it on radical Islamic interpretations of the Qur'an; (2) liberal explanations rest on the belief that social and political conditions foster authoritarianism, to which terrorism is a reaction; (3) others suggest that social and political conditions are burning embers, often silently opposed by people. Those embers are fanned into flames by radical

Islamic ideology, which gives rise and legitimacy to terrorism; and (4) globalization and modernity threatens religions, such as Islam, disregards human rights, fractures traditional values and cultures, and blurs national identity and sovereignty.[17] Those opposed to what they regard as the adverse features of globalization and modernity resort to terrorism in retaliation for the things being forced upon them. Saighal takes a contrary view of this explanation. He argues that Muslims push their communities back into medieval practices that perpetuate a clash of civilizations between the Middle East and the West.[18]

Parenthetically, Muslims also ask "Why?" Illustratively, in India and Myanmar, formerly Burma, there is a history of distrust and hatred between Buddhists and Muslims Episodically, one or the other goes on murderous rampages. In Myanmar during 2012, Buddhists killed 150 Muslims, causing 100,000 of them to relocate to a less hostile place, including refugee camps.[19]

The Prophet Muhammad and the Beginning of Islam

To understand the Middle East, you must have a basic understanding of Islam. It is more than just a religion; it is a prescription for a total way of life, both individually and collectively.[20] It visibly permeates life in the Middle East, including everyday life, business, and government. This is in sharp contrast to nations like the United States (a **secular** nation) where there is a separation of state and religion.

Like Judaism and Christianity, Islam traces its lineage to the "father of all people" Ibrahim (Abraham). According to religious tradition, Abraham was the first of the significant prophets to make covenants (agreements) with God ("Allah" in Arabic). That covenant relationship became the foundation of the three faiths: Judaism, Christianity, and Islam. In Islam, the Old and New Testaments are integral parts of their tradition and most of the Hebrew prophets are revered as messengers from God. Muslims do not believe in the divinity of Jesus, but honor him as an especially esteemed prophet. The ultimate and final messenger within the Islamic tradition is the Prophet **Muhammad**. Muslims often say the phrase "peace be upon him" after speaking or hearing the name of the Prophet Muhammad, to show respect and humility in using the name of their most revered religious founder and leader. "Muhammad" in Arabic means "highly praised."

Islam comes from the Arabic word "aslam," meaning total submission to Allah. A root Arabic word for aslam is "salaam," which has several meanings, but is usually interpreted as "peace."[21] The people of Islam are called **Muslim**, a contraction of two words "Muhammad" and "Islam." The name "Muslim" means one who submits himself/herself to the will of God. This includes obeying Allah in his commandments, doing what is allowed, and avoiding that which is forbidden.

Muhammad was born around 570 A.D. in Mecca, on the western coast of the Arabian Peninsula near the Red Sea. An orphan, Muhammad was raised by his grandfather. After his grandfather died, his uncle, Abu Talib, assumed that duty, raising Muhammad alongside his own son, Ali ibn Abi Talib, who after the Prophet's death became his fourth successor. Muhammad became a successful businessman who rejected the widespread worship of multiple deities and idols. Periodically, he would retreat to the mountains to a cave, "Hira." There, Muhammad meditated, reflected, and prayed alone, seeking truth about religion and life. Allah selected Muhammad to be "Rasul Allah," the final messenger of Allah. According to Muslim belief, Muhammad was 40 when *Jibra'il* (The Archangel Gabriel) visited him in Hira and revealed the first portions of what cumulatively became the **Holy or Noble Qur'an**. Gabriel's revelations continued over a period of 23 years, ending

FIGURE 3–3
Marines near the border Saudi Arabia shares with Iraq. Two of Islam's holiest places, Mecca and Medina, are located in Saudi Arabia.

(Courtesy Sgt. Nathan K. LaForte, United States Marine Corps)

Secular
Separation of church (religion) and state or government.

Muhammad
Born in 570 AD in Mecca, the Prophet Muhammad was believed to be the final messenger of God and the founder of the Islam religion.

Muslim
A derivative of the two words "Muhammad" and "Islam"; westernized to "Moslem" or "Muslim."

Holy or Noble Qur'an
The central book of Islam consisting of 114 chapters developed through the visits of the Archangel Gabriel to the Prophet Muhammad. Simply, the Qur'an or Koran in Western nations.

Box 3-2
Women's Rights in Saudi Arabia

Saudi Arabia is the only country in the world that prohibits women from driving an automobile. The restriction is drawn from the ancestral home of Islam and the male patriarchal traditions of nomadic tribes on the Arabian Peninsula. Saudi law requires a woman to have a male guardian, typically a direct relative (e.g., father, brother, son, cousin) whenever she is away from her home. Further, women must dress modestly by covering all parts of the body except the hands and eyes. The custom of dressing modestly is call "**hijab**," which also refers specifically to a scarf that covers a woman's hair. Women customarily wear a loose-fitting, long garment (abaya). If not wearing a hijab, a "niqab" that covers the head and the face, except for a small opening for the eyes, may be worn. Today, hijab varies from region to region, often reflecting personal taste in color and personality.

Many Muslim women feel that dressing hijab is quite progressive and "liberates" them from the pressures of Western style and influence, breaking the stereotypic roles of "what" women should look like and be. What do you think?

▲ Woman in Dubai wearing niqab
Delphine Goldsztejn/Newscom

▲ Indonesian woman wearing hijab and abaya
Wf Sihardian/NurPhoto/Sipa USA/Newscom

Hijab
Dressing modestly within the Islamic religion; it often refers directly to the veil that covers the head and chest of a Muslim woman.

the year Muhammad died. As he received the revelations Muhammad recited them to his daughter Fatima and an inner circle of friends and companions, which faithfully reduced them to writing.

The Qur'an consists of 114 "suras" (chapters) defining everything from the nature of God and Man to the everyday rituals of cleanliness and bathing. The Qur'an contains Islam's primary instructions and tenets. Muhammad shared the revelations with a growing number of believers. Similar to Jesus (and other religious founders), Muhammad was accepted in some places and denounced in others. A few times he was forced to flee for his life because of opposition to his message.

In early Christian tradition after the death of Jesus, his followers fell into two separate camps. One faction more closely followed the writings of the Apostle Paul and centered primarily in Constantinople (now Istanbul, Turkey) as the Eastern Church. The Apostle Peter was the first leader of the early Christian Church in Rome, which evolved into the Catholic Church, which is led by a "divinely inspired" leader, the Pope. The two camps were more than geographically separated, there were irreconcilable difference (e.g., the Eastern Church rejected the notion of the pope's infallibility in matters of church doctrine). Much later, during the 16th century, the Reformation in Europe resulted in the creation of Protestant churches, which separated from the Roman Catholic tradition.

Quick Facts
Hashimite

The Hashimites are a royal Arab family claiming they are descendants of Haashim ibn Abd al-Manaf, the great grandfather of the Prophet Muhammad, and historically linked to the nomadic groups of eastern Arabia along the Red Sea. Today, the Hashimite Kingdom of Jordon claims to be the largest living segment of this group. It is the same group that revolted against the Ottoman Empire and the British Mandate between 1916 and 1922; the revolt became the subject of the popular movie *Lawrence of Arabia* (1962).

In 632 A.D. Muhammad died, leaving the future of Islam to his followers. Like the early Christian Church, the response of the followers produced profound changes. One unintended consequence was a conflict that produced, again, two factions: **Sunni** and **Shi'a or Shiite**. These Islamic factions have existed continuously since the 7th century and their followers are, respectively, called Sunnis and Shiites. The Islamic scholar Husayn Jafri explains the split within the Muslim world can be much better explained as a political difference rather than a spiritual separation.[22]

Sunni
The "True Path of Allah" and the largest of the two primary Muslim traditions within Islam.

Shi'a or Shiite
One of the two primary Muslim traditions stemming from the "Shi'at Ali" or "The Party of Ali." Followers of the Shi'a tradition believe that Ali was given a divine right of successorship to lead the Muslim community after the death of the Prophet Muhammad.

The Emergence of Two Muslim Traditions: Sunni and Shi'a

The death of the Prophet Muhammad led to a crucial question: Who is the rightful successor to the Prophet Muhammad? Those who came to be called Sunnis called attention to the fact the Prophet did not have a male heir, designate a successor, or establish a procedure for selecting his successor. Sunnis believed that the Prophet's successor should be selected by merit, not by inheritance, or birth of family.[23] Therefore, in their view it was proper for an assembly of distinguished clerics to elect a well-qualified pious person with wisdom who would follow the customs established by the Prophet Muhammad. An assembly of Muslim clerics elected **Abu Bakr** as the 1st Caliph of Arabia and the leader of the Muslim community, or **ummah**. Most of Muhammad's followers accepted Abu Bakr as the new leader. Abu Bakr (573–634 A.D.) was an early convert to Islam. He was a constant and close companion to Muhammad. Their relationship was strengthened by Muhammad's marriage to Abu Bakr's daughter, Aisha. During Muhammad's last illness he gave Abu Bakr the honor of leading prayer.[24] Aisha objected that her father was too frail for that leadership responsibility, but Muhammad insisted.[25] On his deathbed, Muhammad seemingly endorsed Abu Bakr as his successor by instructing his followers to close all doors to the mosque except for the door of Abu Bakr.[26] According to one Muslim tradition, Muhammad's last words were "God, have pity on those who succeed me."[27]

Abu Bakr
The 1st Caliph or ruler of Arabia and the leader of the Muslim community after the death of the Prophet Muhammad.

Ummah
The worldwide community of the Islamic faithful.

A small Hashimite group living in Mecca and the clan of the Prophet Muhammad advocated that Muhammad's cousin and son-in-law, Ali ibn Abi Talib, should be the Prophet's successor. According to early writings,[28] Ali alleged to have been given a divine right to successorship and had received a special mandate from the Prophet to become the next leader of the Islamic community. Ali was also married to Fatimah, the Prophet's daughter. Those calling for the election of Ali became known as the "*Shi'at Ali*" (or "party of Ali") – the Shi'a or Shiites. Although the Shi'a group actually arose several years after the death of the Prophet Muhammad,[29] they contended not only the divinely inspired right of Ali, but also the descendant leadership of the Muslim community through Fatimah, the daughter of the Prophet. Hence, the leadership of Islam should be transmitted exclusively though the Prophet's bloodline.[30]

The Party of Ali objected to Abu Bakr being selected by a vote. They believed that because Allah had selected Muhammad to be the final prophet, Allah intended that the male family member closest to Muhammad should follow. Therefore, the selection of Abu Bakr violated divine order. Ali was Muhammad's cousin and son-in-law by virtue of his marriage to the Prophet's daughter Fatima. Ali in his own right was a substantial candidate to become **caliph**.

Information Link
For more information on the Sunni and Shi'a traditions within Islam, visit the homepage for *The Muslim Observer*, an online periodical that provides news on Islamic issues both within the United States and internationally, at http://muslimmedianetwork.com/mmn/.

Caliph
The political leader or head of a caliphate or Muslim state; a successor to the Prophet Muhammad.

Quick Facts
Islam's Ummah and Caliphate

"Ummah" is used 60 times in the Qur'an.[31] It is also used frequently in the **Hadith**. The Hadith are reports of the words and deeds of the Prophet Muhammad, his closest companions, and the views of luminary Islamic scholars and religious figures.[32] Given its use in different contexts, there is some debate about its meaning. Ummah is the worldwide community of Islamic believers, which transcends race, geography, and national boundaries.[33] It roughly corresponds to those who believe in other transnational religion, such as Catholicism.

"Caliphate" means a single, worldwide Islam nation. In modern time it is conceptualized by some as being ruled by both a religious head and an executive caliph. The last caliphate was dissolved in 1924 upon the founding of the Republic of Turkey. Iran is not a caliphate, but does have a Supreme Leader and a President. The former is a religious figure with control over the military and judicial systems. The President has limited authority as the government's executive officer and is subordinate to the Supreme Leader. The President is elected by a popular vote, but the Supreme Leader is selected by the 86 clerics that form the Assembly of Experts.

Recently, the Islamic State in Iraq and Syria (ISIS) has declared itself as the new Islamic Caliphate, however, its political and religious status as such has not been recognized by the broader Islamic community.

Hadith
A collection of the words and deeds of the Prophet Muhammad, his closest companions, and the views of luminary Islamic scholars and religious figures within the Islamic faith.

Caliphate
An Islamic state where the political and religious leader are the same.

He was a great warrior and greatly respected as "The Leader of the Faithful" and "The Lion of God." Arguably, there was some ambiguity about the Prophet Muhammad's preference for a successor. Although he seemed to endorse Abu Bakr, he also publicly said of Ali: "Whoever has me as a master also has him as a master."[34]

Ali eventually became the fourth caliph, leading Islam from 656 A.D. to 661 A.D. He replaced numerous officials with trusted followers, ultimately provoking an Islamic civil war during his reign. Ali was assassinated in 661, as were his two sons, Hasan and Husayn, who also became caliphs. To avoid persecution, the Shi'a fled east into the mountains of Persia (now Iran). Although Persians are not Arabs, the effect of the Shiites on them has been profound, reflected in every aspect of life from literature and philosophy to politics and, of course, religion.

A key distinction between the Shi'a and the Sunni is that the latter elect separate spiritual and political leaders. For the Shias, leadership belongs to the successors of the Prophet Muhammad as ordained by Allah. Each successor occupies the office of Supreme Imam and selects the next Supreme Imam to maintain the direct lineage from the Prophet to the present time. The Supreme Imam leads not only the spiritual life of his Islamic community, but also the political and temporal aspects of everyday life—a modern caliph. Hence, Shia government is non-secular, combining Islam with the political dimension of rule. On the other hand, the Sunni leader is elected by the leadership of Islam. Sunni government is secular, meaning that religion and government are separated. The Sunni or "True Path of Allah" remain as the majority group in the heart of the Middle East, electing their spiritual leaders after the death of Muhammad by the consensus of Muslim clerics and leaders (see Figure 3–4).

Today the Shi'a tradition remains a much smaller yet vocal minority in the Islamic world. Only 10 to 13 percent of the Islamic population is Shi'a, and those Muslims are primarily located in Iran, Lebanon, Pakistan, India, and Iraq.[35] The remainder of the Islamic community is Sunni and populates the entire Middle East and much of Southeast Asia. The largest Muslim country is no longer in the Middle East, but rather in Southeast Asia—Indonesia, with over 205 million people claiming Islam as their religion.[36] The center of Islamic faith remains in the holy city of **Mecca**, the birthplace of the Prophet Muhammad and the site of the **Kaaba** (Arabic, cube), or alter of Abraham to which millions make pilgrimage each year.

Mecca
The holiest city in the religion of Islam, located in southwest Saudi Arabia near the Red Sea. The birthplace of the Prophet Muhammad and the focus of the Hajj or Pilgrimage to Mecca.

Kaaba
According to Islam, the alter of Abraham (built by Abraham and his son Ishmael) and the focus of Hajj, or the pilgrimage to Mecca.

The Concept of "Jihad"

Some 1.6 billion people embrace Islam in the modern world.[37] It is the fastest growing religion on Earth, with 80 percent of believers now outside the Middle East. Southeastern Asia generally, and Indonesia specifically, represent the concentrated new growth of Islam. For these people, Islam is an intimate personal connection with the same God worshiped by Jews and Christians—a source of strength, a way of life, and hope in a trouble world.[38]

The term *Islam* is Arabic, meaning "submission to the will of God," with roots firmly planted in the common Arabic word for peace: *salaam*. That may come as a surprise to

The Islamic Empire

most Americans, whose perceptions have been tainted by radical terrorists expressing the virtues of jihad against the United States, or the myriad of suicide bombers that have plagued Israel. In fact, the word "jihad" has a very special meaning to those following the Muslim tradition. Derived from the Qur'an, **jihad** means using all of one's strength to overcome adversity and difficulty in the struggle to submit to the will of God. It is a spiritual struggle, not a temporal (or worldly) struggle, to do good over evil. This strife occurs on two fronts: the internal and the external. The internal struggle can be described as the effort to attain one's own essence and perfection, whereas the external one is the process of enabling someone else to attain his or her own essence. In the words of the Prophet Mohammed, the first is the *greater jihad* and the second is the *lesser jihad*. As in Christianity, the body is considered weak, and is often tempted. The struggle for *greater jihad* characterizes a spiritual front over one's own ego and destructive emotions, desires and thoughts (e.g., malice, hatred, envy selfishness, pride, arrogance, and pomp), which prevent man from attaining perfection. It is not a struggle within the world itself. Aboulmagd-Foster observes that the inner struggle's work is within the soul.[39] It is a spiritual cleansing and, as such, an act of worship.[40] The purpose of the inner struggle is living a good life within the teachings of Islam.

The *lesser jihad* is much more materialistic in nature, consisting of physical acts to assist one's family, relatives, neighbors, and country; a call to strengthen the overall "ummah" or community of Muslim believers. Above all else, it is an idealized vision that reminds Muslims of what they should be: unified, connected, profoundly faithful, and practicing high moral standards.[41] Again, in parallel to Christianity, the *lesser jihad* can be acquainted more with acts of mercy and faith, or what are more commonly called "the beatitudes" that Jesus gave during his sermon on the mount. *Jihad* is the means of internal and external balance. It is a "holy war" that is fought within the spiritual context, and winning this war means reaching spiritual perfection and helping other so do the same.[42] In Chapter 4, we discuss the misinterpretation of the word *jihad* by radical Islamic scholars and clerics bent on rallying a war cry against the United States and the West.

In its truest sense, *jihad* was never meant to be associated with physical violence and most certainly not suicide bombing. Today, one of the most intense arguments within Muslim clerics is whether or not the suicide bombers observed worldwide will ever attain the spiritual bliss of Paradise since suicide within the Muslim tradition is strictly forbidden. The perversion of *jihad* began during the 12th century (during the Crusades), with a tribal leader in Morocco rallying his people to repel the European Crusaders invading their land.

FIGURE 3–4
The Shi'a population is primarily concentrated in modern-day Iran, Iraq, Lebanon, and Yemen, whereas the Sunni population is rapidly growing throughout the world, especially in Southeast Asia.

Jihad
Derived from the Holy Qur'an, the word *jihad* represents an internal struggle to overcome adversity and difficulty in submitting to the will of Allah (God). Perverted historically by Islamic fundamentalists to mean "holy war."

FIGURE 3–5
A page from a medieval book depicts
Muslims and Crusaders fighting.

(© Album/Oronoz/Newscom)

Monotheistic
The belief in one God expressed by three
major religions in the world: Judaism,
Christianity, and Islam,

It was a sacred duty to preserve their community, land,
and culture from the invading "infidel" through physical
war ... a "*holy war*" mandated by Allah to safeguard Islam
(see Figure 3–5).

Similarly, other words were perverted and developed,
such as the word "assassin" derived from the radical Shi'a
Ismaili sect in Iran during this same period of time, the
Ismailis. Literally translated, "assassin" means "hashish-
eater"—in reference to the ritual intoxication the assassins
undertook before embarking on their mission of murder.
Hoffman points out that violence for the assassins was a
sacramental act: a divine duty, commanded by religious
text and communicated by clerical authorities.[43] Similarly,
the assassins were promised that, should they perish in
the course of carrying out their attack, they would ascend
immediately to Paradise. The same ethos of self-sacrifice
and suicidal martyrdom can be seen in modern, radical
Islamic terrorist organizations today (e.g., Hamas, Islamic
Jihad, Jemaah Islamiya, al-Qaeda).[44]

Islam and Terrorism

The connectivity between religion and terrorism has not
been without controversy. Several scholars have argued
the role that religion plays in terrorism,[45] yet few accurately depict the immense complexity of a decision to
commit oneself to violence and/or suicide. Religion may
not be the reason or motivator for terrorism, but rather a means to understanding, and
even accepting, political and social crisis. Without the crisis of living in dire poverty, in
disease, in famine, and in suppression, Juergensmeyer argues there can be no suicide
bombing, for such acts lose cosmic meaning without crisis.[46] Essentially, when people
lose power in the present, they also lose hope for the future. It is in these conditions that
the cosmic states of the afterlife (heaven, hell, paradise) take serious meaning in the
justification of radical action, so often observed in terrorism and suicide bombing.

The words *jihad* and *assassin* have both been associated with Islamic terrorism today.
Unfortunately, the spiritual and historical roots of these words are often forgotten and dismissed in our relatively weak understanding of the concept. This is particularly true in the
West, as we struggle to understand such a different culture with such a vastly different
historical and religious heritage. Unfortunately, it is often much easier to appeal to our
emotional aspects by declaring the fanaticism of a religion that we do not understand or
know, and that has been distorted by minority and radical perspectives for the last several
centuries. Remember, religion like terrorism is evocative; it often appeals to emotion rather
than intellect. Islam is a peaceful and beautiful religion that is *not* responsible for terrorism. The likes of Aymen al-Zawari and Usama bin Laden from al-Qaeda, Hassan Nasrallah
from Hezbollah, Sheik Ahmed Yassin from Hamas, and Sheik Abu Bakr Bashir from Jemaah
Islamiya, as well as other leaders of radical Muslim groups in the Middle East that promote
suicide bombing and the escalation of civilian casualties, no more represent Islam than Eric
Rudolph, David Koresh, or Jim Jones represented Christianity.

The Five Pillars of Islam

Islam is not a violent religion. It is a cousin to Judaism and Christianity in that all three
have a **monotheistic** belief in one God. Islam emphasizes that all people are equal through
the love of God (Allah) and it is based on five major principles or pillars of faith. These "pillars" represent the essential tenets of Islamic faith (see Figure 3–6). They are the primary
obligations that Muslims must satisfy in order to live a good and responsible life according
to Islam.[47]

Pillar 1: Testimony of Faith (Shahada)

Shahada means to testify or bear witness, and it is often cited as the most important of the pillars.[48] The Shahada is a testimony of faith in an eloquent yet simple prayer, similar to the Apostles Creed in Christian communities. It is the Muslim profession of faith, expressing its two most fundamental beliefs in a single statement.

> "La ilha illa Allah, Muhamadur rasoolu Allah"
> "There is no true god but Allah, and Muhammad is his Prophet."

A sincere recitation of this confession of faith before two Muslims is the sole requirement for those who wish to join the Muslim community. It must be correctly recited aloud with full understanding, sincerely, and without reservation. Although there is no requirement for the Shahada to be said publicly, there is some sentiment that it should be.[49] Others take the position that Allah is the best witness.[50]

The Shahada declares that Allah is without equal and the only true God. He is all-knowing, all-powerful, and all-merciful. Allah is the Creator of all things seen and unseen and everything is under His Control and His Command.[51] Only Allah deserves to be worshiped. Also acknowledged by the Shahada is that the Prophet Mohammad is Allah's servant and messenger. Muslims believe that understanding what Allah wants from us can be learned by adhering to the message sent to the Prophet by Allah through the Archangel Gabriel.[52]

The Shahada is recited in the Adhan (call for prayer) by the Mussein (the person selected by each mosque to perform the Adhan) and is part of Salat (daily prayer).[53] It is whispered in the ear of the newborn and recited in anticipation of those immediately dying.[54]

Pillar 2: Prayer (Salat)

Muslims perform prayers five times each day. They do so at dawn, noon, mid-afternoon, sunset, and night wherever they happen to be (see Figure 3–7). Although each prayer takes only a few minutes, it is an acknowledgement by the supplicants of the importance of Allah in their lives. It is a quiet time, a time for reflection, a time of peace, and a time of prayer to Allah for

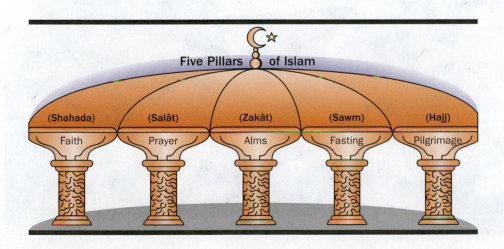

Five Pillars of Islam

| (Shahada) | (Salât) | (Zakât) | (Sawm) | (Hajj) |
| Faith | Prayer | Alms | Fasting | Pilgrimage |

FIGURE 3–6
The Five Pillars of Islam represent the essential tenets of the Islamic faith.

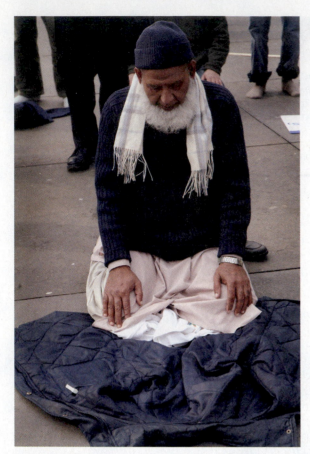

FIGURE 3–7
An elderly Muslim man at prayer.
(© Vehbi Koca/Alamy)

Mosque
A holy place of worship in Islam.

Imam
Local spiritual leader of the Islamic faith, similar to a priest, rabbi, or pastor in other religion.

Nisaab
Arabic for "portion," the threshold after which a person is obliged to pay zakat; varies throughout the Middle East.

guidance and mercy. When possible, Muslims go to a place of worship (a **mosque**) on Fridays for the noon prayer. Here, they listen to the local cleric (**imam**) discuss interpretations of the Qur'an or other topics which pertain to daily life and Islam. This sermon is known as the "khutba." The imams sing their praises to Allah over loudspeakers or raise their voices across wind-swept sands. Many Muslims carry prayer beads on which they murmur the phrase, "Allah u akbar!"—God is great!—as well as other phrases. In the Middle East, people actively engage with their religion five times a day. In contrast, in most western Christian nations (like the United States) worship is neither as public nor as visibly pervasive in daily life.

Although Islam is the dominant religion in the Middle East, it is by far not the only religion. By most standards, Islam is a very tolerant religion. As a reflection of the numerous and diverse ethnic population residing throughout the Middle East, it is not uncommon to see Christian churches of almost every denomination, Catholic cathedrals, Jewish synagogues, and even the occasional Buddhist temple all existing within the same neighborhood in a Middle Eastern city. Potentially, radical Muslim extremists will impact negatively on this harmony.

Pillar 3: Giving Alms (Zakat)

"Zakat" denotes both purification and growth. Zakat is not a tax system that everyone pays in exchange for the delivery of some governmental service, such as the maintenance of roads. The compulsory annual payment of zakat by all adult Muslims and businesses that are able is both a reminder that what they have is a gift from Allah and of their obligation to help the needy and support Islam. Muslims owe zakat when they have or exceed more than a certain amount of money, called the **nisaab**. The zakat is calculated as 2.5 percent or 1/40th of a percent of the amount that exceeds the nisaab. The collection of the zakat varies across Islamic nations. The state, zakat committees, charitable organizations, and mosques are all used to collect zakat.

A list of people in need, such as orphans, the poor, and others, are detailed in the Qur'an. However, Muslims may also give other amounts on a daily basis to those in observable need, for example, the hungry, maimed, orphaned, or others that are reduced to begging (see Figure 3–8). This act is known as "sadaqah," which is voluntary charity that can be done in addition to the mandatory zakat per year. As one Muslim scholar noted, without beggars

FIGURE 3–8
Afghan beggers pray outside of a mosque. Their appearance suggest a hard life and great need.
(Courtesy JalilRezayee/EPA/Newscom)

and paupers there could be no perfection for people striving to see Allah.[55] They provide the means by which the more fortunate can give, and hence grow in their own faith.

Pillar 4: Fasting (Sawm)

Every year in the month of Ramadan, the ninth month of the Arab calendar, all Muslims fast from dawn until sundown, abstaining from food, drink, and sexual relations. Like many religions, fasting is regarded as a method of spiritual self-purification. By depriving one's self of worldly comforts, even for a short time, a fasting person gains true sympathy with those who go hungry, as well as achieve spiritual growth. Ramadan is similar to the Christian tradition of Lent or the Jewish tradition of Yom Kippur, wherein fasting and prayer often combine with spiritual reflection and purpose. The nights of Ramadan are often spent in congregational prayer at the mosque.

Pillar 5: Pilgrimage to Mecca (Hajj)

The final pillar of the Islamic faith is the pilgrimage to Mecca that takes place in the twelfth month of the Islamic calendar. This is a once-in-a-lifetime pilgrimage to the Holy Kaaba in Mecca. The Kaaba is a holy site built by Abraham and his son, Ishmael, according to Islamic tradition. It was the first mosque built by Abraham for worship. Again, the similarity to Judaism and Christianity in that Abraham is revered as the "father" of each religion is reinforced through the hajj.[56] Over two million people go to Mecca each year from every corner of the Muslim world. Most of the pilgrims wear simple clothes (usually two white pieces of cloth) that strip away distinctions of class and culture so that all stand equal before Allah. Symbolically, the hajj represents the spiritual journey that all Muslims are on, growing ever closer to Allah.

Chapter Summary

SUMMARY BY LEARNING OBJECTIVE

1. **Describe the geographical, historical, and cultural aspects of the Middle East.**

   The geographical and cultural area of the Middle East extends from the western Saharan Plans of Africa to the eastern mountains of ancient Persia—current day-Iran, Afghanistan, and Pakistan. The area is bordered on the north by the Mediterranean Sea and to the south by the beginning of the jungles of Africa. It also has significant historical sites, some of which are referred to as "the cradles of civilization," in the Nile River Valley in Egypt and Mesopotamia on the plains between the Tigris and Euphrates Rivers in Iraq. The area historically represents some of the earliest and most advanced civilizations known to mankind and is the birthplace of the world's three major monotheistic religions—Christianity, Judaism, and Islam. Several countries compose the Middle East, including the recognized and major countries of Western Sahara, Morocco, Algeria, Libya, Tunisia, Egypt, Israel, the State of Palestine, Saudi Arabia, Lebanon, Syria, Jordon, Kuwait, Iraq, Iran, Oman, Bahrain, Yemen, Oman, Qatar, United Arab Emirates, Turkey, and Iran.

2. **Explain the misconceptions of Westerners over Muslims and vice versa and the political instability in some of the Middle East countries.**

Terrorism is evocative—"it plays to emotion not intellect." It strikes at the very heart of who we are as Americans and forces many people to have misconceptions about other people, cultures, and religions. For instance, Usama bin Laden (UBL) claimed that the attack on 9/11 was made in order to reveal America's lack of knowledge about the true political and economic conditions of the Middle East. He attempted to justify 9/11 as a response to America and its allies which "disrespected" Islam by stationing troops near Holy sites like Mecca and Medina in Saudi Arabia, exploiting the riches of the region, and supporting puppet right-wing dictators, for example, Egypt under former President Hosni Mubarak, who helped to further subjugate Muslims. UBL made it very clear that he believed Western goals in the Middle East were much more motivated by its self-interest and quest for oil than in safeguarding the human rights of the people in that land. Kingsley identifies four common misconceptions that explain terrorism, particularly involving Westerners and Muslims: (1) Western scholars tend to blame terrorism on radical Islamic interpretations of the Noble Qur'an; (2) liberal explanations rest on the belief that social and political conditions foster authoritarianism, to which terrorism is a reaction; (3) others suggest that social and political conditions are burning embers, often silently opposed by people. Those embers are fanned into flames by radical Islamic ideology, which gives rise and legitimacy to terrorism; and (4) globalization and modernity threatens religions, such as Islam, disregards human rights, fractures traditional values and cultures, and blurs national identity and sovereignty. Those opposed to what they regard as the adverse features of globalization and modernity resort to terrorism in retaliation for the things being forced upon them. Others takes a contrary view of this explanation, arguing that Muslims push their communities back into medieval practices that perpetuate a clash of civilizations between the Middle East (Islam) and the West.

3. **Give a brief history of the development of Islam in the Middle East.**

Islam is one of the three great monotheistic religions of the world (along with Judaism and Christianity) believing in one God. The religion traces its roots directly to the Prophet Muhammad during the late 500s A.D. Muslims believe that Muhammad was visited by the Archangel Gabriel and presented with the Word of God—that there is but one God—Allah. The communications between Muhammad and the Angel Gabriel were compiled into the Qur'an, defining everything from the nature of God and Man to the mundane rituals of cleanliness and bathing. In 632 A.D., Muhammad died and a struggle ensued between two primary traditions: Sunni and Shi'a. Both traditions maintain rightful successorship of the faith; however, the Sunni tradition has vastly outnumbered the Shi'a over the centuries.

4. **Describe the differences between the Sunni and Shi'a traditions within Islam.**

The Shi'a stem from a group of followers of Ali, the son-in-law of the Prophet Muhammad who believed that Ali was divinely chosen to be the leader of the Islamic community after Muhammad's death in 632 A.D. They argue that the leader of Islam must provide political, governmental, and spiritual leadership to Islam as well as be directly descended from the Prophet. On the other hand, the Sunni or "True Path of Allah" tradition believes that the leadership of Islam should be elected, and segregated from temporal and political life. Government should be secular, meaning that religion and government are separate. Sunnis represent about 85 to 90 percent of the Muslim population in the world; the Shi'a represent the minority and are primarily located in Iran, southeastern Iraq, and Lebanon.

5. **Describe the concept of "jihad" from both an Islamic and Western perspective.**

From an Islamic perspective, the term "jihad" is derived from the Qur'an. The word represents an internal struggle to overcome adversity and difficulty in submitting to the will of God. The *greater jihad* characterizes a spiritual front over one's own ego and the destructive emotions often associated with malice, hate, envy, and pride that prevent man from attaining perfection; the *lesser jihad* is much more material and consists of acts of mercy and faith that are designed to help others. The Western perspective of "*jihad*" is based on a Middle Eastern perversion of the word meaning "holy war," and is often associated with violent actions and attacks by Islamic radicals and terrorists as exemplified by Usama bin Laden and al-Qaeda.

6. **Name the five essentials of Islamic faith.**

The Five Pillars of Islam represent the five essentials of Islamic faith. They are: (1) Testimony of Faith (Shahada), (2) Prayer (Selah), (3) Giving Alms (Zakah), (4) Fasting (Sawm), and (5) Pilgrimage to Mecca (Hajj).

REVIEW QUESTIONS

1. Why is it important to understand the concept of terrorism from a Middle Eastern perspective?
2. How did Usama bin Laden view the United States (and other Western countries) and terrorism in the Middle East?
3. What does the word "Islam" mean?
4. Who was the Prophet Muhammad? And what role did he play in the development of Islam?
5. What is the "Qur'an"?
6. Describe the differences between the two Muslim traditions of Sunni and Shi'a.
7. What does the word "jihad" really mean to a Muslim, and how was it perverted to more contemporary Western perspectives?
8. What is the Kaaba?

CRITICAL THINKING QUESTIONS

1. **Monotheistic Religions.** As a class discussion, compare and contrast the three great monotheistic religions of Islam, Judaism, and Christianity. List the similarities of these three religions that all believe in one God. Then list the differences. Interestingly, they all tend to be exclusive in nature, meaning that they don't simply believe in and worship one God, but also deny the existence of the gods of any other religious faiths. Do you think that this trait has made the monotheistic religions historically less tolerant than polytheistic religions?
2. **Compare and Contrast Islam with Judaism and Christianity.** Visit an Islamic mosque and talk with the local imam, visit a Jewish synagogue and talk to the rabbi, and visit a Christian or Catholic Church and talk to the local minister or priest. Ask them what they may know about the opposing monotheistic religions. Are the aware of each other's existence in the same community? Do they schedule meetings or events to share ideas and thoughts about the one God? Do the different faiths commonly mingle or worship with each other? Why not? How tolerant are they of each other?
3. **The Impact of the Crusades.** Explore the History website at www.history.com/topics/ crusades. Watch the videos and read the articles relating to the Crusades. Were the Crusades sparked more by political and economic motivations or by religion? How do you think the Crusades of the 11th through 13th centuries impact current events in the Middle East, and relations between Muslims and Christians?

NOTES

1. Omar Tewfik, "Poll: Egyptian Support for Morsi and the Muslim Brotherhood Plummets," Arab American Institute, June 17, 2013, www.aaiusa.org/index_ee.php/blog/entry/poll-egyptian-support-for-morsi-and-the-muslim-brotherhood-plummets.
2. This account is drawn with restatement from Jack Healy, "Soldier Sentenced to Life for Killing 16," *The New York Times*, August 23, 2013; and Eric M. Johnson, "U.S. Soldier Who Killed Afghan Villagers Gets Life Without Parole," *Reuters*, August 23, 2013.
3. Abigail Hauslohner, "Ravaged Churches Reveal Sectarian Split Feeding Egypt's Violence," *The Washington Post*, August 20, 2013.
4. Raja Abdulrahim, "In Egypt, More Than 35 Muslim Brotherhood Prisoners Reported Killed," *The Los Angeles Times*, August 19, 2013.
5. David D. Kirkpatrick, "Egyptian Court Shuts Down Muslim Brotherhood and Seizes its Assets," *The New York Times*, September 24, 2013.
6. Loc. cit.
7. Loc. cit.
8. The information in this short paragraph is taken with restatement from "Usama bin Laden Largely Discredited Among Muslim Publics in Recent Years," Pew Research Center,

May 2, 2011, www.pewglobal.org/2011/05/02/osma-bib-laden-largely-discredited-among-muslim-publics-in-recent-years.

9. See "On Anniversary of bin Laden's Death, Little Backing of al Qaeda," Pew Research Center, April 30, 2012, www.pewglobal.org/2012/04/30/on-anniversary-of-bin-ladens-death-little-backing-of-al-qaeda.

10. "Opinion of the United States," Pew Research Center, Global Attitudes Project, 2013, www.pewglobal.org.

11. The dollar amounts are given in 2005 value. See Nina Serafino, "U.S. Occupation Assistance: Iraq, Germany, and Japan Compared" (Washington, D.C.: Congressional Research Service, March 23, 2006), p. CRS-1. The reason 2005 dollars are used is because the 2006 report was for Congress and the author wanted to use contemporary dollars for all three countries to make the comparison even.

12. Rhoda Margesson, "International Crisis and Disasters" (Washington, D.C.: Congressional Research Service, August 1, 2013), from the Executive Summary.

13. In part, the information is provided by "Fact Sheet: The U.S. Budget and Humanitarian Aid," www.care.org/getinvolved/advocay/budget_factsheet.asp.

14. On the notion of critical mass applied to social situations, see Gerald Marwell and Pamela J. Oliver, "Social Networks and Collective Action: A Theory of Critical Mass. III," *American Journal of Sociology*, Vol. 94, No. 4, January 1989.

15. An informative article on the causes of terrorism is Edward Newman, "Exploring the Root Causes of Terrorism," *Studies in Conflict and Terrorism*, Vol. 29, Issue 8, December 2006, pp. 749–772.

16. Robert W. Taylor and Harry E. Vanden, "Defining Terrorism in El Salvador: 'La Matanza,'" *The ANNALS of the American Academy of Political and Social Sciences*, Vol. 463, September 1982, pp. 106–117.

17. Okoro Kingsley, "Religion and Terrorism: A Socio-Historical Re-Consideration," *Journal of Alternative Perspectives in the Social Sciences,* Vol. 2, Issue 2, December 2010, pp. 550–576.

18. Vinod Saighal, *Dealing With Global Terrorism: The Way Forward* (Chicago: Independent Publishers Group, 2003), p. 20.

19. Thomas Fuller, "In Myanmar, Revival of Attacks on Muslims," *The New York Times*, October 3, 2013.

20. T. R. Copinger-Symes, "Is Osama bin Laden's Fatwa Urging Jihad Against Americans Dated 23 February 1998 Justified by Islamic Law?" *Defence Studies*, Vol. 3, Issue 1, Spring 2003, p. 46.

21. Etim E. Okon, "Jihad: Warfare and Territorial Expansion in Islam," *Asian Social Sciences*, Vol. 9, Issue 5, May 2013, p. 171.

22. Husayn M. Jafri, *The Origins and Early Development of Shi'a Islam* (Cairo, Egypt: Qum, 1982).

23. "Islam-Sunni and Shia," London Inter Faith Center, www.londoninterfaith.org.uk/resources/islam-sunni-and-shia.

24. Wilferd Madelung, *The Succession of Muhammad: A Study of the Early Caliphate* (Cambridge, England: Cambridge University Press, 1997), p. 25.

25. Loc. cit.

26. Loc. cit.

27. Lesley Hazleton, "The Chosen Ones of Allah," *New Statesman*, Vol. 140, Issue 5058, June 20, 2011, p. 24.

28. According to the Shi'a tradition.

29. This group arose only after the death of the 3rd Caliph Uthman ibn Affan (656), at which point there was a great debate as to who would be the successor and leader of the community of Muslims.

30. Christopher M. Blanchard, *Islam: Sunnis and Shiites* (Washington, D.C.: Congressional Research Service, January 28, 2009), p. 1.

31. Robert A. Saunders, "The Ummah as Nation: A Reappraisal in the Wake of the Cartoons Affair," *Nations and Nationalism*, Vol. 14, Issue 2, pp. 303–304.

32. Ibid., p. 306.

33. Ishtiaq Hossain, "The Organization of the Islamic Conference (OIC): Nature, Role, and the Issues," *Journal of Third World Studies*, Vol. 29, Issue 1, Spring 2012, p. 291.

34. Lieutenant Colonel Adam Oler, "A Brief Introduction to the Sunni-Shi'ite Struggle: Six Key Points," *The Reporter*, Vol. 35, No. 2, June 2008, p. 3. Elsewhere this statement appears as "Whoever has me for a master, Ali is his master."

35. "Mapping the Global Muslim Population," Pew Research Center, October 7, 2009, p. 1, www.pewforum.org/2009/10/07/mapping-the-global-muslim-population.

36. "Muslim Population of Indonesia," Pew Research Center, November 4, 2010, www.pewforum.org/2010/11/04/muslim-population-of-indonesia.

37. "Muslims," Pew Research Center, December 18, 2012, p. 1, www.pewforum.org/2012/12/18/global-religious-landscap-muslim.

38. Don Belt, ed., *The World of Islam* (Washington, D.C.: National Geographic, 2001).

39. Brian Handwerk, "What Does Jihad Really Mean to Muslims," *National Geographic News*, October 24, 2003, p.1, www.news.nationalgeographic.com/news/2003/10/1023_0310023_jhad.html.

40. See Emad M. Al-Saidat and Mohammad Al-Khawalda, "Jihad: A Victim of Policy and Misinterpretations," *Asian Social Science*, Vol. 8, Issue 7, June 2012, pp. 202–207.

41. Garbi Schmidt, "The Transnational Umma: Myth or Reality? Examples of Western Diasporas," *Muslim World*, Vol. 95, Issue 4, October 2005, p. 575.

42. Fethullah Gulen, *Questions Put to Islam by the Ages* (Izmer, Turkey: TOV Yaymevi, 1997), pp. 186–219; and Ayatullah Kashif al Ghita, *The Ja'fari Sect and Its Essentials* (Istanbul, Turkey: Addulkbaki Golpinarli, 1979), pp. 70–79.

43. Bruce Hoffman, *Inside Terrorism* (New York: Columbia University Press, 1998), p. 89.

44. Ibid.

45. The role of religion as a motivator or causation of terrorism has been argued by several scholars. See David C. Rapport, "Fear and Trembling: Terrorism in Three Religious Traditions," *American Political Science Review*, Vol. 78, No. 3 (September 1984); Walter Laqueur, *The Age of Terrorism* (Boston: Little, Brown, Inc., 1987); Mark Juergensmeyer, "Terror Mandated by God," *Terrorism and Political Violence*, Vol. 9, No. 2 (Summer 1997); Mark Juergensmeyer, *Terror in the Mind of God: The Global Rise of Religious Terrorism* (Berkeley, CA: University of California Press, 2000); and Jonathon White, *Terrorism: An Introduction* (Belmont, CA: West/Wadsworth Publishing, 2003).

46. Mark Juergensmeyer, *Terror in the Mind of God: The Global Rise of Religious Terrorism* (Berkeley, CA: University of California Press, 2000).

47. "Five Pillars of Faith," BBC, September 9, 2009, www.bbc.co.uk/religion/religions/islam/practices/fivepillars.shtml.

48. "What are the Five Pillars of Islam?" Islam Guide, p.1, www.islam-guide.com/ch3-16.htm.

49. "The Shahada Explained," August 28, 013, p. 1, www.therevert.com/articles/the-shahada-explained.html.

50. Loc. cit.

51. Ibid., p. 2.

52. Loc. cit.

53. Loc. cit.

54. Loc. cit.

55. Ala al-Din 'Ali al-Muttaqi al-Hindi, *A Treasure of the Laborers for the Sake of the Prophet's Sayings and Deeds* (Beirut, Lebanon: Muassasat al-Risala, 1985).

56. See Bruce Feller, *Abraham: A Journey to the Heart of Three Faiths* (New York: Harper Collins Publishers, 2005) and David M. Kay, *The Semitic Religions: Hebrew, Jewish, Christian and Moslem* (Harper Collins Publishers, Originally published in 1923 and reprinted in 2007).

The Rise of Radical Islam

Learning Objectives

After completing this chapter, you should be able to:

1. Define fundamentalism, and provide a number of common assumptions observed in various fundamental groups, including Islamic fundamentalist groups.

2. State and discuss the similarities between Islamic and other fundamentalist movements easily observed in groups operating in the United States.

3. Provide an historical overview of the Wahhabi movement in Saudi Arabia and the rest of the Middle East.

4. Describe the development and importance of the Muslim Brotherhood in Egypt, including the contributions of Hassan al-Banna and Sayyid Qutb.

5. Discuss and identify the major Palestinian Jihad organizations. How are they different from earlier groups?

6. Describe the differences between the Wahhabi, Salafi, and Jihadist Salafi movements.

7. Describe the roots of radical Islam from the Shi'a perspective and describe the group known as Hezbollah.

8. Discuss the political and historical dimensions of Islamic fundamentalism.

An extremist group, "Muslims Against the Crusaders" burns an American flag because a small church pastor in Florida threatened to burn the Qur'an.

(© Janine Wiedel Photolibrary/Alamy)

Introduction

As discussed in the previous chapter, Islam is the most rapidly growing religion in the world and radical Islam, as exhibited by certain terrorist groups operating throughout the world, represent dangerous threats to Western interests. Marty and Appleby describe **fundamentalism** as a "strategy or set of strategies in which beleaguered believers attempt to preserve their distinctive identity as a people or group. Feeling this identity to be at risk, fundamentalists fortify this identity by a selective retrieval of doctrines, beliefs and practices from a sacred past."[1] There are similarities between Islamic fundamentalists and other extremist ideologies that are seen in domestic terrorist groups found within the United States. These groups are discussed further in Chapter 8.

Fundamentalism
A strategy in which beleaguered believers attempt to preserve their distinctive identity as a people or group.

Selective Interpretation of Scripture and Doctrine

Both Islamic fundamentalist and many extremist or domestic terrorist groups rely on selective interpretation or misinterpretation of important documents. In the United States, the Bible and the U.S. Constitution with its amendments are selectively "twisted" to form the ideological basis seen in right-wing, neo-Nazi groups such as the Skinheads, Phineus Priesthood, and the Ku Klux Klan (see Box 4–1). An example of this selectivity is the interpretation of the Bible's account of human creation by churches belonging to the fundamental Christian Nation. These churches believe that when God created man, he made several "false starts." In this view, God used "mud" that became people of color. Although they had well-developed bodies, their intelligence was lower. Thus, these "false starts" were made by God to serve man. From clay, God created "true people" in his image and endowed them with superior intellect and gave them the Promised Land of the United States. Fundamentalist Christian churches also believe that Satan's temptation of man in the Garden of Eden resulted in the sexual union of Satan with Eve, which produced the Jewish race. This interpretation leads to the conclusion that the United States and the rest of the world are controlled by Jews, who are further demonized as the "killers of the Christ."[2]

Fundamentalist Christians believe they are locked in a vicious war (between good and evil) that will eventually culminate in an apocalyptic Armageddon pitting the Christian white race against people of color and Jews. The U.S. Constitution and its amendments are similarly misinterpreted. Although fundamental and radical Christian groups strongly believe that the founding fathers of this country were divinely inspired, they only support the portions of the Constitution and its amendments that serve their purposes. The Second Amendment is interpreted as an inalienable right not only to own firearms, but automatic weapons as well. On the other hand, the Thirteenth Amendment, ending slavery, and the Fourteenth Amendment, requiring due process of law for all people, are dismissed by these groups as "fraudulent."

Misinterpretation of Symbolic Words

Fundamental and extremist Christian movements carefully select the words with which they identify themselves, such as "Christian Patriot," "free man," and "constitutionalist." These self-identifiers are intended to appeal to nationalistic and religious beliefs held by people for two purposes: (1) to soften the public image of fundamentalist and radical groups and (2) to attract new members who define themselves in similar terms.

Just as the fundamental and extremist Christians churches within the United States have misinterpreted certain passages within the Bible, fundamentalist and extremist Islamic clerics have done the same thing with portions of the Qur'an. Illustratively, the Arabic word "jihad" is a symbolic word focusing on an individual's inner struggle to submit to the will of God. In the Qur'an jihad has little to do with physical war and nothing to do with a religious duty to kill Westerners. Fundamental and extremist Islamic scholars and clerics have misinterpreted jihad to fire the emotional response of people to fight for their personal identity, religion, culture, and the establishment of a worldwide caliphate. This chapter discusses the radical and fundamental Islamic movements that misinterpret the word "jihad" to serve their own violent purposes. And similar to their Christian counterparts, Islamic fundamentalists view their struggle as battle between the "pure" state of Islam that existed centuries ago with the "adulterated" world of today.

Box 4–1
Memphis and the Three Parks

In 2013, the KKK Grand Dragon rallied members of the KKK, Aryan Nation, National Socialist Movement, and the Sadistic Souls Motorcycle Club in Memphis, Tennessee. The Memphis Rally protested renaming parks that formerly honored the Confederacy and two of its prominent figures: Confederate, Nathan Bedford Forrest, and Jefferson Davis parks became, respectively, Health Sciences, Mississippi River, and Memphis parks. Forrest was a controversial Confederate General and Jefferson Davis was the President of the Confederacy. In Memphis, African-Americans are a majority.

Organizations such as the Sons of Confederate Veterans and United Daughters of the Confederacy want to preserve and honor the history of their ancestors. These organizations are not hate groups. Is it right to simply erase their heritage? If you were defending the renaming of the parks what would you say? What argument can you construct not to rename them? Is there any middle ground?

(Jim Weber/The Commercial Appeal/Zuma press/Alamy)

The Justification and Use of Violence Called by God

Demonstrations, counterdemonstrations, and violence are common denominators among fundamentalists and radicals on both sides of the religious equation (see Figure 4–1). They believe God is calling upon his faithful to challenge, refocus, and/or direct violence at the unworthy, non-believers, or other symbolic words they apply to justify their violence. Two benefits are derived from demonizing the group(s) at which they direct violence: (1) It conforms their identities as a "good people" because they are doing God's work and (2) psychologically and emotionally within their movements they are absolved of any culpability or sin, for their actions are required by God and therefore not optional.

The misinterpretation of important documents by fundamentalist and extremist Islamic and Christian groups creates a problem. Uninformed people assume these characterizations are true and that they really represent Islam or Christianity. However, these extremist groups and their leaders represent an extremely small portion of the mainline religions they purport to be a part of: There are more than 2 billion Christians and 1.6 billion Muslims.

Eschatology
A part of religion that focuses on the last days, or ultimate destruction, of the world.

White's work on the **eschatology** of terrorism accurately depicts another commonality between fundamental and extremist movements, whether they are Islamic or Christian in origin.[3] Eschatology is derived from an ancient Greek word that essentially describes the end of the physical world. For many Christian extremists, the end of the world is shaped by their misinterpretation of the Battle of Armageddon as depicted in the Bible. These individuals often view themselves as the "last warriors" or "saviors of the White Christian race." In Islamic extremism, the oppressed Muslim views his or her culture, religion, and way of life as seriously jeopardized by Western ideology, and hence without future. There is only one choice before the end ... the use of extreme violence and terrorism. White and others accurately point out that when violent eschatology is politicized on a cosmic battlefield in

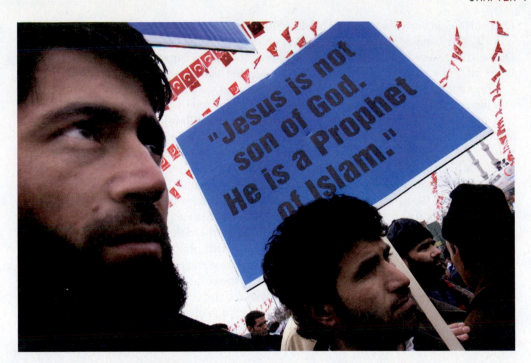

FIGURE 4–1
The clash of religions is readily seen as radical Muslims demonstrate in Turkey against a forthcoming visit of the Pope. About 25,000 radical Muslims of the Islamic Welfare Party participated in the demonstration. Paradoxically, the belief that Jesus is not the Son of God is as offensive to Christians as the assertion that he is to Muslims.

(© Alessandra Benedetti/Corbis)

the mind of the religious extremist, all actions are justified in the eyes of their God.[4] The consequences are potentially devastating, with significant loss of innocent life and property. In the United States, we have seen two such events: the bombing of the Alfred P. Murrah Building in Oklahoma City (August 19, 1995) and the attacks on the World Trade Centers and Pentagon on September 11, 2011.

Charismatic Leadership

Both Christian and Islamic fundamental movements have been heavily influenced by charismatic leaders. Within the Christian right, examples of charismatic fundamentalists include (1) David Koresh (1959–1993) and his Branch Davidian movement that ended after a 51-day standoff in Waco, Texas (see Figure 4–2); (2) Reverend Richard Butler (1918–2004) of Hayden

FIGURE 4–2
In 1993, the Branch Davidian compound bursts into flames during the final assault by the FBI.

(Jerry W. Hoefer/Fort Worth Star-Telegram/MCT/Alamy)

Lake, Idaho, an early leader of the fundamental Christian ideology called the Aryan Nations; and (3) the flamboyant writings of William Pierce (1933–2002), for example, the *Turner Diaries*, that were found in Timothy McVeigh's (1968–2001) car when he was arrested within hours after bombing the Alfred P. Murrah Building in Oklahoma City in 1995.

Fundamental Islam has been led by the writings of various fundamentalist philosophers and ideologues. Several of these individuals wrote centuries ago about European colonization and the exploitation of their land, conditions that have long passed. Yet their philosophical ideology is given renewed credibility by charismatic religious leaders such as (1) Sheik Omar Abdel-Rahman (1938–), the "Blind Sheik," who was convicted and given a life sentence for his role in the 1993 bombing of the World Trade Center; (2) Sheik Ahmed Yassin (1937–2004), who as the former leader of Hamas (The Islamic Resistance Movement in the West Bank and Gaza) was responsible for hundreds of suicide bombings; and (3) Usama bin Laden and Aymen al-Zawahiri, both key leaders in al-Qaeda and the attacks on 9/11.

In each fundamentalist case, we see similar patterns. Selective interpretation of scriptures and misuse of symbolic words, combined with philosophical writings from years ago, are married to current political conditions by very charismatic writers and leaders. Usama bin Laden not only had the ability to speak quite eloquently, but also had the financial means to support his ideological sentiments. Unfortunately as a government, we have grossly underestimated the power of such charismatic leaders and writers to influence other people and sustain such fundamental movements, whether they are Christian, Islamic, or any other religion.

> **Information Link**
> Visit the Peabody Award–winning portrait of the standoff between FBI and ATF agents and David Koresh at the Branch Davidian compound in Waco, Texas, in 1995 at www.vimeo.com/13978271.

The Political Dimension of Islamic Fundamentalism

Essentially, Islamic fundamentalist organizations attempt to "re-Islamize" societies that are already politically and economically ruled by powerful secular governments.[5] These governments are often allied with Western powers, including the United States, and often internally suppress their own people. In the past, some countries of the Middle East (e.g., Libya, Iraq, Egypt, Syria, Saudi Arabia) represent suppressive governments or sheikdoms (kingdoms) where the tenets of democracy were non-existent. There were no free elections, there were huge differences in socioeconomic classes within the population, and there was a concentration of wealth in the hands of only a few families, which often ruled the country and controlled all aspects of business and economic life. Many people in these countries lived in poverty, had no education, suffered from diseases and malnutrition, lacked access to medical care, and had no real political power. Most Arabs argue that this is the case in the West Bank and Gaza, where Palestinians live under the occupation of Israeli forces—freedom of movement is limited through imposed curfews, expression of divergent politics is often suppressed, and opportunities for a better lifestyle are severely limited. Faced with an unattractive future if nothing changes, some people are attracted to radical, fundamental, and extremist causes. Unfortunately, desperate situations spawn desperate actions, and the history of the Palestinian people as discussed in Chapter 2 highlights this type of desperation. Where there is no political power in the present, there is no hope in the future. For some, embracing fundamental Islam offers hope, if not in this world, in the next, for example, because of dying as a suicide bomber. The consequences of such desperation results in an opposing radicalization as well and the two sides are locked in a cycle of tit-for-tat marked by violence, terrorism, and military intervention.

The Arab Revolution

Arab Spring
Refers to a series of recent revolutions beginning in December 2010 in Tunisia aimed at increasing individual rights and freedoms for the people living in Middle Eastern countries.

Beginning in spring 2010 in Tunisia, Egypt, Libya, and Yemen, events have yielded unprecedented changes in governments though out the Middle East and North Africa. Many of these changes have come at the hands of violent uprisings, which frightened tourists away and deepened the poverty of the Middle East (see Figure 4–3). The **Arab Spring** is the term given to these events (see Box 4–2). Civil protests, demonstrations, and in many cases violent uprisings from the masses have forced suppressive governments and dictatorships into exile or surrender. For instance, in 2011 one of the longest serving rulers in the Middle

Box 4–2
The Evolution of "Arab Spring": Chaos in Syria

—By Jamison Tolbert

The modern Arab revolution struggling for self-rule, autonomy, and freedom that began in Tunisia in December 2010 appears to have ended in a bloody civil war in Syria. What was denoted happily as the "Arab Spring" originated as a protest for human rights and freedom has evolved into a bloody civil war, pitting old enemies against each other and forming new alliances that threaten the stability of the entire Middle East.

In early 2011, the Syria rebels demanded that President Bashar al-Assad step down from his leadership role. Rather than abdicate his power, he ordered open fire against demonstrators and stepped-up his military crackdown on the general public. What started as an internal group of protestors has now matured into a number of large rebel army encampments, collectively called the Free Syrian Army (FSA). Unfortunately, the Syrian Free Army is *not* primarily composed of Syrian rebels but rather of fleeing fighters from other countries like Iraq and Afghanistan. With new blood and strength in numbers, new alliances have also formed, ones with terrorist groups well-known to the United States. The largest of these unlikely alliances joined the Jabbat al-Nusra rebel army (part of the FSA) with the remnants of al-Qaeda (from Iraq). The new group has been successful, taking credit for some of the most effective military victories against the al-Assad army and regaining control of northern Syria, including the city of Aleppo. In return, the al-Nusra have pledged their allegiance to al-Qaeda and their new leader, Egyptian jihadist Ayman al-Zawahiri.

The alliance has signaled the loss of international support for Syrian rebels and caused a significant and unforeseen backlash. Shi'a terrorist groups in the region have now linked with the al-Assad regime, pitting Sunni against Shi'a in a reflective war of historic proportions. Hezbollah, from Lebanon now sends armed troops to the al-Assad government, backed by the powerful government of Iran. With Hezbollah and Iran supporting the al-Assad regime, capitulation on the part of the Syrian government is doubtful. The United States is caught in the middle. Not wanting to support al-Assad, the United States has embraced funding for the FSA; unfortunately, this includes funding for members of al-Qaeda, the very fighters that were previously in conflict with U.S. forces in Iraq. Sadly for the people of Syria, the bloodshed and chaos continues in a stalemate.

Discuss how you think the United States can help in resolving the Syrian crisis. What do you think the U.S. policy toward Syria should be?

East (41 years), Muammar Gaddafi in Libya, was killed and replaced by a Transitional National Council that installed a Constitution giving equal authority to various religious and ethnic groups in the country. And in 2011 in Egypt, the most populous nation in the Middle East, Hosni Mubarak resigned under siege and was replaced by a parliamentary government including newly elected members of the Muslim Brotherhood (a group designated as "terrorist" by the United States).

Stability in Egypt continues to be a problem as the newly elected leadership was ousted by the military in 2013. Similar changes have occurred throughout the Middle East; however, the oil-rich nations of Saudi Arabia, the United Arab Emirates, Qatar, Kuwait, and Oman have continued to maintain governments ruled by powerful families and/or sheiks in the form of **constitutional monarchies**.

Constitutional monarchies
A form of government commonly observed in the Middle East when a country has a ruling family or kingdom versus a democratically elected republic or dictatorship.

The Historical Roots of Islamic Fundamentalism

Islamic fundamentalism is not a new phenomenon in the Middle East. Drawing on the early writings of Sayyid Qutb, Muhammad ibn Abd al-Wahhab, and Hassan al-Banna, radical fundamentalism can be traced to the early 16th century.

According to Murphy, the formation of Islamic fundamentalist movements can be historically attributed to a number of factors. These factors are the opposition to state authority; sociocultural and economic strife, which are associated with rapid urbanization and modernization; and the opposition to foreign occupation (colonization) in the Middle East.[6] Usually, more than one factor is needed for the formation of an Islamic fundamentalist movement.

FIGURE 4–3
Recent studies indicate that Islamic fundamentalism is most prevalent in poor, neglected and impoverished rural cities in the Middle East. Here, a mother warms her two children near a bomb crater in Iraq.

(© Mike Goldwater/Alamy)

Quick Facts
The Arab Spring (Timeline)

Country	Date	Revolutionary Actions
Tunisia	December 2010–January 2011	Existing government dissolved; new Constitutional Assembly elected
Algeria	December 2010–January 2012	Military government ousted; change in government
Libya	February 2011–August 2012	Muammar Gaddafi killed; new rebel government
Morocco	February 2011–April 2012	Protests and peaceful changes in the existing government
Egypt	January 2011–	Hosni Mubarak replaced; Muslim Brotherhood elected to power; military junta oust (2013)
Lebanon	February 2011–	Civil war continues with protests and widespread violence
Syria	March 2011–	Violent civil war attempts to replace ruling Bashar al-Assad family; civil war persists and spreads to neighboring Lebanon and Iraq
Iraq	December 2006–	Saddam Hussein executed in Iraq; new Parliamentary government developed
	December 2011–	U.S. forces leave Iraq; open violence remains in many provinces
Jordan	January 2011–August 2013	King Abdulla Hussein monarchy continues with minor changes in governmental policies
Kuwait	February 2011–	Isolated protests; the constitutional monarchy continues
Bahrain	February 2011–	Isolated protests; al-Khalifa monarchy continues
Saudi Arabia	March 2011	Minor protests and no real government changes; al-Saud monarchy continues
Oman	January 2011–May 2011	Widespread protests yield government policy changes
Yemen	January 2011–February 2012	Violent protests succeed in change of government; still significant unrest in the country; al-Qaeda resurgent groups very active in country.

Islamic fundamentalism is divided into two phases, which are represented throughout the history of the Middle East and the Muslim people.[7] Muslims and Islamic fundamentalists interpret the first phase as a positive period. During this positive period, the first Islamic state was created on the Arabian Peninsula and Islam was expanded outside of the Middle East (about 600 A.D. to the early 1900s). In addition, the Muslim culture and civilization was brought to its height with the spread of great Middle Eastern empires, such as the Hashemite and Ottoman Empires.[8] This positive period was soon followed by a second phase, which was the decline of Islam, marked by the Industrial Revolution of the West in the late 1800s and early 1900s. During this era, Muslims witnessed military defeat, loss of territory, and the insurgence of Western colonialism (especially after World War I), which continues to play a major role in the way Islamic fundamentalists interpret the world. According to radical Islamic leaders and writers, these conditions continue today, as witnessed by the **diaspora** of the Palestinian people and the establishment of Israel within the heart of the Middle East. Further, continued U.S. military involvement in Iraq, Afghanistan, and Qatar escalate radical beliefs that Western countries continue to destroy Islamic culture. These same radical clerics focus on the collusion of some governmental leaders with the West (primarily the United States) in an effort to exploit Middle East resources, especially oil. Again, these are not new concepts. Indeed for Islamic fundamentalism, history holds the key to understanding not only the past but the future as well.[9]

Diaspora
The scattering or dispersion of people from their native homeland, often to a different, smaller, or less desirable geographic area.

Islamic Ideologies

Much like Christianity, Islam is a religion of "commandments," and most of them appear to be quite practical. As we learned in the previous chapter, these commandments shape all aspects of life. Islam not only deals with relations between God and man but also with everything that an individual believer or groups of believers encounters in everyday life, from politics to marital affairs to everyday eating and bathing.[10] The separation of religion and state (secular government) is primarily a Western perspective. However, in the Middle East and the world of Islam, it has been traditionally supported by the Sunni tradition. Conflict over secularism can be traced to the early split between Sunni and Shi'a traditions after the death of Muhammad. In the Shi'a tradition, as represented in Iran, strong emphasis is placed on the union of Islam and government, and enforcement of strict **Sharia** or Islamic

Sharia
Islamic law; the moral and religious code of Islam as proscribed by the Prophet Muhammad.

Quick Facts
Mustafa Kemal Ataturk

His father was a minor local official and his mother was religious and, unusual for women of that time, could read and write.[11] They named him "Mustafa" and he later graduated from a military academy (1905). While at the academy, one of his teachers gave him the name Kemal ("perfection") because of his academic record. After graduating he compiled an excellent combat record.

In 1923, Kemal Ataturk became the first president of the new country of Turkey and he became a comprehensive reformer. He abolished the office of the Muslim Caliphate, encouraged people to wear western-style clothes, discouraged Muslim women from wearing veils, abolished Islamic courts, and replaced Arabic script with a new alphabet based on Latin. The name "Ataturk" means father of the Turks; it was bestowed on him by the Grand National Assembly.

Secularism
The separation of church and state; the form of government where persons mandated to represent the state are not members of religious institutions nor are religious dignitaries.

Modernity
An epoch of time, usually referring to post-traditional and post-agrarian (feudal) states toward capitalism, industrialization, secularization, and technological innovation.

law. Sunni radicalism is much more politically dynamic and focused on the development of puppet governments, the exploitation of people and natural resources (specifically oil), and other common conditions observed in colonialism. As discussed in Chapter 2, several non-Islamic philosophers such as Frantz Fanon[12] have also addressed these same issues as they relate to colonialism.

Muslim reactions to the term secularism have been influenced by Western history, politics and religion, and by the fear that **secularism** leads to the marginalization of their religion. Many Muslims interpreted European colonialism and attempts to introduce **modernity** as an attempt to impose Western customs, including secularism—separating religion from state and society—thus weakening the moral fabric and religious power of the Muslim community.[13] Other Muslims believed that secularism, and hence association with Western-developed countries, was necessary to build strong modern societies. Turkey, under the leadership of Kemal Ataturk during the 1920s and 1930s, illustrates this point (see Figure 4–4). Under his leadership, the country of Turkey was able to escape the strong secular beliefs of the time and has evolved into one of the only secular, democratic, stable Islamic countries in the world. Today, with a vibrant Islamic culture and a western economic sentiment blending east and west, Turkey offers the Middle East a viable alternative to radical fundamentalism.

For others in the Middle East, Western ideologies and inventions such as democracy, capitalism, technology, and secularization are viewed as a direct challenge to Islamic existence. Secularism has been and continues to be equated (by most Islamic fundamentalists) with unbelief and thus seen as a direct threat to the religious identity and values of a Muslim society.[14] Today, radical Sunni philosophers and traditional Shi'a beliefs merge to support the idea that government and religion should be one. This is a phenomenon that still rattles most scholars of the Middle East, as the Sunni and Shi'a traditions have been bitter enemies historically since their original split in the 4th century after the death of Muhammad.

The Ideologies of Islamic Fundamentalists

The inability of modern Islamic philosophers to resolve divisions within the Muslim world has created an opportunity for Islamic radicalism and fundamentalism. Islamic thinkers have borrowed various models of political, social, legal, and educational ideas from the West and adapted them to reflect and reaffirm Muslim goals.[15] Essentially, they have attempted to adopt Western organizational structure and mold it to fit Islamic values. Throughout the 19th century, often considered a period of Western colonial intrusion in the Middle East, the majority of people in the Muslim world watched as non-Muslim influences and ideologies eroded their religion, culture, values, and governments.[16] It was later, specifically during the early 1980s, that religious, economic, and cultural issues became the primary motivations of anti-Western Islamic fundamentalist movements.

FIGURE 4–4
A 1923 photograph of Kemal Ataturk (1881–1938) with his well-educated wife Latife Usakizade (1898–1975). They divorced in 1925 and she lived in seclusion, never discussing her marriage.

(Courtesy of the Library of Congress)

According to Davidson,[17] Islamic radicalism and fundamentalism is rooted in the following assumptions:

1. The Muslim world has turned into a state of disorder because of centuries of political and moral decay. Islamic fundamentalists believe this decay began when the values within the Muslim religion were not respected or practiced diligently.

2. Islamic fundamentalists believe the Muslim world has been infected with immoral, secularist values and behaviors because of Western intrusion. These ways were an inherent part of the various Western inspired governmental experiments of the 19th century, as well as the secularizing of legal, jurisprudence, and educational systems. Fundamental Islam viewed new trade and the potential for economic prosperity as a means to covet Western goods and adopt Western dress. They perceive these cultural changes as a direct threat to Islam and to the culture of the Middle East. New Western ideas of gender equality, sexual inhibition, and globalization are seen as further eroding Muslim society.

3. Fundamentalists believe that they need to fight this perceived decay by "re-Islamizing" the Muslim world. In order to re-Islamize the Muslim world, the Sharia (Muslim law) must be reintroduced (and strictly enforced) and most aspects of Western cultural and political influence must be purged, in most cases, violently.

4. The only way to re-Islamize society is to re-politicize Islam itself.

5. The West is seen as evil, as "adulterous nations" that pray to false gods, filled with men that abandon their families during divorce, are overly obsessed with sex, and adhere to corrupt practices that worship money above all else.

The radical movements active in most Muslim countries today work on these assumptions. Many of these movements began as fraternal orders, self-help groups, community action committees, or religious groups of clerics (such as the Muslim Brotherhood) that eventually evolved into political parties. Many of these fundamentalist groups have initiated some positive changes such as providing health care, education, and basic needs to the poor; for example, the Muslims Brotherhood operates hospitals in Egypt and Jordan. Others have been the spawning grounds for violent action and terrorism against many Middle Eastern governments as well as the West.

As previously discussed, jihad is a concept with multiple meanings that has been used and abused throughout Islamic history. Although jihad has always been an important part of the Islamic tradition, more recently, some Islamic fundamentalists and extremists have maintained that it is a universal religious obligation for all true Muslims.[18] Most Islamic fundamentalists believe that the restoration of Muslim power and prosperity requires a return to traditional Islam, and a political or social revolution to create a new caliphate, or Muslim-dominated state throughout the world. This revolution will undoubtedly be violent in nature.

Radical Islamic fundamentalists combine militancy with visions to inspire and mobilize an army of Allah, whose manifestation of a physical jihad they believe will liberate Muslims at home and abroad. Although the Qur'an states jihad is not to be used for justifying aggressive warfare, it has been and continues to be interpreted by some rulers, governments, and individuals as justifying extreme violence and terrorism. The scriptures of Islam have been misinterpreted to justify resistance and liberation struggles, extremism, suicide bombing, violent beheadings and executions, and unholy wars. Fundamentalist movements and groups, such as the Wahhabi and Salafi movements and the Muslim Brotherhood, go beyond classical Islamic interpretation of jihad and recognize no limits but their own.

Wahhabism

A fundamentalist interpretation of Islam stemming from the teachings of Ibn al-Wahhab in the late 1700s; widely adopted throughout the Arabian Peninsula expressing the radicalization of Islam and the alternative meaning of "jihad" as "holy war" against those that do not accept strict adherence to Sharia.

The Wahhabi Movement

Among the more interesting movements in Islam is **Wahhabism**. It is the official form of Islam practiced in Saudi Arabia, other countries on the Arabian Peninsula, and elsewhere in the world. Wahhabi Islam was articulated by *Muhammad ibn Abd al-Wahhab* (1703–1792), who is recognized as the first modern Islamic fundamentalist.[19] In 1744, after receiving his religious education in Medina, he became the spiritual guide to the House of Saud (see Box 4–3).

BOX 4-3
The Founding of the House of Saud: The Holy Alliance of Abd al-Wahhab and Muhammad Ibn Saud

In the late 1700s, al-Wahhab joined forces with a young tribal chief, Muhammad ibn Saud, to lead a militant reform movement in Arabia. They united together to rebel against the Turkish Ottoman rule in Arabia. Muhammad ibn Saud hoped to harness al-Wahhab's religious passion and popular appeal to advance his own goal of political and territorial dominance in central Arabia.[20] In return, al-Wahhab sought ibn Saud's help for his own mission of reform, and an alliance of faith and power were born. They called themselves *muwahhidun*, "those who advocate openness" within the Islamic doctrine of the *Tawid*, interpreted by al-Wahhab as "exclusiveness of the One God."[21] Islam is one of the three monotheistic religions, and it is believed that all is possible through unity with the one God (Allah).

In 1788, with the help of al-Wahhab, the House of Saud ruled over the entire central plateau of the Arabian Peninsula, known as the *Najd*. There were literally hundreds of individual tribes of Arabs and Bedouins throughout the central Arabia plateau. Ibn Saud was the first to unite them under one ideology, and hence one leader. By the early 19th century, the entire Arabian Peninsula was under the rule of the House of Saud practicing the strict Wahabbi brand

of Islam. Ibn Abd al-Wahhab did not live long enough to witness his vision as he died in 1792.

The House of Saud has ruled the Arabian Peninsula for nearly four centuries. All of the leaders have been direct decedents of Muhammad ibn Saud. In 1932, Abdul Aziz ibn Saud (known simply as ibn Saud) declared himself King of the Kingdom of Saudi Arabia. Ibn Saud fathered dozens of sons and daughters by his numerous wives. He divorced and married several times; however, in accordance with strict Wahabbi law, never had more than four wives at any one time. The Head of the House of Saud is the king of Saudi Arabia who serves as the head of state and monarch of the Kingdom of Saudi Arabia. In 1953, Ibn Saud died and leadership of Saudi Arabia was passed to his son. Today, the leader of Saudi Arabia is King Abdulla bin Abdul Aziz, the fifth son of Abdul Aziz and a direct descendant of Muhammad Ibn Saud.

What do you think are the "pros" and "cons" of long-lasting monarchies such as the House of Saud? Can you name any Western monarchies that continue today? How do monarchies differ from country to country?

Al-Wahhab labeled all who disagreed with him as heretics and apostates. He justified the use of force and violence in imposing both his beliefs and his political authority over neighboring tribes as the desire of God. These labels permitted him to declare a jihad, which he interpreted as a "holy war" on other Muslims perceived to not be practicing Islam as he interpreted it.

The central point of al-Wahhab's fundamentalism movement was that absolutely every tenet added to Islam after its establishment by the Prophet Muhammad was false and should be eliminated. Because of this, even today the people and government of Saudi Arabia, as well as some other Arab countries, wear traditional Arab clothing prevalent in the 4th century. These countries also maintain Islamic practices consistent with that time period, for example, having four wives simultaneously. Wahhabism rejects any attempt to interpret Islamic law from a historical, contextual perspective and treats the vast majority of history as a corruption of the true and authentic Islam.[22] Hence, Wahhabism is a very conservative, closed society tradition that is intolerant to non-believers.

Al-Wahhab also emphasized the unity of God. He was upset at the widespread laxity in adhering to traditional Sharia (Islamic law) such as adultery, lack of attention to obligatory prayers, and the failure to allocate shares of inheritance fairly to women. According to al-Wahhab, only those who followed his teachings were true Muslims because they still followed the path laid out by Allah to Muhammad in the Noble Qur'an.[23] Many followers of Wahhabism prefer to be called "muwahhidun," or the unifiers of traditional Islamic practice.

The Wahhabis went on an unrelenting campaign against all others, for example, the Sufis, Shiites, and other tribes on the Arabian Peninsula deemed unfaithful to the Wahhabis' strict interpretation of the Prophet Muhammad. During the course of the late 18th and early 19th centuries, the House of Saud-led Wahhabis succeeded in conquering most of the Arabian Peninsula and much of what is present-day Israel, Jordan, and Syria. The Wahhabis occupied Mecca and Medina in 1802 and proceeded to destroy the shrines and tombs of the two holy cities. They continued their raids north and east into Syria and Iraq, destroying the Shi'ite shrines in the holy city of Karbal. These invasions and acts of violence still remain as points of hostility between Saudi (Sunni Wahabbi) and Iranian (Shi'a) communities.[24]

Today, Wahhabism continues to be the dominant form of Islam practiced on the Arabian Peninsula, although its influence has been greatly diminished and its strict obedience vastly relaxed. Although Wahhabism is a minority position within the Middle East, it has nevertheless been influential in the formation of other extremist philosophies. The strict Wahhabi

Information Link
For more information on the life and history of Muhammad Ibn Abd al-Wahhab, read the article on the website hosted by Princeton University: www.princeton.edu/~achaney/tmve/wiki100k/docs/Muhammad_ibn_Abd-al-Wahhab.html.

opposition to any reinterpretation of traditional Islamic law demonstrates a major influence throughout the Middle East. Radical and fundamental Islamists follow the Wahhabi example by opposing any attempt to reconcile traditional Islam with modern or Western culture, including issues such as gender and family, or the acceptance of modernity.[25] The Wahhabi movement has led not only to today's Saudi Arabia, but it has also encouraged Muslims to be concerned about society, politics, and the nature of the state (government). It was this growing concern among Muslims that set the stage for Salafism—another Islamic fundamental movement that has expressed violence as a methodology for reform and revolution.

The Muslim Brotherhood and the Beginning of the Salafi Movement

Muslim Brotherhood
An Islamic fundamental movement stemming from the writings of Hassan al-Banna and Sayyid Qutb in 20th century Egypt.

The **Muslim Brotherhood** movement was a political-religious movement beginning in Egypt in the 20th century; its motivations and religious objectives were an ideological return to the 19th-century militant Wahhabism.[26] *Hassan al-Banna* (1906–1949) began the Muslim Brotherhood in 1928, specifically in reaction to British colonial presence in Egypt and its growing presence in the Islamic world (particularly in the Middle East).[27] (See Figure 4–5.) In 1927, al-Banna took a position as a teacher in the Suez Canal Zone of eastern Egypt, which was then controlled under the British mandate. It was a critical time for the Middle East as European colonial powers took hold of much of the area through the mandate system described in Chapter 2. Al-Banna contended that the presence of the British and other European countries was eroding the Islamic values established by the Wahhabi movement in Egypt and elsewhere in the Middle East.

Through the Muslim Brotherhood, al-Banna had two basic goals: to liberate the Egypt from all foreign powers and to develop a free state functioning under the rules of Islam. He believed that the Islamic faith was not just a religion, but an all-encompassing way of living and governing. By the late 1940s, the Muslim Brotherhood had become the most powerful Islamic movement in the world.[28] With over a half million members involved in a complex network of businesses, schools, universities, and clinics in Egypt, the Muslim Brotherhood began to engage populations throughout the Middle East (e.g., Syria, Lebanon, and Saudi Arabia).

The Muslim Brotherhood organized its followers into a close-knit, Islamic-oriented community designed to serve as the dynamic nucleus or vanguard in transforming the broader society from within.[29] All members comprised tight, socio-religious organizations with a network of branches and cells. Members were trained and reinforced in their faith and commitment to a stricter Islamic-oriented state and way of life. Religious instruction, youth work, schools, hospitals, religious publications, and social welfare projects were among the activities utilized to create a new generation of leaders within the new Islamic state to be

FIGURE 4–5
Members of al-Gama'a al-Islamiya (Islamic Group) demonstrating against Egypt's then-President Mubarak carry a picture of Hassan al-Banna. It is believed Egyptian security agents assassinated al-Banna in 1949 because he was getting too popular and was considered a threat to the oppressive government. The United States designated the Islamic Group as a foreign terrorist organization in 1997.
(© Sharif Karim/Reuters/Corbis)

created in Egypt. The Muslim Brotherhood grew rapidly as a mass movement, soon expanding from rural to urban areas throughout the Middle East, but particularly remaining very strong in Egypt, even to this day.

The Muslim Brotherhood regarded Islam as "the all-embracing ideology."[30] Again, Western secularization and modernity, with its separation of church and state, and the materialism often associated with capitalism, were seen, and still are seen, as evils that corrupt the very essence of man. The Muslim Brotherhood was not originally designed to be a political party, but its beliefs that the Islamic community was to exist in a state and society governed by Islamic law, soon became drawn into the political arena. According to Munson,[31] the Muslim Brotherhood wanted to initiate several political, judicial, and administrative changes within Islamic countries including ending Arab rivalry, reforming the law so that it would conform to Islamic beliefs, strengthening the armed forces of many Middle Eastern countries, building mutual bonds and cooperation between all Islamic countries, and infusing the Islamic spirit throughout all governments.

In the years after 1936, the Brotherhood gained so much momentum that several leading politicians hoped to use it for their own political agendas.[32] In the pre–World War II era, the organization reached its height of power through violence, student demonstrations, political murders, riots, and the bombing of public places. Unable to use the Muslim Brotherhood for their purposes and confronted by its violence, Egyptian politicians became fearful and began listening seriously to its demands. By the time World War II broke out (1939), the Muslim Brotherhood was one of the most active and popular organizations in Egypt.[33] World War II provided a significant opportunity to extend the Muslim Brotherhood not only throughout Egypt, but the rest of the Middle East as well.

By the end of 1948, the Muslim Brotherhood became a hidden nation inside Egypt, with its own leadership, military, factories, weaponry, schools, and hospitals. Its members prepared themselves to take over Egyptian politics after the war. But Prime Minister Mahmud Fahmi al-Nugrashi Pash reacted to this threat by quickly jailing much of the Brotherhood's leadership, as well as other political adversaries.

The Muslim Brotherhood's dissatisfaction with the failure of Egypt's government to establish an Islamic state escalated into violence, armed conflict, civil war, and the assassination of its founder (al-Banna) in 1949.[34] Government repression drove the Brotherhood underground, but it could not escape the imprisonment and executions of its leaders and members in the mid-1960s. As in many movements, the suppressive tactics of the ruling government infuriated the Brotherhood, further radicalized its members, and to some degree increased its membership in the broader population. Although the Brotherhood was officially banned in Egypt and individual members were arrested and imprisoned, the Muslim Brotherhood continued to grow in many parts of the Muslim world. At the time of Hassan al-Banna's assassination, the group had over 70,000 members. Decades later, membership reached well into the hundreds of thousands and expanded into Sudan, Syria, Jordan, Palestine, and Kuwait.[35] The impact of the Brotherhood on Egyptian and Middle Eastern politics has been enormous as it maintains a majority of parliamentary seats in the government of Egypt and aligns itself with Hamas in the West Bank and Gaza against the country of Israel. Currently, the Brotherhood runs an extensive network of banks, investment companies, and schools focused in Egypt and the surrounding countries. It continues to serve as a catalyst for Islamic fundamentalism and radicalism, and has had a major impact on the interpretation and implementation of Islam in recent years. Almost every country in the Muslim world has an active chapter of the Muslim Brotherhood, fashioned on the model established by Hassan al-Banna in the 1930s.[36]

Today, the FBI reports that the philosophical father of all militant Islamic groups, the Muslim Brotherhood, has established cells in the American Islamic community as well, predominantly among students. For instance, the Muslim Brotherhood co-sponsored a convention in Phoenix, Arizona. The leaders of these groups urged their American supporters to "await an order to attack."[37] Nearly five years before 9/11, after the attacks on the American Embassies in East Africa, American intelligence sources discovered that other radical groups such as al-Qaeda may have merged with members of the Muslim Brotherhood.[38]

The Great Philosopher: Sayyid Qutb

Sayyid Qutb (1906–1966) has been called the "architect of radical Islam" and the "father of modern terrorism."[39] Qutb transformed the ideological beliefs of Hassan al-Banna and the Muslim Brotherhood into a revolutionary call to arms throughout the Middle East. He is remembered not only as a martyr of the Islamic revival, but one of the greatest of all revolutionary philosophers.

Qutb was a devout Muslim and, like Hassan al-Banna, memorized the Qur'an as a child. Qutb was born in 1906 into a family of moderate means living in the village of Musha in Upper Egypt. He was sent to Cairo for an education that was largely of Western orientation.[40] Qutb served with Egypt's Ministry of Education until 1953 after his ministry had sent him as a representative to the United States. Visiting the United States was an experience that proved to be a turning point in his life. After his visit he became a harsh critic of the West, and shortly after his return to Egypt he joined the Muslim Brotherhood. During the 1930s and 1940s, Egypt was involved in the struggle to free itself from British imperial control. This struggle shaped Qutb's outlook much as it had that of his predecessor, Hassan al-Banna.[41]

Information Link
For more information on Sayyid Qutb, visit the website at www.liveleak.com. Explore articles online about Sayyid Qutb as "the Father of Modern Terrorism."

Qutb was disgusted by what he judged to be racial prejudice toward Arabs in the United States. The sexual permissiveness and promiscuity of American society, the free use of alcohol, and the free mingling of men and women in public violated his sense of Islamic law. He often referred to the United States as an "adulterous nation"; interestingly, Usama bin Laden was to later use the same terms in several of his video messages to the world shortly after 9/11. During the fifties, Qutb emerged as a major voice for the Muslim Brotherhood. His commitment, intelligence, and literary style made him especially effective within the group. His radicalization and confrontational views increased after being imprisoned and tortured in 1954 for his alleged involvement in an attempt to assassinate then-Egyptian President Gamal Nasser.[42] Qutb viewed society as being strictly divided into two camps, the party of God and the party of Satan.[43] There was no middle ground—only good and evil—a reoccurring theme in fundamental and radical religious doctrine. Qutb emphasized the development of a group of "true Muslims" within the broader corrupted society—the vanguard of Muslim revolution and militancy. He concluded that attempts to bring about changes from within the existing repressive Muslim political systems were futile and that a "jihad"—interpreted by Qutb as a physical "holy war"—was the only way to implement a new Islamic order.[44] In this manner, violence and terrorism were justified by Allah (God) as sanctified acts necessary for the re-establishment of Islamic order in Egypt and the rest of the Middle East.

Qutb's formulation became the starting point for many radical groups. In 1965, the Egyptian government massively and ruthlessly suppressed the Muslim Brotherhood after it was blamed for an attempt on Nasser's life.[45] Qutb and several other leaders were arrested and executed. Thousands of other Brothers were arrested and tortured as well. Some were able to escape this massive governmental crackdown by going underground or fleeing to other Middle East countries. Qutb became a martyr to the cause of Islamic reform. His writings and books, which number in the hundreds, continue to inspire fundamental and radical Islamic clerics and leaders who feel the need for confrontational action in the face of what they perceive as corrupt and un-Islamic regimes, backed and influenced by Western power and culture. Today, Qutb's writings are read throughout the Middle East, and his interesting commentary on life as a member of the Brotherhood, *Milestones*,[46] is one of the most influential works in Arabic today.

The Rise of Palestinian "Jihad"

In Chapter 2 we discussed the complex history and development of Palestinian resistance that gave way to several radical groups within the Palestinian Liberation Organization: al-Fatah, the Popular Front for the Liberation of Palestine, the Black September Organization, and the Abu Nidal Organization. Much of their rhetoric focused on the liberation of Palestine and the destruction of Israel through Arab unity. These previously identified Palestinian groups were described as politically motivated and revolutionary, not rooted in religious ideology. They were ground in leftist ideologies expressed in the writings of Karl Marx, Che Guevara, and Carlos Marighella. Three important groups, however, emerged from the Palestinian cause that broke this mold, claiming that the liberation of Palestine is a religious mandate and the key to uniting all Arab countries into one great Islamic state. Israel and its supporters, such as the United States, were seen as major obstacles to not only the liberation of Palestine but also the establishment of an Islamic state throughout the Middle East. Violent actions taken in support of an independent and free Palestine are seen as a part of a much larger "holy war" or "holy jihad" within a worldwide Islamic revolution, beginning in the Middle East.

The **al-Aqsa Martyrs Brigade** grew out of the Palestinian-Israeli struggle, aligning itself with the original principles of al-Fatah—that armed struggle against Israel was the only way to achieve a Palestinian state (see Figure 4–6). The group considered terrorist attacks and the murder of Israeli citizens to be a legitimate means of accomplishing this goal, and believed that any Arab concession to Israel was treason to the Palestinian cause.[47]

The al-Aqsa Martyrs Brigade started as a radical nationalist movement within al-Fatah, but soon became ideologically aligned with the radical Islamic thoughts expressed by Sayyid Qutb and others. Some of the earliest suicide bombings were reportedly conducted by this group against the Israeli military. Initially, their operations were targeted against Israeli military roadblocks and settlers in the West Bank. However, the religious radicalization of its members combined with an overwhelming nationalist cause gave way to increased suicide bombings and sniper attacks against Israeli civilians.[48] Since 2002, the group has been responsible for some of the bloodiest attacks in Israel, attacking innocent citizens as they sit in cafes, wait for public transportation, attend synagogue, shop in crowded malls, or ride buses.

Al-Aqsa Martyrs Brigade
One of the first Palestinian terrorist groups to move from a secular to a radical Islamic ideology.

FIGURE 4–6
Members of the al-Aqsa Martyrs Brigade march in the streets of the Gaza Strip, declaring allegiance to Hamas.
(© Mohamed Atta/Zuma Press/ Newscom)

Palestinian Islamic Jihad (PIJ)

One of the early terrorist groups to adopt a radical Islamic ideology that justified violence and suicide bombing as a means to liberate Palestine.

The **Palestinian Islamic Jihad (PIJ)** is another of the primary Palestinian jihadist groups. Two men were particularly important to the development of the PIJ. Fathi Shaqaqi was expelled from Egypt with other Islamic radicals after the assassination of President Anwar Sadat in 1981. He relocated to the Gaza Strip, where he formed the PIJ. In 1988, Israeli authorities expelled Shaqaqi to Lebanon where he gained the support of Syria and Iran. Through the Iranian association, Shaqaqi enlisted the support of Hezbollah, the largest Shiite terrorist group in the world. Hezbollah perfected the use of suicide bombers to inflict mass casualties, for example, in 1973 at the Marine Barracks in Beirut, Lebanon. Shaqaqi was assassinated by Israeli forces in 1995 after the group began to dramatically increase its suicide bombing attacks against Israel. After Shaqaqi's death, Dr. Ramadan Abdallah Shalah stepped into the leadership role of the PIJ. Shalah was formally educated in England, earning a Ph.D. in Banking and Economics. He is most known for his activities within the United States during the 1995–2008 investigation of a University of South Florida professor, Sami al-Arian.[49] Shalah and several others were indicted on 53 counts alleging involvement in a designated terrorist group (PIJ) and conducting a pattern of racketeering activities, such as bombings, murders, and money laundering, in support of that group. It was one of the first criminal indictments in the United States against a Middle Eastern terrorist using the federal Racketeer Influence and Corrupt Organizations Act (RICO).[50] Today, Shalah remains on the FBI's Most Wanted Terrorist list and is reportedly headquartered, along with other members of the Palestinian Islamic Jihad, in Syria as a long-standing ally of Hezbollah and the al-Assad regime.

Palestinian Islamic Resistance Movement (Hamas)

The largest and most politically powerful group expressing radical Islamic ideologies to justify the liberation of Palestine and the destruction of Israel.

The **Palestinian Islamic Resistance Movement (Hamas)** is clearly the largest and most successful of the Islamic fundamentalist groups identified within the Palestinian movement. Springing from the doctrine expressed by the Muslim Brotherhood, the Palestinian Islamic Resistance Movement was developed in the summer 1986. The ideology of Hamas was first observed in its charter, reflecting the common theme for the liberation of Palestine and support of all Palestinian nationalist efforts. However, the document also expresses its belief that Palestine is an Islamic holy land and therefore no part of it may be inhabited by Israel. The charter is strongly anti-Jewish, peppered with stereotypes and bordering on paranoia in its description of Zionist conspiracies. Hamas rejects all peaceful solutions and accords, deeming them a retreat to its primary goal. Its charter reflects its closeness to Muslim Brotherhood doctrine and the writings of Sayyid Qutb, in that the only solution to the Palestinian problem is "jihad." It interprets this concept in a similar radical and fundamental way as meaning "a holy war" in which all Muslims are pitted against Israel and the West in a desperate fight for Islamic culture, land, heritage, and identity.[51] Specifically, the Hamas charter states "The day that enemies usurp part of Muslim lands, Jihad becomes the individual duty of every righteous Islamic person. In the face of Jews usurping Palestine, it is compulsory Islamic law that the banner of Jihad be raised."[52] Hamas calls for not only the liberation of Palestine, but also the destruction of Israel. Although Hamas recognized the Palestinian Liberation Organization (PLO), it rejected Arafat and any attempt at peace. During the **Oslo Accords**, a set of agreements between Israel and the PLO in 1993, Hamas rebelled against Arafat and conducted a flurry of bloody and destructive suicide bombings in Israel, effectively stopping negotiations during the Oslo process. As a result of the bombings and the ensuing Oslo Accords in 1993 and 1995, Arafat lost much ground to the Israelis, further destabilizing the political structure of the PLO. Hamas stepped in to fill the void left by Arafat's crumbling PLO, winning the loyalty and popularity of many Palestinians, especially young Palestinians facing a lifetime of perceived occupation by Israel.[53]

Oslo Accords

In 1993, the negotiation of a bilateral peace agreement between the Palestinian Liberation Organization (PLO) represented by Yassir Arafat and Israel represented by Prime Minister Yitzhak Rabin, moderated by President Bill Clinton.

The primary modus operandi of Hamas has been suicide bombing against civilian targets in Israel. Hamas used this tactic frequently, especially during the late 1990s through 2005. This tactic was encouraged by Hamas founder *Sheikh Ahmed Yassin* (see Figure 4–7). In 2003, after the first U.S. invasion of Iraq, he urged Muslims to strike at Western interests anywhere in the world. His statements sparked concerns that suicide bombing might occur in the United States, because the FBI had long suspected linkages between Hamas and various sympathizers in the United States. Federal and local police began closely tracking thefts of explosives, such as those similarly used in Hamas backpack bombs, and unusual sales of fertilizer, chemicals, and fuel that could be used to make a truck or "personal" bomb.[54]

Israeli and American politicians were astounded and concerned when Hamas won a majority of the seats in the newly developed Palestinian Parliament in June 2007. Hamas had been formally designated as a "terrorist organization" by Israel, the United States, Canada, and the European Union. However, now they had to recognize Hamas as a freely elected representative of the Palestinian people—a group that has at the core of its charter the destruction of the country of Israel. Current leader Kaled Meshai refuses to change the Hamas charter; however, has acquiesced in talks for peace with Israel. The election of *Mahmoud Abbas* as the President of the Palestinian Authority by the Palestinian Legislative Council has caused significant internal conflict between Hamas and the remnants of the PLO and al-Fatah organizations in which Abbas leads. Abbas is the only recognized leader within the Palestinian government by Israel and the United States, yet Meshai (and the rest of Hamas) remain a powerful internal force in Palestinian politics. Similar problems existed in Egypt in 2012 when the Muslim Brotherhood (the philosophical parent to Hamas) came to power in that country.

Salafism

Salafism is an Islamic philosophy founded in the late 19th century by Muslim reformers, such as Muhammad Abdu, Jamal al-Afghani, and Rashid Rida.[55] Salafism (al-Salafiyya in Arabic) comes from the word al-Salaf, which refers to the companions of the Prophet Muhammad. Salaf means "the first" or the earliest, which in their movement is regarded as the first generation of believers who were the companions of the Prophet Muhammad. Jamal al-Din al-Afghani (1838–1897) was born and educated in Iran and British India. Afghani was a teacher and political activist who traveled throughout the Muslim world from Egypt to Pakistan, calling upon Muslims to "arise from their lethargy and reclaim their God-ordained purpose and identity."[56] While he lived and taught in Egypt, he served as an adviser to the Shah of Iran, and traveled Europe preaching a message that "challenged both Muslim and European authorities, the need for national unity to resist the danger of European intervention, the need for a broader unity of Islamic peoples, the need for a constitution to limit the ruler's power."[57] Themes of anti-imperialism, anti-colonialism, Arab unity, and Islamic solidarity were a major part of his legacy, as well as basic tenets of Salafism.

Afghani and his disciples were involved in the nationalist struggle against British and French influence in Egypt in 1882. Afghani was placed under house arrest in 1896, when Iran's, Nasir al-Din Shah was assassinated by a reputed follower of Afghani's.[58] Afghani preached political ideas such as constitutionalism and political participation through elected assemblies. The revitalization of Islam and Muslim solidarity were the keys, according to Afghani, to attain the ultimate goal, independence from the West and the restoration of Muslim independence.

Afghani's protégé Muhammad Abduh (1849–1905) was the developer of the intellectual and social reformist dimensions of Islamic modern thought.[59] Abduh was responsible for beginning the Salafi movement, which sought legitimacy through identification of its Islamic modernist reformist with the elders of the early Muslim community, those who followed the example of the Prophet. Abduh was also an Egyptian trained scholar and taught at Azhar University, the oldest center of Islamic learning in the Middle East. Abduh was the most enthusiastic of Afghani's early students and worked closely with Afghani, publishing articles on sociopolitical reform, and was exiled to Paris with Afghani for his participation in early Egyptian insurgency. After his return from exile, Abduh turned away from political activism and focused on intellectual, religious, and educational reform. He was a critic of the Wahabbi movement and particularly polygamy and its negative effect on the Muslim family. Abduh argued that polygamy had been allowed as a concession to the prevailing social customs within Arabia at the time of the Prophet Muhammad. He also offered new interpretation of the Qur'an for application in a modern world, a concept that countered more radical and fundamentalist concepts Wahhabism and the Muslim Brotherhood.[60]

Rashid Rida, carried on the reformist tradition of Abduh, accepting the reality of modern states, technology, invention, and nationalism while maintaining the Islamic state and

FIGURE 4–7
Sheikh Ahmed Hassan Yassin was an original founder of the Palestinian Islamic Resistance Movement, in Arabic *Harakat al-Muqawamah al Islamiyyah*—Hamas. He was a formally educated man and an inflammatory speaker; confined to a wheelchair as a quadriplegic stemming from an early childhood accident, he was quoted as saying that Israel "must disappear from the map." On March 22, 2004, while still on the steps of a mosque after an early morning prayer service in the Gaza Strip, Yassin was assassinated by an Israeli helicopter gunship that fired two Hellfire missiles at him and his bodyguards. The attack killed Yassin and his bodyguards as well as nine other bystanders and wounded another twelve people. The assassination escalated tensions in the West Bank and Gaza, sparking more suicide bombings against Israeli civilians and mass demonstrations in political support of Hamas.
Source: Hatem Moussa/AP Images

Salafism
A broad intellectual movement spawned by the writings of Egyptian scholars such as Muhammad Abdu, Jamal al-Afghani, and Rashid Rida, focusing on the adoption of modernity and technology within Islam; soon became corrupted and blended with Wahhabism.

Quick Facts
The Evolution of Terrorist Groups

Many of the same individuals that were involved in early Palestinian terrorist groups that expressed Marxist Revolutionary ideologies are now involved in leadership positions of radical Islamic fundamentalist groups. The evolutionary nature of group names has caused significant problems for police and intelligence personnel within the United States to monitor and identify specific individuals.

One group of individuals that has had an especially interesting evolution started out as young teenagers in the Arab Nationalist Movement, then joined the al-Fatah Revolutionary Brigades that soon changed its name to the Arab Revolutionary Brigades (ARB). The Black September Organization (BSO) grew from members in the ARB and many joined the Abu Nidal Organization (ANO) after the 1972 Olympic Massacre. As the leader of ANO, Sabri al-Banna, moved more toward mercenary actions without an ideology, these same individuals joined another group simply known as the Socialist Muslims. Today, these same individuals, now more experienced, are active in Hamas as spiritual and political leaders. The group names have changed but the actors and the terrorist methodology are the same.

---

self-identity for all Muslims.[61] Afghani and Abduh influenced Rida's growing admiration for Saudi-Arabia's self-proclaimed Islamic state or caliphate. He emphasized the self-sufficiency and practical lifestyle of Islam, and in his later writings took a more critical attitude toward the threat of the West in the Middle East. He particularly focused on problems that he believed would stem from Saudi Arabia and the growing importance of oil to Western countries.[62]

Jihadist Salafism: The Ideology of al-Qaeda

Jihadist Salafism
The ideology of al-Qaeda; a second generation of Islamic Salafism that justifies violence and revolution as the means to an end.

Jihadist Salafism[63] is a label that has been given by many scholars to a second generation of Salafism. This group is a radical form of Salafism that emerged during the 1980s, rose in influence during the 1990s, and continues to dominate Middle Eastern and Islamic radical thought. Unlike traditional Salafis, Jihadists Salafis embrace violence as their *only* means to return to the original message of Islam. Jihadist Salafis are also distinct from the traditional Salafis because they have identified new enemies in the West and tend to see "jihad" as a global war that knows no boundaries. The Soviet-Afghanistan War (1980–1989) served as the catalyst for this explosive mixture of Salafi outlook and call to violence. The Soviet invasion of Afghanistan radicalized many Arab Salafis and had the effect of converting to the cause of "jihad" an entire segment of the transnational Salafi movement. Jihadist Salafis embrace a strict, literal interpretation of Islam, but combine it with an emphasis on "jihad," understood again as "holy war" against all those that threaten the historical, cultural, and religious existence of Islam in the Middle East. To them, violence becomes the prime instrument through which the Salafi desire to return to the original "purity" of Islam that controls all aspects of life.

The prime targets of Jihadist Salafi organizations vary according to the country and organization involved. Some concentrate their attacks on the "infidel regimes." These regimes, such as Saudi Arabia and Jordan, are denounced as Muslim in name only and for being subservient to the West. Jihadist Salafis also may engage in random violence against an entire society seen as having reverted to a state of pre-Islamic ignorance and for not siding with "true Muslims" in their struggle against the regime. For most Jihadist Salafi organizations (most prominently al-Qaeda) the main enemy is the United States. The United States is singled out because of its support for Israel and because of its support for Middle Eastern regimes and leaders that are perceived as betraying Islam and repressing Muslims. The charismatic and instrumental leader of the Jihadist Salafi movement was Usama bin Laden, emerging from the 1989 Soviet-Afghan War as a hero and religious icon strong enough to challenge the West. Bin Laden masterminded the 9/11 attacks, which surely excited all fundamentalist Islamic groups. All other Western nations learned a valuable and frightening lesson: If Jihadist Salafists can successfully attack America in its homeland, they are also vulnerable to such attacks.

Islamic fundamentalist movements such as Wahhabism, Salafism, Jihadist Salafism, and the Muslim Brotherhood all attempt to pursue change—many times through violence. These movements have created a cycle of violence and the insurgence of modern-day terrorism. Their goal is to re-Islamize the Muslim world. The fundamentalists view the Muslim world as being "infected" by the West's immoral, secularist values and behaviors. In addition, many Islamic fundamentalists embrace a strict, literal interpretation of Islam and combine it with an emphasis on "jihad," misinterpreted but understood by them as a "holy war." Although "jihad" as an inner struggle has always been an important part of Islam, many Islamic fundamentalists have restated it as a universal religious obligation for all "true" Muslims to join their war against the West in a worldwide Islamic revolution.

The Wahhabi movement has not only led to today's Saudi Arabia but has also encouraged Muslims to be concerned about politics and government. The Muslim Brotherhood, which emerged as a response to the Wahhabi movement, has grown in to be one of the largest and strongest fundamental Islamic organizations in the world. Sayyid Qutb's writings continue to inspire fundamental and radical Muslims who feel the need for confrontational action in the face of what they perceive as corrupt and non-Islamic regimes in the Middle East, backed and influenced by Western power and culture. Salafism has expressed itself in a multiplicity of movements that have given rise to historical self-reflection and hence created a foundation for Jihadist Salafis. Jihadist Salafis, acting through a variety of terrorist organizations such as al-Qaeda, al-Qaeda in the Arabian Peninsula (AQAP), the Islamic State in Iraq and Syria/Islamic State of Iraq and the Levant (ISIS/ISIL), and Jemaah Islamiah (based primarily in Indonesia and the Philippines) pose an enormous threat to Western nations and specifically the United States (see Table 4–1).

TABLE 4–1
Jihadist Salafist Groups Active Throughout the World

The Jihadist Salafist ideologies represent a significant threat to Israel, Europe and other Western nations (including the United States). The philosophy represents the most virulent of radical Islamic fundamentalism and has been the foundation for several active terrorist groups throughout the world. These groups remain active and continue to pose a significant threat of attack in the United States and against American interests abroad.

Abu Sayyaf Group (ASG). ASG is a violent Islamic separatist group operating in the southern Philippine island of Mindinao. Split from the Moro National Liberation Front, the group has been active in narcotics, arms and human trafficking, as well as kidnapping as a means to fund its operations in Southeast Asia.

Al-Qaeda. Established in 1988 by Usama bin Laden in Afghanistan as a resistance movement against the invasion by the Soviet Union, al-Qaeda remains a viable terrorist group aimed at destroying Western influence (particularly the United States) and establishing a worldwide Islamic state. The group has been significantly reduced in number and resources due to military involvement in Iraq and Afghanistan. Al-Qaeda is currently headed by its longtime spiritual leader, Ayman al-Zawahiri, and remnants are still committed to their Jihadist Salafist cause.

Al-Qaeda in the Arabian Peninsula (AQAP). AQAP is a militant group following the ideological philosophies of the larger al-Qaeda. AQAP is based primarily in Yemen, and has been linked with other radical Islamic groups in that country, such as the Yemeni Islamic Jihad and the Aden-abyan Islamic Army. It has been strongly opposed to the House of Saud in Saudi Arabia and has been involved in several terrorist attacks in Saudi Arabia and Yemen. Interestingly, AQAP claimed responsibility for the Christmas Day attempted bombing of Northwest Airlines Flight 253 on December 25, 2009, by Umar Farouk Abdulmutallab. In that incident, Abdulmutallab attempt to set off plastic explosives sewed into his underwear. The explosives failed to detonate and Abdulmutallab was arrested.

Al-Qaeda in Iraq (AQI) or the Islamic State in Iraq and the Levant (ISIL), or the Islamic State in Iraq and Syria (ISIS), or simply the Islamic State. AQI is also known as the Islamic State in Iraq and more recently as the Islamic State in Iraq and the Levant (ASIL). It was established in 2004 by Abu Musab al-Zarqawi, a longtime and strong supporter of Usama bin Laden. AQI and ISIL/ISIS were primary forces against the U.S. military in Iraq, even after al-Zarqawi and other leaders were killed; a new revival of ISIL in Iraq and Syria under the leadership of Abu Bakr al Baghdadi continue to perform acts of terrorism against the established government of Iraq and threaten U.S. interests in the area. Attempting to identify all of the al-Qaeda cells and groups within Iraq is a difficult task as the names of groups often change and merge with new events. For instance, the Khorasan Group was relatively unknown until late 2014 when an American airstrike was directed against it within Syria. The group was headed by Muhsin al-Fadhli, a close associate of Ayman al-Zawahiri, and a strong supporter of al-Qaeda throughout the Middle East.

(continued)

TABLE 4–1
Continued

Al-Qaeda in Islamic Maghreb (AQIM). The Maghreb is a geographical region of northwest Africa, comprising the Atlas Mountains and the modern-day countries of Mauritania, Morocco, Algeria, Tunisia, Western Sahara, and Libya. AQIM has declared itself as an affiliate of the original al-Qaeda and carries out operations in an attempt to overthrow the Algerian government and institute an Islamic state throughout the Maghreb.

Harakat ul-Mujahidin (HUM). Formerly part of the larger radical Islamic movement in Pakistan and Afghanistan called Harakat al-Ansar, HUM operates primarily in Kashmir and can link direct associations with bin Laden and original al-Qaeda fighters in Afghanistan and Pakistan. The group maintains close ties to Jaish e-Mohammad (JEM) or the "Army of Muhammad" in istan. These groups have maintained significant training camps in Pakistan and represent the primary groups that fight against U.S forces in Afghanistan.

Islamic State (IS). See Al-Qaeda in Iraq (AQI).

Jemaah Islamiya (JA). JA is an Indonesia-based terrorist group active throughout Southeast Asia. JI is headed by Abu Baker Bashir, an Indonesian of Yemini descent, and a highly charismatic cleric and leader. The group has active cells in Thailand, Singapore, Malaysia, and Indonesia, and has been linked to the Moro Islamic Liberation Front in the Philippines. The group has been responsible for several high-profile terrorist incidents in Southeast Asia including the 2002 bombing of a nightclub in Bali killing 202 people and the 2003 car bombing of the JW Marriott Hotel in Jakarta, Indonesia, that killed 12 people.

Lashkar-i-Tayyiba (LT). The Lashkar-i-Tayyiba, or "Army of the Righteous," is one of the largest and best trained fighting groups in the Pakistan-Afghan region. It is headed by Hafiz Mohamed Saeed, and has conducted a number of terrorist attacks against India (Mumbai).

Source: The National Counter Terrorism Center (NCTC) website, http://www.nctc.gov/site/index.html.

Khomeinism

Khomeinism
A Shi'a ideology that embraces Islamic worldwide revolution as well as Islamic unity and strict adherence to Sharia; based on the teachings of Ayatollah Ruhollah Khomeini.

As discussed in Chapter 3, the religion of Islam is divided into two primary traditions: Sunni and Shiite. The fundamentalists movements discussed to this point (e.g., Wahhabism, Salafism, and Jihadist Salafism) have been exclusively Sunni developments. There are also fundamentalist movements in the Shiite (or Shi'a) tradition; the most noted is **Khomeinism**. The most prominent of these radical movements stems from the teachings of *Ayatollah Ruhollah Khomeini* (known in the West as simply Ayatollah Khomeini), the conservative and radical cleric that led the 1979 Iranian Revolution against Shah Mohammad Reza Pahlavi. Khomeini strongly believed in Muslim unity and solidarity, and preached the union of all Muslim traditions. He also believed that secular states ultimately lead to the marginalization and ultimate destruction of Islam. Accordingly, he preached that government and religion must be united.[64] Khomeini viewed the development of the Islamic state on a worldwide basis as the revolutionary duty of all Muslims. Khomeini saw this revolution as starting in Iran and moving first throughout the Middle East, reclaiming the holy sites of the Islamic faith, and then on to the rest of the world.

Khomeini successfully led the downfall of the monarchy in Iran and subsequently rose to power in 1979 as the Supreme Leader of the new Islamic Republic of Iran. Under his rule, Sharia was strictly enforced by a new group of radical soldiers called the Islamic Revolutionary Guard. This military unit acted more as an internal police force that focused on the strict enforcement of Sharia law as interpreted by Ayatollah Khomeini, such as the establishment of new Islamic dress codes for men and women; the banishment of all alcoholic drinks; and the banishment of any music, television, or movies produced in the West. Communications and broadcasting within the country were strictly controlled by the government and the threat of surveillance and subsequent arrest by the secret police was always present. Life was harsh in Iran, marked by the execution of thousands of political prisoners and the persecution and torture of untold numbers in Khomeini's prisons. The oppressive government lasted for an entire decade while Ayatollah Khomeini remained as Supreme Leader. He died in 1989 at the age of 86, giving rise to a more moderate, yet still very conservative, leadership under the current Supreme Leader of Iran, Ayatollah Ali Khamenei.

Hezbollah

Similar to other ideologues, Khomeini's radical philosophies of strict enforcement of Sharia law and the continuation of a world Islamic revolution did not die with him. Several of his edicts still permeate the Iranian government and way of life. However, the most visible of Khomeini's follows are observed in Lebanon—a small country adjacent to the north of Israel having a relatively large population of Shi'a Muslims (nearly 1/3 of the total population). As discussed in Chapter 1, **Hezbollah** (Arabic for "Party of Allah or God") is a paramilitary organization headed by Hassan Nasrallah, and originally developed by conservative Lebanese Shi'a clerics loyal to Ayatollah Khomeini. Trained by members of the Iranian Islamic Revolutionary Guard, Hezbollah members continue to wage the revolution of world Islamic order. The 1985 charter of Hezbollah focuses on Islamic unity, the destruction of Israel, and the expulsion of Western powers, including the United States, from the Middle East, "putting to an end any colonialist entity in our land."[65]

Hezbollah
"The Party of God (Allah)"; the largest Shi'a terrorist group in the world, led by Hassan Nasrallah and headquartered in Lebanon.

Backed by Iran, Hezbollah has been extensively involved in Lebanese and Syrian politics for years. Although it has not claimed responsibility for any attack, it has been widely suspected in a number of bloody and vicious suicide bombings, as well as open missile attacks and military raids against Israeli forces from their strong base in Lebanon. Acting in concert with other groups in Lebanon, Hezbollah was the group primarily responsible for the 1983 barracks bombing that killed 241 U.S. Marines, 59 French paratroopers, and 6 civilians in Beirut.[66] More recently, Hezbollah has been an active ally (along with Iran) of Bashir al-Assad's regime, carrying out significant military actions against rebel forces in Syria.[67]

Similar to fundamentalist groups and ideologies from the Sunni tradition, the tenets of Khomeinism, as expressed by Hezbollah, pose a significant threat to not only Western countries, but also those Middle Eastern countries that are predominantly Sunni. The enmity between Sunni and Shi'a tradition is only exacerbated by Iranian rhetoric of a new Islamic world order that begins with Shi'a domination of the holy Islamic sites in Mecca and Medina, Saudi Arabia. To be sure, Khomeinism also poses a significant threat to Israel, the United States and any other Western country with interests in the broader Middle East.

Chapter Summary

SUMMARY BY LEARNING OBJECTIVE

1. **Define fundamentalism, and provide a number of common assumptions observed in various fundamental groups, including Islamic fundamental groups.**

   Fundamentalism is a strategy in which believers attempt to preserve their distinctive identity as a people or group. Feeling this identity to be at risk, fundamentalists fortify this identity by a selective retrieval of doctrines, beliefs, and practices from a perceived sacred past. Common assumptions observed in various fundamental groups, including Islamic fundamentalism, include (1) the selective interpretation of scripture and doctrine, (2) the misinterpretation of symbolic words, (3) the justification and use of violence called by God, (4) an apocalyptic or "end of the world" mentality, and (5) charismatic leadership.

2. **Discuss Islamic fundamentalism and identify some of the key historical writers, philosophers, and leaders that advocate radical Islamic fundamentalism that forms a philosophical base for the ideology.**

Islamic fundamentalism attempts to "re-Islamize" societies that are politically and economically ruled by powerful secular governments. The concept is not new in the Middle East and can be traced to radical fundamentalist writings in the early 16th century. The common elements of Islamic fundamentalism include a return to the Sharia (Islamic laws, values, and rules) within the Muslim religion, a purging of Western cultural and political influence in the Middle East (especially the Western concepts of secularism and modernity), and a re-politicization and reuniting of Islam within governments in the Middle East. At its most radical position, Islamic fundamentalism advocates revolution in order to establish a worldwide, Islamic state. Some of the key writers, philosophers, and leaders that advocate radical Islamic fundamentalism that forms a philosophical base for the ideology are Sayyid Qutb, Muhammad Ibn Wahhab, Hassan al-Banna, Sheikh Ahmed Yassin, Usama bin Laden, Aymen al-Zawarahi, Hassan Nasrallah, and Ayatollah Ruhollah Khomeini.

3. **Provide an historical overview of the Wahhabi movement in Saudi Arabia and the rest of the Middle East.**

The Wahhabi movement or Wahhabism is based on the writings of Muhammad ibn Abd al-Wahhab in the late 1700s. He believed that the only acceptable model for government in the Middle East was established by Muhammad in the 4th century, hence people should live like Muhammad and his followers during that time. Al-Wahhab teamed with a young and talented tribal chieftain in central Arabia named Muhammad ibn Saud. The two were able to unite the disparate tribes of the central plateau of the Arabian Peninsula called the Najd. Although al-Wahhab died in 1792, the House of Saud continues to govern the Arabian Peninsula. In 1932, a direct descendent of Muhammad ibn Saud, Abdul Aziz ibn Saud (simply known as ibn Saud), declared himself King of Saudi Arabia. Today, leadership of the kingdom and state of Saudi Arabia has passed to the sons of ibn Saud (now King Abdullah) and continues to follow the strict teachings of al-Wahhab.

4. **Describe the development and importance of the Muslim Brotherhood in Egypt, including the contributions of Hassan al-Banna and Sayyid Qutb.**

The Muslim Brotherhood represents a political-religious movement starting in Egypt in the 1920 with the writings of Hassan al-Banna. As proscribed by al-Banna, there were two primary objectives of the movement: The liberation of Egypt from all foreign powers and the development of a free state functioning under the rules of Islam. The Muslim Brotherhood grew to the largest and most powerful movement in the world and developed similar movements throughout the Middle East. Another of the influential writers from the Muslim Brotherhood and Egypt was Sayyid Qutb. He is often called the "architect of radical Islam" and the "father of modern terrorism." Qutb transformed the ideological beliefs of Hassan al-Banna into a revolutionary call for arms throughout the Middle East. He was particularly focused on revolutionary change in his home country of Egypt, and concluded that the only viable way to make such changes was through revolution, often led by groups of "true Muslims" that acted as a vanguard of Muslim militancy. Violence and terrorism were justified as sanctified acts under Qutb's new interpretation of "jihad" as a physical "holy war" designed to re-establish Islamic order in Egypt and the rest of the Middle East. Although Qutb spent much of his adult life in prison and was eventually executed in 1965, his writings were very influential in the development of future radical Islamic groups including the Muslim Brotherhood, various Palestinian organizations, Shi'a revolutionary groups in Iran, and al-Qaeda under the leadership of Usama bin Laden.

5. **Discuss and identify the major Palestinian Jihad organizations. How are they different from earlier groups?**

The major Palestinian Jihad organizations are the al-Aqsa Martyrs Brigade, the Palestinian Islamic Jihad (PIJ), and the Palestinian Islamic Resistance Movement (Hamas). These groups have engaged in a bloody and violent "holy war" against Israel marked by attacks, suicide bombings, and assassinations of innocent Israeli civilians. The Palestinian Jihad organizations are different from earlier groups. These groups do not follow secular ideologies as expressed by Marx, Guevara, and others, but rather are part of the much larger radical and fundamentalist Islamic movement throughout the Middle East. Their philosophical roots are based in the teachings of fundamentalist Islam as expressed by al-Banna and Qutb. Hence, they are focused not only on the liberation of Palestine but on the complete destruction of Israel and the development of an Islamic unified state throughout the Middle East.

6. **Describe the differences between the Wahhabi, Salafi, and Jihadist Salafi movements.**

Philosophically, Salafism is nearly identical to Wahhabism, except that Wahhabism is far less tolerant of diversity and differences of opinion. Whereas the liberal age of Salafism came to an end in the 1960s, Wahhabism was able to rid itself of its extreme intolerance and continues to be a major political and religious force throughout the Middle East, but most specifically on the Arabian Peninsula. Wahhabism has essentially co-opted Salafism until the two have become indistinguishable. Jihadist Salafism is a label that has been given to second-generation Salafists that express extreme radicalism. Jihadist Salfists embrace violence and revolution as their only means to an end. This is the ideology of al-Qaeda that has identified enemies not only in the Middle East but also in the West (particularly the United States). Jihadist Salafists believe that "jihad" is not just a physical "holy war" in the Middle East, but rather a global war that knows no boundaries.

7. **Describe the roots of radical Islam from the Shi'a perspective and describe the group known as Hezbollah.**

Radical Islam from the Shi'a perspective is embraced in the fundamentalist movement as expressed by Ayatollah Ruhollah Khomeini, known simply as Khomeinism. Khomeini was the conservative and radical cleric that led the 1979 Iranian Revolution against the monarchy of Shah Pavlavi. Khomeini strongly believed in Muslim unity and solidarity and preached against the secular state. He believed that government and religion must be united. Further, he believed in the development of a worldwide Islamic state that would begin in Iran, move to the Middle East, and extend to the rest of the world. Hence, the country of Iran is led by a Supreme Leaders of the government as well as the Shi'a Islamic faith. Like so many other radical philosophers, his ideas did not die with him, but continue today in Iran as well as in various groups that practice the Shi'a tradition of Islam. The largest of these groups is in Lebanon and is called Hezbollah, meaning "the Party of Allah (God)," The group is headed by Hassan Nasrallah and is focused on the destruction of Israel and the expulsion of Western powers (including the United States) from the Middle East. Hezbollah is heavily funded and supported by Iran and has been suspected in a number of bloody and vicious suicide bombings, including the 1983 barracks bombing in Beirut, killing 241 Marines.

8. **Discuss the political and historical dimensions of Islamic fundamentalism.**

Fundamental Islam has been led by the writings of various philosophers and ideologues, including Ibn al-Wahhab, Sayyid Qutb, Ahmed Yassin, and Hassan al-Banna. Some of these individual wrote centuries ago about European colonization and the exploitation of the Middle East, conditions that have long passed. Islamic fundamentalist organizations attempt to "re-Islamize" societies that are already politically and economically ruled by powerful secular governments. These governments are often allied with Western powers, including the United States, and internally they often suppress their own people. In the past, some countries of the Middle East (e.g., Libya, Iraq, Egypt, Syria, Saudi Arabia) represent suppressive governments or sheikdoms (kingdoms) where the tenets of democracy were non-existent. There were no free elections, there were huge differences in socioeconomic classes within the population, and there was a concentration of wealth in the hands of only a few families, which often ruled the country and controlled all aspects of business and economic life. Many people in these countries lived in poverty, had no education, suffered from diseases and malnutrition, lacked access to medical care, and had no real political power. Faced with an unattractive future, some people are attracted to radical, fundamental, and extremist causes. For some, embracing fundamental Islam offers hope, if not in this world, in the next, for example, because of dying as a suicide bomber. In part, the Arab Spring (beginning in 2010) was a result of a much wider Islamic fundamentalist movement. Civil protests, demonstrations, and in many cases violent uprisings from the masses forced suppressive governments and dictatorships into exile or surrender, such as those in Libya, Egypt, and Syria.

REVIEW QUESTIONS

1. What is fundamentalism and what are the similarities between Islamic fundamentalism and other extremist ideologies?
2. What is eschatology? How does it relate to religious fundamentalism?
3. What was the Arab Spring? Where did it begin and is it still continuing today? Give examples of countries where the Arab Spring was a prominent factor.
4. What are the common assumptions within Islamic fundamentalism and radicalism?
5. Who was Muhammad Ibn Abd al-Wahhab, and what are the basic tenets of Wahhabism?
6. Who was Hassan al-Banna and what was his contribution to fundamental Islam?
7. Who was Sayyid Qutb and why is he often referred to as "the father of modern terrorism"?
8. What are the differences between Salafism and Wahhabism?
9. Who was Ayatollah Ruhollah Khomeini and what was his significance to radical Islamic thought?
10. Who is Hassan Nasrallah and what is Hezbollah?

CRITICAL THINKING EXERCISES

1. **MEMRI and al-Jazeera America.** Visit the homepage for the Middle East Media Research Institute (MEMRI) at www.memri.org. MEMRI is a non-profit research institute that provides timely translations of Arabic, Farsi, Urdu-Pashu, and Dari media for an American and worldwide audience. Popular as well as scholarly media from the Middle East is translated into English, French, Polish, Japanese, and Hebrew. It is one of the most widely respected and utilized online media resources relating to the Middle East. Study the website and read newspaper articles from Cairo, Baghdad, and Istanbul as well as listen to news broadcasts from Mecca, Beirut, and Damascus. Visit the "Jihad and Terrorism Threat Monitor" on the site as well. How do you think MEMRI serves an American audience in understanding the Middle East? How much meaning do you think is lost in the translation of an article from one language to another? Next visit the homepage for al-Jazeera America at www.america.aljaeera.com. Compare the two news media websites. How do they differ, or do they? How much of the media presented is formatted in an unbiased and fact-based style? What agenda does each site have, and how does this agenda impact fact-based reporting?

2. **Historical Problems in the Levant.** Research the Middle Eastern area known as the Levant—an area of land between Egypt, Anatolia, Mesopotamia, and the Arabian Desert. The Levant is an ancient land of great historical civilizations. From the center of the Ur civilization (2100 B.C.) to the kingdom of Babylonia (1700 B.C.), to the ancient Greek and Roman Empires (300 B.C. to 400 A.D.), to the great Ottoman Empire of the 20th century, the Levant has been the crossroad for communication, trade, and commerce between the Middle East to the rest of the world (Europe). The Levant is a geographical area composed of the modern-day countries of Israel, the Palestinian territories of the Gaza and the West Bank, Syria, Jordan, and Lebanon. It is a fertile area located on the southeastern shores of the Mediterranean Sea. Great spiritual meaning has also been given to the area of the Levant as it represents the lands of Abraham, Moses, Jesus, and Muhammad. It is also an area that has witnessed significant historical conflict. Study the countries of the Levant and focus on the current conflict in Syria. Try to identify which groups discussed in this chapter are actively fighting or supporting a specific side in Syria. Next research the history of the al-Assad family in Syria. Who is Bashar al-Assad and do you think he will abdicate his monarchy in the near future? Why or why not?

NOTES

1. Martin E. Marty and R. Scott Appleby directed *The Fundamentalism Project* at the University of Chicago, funded by the American Academy of Arts and Sciences, from 1987 to 1996. Together, they published five volumes as series on conservative fundamentalism between 1991 and 1995 distributed through the University of Chicago Press. See www.press.uchicago.edu/ucp/books/series/FP.html. This definition of fundamentalism is quoted from Volume 4, see Martin E. Marty and R. Scott Appleby (eds.), *Accounting for Fundamentalisms: The Dynamic Character of Movements* (Chicago, IL: University of Chicago Press, 1994), p. 1.

2. Much of the discussion on Christian Identity theology was informed by early writings of prominent leaders in the movement, such as William Pierce, author of the *Turner Diaries* and a leader in the National Alliance and American Nazi Party, and the Reverent Richard Butler, pastor of the Church of Christ's Christians of Hayden Lake, Idaho. Both Pierce and Butler are now deceased.

3. See Jonathon R. White, "Political Eschatology: A Theology of Antigovernment Extremism," *American Behavioral Scientist*, Vol. 44, pp. 937–956 and *Terrorism: An Introduction*, 3rd Edition (Belmont, CA: Wadsworth Thomson Learning, 2002) pp. 46–61.

4. See J. R. White, *Terrorism: An Introduction,* pp. 53–54; and Bruce Hoffman, "Holy Terror: The Implications of Terrorism Motivated by a Religious Imperative," *Studies in Conflict and Terrorism*, Vol. 18, pp. 271–284.

5. Weitzman, *Religious Radicalism in the Greater Middle East.*

6. John Murphy, *The Sword of Islam* (Amherst, MA: Prometheus Books, 2002).

7. Lawrence Davidson, *Islamic Fundamentalism* (Westport, CT: Greenwood Press, 1998).

8. Ibid.

9. John Esposito, *Islam and the Straight Path* (New York: Oxford University Press, 1991).

10. Ibid.

11. This quick facts box is based on restated and reorganized information in Biography: Mustafa Kemal Ataturk, 2014, pp. 1–3, www.biography.com/people/mustafa-kemal-ataturk-20968109#synopsis, accessed August 19, 2014 and "Ataturk, Founder of The Turkish Republic and First President of the Republic," 2005, pp. 1–3, http://www.kultur.gov.tr/EN,31350/biography-of-ataturk.html, accessed August 19, 2014.

12. See Frantz Fanon, *Black Skins, White Masks* (1961); *The Wretched of the Earth* (1963); and *A Dying Colonialism* (1965) (all translated from the French and published by New York: Grove Press, Inc.).

13. John Esposito, *The Islamic Threat: Myth or Reality?* (New York: Oxford University Press, 1965).

14. Ibid.

15. Esposito, *Islam and the Straight Path.*

16. Davidson, *Islamic Fundamentalism.*

17. Ibid.

18. Much of this section is derived from the works of John Esposito, *Islam and the Straight Path*, 1991.

19. Lansine Kaba, *The Wahhabiyya* (Evanston, IL: Northwestern University Press, 1974).

20. Lawrence Davidson, *Islamic Fundamentalism* (Westport, CT: Greenwood Press, 1998).

21. See Kaba, *The Wahhabiyya.*

22. Ibid.

23. Ibid.

24. David Benjamin, *The Age of Sacred Terror* (New York: Random House, 2002).

25. Ziyad Abu Amr, *Islamic Fundamentalism in the West Bank and Gaza* (Indianapolis, IN: Indiana University Press, 1994).

26. Henry Munson, *Islam and Revolution in the Middle East* (New Haven, CT: Yale University Press, 1989).

27. Fluehr-Lobban (ed.), *Against Islamic Extremism* (Gainesville, FL: University of Florida Press, 1998).
28. Ibid.
29. John Murphy, *The Sword of Islam*.
30. Ibid., p. 103.
31. Henry Munson, *Islam and Revolution in the Middle East* (New Haven, CT: Yale University Press, 1989).
32. David Benjamin, *The Age of Sacred Terror*.
33. Ibid.
34. Munson, *Islam and Revolution in the Middle East*.
35. Ibid.
36. Esposito, *Islam and the Straight Path*.
37. David Benjamin, *The Age of Sacred Terror*, p. 124.
38. David Benjamin, *The Age of Sacred Terror*.
39. David Benjamin, *The Age of Sacred Terror*, p. 17.
40. Bruno Leone, *The Spread of Islam* (San Diego, CA: Greenhaven Press, 1999).
41. Ibid.
42. Davidson, *Islamic Fundamentalism*.
43. David Benjamin, *The Age of Sacred Terror*.
44. Ibid.
45. Davidson, *Islamic Fundamentalism*.
46. Sayyid Qutb wrote over a hundred books mainly focusing on social justice and Islam. One of his central themes is the Islamic concept of *tawhid* (the singularity of God and, therefore, of the universe). See Sayyid Qutb, *Milestone*s (Beirut, Lebanon: The Holy Quoran Publishing House, 1980).
47. International Policy Institute for Counter-Terrorism, "Terrorist Organizations: Martyrs of Al-Aqsa," www.ict.org.il/; and Council on Foreign Relations, "Al-Aqsa Martyrs Brigade: Palestinian Nationalists," www.terrorismanswers.om/groups/alaqa.html.
48. Ibid.
49. The case against Sami al-Arian has been well publicized for the last decade. After his indictment on charges under the USA Patriot Act, a 13-day tumultuous trial was conducted in November 2005 under much media attention. The government's case was built on over 20,000 hours of surveillance and years of wiretaps on al-Arian. A jury acquitted al-Arian on the majority of the 17-count indictment and was deadlocked on the remaining charges. The case was viewed as a major defeat and embarrassment to the government and led to extensive review and commentary of the USA Patriot Act. The case has had international impact and been the subject of books and movies. See *USA vs Al-Arian*, an award-winning 2007 documentary film by Norwegian director Line Halvorsen.
50. The Racketeer Influenced and Corrupt Organization Act (RICO) is a U.S. federal law (Chapter 96, 18 USC, Section 1961–1968) that allows civil as well as criminal charges against individuals engaged in activities of an ongoing criminal organization. Enacted through the Organized Crime Control Act of 1970, the law was primary developed to assist in the prosecution of organized crime figures and cartels.
51. Don Peretz, *Intifada: The Palestinian Uprising* (Boulder, CO: Westview Press, 1990), pp. 104–106.
52. See *The Charter of the Islamic Resistance Movement*, August 18, 1988, Article 15. English interpretations can be located at http://avalon.law.yale.edu/20th_century/hamas.asp
53. See British Broadcasting Company (BBC) News, "Who Are Hamas?" http://news.bbc.co.uk/2/hi/in_depth/middle_east/2001/israel_and_the_palestinians/profiles/1654510.stm
54. UPI, "Report: Hamas Attacks Possible in the U.S." March 16, 2003.
55. John Murphy, *The Sword of Islam*.
56. Ibid., p. 69.
57. Esposito, *Islam and the Straight Path*, p. 84.
58. For a more in-depth discussion of Salafism, refer to John Murphy, *The Sword of Islam*. Much of this section has been derived from his original work.
59. Munson, *Islam and Revolution in the Middle East*.

60. Ibid.

61. See: John L. Esposito, *Islam and Politics*, 4th edition, www.docstoc.com/docs/68724700/esposito-islamic-threat

62. Ibid.

63. Ibid.

64. See Bager Moin, *Khomeini: Life of the Ayatollah* (New York: Tauris Publishing, 2009); and Edward Willett, *Ayatollah Khomeini* (New York: Rosen Publishing, 2003).

65. See "The Hizballah (Hezbollah) Program," *The Jerusalem Quarterly,* No. 48, Fall 1988, http://www.ict.org.il/Articles/Hiz_letter.htm

66. Matthew Levitt, *Hezbollah: The Global Footprint of Lebanon's Party of God* (Washington, D.C.: Georgetown University Press, 2013).

67. Bassem Mroue, "Hezbollah Chief Vows to Continue Fighting in Syria." *USA Today*, November 14, 2013.

Terrorist Organizations and Structures

Learning Objectives

After completing this chapter, you should be able to:

1. State the key dilemmas facing terrorist organizations.

2. Identify the levels of involvement with a terrorist organization.

3. Explain why it is important for terrorist organizations to retain current members.

4. Provide the three main reasons why people join terrorist movements.

5. Identify the factors that affect what organizational structure terrorists adopt.

6. Identify six types of cells and briefly describe their diverse missions.

7. Identify the main advantages of the hierarchical model.

8. Explain how ideology helps terrorists identify targets and view victims.

9. State the ways Cronin sees terrorist organizations ending.

Security officials in Karachi, Pakistan, arrest alleged Taliban Commander Abdullah, who also uses the alias Abu Waqas. Abdullah was involved in recruiting female suicide bombers and planning terrorist activities.
(Xinhua Zuma/America/Newscom)

Introduction

Organizations have existed for centuries. Alexander the Great (356–323 B.C.) used one to conquer much of the known world, and the first Bishops created the Catholic Church, and Catholicism became a worldwide religion.[1] These examples illustrate an important characteristic of organizations: They are oriented toward achieving goals. Organizations exist to do the things a single person or a few people are unwilling or can't do by themselves.[2] To illustrate, for a terrorist movement to launch a complex attack on a "hard" target, such as a military base, requires an organization that can effectively collect and evaluate intelligence; plan the attack; collect the equipment needed; train the attackers; get them to the point of the attack; make the assault; collect arms, intelligence, supplies (e.g., medical), and any prisoners; withdraw; and move to a safe position.

Even well-established organizations do not always run smoothly, and for new, "start-up" terrorist organizations "life" is very hazardous. Regardless of what organization model or structure is adopted, dilemmas invariably "pop up." This chapter examines a variety of topics, including the dilemmas facing "start-up" terrorist organizations, the types of organizational structures they might use, the selection of targets, suicide bombers and martyrdom, and how terrorist organizations end.

Dilemmas of Terrorist Organization

Terrorist movements have to develop some form of organizational structure. They need one to ensure their continued existence and to progress toward achieving their goals. Frisch notes that in choosing an organizational structure terrorist movements face five key dilemmas.[3]

Action versus Secrecy

All terrorist movements are caught between two organizational imperatives: (1) taking action and (2) maintaining internal secrecy.[4] Action is necessary to advance the cause, publicize it, and gain recruits and supporters (see Figure 5–1 and Table 5–1). The dilemma is that as more attacks are made, it becomes more difficult to maintain internal secrecy because the success attracts more attention from security services. Internal secrecy means such things as protecting the location of operatives, the identity of future targets, and how the movement is financed. However, internal secrecy also complicates the task of communicating with and coordinating the various parts of the terrorist movement.[5]

In contrast to internal secrecy, a terrorist organization is not concerned about external security. A terrorist movement wants the public to know its name and cause and to fear it. Ironically, this publicity is provided for free by the news media. The Palestinian terrorist group Black September massacred Israeli athletes at the 1972 Olympics in Munich, Germany. Cronin recalls that Abu Daoud, one of the surviving gunmen, claimed that the murder of eleven Israelis forced "our cause" into the homes of 500 million viewers.[6]

Growth versus Control

As a terrorist organization attracts new recruits, its numbers increase and there may also be a growth in the geographic area it can control or have an impact upon. To facilitate growth, the leader of a movement must relinquish a great deal of the operational control he or she had when the movement was smaller.[7] At some point the leader has to delegate some tasks for running the organization to lower ranking leaders. One result of this is the leader has less actual contact or "face time" with fighters. This is because the overall leader is increasingly busy with administrative tasks, such as securing financial supporters. As growth occurs, one of the key decisions is determining what organizational model the movement will adopt. This topic is discussed in a subsequent section of this chapter.

Hardcore Leadership

Cadre

Active Supporters

Passive Supporters

FIGURE 5–1
Levels of involvement in terrorist organizations

Source: "A Military Guide to Terrorism in the Twenty-First Century," United States Army, Fort Leavenworth, Kansas: TRADOC G2, August 15, 2007, p. 3-3, with minor changes.

Hardcore leadership

The hardcore leadership of a terrorist movement may have helped to establish the terrorist organization or come up through its ranks by promotions. It establishes vision, policy, and rules, as well as approves goals and operations. Finally, it ensures that the focus and execution of violence supports ideology and goals.

Cadre

Overall, the dependable nucleus or core group in a terrorist organization. Directs functions such as intelligence, finances, logistics, propaganda, and communication functions. Plans and conducts operations. Mid-level cadre tend to be trainers and technicians, such as surveillance experts. Low-level cadre are direct action specialists, for example, snipers.

Active supporters

Participate in fund raising and other activities, such as providing safe houses, medical care, and transportation. They are fully aware of their relationship with the terrorist organization. They may or may not be known to those outside of the terrorist organization.

Passive supporters

These types of supporters are sympathetic to the goals of terrorist organization, but not committed enough to take an active role. They may assist a front for the terrorist organization and not be fully aware of their relationship to the terrorist organization.

Omar Hammami

In 2006, the 27-year-old Hammami left Alabama and went to Somalia where he joined the clan-based Islamic terrorist movement al-Shabaab. Seven years later, after a series of disagreements with al-Shabaab, the movement killed him in an ambush.

TABLE 5–1
Levels of Involvement in a Terrorist Organization

Level of Involvement	Actions Taken
Hardcore Leadership	May have helped to establish the terrorist organization or come up through its ranks by promotions. Establishes vision, strategy, policy, and rules. Approves goals and operations. Ensures that the focus and execution of violence supports ideology and goals.
Cadre	Overall, the dependable nucleus or core group. Directs functions such as intelligence; counterintelligence; and targeting, finances, logistics, propaganda, and communication functions. Plans and conducts operations. Mid-level cadre tend to be trainers and specialists, such as surveillance experts. Lower-level cadre are direct action specialists, for example, snipers.
Active Supporters	Participate in fund raising and other activities, such as providing safe houses, medical care, and transportation. They are fully aware of their relationship with the terrorist organization. They may or may not be known to those outside of the terrorist organization.
Passive Supporters	Sympathetic to goals of terrorist organization, but not committed enough to take an active role. May assist a front for the terrorist organization and not be fully aware of its true purpose.

Source: A Military Guide to Terrorism in the Twenty-First Century, United States Army, Fort Leavenworth, Kansas: TRADOC G2, August 15, 2007, p. 3-4, with minor changes.

Recruitment versus Retention

In 2012, the terrorist movement Harakat Shabaab al-Mujahidin (al-Shabaab) organized a press conference in Somalia. Its purpose was to "show off" an American-born recruit (see Figure 5–2). The 27-year-old **Omar Hammami** (1984–2013) left Alabama in 2006 and joined the clan-based terrorist group al-Shabaab. Later, Hammami took the name of Abu Mansur al-Amriki (The American). Only a handful of American Muslims have joined FTOs.

The consequences of poor recruitment choices are severe for terrorist organizations. It may result in arrests, casualties, and having entire operations terminated or "rolled up" by governmental agents. Frisch argues that there are three main reasons why individuals choose to join a terrorist movement. First, family members, friends, or individuals in the recruit's social network are going to join or have already done so. Second, the recruit, family members, or members of the recruit's social network have strong grievances against the government. Three, deep religious and/or political beliefs inspire the recruit to fight for a cause.[8]

In addition to those three reasons there are also much more pragmatic reasons: Often there are no other jobs, the recruit needs money to support himself and his family, and joining provides the family with services and assistance that the government does not. Occasionally, some terrorist groups coerce people to join, an unwise strategy because they are candidates to leave the movement and become informers. Some fighters switch from one movement to another because they will be paid better. In 2013, al-Nusra, an al-Qaeda affiliate, was waging war against the Syrian government. It was the most effective rebel force in that country because of its financial resources. It attracted fighters with the highest pay and the opportunity to use the best weapons.

Although there may be a primary reason for joining terrorist organizations, there are others as well. Hezbollah has released a number of violent Internet games, such as Special Force and Ash. Al-Nusra produces and distributes comic books, generates graphic novels, and releases online videos such a Mustafa Hamdi that extoll the virtues of Islam and jihad. The purpose of these games, comics, graphic novels, and videos is to indoctrinate children and attract recruits.[9]

Retention of current members is essential because they have already been trained. Current members may also be experienced and proven themselves to be reliable. Some of them will be groomed for, or assigned, important, organizational roles, for example, making "pitches" to potential recruits, training them, or becoming couriers, reconnaissance specialists, and operational leaders. Recruiting is discussed in greater detail in Chapter 6.

Success versus Longevity

Terrorist organizations must balance the risks associated with conducting operations with the need to ensure their own long-term survival.[10] The use of terror tactics against unarmed, defenseless civilian targets fulfills both of these needs. Terrorists feel assured their casualties will be light. If mass casualties can be inflicted in an attack, it will attract financial supporters and new recruits to the terrorist group. These supporters and new recruits are essential for the continued life of the movement.

One way for an organization to ensure longevity is to reinvent itself. The classical example of this is the March of Dimes. In 1938, President Roosevelt created the Foundation for Infantile Paralysis (polio). It quickly became known as the March of Dimes because people were asked to contribute 10 cents by slipping a dime into a pouch on a card. When the Salk vaccine became available in 1955, polio cases dropped quickly. In 1958, the March of Dimes announced a new goal: the prevention of birth defects, which it continues to pursue.

Another potential way of acquiring longevity is to adopt long-term goals toward which the terrorist organization can work in perpetuity, but may not be able to ever achieve.[11] Al-Qaeda's stated goal is to establish a worldwide Muslim community. The neo-Nazi National Socialist Movement (NSM) wants to prevent all non-White immigration into the United States. Organizations that achieve their goals either go out of business or must reinvent themselves.

Gaibulloev and Sandler's statistical analysis of the longevity and demise of terrorist organizations over an eight-year period revealed some important patterns. Religious-based terrorist movements have longer longevity,[12] perhaps because it is easier to maintain ideological fervor. A homogenous society is hostile to the excessive actions of terrorist groups, whereas a heterogeneous one may to some degree be more tolerant about such "dissent."[13] Geography and terrain may also play a role in longevity: North Africa is conducive to durable movements,[14] although that finding may be a surrogate for the dense Islamic population from which some terrorist groups can recruit and the terrain in which bases can be hidden.[15] Conversely, landlocked nations are an adverse factor, because it is harder for terrorists to import weapons and fighters.[16]

Other features of durable terrorist organizations include an emphasis on diverse methods of domestic attacks, multiple bases from which to operate, and inflicting high casualties with their attacks.[17] A lack of one or more of these conditions could be fatal to a movement. Perhaps

FIGURE 5-2
A federal warrant was issued for Omar Hammami in 2007. It alleged several crimes related to supporting a terrorist organization. Fluent in Arabic, he rapped songs about the "glory of martyrdom." He was also known as Abu Mansoor Al-Amriki (the American).

(*Feisal Omar/Reuters/Newscom*)

the most ominous sign for a terrorist group is experiencing high casualities in each attack it makes, causing fighters and supporters to fade away.

Resource Acquisition versus Constituencies

Olson described how ancient Chinese bandit gangs got their resources. He noted they used two strategies to obtain them: roving and stationary. Roving bandits go into a village, take everything they can, and leave. Stationary bandits settle down and receive something like steady tribute from the village. These bandits get small amounts over a longer period of time, creating a continuing flow of resources.[19] Modern terrorist organizations must also make decisions about how they obtain resources. Ones that select a stationary approach and use violence sparingly are able to attract more highly committed, ideologically motivated recruits while maintaining popular support.[20]

Terrorist Organizational Models

Terrorist movements do not have total discretion about what organizational form they adopt. Many factors shape that decision, including (1) the number of active followers; (2) the geographical locations in which they will locate; (3) the operational pace[21] they intend to pursue; (4) the preferences of supporters; (5) their financial resources; and (6) the capabilities, intentions, and anticipated type of operations of opposing forces.[22]

The structure or "bones" of terrorist organizations may be selected by (1) a proactive and deliberate and process, (2) using a limited amount of effort by selecting the first one which is "good enough," (3) intermittently reacting to the changing needs of the terrorist group and making incremental changes as needed from time to time, and (4) a reaction to drastic changes, such as significant combat losses, and unceasing pressure from adversaries. Terrorist forms of organization covered in this section included the lone wolf, cells, networks, hierarchical, umbrella, and virtual models.

Lone Wolf Organizational Model

The smallest terrorist unit or "organization" is the lone wolf. The lone wolf's attack seemingly comes out of nowhere, with no warning. A lone wolf is one person acting alone and he or she can be every bit as dangerous or lethal as any major terrorist organization. Simon notes there are no constraints on their level of violence because lone wolves are not beholden to a financial or other type of supporter who might mediate their degree of lethality.[23] Lone wolves have no group decision-making process, peer pressure, or supervisor to stifle their inclinations. Simon notes that lone wolves were responsible for the first midair plane bombing, vehicle bombing, hijackings, product contamination, and anthrax attacks in the United States.[24] As Simon speculates, a lone wolf could deliver a crippling attack to our infrastructure by a cyber-attack.[25] Box 5–1 illustrates violence done by people acting alone.

A lone wolf may have a personal grudge or may have some affinity for a domestic or foreign ideology. However, the lone wolf is not controlled by nor receives material assistance from domestic or foreign terrorist movements, although their websites may be visited. Whether a citizen of the United States or a legal resident living here, the lone wolf is a "homegrown terrorist." An American lone wolf is self-radicalized and ordinarily shows little stomach for suicide attacks.[26] A homegrown terrorist who uses Islam as the ideological

Homegrown jihadist
A homegrown terrorist who uses Islam as the ideological basis for his or her attacks may be referred to as a "homegrown jihadist."

Going postal
The phrase "going postal," means becoming uncontrollably mad. It originated at the Edmond, Oklahoma, Post Office. In 1986, a disgruntled postman entered the Post Office and killed 10, wounded 6, and then committed suicide.

Operational security
A process to deny potential adversaries information about capabilities and/or intentions by identifying, controlling, and protecting unclassified information that gives evidence of the planning and execution of sensitive activities, such as future operations (OPSEC).

Box 5–1
The Carnage of "Loners"

Walter Laqueur notes that all terrorism is violence, but not all violence is terrorism.[27] None of these decades-spanning examples of violent loners were charged with terrorism. However, their actions demonstrate how much carnage a single person can cause. These violent loners are distinguished from serial murderers in that the former's actions are committed publically, usually during one violent outburst or shooting rampage that ends with the capture or death of the loner.

From 1940 to 1957 in New York City, George Metesky (1903–1994) planted 33 pipe bombs in places such as theaters, restrooms, phone booths, music halls, and libraries. Although the so-called "Mad Bomber" didn't kill anyone, he wounded at least 15 people. A Marine during World War I, he "patriotically" halted his bombing campaign while the United States was involved in World War II. Metesky's personal grudge stemmed from a work-related injury at the Consolidated Edison electrical plant which caused him to lose his job. Metesky was only allowed 26 weeks of benefits. These events turned him bitter. Following his arrest, Metesky was declared incompetent to stand trial. He was confined in a mental hospital until his release in 1973.

In 1966, Charles Whitman, armed with several high-powered rifles and a shotgun, climbed to the top of a 307-foot tower on the campus of the University of Texas and barricaded himself. Earlier in the day he murdered his wife and mother-in-law. A former Marine, he killed 17 people and wounded another 32 before an Austin police officer went to the top of the tower and shot him dead.

A 12-year-old girl was among seven people in the Chicago area who died from unknowingly taking an extra strength Tylenol laced with cyanide. Investigation revealed that the deadly drug had not been added in its production. Someone bought the Tylenol, added the cyanide, and returned it to the shelf of a store to be sold again. This 1982 incident resulted in many manufacturers adding tamperproof features, which previously had been non-existent. Although these seven murders were never solved, investigators believe only one perpetrator was involved. This conclusion was based on the theory that if it was more than one, word would have slipped out and a suspect with knowledge of it arrested for an unrelated crime would have used it to bargain for leniency. Alternatively, the perpetrator may have murdered any co-conspirator to prevent being identified.

The phrase "**Going postal**," becoming uncontrollably mad, originated in the Edmond, Oklahoma, Post Office. Patrick Sherrill, a disgruntled postal worker and former Marine, was a loner and socially inept.[28] In 1986, Sherrill entered the Post Office with three semi-automatic pistols. Apparently upset about a reprimand he had received, Sherrill walked through the facility, killing 14 people and wounding 6 before killing himself.[29]

A 23-year old South Korean senior majoring in English at Virginia Polytechnic Institute (VPI) bought guns and methodically killed people in several buildings on the VPI campus during 2007. Cho Seung-Hui murdered 32 people and also wounded a number of others before killing himself. Some people were injured jumping out of buildings to avoid contact with the shooter.

In 2010, Joseph A. Stack loaded a light airplane with a 50-gallon drum filled with gasoline. He flew the plane into an IRS office in Austin Texas. That attack killed Stack and an Internal Revenue Service (IRS) employee (see Figure 5–3). Several other people were injured. He left behind a rambling manifesto against the federal government, calling for "American zombies to wake up and revolt."[30] Stack is that rare example to the general proposition that American lone wolves have no appetite for suicide attacks.

In Newton, Connecticut, 20-year-old Adam Lanza got dressed the morning of December 14, 2012, and killed his mother with a shot to the head as she was lying in bed. Armed with a semi-automatic rifle and two handguns, he went to the nearby Sandy Hook Elementary School. He shot up a security door to gain entrance to the school and quickly killed 20 children and 6 adults before shooting himself as the police closed in on him. All of the children were six or seven years old. The motive for Lanza's brutal massacre was not established by investigators.

In 2013, Aaron Alexis gained access to the Washington Naval Yard and allegedly killed 12 people with a shotgun. As is often the case in such crimes, a portion of the initial report was wrong; Alexis was not armed with a military-style assault rifle (AR-15), but a 12-gauge shotgun (Remington 870 pump), commonly used for hunting.

On April 2, 2014, Army Specialist Ivan Lopez opened fire on military and civilian personnel at Fort Hood, Texas. The eight-minute rampage ended with 3 people being killed, and another 16 being wounded by Lopez. Lopez, who was armed with a single Smith and Wesson 45-caliber pistol. He had a history of mental problems and had just recently completed a tour in Iraq the previous year (2013). According to the ensuing investigation, Lopez was upset that he had only been given a 24-hour pass to attend his mother's funeral in November 2013.

Lopez subsequently committed suicide when confronted by a female military police officer. The event marked the second time in five years that a mass shooting had occurred on the grounds of Fort Hood Army Base in Killon, Texas. The first was by an Army Psychiatrist and Medical Corps officer, Major Nidal Malik Hasan. Coincidentally, Lopez and Hasan purchased their weapons at the same gun store just days before their shooting rampages.

Do the actions of these "loners" represent a form of terrorism? Would controlling public access to guns reduce these types of events? Why or why not?

---

basis for his or her attacks may be called a "**homegrown jihadist**." When religion is the driving ideology for an attack it is sometimes referred to as "deified terrorism."

A discrete lone wolf is hard to detect because he or she identifies the target; plans the attack; assembles the materials needed; doesn't have to communicate, coordinate, or get the approval of anyone; and executes the attack. Thus, the lone wolf is self-contained, which enhances **operational security** (OPSEC). Lone wolf attacks are more prevalent in the United States than elsewhere. Of all such attacks that occurred worldwide from 1968 to 2007, 42 percent happened in America.[31] Lone wolves are considered a very significant problem in the United States. This problem is heightened because of al-Qaeda's continuing emphasis on recruiting Americans.

Information Link
Visit the website at the International Institute for Counter Terrorism at www.ict.org.il/LinkClick.aspx?fileticket=qAv1zlPJIGE%3D&tabid=66. Read Sara Teich, "Trends and Development in Lone Wolf Terrorism in the Western World: An Analysis of Terrorist Attacks and Attempted Attacks by Islamic Extremists."

Quick Facts
How Alone Is a Lone Wolf?

While lone wolves act alone, they are not truly alone because of the Internet. Terrorists use Facebook, Twitter, and YouTube to lure people to their websites, where some will gradually become radicalized by audio and video recordings.[32] Illustratively, in 2012, Arif Uka, a Muslim, shot and killed two American servicemen at the Frankfurt, Germany, Airport. Uka said he was motivated to do so by a YouTube video that purported showing American soldiers raiding a home in Afghanistan and raping a daughter.[33]

Also on the Internet, lone wolves have access to terrorist training manuals on reconnaissance, bomb making, target selection, and related skills. They also find social support in digital chatrooms.

The main advantage of the lone wolf is that he or she is totally independent and ordinarily has high OPSEC. The flip side of that advantage is the arrest of a lone wolf "rolls up" all pending operations. The lone wolf usually has to rely on his or her own resources, which may limit attacks to the use of pistols, rifles, or rudimentary explosive devices.

Cell Organizational Models

A **cell** is multiple terrorists working cooperatively toward achieving a particular goal, such as raising funds, gathering intelligence, or executing an attack. Alternatively, a cell may not be specialized and all of these functions may be performed within a single cell. Various sources assert that there are three to seven, four to twelve, or even more members in a cell. As a practical matter, the number of a people in a cell must be large enough to acquire all of the skills needed, but kept as small as possible to enhance OPSEC. A cell trying to manufacture explosives may consist of only one to three people. A cell assigned to executing a major attack will have more members and be supported by several different types of specialized cells, which are discussed later in this chapter.

Cell members do not necessarily have to be located in close physical proximity. However, this is frequently the case. Alternatively, they could be located in several localities or even different countries[34] and only meet face to face if necessary.

Al-Qaeda has adopted the concept of "**taqiyya**." This absolves cell members from religious condemnation for shaving off their required beards, not praying five times a day, and adopting a Western lifestyle as part of OPSEC.[35] Taqiyya allows Arabic terrorists to move with less scrutiny in Western societies.

A group of lone wolves that form a cell are sometimes called a "**wolf pack**." Similarly, a group of homegrown jihadists working collectively make up a "**homegrown jihadist cell**." Animal Liberation Front (ALF) and Earth Liberation Front (ELF) members may also act

Cell
A cell is multiple terrorists working cooperatively toward achieving a particular goal, such as raising funds, gathering intelligence, or executing an attack. Alternatively, a cell may not be specialized and all of these functions may be performed within a single cell.

Taqiyya
Al-Qaeda has adopted the concept of "taqiyya." It absolves Islamic fighters from religious condemnation for shaving off their required beards, not praying five times a day, and adopting a Western life style as part of OPSEC.

Wolf pack
A group of lone wolves that form a cell are sometimes called a "wolf pack."

Homegrown jihadist cell
A group of homegrown jihadists working collectively make up a homegrown jihadist cell. See homegrown jihadist.

FIGURE 5–3
Joseph Stack set his home on fire and then flew his light plane into these offices, some of which were occupied by the U.S. Internal Revenue Service. The building was racked by 50-foot flames for three hours before the fire was brought under control.

(© Ralph Barrera/Austin American Statesman/PSG/Newscom)

Quick Facts
A Homegrown Jihadist Cell's Activities

In 2007, six foreign-born Muslims from Jordan, Turkey, and the former Yugoslavia met in the United States. They eventually formed a cell in New Jersey because they all shared an interest in Internet images of jihad.[36] They acquired firearms and practiced shooting in the Pocono Mountains in northeastern Pennsylvania and played paintball to hone their military skills. Their intent was to murder as

many soldiers as possible at Fort Dix, New Jersey. They had no leader and the cells members just "fed off of each other." The "Fort Dix 6" had no apparent connection to any foreign terrorist organization. They were arrested and convicted of terrorism-related charges. This cell can be characterized three ways: "a homegrown terrorist cell," homegrown jihadists," and using the "leaderless resistance" model.

Box 5–2
Terrorism and Passport Fraud

The greatest prize for transnational terrorists is a genuine passport issued in a false name.[37] South Africa and Venezuela have been two sources for them. A corrupt official in South Africa was arrested in conjunction with 4,000 stolen passports that were being sold on the black market.[38] Until South Africa recently instituted new security features in its passports they were also forged with ease.

Venezuela has issued passports to terrorists,[39] a move that begun under its rabidly anti-American President, the late Hugo Chavez. A variety of false identification papers can be bought at many open-air markets around the world, although the quality varies considerably. One of the largest of these markets is in Lima, Peru. There are also reports of transnational criminal organizations (TCOs) providing identification papers to terrorists.

Examples of other ruses used by terrorists to obtain passports include getting them issued in the name of a dead person, but using the terrorists' photographs and descriptions in them. Passports are also stolen and the terrorists' pictures substituted for the actual bearer. A stolen passport may also be used if the fraudulent user sufficiently resembles the person to whom it was issued. The Department of Homeland Security (DHS) intercepted 30,799 passports in one recent year that were false in one or more aspects.[40]

Do you see any possibilities for reducing the number of stolen, forged, or otherwise fraudulent passports? What would you do about it?

as cell members that have coalesced around a leader or be in a **leaderless resistance cell**. This type of cell is characterized by no leaders and equality of members who share the leadership functions.[41] Leaderless resistant cells are autonomous, self-enrolling, and self-organizing. Former Vietnam veteran Louis Beam popularized the leaderless resistance concept and although at one time he associated with right-wing, racist groups he has since kept a low profile.[42]

Foreign terrorist organizations (FTOs) infiltrate individuals into the United States and other countries. Some may form as a cell after entry. Those infiltrated may enter a country illegally under assumed names or with forged identification papers. Terrorists entering under their legal names with student or tourist visas may have been issued "clean" passports by states sympathetic to their cause. Their "old" passports may have revealed travel to Yemen, Afghanistan, or Iran. Stamps on their old passports from those countries would have invited closer scrutiny by security services because terrorist camps are operated in them. Therefore, the terrorists are given a "clean" passport that doesn't reveal such travel.

There are different types of cells due to the fact that they are created under dissimilar circumstances and they can also have diverse responsibilities. Examples of cells with diverse missions include the following:

1. **Sleeper cells**: Members of FTO sleeper cells lead normal lives, engaging only in lawful employment and activities that call no attention to themselves. The jobs they select may facilitate future terrorist activities. Illustratively, a taxi driver will learn a great about a city's geography and can identify potential targets and move terrorists around. A sleeper cell may receive a signal that "awakens" it for a specific purpose, such as providing a safe house or sabotage. Iran has been inserting sleeper cells in Latin America with the goal of committing, fermenting, and fostering acts of international terrorism.[43]

2. **Command and Control Cells**: C2 cells make all of the final decisions about the execution of an attack and other matters pertaining to the activities of a cell.

Leaderless resistance cell
This type of cell is characterized by no leaders and equality of members who share the leadership functions.

Information Link
For more information on Passport and Visa Fraud, visit the U.S. Department of State website at www.state.gov/m/ds/investigat/c10714.htm. Read the article entitled, "Passport and Visa Fraud: A Quick Course."

Sleeper cells
Members of sleeper cells lead normal lives, engaging only in lawful employment and activities that call no attention to themselves. The jobs they select may facilitate future terrorist activities. Illustratively, a taxi driver will learn a great about a city's geography and can identify potential targets and move terrorists around. A sleeper cell may receive a signal that "awakens" it for a specific purpose, such as sabotage or an assassination.

Command and control cells
C2 cells make all of the final decisions about the execution of an attack and other matters pertaining to the activities of a cell.

Quick Facts
A Hezbollah Fund-Raising Cell

An off-duty deputy sheriff noticed Arabic-speaking men buying 300 cartons of cigarettes each at a tobacco wholesaler and paying for them from wads of cash. A four-year investigation revealed that the men paid the North Carolina cigarette tax of $0.50 per pack, sold to them by the truckloads in Michigan where the tax was $7.50 per carton, and pocketed the difference. The cell raised millions of dollars for Hezbollah.[44]

Tactical operations cells
TAC-OPS cells execute attacks under the guidance of C2 cells.

Intel cells
ICs collect data, make recommendations, may select targets, and provide information about the best routes for ingressing to and egressing from targets.

Logistics cells
LCs provide supplies and various types of support to other cells.

Fund-raising cells
FRCs almost exclusively commit illegal acts to raise funds for their terrorist organization or to be used in support of a particular attack. Examples of these illegal activities include kidnapping for ransom, arms and drug smuggling, operating bogus charities, extortion, credit card fraud, and pirating music and videos.

Network models
Network models include the chain, hub or star, spoke or wheel, and all channel structures.

Dead drop
A dead drop is a secret place where one courier hides documents, often encrypted, for the next courier to pick up.

Hubs
In terrorist network language, "hubs" are "chiefs," from local operational commanders to ideological leaders. The lines between nodes in a cell are called links or edges and represent a communication channel.

3. **Tactical Operations Cells**: TAC-OPS cells actually execute attacks under the guidance of C2 cells.

4. **Intel Cells**: These cells collect data, make recommendations, may select targets, provide information about the best route to approach the target (ingress), and, if not a suicide attack, the best route to follow to when leaving (egressing) the area of the attack.

5. **Logistics Cells**: LCs provide supplies and other support to other cells, especially TAC-OPS, including bomb-making materials and the names and locations of sympathetic doctors to use if there is a medical emergency.

6. **Fund-Raising Cells**: FRCs almost exclusively commit illegal acts to raise funds for the terrorist movement or to be used in support of a particular attack. Illustrations include kidnapping for ransom, arms and drug trafficking, operating bogus charities, extortion, credit card fraud, and pirating music and videos.

Network Organizational Models

The most important advantage of networks is that they are resilient against disruptions and attacks.[45] They are also effective in repairing damage to them and are highly effective in processing communications. Cells are the "building blocks" of **network models** that are illustrated by the (1) chain, (2) hub or star, (3) wheel, and (4) all channel structures.

The Chain Network

The simplest type of network model is the *chain network* (see Figure 5–4), which has no hierarchy. In its simplest form, each courier passes information, material, or encrypted documents to the next courier. In this form of the chain network, each courier knows the courier from whom they received the "package" and the courier to whom he or she gave it. OPSEC is improved when a dead drop is substituted for a face-to-face exchange by the couriers. A **dead drop** is a secret, innocuous place where the "package" the courier carries is left, to be later retrieved by the next courier. The dead drop can be as simple as a loose brick in a wall behind which a flash drive can be hidden.

Unless a courier runs surveillance on the dead drop, the identity of the retrieving courier is unknown to the courier who placed the material in it. It may be possible to take out a few couriers in a chain, but it is more difficult to "roll up" the entire network. However, the chain network is disrupted when some members go missing. Criminal groups and gangs also rely on the chain network when they smuggle goods and humans, or launder money.[46]

The Hub or Star Network

In a terrorist hub or star network, the central "**hub**" may be a local operational commander, ideological leader, or other figure. In contrast, the outer "**nodes**" are more expendable members, such as fighters, whose loss is less critical to the terrorist movement. The lines between nodes in a cell are called **links or edges** and represent a communication channel between nodes and/or the hub.

Figure 5–5a depicts the hub or star network. The hub at the center (a) represents is the leader who has substantial responsibilities. The leader is the only person communicating with higher levels of the terrorist movement and interacts directly with nodes B, C, D, E, and F, who have no contact with each other and may not be aware

The Chain Network

FIGURE 5–4
A chain network.

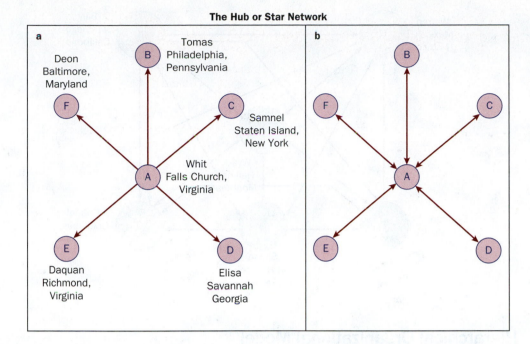

The Hub or Star Network

FIGURE 5–5
A hub or star network.
(A) The hub or star with one-way communication.
(B) The hub or star with two-way communication.

of how many other nodes there are or what their function is—this is an example of a high level of **compartmentalized information**.

In Figure 5–5a, the hub/leader can contact the members of his or her network, but they don't know how to contact their leader. Some hub networks allow two-way communication between the hub and its members, as is shown in Figure 5–5b. In both 5–5a and 5–5b the hub ensures that all outer nodes remain ideologically committed, are fully trained, maintain OPSEC, and makes sure the attack is a success.

A key advantage of a hub or star is that OPSEC is high when only the leader knows the identification of all of its members. This is also its disadvantage: If the leader is apprehended the whole operation may be rolled up. Even if the leader discloses nothing during inter-rogation cell members have no direction and may be isolated from each other until the higher-level command and control function establishes that the cell leader has "gone missing." There are several options for replacing a missing terrorist leader: train and infiltrate a new leader, which may take months; awaken a qualified sleeper; or if there is a **redundant leader protocol**, one of the cell members will assume command of the cell.

The Wheel Network

A variant of the hub or star is shown in Figure 5–6, which is called a wheel network. It primarily differs from Figure 5–5b in that nodes can communicate with the member to their "left" or "right" because of a link. This quickens the pace of sharing information, but increases OPSEC vulnerability.

The All-Channel Network

The all-channel model (see Figure 5–7) is highly decentralized and all nodes can communicate with each other and the hub. The advantage of this model is that it reduces the nodes' feelings of isolation and has great potential for collaboration in problem solving and other activities. The disadvantage is that it is the most difficult to create and maintain because so many horizontal communication channels are required, which also poses a greater threat to OPSEC.

Nodes
In terrorist network language, "nodes" are more expendable members, such as fighters, whose loss is less critical to the terrorist movement.

Links or edges
In terrorist network language the lines between nodes in a cell are called links or edges and represent a communication channel between nodes and/or hubs.

FIGURE 5–6
A wheel network.

FIGURE 5–7
An all-channel network.

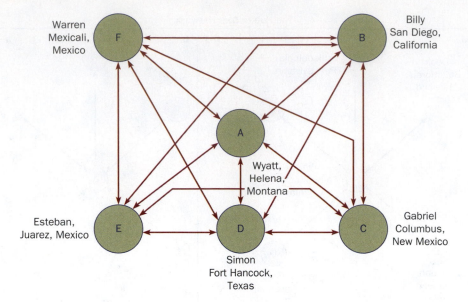

Compartmentalized information

Information to which access is restricted to those with a need to know.

Redundant leader protocol

If the leader of a cell is captured, killed, or otherwise not available, a designated member of the cell will assume the leadership role.

Principle of hierarchy

This principle dictates that each lower organizational unit is under the direct control and supervision of a superior organizational unit. This produces a pyramid shaped form.

Chain of command

The chain of command is a clear and unbroken line of authority and responsibility from the top to the bottom of the organization, which makes it possible to establish accountability.

Hierarchical Organizational Model

"Hierarchy" comes from the 6th century Greek words "hireros" (sacred) and "arkhia" (rule), meaning the governing of scared things. By the early 1600s it signified the differences in rank for the Catholic clergy, from the lowest parish priest to the pope.[47] The hierarchical model incorporates this idea of grades of rank and has the following characteristics:[48] (1) There is a **principle of hierarchy**—each lower organizational unit is under the direct control and supervision of a superior organizational unit. This produces a pyramid-shaped form with a single leader at the top of the pyramid (see Figure 5–8); (2) these organizational units are led by persons whose rank and authority ascends as we go from the lower to higher units, referred to as the **chain of command**; (3) organizational units are essentially stacked horizontal layers and the more there are, the "taller" or more hierarchical the organization will be. "Tallness" may be produced by the organization growing in numbers and creating new units in which to place them, becoming geographically dispersed, or from the need to create specialized units, for example, snipers, hostage takers, financial experts, and identification forgers. This creates the need for more hierarchy to coordinate the many parts of the organization; and (4) there is also an expectation that when lower ranking members of the organization receive a "lawful" order from a superior authority in their chain of command that the orders will be followed. Members may be disciplined for not carrying out orders.

The chief advantages of the hierarchical model are that the chain of command is clearly understood, people know what their jobs are, specialization can be accommodated, and control is normally high. The disadvantages are that horizontal communication between units may be difficult or impossible; groups may compete for the leader's favor, causing goals to be distorted; there is low flexibility; if communication channels are clogged decisions may not be received on a timely basis; and more geographically distant units may become more interested in their own interests versus the organization's goals.

Umbrella Organizational Model

The umbrella organizational model (UOM) has a core group that to some degree assists the groups that voluntarily associate with it. The UOM is a relatively recent hybrid organizational structure that is made up of two other organizational structures, the hierarchical and the networked. An internal (core) hierarchical group is at the top and provides some types of support to the organizations that are

FIGURE 5–8
A simple hierarchical model with three "layers." More complex hierarchical organizations may have seven or more layers, making them much taller than this illustration.

FIGURE 5–9
The umbrella model.

affiliated with it. The affiliated groups are networked or tied together by continuing vertical communication from the core and by horizontal communication between the affiliated movements (see Figure 5–9). The UOM is loose and decentralized in the sense that the affiliated organizations continue to have their own leaders and are to some degree autonomous.

In its beginning al-Qaeda was a small, hierarchical organization with tight controls, but it has evolved into a UOM. Over a period of years militant Islamic organizations joined forces with the "premier terrorist brand" and were "rebadged" as al-Qaeda. Illustrations include the former Tawid wal Jihad, now al-Qaeda in Iraq (AQI), the Algerian group Global Salafist for Preaching and Combat, renamed as al-Qaeda in the Islamic Maghreb (AQIM, Maghreb is Arabic for northwest Africa, the area west of Egypt),[49] and Islamic Jihad in Yemen, one of the predecessors of al-Qaeda in the Arabian Peninsula (AQAP).[50]

Services provided by al-Qaeda include ideological encouragement, articulating strategic goals, occasional operational funds, logistics support, advice from seasoned terrorist commanders, and radical Islamic propaganda from the Global Islamic Media Front (GIMF), founded by al-Qaeda around 2003. GIMF made a broadcasted video calling for the withdrawal of Austrian and German forces from Afghanistan and threatened terrorist attacks for the failure to do so.[51]

The shift to an UOM raises the question of whether al-Qaeda is still an operational terrorist organization or whether it has been reduced to just a support movement, roughly equivalent to a MacDonald's central office supporting its far-flung hamburger franchises.[52] The answer is that al-Qaeda retains some core operational capacity in its special operations unit, but it is substantially an umbrella organization, suggesting operations to affiliates. Because of this Johnsen argues that al-Qaeda's core has ceased to be the most important part of the organization.[53] However, this argument may give insufficient weight to the fact the core is the cement that keeps the overall organization together and functioning.

The primary advantage of the UOM is its flexibility, allowing affiliates to conduct locally important operations and still participate in transnational terrorist attacks. The disadvantages are that affiliates have varying ideologies and they squabble with the core about strategic goals, the allocation of scarce resources, and because they are voluntarily associated with al-Qaeda they can leave whenever they choose. An ongoing al-Qaeda squabble was whether to attack "near enemies," rulers of Islamic countries who do not support

FIGURE 5–10
Virtual organization.

Virtual terrorist organization

A virtual terrorist organization exists in cyberspace. It members can be dispersed geographically, but work together exploiting information technology to achieve their common goals by sharing their skills and knowledge collaboratively.

the radicalized interpretation of the Koran or the "far enemies," Western nations in general and the United States in particular. The single most important disadvantage of the UOM is that the core does not have full authority over its affiliates. When AQI began beheading civilians and prisoners al-Qaeda told it to stop using such harsh tactics because it was alienating people. AQI simply ignored the order.

Virtual Organizational Model

A **virtual terrorist organization** (VTO) exists in cyberspace (see Figure 5–10). It has no headquarters and needs no physical meeting space. Instead, the VTO exists in cyberspace by taking advantage of technology. There is no known large terrorist group that is completely virtual. VTOs are based on cell structures. They may be part of a large terrorist movement or be locally inspired and more independent.

The increased reliance on information technologies by terrorist movements is to some degree caused by (1) The growing number of physical safe havens for terrorists that have been disrupted or eliminated.[54] Diplomacy, foreign aid, military weapons, training, raids, and drone attacks have all played a role in reducing the availability of physical safe havens, although they certainly have not been totally eliminated; and 2) simultaneously, terrorist organizations have been calling for the development of autonomous terrorist cells to attack whoever they consider their enemies to be.

A VTO may be temporary (gathering intelligence for a specific attack) or longer lasting, and requires a high degree of trust between its members. As an example, work by a VTO can be substantially substituted for a physical reconnaissance. A captured al-Qaeda manual asserts that 80 percent of the information needed for operations is available on the Internet in publically accessible sources.[55]

VTO members may be dispersed geographically, but can achieve their goals by sharing their skills and knowledge collaboratively through information technology.[56] Judy's list of the technologies exploited by VTOs include computer networks, mobile phone systems, social media outlets, password protection, message encryption, messages embedded in photographs, online chat rooms, and electronic drop boxes.[57] Experts are wary that as terrorists gain greater cyberspace experience that it will lead to system disruption/netwar, for example, committing highly disruptive attacks on power, transportation, and other computer systems. The main advantages of the virtual organization is that it provides greater security and convenience than face-to-face (F2F) operations.[58] Illustratively, Israel reportedly has been unable to crack Hamas encoded communications sent on the Internet.[59]

Target Selection and Attacks

Terrorist movements have a core set of beliefs and goals that define their ideology and focus their violence.[60] One way or another, ideology identifies "acceptable" targets and acts as a constraint against attacking other targets. Acceptable targets serve another important purpose. In the ideological framework of terrorist movements, victims are blamed for the violence inflicted on them. The essence of this argument is "They brought it on themselves." This construction both relieves terrorists of their moral responsibility for the deaths they have caused and glorifies them for doing so.

As a practical matter, some targets selected may have little to do with a group's ideology. For example, raids on police stations may be triggered by the need to avenge a popular terrorist leader who died while in police custody. Likewise, a target may be selected to meet several goals, for example, a terrorist attack inflicts mass casualties, which in turn provokes an unwise massive retaliation that causes the deaths of many Muslims,

Quick Facts
Center of Gravity, System Disruption, and Terrorist Selection of Targets

Center of gravity refers to the *primary* sources of strength, power, and resistance for a nation or organization and that of an adversary.[61] These sources are identified through an analytical process. Ideally, when the vulnerabilities of a center of gravity are identified and successfully attacked, decisive results are produced.[62] This concept is similar to Robb's system disruption.

During World War II, Americans sent badly needed war goods and troops across the Atlantic Ocean to England by convoys, which usually consisted of 45 or more ships. To prevent this, Germans deployed U-boats (submarines). In 1942, 1,664 ships were lost in the Atlantic to U-boats.[63] America was losing ships faster than they could be replaced.

Although warships and planes protected the convoys, losses remained high. The heart of the problem was that there was an area in the North Atlantic, the air-gap, which was beyond the range of the Allied Powers' aircraft.

The Germans' center of gravity in the Battle of the Atlantic was that area that could not be patrolled by the Allied Powers' aircraft. America's development of the very long-range B-24 bomber (The Liberator) contributed substantially to a decisive reduction of ships lost to the German submarines. The B-24s provided a decisive victory that destroyed the Germans' center of gravity. By 1944, German submarines sank only 67 ships.[64] The result was that much-needed weapons, munitions, food, petroleum, and other essentials would reach England and be used in the war against the Axis Powers.

The major terrorist groups are sophisticated, and their recent announcements about attacking infrastructures reveal a well-developed targeting capability. These groups are developing and recruiting cyber experts, possibly to develop the tools needed for infrastructure attacks. The absence of infrastructure attacks against the United States (The "Great Satan") may reflect an absence of opportunity due to our vigilance. Alternatively, terrorists may not have a real intent to attack the infrastructure because just their announcements may cause us to spend perhaps billions to harden infrastructure targets. The lack of infrastructure attacks could also indicate that terrorists do not yet have the capability to do so. If such attacks do come they are likely to cause Robb's system disruption or weaken our centers of gravity. If their future attacks do strike infrastructures, people might be illuminating their lives with candles for an unknown period of time. Note that netwar and system disruption essentially refer to the same actions.

---

reinforcing the perception that Israel and Western powers nonchalantly kill them.[65] During 2014, Hamas fired at least 2,200 rockets from the Gaza Strip into Israel, breaking several truces of up to 72 hours to provoke a reaction. Hamas allegedly hid rocket launchers and rocket munitions in schools, hospitals, and government buildings, ensuring that to protect their citizens Israel would have to attack them, causing some civilian casualties. In some eyes, the retaliation caused the deaths of civilian Palestinians and provided Hamas with the opportunity to claim that the Israeli Defense Forces (IDF) was committing genocide. A devil's choice is a situation in which there are only unattractive alternatives to a decision. The devil's choice faced by the IDF was to protect its citizens or risk producing some civilian casualties.

Other variables impacting target choices include the symbolism of the target; the terrorist group's size, weapons, planning, and operational capabilities; ability to ingress and egress from the target; and the need to make a demonstration for financial supporters who are impatient for results or from whom support is dwindling. Habash, founder of the terrorist Popular Front for the Liberation of Palestine (PFLP), asserts that when selecting a target the main point is to pick one which is 100 percent guaranteed to be successful.[66] Clarke and Newman use the acronym EVIL DONE to identify the characteristics that make a target attractive to terrorists. Attractive targets are:[67]

Center of gravity
The primary source of strength, power, and resistance for a nation or organization and that of an adversary.

1. *Exposed and publically visible.* Damage done to hidden targets don't produce visually compelling images for the news media to broadcast;

2. *Vital to a society's day-to-day functioning or perhaps even survival.* Such targets are the elements of a country's infrastructure, such as electrical grids, pipelines, computer networks, water supply, and transportation systems;

3. *Iconic or symbolic.* When a picture of it is shown many people can instantly identify it. Illustrations of icons in the United States include the Statue of Liberty, the White House, the Pentagon, and the Golden Gate Bridge. Global examples include the Eiffel Tower, the Colosseum, and the Taj Mahal;

4. *Legitimate, meaning that attacking them will not result in universal condemnation.* The 9/11 attacks were condemned, but they also were widely applauded. Children generally rank as the least legitimate target, but there is no ironclad protection for them. Tim McVeigh knew there was a nursery in the Oklahoma City federal

Quick Facts
Why Do Terrorists Attack Tourists?

Terrorist groups attack tourists and resorts for foreigners for two main reasons: (1) For many countries, tourism is a multibillion industry. Depriving a country of some or a substantial portion of the revenue generated by tourists weakens a target country; and (2) tourists can be held hostage until a substantial ransom is paid. Secondary reasons are the terrorists can feel fairly certain they will get paid and operations need not be large or costly. "Flash kidnappings" are increasing. Only a handful of people are captured and quickly released because terrorists settle for a lower ransom. Kidnapping has signs of becoming a volume business.

Egypt's Red Sea tourism produces $10 billion annually. However, after a series of attacks that sum was reduced to $4 billion. In Mali during 2014, three suitcases filled with five million euros was delivered to an obscure Islamic terrorist group to release 32 European hostages.[68] The funding source was from a German account labeled Humanitarian Aid.[69] Not all ransom paid comes from governments. Insurance companies offer "K and R" (kidnap and ransom) policies.[70] A businessperson in Iraq pays an annual premium of $3,000 to $6,000 for a K and R policy; shipping firms may pay as much as $7 million annually to cover large fleets in dangerous areas.

building, but parked a truck eight feet from the building's door to ensure maximum destruction and lethality. The blast killed 19 children.

5. *Destructible.* Targets cannot merely be damaged; this is a failed attack and results in a lowered opinion of a movement's capabilities. Substantial damage to a target lessens, but does not eliminate, this response.

6. *Occupied, because mass casualties are essential to creating continuing fear.* What kind of people are occupying a potential target may also be important, for example, Buckingham Palace, the London residence and administrative space of Britain's sovereigns since 1837.

7. *Near,* as illustrated by the fact that the IRA in Northern Ireland struck many more targets there than on the British mainland; and

8. *Easy,* without significant and layered defense/security features.

Few, if any, targets will satisfy all of the elements of EVIL DONE, but Clarke and Newman maintain that the final target selected will rank high on most of them.

Proximity to the target for a terrorist group may also play a role in selecting some targets. Although some notable terrorists have lived hundreds of miles from where they attacked, many others do not travel far. Examples of terrorists who traveled some distance to their targets include Tim McVeigh, the Oklahoma City bombing in 1995; Eric Rudolph, anti-abortion and anti-gay bombings and the 1995 Atlanta Olympic Park bombing; and the September 11, 2001 "9/11" hijackers.[71] An analysis of 60 cases determined that 44 percent of attackers lived with 30 miles of their target and 71 percent of attackers who were motivated by a single cause travel only 12 miles.[72] These and other empirical studies of terrorism must be carefully considered: (1) they may be based on a small, non-representative data set or (2) an available data set is analyzed that may be older and the researcher is "stuck" with whatever variables it examined.

Terrorist attacks come in all sizes and degrees of complexity. The 9/11 attacks required years of intelligence gathering, planning, and preparation. In 2001, less planning and preparation was used by Richard Reid, the "shoe bomber." He was caught trying to lite a fuse that would explode his sneakers aboard American Airline Flight 63 from Paris to Miami. Passengers smelled smoke in the cabin and overpowered Reid, a British citizen who converted to Islam. On Christmas Day 2009, a Muslim from Nigeria, Umar Farouk Abdulmutallab, boarded Northwest Airlines Flight 253. The plane was flying from the Netherlands to Detroit, Michigan, when he attempted to light explosives sewn into his underwear and was subdued by passengers. Both Reid and Abdulmutallab had ties to al-Qaeda and received life sentences.

Suicide Bombing Attacks

For most Americans, trying to understand the motivation behind suicide bombing is very difficult. In our culture, such actions are often labeled unpredictable, irrational, and fanatical. However, a careful analysis of the phenomenon shows that suicide bombings are not

FIGURE 5–11
Richard Reid (1973–), the "Shoe Bomber." An Englishman, he became a Muslim while in prison. In 2001, he boarded American Airlines 63, scheduled to fly from Paris to Miami. During the flight he attempted to light the explosives in his shoe with matches, but was noticed and overcome by passengers.
(*Courtesy FBI Law Enforcement Bulletin*)

spontaneous outbursts of emotion, but rather calculated, strategic moves by a particular group for a specific purpose. Deploying suicide bombers is not haphazard; they are carefully trained for their missions. They undergo a relatively long period of indoctrination filled with group pressure, pep talks, and organizational support, which fosters a personal commitment. Suicide is strictly forbidden in the Quar'an. However, some Islamic clerics have issued opinions that it is not forbidden when the act is committed in defense of Islam.

Between 2001 and 2004, Israel was the victim of rampant suicide bombers. Nearly half the attacks were attributed to Hamas. The radical Sheikh Ahmed Yassin* encouraged the bombings by publically proclaiming that Muslims who engaged in suicide bombing against Israel became a "**shahid**," or martyr fulfilling a religious command.[73] A study that covered completed suicide bombings for 1993–2004 determined the bombers were overwhelmingly male; predominately younger, although there was a range from 17–53 years of age; unmarried; had more than a high school education; and 81 percent came from households with eight or more members.[74] The motives for these suicide bombers was mixed. Some wanted to avenge some personal humiliation or wrong done to their family by Israeli officials, while others did it for nationalistic reasons, for example, to do something for their country, or for religious reasons, to be assured of a place in paradise.[75]

The effectiveness of suicide attacks is staggering. Between 1981 and 2008, there were 1,857 such attacks that killed 20,603 people and wounded another 48,209.[76] The first recorded car bombing, which was not suicidal, was in New York's financial district during 1920 by Italian anarchists. Modern terrorist suicide attacks date from two 1983 attacks in Lebanon. The American Embassy was partially destroyed on April 18 when a suicide bomber in a truck killed 34 staff members. Later, on October 23, a suicide bomber driving a yellow Mercedes truck blew up a portion of a peacekeeping compound in Beirut, killing 241 service members, most of them American Marines. Hezbollah was responsible for both attacks. Suicide attacks communicate to supporters and the wider public that the members of a movement hold their cause more dearly than their lives.

Shahid
A Muslim "martyr" who dies in defense of their faith; often inappropriately associated with those that conduct suicide bombings. Originates from the Qur'anic Arabic word for "witness."

---

*On March 22, 2004, Yassin was killed by the Israeli Moussad as he was returning from prayer services at a West Bank mosque.

Quick Facts
A Donkey and Dogs Used as Suicide Bombers

In 2014, Israel invaded the Gaza Strip after being shelled for days by Hamas. In response, Hamas announced that it would have "surprises" ready for the invading Israel Defense Force (IDF). In Rafah, near the Egyptian border, Hamas loaded a donkey with explosives and sent it toward IDF lines. The IDF fired on the approaching donkey to protect themselves, causing it to explode. Similar incidents with dogs also occurred.[77]

A worldwide poll conducted by the Pew Research Center's Forum on Religion and Public Life of Muslims in 2013 revealed that in war war-torn countries like Afghanistan, Iraq, and Palestine, 40 percent of the population supported the use of suicide bombing.[78] This high percentage was countered by less than 20 percent support in the vast majority of more moderate and economically stable Muslim countries.

Women are increasingly making the way into terrorist tactical roles, such as suicide bombings.[79] Nacos estimates that perhaps 20 to 30 percent of all terrorists are women, and they are well represented in regional movements.[80] The earliest record of a female suicide bomber is 1978.[81] In general, women are not viewed as threats or combatants, which may give them tactical advantages in avoiding detection and conducting a surprise attack.[82] In 1991, a woman approached former Indian Prime Minister Rajiv Ghandi, placed a garland on him, bowed at his feet, and killed both of them by detonating a bomb hidden in a basket of flowers.[83] The Liberation Tigers of Tamil Eelam (LTTE) of Sri Lanka was responsible for the assassination. Ghandi earned the wrath of LTTE when he sent Indian troops to help quell violence in Sri Lanka in 1987. Table 5–2 summarizes the work of Clarke and Newman, which examined suicide bombing from the key perspectives of both the bomber's handler and the bomber.

Although some research psychologists have described suicide bombers as loners, depressed, and suicidal, others researchers have rejected this position.[84] Radical Muslims reject the "suicide bomber" label as an attempt by Western journalists to limit the number of bombers. Studying bombers presents unique challenges. The bombers are dead and cannot be interviewed, although they may have made a martyr's video that provides some information.[85] Interviews with family and friends of suicide bombers must be carefully scrutinized: All of them may have a need to cast the deceased in the best light, but may not personally have knowledge of the bombers' true motivations.[86]

TABLE 5–2
Requirements of Handlers and Suicide Bombers

The Handler's Requirements	The Suicide Bomber's Requirements
• A safe house for operations	• Concealable explosives, preferably in the bomber's clothes
• Community support to maintain secrecy	
• A network to identify candidates	• Means of detonating bomb
• Skilled personnel to: (1) train candidates (e.g., rehearse route and means to travel to target, dressing to blend in with area, how to use detonator) and (2) indoctrinate candidates	• Unless walking, means of getting to target
	• Cell phone or other means of communicating with handler
• Select suicide bombers	• Map or memorize route to target
• Reconnaissance tasks: acquire maps, gather intelligence (e.g., security vulnerabilities)	• Preferable a visit to target so can dress accordingly
• Skilled personnel to write, shoot, and edit suicide bomber's last statement	• Knowledge of alternative target if thwarted in attacking primary
	• Dedication to task

See Ronald V. Clarke and Graemer R. Newman, *Outsmarting the Terrorists* (Westport, CT: Praeger Security International, 2006), pp. 64–68 for an extended version of this chart.

Box 5-3
Suicide Bombing and the Shahid: Of Islamic Martyrdom

The Qur'an (2:195 and 4-29) forbids ordinary suicide (Arabic: *intihar*) and those who commit it will be driven into a fire (Qur'an 4:30). It is, therefore, unsurprising that Muslim countries traditionally have the world's lowest suicide rates.[87] Following the 9/11 attacks, some Muslim scholars issued religious rulings condemning suicide attacks, while others issued opinions supporting "martyrdom operations."[88]

Currently, radical segments of Islam see suicide bombers as heroic martyrs or *shahids*. Unlike those who will be driven into the fire, those who fight in the cause of Allah will receive a "great reward" in Paradise (Qur'an 4:74).

Members of Hamas have accounted for over 90 percent of all suicide bombings in Israel and have certainly encouraged this type of radical Islamic tactic. The groups praise suicide bombers as dying in the most noble of causes . . . a misinterpreted perspective of "holy jihad."[89] Those who are martyred during jihad are told they will receive six bounties:[90]

1. their sins are immediately forgiven;
2. they are immediately accepted into Paradise and spared the judgment of the grave;
3. they avoid the great terror (A great frightening sound, all the dead will be made alive and the those alive will die except those who God wishes to spare, the sky will fragment, the mountains scattered, and all hearts will beat rapidly)
4. a great crown is placed on their head, one ruby in which is worth more than all there is in this life;
5. they are married to 72 maidens of Paradise; and
6. they may intercede for 70 relatives.[91]

Do you think that suicide bombing is a viable tactic to win greater public support for a cause? Why or why not?

Quick Facts
Beyond the Six Bounties: Payments to the Family of Suicide Bombers

In addition, in the current era of radicalized Muslim suicide bombing, women who conduct such acts in the name of Allah receive one husband that will please them. Under Saddam Hussein, Iraq paid $25,000 to the families of suicide bombers.[92] Presently, both Syria and Iran make payments to the families of suicide bombers.

How do Terrorist Organizations End?

In America, the failure rate for new small businesses is 50 to 70 percent in the first 18 months.[93] Similarly, Rapoport speculates that 90 percent of all terrorist groups don't survive their first year.[94] Intuitively, a high percentage of "start-up" terrorist groups failing in the first year makes sense. There are powerful forces and technological capabilities deployed against movements. To illustrate, start-up terrorist organizations are more at risk when recruiting because much of it must be done face-to-face. In contrast, more established movements recruit over the Internet. They can contact many candidates simultaneously while also reducing their risk exposure.[95]

"Start-up" small businesses and terrorist movements appear to be at significant risk of failure by four common factors. Stated in terrorist terms, those four factors are (1) inexperience, for example, leaders may not be able to sustain the zeal of followers because they neither know how to do so or don't recognize its importance; 2) bad operational decisions, such as attacking "hard" targets beyond the capabilities of the group; 3) a lack of capital, for example, either they cannot attract well-heeled financial supporters or such supporters are convinced by bad operational decisions the group does not have a future and stop contributing; and (4) an environment in which mistakes may lead to catastrophic failure, illustrated by failing to carefully vet followers which results in penetration of the terrorist organization by informers or security agents.

Cronin envisions terrorist organizations ending in six different ways:[96†]

- *The group's leader is captured or killed.* This is referred to as the "decapitation" strategy and its results are inconsistent. Capturing terrorist leaders is a better option than killing them because the leaders are cut off from the group; the group may be in

---

†We have used Cronin's endings and cited her work appropriately. In addition, we have added our own additional research and comments. Therefore, to avoid misrepresentation of her work, it will be useful to read it.

turmoil while deciding what to do about their leadership; and the captured leaders are humiliated as they are paraded in chains to court before the news media.[97] In balance, an imprisoned leader is a liability and there are some cases where hostages were taken to exchange for the release of the leader.[98] If a terrorist leader is killed, the group may go into decline or even split into factions, leaving no central figure with whom to negotiate, and if the group remains intact, a new leader may emerge who is much more effective than his predecessor.[99] In 1973, Israel killed Mohamed Boudia, who was a PFLP leader in Europe, apparently for his role in the Olympic Massacre the year before. On a temporary basis Illich Sanchez (Carlos the Jackal) filled his shoes.[100] Two years later, the Jackal led a sensational attack on a summit meeting in Vienna, Austria, of the Organization of the Petroleum Exporting Countries (OPEC), killing 3 and taking 63 hostages, including 11 oil ministers.[101] OPEC didn't hold a summit for another 25 years.[102] There may be times when exercising tactical restraint and leaving a terrorist leader in place is the best course of action.[103]

- *The group enters into negotiations.* All democracies publically maintain they do not negotiate with terrorists, but virtually all do so secretly.[104] Before agreeing to go to the table governments must conclude what prospects there are for a reasonable outcome; groups with absolute goals are likely to demonstrate little flexibility while those with political or narrower goals offer better prospects for negotiation.[105] Moreover, a determination must be made whether the organization is sufficiently centralized that the terrorist negotiators can actually get others to "toe the line" of any agreement.[106] State-sponsored terrorist groups offer a similar issue.[107] A precondition to all negotiations is a cessation of hostilities; if a group is not able to deliver on this issue it suggests a lack of internal cohesion in it,[108] for example, a faction opposed to negotiating may use attacks to disrupt the process. Negotiations can be conducted indirectly through a third party.[109] A government will learn useful things about a terrorist group while negotiating, such as details about its structure, the identity of key figures, and something about the relative importance of those at the table.[110] Negotiations seldom end terrorism, but may be associated with producing a decline in terrorist operations.[111]

- *The group's aims are achieved.* If a group claims success, saying it has "achieved its aims," the statement needs to be closely scrutinized. As the saying goes, "The devil is always in the details." For example, it may have accepted concessions granting it the achievement of some goals, but in exchange dropped other demands that may have been impossible to achieve. A Rand Corporation study found that only 10 percent of terrorist groups actually "achieve their goals."[112]

- *There is an implosion or loss of the group's public support.* Cronin asserts that most terrorist movements end because the group eventually disintegrates.[113] A significant factor in this is the loss of support, for example, the ideology loses its relevancy, the group "loses the bubble" in understanding what its constituency wants or needs, and targeting errors provoke a backlash.[114]

- *The group is defeated by force.* The application of military force accounts for 7 percent of the defeats of terrorist groups.[115] It is more effective with insurgency terrorism, whereas using the police is more effective with other groups. Policing produces 40 percent of terrorist endings.[116]

- *There is a transition by the group from terrorism into other forms of violence.* Most commonly, terrorist groups shift to criminal acts, which implies a shift away from political or religious goals and toward acquiring goods and profits that are an end in themselves.[117] To illustrate, Rollins and Wyler note that the Philippines-based Abu Sayyaf Group (ASG) has sometimes prioritized criminal activities over ideological operations.[118] During its periods of high criminality, ASG focuses on maritime piracy, arms trafficking, and kidnappings for ransom.[119] Recruits seem less attracted by ideology and more motivate by promises of financial wealth.[120]

Information Link

For more information on the impact of negotiations and the arrest of leaders on the viability of a terrorist group, refer to the website article and short videos entitled, "Peru Marks 20 Years Since the Capture of Shining Path leader Abimael Guzman" on the *Peru this Week* website at www.peruthisweek.com/blogs-peru-marks-20-years-since-capture-of-shining-path-leader-abimael-guzman-50196.

Two important questions about how terrorist organizations end are (1) what becomes of the military arms and supplies? If the terrorists "win" there is no issue, but if defeated by force or the group's aims are achieved, how much certainty can there be that all arms have been collected or otherwise accounted for? and (2) What becomes of the terrorist fighters? Do they join another cause? Start a new one elsewhere? Will they need to be treated for Post Trauma Stress Syndrome? Will they willingly "retire" to a life of peace?

Chapter Summary

SUMMARY BY LEARNING OBJECTIVE

1. **State the key dilemmas facing terrorist organizations.**

   These dilemmas are (1) action vs. secrecy, (2) growth vs. control, (3) recruitment vs. retention, (4) success vs. longevity, and (5) resource acquisition vs. constituencies.

2. **Identify the levels of involvement with a terrorist organization.**

   Those levels are (1) passive supporters, (2) active supporters, (3) cadre, and (4) hardcore leadership.

3. **Explain why it is important for terrorist organizations to retain current members.**

   Retention of current members is essential because they have already been trained. Current members may also be experienced and proved themselves to be reliable Some of them will be assigned important organizational roles, for example, making "pitches" to potential recruits; training them; or becoming couriers, reconnaissance specialists, and operational leaders.

4. **Provide the three main reasons why people join terrorist movements.**

   First, family members, friends, or individuals in the recruiters' social network are going to join or already have done so; second, those same people have strong grievances against the government; and third, deep religious and/or political beliefs inspire the recruit to fight for a cause.

5. **Identify the factors that affect what organizational form terrorists adopt.**

   These factors are (1) the number of active followers, (2) the geographical locations in which they will locate, (3) the operational pace they intend to pursue, (4) the preferences of supporters, (5) their financial resources, and (6) the capabilities, intentions, and anticipated type of operations of opposing forces.

6. **Identify six types of cells and briefly describe their diverse missions.**

   (1) *Sleeper Cells:* Members lead normal lives, engaging only in lawful employment and activities that call no attention to themselves. The jobs they select may facilitate future terrorist activities. Illustratively, a taxi driver will learn a great about a city's geography, can identify potential targets, and move terrorists around. A sleeper cell may receive a signal that "awakens" it for a specific purpose, such as providing a safe house or sabotage. Iran has been inserting sleeper cells in Latin America with the goal of committing, fermenting, and fostering acts of international terrorism. (2) *Command and Control Cells:* C2 cells make all of the final decisions about the execution of an attack and other matters pertaining to the activities of a cell; (3) *Tactical Operations Cells*: TAC- OPS cells actually execute attacks under the guidance of C2; (4) *Intel Cells:* These cells collect data, make recommendations, may select targets, provide information about the best route to approach the target (ingress), and, if not a suicide attack, the best route to follow to when leaving (egressing) the area of the attack; (5) *Logistics Cells:* LCs provide supplies and other support to other cells, especially TAC-OPS, including bomb making materials and the names and locations of sympathetic doctors to use if there is a medical emergency; and (6) *Fund-Raising Cells:* FRCs almost exclusively commit illegal acts to raise funds for the terrorist movement or to be used in support of a particular attack. Illustrations include kidnapping for ransom, arms and drug trafficking, operating bogus charities, extortion, and credit card fraud.

7. **Identify the main advantages of the hierarchical model.**

   The chief advantages are that the chain of command is clearly understood, people know what their jobs are, specialization can be accommodated, and control is normally high.

8. **Explain how ideology helps identify targets and view victims.**

   Terrorist movements have a core set of beliefs and goals that define their ideology and focus their violence. One way or another, ideology identifies "acceptable" targets and acts as a constraint against attacking other targets. Acceptable targets serve another important purpose. In the ideological framework of terrorist movements, victims are blamed for the violence inflicted on them. The essence of this argument is "They brought it on themselves." This construction both relieves terrorists of their moral responsibility for the deaths they have caused and glorifies them for doing so.

9. **State the ways that Cronin sees terrorist organizations ending**

   Cronin's endings are (1) the group's leader is captured or killed, (2) the group enters into negotiations, (3) the group's aims are achieved; (4) there is an implosion or loss of the group's public support, (5) the group is defeated by force, and (6) there is a transition from one terrorism to another form of violence.

REVIEW QUESTIONS

1. What are passive supporters of terrorist organizations?
2. Lone wolf terrorists are hard to detect. Why?
3. What is a cell?
4. How does a "leaderless resistance cell" function?
5. What are "sleeper cells?"
6. What is a "redundant leader protocol" in a cell?
7. The hierarchy organizational model has what major features?
8. What is the meaning of the acronym EVIL DONE?

CRITICAL THINKING EXERCISES

1. **Interview an FBI Agent or a Local Police Officer assigned to a Joint Terrorism Task Force (JTTF).** Contact your local office of the FBI and set up an appointment to interview a member of a Joint Terrorism Task Force in your area, or have such a member of the law enforcement community visit your class. Ask the agent or officer what types of terrorist organizations may be operating in your community, and more importantly, how are they structured. Ask the agent or officer to describe the types of structure of terrorist organizations that are commonly observed in domestic as well as FTO groups. What type of tactics does the JTTF use to infiltrate and subsequently thwart activities within these groups? Does the type of structure of the group impact the strategy and tactics that might be employed by the JTTF in monitoring these groups?

2. **Mass Shooters and Lone Wolves.** Scour the Internet for mass shooters and lone wolf attacks in the United States. Are there any common denominators between the shooters and their horrific events of the past decade? Review the CNN story and videos entitled "The 25 Deadliest Mass Shooting in U.S. History Fast Facts" at www.cnn.com/2013/09/16/us/20-deadliest-mass-shootings-in-u-s-history-fast-facts/. Next review the article entitled "A Guide to Mass Shootings in America," at www.motherjones.com/politics/20 /07/mass-shootings-map. Note that both articles make a difference between mass murders (single incident) and Spree killing (multiple incidents). View the map presented in the second story, and try to identify any patterns that can be made geographically about these events. Also note the stories are dated October 26, 2013, and April 2, 2014, respectively. Can other events be added to the story since those dates? Discuss the problem of mass shootings and spree killings in class. What do you think can be done to prevent such horrific problems in the future?

NOTES

1. Amitai Etzioni, *Modern Organizations* (Englewood Cliffs, New Jersey: Prentice Hall, 1964), p. 1 with restatement.
2. Charles R. Swanson, Leonard Territo, and Robert W. Taylor, *Police Administration: Structures, Processes, and Behaviors* (Upper Saddle River, New Jersey: Pearson, 8th Edition, 2012), p. 174.
3. These five dilemmas are drawn with substantial restatement and some additions from Ethan Frisch, "Insurgencies Are Organizations Too: Organizational Structure and the Effectiveness of Insurgent Strategy," *The Peace and Conflict Review*, Vol. 6, Issue 1, 2010, pp. 19–24.
4. Ibid., p. 19.
5. Loc. cit.
6. Audrey Kurth Cronin, *How Terrorism Ends* (Princeton, New Jersey: Princeton University Press, 2009), p. 4.
7. Ibid., p. 20.
8. Ibid., p. 22.
9. Bruce W. Don, *Networked Technologies for Networked Terrorists* (Santa Monica: RAND Corporation, 2007), pp. 12–13.
10. Ibid., p. 23.
11. Ibid., p. 24.
12. Khusrav Gaibulloev and Todd Sandler, "Determinates of the Demise of Terrorist Organizations," November 2012, www.utdallas.edu/~tms063000/website/Demise%20of%20Terrorist%20Organizations.pdf, p. 3.
13. Ibid., p. 8.
14. Ibid., p. 15.
15. Loc. cit.
16. Ibid., p. 8.
17. Ibid., p. 7.
18. Faisal Irshaid, "How ISIS Is Spreading Its Messages On-Line," *BBC News Middle East*, June 19, 2014, www.bbc.com/news/world-news-middle-east-27912569.
19. Don, *Networked Technologies for Networked Terrorists*, p. 24.
20. Loc. cit.
21. Operational space is mentioned in Joshua Kilberg, "A Basic Model Explaining Terrorist Group Organizational Structure," *Studies in Conflict and Terrorism*, Vol. 35, Issue 11, 2012.
22. Resources and ideological preferences of supporters are identified in Luis De la Calle and Ignacio Sanchez-Cuena, "The Production of Terrorist Violence: Analyzing Target Selection with the IRA and ETA," *Centro de Estudios Avanzados Ciencias Sociales, Instituto Juan March de Estudios e Invstigaciones*, Madrid, Spain, 2006, p. 1.
23. For an excellent analysis of this subject see Jeffrey D. Simon, *Lone Wolf Terrorism: Understanding the Growing Threat* (Amherst, N.Y.: Prometheus Books, 2013). Also see Mark Thompson, "The Danger of the Lone-Wolf Terrorist," February 27, 2013, p. 1, www.nation.time.com/2013/02/27/the-danger-of-the-lone-wolf-terrorist.
24. Loc. cit.
25. Ibid., p. 4.
26. Jerome P. Bjelopera, "American Jihadist Terrorism: Combating a Complex Threat" (Washington, D.C.: Congressional Research Service, January 23, 2013), p. 34. This statement was made with respect to Americans who are motivated by Islamic jihad, but by observation it also applies to American lone wolves.
27. Walter Laqueur, *The New Terrorism* (New York: Oxford University Press, 1999), p. 8.
28. "Edmond Post Office Massacre," Oklahoma State University Digital Library, undated, www.digital.library.okstate.edu/encyclopedia/entries/e/ed003.html.
29. Loc. cit.
30. Neil Katz, "Joe Stack Suicide Note Full Text: American Zombies Wake Up and Revolt," February 18, 2010, www.CBSNews.com/8301_504083_162_6220533_504083.html.

31. Lone Wolf Terrorism (Rotterdam, Netherlands: Instituut Voor Veiligheids-en Crisis Management), June 6, 2007, p. 17.

32. See Evan F. Kohlmann, "Home Grown Terrorists: Theory and Cases on Terror's Newest Front," *The Annals of the American Academy of Political and Social Science*, Vol. 618, No. 1, pp. 95–109.

33. Mark Hallam, "Frankfurt Shooter Described as Islamist-Influenced Solo Attacker," *DW News*, April 3, 2011, www.dw.de/frankfurt-shooter-described-as-islamist-influenced-solo-attacker/a-14889904.

34. Loc. cit.

35. John Roach, "Estimation of Operations Security (OPSEC) in al Qaeda Operation," *Newsletter of the OPSEC Professional Society*, Vol. 3, Issue 2, July 2012, p. 12.

36. The account in this paragraph is taken with restatement from Dale Russakoff and Dan Eggen, "Six Charged in Plot to Attack Fort Dix," *Washington Post*, May 9, 2007, www.washingtonpost.com/wp-dyn/content/article/2007/05/08/ar2007050800465_2.html.

37. Richard Greenberg, Adam Ciralsky, and Stone Phillips, "Enemies at the Gate," NBC News Today, December 28, 2007, www.today.com/id/22419963/ns/today/t/enemies-gate/#.UjW30xavszY.

38. Emily Smith, "Terrorists Drawn to South African Passports," CNN, June 15, 2011, www.security.blogs.cnn.com/2011/06/15/terrorists-drawn-to-south-african-passports.

39. Luis Fleischman, "Venezuela: Anatomy of a Dictator," *The Journal of International Security Affairs*, No. 11, Fall 2006, www.securityaffairs.org/issues/2006/11/fleischman.php.

40. Greenberg, Ciralsky, and Phillips, "Enemies at the Gate."

41. Chris Dishman, "The Leadership Nexus: When Crime and Terror Converge," *Studies in Conflict and Terrorism*, Vol. 28, Issue 3, 2005, p. 243, www.cerium.ca/img/dishman_2005_the_leadership_nexus.pdf.

42. "Louis Beam," Anti-Defamation League, www.archive.adl.org/learn/ext_us/beam.asp?.xpicked=2&item=beam.

43. "Iran 'Sleeper Cells' are Infiltrating South America, Argentine Prosecutor Says," Fox News Latino, May 30, 2013, www.latino.foxnews.com/latino/news/2013/05/30/iran-terror-sleeper-cells-are-infiltrating-south-america-argentine-prosecutor-says.

44. See David E. Kaplan and Monica M. Ekman, "Homegrown Terrorists," *U.S. News and World Report*, Vol. 134, Issue 7, March 3, 2003, pp. 30–34.

45. Markus Sabadello, "Comparing Terrorist and Internet Networks," Project Danube, Fall 2010, www.projectdanube.org/wp-content/upload/2012/02/comparing-terrorist-and-internet-networks.pdf.

46. A Military Guide to Terrorism in the Twenty-First Century (United States Army, Fort Leavenworth, Kansas: TRADOC G2, August 15, 2007), pp. 3–8.

47. Nicholas Verdier, "Hierarchy: A Short History of a Word in Western Thought," in Denise Pumain, ed., *Hierarchy in Natural and Social Sciences* (New York, N.Y., Springer, 2005), p. 13.

48. The hierarchical/ bureaucratic model is the centerpiece of organizational theory's traditional stem. It existed for centuries and was systematized by Max Weber. The bureaucratic model is compatible with administrative theory. For more information see Charles Swanson, Leonard Territo, and Robert W. Taylor, *Police Administration: Structures, Processes, and Behavior* (Upper Saddle River, New Jersey: Pearson, 8th Edition, 2012), pp. 174–208.

49. Rohan Gunaratna and Aviv Oreg, "Al Qaeda's Organizational Structure and Its Evolution," *Studies in Conflict and Terrorism*, Vol. 33, Issue 12, November 2010, p. 1052.

50. Jonathon Masters, "Al-Qaeda in the Arabian Peninsula," Council on Foreign Relations, May 24, 2012, www.cfr.org/yemen/al-qaeda-in-the-arabian-peninsular-aqap/p9369.

51. "The Global Islamic Media Front Issues Caliphate Voice Channel Video, Threatening Governments of Germany and Austria Over Role in Afghanistan," Christian Action Network, March 12, 2007, www.christianactionnetwork.wordpress.com; and "Pair Sentenced for Terrorist Threat to Austria, Germany," DW (Deutsche Welle) March 13, 2008, www.dw.de/pair-sentenced-for-terrorist-threat-to-austria-germany/a-3189925-1.

52. See Peter Grier, "The New al Qaeda: Local Franchises," *The Christian Science Monitor*, July 11, 2005, http://www.csmonitor.com/2005/0711/p01s01-woeu.html.

53. Siobhan Gorman, "Terror Links Spurred Alert," *The Wall Street Journal*, August 6, 2013, quoting interview with Gregory Johnsen.

54. Major David M. Williams, "Nothing Virtual About It: An Emerging Safe Haven for an Adaptive Enemy" (Fort Leavenworth, Kansas: Monograph for the School of Advanced Military Studies, U.S. Army Command and General Staff College, 2010), p. 2.

55. Williams, "Nothing Virtual About It," p. 40.

56. Michale Judy, "Terrorism's Virtual Safe Havens and the Effects on Terror Organizations," *Global Security Studies*, Vol. 2, Issue 1, Winter 2011, www.globalsecuritystudies.com/judy%20virtual.pdf.

57. Loc. cit.

58. Loc. cit.

59. Loc. cit.

60. This paragraph, with restatement and new material, is drawn from Austin L. Wright, "Terrorism, Ideology, and Target Selection," March 5, 2013, www.princeton.edu/politics/about/file-repository/public/wright_on_terrorism.pdf. It does not appear to have been published other than on this Princeton University site.

61. Dale C. Eikmeier, "Center of Gravity Analysis," *Military Review*, Vol. LXXXIV, No. 6, August 2004, p. 2.

62. Loc. cit.

63. Joe Strange and Richard Iron, "Understanding Center of Gravity and Critical Vulnerabilities," Air War College, Maxwell Air Force Base, undated, p. 2.

64. Battle of the Atlantic Statistics, United States Merchant Marine, www.usmm.org/battleatlantic.html.

65. Dallas Boyd and James Scouras, "The Dark Matter of Terrorism," *Studies in Conflict and Terrorism*, Vol. 33, No. 12, December 2010, p. 128.

66. Terrorism in the Twenty-First Century (Ft. Leavenworth, Kansas: U.S. Army Training and Doctrine Command (TRADOC) G2, Handbook No. 1, December 10, 2010), p. A-1.

67. The discussion of EVIL DONE is drawn from Ronald G. Clarke and Graeme R. Newman, *Outsmarting the Terrorists* (Westport, CT: Praeger Security International, 2006), pp. 93–97.

68. Rukmini Callimachi, "Paying Ransoms, Europe Bankrolls Qaeda Terror," *The New York Times*, July 29, 2014.

69. Loc. cit.

70. "I'm a Client … Get Me out of Here," *The Economist*, June 27, 2013, www.economist.com/blogs/schumpeter/2013/06/kidnap-and-ransom-insurance.

71. Brett Smith, "A Look at Terrorist Behavior: How They Prepare, Where They Strike" (Washington, D.C.: National Institute of Justice, July 2008), *NIJ Journal* 280, www.nij.gov/journals/260/pages/terrorost-behavior.aspx.

72. Loc. cit.

73. Ewen MacAskill, "Suicide Bombs Restarts Hamas Campaign," *The Guardian* (England), July 9, 2001, www.theguardian.com/world/2001/jul/10/israel.

74. Sean Yom and Basel Saleh, "Palestinian Suicide Bombers: A Statistical Analysis," *Economists for Peace & Security*, 2004, http://www.epsusa.org/publications/newsletter/2004/nov2004/saleh.pdf.

75. Riaz Hassan, "What Motivates Suicide Bombers," *Yale Globe On-Line*, September 3, 2009, p. 1, http://yaleglobal.yale.edu/content/what-motivates-suicide-bombers-0.

76. Assaf Moghadam, "Motives for Martyrdom," *International Security*, Vol. 33, Issue 3, Winter 2008/2009, p. 49.

77. Robert Tait, "Donkey Suicide Bomb Stopped by Israeli Troops on Gaza," *The Telegraph* (England), July 18, 2014.

78. The Pew Research Center Forum on Religion and Public Live, *The World's Muslims: Religion, Politics and Society* (Washington, D.C.: April 30, 2013).

79. Jessica Davis, "Evolution of the Global Jihad: Female Suicide Bombers in Iraq," *Studies in Conflict and Terrorism*, Vol. 36, Issue 4, 2013, pp. 279–291, online copy has no page

numbers, www.tandfoline.com.proxy-remote.galib.uga.edu/dol/abs/10/1080/105763598# .uvgxhbavvur.

80. Brigette L. Nacos, "The Portrayal of Female Terrorists in the Media," *Studies in Conflict and Terrorism*, Vol. 28, Issue 5, September 2005, p. 436.

81. Davis, "Evolution of the Global Jihad."

82. Loc. cit.

83. Nacos, "The Portrayal of Female Terrorists in the Media," p. 447.

84. See Robert J. Brym and Bader Araj, "Are Suicide Bombers Suicidal?" *Studies in Conflict and Terrorism*, Vol. 35, Issue 6, pp. 432–443.

85. Ibid., p. 438.

86. Loc. cit.

87. David Cook, "The Implications of Martyrdom Operations for Contemporary Islam," *Journal of Religious Ethics*, Vol. 32, Issue I, Spring 2004, p. 130.

88. Ibid., p. 131.

89. Ibn Warraq, "Virgins? What Virgins?" *The Guardian*, January 11, 2002, www.theguardian .com/books/2002/jan/12/books.giardianreviews5.

90. Some of the current list of bounties do not comport to early descriptions. For example, the Prophet told a companion that those who are martyred will receive six bounties: (1) they shall be forgiven when the first drop of their blood is spilt; (2) they shall see Paradise upon their death; (3) they will be spared the torment of the grave; (4) they will be kept safe from the great fright (A great frightening sound, all the dead will be made alive and the those alive will die except those who God wishes to spare, the sky will fragment, the mountains scattered, and all hearts will beat rapidly), (5) they will be married to wives from among the wide-eyed houris in Paradise (splendid, light skinned, dark-eyed women); and (6) they will be able to intercede for 70 members of their family (see the English Translation of Sunan Ibn Majah, Compiled by Imam Muhammad Bin Yazeed (Riyadh, Saudi Arabia: Darussalam Books, 2007), Volume 4, Hadith 2799, p. 67. When Gabriel took Muhammad on a visit to Paradise, mention was made of 70 beds and on each of which was a (beautiful) woman, but there was no connection to martyrdom. Elsewhere, Muhammad was reported to have said that the least reward for a faithful Muslim in Paradise would be 80,000 servants and 70 houris.

91. These bounties are commonly found in a variety of sources. There may be minor variations in their wording. See Shaykh Faraz A. Khan, "72 Virgins for Martyrs: Making Sense of One of the Rewards of Paradise," *Seeking Guidance*, July 29, 2011, www.seekersguidance.org/ans-blog/2011/07/29/72-virgins-for-martyrs-making-sense-of-one-of-the-rewards-of-paradise.

92. Suicide Bombing During the Current Israeli-Palestinian Confrontation, January 1, 2006, http://www.terrorism-info.org.il/data/pdf/PDF_19279_2.pdf.

93. Pamela Engel, "Small Business Owners Don't Fear the Devastatingly High Failure Rate," *Business Insider*, June 5, 2013, www.businessinsider.com/ small-business-owners-are-optimistic-2013-6.

94. David C. Rapoport, "Terrorism," in Mary Hawkesworth and Maurice Kogan, editors, *Routledge Encyclopedia of Government and Politics* (London, England: Routledge, 1992), p. 1067.

95. Don, *Networked Technologies for Networked Terrorists*, p. 12.

96. These six ways of ending are drawn from Cronin's excellent book, *How Terrorism Ends*. We have added commentary and other research to these ways. Serious students of terrorism should carefully read Cronin's entire work.

97. Don, *Networked Technologies for Networked Terrorists*, pp. 14–15.

98. Ibid., p. 17.

99. Ibid., p. 26.

100. See John Follian, Jackal: *The Complete Story of the Legendry Terrorist, Carlos the Jackal* (London, Orion, 1999).

101. "Carlos the Jackal Attacks OPEC Headquarters," History, This Day in History (December 21, 1975), www.history.com/this-day-in-history/ carlos-the-jackal-attacks-opec-headquarters.

102. Loc. cit.

103. Cronin, *How Terrorism Ends*, p. 34.
104. Ibid., p. 35.
105. Peter R. Neumann, "Negotiating with Terrorists," *Foreign Affairs*, January/February 2007, www.foreignaffairs.com/articles/62276/peter-r-neumann/negotiating-with-terrorists.
106. Loc. cit.
107. Loc. cit.
108. Loc. cit.
109. Cronin, *How Terrorism Ends*, p. 37.
110. Loc. cit.
111. Ibid., p. 34.
112. Seth G. Jones and Martin C. Libicki, "How Terrorist Organizations End, Lessons for Countering Al Qaeda" (Santa Monica, CA: RAND Corporation Summary, 2008), p. xiv, www.rand.org/content/dam/rand/pubs/monographs/2008/rand_mg741-1.sum.pdf.
113. Cronin, *How Terrorism Ends*, p. 34.
114. Ibid., pp. 105, 107, and 108.
115. Jones and Libicki, *How Terrorism Ends, Lessons for Countering Al Qaeda*," p. xiv.
116. Seth G. Jones and Martin C. Libicki, "How Terrorist Organizations End," Rand Research Brief (Santa Monica, CA: RAND Corporation, 2008), p. 1.
117. Cronin, *How Terrorism Ends*, p. 146.
118. John Rollins and Liana Sun Wyler, "Terrorism and Transnational Crime: Policy Issues for Congress" (Washington, D.C.: Congressional Research Service, June 11, 2013), p. 17.
119. Loc. cit.
120. Loc. cit.

Critical Processes of Terrorist Organizations

CHAPTER
6

Learning Objectives

After completing this chapter, you should be able to:

1. Explain what restrains a terrorist movement's capability to launch certain types of attacks.

2. State why it is important for terrorist groups to become learning organizations.

3. Identify and briefly describe a terrorist movement's four organization tools.

4. Explain why adopting an ideology is important to a terrorist organization.

5. Provide four reasons why recruiting is so important to terrorist organizations.

6. State the reasons for voluntary turnover in terrorist organizations.

7. Identify and briefly explain a terrorist movement's six operational skills.

8. Identify and briefly describe Lamb's four settings for safe havens.

An Afghan National Army soldier holds a poppy near the village of Karizonah, Afghanistan. Poppies are used to manufacturer heroin. Like many other insurgent and terrorist groups, the drug trade is a major source of funding for the Taliban.

(*Courtesy U.S. Air Force by Staff Sergeant Joshua L. Demotts*)

Introduction

Asal and Rethemeyer studied 395 terrorist organizations over an eight-year period.[1] During that time 68 (17 percent) of them killed 10 or more people and only 28 (7.1 percent) killed 100 or more in operations.[2] Clearly there is wide variance in how terrorist organizations behave. Ganor explains their actions by dividing them into groups based on their (1) motivations, meaning their intentions and (2) their capabilities to achieve specific objectives, for example, actually destroy a target.[3]

Table 6–1 profiles six terrorist behavioral characteristics on the basis of their motivations and capabilities. The six groups are not a progression through which terrorist

TABLE 6–1
Behavioral Groups for Terrorist Organizations

Group	Description
A	Group A maintains terrorist motivations (intentions), such as destabilizing American allies. However, its low operational capabilities cannot fully support them (e.g., cannot mount more than local small attacks on "soft" targets; possess a low level of tactical and technical competency; primarily have hand-held firearms; cannot produce false identification papers that will pass close scrutiny; and lack the resources to deploy personnel to attack distant targets). May be in movement's early development stages. Lacks or has lost state or other sponsorship. May have experienced significant losses that have degraded its capability. Possibly seeking a safe haven from which to operate. Perhaps the smallest and shortest running terrorist movement in history was the Belgium-based Communist Combat Cells (CCC). The CCC espoused a violent communist ideology and carried out some two dozen bombings that resulted in two deaths between October and December 1985. The arrest of all four CCC members that same December put a permanent end to the group. Several small cells discovered in Pakistan during 2011–2013 could also be included in Group A (e.g., al Furqan, Kharooj, and al Mukhtar). They are examples of groups with terrorist motivations and low operational capabilities. Such groups are thought to be responsible for the increase in Pakistan's bank robberies as they seek funds to build operational capabilities. In Northern Island, the Real Irish Republican Army (RIRA) uses terrorist tactics to support its ideology of a unified Ireland; RIRA is a successor to the original IRA. Its intentions exceed its low capabilities.
B	Possesses motivations and greater operational capabilities than Group A. However, Group B still lacks the full range of resources needed to conduct the kinds and scope of attacks it desires. Following 9/11, the United States and its allies have waged war against al-Qaeda. They have killed many of its key leaders and cadre and denied Iraq, Afghanistan, Somalia, and parts of Pakistan as safe havens. Drone strikes and special operations personnel have also been used to kill leaders, diminish command and control capabilities, and have disrupted training in a number of countries, including Yemen, Somalia, Burkina Faso (Burkina), other African countries, and the Philippines, These actions have degraded al-Qaeda capabilities from Group C to Group B.
C	Motivation is high (e.g., attack the "Great Satan" within the United States) and so are capabilities (e.g., able to mount simultaneous and complex operations). Al-Qaeda's four attacks on 9/11 illustrate this situation. Since then, as noted immediately above, al-Qaeda's capabilities have been systematically degraded, but not eliminated.
D	Capabilities exceed motivation because they cannot carry out a full range of attacks due to Internal and external considerations. For example, due to *external considerations* a terrorist group *might* refrain from using biochemical attacks out of fear of overwhelming reprisals, loss of public support, and/or potential loss of sponsors. An example of an *internal consideration* is when Osama bin Laden directed followers not to attack Western civilians because it was not having the desired effect on their governments.
E	Has the operational capabilities, but not the motivation to use them. Whereas Group D refrains from certain types of attacks, Group E has suspended all operations for some specific purpose (e.g., Hamas has been violently opposed Israel in the Middle East for decades, but episodically agrees to a ceasefire while restraining its military arm, the Izz-al-Din al-Qassam Brigades).
F	Lacks both motivation and operational capabilities. It has abandoned using violence to achieve its goals in favor of the political process. Essentially it has morphed into a political organization. In South Africa, Nelson Mandela, a member of the revolutionary, nationalist, and anti-apartheid African National Congress (ANC), was convicted of sabotage and conspiracy to overthrow the government. He was imprisoned during 1964–1990. Following the abandonment of the anti-apartheid policy, Mandela became the next South African president. In 2008, the ANC was removed from the U.S. Department of State's terrorism watch list. The ANC is now a major political party in that country. The Bodo Liberation Tigers (BLT) laid down its arms and left the path of terrorism when it signed a memorandum of settlement with India's government in 2003, which created an area to be administered by BLT's successor, the Bodoland Territorial Council (BTC). The Bodos are an ethnic people living in northeast India.

Source: Boaz Ganor, "Terrorist Organization Types and the Probability of a Boomerang Effect," *Studies in Conflict and Terrorism*," Vol. 31, Issue 4, April 2008, pp. 279–280, with substantial restatement, more narrative and examples, and the addition of Group C.

Quick Facts
Are There Limits on the Types of Violence the Islamic State Would Use?

In 2006, a former al-Qaeda terrorist group began evolving. Previously known as the Islamic State in Iraq, then the Islamic State of Iraq and Syria, and the Islamic State of Iraq and the Levant, it re-badged itself in 2014 as simply the Islamic State (IS) and announced it was a caliphate with authority over all Muslims in the world.

It is unique among terrorist groups in that it presently controls a substantial area in Iraq, Lebanon, and Syria. IS is extremely brutal, carrying out mass executions of captured Iraqi soldiers

and Christians. It has substantial financial resources from looting banks in captured cities and also by selling oil on the black market from captured oil-producing areas and refineries. This provides IS with the capability to buy weapons systems to supplement those captured from retreating Iraqi forces. In 2014, to protect ethnic groups marked for death by the Islamic State, the United States began an air campaign to protect them, which may provoke attacks on American interests or its homeland. Given its brutality, no one can predict the mode of an IS retaliation attack.

Quick Facts
The Taj Mahal Hotel and Benghazi Attacks

These two attacks represent very different tactics and targets. The Taj Mahal was a soft target that terrorists held for several days, while Benghazi was a raid, following which the terrorists withdrew.

Globally, the Taj Mahal Palace Hotel ranks twentieth among the most elite hotels. In 2008, terrorists attacked multiple targets in Mumbai including the Taj Mahal, which they held for three days. Despite the remarkable efforts of Taj employees to protect guests, 31 people died and 26 were injured. In the end, all

terrorists except one were killed, and the lone survivor was convicted and executed.

The deadly 2012 attack on the American consulate in Benghazi, Libya, was carried out by a group that had connections to three radical Islamic movements. Ambassador Stevens and three other men were killed and 10 injured. The failure to immediately send a quick reaction force (QRF) to the assistance of the beleaguered consulate remains controversial. The Benghazi Raid is an example of a Black Swan event.

movements inevitably progress. They may get stuck at any stage, advance, regress, or their motivations and capabilities may change. Describing a terrorist organization is much like a photograph; it portrays what exists in a particular point in time, but a second photograph, even one taken soon after the first, may show subtle to substantial differences as compared to the first photograph.

Beyond motivation and capabilities, there are many other ways to look at terrorist organizations. Examples include the driving ideology, quality of leadership, demands made, stage of development, size, degree of specialization, sponsorship, and extent of public support. Other factors include tactics used, the selection of targets, whether they hit "soft" or "hard" targets (e.g., bombing a hotel in India popular with Westerners versus a closely guarded military facility), and ability to conduct a rapid series of attacks or complex multi-pronged attacks, degree of independence or subordination to another body, ability to control a territory as a safe haven, the numbers of casualties caused in individual attacks and cumulatively, and the organization's longevity.[4]

To achieve some longevity terrorist movements must become learning organizations. These are characterized by prizing the acquisition of new knowledge, being nimble when faced with new situations, and thinking "outside of the box." According to interrogated prisoners, by 2009 the success of drone attacks was being countered by the al-Qaeda strategy of decentralizing training. Groups of roughly 10 trainees were assigned to remote locations that consisted of a single shack that would not attract attention. Although effective, this strategy cost al-Qaeda some trainees who objected to the primitive conditions under which they were forced to live.[5]

Becoming a learning organization is a survival mechanism for terrorist organizations. For terrorists and other organizations being a learning organization is a survival mechanism. In the Port of Aden, Yemen, al-Qaeda's January 2000 attack on the USS *The Sullivans* failed. The small boat that was to be used as a floating bomb was packed with too many pounds of explosives. As a result, it sank while accelerating toward *The Sullivans*. Although information about the failed attack was widely distributed by the Navy, it failed to foil a second attack. Nine months later, in the same harbor, al-Qaeda successfully heavily damaged the **USS Cole** by simply loading another launch with a manageable payload of explosives (see Figure 6–1).

USS Cole
Successfully attacked in 2000 by al-Qaeda in the Port of Aden, Yemen, by a suicide "bomber" piloting a launch loaded with explosives.

FIGURE 6–1
The terrorist-damaged hull of the USS *Cole*. Both terrorists in the attacking boat were killed by the explosion. The USS *Cole* rode back to the United States "piggyback style" on the Norwegian *Blue Marlin*.

(© Everett Collection Inc./Alamy)

The Two Essential Sets of Terrorist Organizational Tools

During the 1930s the body of knowledge known as administrative theory emerged. Theorists and practitioners sought to identify "universal" methods of administration that could be applied in all organizational settings. In 1937, Luther Gulick coined the most enduring acronym of the functions of administration: POSDCORB: **P**lanning, **O**rganizing, **S**taffing, **D**irecting, **Co**ordinating, **R**eporting, and **B**udgeting.[6] In 2004, Cragin and Daly, either directly or indirectly, accounted for all of these functions and reframed them in the particular needs of terrorist organizations. They determined that there are two essential sets of terrorist organization tools, four of which are organizational and six that are operational (see Table 6–2).

The Four Organizational Tools

Broadly, "organizational tools" refers to the things an organization must accomplish to foster its viability. Cragin and Daly identified four organizational tools: (1) ideology, which represents the reason for existing; (2) leadership, which provides the oversight that steers the organization; (3) recruiting, which is acquiring followers; and (4) publicity, which calls attention to what the terrorist organization broadly intends to do and heralds its successes. In no particular order, a discussion of these factors follows.

1) Adopting a guiding and motivating *ideology* is the key decision because it plays the central role in communicating what "We are about." It must also be powerful enough to motivate members to make sacrifices. Ultimately, it is at the heart of getting someone to "pick up the gun."[7] Al-Qaeda's ideology inspires its followers to believe that the violent acts they are committing fulfills the ordained will of Allah.[8] Skinheads believe they are preserving the "White way of life." Terrorism occurs when opportunity, motivation, and ideology intersect.[9] Ideologies grow out of one of more conditions, such as human rights abuses, economic inequality, a sense of injustice, religion, and political repression.[10] Like radical Muslims,

TABLE 6–2
Terrorist Organizational Tools

The Four Organizational Tools	The Six Operational Tools
• Ideology	• Command and Control System
• Leadership	• Weapons
• Recruiting	• Operational Space
• Publicity	• Training
	• Intelligence and Counterintelligence
	• Finance

Source: Kim Cragin and Sara A. Daly, *The Dynamic Terrorist Threat* (Santa Monica: RAND Corporation, 2004), p. xiv. We have combined some tools from this source.

both the Ku Klux Klan and neo-Nazis focus their hatred, to some degree, out of a warped interpretation of religion that becomes part of their core ideologies.

Following 9/11, terrorism was widely commented on and occasionally studied. One of the early intuitive assertions was that poverty was one of the important root causes of terrorism. If this is true—and admittedly this is just one example—why of eight suspects arrested in Great Britain in 2007 for failed car bombings were six of them foreign-born physicians?[11]

Several empirical studies also assert that poverty causes terrorism. However, the accuracy of this assertion is questionable. Abadie concluded that terrorism is not significantly higher in poor countries and that the degree of political freedom was a better explanation for terrorism.[12] Countries with an intermediate level of political freedom or which are transitioning from an authoritarian to a more democratic model—for example, Iraq, Spain, and Russia—are more prone to terrorism than countries with a high level of political freedom or a highly authoritarian government.[13]

There may be a single factor that drives a terrorist ideology or there may be multiple factors. Regardless of the causes(s), all ideologies share three common characteristics: (1) a belief system that instructs people to do certain things (e.g., drive people of color and the "crusaders" out of "our" lands); (2) the belief cannot be questioned or violated; and (3) the things to be done must be directed toward achieving some objective or cause that resonates both with the general population, to ensure their support, and with potential recruits, so they can be brought into the organization.[14]

The **Kurdistan Workers Party (PKK)** (Partiya Karekeren Kurdistan) has an ideology that resonates and is both separatist/nationalist and Marxist-oriented. Kurds are one of the world's largest ethnic populations without a homeland, numbering some 22 million people.[15] There is often an ethnic component to separatist/nationalist movements. The Bodo Liberation Tigers mentioned in Table 6–2 also illustrate this point. The PKK is seeking a homeland for ethnic Kurds, making its ideology popular with that population. The PKK operates out of portions of Turkey, Iran, and Iraq. There have been episodic peace talks between Turkey and the PKK, but no agreement about a homeland has been produced.

In Figure 6–2, PKK fighters are moving out of Turkey into their safe haven in northern Iran. Several women are in the group; they often serve as snipers in PKK units. These fighters are not expecting contact with their enemy or there would be greater distance between the fighters. Under military Western doctrine, if there was a possibility of contact with the enemy they would be in several shorter columns so maximum firepower could be rushed to the front quickly. Several of the people in photograph are looking up and to their right and a woman is smiling, suggesting the column may be approaching a guide, meeting a PKK patrol, arriving at a place where trucks will pick them up, or are near or entering a base camp. In short, they are feeling safe.

In 2014, the military successes of the Islamic State, particularly in northern Iraq, created thorny public policy problems for the United States. There was no interest in putting large numbers of troops back into Iraq, but the Islamic State was murdering people who did not share in and refused to join their faith. The minority Yazidi were given harsh treatment; reports circulated that perhaps many as 500 of them were buried alive. The Yazidis and other refugees fleeing the Islamic State retreated to Mount Sinjar, where American air strikes kept the Islamic State forces at bay, allowing many of the trapped refugees to travel to safer locations, such as areas controlled by the Kurds and Syria. The PKK fought the Islamic State on the ground, although they badly needed heavier weapons. However, because the PKK is designated as a foreign terrorist organization, the United States was reluctant to provide them. Moreover, doing so would be likely to anger Turkey, a strong American ally, who might later see the PKK use those weapons against it in the PKK's drive for a Kurdish homeland.

Although Chapter 2 discussed the **Revolutionary Armed Forces of Columbia People's Army (FARC)**, a few additional comments are relevant. Although FARC wages a war against the Columbian national government it is unlike the PKK. FARC is neither separatist nor

Kurdistan Workers Party (PKK)

An ethnic Kurdish terrorist group fighting to create a homeland for ethnic Kurds in northern Iraq and Southeastern Turkey; responsible for significant deaths of Turkish civilians (over 20,000) during the past two decades.

Revolutionary Armed Forces of Columbia People's Army (FARC)

The FARC in Columbia wages an insurgency against its national government, but that insurgency is not nationalistic. FARC grew out of the Columbian Communist Party of the 1960s.[16] It is therefore unsurprising that traditionally FARC's ideology has been based on seizing control of the government in order to institute socialist reforms.

FIGURE 6–2
The PKKs are carrying AK-47 type assault rifles A thick black stem to the right of the fighter wearing the blue and white shemagh around his neck is too thick to be a gun barrel and may be one end of a rocket-propelled grenade, possibly a RPG-7 or RPG-9.

(Iraq/Reuters/Newscom)

nationalist. Its ideology is based on seizing control of the government in order to institute socialist reforms.[17] However, FARC is not rabidly attached to its Marxist underpinning.[18] Arguably, it has a serious orientation toward gaining some territorial control from which to further its violent for-profit criminal enterprises, including kidnapping, hijacking, extortion, and controlling the illicit drug industry.[19]

In 2014, FARC and the Columbian national government were in peace talks that began in Cuba in 2012. Columbian President Santos accused FARC with "playing with fire" for its continuing attacks while at the peace table. Prospects are not high that this round of talks will finally settle the 50-year old conflict.[20]

2) Providing *leadership* is a crucial enterprise. Terrorist organizations are often embedded in, operate in, or travel through countries that are opposed to them. Even in so-called safe havens terrorist leaders and facilities are vulnerable to special operations raids and drone attacks Moreover, because top leaders in terrorist organizations are subject to special efforts to capture or kill them it is a hazardous occupation. In Afghanistan the United States Joint Special Operations Command (JSOC) maintained a list of people it wanted to capture or kill.[21] The Joint Prioritized Effect List (JPEL) began with Taliban and al-Qaeda leaders, but it eventually grew to some 2,000 names.[22] As a former member described it, JPEL had the best weapons, the best people, and plenty of money to burn, growing from a tight unit of 200 to several thousand people.[23]

The structure of a terrorist organization will dictate to some degree the importance of top and mid-level leadership. Charismatic leaders have personal qualities and express ideas that attract followers. An excellent public speaker, Hitler projected strength, national pride, and gave the people "enemies" to revile. People with charismatic qualities can draw people into terrorist movements and sustain their fervor.[24] If there are few levels of leadership in the organization, the chain of command is simple and the "Supreme leader" becomes more important because the leader is often present and available to followers. In more complex organizations that are dispersed geographically and that have multiple layers of leadership, the "supreme leader" becomes more of a symbolic or spiritual figure and middle managers take on more substantial face-to-face leadership responsibilities, especially for operations. With reference to al-Qaeda, Neumann, Evans, and Pantucci describe the role of middle managers as being the "connective tissue" that creates the organization's center of gravity.[25]

3) *Recruiting* identifies potential recruits and draws them into the organization, which fulfills four important needs for terrorist organizations: (1) import new energy; (2) acquire new sets of skills; (3) increase operational capabilities; and (4) replace losses caused by fighters being captured (see Figure 6–3), fighters "quitting the cause," defections to other terrorist groups or government forces, and casualties. Some recruitment efforts are aimed at recruiting people who don't fit the profile of a terrorist, for example, recruiting more

FIGURE 6–3

In Afghanistan, Taliban prisoners carry water back from a river to cook their evening meals. Note the AK-47 type rifle in the guard's hand.

(Сергей жуков Itar-Tass Photos/ Newscom)

women to become suicide bombers. A major challenge in recruiting new members is identifying those who can be indoctrinated to the degree that they are willing to risk death or die to help achieve the goals of the terrorist organization. Roughly 3 percent of terrorist movements fail because they cannot replenish their ranks.[26]

There is no single uniform recruiting process used to bring recruits into a terrorism group; the process varies and is tailored to different geographic regions that have their own political, religious, and social histories, to the recruiting pool, and finally, the individual.[27] For example, a "pitch" to young men and women will differ according to the following circumstances: (1) if potential recruits are from a privileged class the appeal might be framed in terms of patriotic or religious duty; (2) members from lower classes can be led to see joining as an advancement in social class; and (3) when parents are disapproving or opposed to their adult children involving themselves with a terrorist organization, recruiters tell their children that it is an opportunity to gain their independence through the "self-discovery" of who they really are.[28] MI5, the British intelligence agency, did a study of several hundred terrorists and extremists known to be involved as fund raisers or planning bombings in Britain and concluded they were mainly males, "demographically unremarkable," radicalized in the early to mid-20s, and did not follow some "typical pathway to extremism." Most were British nationals, not recent immigrants, usually religious novices, and many lacked religious literacy.[29] Many were over 30 years of age, married, and had children. Those studied were neither gullible nor unaccomplished; most were employed in lower level jobs and their educations ran from modest accomplishments to college degrees.[30] Over half of the sample were born in the United Kingdom and acquired radical views there. Both terrorists and extremists tend to be from the second generation of families, children of those who immigrated to Great Britain.[31]

Recruiting may take place in prisons, mosques, refugee camps, coffee shops, soccer games, the Internet, and other places where people come together. Originally, Hamas recruited from refugee camps, but it now takes a longer view. It spends perhaps as much as 60 percent of its annual budget on orphanages, sports clubs, health clinics, and other social institutions, which has a double effect: It creates loyalty toward Hamas, as well as develops deep pools from which to recruit.[32] Recruiting may be conducted to acquire the people or skills needed for a specific mission or for some other purpose, such as simply increasing the number of "foot soldiers."[33]

In addition to recruiting, Hamas uses cartoons to indoctrinate the young. FarFour the Mouse bears a remarkable resemblance to Disney's Mickey Mouse, but is not amusing. He is used to teach children the importance of Islamic domination and hatred toward Israel (see Figure 6–4).

FIGURE 6–4
In his last episode, FarFour is beaten to death by an "Israeli official" for refusing to sell his land.[34] The teen host of the show, Sara, describes the death as being martyred for defending his land, killed by the killers of children.

(*Mohammed Saber/EPA/Newscom*)

The Recruiting Pool

The Recruiting Process

Targets Resist

No Further Contact

Some Targets Respond

Recruitment Successful

Complete Training

FIGURE 6–5
The terrorist recruiting funnel.
Source: Scott Gerwehr and Sara Daly, *Al Qaida: Terrorist Selection and Recruitment* (Santa Monica: RAND Corporation, 2006), p. 77 and in D. Kamien, *Homeland Security Handbook* (New York: McGraw-Hill, 2007), p. 77. This figure represents a process and is not a precise mathematical representation.

The recruiting process can be thought of as a funnel through which potential recruits pass (see Figure 6–5). According to Weimann, who identified some 5,000 terrorist websites, terrorist organizations are technologically sophisticated, using social media sites to recruit, including YouTube, Twitter, Facebook, MySpace, chat rooms, and other sites.[35] The Global Islamic Media Front (GIMF) released an encryption program on the Internet in seven languages to provide secure communication for popular messaging networks including AOL Instant Messenger, Google Talk, and Yahoo Messenger.[36]

The key advantage Internet recruiting provides is that it allows terrorist movements to recruit without any geographical boundaries. Recruiting foreigners is a priority because it reduces the effectiveness of profiles aimed at identifying ethnic terrorists. Therefore, Investigative agencies mine data from Internet sites for intelligence.

With some recruits little or no recruitment is needed; they are already substantially self-radicalized. A Somali citizen legally living in Minnesota illustrates this point. Mahamud Said Omar made arrangements for 20 or more ethnic Somalian men to return to their native land and jihad against government troops with al-Shabaab, an al-Qaeda affiliate. At least two of them are believed to have killed themselves in suicide bombings. Omar received a 20-year prison term plus probation for life following his release from confinement.[37]

Retention of existing members is somewhat akin to the ongoing recruitment of them. Despite such efforts, there is voluntary turnover in the ranks of experienced members which Jacobson explains as (1) disillusionment with the group's strategies and tactics; (2) a lack of respect for the group's leadership; (3) resentment from taking orders from leaders who have never served on the battlefield, particularly when unnecessary casualties are seen to be caused by the leaders' inexperience; (4) a perceived inequity of

Quick Facts
Voices of Those Who Left Terrorist Groups

Recruiters are good at telling you what you want to hear; they push all of your emotional buttons, but life in the training camps is harsh and unexciting, nothing like what you were promised. Then you get used as cannon fodder. Al-Qaeda has interpreted Islam in a way they is reprehensible and illegitimate. There is hypocrisy by leaders. They have abandoned the pursuit of altruistic goals in favor of pursuing their own self-interest.[38]

Quick Facts
Learning How to Make a Suicide Vest on the Internet

Increased bandwidths and new software allows unsophisticated terrorists users to develop and disseminate complex information via the Internet. A militant Islamic group posted a 26-minute video clip on the Internet that teaches how to develop a suicide vest and how to use it on a bus.[39] Once on the Internet the video gave the group a worldwide cyber footprint that also gained it publicity.

compensation as compared to the members' contributions; (5) favoritism by leaders; (6) pleas to leave the group from families and friends outside the movement with whom the member has maintained contacts; and (7) switching from one group to another because they can be paid better, their families will be fed, or for other pragmatic reasons.[40]

4) The cheapest and fastest means of generating *publicity* is by using the Internet to communicate with three different target audiences: (1) reach out to current and potential supporters who can make donations and purchase T-shirts, badges, flags, publications, and compact disks with music or propaganda videos on them; (2) shape favorable international public opinion by the site's content, which may be in a half-dozen or more languages; and (3) demoralize enemy publics by threatening operations, to stimulate public debate about their cause, and to weaken support for enemy regimes.[41]

Terrorist movements use the Internet to distribute their propaganda, to communicate with their followers and supporters, to foster public awareness of their existence and goals, to generate sympathy for their cause, to engage in psychological warfare, to raise funds, to recruit and mobilize, to ferment violence, and even to execute missions/attacks. Tools for self-learning are also available on the Internet, such as conducting counter surveillance.

On the internet, Al Qaeda distributed a 51-page step-by-step manual, "The Art of Recruiting Mujahedeen". At each step instructions are provided and points allowed for how successful the recruiter is in performing them. If in a particular chapter the recruiter doesn't get enough points, all steps needed to be repeated until he/she does. Al-Qaeda also publishes an online magazine, *Inspire*, to communicate its propaganda around the globe.

The Internet has no to little regulation and censorship, it provides global coverage, huge audiences can be reached, it's inexpensive to develop and maintain a website, there is anonymity for the communicator, and it provides a multimedia platform. Moreover, by providing information about their organization, terrorist movements can to some degree influence how the regular news media treats them.[42]

Information Link
Visit https://PublicIntelligence.net and search for "Inspire Magazine" to see a cross section of articles from that source.

Typically a site will provide a history of the organization and its activities; a detailed summary of its political and social background; accounts of notable exploits; biographies of its leaders, founders, heroes, and imprisoned comrades; information about its goals; fierce criticism of its enemies; identification of its allies and competitors; up-to-date news; and press releases.[43] Separatist and nationalist movements generally display a map of the contested geographical area: Hamas displays a map of Palestine and FARC's site shows a map of Columbia. Most sites mention the "armed struggle" in which they are engaged. Even if they discuss the legitimacy of their use of violence, most sites refrain from mentioning their deadly actions and the fatalities caused by them. Two

Since its inception in 2010, Al-Qaeda has periodically released new issues of its online *Inspire* magazine. The Spring 2014 issue calls for car bombs to be used against targets in New York, Washington, D.C., Chicago, Los Angeles, and locations in England and France.[44] Specific targets are suggested, such as the Chicago Board of Trade, the Louvre art gallery (Paris), and the Savoy Hotel (London).[45] Instructions are also provided for making bombs and a suggested disguise of Santa Claus for a Christmas attack.[46] There is concern that *Inspire* will play a role in radicalizing young Americans.[47]

exceptions to this rule are Hamas and Hezbollah, whose sites feature updated statistical reports about their daily actions (daily operations) and tallies of "dead martyrs," and "collaborators" killed.[48]

On the Internet there are also some known password-protected sites believed to be jihadist chatrooms. Two of these, al-Ekhlass and al-Hesbah, are thought to be associated with al-Qaeda, whose propaganda arm releases approximately 80 "official" videos annually to keep al-Qaeda in the public eye and to generate support for it.[49]

The Six Operational Tools

Terrorist movements need operational tools in order to generate attacks. We have modified Cragin and Daly's list of operational tools by combining several categories. The operational tools are:

1) A *command and control system*, which is a necessary step and the mechanism by which terrorist movements plan, staff, train, coordinate, and execute their attacks.[50] This mechanism is also referred to as C and C or C2. The stage of development and size of a terrorist organization influences how this function is executed. The **Provisional Irish Republican Army (PIRA)**, whose members were called "Provos," officially ended its terrorist campaign against Britain for a unified Ireland in 2005; two years later an independent commission concluded PIRA had decommissioned its weapons and was committed to the political path.[51] However, when PIRA declared a ceasefire in 1997, a splinter group, the **Real Irish Republican Army (RIRA)**, broke away from PIRA to continue the fight for a unified Republic of Ireland. Today, both RIRA and the Continuity Irish Republican Army (CIRA) are considered terrorist organizations.[52]

Because RIRA is concentrated in a small geographical area, its C2 needs are limited and directions[53] can often be given face-to-face or by couriers who only have to travel a short distance. Still, British authorities have had great success in penetrating RIRA, imprisoning at least 46 of its members and disrupting operations.[54] In a similar fashion, in the early 1990s Hamas was roughly in the same situation as RIRA, but now its C2 is more sophisticated and includes multiple C2 commands and "replacement teams" in the event that one or more members of a forthcoming operation are arrested or assassinated by Israeli security forces.[55] FARC's present C2 consists of middle managers giving strategic guidance to operational commanders who have discretion in the way they achieve the overall objectives.[56] In terms of disrupting terrorist operations, having intelligence that allows targeting the C2 is a major asset.

2) Acquiring *weapons* and a reliable source of spare parts to repair them—to replace combat losses and to resupply ammunition—is an essential tool for terrorists. The arms in the inventory of a terrorist movement are likely to consist of a mixture of those supplied by individual and state sponsors or by other terrorist organizations; purchased with drugs, money, or gemstones from the illicit weapons black market; or captured. In the first two decades of the last century the Irish Republican Army helped Ireland achieve independence from Great Britain by relying on captured weapons to a substantial degree. This tactic continues to work: In 2000, FARC raided a Columbian naval base and acquired substantial armaments, including mortars and claymore mines.

Provisional Irish Republican Army (PIRA)
The Provisional Irish Republican Army was the first and primary movement in Ireland to use terrorism as a means to justify its revolt against Great Britain and gain world status as a separate nation (Ireland). The group officially ended its campaign against Great Britain for a unified and separate Ireland in 2005, and now continues in political dialogue for the same goal.

Real Irish Republican Army (RIRA)
The Real Irish Republican Army in Northern Ireland uses terrorist tactics to support its ideology of a unified Ireland; RIRA is a successor to the original PIRA.

FIGURE 6–6
Pakistani security officials show vests and ball bearings to be used with them in suicide bomber attacks. In addition to the suicide vest materials, the raid resulted in the arrests of four men and the seizure of guns and ammunition.

(*Rahat Dar/EPA/Newscom*)

Operational space
This term means having a sanctuary or safe haven where attacks can be safely planned, trained for, and rehearsed.

Safe havens
A place or situation that allows illicit actors, including criminals, smugglers, and terrorists, to operate with relative impunity.

Bekaa Valley
Located in Lebanon, it has perhaps the longest continuous history as an operational space for terrorist groups.

The arms inventory of terrorist movements is a crude indicator of their size, intentions, and capabilities. That inventory and the operational terrain also influence the tactics terrorists can use offensively and defensively. The opposing force also influences the weapons needed by terrorists. In 2013, anti-government forces battling the Syrian government were desperate to be supplied with surface-to-air missiles to counter the government's aircraft attacks. The next year in Iraq, the Islamic State captured vast weapons from the Iraqi Army, including some armored personnel carriers and tanks, which enhanced IS's combat capabilities.

At the low end of the spectrum, small terrorist organizations are likely to be limited to small arms, which are primarily pistols, rifles, and light machine guns.* Explosives are also likely to appear in their inventory.

3) Having an **operational space** means a physical sanctuary or safe haven where attacks can be safely planned, trained for, and rehearsed (see Figure 6–7).[57] During the Middle Ages in Europe (Roughly 500 to 1450 A.D.), churches and monasteries could give "sanctuary" to persons fleeing justice or prosecution, a place where they would be safe. The laws regulating sanctuaries varied by period and kingdom, somewhat akin to the present conditions under which some nations tolerate the presence of terrorist movements within their borders.

Safe havens are a place or situation that allows illicit actors, including criminals, smugglers, and terrorists, to operate with relative impunity.[58] Other advantages include that the terrorists can organize, plan, raise funds, communicate, recruit, train, and operate with a reasonable or higher degree of security.[59]

In the modern terrorism period Lebanon's **Bekaa Valley** has perhaps the longest continuous history as an operational space for terrorist groups.[60] Although some think a territory controlled by a terrorists is different from a safe haven,[61] we view it is being a special case of a safe haven, an area tightly patrolled and policed by a terrorist group.

One way of thinking about operational space is the types of settings that are used as safe havens. Lamb identifies four settings for safe havens:[62]

a) The classic *land safe haven* is a region that is remote, possesses rugged terrain, and has a low population density, little or no government presence, and a dense vegetation cover, although even some desert territory might provide adequate cover. A prime example of a remote land safe haven is Waziristan,[63] a mountainous region of 4,500 square miles in northwest Pakistan, bordering Afghanistan. In the 1950s, when Fidel Castro's communist July 26th Movement was waging an insurgency against Cuba's government, his forces used the Sierre Maestra mountains as a remote land safe haven. Those mountains are heavily forested, offering excellent concealment, with deep ravines and steep terrain which provided the insurgents excellent defensive positions and broke up and isolated attacking forces. Safe havens are further discussed in the next chapter.

b) *Urban safe havens* include both traditional urbanized areas and non-traditional suburbs such as squatter villages and shantytowns. Carlos Marighella advocated attacking dictators from urban bases of operation, whereas Fanon argued for the opposite: rural-based fighters entering cities to inflict severe acts of terrorism to inspire fear. The sheer size of cities provides a degree of anonymity to terrorists because they can "hide in plain sight." Some European and Asian cities also have "no go" areas seldom visited by the police, such as the Islamic Sharia zones, which can provide safe houses for terrorists.

*Light machineguns fire a round that is 7.62 mm or less.

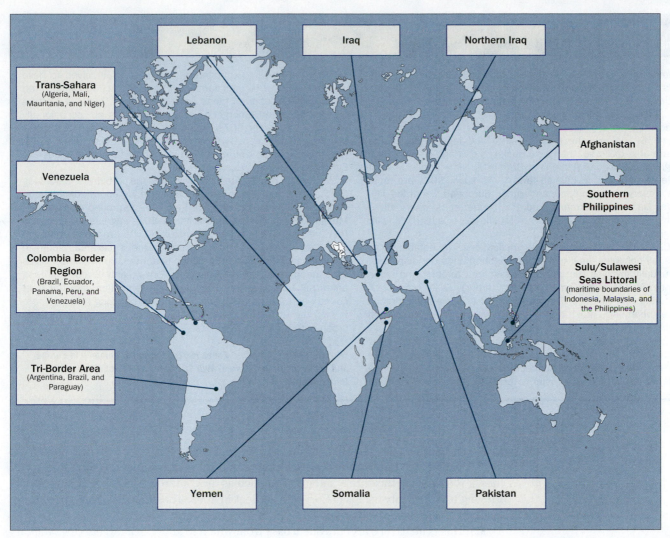

FIGURE 6–7
Remote land safe havens.

Source: Jacquelyn L. Williams-Bridger, "Combating Terrorism." Statement before the House of Representatives Subcommittee on Oversight, Investigations, and Management of the Committee on Homeland Security, June 3, 2011, p. 5.

The Provisional Irish Republican Army established no-go areas in the minority Catholic sections of some Northern Ireland cities, openly patrolling the streets and manning roadblocks while carrying weapons. If British soldiers entered the area, "Hen Patrols" would warn of their approach and movement by rattling the tops of garbage pails while children blew whistles.[64]

In 2005, a series of bomb attacks by a homegrown jihadist cell in London, England, killed 53 people and wounded more than 700. The attacks demonstrate that an urban setting can be a safe haven. All four suicide bombers lived in cities near London.[65] Three men were second-generation British citizens of Pakistani parents. The fourth man was born in Jamaica and converted to Islam. In England, he met and married a British citizen who had also adopted Islam as her religion. The men apparently met in Muslim circles and bonded. On the day of the bombings fixed video cameras recorded the men meeting and hugging, then going their separate ways. One of them entered a shop and bought a battery for his detonator. Soon bombs exploded on trains and a double-decker bus. Al-Qaeda claimed credit for the attacks. One of bombers left behind a video in which he claimed the attacks were because democratically elected governments continuously perpetrated atrocities against Muslim people.

Some terrorist movements have no substantial alternative to using an urban sanctuary because the geography in which they are located has few or no remote land safe areas. The Real Irish Republican Armey in Northern Ireland illustrates this point.

c) *Maritime safe havens* are situated on lands bordering littoral or shallow waters, such as the 7,100 islands in the Philippines,[66] as well as along rivers that flow to the ocean.

Box 6-1
Sharia Controlled Zones

Extremist Islamic Sharia Controlled Zones (SCZs) are neighborhoods in Western nations where extremist Muslims have substantially or totally driven out non-Muslims to establish their own social, political, and legal control.

The extremists' goal is to rule an area in which they can administer Sharia law, the Islamic moral and legal code. Where they are able to do so, the larger society's civil and criminal laws are ignored. Sixty-one percent of British Muslims surveyed want Sharia as opposed to English laws.[67] As such, SCZs are most often observed in England and other European countries like France, Denmark, Germany, and the Netherlands where there is a high percentage population of Muslims, particularly Muslim immigrants.

SCZs have immediate crime implications. To establish the zones, all non-Muslims living in the neighborhoods are displaced. This usually involves the use of harassment, threats, and some violence. Non-Muslim women passing through SCZs have been threatened with violence. They are told not to come back through the neighborhood unless their face is covered. Those suspected of being gay have also been threatened.

These extremist Muslims reject integration into the larger society. In the end, they want to supplant the larger society. For instance, British authorities suspect that 117 Muslim women were murdered as "honor kills." Islamic practice permits fathers and brothers to kill wives, daughters, and sisters perceived to have brought dishonor to their families.[68] A lack of cooperation often thwarts investigation of these and other crimes. To make matters worse, police and emergency services vehicles are occasionally stoned if they enter SCZs. Radicalized Muslims are not tolerant of other lifestyles, cultures, and religions in designated SCZs. They represent an entirely different culture than their moderate European Muslim counterparts.

In France, there are some 717 Zone Urbaines Sensibles (ZUSs, Sensitive Urban Zones) that are deteriorated neighborhoods. An unknown number of them are controlled by extremist Muslims. Police may not patrol these SCZs aggressively because they are wary of a Muslim response if arrests are made. Although SCZs are not present in the United States, such areas seem to be increasing throughout European countries. In 2014, new SCZs have been observed in Belgium, Norway, and Sweden. These areas set up the prospect of continuous conflict with the host country and diverts resources from other pressing issues. There is also the unsettling prospect of SCZs providing a comfortable urban safe haven for terrorists.

Why are Sharia Controlled Zones (SCZs) somewhat common in Europe and not in the United States? Will SCZs ever be established in the United States?

Such safe havens allow terrorists to move equipment and personnel from one country to another rapidly on the vastness of oceans and to take advantage of poorly monitored coastlines.[69] Recognizing this threat and missions such as drug interdiction, the U.S. Navy began bringing littoral combat ships (LCSs) into its fleet in 2008. These smaller, high-speed ships can operate in waters of 20 or less feet.

Maritime safe havens also provide a base from which to attack sea targets (e.g., military and civilian vessels, ferries, and oil and natural gas platforms) and to attack resorts and port facilities from the sea.[70] As an illustration, in 2009, Egyptian authorities foiled an al-Qaeda plot to bomb foreign ships in the Suez Canal and the pipelines adjacent to it; the terrorists included 24 Egyptian engineers and technicians lead by a Palestinian man.[71] The plot was funded by contributions to Islamic charities and training was received via a jihad website.[72] The terrorists also robbed and murdered an Egyptian Christian jeweler to help fund their operation.[73]

d) *Virtual safe havens* exist in cyberspace and are used as a strategy to avoid being detected by security forces. As noted in the previous chapter, virtual terrorist safe havens are presently cell-sized and not complete organizations.

4) For most recruits to terrorist groups, *training* begins with an initial emphasis on indoctrination, physical conditioning, small arms familiarization, marksmanship, and basic martial arts.[74] More advanced topics include planting bombs, and tactics for assaulting military convoys and installations. Some terrorists will receive training for specialized functions, such as sniping, bomb building, car hijacking, hostage taking, and eliminating sentries.

The war on safe havens seems to have spelled the end of large training camps, such as al-Qaeda had in Afghanistan under the Taliban pre-9/11. The concurrent shift in al-Qaeda's strategy to small independent cells and regional attacks has resulted in substantial terrorist "e-learning" courses becoming available on the Internet on a variety of courses, including bomb-making manuals by one of al-Qaeda's weapons masters, Abdullah Dhu al-Bajadin, an assumed identity. As part of the effort to monitor terrorist e-learning the University of Arizona collects and analyzes data from 4,300 Islamic terrorist websites.[75]

5) *Intelligence and Counterintelligence*

From a terrorist organization's view, intelligence is the collection, processing, integration, analysis, evaluation, and interpretation of available information on a specific subject, for example, the current intentions of America against the Islamic State. Intelligence must be delivered with conclusions useful to the terrorist "client" in need of it. The mere collection of data without any processing does not constitute intelligence. In contrast, a terrorist's counterintelligence (CI) activities are a security tool comprised of activities dedicated to undermining the effectiveness of the intelligence activities of America and its allies.[76]

During the post-9/11 war in Afghanistan, the Taliban has been repeatedly characterized as having an impressive ability to collect and exploit intelligence.[77] It has advance knowledge of at least some impending allied operations that transcends mere chance.[78] Illustratively, the United Kingdom's Prime Minister David Cameron was forced to cancel a visit to an Afghanistan military outpost because the Taliban was already aware of it.[79] Chapter 9 discusses intelligence and counterintelligence more fully.

> **Information Link**
> Like "terrorism," there are a number of definitions of intelligence. This link to the Central Intelligence Agency explores some of these definitions: https://www.cia.gov/library/center-for-the-study-of-intelligence/csi-publications/csi-studies/studies/vol46no3/article02.html.

6) With few exceptions, such as financially secure lone wolves, *finance* is of continuing concern to terrorist leaders, regardless of whether they are small cells or large transnational organizations that are somewhat akin to international business conglomerates.

Following 9/11, substantial interest quickly developed in denying terrorists the use of normal banking channels. As a result, new banking regulations were put into place, new programs established, such as the U.S. Department of Treasury's Terrorist Finance Tracking Program (TFTP), interagency task forces were formed, and diplomatic pressure placed on countries that were passive supporters of terrorism (e.g., generally not taking actions to create more control over their geographical space and/or financial transactions).[80] Subsequently, the European Union arrested 80 people in a single year for financing separatist groups in Spain and France.[81] As financial intelligence was created, it became a formidable weapon. A sample of 500 FBI terrorist investigations revealed that 42 percent of them were aided by financial intelligence.[82] It also was important in preventing a terrorist attack on in English airport and in tracking down a senior terrorist leader, Hambali, the suspected mastermind of a bombing in Bali.[83]

Hawalas

In response to growing pressure from formal banking systems, terrorists began making greater use of alternative remittance systems (ARSs), particularly the **hawala**. This is an informal and often unregulated remittance system that operates from many countries conducting domestic and international transactions.[84] It was developed in India before formal banking practices were introduced. In some cities of the world Hawala services are openly advertised.[85] Hawalas are a faster and safer means than using a courier who could be arrested for currency violations or another offense while traveling. Illegal aliens also use the hawala or other alternative remittance system to send money home to their families in order to avoid all official contacts that might expose them to deportation.

Hawala
An Asian-based alternative remittance system that is based on trust and which allows users to remain unknown and escape contact with banking and other officials.

Hawalas are distinguished from traditional banks by (1) strong trust; they are illegal in some countries, yet they operate effectively and efficiently without regulatory oversight or any legal recourse; (2) hawala dealers are often bound together by family, business partners, or regional connections; (3) they make minimal use of formal negotiable instruments; (4) no money is actually transferred between hawalas; (5) the transactions take place based on communications between members of a network of hawaladars or hawala dealers; (6) hawalas operate with little paperwork and what exists is minimal and often in codes; (7) they provide better currency exchange rates than banks offer; (8) the person receiving the money gets it fast, within hours to a day or two at most; (9) some hawaladars are open and available 24-hours a day, such as local grocery stores; and (10) all taxes are avoided.[86]

FIGURE 6–8
A hypothetical hawala transaction.

Hawaladars typically charge a 2 to 5 percent transaction fee and operate out of a regular business, such as jewelry store, pawnshop, travel agency, or used car business. Being hawaladars is often not their principal work. Figure 6–8 depicts a hawala transaction.

In Figure 6–8, Ibrahim in Karachi, Pakistan, wants to send $5,000 to his nephew Salim in Baltimore. Ibrahim goes to a Javeria, a Karachi hawaladar, and pays her $5,000, plus a transaction fee of 5 percent. Javeria sends the order by phone, fax, or Internet to Obaid, a hawaladar in Baltimore, but sends no money. In person, Obaid pays Salim in cash. Obaid now has a credit of $5,000 with Javeria for when he wants her to pay someone. For purposes of illustration, we will assume Salim will use the money to buy materials with which to make several bombs.

Among the other ways to disperse money secretly between entities is manipulating invoices with a colluding partner. Assume Company A is a foreign exporter who sends 50,000 scarfs, actually valued at $2 each, to Company B, a domestic importer in another country. However, company A invoices the cost of the scarfs at $1 each. Company B pays Company $50,000 and subsequently sells the scarfs for $100,000, their actual value. Company B then disperses the excess $50,000 made according to the instructions of Company A.

BitCoin
An online money that can be bought, transferred to someone else, or sold. If sold a check is sent to your bank account. Although it is an interesting system, BitCoin is struggling to find even modest acceptance in the marketplace.

In mid-2014, **BitCoin** was being studied by several federal agencies to determine if terrorists could use it as an alternative remittance system or otherwise gain an advantage from using it. The system appeared online in 2009, apparently developed by an anonymous person identified as Satoshi Nakamoto. BitCoins can be bought, transferred to someone else, and sold online. If sold, a check is sent to your bank account, where all transactions are recorded. BitCoins are accepted by a few merchants online. Although it is an interesting system, BitCoin is struggling to find even modest acceptance in the marketplace.

Narco-Terrorism

As the efforts to financially strangle terrorists continued, state and individual sponsorship of terrorists generally declined. An unintended consequence was that it pushed terrorist organizations toward the drug trade. The illegal global drug trade may amount to as much as $1.5 trillion annually and for some time terrorist movements have derived a portion of their income from it.[87] The United Nations estimates that $2.3 billion from the drug trade ends up in the coffers of terrorists, much of it with larger transnational organizations.[88] Interpol concluded that the main source of income for terrorist organizations comes from involvement in the drug trade.[89] The PKK, IRA, Kosovo Liberation Army, ETA, Sendero Luminoso (Shining Path), and other terrorist groups all profit from the drug trade.

Narco-terrorism originally referred to campaigns of extreme violence, including torture, beheadings, bombings, and assassinations by drug traffickers against competitors, the police, and others. Columbian Pablo Escobar (1949–1993) led the Medellin Cartel that controlled 80 percent of the cocaine shipped to the United States and was identified by

Quick Facts
Pablo Escobar

Escobar is described as being both from a poor family or from a lower middle-class family. Reportedly, as a child he was sent home from school because his family was so poor it could not afford the required shoes. He started life as a petty street criminal and later took over a drug trafficking ring. The head of it was reportedly killed on Escobar's orders.

As Escobar amassed wealth, he used some of it to curry favor with the people, for example, building soccer fields, hospitals, and schools, positioning himself as a modern-day Robin Hood.

Escobar also built a private zoo that people could visit for free. Following his death several hippos escaped. They reproduced, and now a small group of them runs wild in Columbia.[90]

After 15 months, Escobar escaped from his luxury prison and was soon on the run from Columbian authorities, who were reportedly aided by a constellation of U.S. law enforcement agencies and a highly skilled U.S. military counterterrorism unit. In 1993, he was killed in a gunfight with his pursuers.

Fortune and *Forbes* magazines as one of the ten wealthiest people in the world.[91] To build and maintain this empire the Medellin Cartel killed three candidates for Columbia's presidency, over 200 judges, and in excess of 1,000 police officers.[92]

A common threat by the Medellin Cartel to public officials was "Plato o plomo" (Silver or lead), meaning accept the bribe or be killed. The mutilated bodies left on the streets of Mexican towns along America's southern border is a manifestation of narco-terrorism as drug traffickers fight each other for dominance. Among the major Mexican drug syndicates are Los Zetas, Caballeros Templarios, and the Sinaloa Cartel.

Narco-terrorism also refers to some nexus or connection of terrorist organizations with the drug trade. To illustrate, terrorists may be (1) at the margin of the drug trade, (e.g., for a fee they protect the coca plants from which cocaine is made or guard the clandestine laboratories that produce cocaine) or 2) they are engaged more fully in the drug trade to maximize their profit. In Columbia, FARC began its involvement with "taxing" coca plant producers for protecting them from government forces and right-wing paramilitary groups. FARC later gradually extended its participation to include production and trafficking in order to maximize its profits. Its earnings are estimated to be $400–$600 million annually. Al-Qaeda and the Taliban control lands in Pakistan and Afghanistan that grow poppies, as well as the laboratories that turn them into heroin. With the help of drug lords, the heroin is moved to Europe and sold, creating an annual income of $20 billion.

To reduce the income of terrorists and criminal organizations, the police adopted the strategy of eradicating poppy fields and coca tree crops. In response, terrorist and criminal organizations began producing synthetic drugs to make up for their lost revenue. Millions of dollars now flow to the Middle East from the sale of synthetic drugs like K-2, Spice, and Blaze.[93] A 2014 nationwide raid on synthetic drug dealers in 29 states resulted in 150 arrests and the seizure of more than $150 million in cash and assets, along with a ton of drugs.[94] At just one store selling synthetic drugs in Birmingham federal agents discovered evidence of $38 million being sent to Yemen, where it is suspected that some portion of it ended up in terrorist hands.[95] Parenthetically, synthetic drugs are also called designer drugs, because new chemical formulations are created. Once a drug compound is banned, the manufacturers change the formula somewhat to make it legal and began selling it under a different name.

Traditional for Profit Crimes

In Mali, a German official exited a military plane with three suitcases filled with 5 million euros.[96] Officially, the money was budgeted in 2014 for humanitarian relief.[97] Instead, it was paid to obscure Islamic extremists for the release of 32 European hostages.[98] Although countries publically proclaim they do not pay ransom, some number of them do: In just 2013, al-Qaeda and its affiliates were paid $66 million to free hostages they had taken.[99]

The U.S. Treasury calculates that in 2013, $165 million was paid in ransom to terrorists worldwide.[100] Each transaction reinforces the terrorists' belief that kidnapping is a good line of business in which to be. One al-Qaeda leader described it as "an easy spoil."[101]

On its face, cooperation between terrorist organizations and criminal groups does not seem likely. Terrorists seek publicity and organized criminal groups prefer to stay in the shadows, avoiding official attention. If terrorists groups are successful in establishing a homeland, or in the case of IS, a caliphate, the markets of transnational criminal organizations for drugs and other goods is likely to be destabilized. Terrorists are ideologically driven and criminal groups operate out of the profit motivation.[102] Terrorists desire to substantially alter the nature of government, replace it with their ideology, or destroy it altogether. Criminal groups want to neutralize government interference with their illegal activities and take money and things of value out of a society.

A salient advantage of cooperation between criminal organizations and terrorists is that in addition to, or in lieu of, money they can provide passports, intelligence, access to smuggling routes, and other things of value to the other party. This is a symbiotic relationship in that the exchanges between these dissimilar organizations are mutually beneficial. For example, terrorists can provide training in bomb making to drug traffickers seeking to eliminate rivals. This reduces competition in the marketplace and also helps to establish longevity.

When terrorist and criminal groups cooperate they both ultimately end up with what they need or want. The terrorists need money to buy better weapons, attract seasoned fighters from other movements, finance attacks, expand their organizations, support their charitable activities, gather intelligence, and other uses. The criminal groups want their profits. While terrorism seeks to destroy ways of life, criminal organizations are a blight on them. They corrupt public officials, weaken the economy by not paying business or personal taxes, threaten the national security of weak nations, promote violence by arms trafficking, destroy families by trafficking in humans, reduce lawful earnings by pirating music and software, and cause societies massive expenditures to fight the importation and distribution of drugs.

Al-Qaeda in the Islamic Maghreb, al-Qaeda in the Arabian Peninsula, and al-Shabaab in Somalia are all abiding by a common protocol: The seizure of the hostages is outsourced to criminal organizations, who get 10 percent of the ransom.[103]

Terrorists are not known to have counterfeited United States currency, although there is a report that a terrorist group counterfeited Indian rupees.[104] The best counterfeiter of the United Sates $100 bill is North Korea, which does so to bring in cash and to try and destabilize the American economy. Because it takes sophisticated examination to detect it, the bill is referred to as the "Super note." Terrorists do traffic in the global $500 billion counterfeit goods market, for example, Louis Vuitton purses and luggage.[105] In a single year, the black market counterfeit sales cost New York an estimated $1 billion in lost tax revenue.[106]

In Somalia, terrorists receive a portion of the money criminal organizations get from maritime piracy. Ever adaptable and quick to seize new opportunities, terrorists have a long-standing interest in using the Internet to raise money.[107] Illustratively, in the United Kingdom, 22-year-old Younis Tsouli became the premier Internet jihadist, referring to himself as "Terrorist 007."[108] Using 1,400 stolen credit card numbers and security numbers, the Moroccan-born man living in England raised and laundered the equivalent of $2.4 million, which was used to support 180 websites playing al-Qaeda propaganda videos and to buy equipment for terrorists.[109] Tsouli was arrested in 2005 and subsequently convicted.

Sponsorship, Donations, Charities, Zakat, and Sadaqah

Although it is accurate to state that state-sponsored funds and individual donations have generally declined, there are exceptions. Notably, the U.S. Department of State has called attention to the increase in Iran's support of Hezbollah, which has reached levels not seen since the 1990s.[110] As another means of growing its financial resources, some terrorist organizations have established shell corporations that claim they are for philanthropic and humanitarian purposes, but the funds collected are used to support terrorism.[111] Examples of overtly charitable organizations used for terrorism include the Global Relief Fund and the Holy Land Foundation for Relief and Development.[112] One of the duties of Muslims is **zakat**, annually giving money to be used for humanitarian purposes. Zakat is 2.5 percent of savings and earnings.[113] Some Muslims made zakat donations to charitable organizations, not realizing that instead of going for good works the money was being funneled to terrorist organizations. In addition to zakat, the Qur'an and Islamic traditions also advocate additional charitable acts of giving, sadaqah, which in some instances has also ended up in terrorist coffers.[114]

Zakat
An annual humanitarian giving by Muslims.

Convergence

There is a significant danger to terrorist organizations becoming too involved in for-profit crimes: They may lose their ideological zeal because of the substantial profits to be made. When this happens, they convert from one type of an organization to another. The Philippines-based and ultra-violent Abu Sayyaf Group (ASG) illustrates this. Nominally, ASG wants to establish an Islamic state. However, it has become so involved in for-profit criminal activities that its ideological foundation appears to be temporally eradicated.[115] Stated simply, ASG is a movement that is at the slippery convergence of terrorism and for-profit crime, a position it shares with FARC.

Chapter Summary

SUMMARY BY LEARNING OBJECTIVE

1. **Explain what restrains a terrorist movement's capability to launch certain types of attacks.**

   Internal and external considerations restrain the launching of certain types of attacks. If, for example, terrorists contemplate using biochemical weapons, they might be *externally* restrained from doing so out of fear of overwhelming reprisals and loss of public support and/or potential loss of sponsors. *Internally*, terrorist leaders might restrain certain types of attacks. As an example, Usama bin Laden ordered followers not to attack Westerns civilians because it was not having the desired effect on their governments.

2. **State why it is important for terrorist groups to become learning organizations.**

   Learning organizations are characterized by prizing the acquisition of new knowledge, being nimble when faced with new situations, and thinking "outside of the box." It is important because it can be a survival mechanism for the terrorist organization: It allows them to analyze their failures and evolve.

3. **Identify and briefly describe a terrorist movement's four organization tools.**

   The four organizational tools are (1) ideology, which represents the reason for existing; (2) leadership, which provides the oversight that steers the organization; (3) recruiting, which is acquiring followers; and (4) publicity, which calls attention to what the terrorist organization broadly intends to do and heralds its successes.

4. **Explain why adopting an ideology is important to a terrorist organization.**

   Ultimately, it is at the heart of getting someone to "pick up the gun."

5. **Provide four reasons why recruiting is so important to terrorist organizations.**

   Recruiting allows terrorist organizations to (1) import new energy, (2) acquire new sets of skills, (3) increase operational capabilities, and (4) replace losses caused by "quitting the cause," defections to other terrorist groups or government forces, and casualties.

6. **State the reasons for voluntary turnover in terrorist organizations.**

   These reasons are (1) disillusionment with the group's strategies and tactics; (2) a lack of respect for the group's leadership; (3) resentment from taking orders from leaders who have never served on the battlefield, particularly when unnecessary casualties are seen to be caused by the leaders' inexperience; (4) a perceived inequity of compensation as compared to the members' contributions; (5) favoritism by leaders; (6) pleas to leave the group from families and friends outside the movement with whom the member has maintained contacts; and (7) some terrorists switch from one group to another because they can be paid better, their families will be fed, or for other pragmatic reasons.

7. **Identify and briefly explain a terrorist movement's six operational tools.**

   These tools are (1) establishing a command and control system, which is the mechanism by which terrorist movements plan, staff, train, coordinate, and execute their attacks; (2) acquiring weapons and a reliable source of spare parts to repair them, to replace combat losses, and to resupply ammunition; (3) securing an operational space, a sanctuary or safe haven where attacks can be safely planned, trained for, and rehearsed; (4) providing training, which begins with an initial emphasis on indoctrination, physical conditioning, small arms familiarization, marksmanship, and basic martial arts. More advanced topics include planting bombs and tactics for assaulting military convoys and installations. Beyond that for some members is specialist training, such as bomb making, car hijacking, sniping, eliminating sentries, and mission-specific training; (5) using intelligence and counterintelligence as key means by which terrorists reduce their risk exposure; and (6) obtaining funds from wealthy individual sponsors or states or acquiring funds from criminal activities such as maritime piracy, bank robberies, extortion, drug and arms trafficking, counterfeiting, kidnapping for ransom, and pirating movies, music, and software.

8. Identify and briefly describe Lamb's four settings for safe havens.

Those four settings are (1) the classic remote land safe haven is a region that is remote;, possesses rugged terrain; and has low population density, little or no government presence, and a dense vegetation cover, although even some desert territory might provide adequate cover; (2) urban safe havens include both traditional urbanized areas and non-traditional suburbs such as squatter villages, shantytowns, and other types of slums that spring up around some cities; (3) maritime safe havens are situated on lands bordering littoral or shallow waters, such as the 7,100 islands in the Philippines, as well as along rivers that flow to the ocean; and (4) virtual safe havens that are like virtual organizations. Virtual safe havens exist in cyberspace and are used as a strategy to avoid being detected by security forces.

REVIEW QUESTIONS

1. Distinguish between terrorist motivations and capabilities.
2. Describe the difference between "soft" and "hard" targets.
3. What ideology characteristics do all terrorist organizations share?
4. The Internet provides what key advantages to terrorist recruiting?
5. The arms inventory of a terrorist organization is a crude indicator of what?
6. How does a Hawala operate?

CRITICAL THINKING EXERCISES

1. **The Benghazi Attack on September 11, 2012.** On the night of September 11, 2012, a large group (over 100 people) of heavily armed insurgents attacked the U.S. Consulate office in Benghazi, Libya, killing Ambassador J. Christopher Stevens, another diplomat, and two embassy security personnel. A second assault occurred the next morning, targeting a CIA compound about a mile away from the Consulate building. The event became a major issue during the 2012 U.S. Presidential elections as President Barak Obama and then-Secretary of State Hillary Clinton were assailed for not preventing nor responding correctly to the attack. Just hours before the incident, Aymen al-Zawahiri had issued a video to coincide with the anniversary of the 9/11 attacks in 2001, which called for attacks on Americans in Libya. Further, within the week before the attack, eight other diplomatic missions in the Middle East, Asia, and Europe had encountered large demonstrations and violent attacks in response to an anti-Muslim video entitled "Innocence of Muslims." The attack in Libya was initially characterized as a spontaneous protest against the video versus a planned terrorist attack launched by radical Islamists linked directly to al-Qaeda. The attack was the subject of congressional and administrative investigations focused not only on the U.S. response to the incident, but also the larger role of the CIA's presence in Libya. Search the web at the following sites to learn details relating to the attack on the U.S. Consulate in Benghazi on September 11, 2012.

Review the following *Congressional Hearings and Reports* as well:

The Security Failures of Benghazi (October 10, 2012) at http://online.wsj.com/news/articles/SB10000872396390444620104578008922056244096

Benghazi and Beyond, Part I (November 15, 2012) and ***Part II*** (December 20, 2012) at http://permanent.access.gpo.gov/gpo33415/pt1.pdf andhttp://permanent.access.gpo.gov/gpo33415/pt2.pdf.

Review of the Benghazi Attacks and Unanswered Questions (September 19, 2013) at http://www.gpo.gov/fdsys/pkg/CHRG-113hhrg85095/pdf/CHRG-113hhrg85095.pdf. Do you think that the attacks in Benghazi could have been prevented? Discuss as a class what types of security failures occurred in Benghazi and what can be done to prevent similar incidents in the future.

2. **The Evolution of Terrorist Tools and Tactics.** Terrorist tools and tactics appear to be evolving over time. Terrorists may favor attack methods that exploit perceived vulnerabilities, such as adopting active shooter tactics and find new methods of concealing dangerous nuclear, biological, or chemical materials. Further, radical Islamic terrorists will likely pursue opportunities to inflict mass casualties, particularly considering recent upheaval in the Middle East (Arab Spring) and the death of Usama bin Laden. Homegrown violent extremism will likely continue to emerge as a significant threat. These are the long-term trends identified by the Strategic Foresight Initiative sponsored by the Federal Emergency Management Agency. Read the "Evolving Terrorist Threat" at www.fema.gov/pdf/about/programs/oppa/evolving_terrorist_threat.pdf.

   In small groups of three or four students, read and discuss the above article. Do you think that our federal, state, and local governments are ready for the changes in terrorist tools and tactics that are identified in this report? How will the roles of police officers, the military, FEMA, local agencies, and first responders change to meet these challenges? Develop a potential training plan for agencies and first responders to the meet the challenges posed by future terrorists. Where are we as a nation most vulnerable, and how do we eliminate or significantly reduce this vulnerability?

NOTES

1. See Victor Asal and R. Karl Rethemeyer, "The Nature of the Beast: Organizational Structures and the Lethality of Terrorist Attacks," *The Journal of Politics*, Vol. 70, Issue 2, April 2008, pp. 437–449.

2. Loc. cit.

3. Boaz Ganor, "Terrorist Organization Types and the Probability of a Boomerang Effect," *Studies in Conflict and Terrorism*," Vol. 31, Issue 4, April 2008, pp. 279–280.

4. Almost all of these are mentioned in Ganor, "Terrorist Organization Types."

5. Nic Roberson and Paul Cruickshank, "Al Qaeda's Training Adapts to Drone Attacks," CNN. Com/Crime, July 31, 2009, www.cnn.com/crime/07/30/robertson.al.qaeda.training/index.html.

6. Charles R. Swanson, Leonard Territo, and Robert W. Taylor, *Police Administration: Structures, Processes, and Behavior* (Boston: Pearson, 2012), p. 188.

7. Kim Cragin, *Understanding Terrorist Ideology* (Santa Monica: RAND Corporation, 2004), p. 1.

8. See Christina Helimich, "Al-Qaeda—Terrorists, Hypocrites, Fundamentalists? The View From Within," *Third World Quarterly*, Vol. 26, Issue 1, February 2005, pp. 39–54.

9. Muhammad Hassan, "Key Considerations in Counter-ideological Work Against Terrorist Ideology," *Studies in Conflict and Terrorism*, Vol. 29, Issue 6, September 2006, p. 531.

10. The first four of these factors comes from Edward Newman, "Exploring the 'Root Causes' of Terrorism," *Studies in Conflict and Terrorism*, Vol. 29, Issue 8, December 2006, p. 751. Newman rejects the notion that poverty is a root cause of terrorism.

11. "6 Doctors Among 8 Held in U.K. Bomb Plot," CBS/AP, February 11, 2009, www.cbsnews.com/2100-224_162-3004644.html.

12. Alberto Abadie, "Poverty, Political Freedom, and the Roots of Terrorism," Working Paper 1085 (Cambridge, Massachusetts: National Bureau of Economic Research, October 2004), pp. 1–2.

13. Loc. cit.

14. Randy Borum, *Psychology of Terrorism* (Tampa: University of South Florida, 2004), p. 40.

15. Amir Hassanpour, "The Kurdish Experience," *Middle East Report (MER)*, 189, Vol. 24, July/August 1994, p. 2.

16. "Revolutionary Armed Forces of Columbia (FARC)," *National Consortium for the Study of Terrorism and Responses to Terrorism*, University of Maryland, p. 1. www.start.umd. edu/start/data_collections/tops/terrorist_organization_profile.asp?id=96.

17. Kim Cragin and Sara A. Daly, *The Dynamics of Terrorist Threat: An Assessment of Group Motivations and Capabilities in a Changing World* (Santa Monica: RAND Corporation, 2004), p. 32.

18. "Revolutionary Armed Forces of Columbia (FARC)," *National Consortium for the Study of Terrorism and Responses to Terrorism*, University of Maryland, p. 1. www.start.umd. edu/start/data_collections/tops/terrorist_organization_profile.asp?id=96.

19. This bones of this paragraph are drawn from Cragin and Daly, *The Dynamics of Terrorist Threat*, pp. 32–34. However, there are substantial restatements and additions.

20. Saumas Milne, "Columbian Peace Talks Will Fail Without Government Concessions FARC Warns," *The Guardian* (England), July 30, 2014, www.theguardian.com/world/2014/ jul/30/colombian-peace-talks-fail-farc-leaders-interview.

21. Jeremy Scahill, *Dirty Wars* (New York: Nations Books, 2013), p. 167.

22. Loc. cit.

23. Loc. cit.

24. Cragin and Daly, *The Dynamics of Terrorist Threat*, pp. 32–34.

25. See Peter Neumann, Ryan Evans, and Raffaello Pantucci, "Locating Al Qaeda's Center of Gravity: The Role of Middle Managers," *Studies in Conflict and Terrorism*, Vol. 34, Issue 11, pp. 825–842.

26. Leonard Weinberg and Arie Perliger, "How Terrorist Groups End," *CTC Sentinel*, Vol. 3, Issue 2, February 2010, from Table1, p. 16.

27. Scott Gerwehr and Sara Daly, *Al Qaida: Terrorist Selection and Recruitment* (Santa Monica: RAND Corporation, 2006), p. 77 and in D. Kamien, *Homeland Security Handbook* (New York: McGraw-Hill, 2007), p. 75.

28. Ibid., pp. 74–75.

29. Alan Travis, "MI5 Report Challenges Views on Terrorism in Britain," *The Guardian*, August 20, 2008, www.guardian.co.uk/uk/2008/aug/20/uksecurity.terrorism1.

30. Loc. cit.

31. Travis, "MI5 Report Challenges Views on Terrorism in Britain."

32. Cragin and Daly, *The Dynamics of Terrorist Threat*, p. 35.

33. Ibid., pp. 36–37.

34. "Mickey Mouse 'Twin' Killed on Hamas TV," *The Washington Post*, June 30, 2007, www. washingtonpost.com/wp-dyn/content/article/2007/06/29/AR2007062902105.html.

35. See Gabriel Weimann, "The Psychology of Mass-Mediated Terrorism," *American Behavioral Scientist*, Vol. 52, No. 1, September 2008, pp. 69–86.

36. "GIMF Develops 'Islamic Encryption Plugin' for Chat Programs," Site Intelligence Group, February 13, 2012, www.news.siteintelgroup.com/component/content/ article/6-jihadist-news/2733-gimf-develops-islamic-encryption-plugin-for-chat-programs.

37. This account is drawn from Amy Forliti, "Man Gets 10 Years in Somali Terror Investigation," *MPR News* (Minnesota Public Radio), May 13, 2013, http://minnesota.pub- licradio.org/display/web/2013/05/13/news/somaili-terror-investigation.

38. Source: Michael Jacobson, *Terrorist Dropouts: Learning From Those Who Have Left* (Washington, D.C.: The Washington Institute for Near East Policy, January 2010), pp. 7–8, 10, 13–14.

39. Irving Lachow and Courtney Richardson, "Terrorist Use of the Internet," *National Defense University Press*, Issue 45, 2nd Quarter, 2007, p. 100.

40. Michael Jacobson, "Why Terrorists Quit: Gaining From al-Qaida's Losses," *CTC Sentinel*, Vol. 1, Issue 8, July 15, 2008, www.ctc.usma.edu/wp-content/uploads/2010/06/vol1iss8-artl.pdf.

41. Gabriel Weimann, "How Modern Terrorism Uses the Internet," *Journal of International Security Affairs*, Number 8, Spring 2005, p. 5, www.securityaffairs.org/issues/2005/08/weimann.php, p. 4.
42. Weimann, "How Modern Terrorism Uses the Internet," pp. 5, 10–11.
43. Loc. cit., the content of this paragraph is drawn from this source with restatement.
44. Chuck Goudie, "Chicago Targets in Terrorist Crosshairs, New Al Qaeda Magazine Inspire Says," March 15, 2014, http://abc7chicago.com/archive/9467587.
45. Loc. cit.
46. Loc. cit.
47. Loc. cit.
48. Weimann, "How Modern Terrorism Uses the Internet," pp. 4–5.
49. "Computer Image Shows Washington, D.C. Devastated by al-Qaeda Nuclear Attack," *The Telegraph* (United Kingdom), May 30, 2008, www.telegraph.co.uk/news/2052575/american-apocalypse-picture-shows-washington-dc-devastated-by-al-qaeda-nuclear-attack.html.
50. Cragin and Daly, *The Dynamics of Terrorist Threat*, p. 40.
51. "Provisional Irish Republican Army (PIRA)," British Security Service, MI5, undated, but written sometime from 2007 forward, p. 5, www.mi5.gov.uk/home/the-theats/terrorism/northern-ireland/provisional-irish-republican-army-pira.html.
52. "Terrorist Designations and State Sponsors of Terrorism," U.S. Department of State, 2013, p. 1, www.state.gov/j/ct/list.
53. Cragin and Daly, *The Dynamics of Terrorist Threat*, p. 40.
54. Loc. cit.
55. Ibid., pp. 40–41.
56. Loc. cit.
57. Cragin and Daly, *The Dynamics of Terrorist Threat*, p. 45.
58. Robert D. Lamb, *Ungoverned Areas and Threats from Safe Havens* (Washington, D.C.: Final Report of the Ungoverned Areas Projects, U.S. Department of Defense, January 2008), p. 6.
59. Loc. cit.
60. "Terrorist Havens: Lebanon," Council on Foreign Relations, May 2007, www.cfr.org/lebanon/terrorism-havens-lebanon/p9516.
61. See Blake W. Mobley, *Terrorism and Counter-Intelligence: How Terrorist Groups Escape Detection* (New York: Columbia University Press, 2012), p. 14.
62. These settings, with additional commentary, are drawn from Robert D. Lamb, *Ungoverned Areas and Threats from Safe Havens* (Washington, D.C.: Department of Defense, January 2008),
63. Ibid., p. 25.
64. Mobley, *Terrorism and Counter-Intelligence*, p. 31.
65. This account is drawn from a preliminary report, Report of the Official Account of the Bombings on 7th July 2005, House of Commons (London: The Stationary Office, 2006).
66. *Terrorist Safe Havens* (Washington, D.C.: Department of State, May 30, 2013), Chapter 5, no page number, www.state.gov/j/ct/rls/crt/2012/2099987.htm.
67. Hearing Before the Subcommittee on the Middle East and Central Asia of the Committee on International Relations, U.S House of Representatives, 109th Congress, 2nd Session, September 14, 2006, p. 27.
68. James Brandon, "Britain Grapples with 'Honor Killing' Practice," *The Christian Science Monitor*, October 19, 2005, www.csmonitor.com/2005/1019/p04s01-woeu.html.
69. Lamb, *Ungoverned Areas and Threats from Safe Havens*, p. 21.
70. Some of these examples are drawn from Michael D. Greenberg, et al., *Maritime Terrorism Risks and Liabilities* (Santa Monica: RAND Corporation, 2006), p. 9.
71. "Egyptian Authorities Foiled al Qaeda Terror Plot Against the Suez Canal," Maritime Terrorism Research Center, July 1, 2009, www.martimeterrorism.com/2009/07/01/egyptianauthorities-foiled-al-qaeda-terror-plot-against-suez-canal.
72. Loc. cit.

73. "Egypt Foils Terror Plot," CBN News, July 9, 2009, www.cbn.com/cbnnews/insideisrael/2009/july/egypt-foils-ssuez-terror-plot.

74. For more on this subject see Joshua E. Keating, "What Do You Learn at Terrorist Training Camp?" *Foreign Policy*, May 10, 2010, www.foreignpolicy.com/articles/2010/05/what_do_you_learn_atterrorist_training_camp.

75. David M. Williams, "Nothing Virtual About It: An Emerging Safe Haven for an Adaptive Enemy," Monograph, School of Advanced Military Studies, U.S. Army Command and General Staff College, 2010, Fort Leavenworth, Kansas, p. 36.

76. Mark L. Reagan, *Introduction to U.S. Counter Terrorism* (Washington, D.C.: Department of Homeland Security, 2005), pp. 6–7.

77. Ben Brandt, "The Taliban's Conduct of Intelligence and Counter Intelligence," *CTC Sentinel*, Vol. 4, Issue 6, June 2011, p. 19.

78. Loc. cit.

79. Loc. cit.

80. Michael Jonsson, "Countering Terrorist Financing: Success and Setbacks in the Years Since 9/11," *CTC Sentinel*, Vol. 3, Issue 7, July 2010, p. 198, www.ctc.usma.edu/v2/wp-content/uploads/2010/08/CTCSentinel-Vol3Iss7-art71.pdf.

81. Loc. cit.

82. Loc. cit.

83. Loc. cit.

84. Patrick M. Jost and Harjit Singh Sandhu, "The Hawala Remittance System and Its Role in Money Laundering," *Financial Crimes Enforcement Network in Cooperation with INTERPOL/FOPAC*, 2013, p. 5.

85. Ibid., pp. 5–6.

86. Loc. cit.

87. Emma Bjornhed, "Narco-Terrorism: The Merger of the War on Drugs and the War on Terror," *Global Crime*, Vol. 6, No. 3–4, August–November, 2004, p. 310.

88. Loc. cit.

89. Nikesh Trecarten, "The Global Convergence of Terrorism and Narcotics Traffick-ng," *Fraser Institute* (Canada), Winter 2014, p. 31.

90. William Kremer, "Pablo Escobar' s Hippos: A Growing Problem," *BBC News Magazine*, p. 1, June 26, 2014, www.bbc.com/news/magazine-27905743.

91. Bio: Pablo Escobar, undated, p. 1, www.biography.com/people/pablo-escobar-9542497#synopsis.

92. Loc. cit.

93. "DEA Takes Aim at Synthetic Drugs with Nationwide Raids," May 7, 2014, p. 1, www.pbs.org/newshour/rundown/dea-takes-aim-synthetic-drugs-nationwide-raids.

94. Loc. cit. and "Drug Busts Add to Suspicion that Profits Fund Terrorist Groups," *CBS News*, May 8, 2014, p. 1, www.cbsnews.com/news/synthetic-drug-busts-add-to-suspicion-that-profits-fund-terror-groups.

95. "Drug Busts Add to Suspicion that Profits Fund Terrorist Groups," p. 2.

96. This account is drawn with restatement from Rukmini Callimachi, "Paying Ransoms: Europe Bankrolls Qaeda Terror," *The New York Times*, July 29, 2014.

97. Loc. cit.

98. Loc. cit.

99. Loc. cit.

100. Loc. cit.

101. Loc. cit.

102. The points in this paragraph are taken with restatement from "Actual and Potential Links Between Terrorism and Criminality," *Canadian Centre for Intelligence and Security Studies*, Vol. 2006-5, pp. 2–3.

103. Loc. cit.

104. No author, "Fake Currency Seized," *The Times of Indian*, July 25, 2014.

105. "Counterfeit Goods Are Linked to Terror Groups," *The New York Times*, February 12, 2007.

106. Loc. cit.

107. *The Use of the Internet for Terrorist Purposes* (New York: United Nations, 2012), p. 7.

108. Loc. cit.

109. Loc. cit.

110. Guy Taylor, "Feds Say Iran's Support for Terrorism Growing," *The Washington Times*, May 30, 2013.

111. Loc. cit.

112. Loc. cit.

113. Juan Miguel del Cid Gomez, "A Financial Profile of the Terrorism of al Qaeda and Its Affiliates," *Perspectives on Terrorism*, Vol. 4, No. 4, 2010, p. 3, www.terrorismanalysts.com/pt/index.php/pot/article/view/113.

114. Callimachi, "Paying Ransoms: Europe Bankrolls Qaeda Terror," pp. 1–2.

115. John Rollins and Liana Sun Wyler, *Terrorism and Transnational Crime: Foreign Policy Issues for Congress* (Washington, D.C.: Congressional Research Service, June 13, 2013), p. 17.

Typologies of Terrorism: State-Involved and Single or Special Issue Movements

CHAPTER

7

Ayatollah Khomeini (1900–1989) was exiled from Iran in 1962 because of his opposition to the existing government. He continued to ferment and plan opposition to it. In 1979, the government finally collapsed and Khomeini returned in triumph. Later that year, he was elected Iran's political and religious leader for life. His radical views on Islam led to the capture of hostages in the American Embassy later that year.
(© Keystone Pictures USA/Alamy)

Learning Objectives

After completing this chapter you should be able to:

1. Differentiate between typologies and taxonomies.

2. Identify and describe the four waves of terrorism.

3. State the two factors that birthed the Islamic Revolution of 1979.

4. Contrast state terrorism and state enabled terrorism.

5. Explain Argentina's "disappeared" program.

6. Describe the advantages that a safe haven provides to a terrorist movement.

7. State the five characteristics of failed states.

8. Briefly describe the Iran-Contra Affair.

9. Explain why single-issue/special-issue movements are so important in the United States.

Introduction

Typologies and taxonomies are both methods of classification. Sometimes they are used synonymously. However, there is a crucial difference. **Typologies** rationally group related concepts and other things into categories. In contrast, **taxonomies** have categories that are formed by empirically studying observable and measurable characteristics.

Typologies bring clarity and patterns out of what otherwise would be a chaotic mass of information.[1] They allow us to quickly see the differences and similarities in concepts by using carefully reasoned categories. The use of typologies allows us to have shared understandings and a common language about the categories.[2] Despite such advantages, typologies have shortcomings. Their categories are artificial creations. They are ideal or pure descriptions that cannot fully account for the rich diversity of reality. Some concepts may fit equally well into more than one category. Cases that cannot be comfortably slipped into any category are forced into the best fitting category despite the fact they have some features of other categories as well. Finally, typologies can lead to stereotyping.

There are many typologies of terrorism because unlike data-driven taxonomies, they are based on the reasoning of their originator. Johnson asserts that there are as many typologies of terrorism as there are analysts.[3] This chapter relies on the use of typologies because there is a dearth of well-developed taxonomies of terrorist organizations.

Typologies
Rationally group related concepts and other things into categories.

Taxonomies
Categories that are formed by empirically studying observable and measureable characteristics.

A Political Orientation Based Typology: The Four Waves of Terrorism

Rapoport analyzed the sweep of terrorism history beginning in the 1880s and identified points at which there were major shifts in terrorism. He called these the **four waves of terrorism**: the anarchist wave, the anti-colonial wave, the new left wave, and the religious wave.[4] Rapoport's four waves provide a good framework in which to summarize the various political, cultural and religious ideologies historically developed to this point.[5] As useful as Rapoport's four waves may be, his work illustrates one of the shortcomings of typologies; his waves could also be categorized as political or historical with equal accuracy. Each of Rapoport's types of terrorism has a range of dates associated with it. However, each type doesn't neatly start and stop on those dates. The dates merely denote a predominate type of terrorism during any given period. For example, terrorism to establish a homeland or new nation for an ethnic minority or to establish a new form of government spans all four waves:

Four waves of terrorism
Typology developed by David Rapoport to better understand terrorism: Anarchist, anti-colonial, new left, and religious.

- *The Anarchist Wave:* Anarchy" comes from the Greek word "anarchos" and means "without a ruler."[6] According to Rapoport, the **anarchist wave** began in the 1880s and continued for some 40 years.[7] Practical anarchy recognizes the impossibility of actually achieving an idealized state of pure anarchy characterized by the absence of a central government. Consequentially, most anarchists are willing to settle for a weak government that is minimally intrusive in the lives of its citizens. Anarchy is inherently anti-authoritarian and revolutionary—it strives to overthrow an existing ruler and/or government. Anarchy is also used to describe chaotic social and economic conditions that are produced by the failure of the central government. A present-day example of this is Somalia. Gettleman described Somalia as "the most dangerous place in the world"[8] because it is a failed government, unable to control its own territory. This makes it an ideal safe haven for terrorists.

  If idealized and practical anarchists knew the writings of American philosopher Henry David Thoreau (1817–1862), they would identify with his notion that the government that governs not at all or least is best. Anarchists have frequently used assassination to pursue their goals.[9] Victims of anarchists include Russian Tsar Alexander II's death at the hands of a bomb-throwing member of Narodnaya Volya (The People's Will) in 1881 and the stabbing murder of French President Carnot in1894. Shooters killed Spanish Prime Minister Canovas in 1897, Italian King Umberto I in 1900, and American President McKinley in Buffalo in 1901. The assassinations of

Anarchist wave
Roughly 1880–1920, anti-authoritarian and revolutionary concept that in pure form exists as a society without any government.

Archduke Ferdinand, heir to the Austrian throne, and his wife Sophie in 1914, triggered the onset of World War I a month later. Concern about anarchism resulted in the United States passing the Immigration Act of 1903. The Act made anarchists an excludable class of immigrants.[10] Although the anarchist wave ended in 1920, assassinations have continued. Most notably, in 1995, Israeli Prime Minister Yitzhak Rabin was assassinated in Tel Aviv by a right-wing orthodox Jew opposed to his policies.

- *The Anti-Colonial Wave:* Colonialism goes back to the early modern era, roughly 1500 to 1800. During that time European nations used their military power to form colonies in other parts of the world that they could control[11] Colonies were created in Asia, South America, the Caribbean, North America, Africa, and the Middle East. During the **anti-colonial wave** (1920s–1960s)[12] colonies sought their independence by negotiating; when that failed they often turned to terrorism.[13] Following the defeat of Germany and Ottoman Turkey in World War I, the League of Nations gave a mandate or authorization to a few member nations to rule the colonies of the defeated powers. Over time, many of these colonies were successful in freeing themselves from their largely European rulers. As the colonies struggled to gain their freedom, they invariably had the support of the people.[14] Some colonies gained independence by helping the allies fight the Axis powers during World War II. As an example, the Philippines separated from the United States in 1946, and the country of Israel became a separate nation under a United Nations plan after the war (1948). India, formerly ruled by the British, was partitioned into India and Pakistan in 1947. Indonesia (1949) separated from the Netherlands. Algiers (1962) broke away from France and the Republic of Kenya and Malaysia (1963) split from England as colonial territories.

- *The New Left Wave:* The Vietnam War ultimately produced widespread opposition to it in the United States and abroad. America and its allies were viewed as engaging in a form of colonial imperialism, which the new left saw as the cause of inequality and oppression throughout the world.[15] Although the **new left wave** (1960s–1990s)[16] concluded that terrorism was a tactic to reform governments, it was notoriously unsuccessful in doing so.[17] For instance, in the United States, the violent leftist revolutionary **Weather Underground** (formerly the *Weathermen*) robbed banks to fund its operations. The group also bombed 12 federal buildings and facilities, including the Capitol Building and the State Department in Washington, D.C. Left-wing movements have often included socialists advocating programs to helping the "underclass," the weak and poor.

According to Rapoport, it is important *not* to overlook that during each wave other extremist movements did not stand still. For example, the American right-wing **National Socialist Movement (NSM)** was formed in 1974 and billed itself as "The premier white civil rights organization" of the time. Its root is the American Nazi Party founded by George Lincoln Rockwell in 1959. NSM membership is open to "heterosexual people of European descent" and its Viking Youth Corps (VYC) shapes the views of adolescents. Membership in NSM cannot be granted to Jews or homosexuals, and its platform calls for ending non-white emigration to the United States.[18] Clearly, right-wing as well as left-wing movements were active during same period of time.

- *The Religious Wave:* There were major acts of secular terrorism prior to the beginning of the religious wave. For instance, the Black September Organization (BSO) was dedicated to creating a Palestinian homeland. In 1972 the BSO murdered Israeli athletes at the Munich Olympics. Israel quickly retaliated with military strikes against several Middle East countries, most notably Lebanon, Jordan, Egypt, and Syria. More importantly, the "Munich Massacre" was counterproductive because worldwide public opinion swung against the Palestinian cause. According to Rapoport, the current **religious wave** began in 1979 with Iran's Islamic Revolution, which overthrew the ruling monarch, Shah (King of Kings) Pahlavi (1919–1980). Ayatollah Khomeini was installed in his place as Supreme Leader, creating the first modern national government based on Islamic beliefs. Two factors in 1979 helped birth the religious wave: (1) the taking of 53 American hostages[19] by radicalized Iranian Muslims at the American Embassy in Tehran,[20] which lasted 444 days (See Figure 7–1) and the subsequent aborted Operation Eagle Claw to

Anti-colonial wave
Prevalent during 1920s-1960s. Colonies sought independence from major powers controlling them.

New left wave
Concluded that terrorism was the way to reform governments.

Weather Underground
Originally called the Weathermen, this group spun off of the Students for a Democratic Society (SDS) in the late 1960s. It issued a "state of war" against the United States and was strongly opposed to the War in Vietnam, calling it an example of American imperialism in Southeast Asia. The group conducted a number of bombings against government buildings and banks; however, it was not responsible for anyone's death. The group disbanded in 1977.

National Socialist Movement (NSM)
Formed in 1974. Roots in the American Nazi Party. Self-billed as the "premier while civil rights organization."

Religious wave
Began with the Islamic Revolution in Iran and continues.

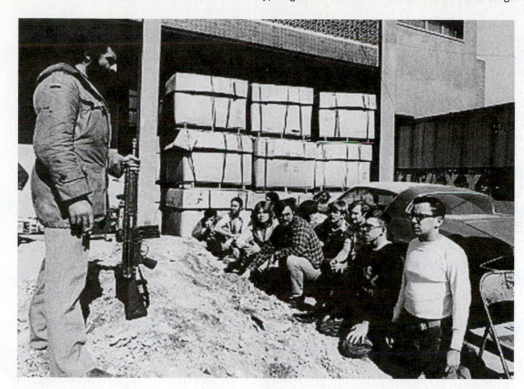

FIGURE 7–1
American hostages from the Embassy in Tehran, Iran, were occasionally let outside in small groups while armed guards watched them closely. The Iranians released them the same day President Reagan was sworn in as president.
(© Moshen Shandiz/Sygma/Corbis)

rescue them, discussed in Chapter 14; and (2) the ill-fated Soviet military entry into Afghanistan.[21] Together, these two events communicated to the developing world that perhaps the superpowers were impotent and vulnerable "paper tigers."

Weinberg and Eubank argue that the current wave of religious terrorism has killed more people, cased more injuries, and spanned the globe more widely in comparison to other waves.[22] Still, they reason that radical Islamic terrorism may be on the wane. After its 34-year-old effort to create a worldwide Islamic state, only one revolutionary Islamic state exists: Iran.[23] Mass movements tend to lose their momentum over long periods of time for two reasons. Governments develop better skills in dealing with them and over a succession of leaders the movement tends to become more moderate, allowing for less violent resolutions.[24] Support for radical Islam and global jihad may be trending downwards. There is some difficulty in a cause being "translated" from one generation of terrorists to the next.[25] Through the use of drones and military raids, the United States and its allies have been systematically killing radical Islam leaders. This "decapitation of the core leadership" strategy has caused some radical Muslims to become more concerned with their own safety than "the cause."

Motivation-Based Typologies

Motivation-based typologies are the most numerous of terrorism typologies. The types of terrorism identified in motivation-based typologies vary from one such typology to another. For the remainder of this chapter, the focus is on state-involved terrorism and single/special issue terrorism. In Chapter 8, the discussion of typologies of terrorism continues, focusing on those movements spawned by separatist or nationalist intentions, left- and right-wing socio-political changes, and radicalized religious causes

State-Involved Terrorism

State-involved terrorism occurs when a national government supports, fosters, or commits acts of terrorism. Briefly, state-involved terrorism has four components: (1) State terrorism is the case in which an established government uses terrorism against its citizens and sometimes visitors within the confines of that country's national borders. (2) state-enabled terrorism occurs when a national government passively allows the presence of terrorists. The state neither provides material assistance nor conducts operations against the terrorists with the expectation that attacks will only be executed in other countries. (3) State-sponsored terrorism results when a government actively supports terrorism, typically as a tool of national foreign policy. (4) State-perpetrated/international terrorism ensues when a government uses its own security force operatives to commit terrorism in foreign countries, such as assassinating their expatriates who are former governmental officials or ferment dissent or rebellion against the government of their home country.

Because terrorism is a tactic used both by governments and other entities, such as insurgents, the question fairly arises as to which, if either, really has the best interests of the people in mind. Long a champion of human rights, the United States has also turned a blind eye to terrorism on occasion as a matter of convenient foreign policy. Illustratively, the United states was well aware of Iraq's Saddam Hussein use of terrorism against his own people to remain in power. However, it was ignored and we provided foreign aid to Iraq from 1980–1988 as it waged war against Iran. As a reminder, in 1978, radicalized Muslims held 53 hostages at the American Embassy in Tehran for 444 days. Beginning in 1980, Iraq kept Iran occupied and expending resources while fighting a war, which was congruent with American foreign policy regarding Iran.

State Terrorism

State terrorism
Terrorism committed by a national government, inside of its national borders and directed at its own citizens and sometimes visitors.

Genocide
The systematic killing of all or part of a racial, ethnic, religious, or national group within a specific country or area; often linked to totalitarian regimes.

State terrorism is terrorism committed by a national government, inside of its national borders and directed at its own people and sometimes visitors. This action contravenes a state's moral and legal duty to protect its citizens. The purpose of state terrorism is to repress and instill fear in citizens and sometimes visitors to consolidate the ruling regime's power and to maintain control over the country's civilian population. **Genocide**, the systematic killing of all or part of a racial, ethnic, religious, or national group within a specific country or area, is often linked to totalitarian regimes. These actions are often carried out by a state's security, police, intelligence, and/or military organizations, usually directed by one leader in an effort to "purge" or "clean" an indigenous population from the targeted group.

Some terrorism experts do not regard state terrorism as terrorism, preferring instead to label it as some form of political violence, or criminal acts such as genocide or murder. Others think that because the state has a legitimate monopoly on the use of force, it cannot be terrorism even if the violence is directed at its own citizens. We hold with other scholars, such as Baserne, who believe a state can turn terrorism inward, and be guilty of both state terrorism and genocide.[26] If a government terrorizes its own citizens as well as citizens of other countries, the character of those acts is the same. Is terrorism less repugnant when the state's victims are also its own citizens? We think not.

Terrorism by totalitarian states is the most extreme and often the most sustained form of state terrorism.[27] Unfortunately, it is the most common as well. The three most widely known names in state terrorism are Adolph Hitler, Josef Stalin, and Mao Tse-Tung (see Box 7–1).

There are numerous other examples of state terrorism, including the death squads in Brazil, El Salvador, Honduras, and Guatemala. In the sections that follow, state terrorism is further explored by examining lesser-known events in several countries.

Parsley Massacre
1937, Dominican Republic dictator Trujillo ordered the military to kill all people immediately who could not pronounce the Spanish word for parsley with the proper Spanish trill on the "r," on the suspicion they were Haitians who had illegally entered the country.

The Dominican Republic—The Parsley Massacre: Ayuso regards the **Parsley Massacre** as "one of the ugliest and least known major events of the twentieth century."[28] Hispaniola, a major Caribbean island, hosts two nations, the Spanish-speaking Dominican Republic and Haiti, which has two official languages, French and Haitian Creole. In 1937, Dominican Republic dictator Rafael Trujillo alleged official outrage that Haitians were illegally crossing the border, taking up residence, using his country resources, and stealing from its citizens.[29] Trujillo directed his military to go the borderland, hold up a sprig of parsley to everyone they encountered, and ask them to say what it was. Those that answered "perejil" (parsley) in Spanish with the proper trill of the "r" were passed by because their answer suggested they were native Spanish speakers. Those who lacked the trill were instantly killed, often with

Box 7-1
Leaders of Totalitarian Governments that Conducted State Terrorism: Adolph Hitler, Josef Stalin, and Mao Tse-Tung

Adolph Hitler (1889–1945) became Chancellor of Germany in 1932 and ruled it as a dictator from the following year until his suicide near the end of World War II in the European Theater (1945). During the Holocaust the Nazis killed millions of Jews from Germany and other European countries without even a pretense of a trial. Hitler imprisoned or executed his own citizens who were mentally ill, physically impaired, homosexuals, gypsies, political opponents, dissidents, Jehovah Witnesses, and Jews. Post–World War II, many German officials were convicted of war crimes for atrocities committed in the concentration camps and elsewhere.

Courtesy © David Cole/Alamy

Courtesy © Pictorial Press Ltd/Alamy

Joseph Stalin (1878–1953) ruled Russia as a dictator (1928–1953). Without any trace of introspection, Hitler remarked of Stalin's murderous dictatorship: "He is probably sick in the brain...his bloody regime can otherwise not be explained."[30] Stalin moved national resources from agricultural to industry. He removed farmers from their lands and seized them as state property. The land was pooled to create large state-owned farming "collectives." Farmers working the land received just a small amount of what was grown. The rest was sold and the profit used to create industries. In doing so perhaps seven million people were killed outright or deliberately starved to death in "troublesome" regions in the great famines of 1930–1933.[31] These victims were characterized as "socially harmful elements...enemies of the people."[32]

Stalin also instituted great "chistkas" (literally cleansing, but meaning purges) of political opponents and dissenters, particularly during 1935–1938, killing five million and sending millions into gulags (penal camps).[33] Russian historian Rogovin reports that during the purges a "court" would dispose of 500 cases in a single evening at a rate of several "trials" a minute.[34] The courts didn't have time to read the summons, let alone read the dossiers.[35] Some defendants were arbitrarily shot while others received various prison sentences.[36] Estimates of how many Russians Stalin killed vary considerably; a common uppermost estimate is 40 million,[37] which represents roughly one in every four Russians. In contrast, the Soviet Union experienced 8.6 million military combat deaths fighting the Germans in World War II.[38]

Mao Zendong (1893–1976), also translated as Mao Tse-Tung, received some formal education, but was largely self-taught.[39] In

1921, Mao helped formed the Chinese Communist Party (CCP). During the 1920s the CCP was forced out of the larger Kuomintang (National People's Party, also known as the Nationalist Party), which was oriented toward a democratic parliament and some socialist programs. The CCP and the Nationalist Party soon were fighting each other militarily. As a left-wing revolutionary devoted to overthrowing the established government, Mao resorted to terror tactics to control his small army; illustrative, on just one occasion he executed 3,000 officers and men who questioned his rule.[40]

The CCP and Nationalist Party called a truce in 1937 to independently fight the Japanese during World War II. Following the war in 1945, they again turned on each other. In 1949, the CCP militarily defeated the Kuomintang, forcing it to flee to Taiwan. Mao Tse-Tung announced the formation of the Communist People's Republic of China on the mainland. Once in power, Mao quickly launched a violent campaign to consolidate his power and executed perhaps 3,000,000 "class enemies."[41] As a totalitarian leader his policies resulted in some 30 million people starving.[42] However, unlike Stalin, Mao did not deliberately set out to starve "troublesome" regions, his policies were simply disastrous.

What compels some government leaders to be so harsh on their own people? Is it is just a coincidental that Hitler, Stalin, and Mao came to power at roughly the same period of time in history? Or is this period of time just unique in the annuals of history? Why?

Courtesy © MARKA/Alamy

Tonton Macoute
A long-standing private force answering only to the president of Haiti. Hacked and shot to death opposition leaders and reformists in extra-judicial executions.

Khmer Rouge
"Red Cambodians," communists who came to power by overthrowing the existing government. See Zero year.

Zero year
Pol Pot, leader of the Khmer Rouge, wanted to "turn the clock back" to "zero year." This "required" emptying the cities and returning to an agrarian society. In doing so 1.7 million Cambodians were killed, often beaten to death because they were Catholics or some other religion, businessmen, intellectuals, and others.

Information Link
For more information on Cambodia under the Khmer Rouge, visit the webpage for Tuol Sleng Genocide Museum in Phnom Penh, Cambodia at www.tuolsleng.com/history.php and The Killing Fields Museum at www.killingfieldsmuseum.com/s21-victims.html. Tuol Sleng Prison was a high school used as the notorious Security Prison 21 during the Khmer Rouge regime from 1975 to 1979. An estimated 20,000 prisoners were tortured and killed at the prison.

Military junta
A government led by a group or committee of military leaders in a specific country; a military dictatorship.

Desaparecidos
From roughly the early 1970s to the early 1980s, a military junta (group) ruled Argentina. The junta labeled anyone who opposed them as communists or subversives. When the junta came to power it had a "kill list" of perhaps 30,000 people who were abducted and placed in concentration camps. Most often they were killed. Their bodies were thrown from aircraft into the ocean or other large bodies of water and the deceased were never found. Therefore, they were called the disappeared. Children born to women in the camps were given to families the junta thought were "reliable." Children were also abducted for the same purpose.

Kurds
A Middle East ethnic minority that does not have a homeland. Kurds live in parts of Iraq, Turkey, Syria, and Iran.

a bayonet, on the presumption they were Haitians.[43] Perhaps as many as 30,000 people were murdered in what the Dominicans call "El Corte," the cutting.[44] Some historians note that Trujillo was an anti-Haitian and imply that he may have been a racist as well. They suggest his real intent was not protecting his citizens or maintaining territorial integrity, but racism: He wanted to "whiten" the Dominican Republic and rid it of the Afro-Haitians.[45]

Haiti—The Tonton Macoute: President Francois Duvalier ("Papa Doc," 1907–1971) ruled Haiti from 1957 to 1971.[46] He survived a military coup in 1959 and quickly took measures to ensure another would not occur, substantially dismantling the Army and staffing its remnants with loyal allies. Papa Doc also created a volunteer private force answerable only to him, the **Tonton Macoute**,[47] which was also the name of a mythological Haitian bogyman that kidnapped disobedient children in a sack and ate them for breakfast.[48] Carrying machetes and some firearms, the Tonton Macoute hacked to death or shot opposition leaders and reformists in extrajudicial executions, often at night, and put their victims' bodies on public display[49] to strike terror in the people. Soon, anyone suspected of harboring anti-Papa Doc sentiments, even in remote villages, were murdered. In 1971, Papa Doc's son, Jean Claude Duvalier ("Baby Doc," 1951–) came to power and ruled Haiti until he was deposed in 1986. By that time the Tonton Macoute had killed an estimated 60,000 Haitians.[50] Aponte describes the Tonton Macoute as "the central nervous system of Haiti's reign of terror."[51] Its violence continued for years even after Baby Doc lost power. Notably, in 1988, the Tonton Macoute invaded a mass at St. Jean Bosco Catholic Church in Port-au-Prince, killing 12 parishioners and wounding another 77 using spears, machetes, and guns.[52] Eventually, Haitians turned on the Macoute, occasionally killing them.

Cambodia—The Khmer Rouge: The communist **Khmer Rouge** (Red Cambodians) ruled during 1975–1979, having come to power by overthrowing the existing government. Its leader, Pol Pot, wanted to turn the clock back to "**Zero Year**," empty the cities, and return to an agrarian society. He set in motion a massacre of Buddhists, Catholics, Muslims, intellectuals, businessmen, foreigners, and other classes, such as people who wore glasses (which suggested they were literate), spoke a foreign language (possibly tainted by outside ideas), or lacked any agricultural or mechanical skills (not useful in the future).[53] Approximately 1.7 million Cambodians died from executions, overwork, starvation, and disease before the Khmer Rouge were overthrown by the intervention of Vietnam.[54]

Argentina—"The Disappeared": State domestic terrorism occurred during Argentina's "dirty war" against opposition leaders and leftists, as well as their families and friends. The dates assigned to the dirty war vary, but it was conducted roughly between the mid-1970s and early-mid 1980s when a **military junta** ruled the country. In the course of combating what the junta described as a subversive Marxist threat, government agents abducted perhaps as many as 30,000 unionists, intellects, reporters, Jews, and others, of which approximately 30 percent were women."[55] The abductees were confined without due process in one of 340 detention camps where they were interrogated, tortured, and sometimes executed.[56] Approximately 500 children were also abducted or taken from their mothers at birth in concentration camps and given to "reliable" parents in favor with junta.[57] Other children were also abducted for the same purpose (see Figure 7–2). Some women arrived at camps pregnant and others became so after rapes by guards. After nursing their babies, the women were "transferred." They were drugged, placed on roughly weekly "death flights," and thrown from aircraft into the Atlantic or other large bodies of water.[58] Because their bodies and those of executed men were seldom found they were collectively referred to as the **desaparecidos**, the disappeared.

Iraq—The Kurds: In 1987, the Iraq-Iran war was winding down. The President of Iraq, Saddam Hussein (1937–2006), ordered planes to drop poison gas on Kurdish civilians living in the Northern portion of his country. Hussein believed the ethnic minority Iraqi **Kurds** had been assisting his enemies, the Iranians, and in retaliation ordered his Air

Force to deploy the gas. Estimates of deaths range from 3,200 to 5,000 with perhaps another 10,000 injured.[60] Hussein also pursued a general policy of ethnic cleansing of both the Kurds and Shiite Muslims and also murdered all who opposed his regime's policies. Numerous mass graves have been found attesting to the butchery authorized by the late Hussein. Although the actual number of those murdered will never be fully known, it was certainly hundreds of thousands.[61] In 2003, Hussein was captured by American forces, tried by an Iraqi tribunal, convicted of crimes against humanity, and hung at an Iraqi Army Base in 2006.

State-Enabled Terrorism

State-enabled terrorism occurs when a state doesn't provide direct support to a terrorist group so long as it conducts no operations against the state or its citizens. The state (1) passively allows its own non-governmental entities and individual supporters to assist it; (2) implicitly condones the existence of the terrorist group by not conducting operations against it; and/or (3) fosters a safe haven for a terrorist group because it cannot govern its own territory, the case of the failed state.[62] **Safe havens** are a place or situation that allows illicit actors, including criminals, smugglers, and terrorists, to operate with relative impunity.[63] Other advantages include that the terrorists can organize, plan, raise funds, communicate, recruit, train, and operate with a reasonable or higher degree of security.[64]

National governments are the primary building blocks of order. To a substantial degree international security relies on states to prevent chaos at home so they do not become incubators for international anarchy and terrorism.[65] Failed states are in default

State-enabled terrorism
A state that tolerates the presence of terrorists in the country so long as they only attack other states and citizens of other states.

Safe havens
A place or situation that allows terrorists and other types of criminals to operate with relative impunity.

FIGURE 7–2
In Buenos Aires during 2012, people continue to search for the babies and children stolen from them. About 100 adults have learned of their real families. Each year, there is a march to commemorate the disappeared and a wall of photographs erected in their remembrance.

(© Imago Stock & People/Newscom)

Quick Facts
Ungoverned Space

Few places in the world are literally "ungoverned;" the term also includes places that are under-governed, misgoverned, areas where governance is contested, and exploitable arenas, such as virtual safe havens on the Internet. Ungoverned areas are not necessarily terrorist safe havens; they are prospective or potential terrorist safe havens.[66]

Failed states

States that cannot govern their own territory. Their governments may be unstable, corrupt, cannot provide basic services, their citizens resent the government, and the government cannot guarantee the security of any weapons of mass destruction in its possession. See Collapsed state and Ungoverned space.

Ungoverned space

A government that cannot control its borders usually ends with space it cannot govern, "ungoverned space." The term also includes space that is misgoverned, under-governed, and where governance is contested. See Failed state and Collapsed state.

Collapsed state

The most extreme example of a failed state. See Ungoverned space and Safe haven.

of meeting this international political obligation. Afghanistan, Angola, Burundi, the Democratic Republic of the Congo, Liberia, Sierra Leone, Somalia, and Sudan are or have been have failed nations.[67]

Characteristically, **failed states** (1) may be in conflict or recently emerged from one; (2) have governments that lack stability, are corrupt, and cannot provide basic services to its citizens; (3) are unable to control their borders or their territory, resulting in "**ungoverned space**" for terrorists to occupy;[68] (4) have civilian populations that resent the central government, which provides a pool of potential terrorism recruits;[69] and (5) lack the capacity to guarantee the security of any weapons of mass destruction weapons or other advanced technologies in their possession.[70]

Other ills that result from failed states include increases in criminal and political violence; rising ethnic, religious, and culture hostilities that can spiral into open warfare; a collapsed health system in which infant mortality rates escalate and life expectancies decline, and increasingly severe food shortages that lead to starvation.[71]

Failed states become the equivalent of a corporation's international headquarters for terrorists.[72] They provide the opportunity to acquire territory on a scale much larger than a collection of scattered safe houses—enough to accommodate entire training complexes, arms depots, and communications facilities.[73] Generally, terrorist groups have no desire to assume complete control over an area they occupy; they just want to be unmolested.[74] IS, with its intention to create a caliphate, is an exception to this observation. The desire of radicalized Muslims, such as the Islamic State movement, to create Islamic states is an exception to this general observation.

Somalia is the most extreme example of a failed state, the **collapsed state**. It is an Eastern African nation that has enabled terrorism. Somalia is a long coastal nation that borders the Indian Ocean and the Gulf of Ayden. Transit from Yemen on the Arabian Peninsula to Somalia is easily made by Islamic jihadists by a boat trip of roughly 100 miles. Somalia has been without an effective central government since Soviet-supported President Siad Barre was overthrown in 1991 by warring clans. The clans then turned on each other and the country was plunged into chaos, famine, and disease. Somalian warlords regularly hijacked humanitarian shipments of food and medicine, using them to pay their troops and secure the loyalty of their local citizens. During 1992–1994, the United States Army put "boots on the ground" in a humanitarian effort authorized by the United Nations to help stabilize the situation.[75] The movie *Black Hawk Down* (2001) depicts the 1993 U.S. raid to arrest a warlord in Mogadishu, which resulted in Army Rangers being engaged with a numerically superior foe. The Ranger casualties in the battle played a key role in the United States subsequently withdrawing from Somalia without stabilizing the situation; Somalia became a failed state and a breeding ground for terrorism.

Subsequent to 1994, there were some promising developments, such as a new constitution and the election of a legislative General Assembly, although it had to meet in neighboring Kenya. However, Somalia seems once more descending toward chaotic conditions largely because of the insurgent radical Islamic al Shabaab movement that affiliated with al-Qaeda in 2012 (see Figure 7–3). Beyond politics and battlefield there has been a humanitarian crisis with perhaps a million or more people who are malnourished and undernourished; in just one four-month period 30,000 children died.[76] There has been some speculation and thinly documented press reports that the United States has been in an alliance with some of the warlords it fought during 1992–1994 to fight al Shabaab, including use of drones armed with Hellfire missiles being flown in from neighboring countries.[77] If true, the effort would be subject to the criticism that the United States erred by using warlords instead of strengthening and working through the central government.

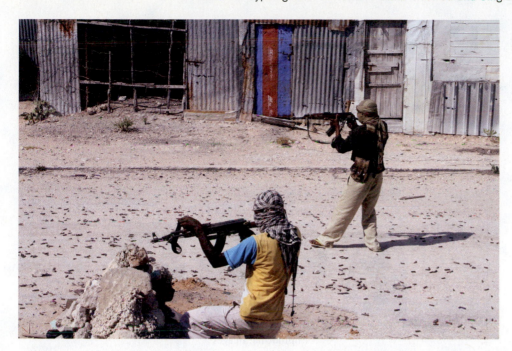

FIGURE 7–3
The violence continues in Mogadishu, Somalia. Members of the extremist group Hezbul Islam trade shots with government forces. Note their covered faces and the ground littered with cartridge cases from fired rounds, suggesting this may be a frequently contested area. Hezbul Islam has suffered defects of fighters to al Shabaab and has been weakened by those losses.

(© Chine Nouvelle/Sipa/Newscom)

State-Sponsored Terrorism

State-sponsored terrorism is a relatively recent development. Historically, terrorism has been between a state and a group of people or organization; however, in the second half of the 20th century state-sponsored terrorism grew as states used terrorist individuals and organizations as their proxies in international affairs. Before its breakup in 1991, Russia was particularly adept at working mischief with proxies for its adversaries. In 2014, Russia apparently had its eye on the Ukraine and was covertly supporting and arming breakaway nationalists rebels in that country.

The U.S. Secretary of State issues a report annually and can designate a country as a state sponsor of terrorism if it has repeatedly provided support for acts of international terrorism; upon such a finding, four main categories of sanctions can be applied: (1) restricting the receipt of foreign assistance, (2) a ban on the sale and export of defense materials to it, (3) limiting the export of dual-use material (i.e., materials that can be used for commercial and military purposes, such as highly advanced computers, or that could be used to develop weapons and technologies of mass destruction), and (4) miscellaneous financial and other restrictions.[78]

As of April 2014, the U.S. Department of State (USDOS) lists only four state sponsors of terrorism: Cuba, Iran, Sudan, and Syria.[79] Our close neighbor Cuba has a long history of unsuccessfully trying to export its style of revolution, supporting terrorists by providing them with sanctuary, and harboring at least 70 American fugitives, including prison escapee Joann Chesimard who was convicted of murdering New Jersey State Trooper Werner Foerster.[80] Cuba has shielded Chesimard since 1984 (see Figure 7–4). The FBI notes that she was an active and prominent member of the Black Panther Party and later the Black Liberation Army, one of the most violent militant organizations of the 1970s.[81] Cuba also provides sanctuary for terrorists from ETA and FARC.

Iran is considered by the USDOS as the "most active state sponsor of terrorism,"[82] providing funding, arms, training, and safe haven to numerous terrorist groups, including those from Afghanistan, Iraq, and Lebanon.[83] Groups backed by Iran include Hamas and Hezbollah; Iran's support just to Hezbollah is estimated at $100 to $200 million annually.[84] Illustrative of Iran's activities is its support of terrorists who in 1996 car bombed the Khobar Towers in Saudi Arabia, killing 19 U.S. servicemen.[85] Since 2001, attacks on U.S. and NATO troops in Afghanistan and on Coalition forces in Iraq have been made with Iranian-produced weapons.[86] In 2011, the United States accused Iran of plotting to assassinate the Saudi Ambassador and to attack the Israeli Embassy in Washington, D.C.[87]

In the past, Sudan has allegedly harbored the late Usama bin Laden, as well as members of other terrorist movements, including Hezbollah, Hamas, the Abu Nidal Organization, and

State-sponsored terrorism
A relatively recent development. States use terrorist groups as proxies to further their agenda in international affairs.

FIGURE 7–4
Wanted poster for Joann Chesimard, the first woman to be placed on the FBI's Most Wanted list.

(Courtesy Federal Bureau of Investigation)

Act of Terrorism - Domestic Terrorism; Unlawful Flight to Avoid Confinement - Murder

JOANNE DEBORAH CHESIMARD

Multimedia: Images

Aliases:
Assata Shakur, Joanne Byron, Barbara Odoms, Joanne Chesterman, Joan Davis, Justine Henderson, Mary Davis, Pat Chesimard, Jo-Ann Chesimard, Joanne Debra Chesimard, Joanne D. Byron, Joanne D. Chesimard, Joanne Davis, Chesimard Joanne, Ches Chesimard, Sister-Love Chesimard, Joann Debra Byron Chesimard, Joanne Deborah Byron Chesimard, Joan Chesimard, Josephine Henderson, Carolyn Johnson, Carol Brown, "Ches"

DESCRIPTION

Date(s) of Birth Used:	July 16, 1947; August 19, 1952	**Hair:**	Black/Gray
Place of Birth:	New York City, New York	**Eyes:**	Brown
Height:	5'7"	**Sex:**	Female
Weight:	135 to 150 pounds	**Race:**	Black
		Citizenship:	American

Scars and Marks: Chesimard has scars on her chest, abdomen, left shoulder, and left knee.

Remarks: She may wear her hair in a variety of styles and dress in African tribal clothing.

CAUTION

Joanne Chesimard is wanted for escaping from prison in Clinton, New Jersey, while serving a life sentence for murder. On May 2, 1973, Chesimard, who was part of a revolutionary extremist organization known as the Black Liberation Army, and two accomplices were stopped for a motor vehicle violation on the New Jersey Turnpike by two troopers with the New Jersey State Police. At the time, Chesimard was wanted for her involvement in several felonies, including bank robbery. Chesimard and her accomplices opened fire on the troopers. One trooper was wounded and the other was shot and killed execution-style at point-blank range. Chesimard fled the scene, but was subsequently apprehended. One of her accomplices was killed in the shoot-out and the other was also apprehended and remains in jail.

In 1977, Chesimard was found guilty of first degree murder, assault and battery of a police officer, assault with a dangerous weapon, assault with intent to kill, illegal possession of a weapon, and armed robbery. She was sentenced to life in prison. On November 2, 1979, Chesimard escaped from prison and lived underground before being located in Cuba in 1984. She is thought to currently still be living in Cuba.

REWARD

The FBI is offering a reward of up to $1,000,000 for information directly leading to the apprehension of Joanne Chesimard.

SHOULD BE CONSIDERED ARMED AND DANGEROUS

If you have any information concerning this person, please call the FBI Toll-Free tip line at 1-800-CALL-FBI (1-800-225-5324). You may also contact your local FBI office , or the nearest American Embassy or Consulate.

Jamaah Islamiyah.[88] In 1998, al-Qaeda operatives based in Sudan were reportedly involved in the bombing of the American Embassies in Kenya and Tanzania. Insurgencies in Uganda, Tunisia, Kenya, Ethiopia, and Eritrea have also received aid from Sudan. In 1999, Sudan signed the International Convention for the Suppression of Terrorist Bombing. Presently, it is

Box 7-2
The Assassination Attempt on Pope John Paul II

In 1981, Pope John Paul II, a native of Poland, was riding in an open car in St. Peter's Square in Vatican City when he was shot four times by Mehmet Ali Agca, a Turkish citizen and a member of the ultra-nationalist "Grey Wolves" in Turkey. Before attacking the Pope, Agca was imprisoned for murdering a newspaper editor. He mysteriously escaped from a maximum prison in Turkey, traveled to Italy, and attempted to assassinate Pope John Paul II on May 13, 1981.[89] For that attempt he served 19 years in an Italian prison, and then was deported back to Turkey and imprisoned for murder (of the newspaper editor) for another 10 years. When released, he shouted "I am the Christ eternal. The Gospel is full of mistakes. I will write the Perfect Gospel. Everyone will die by the end of the century."[90]

Agca originally claimed that he shot the Pope at the behest of Russian and Bulgarian secret service agencies, which wanted to eliminate the Pope's influence in Eastern Europe. Agca later recanted those assertions. Perhaps he was afraid of retaliation against his family for the disclosures[91] or because they were untrue.

Based on Agca's statements, do you think that the assassination attempt on Pope John Paul II should have been classified as an act of "state-sponsored terrorism?"

▲ A Polish statue of Pope John Paul II in the standing position.

(Courtesy Günter Lenz/imageBROKER/ Newscom)

---

thought that with the exception of Hamas, Sudan does not harbor any terrorists. However, because Sudan has accepted Hamas as the legitimate representative of the Palestinian Authority and allows it to raise funds, it remains on the USDOS's state sponsors of terrorism list.

Syria's government continues to allow terrorist organizations such as Hamas and Palestinian Islamic Jihad to maintain headquarters in Damascus.[92] It actively supports Hezbollah and has a covert presence in Lebanon. Syria rejects its designation as a state sponsor of terrorism, saying that the organizations it shields are legitimate movements whose purpose is liberating Arab lands held by Israel.

Some members of Congress believe North Korea should be included in the USDOS's next list of state sponsors of terrorism. It has attacked South Korea numerous times without provocation, provided arms to be used by Hezbollah against Israel, abducted an estimated 180,000 people from 12 countries,[93] committed genocide against its own people, and exported technology that could lead to the proliferation of nuclear weapons.[94] North Korea refers to its own nuclear capability as its "treasured sword."[95]

> **Information Link**
> Visit the U.S. Department of State, Diplomacy in Action webpage at www.state.gov/j/ct/list/c14151 .htm. Read the details as to why Cuba, Iran, Sudan, and Syria are listed on the website in "Overview of State Sponsored Terrorism."

There are different ways of thinking about state-sponsored terrorism, such as (1) the amount of control a sponsor is actually able to exert over a proxy, (2) the amount and kinds of support (e.g., substantial amounts of arms and ammunition), (3) the frequency of such support (e.g., only infrequent sharing of low-level intelligence on anticipated movement of vessels in the region), and (4) the degree of openness with which it assists terrorist organizations.

State sponsors of terrorism generally prefer to act covertly, without other nations being aware of their actions (see Box 7–2). Doing so offers a number of advantages: (1) the use of terror groups as proxies offers an attractive alternative to open, all-out warfare because the state's homeland and conventional forces are not placed at risk; (2) compared to conventional warfare it is a low-cost alternative which may have a high impact, such as destabilizing a rival regime or affecting voting outcomes; (3) if the connection to the sponsoring state is discovered the terrorist attack(s) may not lead to open war (e.g., the attacked state may not be able to stand toe-to-toe with the conventional military forces of the sponsoring nation; it may seek sanctions supported by the international community; or it may simply wait for a more opportune time to seek its revenge, such as waiting until

Sandinistas
Left-wing revolutionary group that overthrew the government of Nicaragua in 1979.

Contras
Nicaraguan counterrevolutionary group battling the Sandinistas for control of the country (See Sandinistas).

Iran-Contra Affair
Reports of human rights violations/atrocities by the Contras caused Congress to prohibit further U.S. funding for them. To secure the release of hostages taken during Iran's 1979 Islamic Revolution, American illegally sold them arms. The profits were then secretly used to fund the Contras. This became known as the "Iran-Contra Affair" and brought significant Congressional criticism of President Reagan's administration.

State-perpetrated/state international terrorism
A state uses its own internal security forces to commit acts of terrorism in another country to promote its own international policy objectives.

the terrorist sponsoring state is waging war with some other state and therefore weakened); and (4) by acting clandestinely sponsoring states have plausible deniability.[96]

Periodically the United States has been accused of being a state sponsor of terror. A common, yet relatively isolated example is our support of the Contras in Nicaragua, which is the largest and least populated country in Central America. In 1979, the left-wing revolutionary **Sandinistas**[97] overthrew President Anastasio Somoza (1925–1980) and began ruling the country; the following year Somoza was assassinated in Paraguay.[98] The Sandinistas were characterized by the United States as puppets of Russia and Cuba that had established a "communist beachhead" in Central America.[99] The American government was soon supporting a counterrevolutionary force dubbed the "**Contras**," some of which had camps in neighboring Honduras (see Figure 7–5). Reports of atrocities, including murder, rape, torture, and mutilation, committed by the Contras resulted in U.S. military aid to them being officially cut off;[100] human rights groups subsequently reported continuing violations.

In the mid-1980s, the United States secretly and illegally arrange the sale of military arms to Iran in return for its help in freeing American hostages held in Lebanon by various factions of Iran's proxy, Hezbollah.[101] The profits from these sales were clandestinely used to support the Contras, in contravention of Congressional legislative actions that forbade such assistance.[102] Ultimately, America's clandestine practices were discovered and the resulting "**Iran-Contra Affair**" brought President Reagan's administration under blistering criticisms from the Congress.

Subsequently, Nicaragua sued the United States in the United Nations' International Court of Justice (ICJ). In 1986, the IJC ruled that the United States had breached its international duty by intervening in Nicaragua's internal affairs by training, arming, equipping, financing, and supplying the Contra forces or otherwise encouraging, supporting, and aiding military and paramilitary actions against Nicaragua and also breached its duty under a friendship treaty.[103] The ICJ noted that although the United States produced a manual on guerrilla war that encouraged the commission of acts contrary to humanitarian law, no such acts were imputable to the United States.[104] The IJC also concluded that the United States had a duty to make reparations to Nicaragua for its breaches of duties and for damages caused, but Nicaragua has never sued to collect damages.

State-Perpetrated/International Terrorism

State-perpetrated/state international terrorism occurs when governments that lack the economic or military resources necessary to achieve their policy objectives use their own internal security forces to commit acts of terrorism on foreign soil to further their agenda or a country with resources chooses to do so using their own operatives. It is this

FIGURE 7–5
Anti-Sandinista forces preparing a raid across the Honduras border into Nicaragua to fight the communist Sandinistas during the Iran-Contra Affair.

(© Mike Goldwater/Alamy)

reliance upon and use of the state's own internal resources that distinguishes this type of terrorism from state-sponsored terrorism's use of proxies.

State-perpetrated terrorism has been used to spy on, harass, and assassinate a state's vocal dissidents and opposition leaders living abroad. Several examples illustrate this point. Orlando Letelier (1932–1976) was Chilean President Allende's (1908–1973) Ambassador to the United States (1971–1973).[105] Allende was overthrown in a coup orchestrated by General Pinochet, who ordered Letelier arrested; he was later released, came to the United States,[106] and became a powerful voice against Pinochet. In 1976, Letelier was assassinated in Washington, D.C. by a bomb planted under his car; his American administrative assistant Ronni Moffitt was also killed in the incident.[107] Two men with ties to the Chilean secret service were later convicted for the bombing.[108]

Since Iran's Islamic Revolution in 1979, at least 83 Iranian exiles living in foreign countries have been murdered by Iranian officials.[109] Iran's former Prime Minister Bakhtiar (1914–1991) fled to Paris, where he led the Iranian government in exile. Although he had survived a previous attempt on his life, he was not so fortunate in 1991. Three Iranian men entered his home and executed Bakhtiar and his secretary.[110] Two killers were apprehended and convicted; French prosecutors alleged they were tied directly to the Islamic Republic of Iran's Ministry of Intelligence and National Security (VEVAK).[111] In 2012, there was a similar incident. Manssor Arbabsiar, who holds dual U.S. and Iranian citizenship, pled guilty to criminal charges involving a plot to assassinate the Saudi Arabia Ambassador to the United States in a Washington, D.C. restaurant. Arbabsiar admitted that he was acting at the direction of Iranian military officials.[112]

State-perpetrated terrorist acts are also illustrated by planting bombs on airplanes and at popular spots, such as foreign discotheques and hotels, frequented by exiles or civilians from enemy states. After the United States bombed Libya in 1986 for supporting terrorism, Muammar Gaddafi knew his country could not stand toe-to-toe with the United States militarily. He responded with state-perpetrated terrorism. In 1988 a Libyan intelligence officer, later convicted of the act, bombed **Pan Am Flight 103**, flying from England to New York City, causing the deaths of all 259 people on board and 11 more in the small village of Lockerbie, Scotland.[113]

Single-Issue or Special-Issue Threats and Extremism

A **homegrown violent extremists (HVE)** is a person who encourages, endorses, condones, justifies, or supports the commission of a violent criminal act to achieve political ideology, religious, social, or economic goals by a citizen or long term resident of a Western country who has rejected Western cultural values, beliefs, and norms[114] and is influenced by a foreign terrorist organization (FTO). HVEs are not to be confused with single-issue/special-issue interest extremists who may be charged with violations of state or federal laws or as domestic terrorists. A key distinction between HVEs and all domestic terrorists is that the influence of a FTO is absent in the latter. At the national level the FBI has primary responsibility for terrorism investigations. Although not part of the domestic terrorism law, the FBI uses the phrase "Influenced by U.S.-based extremist ideologies" to identify cases as domestic terrorism.

There is some ambiguity about what "U.S.-based extremist ideologies" means.[115] Illustratively, some white supremacy groups in the United States reflect themes from Germany's Nazism and the skinhead movement evolved originally in several foreign countries,[116] but criminal acts by extremists from such ideologies will be charged with domestic terrorism or other violations of federal and state laws, but not as HVEs.

Presently, the federal government does not generate an official and public list of domestic terrorism individuals or groups;[117] there is no domestic terror organization counterpart to the Secretary of States' list of foreign terrorist organizations (FTOs). Instead, federal agencies use a more cautious language, describing some causes as "threats" and those who commit criminal acts on their behalf as "extremists." Single-issue/special-issue terrorism is not ordinarily committed to effect widespread societal change. Its purpose is to change policies and practices with respect to a specific cause.

Groups with extreme views enjoy all the protections of the U.S. Constitution, including the free speech right to advocate for their cause.[118] Such groups may have a "front group" that

Pan Am Flight 103
Blown up in 1988 by a Libyan intelligence officer killing 259 people on board, as well as some people on the ground in Scotland, over which the plane exploded. Believed to have been ordered by Libya's dictator Muammar Gaddafi in retaliation for U.S. bombing his country in 1986.

Homegrown violent extremist (HVE)
A person of any citizenship who mostly lives in the United States and who commits terrorist activity to advance an ideology when that person is influenced by a foreign terrorist organization (FTO), but acts alone.

Quick Facts
Who Could Be A Homegrown Violent Extremist?

HVEs are a diverse group of individuals who can include U.S.-born citizens, naturalized citizens, green card holders (permanent residents) or other long-term residents, foreign students, or illegal residents.[119]

Single-issue/special-issue extremists

As rule of thumb, typically attack property as opposed to persons. Most common form of violent political extremism in the United States. May be members of, or loosely affiliated with, extreme group, may never have contacted group, but has an affinity for it, may have their own unique cause. Typically espouse a single issue or narrow range of issues.

Hacktivists

Single-issue/unique cause extremists who use the Internet to attack hate sites and disclose personal information about its members.

Animal Liberation Front (ALF)

ALF rejects the institutional position that animals are property and can be used as test subjects by corporations. ALF members or sympathizers may "liberate" animals and find "good homes" for them or return the to the wild and damage or destroy associated research facilities.

Earth Liberation Front (ELF)

ELF's mission is to cause as much economic loss to persons and other entities whose selfish greed and desire for profits results in the destruction of the natural environment and life. By doing so ELF members and/or sympathizers hope to compel them to discontinue their destructive practices.

performs their "public information" function and may be regarded as terrorist threats, but not as terrorists. They may also have a subgroup that carries out attacks to further their ideology.

Single-issue/special-issue extremists may (1) be members of groups or movements with extreme views; (2) be loosely affiliated with extreme causes; (3) never have contact with extreme causes, but have an affinity for their ideology; or (4) have their own unique ideology, such as "**hacktivists**" who use the Internet to attack hate sites, damage them, and release personal information about their members. As a rule of thumb, single-issue/special issue extremists target property and not people, (e.g., burn federal offices or ski resorts). Nonetheless, large-scale property attacks place emergency responders in dangerous situations. Other tactics include "spiking trees" to make them too dangerous to cut by hammering spikes into them, filing a barrage of frivolous suits, and destruction of research files. Attacks by single-issue/special-issue extremists may range from annoying vandalism to arsons that destroy millions of dollars of property.

Single-issue/special-issue attacks are the most common form of violent political extremism in the United States and most of the industrialized nations of the world.[120] Examples of extremist single-issue/special-issue groups include the **Animal Liberation Front (ALF)** and the **Earth Liberation Front (ELF)**, anti-genetically modified organisms groups, anti-technologists, and anti-abortionists.

The Animal Liberation Front (ALF) and the Earth Liberation Front (ELF)

Although the number of perpetrators in attacks is unknown, ALF and ELF and/or sympathizers committed 2,000 attacks over a 29-year period, causing $110 million in damages (see Table 7–1).[121] In 2005, three people who later claimed to be ALF members

TABLE 7–1
ALF and ELF Missions[122]

ALF	ELF
1. To liberate animals from places of abuse, that is, laboratories, factory farms, fur farms, etc., and place them in good homes where they may live out their natural lives free from suffering;	1. To cause as much economic damage as possible to a given entity that is profiting off the destruction of the natural environment and life for selfish greed and profit;
2. To inflict economic damage to those who profit from the misery and exploitation of animals;	2. To educate the public on the atrocities against the environment and life; and
3. To reveal the horror and atrocities committed against animals behind closed doors, by performing direct actions and liberations; and	3. To take all necessary precautions against harming life.
4. To take all necessary precautions against harming any animal, human, or non-humans; any group of people who are vegetarians or vegans and who carry out actions according to these guidelines have the right to call themselves as part of the Animal Liberation Front.	

Box 7-3
Greenpeace

Greenpeace (GP) incorporated in 1971 with just a small nucleus of supporters. Today, it has 2.8 million supporters, 5 ships, 27 national and regional offices, and a presence in 41 countries. It rarely shows up on databases that list terrorist groups and extremist threats. It takes "direct action" to call attention to the situations it opposes, such as deforestation; nuclear testing; illegal whaling; releases of hazardous chemicals; deep ocean oil drilling; unsustainable fishing methods that needlessly kill baby tuna, sharks, and turtles; protecting seals; and opposing oil pipelines and toxic dumping in oceans.

The techniques used by GP include chaining themselves to equipment to prevent its use and climbing terrain and buildings to place their banners where many people will see them. In Australia, protesters perhaps affiliated with GP attacked a genetically modified wheat plot wearing Hazmat suits and used weed string trimmers to destroy an entire experimental crop.[123] GP has also been accused of interfering with the navigation rights of whalers and conducting their direct actions in ways that are dangerous to the GP personnel and security personnel. In 2013, Greenpeace representatives attempted to board a Russian oil-drilling platform in the Arctic to display a banner calling for an end to drilling in that region. The Russians quickly responded and seized the ship and 30 people on it. By the end of 2013, all personnel had been allowed to leave the country. GP is working to secure the release of the ship.

GP differs from terrorist and extremist groups in important ways. It is incorporated, has legal responsibilities, and largely operates out of the tradition of protest, albeit sometimes over the top. Most often its "direct actions" are intended to change the practices of businesses rather than the policies of governments. GP has a major interest in not harming people and destruction of property is a relatively unusual act, even by sympathizers. It has also been the victim of violence; the French blew up one of its

▲ The Greenpeace movement's Rainbow Warrior ship docked in Pula, Croatia, which is used to transport activists to various locations to demonstrate.

(Carmen Jaspersen/dpa/picture-alliance/ Newscom)

ships and killed a photographer because of GP's opposition to nuclear testing in the Pacific.

Do you think Greenpeace should be labeled as a terrorist group? Why or why not?

---

broke into a facility at the University of Iowa and freed 300 rodents being used for research; broke equipment; and poured acid on computers, papers, and books, producing losses and added expenditures of $875,000. They also publicized the mail addresses and other personal information of the researchers and their spouses, resulting in numerous intimidating calls. Five faculty members also received over 400 unsolicited magazine subscriptions under the "bill me later" option. ELF's term for economic sabotage is "**monkey wrenching**" and is also referred to as **ecotage**, a corruption of eco—pertaining to the environment—and sabotage. Monkey wrenching may involve both destructive acts and acts of obstruction (e.g., tree sitting to avoid clear cutting of forests). In 2012, an ELF arson attack in 2012 on a U.S. Forest Station Research Station in Pennsylvania caused $700,000 in damages and destroyed 70 years of research.[124]

Anti-Genetically Modified Organism (GMO) Groups

GMO extremist groups appeared in the 1980s in Germany in reaction to large-scale research on genetically altered agricultural plants, such as wheat and potatoes, which were resistant to diseases and provided a higher yield per acre. Extremists believed to be associated or have an affinity with lesser-known movements such as "Take the Flour Back" and the "Field Liberation Movement" invaded test plots and destroyed "**Frankenfood**" plants. In contrast, Greenpeace is an internationally recognized name of an environmental protection movement with broad interests. It has also been involved in protests against GMOs. "Concerned Oregon State University Students and Alumni" took credit for destroying 700 poplar trees, some of which were genetically engineered as part of research conducted by an OSU forestry professor; the research was being conducted to determine if the fast growing poplar trees were suitable for use in the timber industry.[125]

Monkey wrenching
Earth Liberation Front (ELF) term for economic sabotage. Involves acts of destruction and obstruction. See Ecotage.

Ecotage
Earth Liberation Front's (ELF"s) corruption of eco (pertaining to the environment) and sabotage; used synonymously with monkey wrenching. See Monkey wrenching.

Frankenfood
Term developed by anti-genetically modified organism (GMO) groups to describe genetically altered agricultural plants, such as wheat and potatoes.

Quick Facts
The Unabomber's Manifesto

In 1995, writing as "KC" to confuse investigators, the Unabomber demanded that *The New York Times*, *The Washington Post*, and *Penthouse Magazine* publish a 35,000-word manifesto explaining his actions or he would strike again. Only *Penthouse* refrained from doing so. It part, the manifesto read "The industrial revolution and its consequences have been a disaster for the human race ... [It has] destabilized society, made life unfulfilling, and subjected human beings to indignities ... the continued development of technology will worsen the situation ... we therefore advocate the overthrow of the economic and technological basis of our society."[126]

Anti-Technologists

Theodore Kaczynski

Nicknamed the "Unabomber," Kaczynski was a mathematician and murderer who carried out a nationwide bombing campaign against people associated with industrialization and modern technology in the United States. Most of his bombs were crude, home-made bombs that were mailed to his victims.

Unabomber

See Theodore Kaczynski.

Army of God

Anti-abortion group, underground Christians, who produced manual on how to attack clinics.

Theodore Kaczynski, a Ph.D. mathematician (see Figure 7–6), became notorious as the **Unabomber** until his identity was established. An anti-technologist, he anonymously sent 16 bombs through the mail that exploded when opened during 1978–1995. Three people were killed and dozens injured.[127] Referred to as the *Unabomber* by the FBI, Kaczynski lived a Spartan, survivalist lifestyle in a remote Montana cabin. The bombs expressed his rage against technology; a key event radicalizing him was when a road was built though a pristine area he enjoyed visiting. His brother came to the conclusion "Ted" was the Unabomber and contacted the FBI. Kaczynski is serving multiple life sentences without the possibility of parole in a Colorado federal prison.

Anti-Abortionists

In *Roe v. Wade* (1973), the U.S. Supreme Court held that abortions were legal, which fueled the anti-abortion movement. The anti-abortion movement fully emerged in the early 1980s, peaked around 1984, and substantially disappeared until another spike in 1996. Since then anti-abortion attacks have trended down, but have never disappeared.[128] Some right-wing movements and individuals may include an anti-abortion element within their multiple cause agendas, which is distinguishable from movements in this section that have it as their single issue.

Planned Parenthood Clinics have been a common target of anti-abortionists, who can be divided into two camps: (1) those who peacefully seek to end abortions through the passage of laws forbidding them, providing education to rally public support, giving financial aid to pregnant women who might otherwise have an abortion, and peaceful demonstrations; and (2) violent extremists who engage in practices such as throwing acid on the property of abortion clinics, bombing them, committing arson of facilities, and assaults upon and murders of abortion providers. The **Army of God** is an underground Christian terrorist organization that produced a manual on how to attack clinics, including the use of bombs. Attacks attributed to the Army of God have virtually disappeared since 1998.[129] Most attacks since then have simply been attributed to "anti-abortion activists." The murder of a physician, George Tiller, provides insight into the minds of violent anti-abortion extremists.

In Wichita, Kansas, Dr. George Tiller performed late-term abortions. While Tiller was passing out bulletins for the Sunday services at his Lutheran Church, Scott Roeder shot him point blank, killing him.[130] The 52-year-old Roeder was subsequently convicted of first degree murder with no possibility of parole for 50 years.[131] Roeder was unrepentant about the murder, claiming he stopped Tiller so he "could not dismember another innocent baby."

FIGURE 7–6
The April 4, 1996, jail booking photograph for Unabomber Theodore Kaczynski.

(Courtesy FBI Law Enforcement Bulletin)

Chapter Summary

SUMMARY BY LEARNING OBJECTIVE

1. **Differentiate between typologies and taxonomies.**

   Typologies rationally group related concepts and other things into categories. In contrast, taxonomies have categories that are formed by empirically studying observable and measurable characteristics.

2. **Identify and describe the four waves of terrorism.**

   These four waves are: (1) anarchist, which predominated during 1880s–1920s. Pure anarchy requires an absence of a central government and people who respect and help each other; (2) colonialism began in the early modern period (1500–1800) when powers used their military might to impose their will on other parts of the world; (3) the new left wave (1960s–1990s) saw America and its allies engaging in a form of imperialism and were opposed to it. They saw revolution as the way to reform governments, but were very unsuccessful; and (4) the religious wave began in 1979 during Iran's Islamic Revolution and continues. It is fundamentally, but not exclusively, Islamic in nature. Its ultimate goal is a world-wide Islamic religion entwined with Islamic government.

3. **State the two factors that birthed the Islamic Revolution of 1979.**

   These two factors are the taking of American hostages at the United States Embassy in Tehran, Iran, and the defeat of the Soviets in Afghanistan. These two events suggested that the two superpowers involved were "paper tigers."

4. **Contrast state terrorism and state-enabled terrorism.**

   State terrorism is terrorism directed internally, inside of its national borders. This action contravenes a state's moral and legal duty to protect its citizens. Defined more broadly, state terrorism is directed at a nation's citizens or residents to repress and instill fear in them, to consolidate the ruling regime's power (e.g., by genocide), and to maintain control over the country's civilian population. It is carried out by a state's security, intelligence, and military organizations, and in some cases volunteers. In contrast, state-enabled terrorism is passive. A country allows one or more terrorist movements to exist within its borders as long as no attacks are directed at the citizens or the government.

5. **Explain Argentina's "disappeared" program.**

   Roughly between the mid-1970s and early 1980s a military junta (group) ruled Argentina. In the course of combating what the junta described as a subversive Marxist threat, government agents abducted perhaps as many as 30,000 unionists, intellects, reporters, Jews, and others—of which approximately 30 percent were women. The abductees were confined without due process in one of 340 detention camps where they were interrogated, tortured, and sometimes executed. So few people returned from the camps that those who were abducted were called the disappeared.

6. **Describe the advantages that a safe haven provides to a terrorist movement.**

   In safe havens terrorists can operate with impunity and organize, plan, raise funds, communicate, recruit, train, and raise funds with a reasonable or higher degree of security.

7. **State the five characteristics of failed states.**

   Characteristically, failed states (1) may be in conflict or recently emerged from one; (2) have governments that lack stability, are corrupt and cannot provide basic services to its citizens; (3) are unable to control their borders or their territory, creating "ungoverned space" for terrorists; (4) have civilian populations that resents the central government, which provides a pool of potential recruits; and (5) lack the capacity to guarantee the security of any weapons of mass destruction weapons or technologies in their possession.

8. **Briefly describe the Iran-Contra Affair.**

   In the mid-1980s, the United States secretly and illegally arranged the sale of military arms to Iran in return for its help in freeing American hostages held in Lebanon by various factions of Iran's proxy, Hezbollah. The profits from these sales were clandestinely used to support the Contras, in contravention of Congressional legislative actions that forbade such assistance. Ultimately, America's clandestine practices were discovered and the resulting

"Iran-Contra Affair" brought President Reagan's administration under blistering criticisms from the Congress.

9. **Explain why single-issue/special-issue movements are so important in the United States.**

Single-issue/special-issue attacks are the most common form of violent political extremism in the United States.

REVIEW QUESTIONS

1. What is the root meaning of anarchy and what does it mean?
2. Who are the three most widely known persons in state terrorism?
3. What were the main factors in the Parsley Massacre?
4. In mythology what did the Tonton Macoute do and what did the Tonton Macoute actually do for Papa Doc?
5. Which nation is the most active sponsor of state terrorism?
6. What are ALF and ELF?
7. What is "frankenfood"?

CRITICAL THINKING EXERCISES

1. **The Holocaust and Genocide.** Visit the homepage of the United States Holocaust Memorial Museum at www.ushmm.org/. Learn about the Holocaust under Adolf Hitler and listen to the survivors and victims of this horrific event. Search the latest news and discover that genocide sadly continues today in several countries throughout the world. How do you think that genocide impacts the development of a country? Can a government ever overcome the history of genocide? Research and discuss as a class some of the more contemporary genocides observed in countries like Sudan, Rwanda, and Bosnia. Has the World Court been successful in preventing such tragedies through the prosecution of war crimes? Why not? Now, compare these contemporary genocides with the loss of Aboriginal people in Australia and Native Americans in the United States during the 18th and 19th centuries. Do you think genocide only occurs in developing nations? What can be done to prevent these types of horrific events?

2. **Greenpeace and PETA.** Search the web for articles on Greenpeace. Notice how many depict the organization as a group of radical environmentalists that potentially use violence and dangerous interventions to stop whaling and pollution in the world's oceans. What motivates some entities to characterize Greenpeace in this manner? How does Greenpeace differ from the groups discussed in the chapter that are commonly referred to as "eco-terrorists," like the Animal Liberation Front (ALF) and the Earth Liberation Front (ELF)? Now, visit the People for Ethical Treatment of Animals (PETA) website at www.peta.org. What is PETA's position on the Animal Liberation Front? Are Greenpeace and PETA alike, or do they differ? How?

NOTES

1. Ruth Lupton, Rebecca Tunstall, Alex Fenton, and Rich Harris, *Using and Developing Place Typologies for Policy Purposes* (London: Department for Communities and Local Government, February, 2011), p. 11.
2. Loc. cit.
3. Chalmers Johnson, "Interpretations in Terrorism," in Walter Laquer, editor, *The Terrorism Reader* (New York: New American Library, 1978), p. 276.
4. David C. Rapoport, "Modern Terror: The Four Waves," in *Attacking Terrorism: Elements of a Grand Strategy*, Audrey Cronin and J. Ludes, editors (Washington, D.C.: Georgetown University Press, 2004), p. 47.
5. We have faithfully cited Rapoport's excellent work that should be read in its original entirety if there any questions about what he and the present authors contribute herein.

6. Jeff Shantz, "Beyond the State: The Return to Anarchy," *Disclosure: A Journal of Social Theory*, Issue 12, 2003, pp. 87–103, http://uknowledge.uky.edu/disclosure/vol12/iss1/7/.

7. David C. Rapoport, "The Four Waves of Rebel Terror and September 11th," *Anthropoetics*, No. 1, Spring Summer 2002, pp. 1–19, www.anthropoetics.ucla.edu/archive/ap0801.pdf.

8. Jeffrey Gettleman, "The Most Dangerous Place in the World," *Foreign Policy*, Issue 171, March/April 2009, p. 60.

9. Rapoport, "The Four Waves of Rebel Terror and September 11th," p. 2.

10. Julia Rose Kraut, "Global Anti-Anarchism: The Origins of Ideological Deportation and the Suppression of Expression," *Indiana Journal of Global Legal Studies*, Vol. 19, Issue 1, Winter 2012, p. 182.

11. Robert Taylor, *History of Terrorism* (San Diego: Lucent Books, 2002), p. 38.

12. Rapoport, "The Four Waves of Rebel Terror and September 11th," p. 2.

13. Loc. cit.

14. Loc. cit.

15. Ibid., p. 59.

16. Rapoport, "The Four Waves of Rebel Terror and September 11th," p. 2.

17. Loc. cit.

18. Taken from the NSM website, www.NSM88.org/25pointsengl.html.

19. At the beginning, there were 66 hostages, but by January 1981 the Iranians had released 14 of them. See Christine Coker, "Planning in Hostage Rescue Missions, U.S. Operation Eagle Claw and U.K. Operation Barras," *Military Technology*, Volume 30, Issue 9, September 1, 2006, p. 66.

20. Six American diplomats escaped being captured and in 1980 were whisked out of Iran by courageous members of the Canadian Embassy. The 2012 movie *Argo* was loosely based on that event.

21. Leonard Weinberg and William Eubank, "An End to the Fourth Wave of Terrorism?" *Studies in Conflict and Terrorism*," Vol. 33, Issue 7, 2010, p. 595.

22. Weinberg and Eubank, "An End to the Fourth Wave of Terrorism?" p. 598.

23. Ibid., p. 598.

24. Loc. cit.

25. Defining Terrorism,, WP 3, Deliverable 4, A Project Funded by the European Commission, October 1, 2008, p. 45.

26. Sertac H. Baserne, "Terrorism with Its Differentiating Aspects," *Defence Against Terrorism Review*, Vol. 1, No. 1, Spring 2008, p. 5.

27. "The State as Terrorist," *Stanford Encyclopedia of Philosophy*, August 8, 2011, www.Plato.stanford.edu/entries/terrorism/#StaFer.

28. Monica G. Ayuso, "How Lucky for You That Your Tongue Can Taste the 'r' in Parsley: Trauma Theory and the Literature of Hispaniola," *Afro-Hispanic Review*, Vol. 30, No. 1, Spring 2001, p. 47.

29. Ezra Fieser, "Haiti, Dominicans Try to Move Beyond the Parsley Massacre's Long Shadow," *Christian Science Monitor*, October 19, 2012.

30. Hiroaki Kuromiya, "Stalin's Great Terror and International Espionage," *Journal of Slavic Military Studies*, Vol. 24, Issue 2, April–June 2011, p. 240.

31. See Arch Puddington, "Denying the Terror Famine," *National Review*, Vol. 44, Issue 10, May 25, 1992, pp. 33–36.

32. Cynthia Haven, "Stalin Killed Millions. A Stanford Historian Answers the Question 'Was it Genocide?'" Stanford (University) Report, September 23, 2010, www.news.stanford.edu/news/2010/september/naimark-stalin-genocide-092310.html.

33. See Robert Conquest, *The Great Terror: A Reassessment* (New York City: Oxford University Press, 2007), which addresses Russia during the 1930s.

34. See Vadim Z. Rogovin, *Stalin's Terror of 1937–1938: Genocide in the USSR* (Oak Park Michigan: Mehring Books, 2009). Rogovin is the author of a highly regarded five-volume history of Russia.

35. Loc. cit.

36. Loc. cit.

37. J. D. Lindy and B. Kolk, "Notes from Moscow (1990): Some Thoughts on the Politics of PTSD During Perestroika," *Journal of Traumatic Stress*," Vol. 4, No. 3, 1991, p. 439.

38. Ria Novosti, "Russia's Losses in WW II Estimated at Some 27 Million People," www.en.rian.ru/russia/20100506/158896419.html, accessed January 15, 2013. This figure varies by source from a low of 6 million to a high of 11 million. The higher figure also includes an unknown number of missing service members.

39. Fox Butterworth, "Obituary, Mao Tse-Tung: Father of the Chinese Revolution," *New York Times*, September 10, 1976, www.nytimes.com/learning/general/onthisday/bday/1226.html.

40. Loc. cit.

41. Loc. cit.

42. Vaclay Smil, "China's Great Famine: 40 Years Later," *BMJ*, 319, December 1999, p. 1619.

43. The account of the "Parsley Test" is taken from Ayuso, "How Lucky for You That Your Tongue Can Taste the 'r' in Parsley," p. 47.

44. Ezra Fieser, "Haitians and Dominicans Remember the Parsley Massacre 75 Years Later," *The Miami Herald*, October 9, 2012. One source places the publication data two days later, although that may have been when it was posted to the Internet.

45. Fieser, "Haiti, Dominicans Try to Move Beyond the Parsley Massacre's Long Shadow," p. 1.

46. "Francois Duvalier," *New York Times Topics*, December 3, 2012, www.topicsnytimes.com/top/reference/timestopics/people/d/francois_duvalier/index.html.

47. See Graham G. Diederich, *Papa Doc & the Tontons Macoutes* (Princeton, N.J.: Marcus Weiner Publishers). Originally published in 1970, re-released in December 2005.

48. David Aponte, "The Tonton Macoutes: The Central Nervous System of Haiti's Reign of Terror," *Council on Hemispheric Affairs*, March 11, 2010, www.coha.org/tonton-macoutes/.

49. Stephen Kurczy, "5 Reasons Why Haiti's Jean Claude Duvalier is Infamous," *Christian Science Monitor*, January 20, 2011, p. 1.

50. Aponte, "The Tonton Macoutes."

51. Loc. cit.

52. Don A. Schanche, "9 Top Haitian Officers Fired, But Action Fails to Halt Military Unrest," *Los Angeles Times*, September 22, 1988.

53. There are a number of sources describing the victims. For example, see Douglas B. Levene, "Reflections on Cambodia," *National Review*, November 12, 2012, p. 1, www.nationalreview.coc/articles/293017/reflections-cambodia-douglas-b-levene?pg=2; "Cambodian Genocide," William Mitchell College of Law (an independent college of law), p. 1, www.worldwithoutgenocide.org/genocides-and-conflicts-/cambodian genocide; and Peter Walker, "Behind the Cambodian Killing Fields," *The Guardian* (Daily newspaper, England), September 19, 2007.

54. "Khmer Rouge," *New York Times Topics*, November 23, 2011, www.topics.nytimes.com/top/reference/timestopics/organizations/k/khmer_rouge/index.html.

55. Stephen G. Michaud, "Identifying Argentina's Disappeared," *New York Times Magazine*, December 27, 1987, www.NYTimes.com/1987/12/27/Magazine/Identify-Argentina-s-disappeared.html.

56. Ernesto Saboto, President, Argentina National Commission on the Disappearance of Persons, Section D, Detention Centers, unnumbered manuscript, 1984. The report was later translated into English as Nunca Mas (Never Again) and published in New York by Farrar, Straus, Giroux, 1986.

57. Alexei Barrionuevo, "Daughter of Dirty War Was Raised by Man Who Killed Her Parents," *New York Times*, October 8, 2011.

58. Francisco Goldman, "Children of the Dirty War: Argentina's Stolen Orphans," *The New Yorker*, March 19, 2012, p. 54.

59. "Rafael Videla Admits His Government Killed and Disappeared Thousands," *Fox News Latino*, April 16, 2012, www.latino.foxnews.com/latino/news/2012/04/16/rafael-videla-admits-his-government-killed-and-disappeared-thousands.

60. "On This Day: 1988: Thousands Die in Halabja Gas Attack," *BBC*, undated, www.News.bbc.co.uk/onthisday/hi/dates/stories/march/16/newsid_4304000/4304853.stm.

61. Heather Pringle, "Witness to Genocide," *Archaeology*, Vol. 62, No. 1, January/February 2009, p. 28.

62. Daniel Byman, "Passive Sponsors of Terrorism," *Survival: Global Politics and Strategy*, Vol. 47, Winter 2005, No. 4, p. 118. These points come from Byman, but we have restated them.

63. Robert D. Lamb, *Ungoverned Areas and Threats from Safe Havens* (Washington, D.C.: Final Report of the Ungoverned Areas Projects, U.S. Department of Defense, January 2008), p. 6.

64. Loc. cit.

65. Robert I. Rotberg, "Failed States in a World of Terror," Council on Foreign Relations, July/August 2002, See www.foreignaffairs.com/articles/58046/robert-i-rothberg/failed-states-in-a-world-of-terror.

66. Robert D. Lamb, *Ungoverned Areas and Threats from Safe Havens* (Washington, D.C.: Department of Defense, January 2008), p. 6.

67. Ibid., p. 5.

68. Liana Sun Wyler, *Weak and Failing States: Evolving Security Threats and U.S. Policy*, (Washington, D.C.: Congressional Research Service, August 28, 2008), pp. 4–5.

69. Most of these factors are discussed in James A. Piazza, "Incubators of Terror: Do Failed and Failing States Promote Transnational Terrorism?" *International Studies Quarterly*, Vol. 52, Issue 3, 2008, pp. 469–488.

70. Robert S. Litwak, "Assessing the Nexus of Proliferation and Terrorism," Ridgway Center on the Determinants of Security Policy in the 21st Century, 2007, p. 3.

71. Rotberg, "Failed States in a World of Terror," p. 5.

72. Rag Takeyh and Nicholas Gvosdev, "Do Terrorists Need a Home?" *The Washington Quarterly*, Vol. 25, No. 3, Summer 2002, pp. 98–99.

73. Loc. cit.

74. Loc. cit.

75. In 1993, Americans went into Mogadishu to arrest warlords and it escalated into fierce fighting that is depicted in the movie *Black Hawk Down*.

76. Ted Dagne, Somalia: *Current Conditions and Prospects for a Lasting Peace*, (Washington, D.C.: Congressional Research Service, August 31, 2011), p. 1.

77. One report in this genre is Mark Mazzetti, "Efforts by CIZ Fail in Somalia, Officials Charge," *New York Times*, June 9, 2006.

78. "State Sponsors of Terrorism," U.S. Department of State, www.state.gov/j/ct/list/c14151.htm.

79. Loc. cit.

80. Congresswoman IIena Ross-Lehtinen, "Cuba Continues to Harbor Over 70 Fugitives Wanted by U.S. Law Enforcement Officials Says Ros-Lchtinen," April 9, 2013, http://ros-lehtinen.house.gov/press-release/cuba-continues-harbor-over-70-fugitives-wanted-us-law-enforcement-officials-says-ros.

81. "Joanne Chesimard, Convicted Murderer and Fugitive," *FBI News Release*, May 2, 2013, p. 1.

82. Greg Bruno, "State Sponsors: Iran," Council on Foreign Relations, October 13, 2011, www.cfr.org/iran/state-sponsors-Iran/p9362.

83. Loc. cit.

84. Loc. cit.

85. Loc. cit.

86. Loc. cit.

87. Loc. cit.

88. The information in this paragraph is taken, with restatement, from Preeti Bhattacharji, "State Sponsors: Sudan," Council on Foreign Relations, April 2, 2008, pp. 1–2, www.cfr.org/sudan/state-sponsors-sudan/p9367.

89. This information is drawn from Ray Moseley, "Pope 'Plot' Central to Trial of Century," *Chicago Tribune News*, May 14, 1981.

90. Sabnem Arsu, "Man Who Shot Pope in 1981 is Freed," *New York Times*, January 18, 2010.

91. Loc. cit.

92. The information in this paragraph is drawn with restatement from Holly Fletcher, "State Sponsor: Syria," Council on Foreign Relations, February 2008, p. 1, www.cfr.org/syria/state-sponsor-syria/p9368.

93. Robert Park, "North Korea's Legacy of Terrorism," *World Affairs*, June 6, 2013, www.worldaffairsjounal.org/article/north-korea's-legacy-terrorism, p. 2.

94. Ibid., p. 3.

95. Ibid., p. 2.

96. Justin Conrad, "Interstate Rivalry and Terrorism: An Unprobed Link" *Journal of Conflict Resolution*, Vol. 55, No. 4, February 21, 2011, http://jcr.sagepub.com/content/55/4/529.

97. The Sandinistas took their name from Augusto Sandino. He was a popular leader, executed by his government, who was opposed to a series of American military interventions in Nicaragua from 1912 to the 1930s. Among the reasons for these interventions was protecting the interests of the American owned United Fruit Company that exported bananas to the United States and Europe. Parenthetically, from 1889 until the mid-1930s America often intervened in the internal affairs of Caribbean and Central America nations to protect its commercial interests, a period referred to as the "Bananas Wars."

98. Guy Gugliotta, "Assassinating a Tyrant: How Somoza Died," *The Chicago Tribune*, July 19, 1989.

99. See Michael J. Schroeder, "Bandits and Blanket Thieves, Communists and Terrorists: The Politics of Naming the Sandinistas in Nicaragua, 1927–36 and 1979—1990," *Third World Quarterly*, Vol. 26, Issue 1, February 2005, pp. 67–86.

100. Loc. cit.

101. The Tower Commission Report (1987) is the official inquiry to "Irangate"; it suggests that the purpose of the sales was for this assistance, but stops just short of plainly asserting it. See John Tower, Chairman, *The Tower Commission Report: The President's Special Review Board* (Washington, D.C.: Government Printing Office, 1987).

102. "The Iran-Contra Affair, www.pbs.org/wgbh,americanexperience/features/general-article/reagan-Iran, accessed April 8, 2013. The Tower Commission Report found considerable evidence, but no hard proof that the arms deal money had gone to the contras.

103. The information in this paragraph is drawn from the 11-page decision "Case Concerning the Military and Paramilitary Activities In and Against Nicaragua (*Nicaragua V. United States of America*) (Merits), Judgment of 27 June 1986, International Court of Justice, The Hague, Netherlands.

104. Loc. cit.

105. Robert Pear, "Chile Agrees to Pay Reparations to U.S. in Slaying of Envoy," *New York Times*, May 13, 1990.

106. Loc. cit.

107. Loc. cit.

108. "TNI and the Pinochet Precedent," August 12, 2009, www.tni.org/primer/tni-and-pincochet-precedent.

109. Ely Karmon, "Counterterrorism Policy: Why Tehran Starts and Stops Terrorism," *The Middle East Quarterly*, Vol. 5, Issue 4, December 1998, pp. 35–44. Karmon records number of deaths by separate periods.

110. Dan Geist, "A Darker Horizon: The Assassination of Shapour Bakhtiar," PBS, p. 2, www.pbs.org/wgbh/pages/frontline/tehranbureau/2011/08/a-darker-horizon-the-assassination-of-shapour-bakhtiar.html.

111. Loc. cit.

112. Chad Bray and Evan Perez, "Guilty Plea in Plan to Kill Saudi Arabian Diplomat," *The Wall Street Journal*, October 17, 2012.

113. Richard Obina Iroanya, "Implications of State and State Sponsored International Terrorism for Africa: The Case of Libya and Sudan," a thesis submitted in partial fulfillment for the Master of Security Studies, Department of Political Sciences, University of Pretoria, South Africa, November 2008, p. 22.

114. Awareness Brief: Homegrown Violent Extremism," (Washington, D.C.: Community Oriented Policing Services, U.S. Department of Justice, 2014), p. 1. The content of the cite is drawn from several sources of the International Association of Chiefs of Police. See "http://www.theiacp.org/portal/0/homegrownviolentextremistawarenessbrief.pdf".

115. Ibid., p. 5.

116. Loc. cit.

117. Jerome P. Bjelopera, *The Domestic Terror Threat: Background and Issues for Congress*, (Washington, D.C.: Congressional Research Service, January 17, 2013), p. 9.

118. Ibid., p. 10.

119. Loc. cit.

120. William Dyson, The Emergence of Special-Interest/Single-Issue Terrorism," State and Local Anti-Terrorism Training (SLATT) Program, (Tallahassee, Florida, Institute for Intergovernmental Research, 2001), p. 1.

121. Federal Bureau of Investigation, "Putting Intel to Work Against ELF and ALF Terrorists," June 6, 2008, www.FBI.gov/News/Stories/2008/June/Ecoterror_200208110011.

122. This table is prepared from information contained in Jerome P. Bjelopera, *The Domestic Terrorism Threat: Background and Issues for Congress* (Washington, D.C.: Congressional Research Service, May 15, 2012), p. 47.

123. Jessica Narim, "GP Destroyed GM Wheat," *ABC News*, July 14, 2011, www.abc.ner.au/news/2011-07-14/20110714-greenpeace-gm-protest/2794272.

124. University of Maryland, Global Terrorism Data Base, Incident Summary Number 200208110011. www.Start.Umd.edu/gtd/Search/Incidentsummary.Aspx?gtdid=200208110011.

125. "Vandals Attack Forestry Research Project," *OSU News and Research Communications*, March 23, 2001.

126. Gordon Witkin and Ian Greenberg, "End of the Line for the Unabomber," *U.S. News and World Report*, Vol. 124, Issue 4, February 2, 1998, p. 34.

127. The Unabomber's manifesto appeared as an 8-page supplement to *The Washington Post*'s September 25, 1995 edition. See www.washingtonpost.com/wp-srv/national/longterm/unabomber/manifesto.text.htm.

128. "Chart of Abortion Attacks," *National Consortium for the Study of Terrorism and Responses to Terrorism*" undated, www.start.umd.edu/gtd/search/results.aspx?Search=abortion&sa.x=0&sa.y=0&sa=search, p. 1.

129. "Terrorist Organization Profile: Army of God," *National Consortium for the Study of Terrorism and Responses to Terrorism*," undated, www.start.umd.edu/start/data_collections/tops/terrorist_organization_profiles.asp?id=28.

130. See Robin Abcarian, "Abortion Doc's Killer Convicted," *Chicago Tribune*, January 30, 2010; and "George R. Tiller," *New York Times*, January 29, 2010.

131. CNN Wire Staff, "Doctor's Killer Sentenced to Life in Prison," www.cnn.com/2010/crime/04/01/kansasabortion.roeder.sentence/index.html.

Typologies of Terrorism: The Right and Left Wings and Separatist or Nationalist Movements

Learning Objectives

After completing this chapter, you will be able to:

1. State what is at the core of American right-wing ideology.

2. Identify three major right-wing ideologies in the United States.

3. Describe the role of racism with respect to the white supremacy movement.

4. Identify and briefly describe the earliest racist organization in America.

5. Explain why the KKK was originally founded.

6. Discuss neo-Nazi groups.

7. Explain the goal of George Lincoln Rockwell.

8. Profile the Hammerskin Nation.

9. Trace the development and present state of the anti-federalist/Christian Patriot movement.

Norwegian terrorist Anders Breivik bombed a government building and attacked people at a youth camp, killing a total of 77 people. The man standing in the foreground has blood on his hands and arms perhaps from trying to help someone or from his own injuries. He is gazing upward, possibly stunned or asking "Why?" Although it is easy to think of terrorism as being committed by radicalized Muslims, it should not deflect us from noting others also commit acts of terrorism—in this case by a person philosophically from the international far right.
(© Kamerapress Sweden/Photoshot/ Newscom)

Introduction

As discussed previously, this chapter represents the balance of the typologies of terrorism identified by leading scholars. This includes groups that are broadly associated with left-wing and right-wing political movements as well as separatist or national movements. Although we have briefly mentioned some of these groups from a historical perspective, we now address them in more detail.

The Right Wing

Right-wing movements and politics are by nature conservative; illustrations of this in the United States include the Tea Party and the American Family Association. However, as used here, "right wing" denotes individuals and groups whose views exceed being merely conservative. They are sometimes characterized as the "far right," "extremist right," or "radical right." This right wing potentially poses a serious threat, both here and abroad.

Movements within the American right wing have different ideas about the "enemies" and ideas they oppose. Illustrations of these include illegal immigrants, the "Zionist Occupied Government" (ZOG) in Washington, D.C., African-Americans, feminist views, lesbians, gay, bisexual and transgender (LGBT) people, and Muslims. Simultaneously, they often share beliefs such as politicians and political parties do not properly represent them, the Constitution is being subverted, the government cannot be trusted and is eating away individual freedoms, the federal government is part of a plot to impose a "one world government" on U.S. citizens, and even a claim that the Federal Emergency Management Agency (FEMA) has 800 concentration camps for people who protest government policies and programs.[1]

Recruits have been flocking to right-wing movements roughly since 2000. The strong gun control measures taken by President Clinton's administration moved some people to join right-wing groups and the 9/11 attacks did likewise as conspiracy theories quickly sprang up (e.g., Jewish people working in the Twin Towers didn't go to work on 9/11 because they knew about the attacks in advance, aluminum planes can't bring down massive steel structures and what actually happened was the government planted bombs to ensure the Twin Towers came down to justify the wars in Iraq and Afghanistan).[2] More recently, the election of an African-American president, disclosures about the breadth of data collection by the National Security Agency (NSA), and renewed efforts for gun control have further swelled the far right's ranks. Patriot groups have rocketed from 149 in 2008 to 1,274 just three years later, and the Southern Poverty Law Center has identified 1,018 hate groups in this country.[3] An alarming development is some men at a few of President Obama's speeches have carried signs reading "The tree of liberty needs to be watered with the blood of tyrants,"[4] a paraphrasing of Thomas Jefferson's (1743–1826) "The tree of liberty must be refreshed from time to time with the blood of patriots and tyrants." Although different meanings could be applied to these signs, one is that they carry an implicit threat.

The increase in right-wing groups and agendas has shifted some security attention away from the left wing, which historically has wanted to replace existing governments with communist or socialist ones. The left wing has had little success in doing this and although monitored by the government it is not presently considered a serious threat. Other terrorist threats discussed in this chapter are separatist/nationalist and religious movements.

The International Right Wing

Europe has a number of right-wing political parties that have aggressive environmental and/or anti-immigration platforms. Examples of these parties include the National Front Party (France), Freedom Party (Austria), and the National Democratic Party (NDP, Germany). The neo-Nazi NDP believes "immigrants should go back to the Middle East on flying carpets"[5] (see Figure 8–1). Italy's Northern League takes positions across the political spectrum, but its strong stances against illegal immigration and Islam are popular with voters.[6]

As in other European countries, the unwillingness of immigrant Muslims in Italy to be assimilated is causing significant social strain. The fact that the Northern League and other right-wing parties have enjoyed moderate success at the polls reflects sentiments loose in

Quick Facts
Right-Wing Violence in Sweden

Anders Breivik bombed a building in Oslo, Sweden—killing eight people—and drove to a youth camp, where he killed another 69 and wounded hundreds more. His personally created ideology combined the hate of the right wing with his own rage against Muslims who were (according to him) engaged in the "Islamic colonization of Europe.[7] He declared his victims were "traitors," guilty of embracing multiculturalism, and deserved to die.

FIGURE 8–1
Followers of the neo-Nazi National Democratic Party participating in an anti-Muslim demonstration near a mosque in Duisburg, Germany.

(© Roland Weihrauch/EPA/Newscom)

English Defence League
The EDL represents a growing phenomenon in Europe: right-wing groups that are not simply racist, but profoundly hostile toward Islam and their immigration into Western Europe. The EDL and other anti-jihad movements are united in their belief that Islam and Muslims are a fundamental threat to the resources, identities, and survival of Western nations.

Xenophobic
a person who manifests xenophobia. See xenophobia.

James Earl Ray
He assassinated civil rights champion Reverend Martin Luther King in Memphis, Tennessee, in 1968.

Nativism
The right wing rests on nativism, the ultra-preference for the traditional culture of a homeland to the exclusion of immigrants and their alien ways, as well as opposition to foreign ideas and influences. Nativism also rejects those in the homeland who champion immigrants, "alien" ways, and non-traditional ways of looking at the world.

the populations of their respective nations. Outside of the political arena there are examples of right-wing violence. In Florence, Italy, a man with reported ties to the right-wing anti-immigration group Casa Pound shot and killed two African street vendors and wounded another before killing himself.[8] In Germany, a three-member group described as neo-Nazis and calling themselves the National Socialist Underground are thought to have killed seven men of Turkish origin and one Greek.[9] In Japan, right-wing movements are substantially nationalistic, anti-Korean, and anti-Chinese. Right-wing movements in Africa include labor groups and white separatists. Right-wing groups from Hindu India and Islamic Pakistan often clash and the violence is fueled by a volatile combination of religious hatred and nationalism.

Although denying any aspiration to become a political party, the **English Defence League** (EDL) represents a growing phenomenon in Europe: groups that are not simply right wing, anti-Muslim, or overtly racist, but **xenophobic**, profoundly hostile toward immigration.[10] Between 2009 and 2012, the EDL organized over 50 street demonstrations, each with 1,000 to 3,000 supporters.[11] It has 80 local divisions in England and 80,000 Facebook followers.[12] Other defense leagues have been established in Belgium, Scotland, Australia, Denmark, and Norway. The public face of EDL is that it exists to peacefully demonstrate against the spread of Islam; however, without assigning any blame, it has been a counterforce at pro-Islamic demonstrations that turned violent. The larger right-wing anti-jihad movement includes the defense leagues and other groups, such as the Citizen's Movement Pax Europa in Germany, Generation Identity in France, and the American Freedom Defense Initiative that are united in their belief that Islam and Muslims are a fundamental threat to the resources, identities, and survival of Western nations.[13]

Issues in Defining the Right Wing

The difficulties in defining terrorism also apply to defining the "right wing." Terminological chaos and the absence of a clear conceptual framework also hinder our understanding of right-wing terrorism.[14] Consider the array of terms used: right wing, the far right, extreme right, radical right, and right-wing populist.[15] Geography and religion also affect what constitutes right-wing extremism. In Europe there frequently isn't a religious component to right-wing extremism, but in Israel and the United States there is often one.[16] In Israel extreme right-wing views are linked to justifications for using extreme measures to maintain control over the West Bank and the Gaza Strip; in the United States religion is part of the ideology of white supremacy and other right-wing movements.[17]

Right-Wing Attacks and Ideology in America

Right-wing attacks in America have risen. Annual attacks by far-right individuals and groups averaged 70.1 during the 1990s, but during 2000–2011 that figure rose to 307.5, an increase of more than 400 percent.[18] Right-wing extremists have caused terrible harm to the United

In Brockton, Massachusetts Keith Luke—who carved a swastika on his forehead while awaiting trial—murdered two immigrants from the Republic of Cape Verde and raped another as part of his plans to deal with African-Americans, Hispanics, and Jews. His motive was to fight for, and help preserve, "a dying race."

It is believed that Joseph Paul Franklin's crime spree in the United States started in 1977. In addition to bank robberies, this racist and anti-Semitic murdered Jews and visitors leaving a synagogue and mixed-race couples, killing 20 people. He also targeted persons who were friendly to minorities. Franklin believed that God wanted him to start a race war. He was convicted of murder in 1980 and executed in 2013.

The most visible American anti-illegal immigration groups are often located in states along the Rio Grande River, the boundary with Mexico; they include the California Coalition for Immigration Reform, Border Guardians, Border Patrol Auxiliary, Texas Border Volunteers, American Freedom Riders, and Mountain Minutemen (see Figure 8–2).

States. In 1968, a lone white supremacist,[19] **James Earl Ray** (1928–1998), set off riots and demonstrations in 100 American cities when he used a rifle to assassinate the civil rights leader Reverend Martin Luther King Jr., who was standing outside of his room at the Lorraine Motel in Memphis, Tennessee.

At its core, American right-wing ideology envisions having a homeland population that is homogeneous with respect to ethnicity, language, culture, and beliefs, as well as a systematic rejection of all those who are different.[20] The right rests on the notion that "being American" equates to emanating from European Anglo-Saxon stock, being Christian, nationalistic, and ruggedly independent.[21] To one degree or another, the right wing rests on **nativism**, the ultra-preference for the traditional culture of a homeland to the exclusion of immigrants and their alien ways, as well as opposition to foreign ideas and influences.[22] Nativism also rejects those in the homeland who support immigrants, "alien" ways, and non-traditional ways of looking at the world.[23] Nativism incorporates **xenophobia**, which involves an irrational fear, hatred, and hostility toward people who are "different," including not only immigrants but those with different lifestyles, sexual preferences, and "strange" ideas; racism rests on the same dynamics, but is rooted in a narrower race-based hatred, driven by the belief that "we" are naturally superior to "them."[24]

The Three Major Ideological Right-Wing Movements in the United States

Perliger identifies three major ideological right-wing movements in the United States: (1) racist/white supremacy, (2) anti-federalist, and (3) religious fundamentalists. Their ideological orientations affect the targets they select, the tactics used, and the operations conducted.[25]

The Racist/White Supremacy Movement

To no small degree the abominable practice of slavery has engendered the lingering *voluntary sickness* of racism in America. Racism essentially birthed the wider white supremacy movement with its volatile mixture of nativism, xenophobia, anti-immigration, **homophobic**, Christianity, and anti-Semitic components. As a society, the United States does not have "clean hands" when it comes to racism/white supremacy. Although not to the same degree as African-Americans, other ethnic groups have also suffered.

In the pre-revolution English colonies in America free Irish immigrants usually arrived here impoverished, joining African-American slaves at the bottom of society's ladder. Ships' captains bringing servants to the colonies were paid a bonus for non-Irish males because Ireland had a long history of rebellion against England and were

FIGURE 8–2
Near Naco, Arizona, a Minutemen volunteer watches the Arizona/Mexico border for illegal aliens crossing into the United States. When observed, Minutemen call the Border Patrol to apprehend the "crossers."
(© Holbrooke/SIPA/Newscom)

Xenophobia
An irrational fear, hatred, and hostility toward people who are "different," including not only immigrants but those with different lifestyles or sexual preferences, and "strange" ideas.

Homophobic
Describes a range of negative attitudes and feelings toward people who are gay, lesbian, bisexual, or transgender (GLBT).

Manifest Destiny

In 1845, as Americans pushed westward, newspaper editor John O'Sullivan coined the term "manifest destiny," meaning the United States had a divine obligation to push its boundaries ever-forward. At the heart of manifest destiny was the pervasive belief in American cultural and racial superiority.

FRANK LESLIE'S ILLUSTRATED NEWSPAPER.

FIGURE 8–3

Racial hatred is often a precursor to racial terrorism. During the 1870s and 1880s there were 153 anti-Chinese riots in the American West. In 1880, anti-Chinese sentiment was loose in Denver, inflamed by a local newspaper that called the Chinese the "Pest of the Pacific" and prophesized that if more arrived white men would starve and women would be forced into prostitution. During Denver's riot one Chinese man was beaten to death, the Chinatown section was burned down, and their laundries were destroyed. Some citizens hid the Chinese in their homes, as did a brothel. No criminal charges were ever filed.[40]

(Courtesy Library of Congress)

Catholics, a religion abandoned by England.[26] If the Irish indentured themselves, they were required to perform more years of service than indentured people from England.[27] Indentured Irishmen were often given more dangerous jobs than slaves because the latter were more valuable.[28] The Irish were so lowly regarded that even slaves could safely tell anti-Irish jokes.[29]

In 1845, as Americans pushed westward, newspaper editor John O'Sullivan coined the term "**manifest destiny**," meaning the United States had a divine obligation to push its boundaries ever-forward.[30] "At the heart of manifest destiny was the pervasive belief in American cultural and racial superiority."[31] The westward movement was particularly fueled by the discovery of gold at Sutter's Mill, California (1848), the availability of free land to settlers under the Homestead Act (1862), and the end of our Civil War (1865), which released large numbers of restless men who sought adventure and fortune in the West.[32] As manifest destiny made the shift from a slogan to unofficial government policy the previous practice of going onto Indian lands, making genocidal war on Native Americans, then treaties, and then more wars when the treaties didn't suit the federal government became virulent. The refrain attributed to General Phillip Sheridan that "The only good Indian is a dead Indian" was commonly voiced. Despite the refrain's endless repetition there is considerable doubt that Sheridan ever said it.[33]

Hispanics were also subject to racism during the westward movement. There were 597 documented lynchings of Latinos, about one-fifth the number for African-Americans for the same period.[34] Although crimes were alleged in many cases, Latinos were also lynched for being "uppity," refusing to leave land coveted by Anglos, being "too Mexican" (Speaking Spanish too loudly), and even a few Mexican woman were lynched for resisting Anglo advances "too vigorously."[35]

Excitement about the discovery of gold at Sutter's Mill led to waves of Chinese coming to America to seek their fortune.[36] However, they were quickly pushed off any productive claims they found and forced into menial laborer jobs, most notably the construction of railroads. Still, within 30 years the Chinese represented 10 percent of California's population.[37] Their "strange" language, Buddhist religion, manner of dress, physical appearance, and living in Chinese enclaves made assimilation in 19th-century America an impossibility. During the economic depression of 1873–1879 the Chinese were considered a threat to white employment[38] and racial violence quickened, including the burning of some "China Towns" (see Figure 8–3). Numerous racist laws regulating the Chinese were passed. For example, in California the Chinese couldn't testify in court or live within incorporated areas because they were considered a dangerous presence to the state.[39] The outcry against them grew so ferocious that in 1882 the Congress enacted the Chinese Exclusion Act, effectively barring Chinese immigration to America. In 1924, the National Origins Act restricted immigration from all Eastern Asian nations, which remained unchanged until the 1960s.

The surprise attack on Pearl Harbor, Hawaii, on December 7, 1941, led the American government to fear an imminent West Coast invasion by Japanese military forces. In 1942, the United States placed 120,000 mainland ethnic Japanese-Americans, two-thirds of whom were native United States citizens, behind barbed wire in 10 guarded **Japanese-American internment camps** located in Western states and Arkansas as a "national security measure" (see Figure 8–4); this action was taken despite the fact that thousands of them had been investigated by federal agents and deemed not to be a threat.[41] The interred were forced to abandon their homes and businesses or sell them at distressed prices. However, it was impractical to inter the Japanese-Americans on Hawaii because they were the majority of the population and they were therefore left in place.

FIGURE 8–4
In 1942, behind the barbed wire at the Manzanar Relocation Camp, California, Japanese-American citizens recognize Memorial Day, which honors the men and women who died while serving in the Armed Forces of the United States. As indicated by their American Legion hats, some of these men were veterans of World War I.

(Courtesy Library of Congress)

In 1942, the Army discharged all Japanese-American citizens from its Reserve Officer Training Corp (ROTC) program and changed their draft status to 4C, "enemy alien."[42] Remarkably, many of the interred Japanese-American men volunteered to serve in the Army and formed the **442nd Regimental Combat Team**, along with volunteer Japanese-Americans from Hawaii. Fighting in the European Theater of Operations, the 442nd became the most heavily decorated unit of its size in military history.[43] We have been unable to find a single case of espionage or sabotage by Japanese Americans during World War II. In 1988, the Congress recognized the "grave injustice" done and awarded each surviving camp member $20,000; each reparation paid was accompanied by a letter of apology from President Regan. Longitudinal health studies showed that incidents of heart disease and premature death among internees were twice that of the general American population.[44]

The **German-American Bund**, a pro-Nazi organization, sprung up in this country in the 1930s to proclaim the virtues of Hitler and the Third Reich and to encourage America to remain neutral in the approaching European war (see Figure 8–5).[45] The anti-Semitic Bund's membership was made up of 25,000 German-American citizens, including 8,000 uniformed Storm Troopers, who occasionally clashed with American Jewish veterans of World War I.[46] Although the Bund was outlawed at the onset of World War II and a few leaders incarcerated, its Anglo-Saxon members, unlike the Japanese-Americans, were not rounded up and incarcerated.

During World War II racist violence toward Chicanos erupted. **Zoot suit** fashion originated out of the African-American jazz movement and jumped to the Chicano culture. The zoot suit featured exaggerated shoulders, long coat tails, a high waist, pleated pants with pegged legs, thick-soled leather shoes, and a long watch chain.[47] On the West Coast, American servicemen saw the style as a not only a waste of materials needed for the war effort; but subversive as well.[48] There were a number of violent clashes between servicemen and Chicano "Zoot Suiters" (see Figure 8–6), including one in 1943 in which the "suiters" were beaten, stripped naked, and their clothing burned in the street.[49]

In the wake of the 9/11, anti-Islamic attacks in America skyrocketed from 28 in 2000 to 481 in 2001.[50] Ten years later, the number of anti-Islamic attacks had fallen to 157, or 12.7 percent of all hate crime that is religion based; the anti-Jewish figure was 62.5 percent of the total.[51] Although "Islamophobic" attacks were down, gruesome violence against Muslims continues. Notably, in 2012, a 31-year-old New York City woman was charged with second degree murder. She allegedly pushed a man, who she mistakenly identified as a

Japanese-American internment camps
At the outbreak of World War II, Japanese-Americans were placed in internment camps for "national security." Some volunteered to serve in the 442nd Regimental Combat Team to demonstrate their loyalty. In 1988, the Congress recognized the "grave injustice" done to those interred and awarded each surviving camp member $20,000; each reparation paid was accompanied by a letter of apology from President Regan.

442nd Regimental Combat Team
A Japanese-American unit that served in the European Theater with great distinction. It consisted of Japanese-American volunteers from Hawaii and the internment camps. The 442nd became the most heavily decorated unit of its size in military history. See Japanese-American internment camps.

German-American Bund
In the 1930s, The GAB emerged in this country as a pro-Nazi movement that sang the praises of Hitler and the Third Reich, encouraged Americans to stay out of the war in Europe, and was anti-Semitic. Its members were largely drawn from German Americans. Unlike the wholesale internment of Japanese-Americans, only a small number of the GAB were incarcerated after it was outlawed.

Zoot suit
A men's fashion that moved from the African-American jazz movement into Chicano style. The exaggerated style was offensive to World War II American servicemen who saw the style wasteful and subversive. The result were some violent clashes between the Chicano "zoot suiters" and servicemen.

FIGURE 8–5
In 1937, German-American Bund members marched in uniforms on Long Island, New York. A portion of a flag bearing the Nazi swastika appears to the right of the first American flag.

(Courtesy Library of Congress)

Slave patrols
The first formal racist organization in America.

Muslim, onto the subway tracks where he was killed by an oncoming train. The woman told investigators: I've hated Hindus and Muslims ever since 2001, when they put down the Twin Towers. I've been beating them up since then.[52] In the wake of the Boston Marathon bombing in 2013 by the two Tsarnaev brothers, both ethnic Chechens and Muslims, many feared a repeat of the widespread anti-Islamic attacks that followed 9/11, but this did not happen. African-Americans continue to suffer disproportionally from reported race-based hate crime, constituting some 71.1 percent of all of it, while Hispanics represent 56.2 percent of all reported ethnicity/national origin hate crimes.[53] Gay, lesbian, bisexual, and transgender (GLBT) persons accounted for 20.8 percent of all reported single-bias incidents.[54] A fundamental truth of these statistics is that African-Americans, Jews, Hispanics, and GLBTs continue to suffer disproportionately from right-wing extremism.

The Ku Klux Klan Movement

Conventionally, the Ku Klux Klan (KKK) is "recognized" as the first formal racist organization in this country. However, that "distinction" actually belongs to the **slave patrols** that began in the colonial era and were highly regulated in some states. Beginning in 1704, South Carolina enacted laws controlling such slave patrol matters as district patrol boundaries, patrol authority, and relief from militia duty if serving on slave patrols.[55] These patrols were not informal, spontaneous, or episodic groups, but organizations created by law and are therefore the earliest formal racist organization in this country. Inasmuch as this section covers the racist/white supremacy portion of the American right wing, the discussion here is focused on its most visible components, the Ku Klux Klan and the neo-Nazis.

Pulaski, Tennessee, was a sleepy town in 1865. The Civil War was over and several former Confederates played in a band to help raise money to buy artificial limbs for some of their maimed comrades. Bored Confederate veterans formed the Ku Klux Klan in 1866[56] to create a stir and excitement at parties. They made up nonsensical names like the Grand Cyclops and Imperial Wizard and rode off to parties wearing costumes and masks.[57] Very quickly the KKK began intimidating former slaves, referred to after the

FIGURE 8–6
Chained together, "Zoot Suiters" are lined up outside of the Los Angeles jail waiting to board the bus that will take them to court after an evening feud with sailors. These encounters were sometimes brutal because servicemen beat the "suiters" with clubs.

(Courtesy Library of Congress)

Civil War as "freedmen," and then jumped to committing violence against them. Many Southerners approved of KKK actions because it restored what they saw as the natural order of things. By 1868 the KKK was a full-blown terrorist organization that its members called the "Invisible Empire of the South."[58] Beginning in 1870, Congress passed a series of laws that were aimed at defeating the KKK.

Originally a Southern phenomenon, the first KKK was substantially eroded and became a marginal movement not later than 1900. In 1915, a second, revitalized KKK appeared that was prominent into the 1930s; its membership extended into regions outside of the South and at its height it had 5,000,000 members.[59] The 1915 KKK was the most successful far–right-wing movement in U.S. history in terms of the power to elect political candidates, recruit dues-paying members, and turn out supporters at rallies.[60] To no small measure the silent film "Birth of a Nation," released in 1915, aided recruitment by portraying African-Americans negatively and the Klan as a heroic force holding back this "threat" to America.

This "second" KKK pursued a national agenda that was virulently anti-immigration, anti-Catholicism, anti-Semitic, and anti-African-American, while at the same time being pro-family, pro-protestant, pro-prohibition, and pro-American white nation (see Figure 8–7). These themes resonated across class lines, causing the regular KKK membership rolls to bulge. The KKK also distributed a magazine to reinforce these messages and allowed for local agendas, such as targeting Mormons and labor radicals. Additionally, there were affiliate organizations, including the Women's Ku Klux Klan (WKKK), the Junior Order of the Ku Klux Klan for boys, and the Tri-K Klan for girls.[61] The Great Depression that began in 1929 and lasted until the late 1930s gutted the ability of many to pay KKK dues and membership declined. The entry of the United States into World War II diverted potential recruits to military service and the Klan substantially disappeared until after the Korean War (1950–1953).

The resurrection of the "third" Klan was inhibited by many states passing anti-Klan laws, the passage of the federal Civil Rights Act of 1964, the enforcement of its provisions by the FBI, arrests made on cold cases, including the bombing of African-American churches, and a series of civil suits that cost the Klan millions of dollars (e.g., the KKK was ordered to pay $38 million because it incited the hatred that resulted in an African-American Church being burned in Manning, South Carolina).[62]

Beginning in the 1970s and continuing into the 1980s, the Klan toned down its racial rhetoric and reframed its messages in a neo-conservatism shift. Jews were at the heart of a conspiracy to destroy America. They were blamed for an increasingly liberal national government that the Klan dubbed the "**Zionist Occupied Government**" (ZOG) and condemned as the "Jewish dominated news media" that espoused the acceptance of "deviant lifestyles," such as homosexuality, the mixing of races, and feminist views. To fight this menace, the Klan appropriated the warped notion of Christianity Identity, which established the Bible as the authority for what they did, while retaining their nativist and xenophobic views of what constituted being "American." In doing so, the Klan morphed from being a hate organization to a "theologically based, patriotic white supremacy movement." The Christian Identity movement is discussed later in this chapter and is sometimes referred to by mainstream theologians as "**Counterfeit Christians**."

The KKK has been fragmented for some time; there are at least 40 different Klan groups of various sizes with perhaps 100 local **Klaverns** or chapters between them. Until recently there was only an estimated total membership of 5,000.[63] As an indication of its impotence, at a 1999 protest in downtown New York the Klan could muster only 16 members in the face of 8,000 New Yorkers who came out to counter demonstrate.[64] Since 2006, the Klan has attempted to exploit fears about immigration, amnesty, gay marriages, crime,

FIGURE 8–7
On August 8, 1925, 35,000 Klansmen marched in Washington, D.C., a substantial display of its power. The white-robed men paraded in orderly military formations as far as the eye could see. Barely visible in the distance is the dome of the United States Capitol building.
(Courtesy Library of Congress)

Zionist Occupied Government
A right-wing term sometimes used to refer to the U.S. government.

Counterfeit Christians
Sometimes used to refer to Christian Identity adherents.

Klaverns
Local chapters of the KKK.

TABLE 8–1

States Notable for Active or Growing Ku Klux Klan Chapters

This table is a snapshot of Klan activity in 2006-2007 and does not reflect developments after that date

South	Midwest	Great Plains	Mid-Atlantic
Alabama	Indiana	Iowa	Maryland
Arkansas	Kentucky	Nebraska	New Jersey
Florida	Michigan		Pennsylvania
Georgia	Ohio		West Virginia
Louisiana			
Mississippi			
South Carolina			
Tennessee			
Texas			

Source: From The Ku Klux Klan Rebounds. Copyright © 2013 by Anti-Defamation League.

George Lincoln Rockwell

Founder of the American Nazi Party who ran for president in an effort to change the U.S. Constitution and laws to align with the racist perspectives of the Nazi Party.

Dr. William Luther Pierce

As Andrew MacDonald authored *The Turner Diaries*, still considered one of the right wing's most influential publications. He also wrote *Hunter*, which did not receive nearly the acclaim that *The Turner Diaries* did.

Andrew MacDonald

See Dr. William L. Pierce.

The Turner Diaries

See Dr. William L. Pierce.

Hunter

See Dr. William L. Pierce.

gun control, and other issues;[65] as a result it is believed there has been a rapid expansion in size (see Table 8–1). Although some Klansmen still wear robes and burn crosses, some younger ones are virtually indistinguishable from racist skinheads and neo-Nazis, adopting their music, dress, tattoos, and imagery.[66]

The Neo-Nazi Movement

"Neo-Nazi groups share a hatred for Jews and a love for Adolf Hitler and Nazi Germany. While they also hate other minorities, gays and lesbians and even sometimes Christians, they perceive 'the Jew' as their cardinal enemy, and trace social problems to a Jewish conspiracy that supposedly controls governments, financial institutions and the media."[67] There is not one neo-Nazi organization; there are many. Estimates vary, but there may be as many as 200 neo-Nazi groups in the United States, many of which share agendas.

The goal of **George Lincoln Rockwell** (1918–1967) was to use his American Nazi Party (ANP) to become President of the United States in 1972 and then "exterminate all treasonous Jews, banish all American Negroes to Africa, and amend the Constitution to suit the Nazi party."[68] The FBI's official 1965 threat assessment of the ANP was "Though small in numbers and influence the ANP is a dangerous organization of misfits … capable of perpetrating acts of violence."[69] In 1967, Rockwell was at a carwash when a sniper killed him; the perpetrator was a man Rockwell had dismissed from the ANP. Despite the hatred it spewed out and the extensive news media coverage it received, the ANP was never a major force. A more recent parallel to Rockwell's political ambitions is Billy Joe Roper, who in 2002 founded the neo-Nazi White Revolution as an Arkansas-based political party that seeks to promote cooperation among supremacy groups.[70] Roper, who was expelled from the neo-Nazi National Alliance (NA) in a leadership struggle, ran an unsuccessful write-in candidacy in the 2010 Arkansas governor's race.[71]

Shortly after Rockwell's death the ANP was rebadged as the National Socialist White People's Party (NSWPP) and **Dr. William Luther Pierce** (1933–2002), a former physics professor at Oregon State University, became one of its principal leaders.[72] Beginning in 1974, Pierce headed the neo-Nazi National Alliance (NA)[73] and it was there that he became the leading figure of the racist/white supremacy movement for nearly 30 years. Pierce envisioned NA as being the vanguard of a white nationalist movement. The NA used right-wing magazines, bands, record companies, music (National Socialist Black Metal, NSBM), weekly radio talks, the Internet, and Internet games to spread its gospel.[74] NA's National Vanguard Press eventually had a list of 700 books to spread the NA's message.[75]

Writing under the name of **Andrew MacDonald**, Pierce wrote two influential racist/white supremacy novels, **The Turner Diaries** (1978) and **Hunter** (1984). The former depicts an Aryan revolution in America that spreads globally, includes nuclear attacks, and results in the elimination of all "impure races." The revolution begins with the truck bombing of the FBI Headquarters in Washington, D.C., a scenario that many think was a model for Tim McVeigh's 1995 attack on the Murrah Federal Building in Oklahoma City.[76] The fictional and McVeigh's attacks occurred at almost the same time of day, both featured truck bombs, and when arrested McVeigh had a portion of *The Turner Diaries* in his car. *Hunter* is considered the prequel to *The Turner Diaries*. In *Hunter*, Yeager assassinates mixed-race couples and, public figures advocating racial civil rights; battles other neo-Nazi enemies, including Jews; and becomes involved with a white nationalist movement.

Under Pierce the NA became the largest and most active neo-Nazi organization in the United States; dozens of violent crimes were attributed to NA members or by those apparently influenced by its propaganda.[77] In 2005, many members defected to the newly formed National Vanguard, weakening the NA. By 2012, 10 years after Pierce's death, the NA had been reduced to a tiny band of small-time propagandists.[78] Although small, the NA is dangerous; four recruits have been accused or convicted of carrying out at least a dozen murders.[79]

In 1974, two members of the ANP left it and formed the National Socialist American Workers Freedom Movement, which became the previously mentioned National Socialist Movement (NSM) 20 years later.[80] Ideologically, the NSM mirrors that of the original American Nazi Party; the NSM openly idolizes Hitler and describes him as the "Our Furher, the beloved Holy Father of our age."[81]

One of the NSM's symbols is "88." The eighth letter of the alphabet is "H" and "88" means "Heil Hitler." The NSM's rhetoric is anti-Jewish, homophobic, anti-immigration, racist, and white nationalist. The NSM demands territory for the creation of a union in which only whites of pure blood may be citizens; Jews and homosexuals are specifically excluded from citizenship.[82] All illegal immigrants must be returned to their homeland; non-whites can live in the white homeland only as guests under the law of aliens, meaning they have no legal right to remain in the country.[83] One of the NSM's leaders asserts "the Constitution was written by white men alone; therefore, it is intended for whites alone."[84] Unlike other neo-Nazi groups the NSM allows members of other groups to join without abandoning their other memberships.[85]

FIGURE 8–8
The Aryan Nations is trying to reorganize. At an undisclosed location in Maryland members set a cross on fire, made speeches, and distributed Aryan Nations literature to those in attendance.

(Jim Lo Scalzo/EPA/Newscom)

Organized in 1977, the Aryan Nations is a white supremacy group that, to some degree, operates as an umbrella organization, holding an annual World Congress for similar groups at its base of operations in Hayden Lake, Idaho. In 2000, it lost substantial assets due to a successful Southern Poverty Law Center civil suit. The death of Aryan Nations' founder in 2004 hastened some further disintegration of the group (see Figure 8–8).[86]

Starting in 2004, the NSM began to overshadow all other American neo-Nazi groups,[87] primarily due to setbacks by other groups between 2002 and 2007.[88] It has members in every region of the United States, although the Northeast has the most local units.[89] NSM members tend to be young and they include some skinheads.[90] It is the most explicit "Nazi-like" movement,[91] specializing in provocative street demonstrations where its members show up in militant black battle fatigues. During the recent past the NSM has emphasized immigration and amnesty issues.

The Skinhead Movement

The Hammerskin Nation (HN), founded in Dallas, Texas, in 1988, is the most violent, best organized neo-Nazi skinhead group in the United States.[92] Although primarily an American movement, HN has chapters in Canada, England, France, Germany, and several other countries.[93] Although not large, American Front (AF) is the oldest continuously active skinhead group in the United States with members in several states.[94] Some local skinhead groups in the United States affiliate with HN or AF to have an umbrella organization to tie them together. Others affiliate with the England-based Blood and Honour organization. In 2011, four members of Tampa's Blood and Honour movement beat a homeless man to death and pled guilty or were convicted of the act.[95]

Blood and Honour members believe white persons of Aryan descent are the superior race and consider the homeless to be an inferior class; "bum rolling" is the term given to targeting and committing acts of violence against homeless persons. Hammerskins and skinheads in general are disillusioned, unhappy young men who find the structure and exclusivity of the Hammerskins appealing; the probationary period for someone aspiring to join may last as long as two years.[96] Members may have shaved heads, be heavily tattooed, wear boots, jeans, and waist-length leather jackets. Like other movements, skinheads have their own language and symbols—for example, "**skinbyrd**" is a female skinhead and **red laces** in the boots means the wearer has shed his blood for the movement; some skinheads will randomly attack people to earn their laces.[97]

There are also groups that don't fit neatly into a violent racist/white supremacy mold. Neo-Confederates represent a revival of pro-Confederate sentiments and they advocate

Skinbyrd
A female skinhead.

Red Laces
Worn in the boots of skinheads, they denote the wearer has shed blood for the skinhead movement.

Box 8–1
The Posse Comitatus and Sovereign Citizen Movements

William Potter Gale founded the Posse Comitatus in 1970.[98] The Latin phrase translates to the "power of the county." It refers to a right-wing movement that opposes the federal government and holds that local authority trumps federal authority. However, the posse did not gain real momentum until Gale added Christian Identity "theology" to the anti-tax stance and spread it to the fiscally stressed farm belt.

In 1983, Posse adherent and tax protester Gordon Kahl killed two federal marshals in North Dakota; as a result, the entire movement became firmly fixed on law enforcement's radar. Kahl died in a gunfight with federal marshals, FBI agents, and local law enforcement officers in Smithville, Arkansas, in 1988. Although fledging remnants of the Posse Comitatus continue today, primarily in rural parts of the Midwest, the group and movement has withered away. Many of the former members left the Posse to join active groups in other right-wing movements.

The Sovereign Citizen movement is classified as a domestic terrorist movement by the FBI and has existed for decades[99] The Sovereign Citizen movement was a natural evolution of the Posse Comitatus ideology. The sovereigns largely operate as individuals and come together in loose groups to provide mutual assistance, train, socialize, and talk about their ideology.[100] Sovereigns refer to themselves as "freemen" or "Constitutionalists" and believe

they are free from all forms of government control because the federal, state, and local governments operate illegally.[101] Sovereigns assert that they have no obligation to pay taxes, get drivers licenses or vehicle tags, or otherwise comply with any governmental regulations or laws. If arrested or called into court they try to clog it with frivolous claims and filings. Contacts with some sovereigns can be deadly. In 2010, a father-son sovereign team killed two West Memphis, Arkansas, police officers who had stopped their vehicle.[102] The Alabama-based Republic for the United States is the largest organized group of sovereigns currently in the United States. However, the Republic of Texas group is also relatively large and active with more than 100 members. In 2011, the Republic groups held a congress with voting members from 49 states to create a new "government in waiting"[103] for the entire United States. While the Republic for the United States and the Republic of Texas do not express a violent means to an end, they do openly advocate for political revolution.[104] Recently, they have received significant political support from more radical factions of the Tea Party, particularly in Texas.

Could there be a connection between periods of economic depression in the United States and growth in anti-government groups, hate groups, and other right-wing domestic followers?

Christian Patriot movement
The collection of various right-wing, conservative groups spawning from the Posse Comitatus group; includes white supremacist organizations, sovereign citizens, and Christian Identity churches, the Ku Klux Klan, neo-Nazi groups, and Skinhead groups.

Posse Comitatus
The Latin phrase translates to the "power of the county." It refers to a right-wing movement that opposes the federal government and holds that local authority trumps federal authority. It was founded by William Potter Gale in 1970, but did not gain momentum until he incorporated Christian Identity (CI). The group was substantially defunct by 1990, several years after Gale's death.

Sovereign Citizen movement
Anti-government extremists who believe they are separate or sovereign from the federal government. Referring to themselves as freemen, or free patriots, the people associated with this movement do not pay taxes or recognize any federal or state authority, including the courts, motor vehicle departments, or law enforcement agencies.

Information Link
For more information on the Sovereign Citizen Movement, visit the FBI story relating to such groups at www.fbi.gov/news/stories/2010/april/sovereigncitizens_041310.

traditional gender roles, display hostility toward democracy, are opposed to homosexuality, favor segregation, and sometimes are openly secessionist from the United States.[105] The Institute for Historical Review (IHR) asserts its purpose is to promote truth and accuracy in history.[106] However reasonable that sounds, the real purpose of the IHR is to promote denials of the Jewish Holocaust and to defend Nazism.[107]

The Anti-Federalist (Christian Patriot) Movement

The original anti-federalist movement opposed the ratification of the U.S. Constitution, but there are other early examples of people being opposed to, or fearing, America's federal government. When the new federal government passed a tax on homemade whiskey that was used as barter, farmers in Western Pennsylvania attacked agents attempting to collect taxes. The situation became serious enough that in 1794, President George Washington rode out at the head of a column of troops to restore order. The protestors disbanded before his arrival. A handful of men were arrested, but with sympathetic local juries hearing the cases there were no convictions.

The anti-federalist movement, sometimes referred to as the **Christian Patriot movement**, has many variations. Some individuals live the movement's tenets without formally joining any organization. The Christian Patriot movement grew out of the **Posse Comitatus** and **Sovereign Citizen movements** that began during the 1970s and 1980s, which were anti-government and anti-tax.[108] Many were also racist and anti-Semitic as well.

The anti-federalists ideology is based on the idea that there is an urgent necessity to undermine the influence, legitimacy, and practical sovereignty of the federal government and its proxies.[109] In this view, America has been hijacked by external forces determined to make it part of a New World Order in which the United States would be embedded in the United Nations or a global government and policed by foreign peacekeeping forces.[110] An initial step toward that is taking up the guns presently in the hands of American citizens so they can't resist. Members see themselves as the successors to the nation's founding fathers, trying to restore America's true identity, values, and way of life.[111] In 1996, there was an 81-day standoff between Montana Freemen and federal agents.[112] Freemen adherents had formed their own township, issued warrants, developed a court and banking system, and recognized no authority higher than their own. The Freemen's land was under foreclosure and a number of Freemen were wanted on various charges. Ultimately, the Freemen surrendered and a blood bath was averted.

The unregulated "volunteer" militias that spring up are solidly anti-federalist. Four Medicare-eligible men were arrested in plots to assassinate public officials, including the U.S. Attorney General, bomb federal buildings, and attack cities with deadly ricin made from plants.[113] The men may have been members of the Georgia Militia that is not fighting the "New World Order" but instead is grounded in racist, anti-Semitic, and neo-Nazi ideology.[114] Four Ft. Stewart, Georgia, soldiers formed a militia-styled group called "Forever Enduring, Always Ready" (FEAR), which wanted to kill President Obama and start a revolution to give America back to the people. As they moved forward with their plans they allegedly killed one of their members and his girlfriend, apparently fearing that they would reveal the plot to authorities. What both of these plots had in common was the killing of senior federal government officials.

The second most deadly terrorist attack in this country was carried out by Timothy McVeigh and his accomplices at the Murrah Federal Building in Oklahoma City. McVeigh, a decorated Army combat veteran, attended a few militia meetings and made a half-hearted attempt to start one in Arizona after being discharged from the Army.[115] On April 19, 1995, McVeigh parked a rental Ryder truck filled with a deadly mixture of agricultural fertilizers, diesel fuel, and other chemicals; set a timer; and drove away.[116] The explosion killed 168 people, including 19 children, and wounded more than 500 others (see Figure 8–9).[117] Ninety minutes after the explosion McVeigh was stopped and arrested by an Oklahoma Highway Patrol Trooper on unrelated minor charges; among his possessions was a portion of *The Turner Diaries*.[118] While still in jail several days later, McVeigh was identified as a suspect in the Murrah Building bombing. McVeigh and his accomplices were convicted of the bombing, but only the unrepentant McVeigh was executed.

In 1992, federal agents tried to arrest Randy Weaver on federal weapons charges of selling illegally sawed off shotguns at his home in **Ruby Ridge**, Idaho.[119] An 11-day standoff ensued and shots were exchanged. Federal agents killed Weaver's son and wife. McVeigh was angered by what he saw as an out-of-control government. Three years later McVeigh was in Waco, Texas, where federal agents laid siege to the Branch Davidian Compound.[120] The Branch Davidians were a religious sect led by **David Koresh**. Federal agents had obtained a warrant to search the compound for weapons stockpiling. Resisted in their attempt to serve the warrant, federal agents besieged the compound for 51 days. Several federal agents were killed by Branch Davidians as they attempted to force entry into the compound. On April 19, 1995, federal agents again assaulted the compound and 76 Branch Davidians died by gunshot or by fire. McVeigh was at Waco and revenging it became his primary motivation. Two years to the day after the final assault at Waco, McVeigh detonated the bomb that gutted the Murrah Building.

The Christian Identity Movement

British Zionism ideology achieved a degree of prominence in 18th century England; ethnic Western Europeans, especially the Anglo-Saxons of Great Britain, believed they were the progeny of the ten lost tribes of Israel[121] who had migrated to the British Isles. This meant the Bible was not written for the Jews, but for the white race.[122] This false form of Christianity placed the white race at the center of God's divine plan and all other ethnicities were lesser beings, soulless "mud people."[123] By the mid-late 1940s, the British Zionism ideology gained traction in America's West. In 1946, Wesley Swift, a Grand Dragon of the Ku Klux Klan, founded the Church of Jesus Christ Christian.[124] It is the root church for the

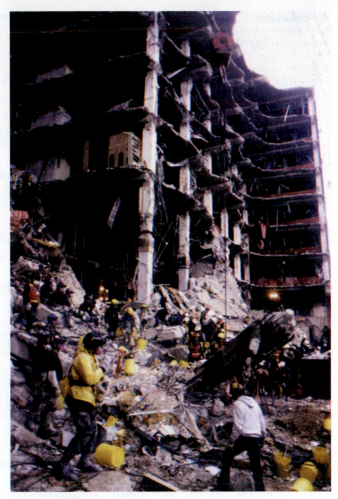

FIGURE 8–9
Search and rescue teams work to save survivors trapped in the bombed Murrah Federal Building.
(Courtesy Federal Emergency Management Agency)

Ruby Ridge (Idaho)
Federal agents went to Randy Weaver's rural home to arrest him on weapons charges. A standoff ensued and eventually gunfire was exchanged, killing Weaver's wife and son. The incident added fuel to the patriot, militia, and right-wing movements.

David Koresh
Leader of the Branch Davidians. Died at their compound in Waco, Texas.

Christian Identity Movement

The CI movement in its most extreme form postulates that the Jews were not God's chosen people, but instead are the spawn of the devil, the mating of Eve and the Serpent in the Garden. Different strands of CI believe it is wrong to mix with other races, interracial marriage is a sin, the Jews are the natural enemies of the Aryan race, racial treason is the greatest crime, and homosexuality should be punished by death. See Counterfeit Christians.

U.S. **Christian Identity Movement**, which in its most extreme form postulates that the Jews were not God's chosen people, but instead are direct descendants of Satan,[125] the physical mating of Eve and the Serpent in the Garden of Eden.

Christian Identity churches are located throughout the United States. The first such church was originally located near Hayden Lake, Idaho, under the direction of Reverend Richard Butler, a former aerospace engineer for Lockheed. Butler combined the ideologies and symbols of neo-Nazism and fundamental Christianity with the racial hatred of the Ku Klux Klan to form the Aryan Nations. He constantly preached to his community the values of a white, Anglo-Saxon country devoid of foreign immigrants and people of color. He was indicted for seditious conspiracy to create a "race war" with 14 other right-wing leaders of the time (1987); however, federal prosecutors failed to prove the conspiracy among all members of the group. In 2000, Butler was successfully sued by Victoria and Jason Keenon, two Native Americans previously harassed and threatened by members of the Aryan Nations. The suit was filed by the Southern Poverty Law Center and a judgment of $6 million was issued against Butler and other members of his Christian Identity movement. The judgment forced the Hayden Lake properties to be sold and Butler shrank into relative obscurity. He died in his sleep of a heart attack in 2004 and the Aryan Nations membership continues to decline.

The Christian Identity movement expresses a strong belief that is wrong to mix races and that interracial marriage is a sin. Further, they believe that Jews are the natural enemies of the white Christian and Aryan race, and that racial treason is the greatest of all sins or crime. The movement is also homophobic and openly advocates against gay rights and homosexuality, arguing that it is an "abomination before God" and should be punished by death.[126]

Benjamin Smith (1978–1999) was a disciple of the Christian Identity movement and member of the World Church of the Creator. He was an ardent follower of Matthew Hale, the son of an Illinois police officer who regularly preached racial hatred as justified through the Christian Identity movement. Smith went on a killing spree in Chicago and Northern Illinois in 1999, shooting people he identified as Jews by their dress. He also shot at African-Americans and Asians simply walking down the street, killing two and wounding nine others before finally committing suicide.[127] The Christian Identity movement, through Matthew Hale, did not take credit for the event. However, it did joyously exalt Smith as a good friend and hero to the Christian Patriot movement. In 2005, Matthew Hale was sentenced to 40 years in a maximum security prison for soliciting an undercover FBI informant to kill a federal judge in the Northern District of Illinois.

The tenets of the Christian Patriot movement have been openly expressed by neo-Nazis, Skinheads, and other far-right groups that have used violence as a means to emphasis their hatred and bigotry. Examples of Christian Identity groups include the Anglo-Saxon Israel, Aryan Nations 88, Christian Patriot and Truth Ministries, Church of True Israel, the Aryan Nations, and the World Church of the Creator, which has been recast as the Creativity Movement.

The Left-Wing Movement

The traditional objective of left-wing terrorism is to overthrow the economic, political, and social structure of a society and replace it with one developed on Marxist-Lenist principles.[128] Groups historically in this category are located across the globe, including Sendero Luminoso (Shining Path) in Peru; the Red Army Faction (RAF) that operated mainly in Germany, but also in France, Switzerland, and the Netherlands; the Red Brigades in Italy; Revolutionary Armed Forces of Columbia (FARC), the Seung fein in China; and the Weather Underground in the United States.[129]

In the United States, the left wing originally sprang from labor/working class movements seeking to eliminate class distinctions,[130] setting the stage for later developments such as the Communist Party USA (CPUSA) that was formed in 1919. There are a variety of communist/socialist political parties. Of greater interest for present purposes is the violent left, which has not received a great deal of attention in recent years because of the federal emphasis on radicalized Muslims and the general demise of the extremist left wing in America.

Quick Facts
The Black Panther Party

In 1966, Huey Newton and Bobby Seale founded the Black Panther Party for Self Defense in Oakland, California.[131] Its name was soon shortened to the Black Panther Party (BPP). The BPP saw Reverend King's non-violent civil rights program as a failure and chartered a new and ultimately violent socialist course. Its original focus was to protect the black community from police brutality by using roving, armed patrols. The BPP also developed an impressive list of activities that included free health, dental, clothing, and children's breakfast programs, as well as legal aid, martial arts, and drama classes.

Because of their confrontational tactics, violent acts, and allegations of criminal acts, the BPP became a police target and many leaders and members were arrested and convicted. FBI Director Hoover called the BBP "the greatest threat to the internal security of this country." By the 1980s the BPP had declined to fewer than 25 members and lost its national prominence. The BPP should not be confused with the New Black Panther Party (NBPP) discussed later in this chapter.

Quick Facts
Patty Hearst and the Symbionese Liberation Army (SLA)

In the 1970s, the SLA wanted to use violent guerilla tactics to overthrow the government of the United States and replace it with a left-wing government. The SLA kidnapped Patty Hearst, a 19-year-old heiress and socialite, to create publicity. They successfully used crude brainwashing techniques to "convince" her to join their movement. She did so, and after being captured she was convicted of bank robbery and sentenced to seven years' imprisonment. After she served some 22 months, President Carter commuted her sentence to time served and she was released from prison. In 2001, President Clinton gave her a full pardon, wiping away her criminal record away.

The beginning of the end for the SLA was a 1974 shootout with police that ended in the death of its founder Donald DeFreeze and several other members. Hearst was away from the house during the siege and escaped arrest for a short time thereafter. The last SLA member who had been "on the run" since the 1975 shootout was James Kilgore. He was finally arrested in 2002, nearly 27 years later, in South Africa by the FBI.[132] Kilgore was convicted of using a dead baby's birth certificate to get a passport under another identity and possessing a pipe bomb, which was found in his San Francisco area apartment in 1975. He served 54 months in a federal facility and was paroled in 2009.[133]

Using 1960 as a starting point, left-wing extremism and nationalism expressed itself through organizations such as the United Freedom Front, Weather Underground, Back Liberation Army, Black Panthers, May 19th Communist Organization (M19CO), and the Republic of New Africa (RNA), which sought a black majority homeland carved out of existing southern states and billions of dollars in reparations from the federal government for the enslavement of African-Americans and the discrimination they have suffered.

Two of the most compelling events of the recent left wing involve the New Year's Gang (NYG) and Patty Hearst, a socialite heiress to a vast newspaper fortune established by her grandfather, William Randolph Hearst. The four-member NYG is often described as anti-war (Vietnam) activists; the FBI has tagged them as left-wing extremists. In 1970, the four men detonated a 2,000-pound bomb in a van at Sterling Hall on the campus of the University of Wisconsin, home to the Army's Mathematical Research Center. One researcher, the father of three children, was killed and others injured by the explosion that did $6 million in damages. It was the largest domestic terrorism attack until the bombing of the Murrah Federal Building led by McVeigh 25 years later. Three of the NYG were captured, convicted, and released after completing prison terms. Defying the odds, the fourth man, Leo Frederick Burt, has eluded capture since 1970.

> **Information Link**
> For more information on the Patty Hearst Kidnapping, visit the FBI website on Famous Cases & Criminals at www.fbi.gov/about-us/history/famous-cases/patty-hearst-kidnapping.

Separatist or Nationalist Movements

Ideally, a nation is a group that shares a common ideology, common institutions and customs, and a sense of homogeneity.[134] The people of a nation have a strong group sense of belonging together. In reality, many nations are not so homogenous; instead, they reflect some diversity in the characteristics of their population.

Episodically, some sub-national groups express a desire for their own national identity. They may seek home rule, in which they can have their own customs, law, and institutions, but remain united with the larger nation in which they are located. Alternatively, they may

During 2014, persons believed to be Muslim ethnic Uighurs reportedly massacred people at a Kumning train station. The victims are thought to be majority Hun Chinese. Twenty-nine people were killed and 143 injured by people wielding large knives and machetes.[135] Uighurs resent increasing government controls on their religious life and believe the growing number of majority Hun Chinese in their province deprives them of jobs, land, and other opportunities.[136] The state-operated Xinhua News Agency blamed the attack on separatist, terrorist Uighurs.[137]

want to establish their own state. A very early step in doing so is the formation of a national liberation organization (NLO), some of which resort to terrorism. NLOs do not possess legal authority over a specific territory; they are seeking to "liberate" it.

Examples of NLOs include (1) the Eritrean Liberation Front (ETA) in Spain, which has successfully obtained a strong measure of autonomy for the ethnic Basques in that country; (2) the Tamil Tigers, who have sought a nation for the Tamil people in northern Sri Lanka; (3) the Kurdistan Workers Party (PKK), which is committed to establishing a Kurdish country from parts of Turkey; and (4) the Liberation Front of Quebec, which desires an independent Quebec for its French-speaking constituencies.

Within the United States there are also examples of groups desiring their own homeland: (1) the late secessionist Thomas Naylor founded The Second Vermont Republic in 2003; he believed that "America has truly lost its way and was no longer sustainable as a nation."[138] Naylor wanted Vermont to return to 1777, when it proclaimed itself an independent nation; (2) the League of the South (LOS) was founded in 1994 and is a nationalist movement whose ultimate goal is a free and independent South;[139] there are a number of affiliated LOSs in southern states. The LOS denies accusations that it is a neo-Confederate white supremacy movement; and (3) founded in 1989, the separatist/nationalist New Black Panther Party (NBPP) has a 10-point plan that has some similarities to the BPP's demands. The NBPP has a list of demands that include a homeland for Black Americans that can make its own laws, as well as reparations for slavery and the release of all black prisoners.[140] The Southern Law Poverty Center describes the NBPP as being "virulently racist and anti-Semitic."[141] Its leaders have encouraged violence against whites, Jews, and law enforcement officers.[142] The original BPP has rejected the NBPP as a "black racist hate group" and has contested its hijacking of the BPP's name and symbol.[143]

Nationalistic Puerto Ricans have made several attacks in Washington, D.C., to call attention to their ambition to have the Commonwealth of Puerto Rico become an independent nation. In 1950, two Puerto Rican men attempted to assassinate President Harry Truman (1884–1972).[144] After a shoot-out, a member of Truman's security detail and one of the attackers were dead. In 1954, Puerto Ricans fired from the balcony of the House of Representatives, wounding several members but killing no one.[145] In 1978 and 1979 President Carter pardoned the men involved in both attacks. Puerto Rico has a long history of revolutionary nationalist organizations, including the Armed Forces for National Liberation, which carried out a series of bombings in Chicago and New York City during the 1970s, Armed Commandos for Revolution, Volunteers' Organization for Puerto Rican Revolution, the People's Boricua Army (also known as Los Macheteros or the Machete Wielders), and more recently, Nueva Lucha (New Struggle).

Case Study: Ireland

Ireland, roughly the size of Maine, looms large in the history of the United States. Although there were earlier Irish immigrations, the Potato Famine of 1845–1851 triggered horrific consequences. During it, one million Irish starved to death and another million immigrated to America. Together, these two events reduced the population of Ireland by some 25 percent.[146] The Irish were the first great wave of unskilled immigrants to the United States. They started life in America at the lowest imaginable rung, but over time became prominent in politics. Nine signers of the declaration of Independence were Irish-Americans[147] and

20 presidents claim Irish ancestry.[148] During the American Civil War (1861–1865), Irishmen came to the United States and enlisted, primarily for the Union Army (see Figure 8–10). Some number of them did so to gain military experience to return to Ireland and continue fighting for Irish independence. Today 39.6 million Americans list their heritage as partially or primarily Irish.[149] Their nationalist drive mirrors our own in many regards (see Table 8–2).

In the early 20th century political party Sinn Fein (Gaelic for We Ourselves) and the Irish Republican Army (IRA) were also NLOs. The island of Ireland hosts the largely Catholic Republic of Ireland in the South, but is substantially protestant in Northern Ireland. How this came to be is a tumultuous history.

One of Ireland's minor kings promised loyalty and lands to England's King Henry II (1133–1189) if he would send a force to help defeat the minor king's foes. Henry II sent a force and some 850 years later the English have still not left. Those that Henry II sent mostly built strongholds in the large cities, sometimes fought the Irish, and at other times fought among themselves. The English occupiers gradually adopted Irish dress, laws, and language and intermarried with them, giving them control over even more lands.[150] Following another Irish rebellion in the northern province of Ulster, the rebels and their followers were granted pardons for leaving Ireland, referred to as the "Fight of the Wild Geese." Ulster was substantially repopulated with English Protestants loyal to England, which set up the dynamics leading to what is now a Protestant Northern Ireland, which is still part of the United Kingdom, and Catholics to the south in what is now the independent Republic of Ireland.

In addition to further forfeiture of lands to punish the Irish, laws were passed at different times that are collectively referred to as the Penal Code. Its purpose was to (1) ensure that the Catholic Irish could never achieve any measure of political or economic power and

FIGURE 8–10
The Union Army's Irish Brigade consisted of the three regiments, the 63rd, 69th, and 88th. The officers of the 69th Regiment assembled for this photograph between 1862 and 1865. The Brigade was known for its valor. At the Battle of Antietam it suffered 60 percent casualties.

(Library of Congress)

TABLE 8–2
Comparison of the American Revolution (1775–1783) and the Anglo-Irish War (1919–1921)

Variable	American Colonies	Ireland
Language Spoken	Primarily English	Primarily English
Goal	Independence	Independence
Adversary	England	England
Scope of Military Capabilities	Limited	Limited
Scope of Adversary's Military Capabilities	World power	World power
Warfare Tactics	Guerilla, conventional	Guerilla, terrorism
Military Resources	Limited, improved with assistance from France. Spain, an informal ally, forced the British from Florida. This enabled Spain to send some supplies to the colonists through its port in New Orleans.	Limited, financial support from other Irish populations, especially in America and Australia, helped finance cause. Irish arms were largely captured by raids and ambushes.
Level of Domestic Support	Limited to moderate support initially. Clumsy and coercive reactions by British led to first Continental Congress (1774) and ultimately to the Declaration of Independence.	Low initially, grew swiftly due to numerous atrocities against civilians by the British. Irish patriots starved themselves to death, causing international opinion to swing against England.
Outcome	Independence	A period of substantial autonomy followed by full independence.

(2) separate the Catholic Irish from their church; among the provisions enacted was the Irish couldn't practice Catholicism, buy land, educate their children, hold public office, own arms, become lawyers, or live in important cities, or own arms.[151] Ultimately these harsh measures were repealed, but not before culturally fixing in the minds of generations of Catholics and Protestants that the other side was villainous.

Although the Protestant majority in Northern Island was content to remain part of the United Kingdom, the "Southern" Irish had national aspirations. How these aspirations were achieved has some similarities to America's revolution, which it makes an important case study.

Sinn Fein was formed in 1905 as a political party that originally advocated for Irish home rule within the British Commonwealth. It was not regarded as a serious threat, although England watched its fermentations. Ever opportunistic, the Irish operated on the principle that "England's difficulty was Ireland's opportunity."[152] So, while England was preoccupied with World War I in Europe (1914–1918), the Easter Uprising (April 24–30, 1916) occurred in Dublin, where the Proclamation of the Republic of Ireland was issued, a document analogous to America's Declaration of Independence.

The three major "military" components of the rising, the Irish Republican Brotherhood, the Irish Volunteers, and the Irish Citizen Army, were ragtag outfits that lacked proper weapons and were essentially untrained. In a week the British Army defeated them. Some in the Dublin crowds lining the streets threw rotten vegetables and others emptied chamber pots (placed under beds and used for night urinals in the era before indoor plumbing) on the surrendered Irishmen as they were marched into captivity.[153] They may have done so because 254 civilians were killed in the fighting or because they had sons serving in the British Army during World War I.[154]

Fifteen of the rising's leaders were executed after perfunctory trials. Padriag Pearse (1879–1916) declared at his sentencing: "You cannot extinguish the Irish passion for freedom. If our deed has not been sufficient to win freedom, then our children will win it by a better deed."[155] James Connolly (1868–1916) was badly wounded in the fighting and could not stand. He was placed before the firing squad while tied to a chair in his hospital pajamas,[156] an ugly image to many leaders in the international community. Joseph Plunkett (1887–1916) was granted his request to marry his sweetheart Grace Gifford and shot hours later.[157] She never remarried. Two leaders of the uprising were initially sentenced to death, but their sentences were commuted to life imprisonment. Countess Markievicz[158] (1868–1927) strongly protested her commutation, claiming she had "done enough to be entitled to an execution,"[159] served a year, and was released; she later served as the Irish Minister of Labor.[160]

Eamon de Valera (1882–1975) was the sole signer of the 1916 Proclamation who was not executed, because his citizenship was in question and because of the politics of World War I. Although born in the New York City, de Valera had lived in Ireland for years.[161] Moreover, the United States, although officially neutral at that time in World War I, was supplying arms and other goods to England. The British were urging the Americans to help them and France by declaring war against the Germans. England had no desire to upset larger plans by executing de Valera, so he was spared. The English plans came to fruition and the United States fought alongside the allied powers from 1917 until the end of the war two years later.

De Valera was released from prison in 1917 and later became President of Ireland. Many of those who surrendered in the 1916 rising were interned in England and released the following year. The executions of the leaders of the Easter Uprising caused the Irish public to take another look at the rising. What they saw stirred them: a poorly armed force with courage taking on a mighty empire and holding it at bay for a week, trying to free the country from foreign domination.

One consequence of the Easter Uprising is that Sinn Fein became a focal point for the newly energized nationalist movement. In 1918, the Sinn Fein party won 73 of 105 seats to represent Ireland in the English Parliament.[162] However, they refused to take their seats and instead formed an Irish revolutionary legislative body, the Dail Eireann (Gaelic for Assembly of Ireland), which proclaimed Ireland an independent republic. The Anglo-Irish War (1919–1921) followed, fought by the newly created Irish Republican Army (1919, IRA).

Quick Facts
Instructions to the Black and Tan

The Black and Tans[163] were mostly former mercenaries and out of work military veterans brought to Ireland by the British government in 1918 to assist the Royal Irish Constabulary in their work. The Irish soon viewed them as thugs opposed to the separatist movement in Ireland.

The attitude of the Black and Tans is best summed up by one of their divisional commanders, Lt. Colonel Smyth, on June 19, 1920, in Listowel, Ireland:

"If a police barracks is burned or if the barracks already occupied is not suitable, then the best house in the locality is to be commandeered, the occupants thrown in the gutter.

Let them die there—the more the merrier. Should the order (Hands Up) not be immediately obeyed, shoot and shoot with effect. If the persons approaching a patrol carry their hands in their pockets, or are in any way suspicious, shoot them down. You may make mistakes occasionally and innocent persons may be shot, but that cannot be helped, and you are bound to get the right parties some time. The more you shoot, the better I will like you. I assure you no policeman will get into trouble for shooting any man."[164]

Source: The Black and Tans from historylearningsite. Used by permission of historylearningsite.

The Irish war in part was funded by solicitations and donations, particularly from the United States, New Zealand, and Australia.[165] The IRA was small and could not fight in a conventional manner. Many of its members came from the same groups involved in the Easter Uprising. The IRA used guerilla tactics, picking the time and places they would strike. The IRA also wisely used selective terrorism because they were fighting on the same ground occupied by the countrymen.

Because the Royal Irish Constabulary (RIC) was used by the British to gather intelligence the IRA assassinated its members, raided their barracks for firearms, and burned over 400 RIC barracks to the ground, as well as many English tax offices. When disguised RIC members killed the Mayor of Cork in front of his family the IRA found out who gave the order and the man was soon dead.

The British decided to supplement the RIC and formed the Royal Irish Constabulary Auxiliary Division, largely made up of out-of-work English veterans of World War I. The first of them reached Ireland in 1920 and because of the colors of their mismatched uniforms they were quickly dubbed the "black and tan." These auxiliaries soon gained a reputation for being undisciplined, drunkenness, and atrocities. They raped Irish women, looting and burning villages. If attacked, the Auxiliaries shot anyone they subsequently saw, such as uninvolved people working in a field or walking down a road, as a reprisal. These actions were encouraged by Auxiliary leaders. The IRA quickly killed Auxiliaries who committed crimes and Smyth was targeted by the IRA for issuing illegal orders and was killed within two weeks.

Late in 1920, the Lord High Mayor of Cork, Terrence MacSwiney, rallied international opinion against the British Commonwealth when after being arrested for sedition he starved himself to death in 74 days.

Wearing of fighting a guerilla war and withering under mounting international opposition to their Irish policies, Britain passed the Government of Ireland Act of 1920 that created the Irish Free State. Primarily Protestant Northern Ireland and its six counties legally opted out of this arrangement to remain in the United Kingdom with home rule. The 26 overwhelmingly Catholic counties of "southern" Ireland rejected the Act so it could pursue full independence and the Anglo-Irish War continued. To some degree this effort was bolstered by Irishmen who had fought for England against Germany in World War I, returning home with combat experience in tactics and weapons.

Both sides in the Anglo-Irish War committed acts of terrorism. For example, when England used its 12-member "Cairo Gang"[166] to spy on the IRA, the IRA responded by sending teams to summarily kill each of them on November 21, 1921. Later that day angry British troops, RIC, and Black and Tans fired at spectators at a hurling match in Dublin, killing 12 and injuring 65 others.[167] When the British announced that henceforth they would execute captured IRA members, the IRA responded they would randomly kill two Englishmen or their allies in return for every member they lost. The IRA also randomly executed members of their opposing forces for crimes committed against the Irish, such as burning parts of Cork.

FIGURE 8–11

Raw recruits of the Irish Free State (IFS) Army taking a break during their training in 1922.

(© Underwood & Underwood/Corbis)

The Anglo-Irish Treaty of 1921 ended the Anglo-Irish War and recognized "Southern" Ireland as the Irish Free State (IFS). The treaty provided greater independence than Northern Ireland enjoyed, for example, the IFS could maintain an army and have foreign embassies around the world, although it also remained tied to England under home rule. Michael Collins, the Big Fella, led the treaty negotiating team. The Republicans, Irish nationalists, felt he had "sold out" to the British and exceeded his bargaining authority by accepting the partition of Ireland and home rule, as opposed to the island becoming one sovereign nation. In the end, Sinn Fein split between pro and anti-treaty factions.

The Irish Civil War (1922–1923) ensued between the Republicans and the "Free Staters" (see Figure 8–11) who supported the treaty. The original IRA split, some joining the Republicans but still using the name of the IRA, while others joined the new national army commanded by Collins.

Like most civil wars, the Irish one was ugly with former comrades killing each other, demonstrating the adage that "revolutions eat their own children."[168] The enormously popular "Big Fella" was among those killed in the Irish Civil War, dying in an ambush by split IRA members in 1922. The next year the Irish Civil War was over. The IRA was banned in the Irish Free State in 1936. The following year Ireland approved a new constitution, shed its identity as the Irish Free State, and declared itself the independent Republic of Ireland, a measure made complete when it officially left the British Commonwealth in 1949.

There has been continued violence in Northern Ireland as Irish Catholics seek reunion with the Republic of Ireland and are countered by British military forces, the Ulster Defense League, and other groups. From Northern Ireland the new IRA has made attacks on the English mainland. Illustratively, in 1974, it set a bomb off at the British Parliament. Although some Irish Catholics in Northern Ireland wish to reunite with the Republic of Ireland in the South, there is only tepid support for that in the Republic of Ireland. The major objection is that many people in Northern Ireland are on social welfare and there is little sentiment to take on that huge cost.

Chapter Summary

SUMMARY BY LEARNING OBJECTIVE

1. **State what is at the core of American right-wing ideology.**

   At its core, American right-wing ideology envisions having a homeland population that is homogeneous with respect to ethnicity, language, culture, and beliefs, as well as a systematic rejection of all those who are different. The right rests on the notion that "being American" equates to emanating from European Anglo-Saxon stock, being Christian, nationalistic, and ruggedly independent.

2. **Identify three major right-wing ideologies in the United States.**

   The three major ideological right-wing movements in the United States are (1) racist/white supremacy, (2) anti-federalist, and (3) religious fundamentalists. Their ideological orientations affect the targets they select, the tactics used, and the operations conducted.

3. **Describe the role of racism with respect to the white supremacy movement.**

   Racism essentially birthed the wider white supremacy movement with its volatile mixture of nativism, xenophobia, anti-immigration, homophobic, Christianity, and anti-Semitic components.

4. **Identify and briefly describe the earliest racist organization in America.**

Although the KKK is frequently cited as the earliest racist organization in America, that "distinction" belongs to the slave patrols. Beginning in 1704, South Carolina enacted laws controlling such slave patrol matters as district patrol boundaries, patrol authority, and relief from militia duty if serving on slave patrols.[169] These patrols were not informal, spontaneous, or episodic groups, but organizations created by law and are therefore the earliest formal racist organization in this country.

5. **Explain why the KKK was originally founded.**

Bored Confederate veterans formed the Ku Klux Klan (KKK) in 1866 to create a stir and excitement at parties. They made up nonsensical names like the Grand Cyclops and Imperial Wizard and rode off to parties wearing costumes and masks to create a little stir. By 1868 the KKK was a full-blown terrorist organization that its members called the "Invisible Empire of the South."

6. **Discuss neo-Nazi groups.**

Neo-Nazi groups share a hatred for Jews and a love for Adolf Hitler and Nazi Germany. Although they also hate other minorities, gays and lesbians, and even sometimes Christians, they perceive "the Jew" as their cardinal enemy, and trace social problems to a Jewish conspiracy that supposedly controls governments, financial institutions and the media.

7. **Explain the goal of George Lincoln Rockwell.**

The goal of George Lincoln Rockwell (1918–1967) was to use his American Nazi Party (ANP) to become President of the United States in 1972 and then "exterminate all treasonous Jews, banish all American Negroes to Africa, and amend the Constitution to suit the Nazi party."

8. **Profile the Hammerskin Nation.**

The Hammerskin Nation was founded in Dallas, Texas, in 1988, and is the most violent, best organized neo-Nazi skinhead group in the United States. Although primarily an American movement, the Hammerskin Nation has chapters in Canada, England, France, Germany, and several other countries.

9. **Trace the development and present state of the anti-federalist/Christian Patriot movement.**

The original anti-federalists were opposed to the ratification of the United States Constitution. The modern anti-federalist movement, sometimes called the Christian Patriot movement, has many variations. Some individuals live the movement's tenets without formally joining any organization. The Christian Patriot movement grew out of the posse comitatus and sovereign citizen movements that began during the 1970s and 1980s.

REVIEW QUESTIONS

1. Why did racial violence against the Chinese increase during 1873–1879?
2. How were Japanese-Americans and members of the German-American Bund treated at the beginning of World War II?
3. Why were there violent clashes between Chicano Zoot Suiters and American serviceman during World War II?
4. What is the history of the 442nd Regimental Combat Team?
5. What American groups disproportionally suffer from right-wing extremism?
6. Is there a connection between *The Turner Diaries* and the bombing of the Murrah Building?
7. What does "88" mean?
8. What are three examples of the Penal Code the English applied to the Irish?
9. What happened following the assassination of the Reverend Martin Luther King?
10. What is the traditional objective of the left wing?

CRITICAL THINKING EXERCISES

1. **Hate on the World Wide Web.** Visit the website of the Southern Poverty Law Center (SPLC) and learn about hate in America at www.splcenter.org/.

    Study some of the available *Intelligence Reports* online and note the high number of active hate groups in the United States. Should you be a partner sharing the mission of the SPLC fighting hate and seeking justice? Think of your community; are there any visible signs of hate or intolerance where you live?

2. **The Provisional Irish Republican Army.** On July 28, 2005, the Provisional IRA (PIRA) made a statement in which it declared a formal end to the armed struggle for Northern Irish independence. Further, on that following September, the group announced that it had decommissioned all weapons and was entering negotiations for peace and independence with the Social Democratic and Labor Party in Northern Ireland and the British Labor Party in London. Sinn Fein, the oldest political movement in Ireland, works toward the right of Irish people as whole to attain national self-determination. Visit the websites of Sinn Fein at www.sinnfein.org and the Provisional Irish Republican Army at www.provos2.webs.com. Also read the article on the Council on Foreign Relations website entitled "Provisional Irish Republican Army (PIRA) aka 'the Provos,'" by Kathryn Gregory (March 16, 2010) at www.cfr.org/separatist-terrorism/provisional-irish-republican-army-ira-aka-pira-provos-oglaigh-na-heireann-uk-separatists/p9240. Review other articles on the CFR website that focus on the PIRA. Finally, search the web for other sites about the violence in Northern Ireland between the PIRA and Great Britain. What were "Bloody Friday" bombings and what was "Bloody Sunday?" Do you think the PIRA was a "terrorist group" or a legitimate revolutionary movement aimed at gaining Irish sovereignty from Great Britain? What do you think differentiated the conflict between Irish separatists versus any other group that separated from the British Empire after World War II, for example, India, Israel, Ghana?

NOTES

1. Illustratively, see www.educate-yourself.org/cn/femaconcentrationcamplocations07sep05.shtml. A Google search locates further "information" on this subject.
2. Mark Potok, "The Patriot Movement Explodes," *Southern Poverty Law Center*, Intelligence Report Issue 145, Spring 2012, p. 1.
3. Loc. cit.
4. Mark Potok, "Rage on the Right," *Southern Poverty Law Center*, Intelligence Report Number 137, Spring 2010, p. 1.
5. Carla Bleiker, "Far-Right NPD Loses State Subsidies," *DW*, February 26, 2013.
6. "Not So Grim Up North," *The Economist*, October 14, 2010, p. 1.
7. "Anders Behring Breivik," *New York Times*, August 24, 2012, www.Topics.NYTimes/Top/Reference/Timestopics/People/Anders_Behring_Breivik/index.html.
8. Nick Squires, "Florence Street Vendors Killed by Lone Gunman," *The Telegraph* (England), December 13, 2013.
9. Marcel Furstenau, "Neo-Nazi Murder Spree Shocks Germany," *DW*, March 13, 2013.
10. Matthew Goodwin, "The Roots of Extremism: The English Defence League and the Counter Jihad Challenger," A Chatham House Briefing Paper, March 2013, p. 1.
11. Ibid., p. 5.
12. Ibid., p. 6.
13. Ibid., p. 3.
14. Arie Perliger, "Challenges from the Sidelines: Understanding America's Far-Right," (West Point, New York: Combating Terrorism Center, West Point, United States Army, November 2012), p. 13.
15. Loc. cit.
16. Loc. cit.
17. Loc. cit.
18. Perliger, "Challenges from the Sidelines," p. 87.

19. Public Broadcasting System Radio Program, "Online Focus: Unanswered Questions," Gerald Posner Asserts Ray Is a Racist, April 23, 1998, www.pbs.org/newshour/bb/race_relations/jan-june98/ray_4_23html.

20. Perliger, "Challenges from the Sidelines," p. 15.

21. Some of these ideas are explored in Lindsay Perez Huber et al., "Getting Beyond the 'Symptom' and Acknowledging the Disease: Theorizing Racist Nativism," *Contemporary Justice Review*, Vol. 11, Issue 1, March 2008, p. 42.

22. Perliger, "Challenges from the Sidelines," p. 16.

23. Loc. cit.

24. Ibid., pp. 16–17.

25. Ibid., pp. 1–2.

26. Bill Rolston, "Bringing It All Back Home," *Race & Class*, Vol. 45, Issue 2, October–December 2003, pp. 39–53. Copy accessed electronically on April 23, 2013, did not have page numbers.

27. Loc. cit.

28. Loc. cit.

29. Loc. cit. One joke was that the Irish didn't know how to walk upright until the wheelbarrow was invented. Shops seeking employees posted signs that read "Vacancy, inquire within. Irish need not apply."

30. U.S. History, "29. Manifest Destiny," undated, p. 1, www.ushistory.org/us/29.asp.

31. Loc. cit.

32. Charles R. Swanson, Leonard Territo, Robert W. Taylor, *Police Administration: Structures, Processes, and Behaviors* (Boston: Pearson, 2011), p. 6.

33. There is some question as to whether Sheridan actually made this statement. He denied it a number of times and there is no contemporary written record that he did.

34. Richard Delgado, "The Law of the Noose: The History of Latino Lynching," *Harvard Civil Rights-Civil Liberties Law Review*, Vol. 44, No. 2, Summer 2009, p. 299.

35. Loc. cit.

36. Walter Ko, "The Blood, Sweat, and Tears of Chinese in 19th-Century America," *Chinese American Forum*, Vol. 28, Issue 3, January 2013, p. 14.

37. Philip Chin, "The Chinese Exclusion Act of 1882," *Chinese American Forum*, Vol. XXVIII, No. 3, January 2013, pp. 7–8.

38. Loc. cit.

39. Ko, "The Blood, Sweat, and Tears of Chinese in 19th-Century America," p. 9.

40. David J. Wishart, "Denver's Anti-Chinese Riot," *Encyclopedia of the Plains*, undated, p. 1, http://plainshumanities.unl.edu/encyclopedia/doc/egp.asam.011.

41. Cliff Akiyama, "When You Look Like the Enemy," *Brief Treatment and Crisis Intervention*, Vol. 8, Issue 2, May 2008, p. 210.

42. "442nd Regimental Combat Team," p. 1. www.goforbroke.org/history/history_historical_veterans_442nd.asp.

43. Ibid., p. 2.

44. Michi Weglyn, "Children of the Camps," Public Broadcasting System, undated, www.pbs.org/childrenofcamp/history/.

45. "German American Bund," *Holocaust Encyclopedia, United States Holocaust Memorial Museum*, p. 1. www.ushmm.org/wic/en/article.php?Moduleid=10005684.

46. Loc. cit.

47. Sarah Elizabeth Howard, "Zoot to Boot: The Zoot Suit as Both Costume and Symbol," *Studies in Latin America Culture*, Vol. 28, 2010, p. 113.

48. Ibid., p. 115.

49. Ibid., pp. 116–117.

50. Tanya Schevitz, "Hate Crimes Against Religious Groups, 2001," *San Francisco Chronicle*, November 26, 2002, www.sfgate.com/news/article/fbi-sees-leap-in-anti-muslim-hate-crimes-9-11-2750152.php.

51. FBI, "Hate Crime Statistics 2011," www.fbi.gov/about-us/cjis/ucr/hate-crime/2011/tables/table-1. Percentages computed from data in Table 1.

52. Marc Santora, "Woman Is Charged with Murder as a Hate Crime in a Fatal Subway Push," *The New York Times*, December 29, 2013.

53. Loc. cit.
54. "Hate Crime Statistics 2011," Federal Bureau of Investigation (Washington, D.C.: Federal Bureau of Investigation), p. 1, www.fbi.gov/about-us/cjis/ucr/hate-crime/2011/narratives/incidents-and-offenses.
55. K. B. Turner, David Giacopassi, and Margaret Vandiver, "Ignoring the Past: Coverage of Slavery and Slave Patrols in Criminal Justice Texts," *Journal of Criminal Justice Education*, Vol. 17, Issue 1, March 2006, p. 185.
56. Elaine Frantz Parsons, "Midnight Rangers: Costume and Performance in the Reconstruction Era Ku Klux Klan," *Journal of American History*, Vol. 92, Issue 3, December 2005, p. 811.
57. Ibid., p. 812.
58. No author, "General Article: Rise of the Ku Klux Klan," Public Broadcasting System, undated, www.pbs.org/wgbh/americanexperience/features/general-article/grant-kkk.
59. Kris Axtman, "How the South Outgrew the Klan," *Christian Science Monitor*, Vol. 93, Issue 112, May 4, 2001, p. 1.
60. Kathleen Blee and Amy McDowell, "The Duality of Spectacle and Secrecy: A Case Study of Fraternalism in the 1920s U.S. Ku Klux Klan," *Ethnic and Racial Studies*, Vol. 36, Issue 2, February 2013, p. 249.
61. Ibid., pp. 254–255.
62. "Klan Must Pay $37 Million for Inciting Church Fire," *The New York Times*, July 25, 1998.
63. "About the Ku Klux Klan," Anti-Defamation League, 2013, http://archive.adl.org/learn/ext_us/kkk/default.html.
64. Alexandra Marks, "The Disruptive Face of a Dwindling KKK," *Christian Science Monitor*, Vol. 91, Issue 230, p. 2.
65. "About the Ku Klux Klan," p. 1.
66. "The Ku Klux Klan Rebounds," *Anti-Defamation League*, 2013, p. 1. http://archive.adl.org/learn_us/kkk/intro.asp?learn_cat=extremism&learn_subcat=extremism_in_america&xpicked=4&item=kkk.
67. "Neo-Nazi," *Southern Poverty Law Center*, 2013, www.splcenter.org/get-informed/intelligence-files/ideology/ne0-nazi#.uyux16vgofi.
68. "American Nazi Party," Confidential FBI Report, June 1965, p. 8. The document has typed and handwritten page numbers that do not coincide; we have used the handwritten page numbers.
69. Ibid., p. 98.
70. "White Revolution/Billy Roper," *Anti-Defamation League*, undated, © 2013, p. 1, http://archive.adl.org/learn/ext_us/w_revolution.asp.
71. Dianne Dentice, "The Nationalist Party of America," *Social Movement Studies*, Vol. 10, Issue 1, January 2011, p. 107.
72. "Extremism in America: William Pierce," *Anti-Defamation League*, 2005, http://archive.adl.org/learn/ext_us/pierce.asp.
73. Ibid., p. 2.
74. Ibid., pp. 4–5 with a few additions.
75. This information was taken from the National Vanguard Books website; see www.natvan-books.com.
76. "Extremism in America: William Pierce," p. 3.
77. "Poisoning the Web: Hatred On-Line," *Anti-Defamation League*, 2001, p. 1, http://archive.adl.org/poisoning_web/national_alliance.asp.
78. Mark Potok, "Ten Years After Founder's Death, Key Neo-Nazi Movement a 'Joke,'" *Southern Poverty Law Center*, July 23, 2012, p. 1.
79. Loc. cit.
80. "National Socialist Movement," *Southern Poverty Law Center*, undated, © 2013, p. 2, www.splc.org/ger-informed/intelligence-files/groups/national-socialist-movement#.uyuzikvgofi.
81. Loc. cit.
82. Taken from the NSM website, "25 Point Party Thesis," undated, www.nsm88.org.
83. Loc. cit.
84. "National Socialist Movement," p. 2.

85. Loc. cit.
86. "Aryan Nations," *Southern Poverty Law Center*, undated, p. 1, www.splcenter.org/get-informed/intelligence-files/groups/aryan-nations.
87. Loc. cit.
88. "The National Socialist Movement," Anti-Defamation League, 2013, p.1, http://archive.adl.org/learn/ext_us/nsm/default.asp?learn_cat=extremism&learn_subcat=extremism_in_america&xpicked=3&items=nsm.
89. Loc. cit.
90. Ibid., p. 2.
91. Loc. cit.
92. "Hammerskin Nation," *National Consortium for the Study of Terrorism and Responses to Terrorism*, undated, © 2013, p. 1, www.start.umd.edu/start/data_collections/tops/terrorists_organization_profile.asp?id=3483.
93. Loc. cit.
94. "American Front," *Anti-Defamation League*, undated, but © 2013, p. 1, www.adl.org.
95. See "Skinhead Convicted of Murder of Two Homeless Men in Tampa," *FBI Press Release*, October 18, 2011.
96. "Hammerskin Nation," p. 2.
97. "Racist Skinhead," *Southern Poverty Law Center*, undated, © 2013, p. 3, www.splcenter.org/get-informed/intelligence-files/ideology/racist-skinhead#.uyjliavgofi.
98. This content is drawn with restatement from "Hate Group Expert Daniel Levitas Discusses Posse Comitatus, Christian Identity Movement and More," *Southern Poverty Law Center*, Intelligence Report, Spring 1998, Issue 90, p. 1.
99. FBI Counterterrorism Section, "Sovereign Citizens: A Growing Threat to Law Enforcement," *FBI Law Enforcement Bulletin*, September 2011, p. 1
100. Ibid., pp. 1–2.
101. Ibid., p. 1.
102. Potok, "The Patriot Movement Explodes," p. 3.
103. Ibid., pp. 3–4.
104. Loc. cit.
105. "Neo-Confederate," *Southern Poverty Law Center*, 2013, www.splcenter.org/ger-informed/inteligence-files/ideology/neo-confederate#.uygv_avgpfi.
106. "Institute for Historical Review," *Southern Poverty Law Center*, undated, © 2013, p. 1, www.splcenter.org/get-informed/intelligence-files/groups/instutute-for-historical-research#.uyfhw6vgpfi.
107. Loc. cit.
108. Michael Kimmel and Abby L. Ferber, "White Men Are This Nation: Right Wing Militias and the Restoration of American Masculinity," *Rural Sociology*, Vol. 65, Issue 4, December 2000, p. 586.
109. Perliger, "Challenges from the Sidelines," p. 28.
110. Loc. cit.
111. Ibid., pp. 30–31.
112. "Montana Freemen," *National Consortium for the Study of Terrorism and Responses to Terrorism*, University of Maryland, September 1995, p.1.
113. Bill Morlin, "Georgia Militia Members to be Tried Later This Year in Movement's Latest Murder Plot," *Southern Poverty Law Center*, Intelligence Report, Issue 145, Spring 2012, p. 1.
114. Ibid., p. 2.
115. "Timothy McVeigh: The Oklahoma City Bomber," *Anti-Defamation League*, 2001, http://archive.adl.org/McVeigh/faq.asp.
116. "Terror Hits Home: The Oklahoma City Bombing," Federal Bureau of Investigation, undated, www.fbi.gov/about-us/famous-cases/oklahoma-city-bombing.
117. "From Decorated Veteran to Mass Murderer," CNN.Com Programs, hosted by Paul Zahn, 2001, p. 1, www.cnn.com.cnn/programs/people/shows/mcveigh/profile.html.
118. Jo Thomas, "Behind a Book That Inspired McVeigh," *The New York Times*, June 9, 2001.
119. "From Decorated Veteran to Mass Murderer," p. 4.
120. Loc. cit.

121. Martin Durham, "Christian Identity and the Politics of Religion," *Totalitarian Movements and Political Religions*," Vol. 9, No. 1, March 2008, p. 79.

122. Loc. cit.

123. Loc. cit.

124. Rosemary Bradford Ruether, "Racist Extremists Use Bible Verse to Justify Killing," *National Catholic Reporter*, Vol. 35, July 27, 1999, p. 13.

125. Loc. cit.

126. To examine different CI websites use the hyperlinks at www.thechristianidentotyforum. com/forum.net/index.php?/topic/94/-big-list-of-christian-identity.

127. Ruether, "Racist Extremists Use Bible Verse to Justify Killing," p. 13.

128. Concepts of Terrorism, Deliverable 5, Work Package 3, December 2008, p. 126, www.transnationalterrorism.eu.

129. Jeffrey M. Bale, "Definition of Terrorism, *Monterey Terrorism and Research Center Education Program*, undated, www.mils.edu/academics/researchcenters/terrorism/about/ terrorism_definition.

130. Karl A. Seger, *Left Wing Extremism: The Current Threat* (Washington, D.C.: U.S. Department of Energy, April 2001), p. 1.

131. Much of this paragraph is drawn from information in D.J. Mulloy, "New Panthers, Old Panthers and the Politics of Black Nationalism in the United States," *Patterns of Prejudice*, Vol. 44, Issue 3, July 2010, pp. 217–238; Joe Street, "The Historiography of the Black Panther Party," *Journal of American Studies*, Vol. 44, Issue 2, May 2010, pp. 351–375; and Hugh Pearson, *Shadow of the Panther: Huey Newton and the Price of Black Power in America* (Cambridge, Massachusetts: De Capo Press, 1995).

132. Many of the facts herein are drawn from "The Patty Hearst Kidnapping," www.fbi.gov/ about-us/history/famous-cases/patty-hearst-kidnapping.

133. Don Thompson, "Former SLA Member James Kilgore Paroled," S*FGate*, May 11, 2009, p. 1, www.sfgate.com/bayarea/article/Former-SLA-member-James-Kilgore- paroled-3162180.php.

134. The information in this paragraph is draw from *Nationalist-Separatist Movements* (New York: United Nations, 2003), www.munfw.org/archive/47th/gal.htm.

135. "Death Toll Rises to 33 in Knife Attack on China Train Station," www.foxnews. com/2014/03/02/gang-knife-weilding-men-in-deadly-attacks-on-chaina-train-station.

136. Chris Buckley, "Attackers with Knives Kill 29 at Chinese Rail Station," *The New York Times*, March 1, 2014.

137. Loc. cit. and "Dozens Stabbed to Death in Chinese Attack," *CNN News*, www.cnn.com/ 2014/03/01/world/asia/china-railway-attacks.

138. "Thomas Naylor, Controversial Vermont Secessionist, Dies," *Southern Poverty Law Center*, © 2013, www.splcenter.org/home/2012/spring/ thomas-naylor-controversial-vermont-secessionist-dies#uyryqqvgpf.

139. See the League of South website at www.dixienet.org/rights/whatisthels.shtml.

140. "New Black Panther Party," *Southern Poverty Law Center*, undated, © 2013, p. 2, www.splcenter.org/get-informed/intelligence-files/groups/new-black-panther-party# .uyv9vqvgpfi14.

141. Ibid., p. 1.

142. Loc. cit.

143. Loc. cit.

144. Allen Pusey, "November 1, 1950: Truman Escapes Assassination," *ABA Journal*, November 1, 2012, p. 1, www.abajournal.com/magazine/article/ November_1_1950_truman_escapes_assassination.

145. Emma Brown, "Lolita Lebron, Jailed for Gun Attack at U.S. Capitol in 1954, Dies at 90," *The Washington Post*, August 2, 2010.

146. "The Famine of 1845," *The History Learning Site*, undated, www.historylearningsite. co.uk/ireland_great_famine_of_1845.htm.

147. Brendan Patrick Keane, "The Irish Who Signed the Declaration of Independence," *Irish Central*, July 4, 2014, www.irishcentral.com/opinion/others/the-irish-side-of-the-american- declaration-of-independence-97713259-238038151.html#.

148. Sean Murphy, "American Presidents with Irish Ancestry," *Directory of Irish Ancestry*, undated, http://homepage.eircom.net/~seanjmurphy/dir/pres.htm.

149. Irish Central Staff Writers, "U.S. Census Shows Seven Times More Irish Americans than Population of Ireland," *Irish Central*, August 5, 2013, www.irishcentral.com/news/-census-shows-almost-seven-times-more-irish-americans-than-population-of-ireland-218344001-237779801.html.

150. Michael D. Greaney, "Last of the Norman Invasions," *Military History*, Vol. 15, Issue 5, December 1998, pp. 42–51.

151. *A Short History of Ireland: The Penal Laws* (London: BBC Home, undated), URL no longer available.

152. Richard F. Welch, "The IRA's Guerilla Wars," *Military History*, Vol. 20, Issue 1, April 2003, p. 58.

153. Peter De Rosa, *Rebels: The Irish Rising of 1916* (New York: Fawcett Columbine, 1990, p. 391.

154. Higher numbers are also cited; De Rosa claims 450 deaths and 2,614 wounded, which may include British casualties. See Ibid., p. 1

155. De Rosa, *Rebels: The Irish Rising of 1916*, p. 417.

156. Ibid., p. 538.

157. Ibid., pp. 444, 452.

158. She was born in England as Constance Gore-Booth and became a countess by virtue of her marriage to a Polish count. They settled in Dublin in 1903. Countess Markievicz became an active Irish Nationalist around 1908.

159. Ibid., p. 464. For a closer examination of her life see Suzanne Kennedy Flynn, "Countess Courageous," *World of Hibernia*, Vol. 4, Issue 3, Winter 1998.

160. De Rosa, *Rebels: The Irish Rising of 1916*, pp. 506–507.

161. See Phil Chapple, "'Dev': The Career of Eamon de Valera," *History Review*, Issue 53, pp. 28–33, December 2005.

162. "The Irish War," www.Theiririshwar.com/history/irish-war-of-independence/.

163. See "The Black and Tans" at www.historylearningsite.co.uk/black_and_tans.htm.

164. "The Black and Tans," *BBC Home*, www.bbc.co.uk/history/easterrising/aftermath/AF05/shtml.

165. A fuller accounting of this point is found in Caoimhe Nic Dhaibheid, "The Irish National Aid Association and the Radicalization of Public Opinion in Ireland, 1916–1918," *Historical Journal*, Vol. 55, Issue 3, September 2012, pp. 705–729.

166. The reason for the unit being named the Cairo Gang is disputed. One version is that many of the people in the unit were military veterans who served in the Middle East. The second reason offered is that the group occasionally met at the Cairo Café in Dublin.

167. Loc. cit.

168. Welch, "The IRA's Guerilla Wars," p. 62.

169. K. B. Turner, David Giacopassi, and Margaret Vandiver, "Ignoring the Past: Coverage of Slavery and Slave Patrols in Criminal Justice Texts," *Journal of Criminal Justice Education*, Vol. 17, Issue 1, March 2006, p. 185.

Intelligence and Terrorism

CHAPTER

9

Learning Objectives

After completing this chapter, you should be able to:

1. Explain the impact of the Gilmore Commission and provide a brief statement regarding its major findings.

2. Define intelligence and counterintelligence.

3. Provide a brief overview of the U.S. Intelligence Community and discuss the role of the Office of the Director of National Intelligence.

4. Describe the National Counterterrorism Center (NCTC).

5. Explain the differences between the CIA and the FBI relating to terrorism and intelligence.

6. Discuss the differences between investigation and intelligence.

7. Define JTTFs and discuss the importance of their role and mission.

8. Discuss the role of the National Security Agency as an intelligence agency.

9. Define the concept of "cyberterrorism" or "digital terrorism."

10. List the other agencies within the intelligence community.

11. Describe the intelligence cycle.

12. Define and describe the four goals of a fusion center.

The U.S. Department of Homeland Security has spent nearly $1.5 billion since 2003 to build state and local fusion centers throughout the country. MOSAIC in the Dallas, Texas, Police Department represents state-of-the-art in high-tech equipment and integrated information processing systems and is used tactically to fight everyday crime as well as more strategic activities designed to prevent terrorist attacks in the future.

Zuma Press/Alamy

Introduction

The terrorist attacks on September 11, 2001, had a major impact on national homeland security policies and law enforcement strategies at the federal, state, and local levels. A recent report indicates that there are over 1,271 government organizations and 1,931 private organizations involved in homeland security, intelligence gathering, and counterterrorism issues.[1] The U.S. Department of Homeland Security (DHS) alone has contributed more than $500 million toward the development of new local and state agencies centered on the goal of improving the coordination of policing through intelligence sharing.[2] A deficiency that was quickly identified following the 9/11 attacks was that coordination and intelligence sharing between agencies and levels of government was nearly nonexistent.[3]

Several post 9/11 studies have been critical of the U.S. intelligence community's ability to collect and analyze important intelligence information on terrorist groups.[4] The most important of these inquiries was known as the **Gilmore Commission**, named after the Virginia Governor, Jim Gilmore, chair of the Congressionally sponsored commission to assess the domestic response of federal law enforcement and intelligence agencies against terrorism between 1999 and 2003. Five key issues were identified as problems: (1) failure to emphasize traditional human intelligence gathering and analysis in favor of an overreliance on technological tools such as satellites and computer programs; (2) failure to provide timely, accurate, and specific intelligence information to law enforcement agencies; (3) an overly bureaucratic and decentralized structure, particularly within the FBI, that hindered counterterrorism efforts; (4) outdated and obsolete computer systems that prevented the timely sharing of critical information with and between law enforcement agencies; and (5) overly restrictive guidelines and laws that hindered the effective use of informants and intelligence gathering on terrorists.[5]

Complicating these five potential problems is the structure of American government, which includes the cities and counties that form local government, state governments, and the federal government. Just what terrorism responsibilities should these different levels of government have and which of their agencies should have what responsibilities? To illustrate, should acts of terrorism be investigated only by the FBI and the appropriate state and/or local law enforcement agencies? Should ferreting out terrorist plots be the exclusive jurisdiction of the Central Intelligence Agency and the military? Within the military, which units should be involved? The answers to these questions are not simple. This chapter will define the role and scope of intelligence in combatting terrorism and describe the various agencies that make up the U.S. intelligence community.

Gilmore Commission
Congressionally sponsored inquiry after 9/11 to assess the domestic response of federal law enforcement and intelligence agencies against terrorism.

Defining Intelligence and Counterintelligence

The term "intelligence" often refers to information that is significant or relevant to an impending event and that will be a contribution to the positive outcome of that specific incident. It is paramount to understand the monumental differences between information and intelligence. Information is nothing more than data that has yet to be screened and interpreted through professional analysis. Once information has been analyzed, then it *may become* legitimate intelligence.

The analytical step toward processing gathered information into intelligence is often a misunderstood concept as well. Technology has offered analysts the comfort of reducing the number of people that can be responsible for categorizing and storing data. However, complete analysis of gathered information requires critical thinking that results in conclusions and recommendations stemming from the analyzed information. It is through effective analysis that government leaders and officials make informed decisions and base important responses to potential terrorist attacks (e.g., the deployment of police officers).[6]

Historically the missing dimension in quality intelligence has been *analysis*. The transformation of raw data, whether acquired through human, technical, or open sources, must be collated, scrutinized, and processed accurately and timely. The ultimate goal of this analytic process is a finished product more intelligible, accurate, and usable than the data and information drawn upon to prepare it. **Intelligence**, then, is a product derived from systematic and thoughtful examination, placed in context, and provided to governmental executives and military leaders with facts and alternatives that can inform critical decisions.[7]

Intelligence
An information process and product derived from systematic and thoughtful examination (analysis).

Quick Facts
The Son Tay Raid: Well Executed, but an Intelligence Failure

In 1970, during the Vietnam War, intelligence was developed that American prisoners were being held under harsh conditions at the Son Tay POW Camp in North Vietnam. Army Colonel Arthur "Bull" Simons lead Operation Ivory Coast to free them. His ground force consisted of 56 Special Forces volunteers. Despite the operation being extremely well run, no prisoners were freed because they had been moved to another camp—an intelligence failure. Some military commanders believe that the 1976 Israeli raid to free civilian prisoners being held by terrorists in Entebbe, Uganda, was planned on precepts established by the Son Tay raid.

Counterintelligence (CI)
Activities intended to prevent adversaries from acquiring accurate information about another organization's capabilities.

FIGURE 9–1
The condition of this former POW underscores why freeing POWS is an urgent mission. This 23-year-old man was a former communist in the Vietnam War. He defected to allied forces and then was captured by the Viet Cong, who were deliberately starving him to death.
(© Historical/Corbis)

Intelligence is both a process and a product. Information is collected and analyzed and a finding is produced to meet the needs of a specific "customer."[8] Among the sources from which intelligence can be collected are humans (HUMINT), signals (SIGINT), geospatial (GEOINT), technical (TECHINT), imagery (IMINT), photographs (PHOINT), and open source (OSINT). Intelligence can be used for broad purposes, for example, shaping policy and doctrine. In those applications intelligence is not time sensitive, but in others it may be.

On rare occasions during the Vietnam War a Viet Cong defector would reveal where prisoners of war (POWs) were being held (see Figure 9–1). Because those camps were often moved, raids had to be launched quickly. That situation describes tactical intelligence, which is perishable and therefore requires rapid action. On the other hand, **counterintelligence (CI)** is a constellation of activities, analyses, and decisions intended to prevent adversaries from acquiring accurate information about an organization's capabilities, intentions, personnel, and plans.[9] Counterintelligence is used by the U.S. intelligence services to disrupt the activities and operations of terrorist groups, and conversely, terrorist groups use counterintelligence to learn more about the methods used by the U.S. government to thwart their activities.

Pre-9/11, the Taliban ruled Afghanistan and had a substantial HUMINT collection capability: 20,000 spies and over 100,000 informants, at least one on every block, as well as in hospitals, military units, and aid agencies.[10] Following the 9/11 attacks, the Taliban refused to hand over Usama bin Laden and the United States and its allies waged war on both the Taliban and al-Qaeda, deposing the Taliban as the government of Afghanistan. It is widely believed that subsequently units of both terrorist groups evaded capture or destruction on a number of occasions based on their informants in Pakistan's Inter-Services Intelligence (ISI) unit.[11] The Taliban is also thought to have gathered intelligence from an Air Force officer's blog that discussed screening of passengers at airports, had photographs of his base, and pictures of his Afghanistan counterparts.[12] The Taliban continues to have a wide circle of informants and uses them to identify and eliminate suspected spies for Afghanistan security forces.[13]

As with intelligence, terrorists' counterintelligence practices are shaped by their numbers, the degree of popular support, and other resources. However, counterintelligence can be as simple as a thorough vetting of recruits to avoid being penetrated by government agents or potential informants.[14] The Provisional Irish Republic Army (PIRA) employed a variety of effective, but not necessarily costly, practices to thwart the British and the Royal Ulster Constabulary (RUC), Northern Ireland's police force. As an example, PIRA, which usually killed informants they discovered, undercut the effectiveness of British recruitment of informants by declaring an informer amnesty:[15] Come and tell us everything you gave up, what procedures were used to recruit you, what questions you asked, and no harm will come to you. This program revealed that the British were covertly operating a laundry so it could test the clothes of suspected PIRA members for explosive

Quick Facts
Counter Forensics Manual

The Provisional Irish Republic Army (PIRA) developed a "counter forensics" manual for its members that described the kinds of conclusions that could be reached by the forensic examination of different types of physical evidence.[16] One tip was not to wear wool clothes because wool picked up other materials and shed easily. The goal of the program was to limit the forensic evidence available to the British.

residues.[17] Also discovered was a bogus radio contest operated by the British Security Service MI5. It was rigged so targeted PIRA members "won" and when they left on their vacation, MI5 entered the homes and planted microphones.[18] In addition to reducing the number of informants, the PIRA program was able to assess the damage done and make adjustments to prevent further damage.[19]

Overview of the U.S. Intelligence Community

In order to address the problems identified by the Gilmore Commission, the Intelligence Reform and Terrorism Prevention Act of 2004 (IRTPA) established the **Office of the Director of National Intelligence (ODNI)**. The creation of the ODNI centralized all intelligence information from the myriad of agencies that had a mission to gather specific intelligence relating to their function. There are currently 16 different agencies that report directly to the ODNI, including the Central Intelligence Agency and the FBI National Security Branch. These 16 agencies represent the primary groups of federal government responsible for national security, including each branch of the military (i.e., Air Force, Army, Navy, Coast Guard, and the Marine Corps), the primary national intelligence agencies (e.g., National Security Agency and Central Intelligence Agency), and federal law enforcement (e.g., Federal Bureau of Investigation, Drug Enforcement Administration, and Department of Homeland Security). These agencies and the Office of the Director of National Intelligence are referred to as the **intelligence community (IC)** of the United States (see Figure 9–2).

The primary purpose of this new structure is to better coordinate, integrate, and manage the collection, analysis, and dissemination of intelligence information, including the intelligence that relates directly to international and domestic threats posed by terrorism. The ODNI administers the **National Intelligence Program (NIP)**, which funds the intelligence activities of the entire federal government. The estimated 2013 budget is nearly $60 billion per year and is critical in strengthening the nation's intelligence agencies.[20]

The National Counterterrorism Center (NCTC)

The integration and analysis of terrorist threat information from various sources and the dissemination of that information to other members of the intelligence community, as well as other important state and local law enforcement partners, is accomplished through the National Counterterrorism Center (NCTC). The Center serves as the nation's "hub" for intelligence activity both domestically and internationally, coordinating intelligence information derived by individual members of the intelligence community. It also serves as a single point for the strategic and operational planning of counterterrorism activity. This is often accomplished through interagency meetings and secure teleconferences about terrorist groups, capabilities, plans and intentions, and emerging threats to U.S. interests.[21] The Center also operates a secure website (NCTC Online CURRENT) that serves as the primary dissemination mechanism for terrorist information to and from operational elements such as local FBI Joint Terrorist Task Forces (JTTFs) and military combatant commands. Located in Washington, D.C., the NCTC is part of the Office of the Director of National Intelligence and maintains the national repository of known and suspected terrorists and administers the Joint Counterterrorism Assessment Team (JCAT).* The JCAT is composed of public safety personnel from around the country. The goal of this coordination body is

Office of the Director of National Intelligence (ODNI)
The national office created to centralize all intelligence information function from all federal, state, and local agencies.

Information Link
For more information on the Office of the Director of National Intelligence, visit the website at www.dni.gov/index.php.

Intelligence community (IC)
Sixteen federal agencies representing various governmental groups reporting to the Office of the Director of National Intelligence.

National Intelligence Program (NIP)
The primary funding budget for the strengthening the nation's intelligence agencies.

*JCAT was previously named as the Interagency Threat Assessment Coordination Group (ITACG).

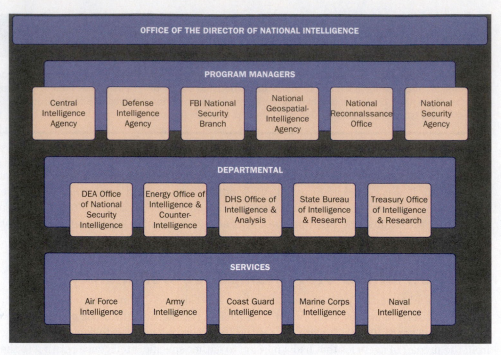

FIGURE 9–2
The Intelligence Community under the Office of the Director of National Intelligence (ODNI).
United States Intelligence Community Seal and Organizational chart
Source: National Intelligence Community

to inform public safety personnel in an effort to better identify, respond to, mitigate, and, most importantly, prevent the next terrorist attack against the homeland.[22] The National Counterterrorism Center also develops and distributes the *Counterterrorism Calendar* (see Figure 9–3) that commemorates particular events, traces the development of terrorist groups, has interactive timeline maps, and provides technical information on various topics

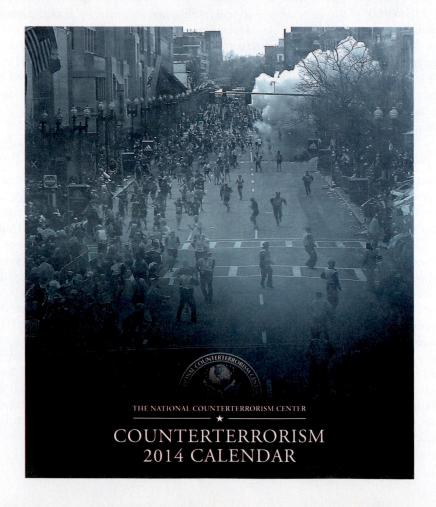

FIGURE 9–3
The NCTC maintains the Counterterrorism Calendar, which can be downloaded from the Internet and used by members of the general public. See www.nctc .gov/calendar.html.
Source: NCTC

such as biological and chemical threats.[23] The JCAT improves information sharing and public safety. It collaborates with other members of the intelligence community to research, produce, and disseminate products for federal, state, local, tribal, territorial, and private-sector partners and advocates for the needs of those partners.[24]

The Central Intelligence Agency (CIA)

The framework for U.S. intelligence was created in a different time to deal with different problems other than terrorism. The National Security Act of 1947, which established the Central Intelligence Agency (CIA), envisioned the enemies of the United States to be nation-states such as Russia, North Korea, Iran, and China. The result was organizations and authority based on strict distinctions between domestic versus foreign threats, law enforcement versus national security concerns, and peacetime versus wartime operations.[25] The Federal Bureau of Investigation (FBI) was given responsibility for domestic intelligence inside the United States, and the CIA was charged with developing foreign intelligence outside the country. In contrast to the FBI and other law enforcement agencies (e.g., Drug Enforcement Administration, Secret Service), the CIA collects and analyzes information regarding national security in order to forewarn our government before an act occurs. The CIA, relegated to working outside the United States, has no arrest powers, and its activities are proactive in nature. Figure 9–4 compares the responsibilities of the CIA and FBI.

The Central Intelligence Agency is the principal foreign intelligence gathering agency for the United States. For the most part, the focus of the CIA historically has not been on thwarting potentially violent groups in foreign lands (such as al-Qaeda) but rather on individual nation-states that had the potential to conduct military attacks against the United States. The mission of the CIA is threefold: (1) Stop activities from terrorist organizations and nation states that threaten the U.S. homeland or U.S. interests abroad by collecting intelligence information vital to U.S. decision makers; (2) conduct effective covert actions against enemies of the United States as directed

FIGURE 9–4
Comparison Chart between the CIA and FBI

	CIA	**FBI**
	Source: Central Intelligence Agency	Source: Federal Bureau of Investigation, US Department of Justice
Stands for:	Central Intelligence Agency	Federal Bureau of Investigation
Motto:	Ye shall know the truth and it shall set you free.	Fidelity, Bravery, Integrity
Formed:	September 18, 1947	July 26, 1908
Employees:	Classified. Estimated 20,000 agents and 35,000 staff in 2013	Classified. Estimated 13,785 agents and 22,117 staff in 2013
Headquarters:	George Bush Center for Intelligence Langley, Virginia	J. Edgar Hoover Building, Washington, D.C.
Agency Executives:	John O. Brennan, Director Mission executives (Chiefs of Station) are based in major embassies around the world and manage global operations on a regional or country basis.	James Comey, Director Other directors (or Special Agents in Charge – SAC) are located in major large cities domestically and are responsible for regional geographic districts.
Website:	www.cia.gov	www.fbi.gov
Annual budget:	Classified	$8.1 billion (2013)

Source: CIA vs FBI from Diffen.com. Used by permission of Diffen.com.

Box 9–1
Spies, Secret Messages, and Steganography

The earliest record of sending a secret message occurred in Greece in 5 B.C.[26] A man wanted to incite his son-in-law to revolt against the government. He shaved the head of one of his slaves, tattooed the message on his head, and when the hair grew back sent the slave to his son-in-law. During the American Revolution invisible inks were used to send important messages. When treated chemically or with heat by the recipient the hidden message would be revealed.[27]

Another method of sending secret messages during that war was based on books. If two people had the same edition of a book they could exchange secret messages. Upon receiving a message that began "43.21.6" the first word of the message could be found on page 43, line 21, word 6 of the agreed upon book.[28] Obviously, the book selected had to contain a vocabulary that included the words that would commonly be used in messages.

In 1924, Thomas Dyer graduated from the U.S. Naval Academy and was assigned as an ensign to the battleship *New Mexico*.[29] Crossword puzzles had gained popularity during the 1920s. The Navy's Communications Research Desk (CRD) distributed crossword puzzles with "secret" messages hidden in them (steganography). Naval personnel were encouraged to work the crossword puzzles, find the hidden messages, and send their "solution" to CRD. Dyer routinely was able to find the hidden messages. As a consequence, he was transferred and trained in "making and breaking codes." The CRD crossword program was successful: It identified the few people with an aptitude for that kind of work.

In early 1942, Japan dominated the war in the Pacific Theater, enjoying an unbroken string of victories. That same year Japan planned to attack American forces on Midway Island. By then a lieutenant commander, Dyer was a member of Commander Rochefort's cryptanalysis ("code breaking") team. Dyer broke the Japanese naval code and Rochefort, fluent in Japanese, was able to read the subtle nuances in Dyer's translation and understood their foe's plans. The result was a stunning American naval victory at the Battle of Midway that reversed the tide of war in the Pacific Theater.

The steganography with which Dyer struggled in the 1920s was rudimentary and manually driven. However, the technological capabilities currently possessed by some terrorist groups has allowed them to exploit the new generation of digitally driven steganography to send secret messages that pose significant challenges.

Any picture, or other matter that can be reduced to a digital form, can be included in an altered file, creating a steganographic or hidden message. Consider the following:

1. There are 8 bits in a byte: 0-1-01-01-01;
2. The 8th or last bit always adds the smallest amount to the overall identity of a file;
3. Replacing the last bit can be done without causing an immediately detectable difference in an text, image or auditory file; and
4. A PowerPoint file might easily contain 10 megabytes. This provides the opportunity for a hidden message of 1.25 megabytes (1/8 of 10 megabytes).[30]

In 2012, German police questioned Maqsood Lodin, who had just returned from Pakistan.[31] Digital storage devices were discovered in his underwear that included a pornographic video, "Kick Ass." Contained within the video were al-Qaeda plans to hijack a cruise ship, dress passengers in orange jumpsuits like the ones worn by Islamic prisoners at the U.S. naval base at Guantanamo Bay, Cuba, and apparently videotape them being executed to pressure governments for concessions. Other plans included a series of attacks in London England.

Do you think the government still runs secret programs to identify people that have certain abilities?

What tradeoff would you be willing to accept: Keeping intelligence safe versus sharing it more broadly with agencies that might be able to make use of it and potentially add to the intelligence you have, but increasing loss of security? Given the high-speed code breaking capabilities of super computers, how safe is any encrypted data?

National Clandestine Service
The operational wing of the CIA that carries out covert paramilitary operations against terrorist groups and cells outside the United States.

Information Links
For more information on the CIA, FBI, and NSA relating to the collection, analysis, and dissemination of terrorist intelligence information, refer to their websites at:
Central Intelligence Agency (CIA): www.cia.gov/index.html
Federal Bureau of Investigation (FBI): www.fbi.gov/
National Security Agency (NSA): www.nsa.gov/

by the President; and (3) safeguard national secrets that maintain the security of the United States (see Box 9–1). The **National Clandestine Service**, formerly known as the Directorate of Operations, is a major part of the structure of the CIA. It is the operation wing that carries out covert paramilitary operations against terrorist groups and cells outside the United States. It is also the part of the CIA that is most often romantically depicted in the popular media. The adventures of spies and secret agents have been depicted throughout literature as well as television and the movies. Recently however, the CIA has shifted focus from traditional counterterrorism activities to cyber intelligence and more offensive cyber operations.[32] Agencies that have intelligence responsibilities also have cryptanalysis (code breaking). The National Security Agency (NSA) globally monitors communications and collects, analyzes, and disseminates it as needed.

The Federal Bureau of Investigation (FBI)

Headquartered in Washington, D.C., at the J. Edgar Hoover Building, the FBI is the largest investigative agency in the U.S. Department of Justice. It represents the nation's premier law enforcement agency. It has two distinct missions relating to terrorism: (1) The Federal Bureau of Investigation (FBI) is the primary criminal investigative body on any terrorist attack against the United States both domestically and internationally, and

(2) the FBI collects, analyzes, and disseminates all domestic intelligence information relating to terrorist threats. The National Security Branch of the FBI houses the Directorate of Intelligence and is responsible for ensuring that accurate and timely intelligence is embedded into all counterterrorism activities. The FBI is an **intel-driven organization**; that is, it combines investigation and intelligence operations to be more predictive and preventative in nature—more aware of emerging threats and better able to prevent them from occurring.[33]

The primary vehicle for the collection of intelligence information relating to potential terrorist attacks and specific intelligence on individual terrorist groups is derived from the **Joint Terrorism Task Forces (JTTFs)** located throughout the United States (see Figure 9–5). The FBI is the lead agency in managing and directing these task forces. JTTFs represent a collage of highly trained federal, state, and local law enforcement officers and agents committed to gathering intelligence, investigating specific activities, making arrests, and responding to threats at a moment's notice. The task forces are based in 102 cities nationwide, including one in each of the 56 FBI field offices. As of 2014, a total of 71 of these JTTFs have been created since 9/11, composed of more than 4,200 members from over 600 state and local agencies and 50 federal agencies (e.g., U.S. Marshals Service, Secret Service, Immigration and Customs Enforcement, Drug Enforcement Administration, Transportation Security Administration, U.S. Military).[34]

FIGURE 9–5

A member of a JTTF enters a home in North Bergen, New Jersey. Along with others, he conducted a search of the home. It is believed the home was connected to terrorist suspect, Mohammed Hamoud Alessa, who was arrested before he could board a plane at JFK Airport in New York in 2010.

(© John Munson/Star Ledger/Corbis)

Blurred Lines and Conflicting Roles

The FBI and local and state police agencies within this country have a different role than the CIA, one that focuses on crime most often committed by citizens within the United States. With the passage of the USA PATRIOT Act in 2001,[35] the hard-and-fast distinctions between the FBI and the CIA, and hence the role of the police in combating terrorism, have become somewhat blurred. Law enforcement's primary focus has been to collect evidence *after* a crime was committed in order to support prosecution in a court trial. This process, called investigation, is reactive in nature (see Figure 9–6). Traditionally, police intelligence activity has been severely limited by law. A long and controversial history of abuse, particularly on the part of the FBI during the 1960s and 70s, led to the issuance of various Attorney General guidelines limiting the ability of the police to collect intelligence information.[36] The Church Senate Investigative Committee, named after Idaho Senator Frank Church in 1975, revealed a host of constitutional and human rights violations on the part of the FBI Counterintelligence Program (commonly referred to as COINTELPRO) designed specifically to disrupt and intimidate legitimate civil rights groups including the National Organization for Women (NOW), the American Indian Movement (AIM), and the National Association for the Advancement of Colored People (NAACP). These illegal activities (ranging from personal intimidation and threats, illegal eavesdropping, and even burglary) were detailed in the FBI's own internal documents.[37] As a result, the FBI and police were allowed to use intelligence information *only* to develop probable cause that would justify arrest and prosecution. In most incidents, a suspect had to actually break the law or threaten to break it before the police or the FBI could act on intelligence information. This was a frustrating predicament—police agencies could not act without probable cause, but at the same time they were prevented from engaging in the very activities that could establish probable cause![38]

Intel-driven organization

An organization that combines investigation and intelligence operations to be more predictive and preventative in nature.

Joint Terrorism Task Forces (JTTFs)

A group of highly trained federal, state, and local law enforcement officers and agents focusing on terrorism-related intelligence and investigations.

- **Investigation:**

  Reactive; occurs after the event, incident, or crime
  Reports are generally open
  Sources are generally known and open
  Arrests are made based on probable cause: evidence and facts

- **Intelligence:**

  Proactive; information gathered before the event or incident
  Reports are almost always closed
  Sources are confidential and closed
  Arrests are rarely made

FIGURE 9–6

The Differences between Investigation and Intelligence

Source: Robert W. Taylor, Eric J. Fritsch, and John Liederbach, *Digital Crime and Digital Terrorism*, 3rd edition (Upper Saddle River, NJ: Pearson, 2015), p. 234.

The USA PATRIOT Act now allows the FBI and state or local police to engage in covert intelligence operations, greatly expanding the use of police surveillance through roving wiretaps, "sneak and peak" warrants, "trap and trace" pen registers on telephones, and the like. The police can now monitor surreptitiously your use of the Internet and receive a list of all sites visited by your IP address—all without a warrant or other judicial oversight mechanism. Arguably, the FBI and other police organizations indicate that they must have these tools to ferret out would-be terrorists living inside the United States, essentially to protect us from another terrorist attack.

On the other hand, many argue that our laws mandate civil liberties and constitutional rights for each individual citizen. These laws were developed to protect the individual and to balance the power of the police during an investigation...the police have never been given the right to collect intelligence information on individuals without judicial oversight. The right to be free from unwarranted searches and seizures as developed under the Fourth Amendment of the Constitution and to check illegal intrusions into our privacy without probable cause are two of the most basic and enduring rights enjoyed by all citizens of the United States. See Chapter 10 for a more thorough discussion of the issues presented by the collection of intelligence in a free society.

The National Security Agency (NSA)

The National Security Agency (NSA) bills itself as the nation's preeminent "cryptologic organization." In more familiar language, the NSA is primarily responsible for designing and maintaining computerized coding systems designed to protect the integrity of U.S. information systems.[39] (See Figure 9–7.) It has also become the lead agency responsible for monitoring and protecting all of the federal government's computer networks from acts of cyberterrorism.[40] In direct relation to these responsibilities, NSA agents are also responsible for detecting and exploiting weaknesses in an adversarial country's computerized secret coding systems. Headquartered in Fort Meade, Maryland, the NSA has been providing the nation with "code-breaking" capabilities since these operations began against the Japanese in the Pacific theater of World War II. The NSA's role in providing information system security and information assurance has expanded with the parallel growth in computerized communications technology during the Cold War and the ensuing decades.[41]

The NSA's role in protecting classified computer data demands an eclectic mix of agents who specialize in a wide range of professional fields, including researchers, computer scientists, mathematicians, and engineers. Though much of the work of NSA agents remains secretive in nature, the agency's expertise in the area of information systems has led to a number of collaborative initiatives intended to improve information security research, knowledge, and expertise through the federal law enforcement system. For example, the NSA has recently created the INFOSEC Service Center designed to increase research initiatives concerning computer security by the federal government. The NSA has also helped to form the National Computer Security Center (NCSC), which is designed as an avenue to create partnerships among the federal law enforcement and intelligence communities.[42]

FIGURE 9–7
The National Security Agency uses satellites, as well as other information system technologies to collect data, information, and intelligence about potential terrorist groups and attacks. Recently, the agency has come under attack for eavesdropping on foreign telephone communication.

Source: NASA

Source: National Security Agency

Source: NASA

The NSA has also assumed an active role in providing information security training to both government and private entities through the National INFOSEC Education and Training Program. This program provides training for security specialists, including risk assessment, security design, and information security evaluation. Through these initiatives, the NSA aims to provide government agencies and the private sector information system security expertise.[43] Additionally, the NSA works to provide information security through security tools, security products, threat warnings, analysis of potential attacks by terrorists, and security bulletins.[44] In 2013, the NSA came under considerable attack for spying on several U.S. citizens and foreign leaders (see Figure 9–8). In addition, the security of the agency appears to have been compromised by the effort of Edward Snowden, a former CIA employee and NSA contractor who disclosed classified NSA documents to several media outlets and revealed the agency's global surveillance activities.[45] These activities are further discussed in Chapter 10.

FIGURE 9–8
An aerial view of the NSA's Data Center in Bluffdale, Utah. Under a secret court order the NSA has been collecting the telephone records of millions of U.S. citizens. Defenders of the program cite national security requirements and critics point to the lack of need to simply collect the records of citizens who are not under any suspicion.

(© Rick Bowmer/AP/images)

Intelligence and Cyberterrorism

Teams from the FBI, the CIA, and the NSA work together in a secure location known as the Remote Operation Center, the "ROC" ("rock"). With overlapping missions and legal authorities combined with the best high technology equipment available, these teams have a dual mission:

- *Cyber Defense:* Protect current U.S. military and intelligence systems, as well as other critical infrastructure and information systems within the United States from foreign or terrorist attack; and

- *Cyber Offense:* Covertly exploit and infiltrate, via virtual methodologies, foreign systems and create a presence inside these targeted systems for advancing the interests of the United States.

These two missions provide a strong base in which to combat **cyberterrorism or digital terrorism**. These terms are often used interchangeably and can be defined as the premeditated, politically or ideologically motivated attack against information networks, computer systems, computer programs, and/or data that can result in violence against civilian targets.[46] According to Barry Collin of the Institute for Security and Intelligence, cyberterrorism is "hacking with a body count."[47] An early assessment by RAND's National Research Defense Institute concluded that cyberterrorism may also include attacks motivated by political or ideological objectives that can cause serious harm, such as a prolonged loss of infrastructure, like electricity or water (see Chapter 11 for a discussion of the vulnerabilities of critical infrastructure).[48] Yet another definition includes severe economic loss as a qualifier for cyberterrorism: If economic loss is harsh enough, a destabilization may occur that can result in serious harm to a society.[49] To muddy the waters even more, a less significant activity designed to protest, "spread the truth," or otherwise emphasize a particular belief or political bent without intentional harm to human life is referred to as "hacktivism."[50] In these cases, mostly involving website defacement, the actor is involved much more in vandalism and chaos versus economic gain and/or destruction—terrorism *without* the body count.

Cyberterrorism (or Digital terrorism)
The premeditated, politically, or ideologically motivated attack against information networks, computer systems, computer programs, and/or data that can result in violence against civilian targets.

Other Agencies within the Intelligence Community

As previously mentioned, there are 16 separate agencies reporting to the Office of the Director of National Intelligence (ODNI). Although the CIA, FBI, and NSA remain the largest and most well-known of these agencies, there are a still a number of smaller, lesser known agencies that collect, analyze, and disseminate intelligence related to potential terrorist activities, including the following.

Box 9–2
Al-Qaeda and the Potential for Cyberterrorism

Much of the current interest in cyberterrorism sprung from the use of information technology by al-Qaeda in planning the events of September 11, 2001. Under the present direction of Egyptian cleric Ayman al-Zawahiri, al-Qaeda appears to have a sophisticated system of communication, surveillance, and coordination via computer networks and other information tools. In addition, members of al-Qaeda pose a major threat via the Internet. Al-Zawahiri is presumed to be hiding in Pakistan and has released numerous propaganda videos via the Internet since bin Laden's death (in 2011), exhorting followers to violence and "personal jihad."

In an interview with *Computerworld*, Sheikh Omar Bakri Muhammed, an Islamic cleric with proven ties to bin Laden, said that al-Qaeda was actively planning a "cyber jihad" against the United States and its allies. Bakri identified the stock market as a major target and described how the fundamentalist Islamic groups are assembling cadres of computer science students sympathetic to al-Qaeda's cause in places like Pakistan and Malaysia.[51]

Since that time, the FBI noted a series of network intrusions into emergency telephone and electrical generation systems, water storage facilities, nuclear power plants, and gas facilities. Each of the probes had been routed through telecommunications centers in Saudi Arabia, Pakistan, and Indonesia—all known operational centers for al-Qaeda. Subsequent computers seized in Afghanistan by U.S. troops contained information about these probes.[52] In 2011, Seal Team 6 killed bid Laden in his home in Abbottabad, Pakistan. Perhaps at least as important was seizing computers in bin Laden's home for intelligence exploitation. The intelligence information derived from these computer systems helped target terrorists, as well as thwart future attacks. Additionally, it may have left al-Qaeda on the defensive because they are not sure just what information was captured. The destruction of the al-Qaeda communication network may not have been as symbolic as the killing of bin Laden, but nonetheless, much more important and effective in actually disrupting the future of al-Qaeda as a terrorist organization.

U.S. officials found evidence on bin Laden's computers that al-Qaeda operatives spent considerable time on websites that offer software and programming instructions for the digital switches that run critical infrastructure such as transportation and power grids. Because the switches are not meant for public access, they have few security safeguards built into them. An attack using these switches could produce devastating results. Some captured al-Qaeda operatives have confessed their intentions to use switch information for attacks on the United States.[53] This information is further confirmed by reports from the FBI (in 2013) that directly point to al-Qaeda targeting commuter rail and airline systems within the United States.

Simple hacking tools, such as "LOphtCrack," were also found on al-Qaeda computers. LOphtCrack allows a hacker to run combinations of characters at lightning speed in order to try and replicate a password. Other more sophisticated information technology tools, such as data hiding and encryption, were also a common theme in captured al-Qaeda caches.[54] Additionally, terrorist groups have developed hacker tools to engage in credit card theft and rootkits that would allow hackers to remotely command victim machines. These resources are available for download, including a resource titled the "al-Qaeda University for Jihad Studies."[55] This page provides access to propaganda, hacker tools, requests for money and support, and instructional materials to train new generations of hackers to continue the mission of this terrorist network.[56]

Many terrorism experts predict that the next major attack on the United States will be an attack on the digital and electronic resources of the country. Do you think that terrorist groups like al-Qaeda have the capability to conduct acts of cyberterrorism?

Geospatial intelligence (GEOINT)
Intelligence information derived from maps, imagery, charts, and/or satellite data.

Information Links
For more information on these agencies, visit their home pages at:
The Defense Intelligence Agency (DIA): www.dia.mil/
The National GeoSpatial Intelligence Agency (NGIA): www.nga.mil/Pages/default.aspx
The National Reconnaissance Office (NRO): www.nro.gov/
Department of State Bureau of Intelligence and Research (INR): www.state.gov/s/inr/
Department of Homeland Security, Office of Intelligence and Analysis (ONI): www.dhs.gov/about-office-intelligence-and-analysis

The Defense Intelligence Agency (DIA)

The Defense Intelligence Agency provides intelligence in support of U.S. military planning and operations. It is the primary intelligence agency for the U.S. Department of Defense and focuses on preventing strategic surprise from a nation-state (similar to Pearl Harbor in December 1941) or an attack on U.S. military forces overseas (similar to the terrorist attack of the U.S. Marine Barracks in Beirut, Lebanon in 1983). The DIA houses the Office of the Inspector General that conducts audits, inspections, investigation, and intelligence oversight focused on preventing and detecting fraud, waste, and abuse within the defense industry.[57] The DIA also conducts security background investigations on all military or defense personnel relating to security clearances.

National Geospatial-Intelligence Agency (NGA)

Using **geospatial intelligence (GEOINT)** derived from maps, imagery, charts, and satellite data, the NGA provides a foundation for the intelligence discipline (see Figure 9–9). Using high-level geographic information systems (GIS)[58] and remote sensing techniques provides NGA analysts with critical information relating to terrain, elevation, and gravity.[59] Such information provides immediate intelligence relating to any physical or geographical point in the world, allowing strategic and tactical advantage to warfighters during combat as well as support for various types of counterterrorism operations.

National Reconnaissance Office (NRO)

The NRO is the government agency responsible for designing, building, launching, maintaining, and monitoring America's intelligence satellite system.[60] The NRO works closely with other members of the intelligence community and particularly those associated with the U.S. Department of Defense and the military.

State Bureau of Intelligence and Research

The primary intelligence division within the U.S. Department of State is the Bureau of Intelligence and Research (INR). Its mission is to provide intelligence information in support of U.S. diplomacy and is often the focal point for actions involving counterintelligence and law enforcement activities outside the United States.[61] The State Bureau of Intelligence and Research also provides intelligence support for the safety and security of embassies located throughout the world.

U.S. Department of Homeland Security, Office of Intelligence and Analysis

The Office of Intelligence and Analysis (I&A) is an agency that manages the collection, analysis, and dissemination of intelligence through the entire U.S. Department of Homeland Security. The Office tracks individual terrorist and groups as well as monitors threats against critical American infrastructure. One of the primary missions of the Office is to integrate the intelligence elements within DHS and to share this information with state and local governments as well as the private sector.[62] To this end, the I&A has been instrumental in establishing and funding intelligence fusion centers throughout the United States. Fusion centers are discussed later in this chapter.

Other members of the intelligence community include smaller units within various governmental departments and agencies such as the Drug Enforcement Administration Office of National Security Intelligence, the U.S. Department of Energy Office of Intelligence and Counterintelligence, and the U.S. Department of Treasury Office of Intelligence and Research. The final members of the intelligence community represent the intelligence services within each branch of the military: Air Force, Army, Coast Guard, Marine Corps, and Navy.

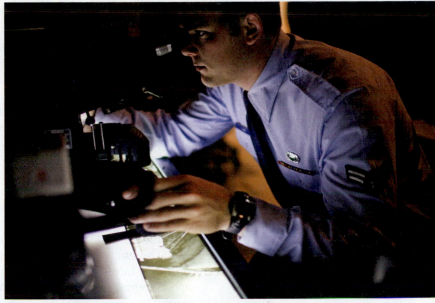

FIGURE 9–9
Geospatial data has both military and civilian applications. A U.S. Air Force geospacial intelligence analyst studies images of the damage done by a large hurricane on the Gulf Coast. Information from such analyses allows for the rapid examination of damages and where resources need to be directed and prioritized.

(© Max Whittaker/Corbis)

Intelligence at the State and Local Level

In addition to federal effort, state and local police departments are implementing their own brand of intelligence gathering and analysis through the planned networking of large databases that seek to contribute to the national process of intelligence gathering and sharing. This new strategy, the **National Criminal Intelligence Sharing Plan (NCISP)**, combines the public partnership concepts of community policing with problem-solving tactics that aim to enhance police efficiency and draw attention to the primary concern of preventing terrorist attacks through effective communication and coordination. The strategic integration of intelligence, with an emphasis on predictive analysis–derived real data defines a new style of policing called **intelligence-led policing (ILP)**. An important hallmark of ILP is the reliance on sophisticated computers and software programs to assist police decision makers in their daily duties. Ultimately, the goal of intelligence-led policing is to provide an expansive intelligence system involving local police that not only helps coordinate agency responses, but again, also informs objective decision making on how to prevent and combat both crime and terrorism.[63]

National Criminal Intelligence Sharing Plan (NCISP)
A national effort that combines public partnerships with problem-solving tactics aimed at enhancing police efficiency in preventing terrorist attacks through effective communication and coordination.

Intelligence-led policing (ILP)
A new style of policing that integrates intelligence, with an emphasis on predictive analysis derived from the discovery of hard facts, information, patterns, and traditional crime analysis.

FIGURE 9–10
The Intelligence Cycle
The intelligence cycle is the process of developing unrefined data into polished intelligence for the use of policymakers.

Source: http://www.fbi.gov/about-us/intelligence/intelligence-cycle

The Intelligence Process and Cycle

The National Criminal Intelligence Sharing Plan (NCISP) contained 28 specific recommendations for major changes in local policing. However, the key concept from the document emphasized the strategic integration of intelligence into the overall mission of the police organization. Rather than react and respond to past calls for service, the plan placed much more emphasis on predictive analysis derived from the discovery of hard facts, information, patterns, intelligence, and good crime analysis. Accurate and timely intelligence information, then, becomes a critically important element of the plan. In order to protect the civil liberties of all individuals, the intelligence process (from collection through analysis to dissemination) is developed with key evaluation points aimed at verifying source reliability and validity at the beginning of the collection cycle. The goal was to develop a universal process that would integrate both law enforcement and national security intelligence agendas, while at the same time provide mechanisms for securing individual freedoms, yet allow law enforcement agencies to be proactive in preventing and deterring crime and terrorism. The end result was the "intelligence cycle" presented in an effort to bring varied pieces of information together in an effort to draw logical conclusions from a thorough and systematic process (see Figure 9–10). The intelligence cycle also provides the crucial means to communicate and share intelligence information between individuals and agencies through the dissemination process.

The intelligence cycle consists of six steps. The graphic in Figure 9–10 shows the circular nature of this process, although movement between the steps is fluid. Intelligence uncovered at one step may require going back to an earlier step before moving forward. The six steps of the intelligence cycle are:

Requirements are identified information needs—what we must know to safeguard the nation. Intelligence requirements are established by the Director of National Intelligence according to guidance received from the president and the national and homeland security advisors. Requirements are developed based on critical information required to protect the United States from national security and criminal threats. The attorney general and the director of the FBI participate in the formulation of national intelligence requirements.

Planning and Direction is management of the entire effort, from identifying the need for information to delivering an intelligence product to a consumer. It involves implementation plans to satisfy requirements levied on the FBI, as well as identifying specific collection requirements based on FBI needs. Planning and direction also is responsive to the end of the cycle, because current and finished intelligence, which supports decision making, generates new requirements. The executive assistant director for the National Security Branch leads intelligence planning and direction for the FBI.

Collection is the gathering of raw information based on requirements. Activities such as interviews, technical and physical surveillances, human source operation, searches, and liaison relationships result in the collection of intelligence.

Processing and Exploitation involves converting the vast amount of information collected into a form usable by analysts. This is done through a variety of methods including decryption, language translations, and data reduction. Processing includes the entering of raw data into databases where it can be exploited for use in the analysis process.

Analysis and Production is the conversion of raw information into intelligence. It includes integrating, evaluating, and analyzing available data, and preparing intelligence products. The information's reliability, validity, and relevance is evaluated and weighed. The information is logically integrated, put in context, and used to produce intelligence. This includes both "raw" and finished intelligence. Raw intelligence is often referred to as "the dots"—individual pieces of information disseminated individually.

According to the U.S. Department of Homeland Security, **data fusion** is defined as the exchange of information from different sources—including law enforcement, public safety, and the private sector—and, with analysis, can result in meaningful and actionable intelligence and information that can inform both policy and the tactical deployment of resources.

Sources: U.S. Department of Homeland Security, Fusion Center Guidelines: Developing and Sharing Information and Intelligence in a New Era (Washington, D.C.: 2006) and David Lambert, "Intelligence-Led Policing in a Fusion Center," *FBI Law Enforcement Bulletin* (Washington, D.C.: Federal Bureau of Investigation), www.fbi.gov/stats-services/publications/law-enforcement-bulletin/Dec2010/intelligence_feature.

Courtesy Toria/Shutterstock

Finished intelligence reports "connect the dots" by putting information in context and drawing conclusions about its implications.

Dissemination—the last step—is the distribution of raw or finished intelligence to the consumers whose needs initiated the intelligence requirements. The FBI disseminates information in three standard formats: Intelligence Information Reports (IIRs), FBI Intelligence Bulletins, and FBI Intelligence Assessments. FBI intelligence products are provided daily to the attorney general, the president, and to customers throughout the FBI and in other agencies. These FBI intelligence customers make decisions—operational, strategic, and policy—based on the information. These decisions may lead to the levying of more requirements, thus continuing the FBI intelligence cycle.[64]

Data fusion
The exchange of information from different sources, with analysis, that results in meaningful and actionable intelligence.

Fusion Centers

The transformation of state and local police agencies into intelligence-led organizations involves several key objectives: (1) the creation of a task and coordination process, (2) the development of core intelligence products to lead the operation, (3) the establishment of standardized training practices, and (4) the development of protocols to facilitate intelligence capabilities.

This approach is intended to improve the capability of local law enforcement to respond to terrorist threats and the imperative to "fight crime." Intelligence-led policing blends community partnerships with crime fighting and police accountability in an effort to maximize police efficiency and effectiveness toward terrorism prevention and crime reduction. There is evidence to suggest that this initiative has started to alter the face of traditional policing in the United States. A national study found that a majority of local and state police agencies have conducted terrorism threat assessments since 9/11, and about one-third of these agencies have collaborated with the FBI's joint terrorism task force to assist in local crime investigations.[65] The movement toward intelligence-led policing has also been pushed by the creation of fusion centers inside local and state police agencies that serve as "clearinghouses" for all potentially relevant homeland security information

Fusion center
A "clearinghouse" or information "hub" that blends the power of information technology with terrorism prevention and crime fighting.

that can be used to assess local terror threats and aid in the apprehension of more traditional criminal suspects.

Originally launched in New York City under the direction of Raymond Kelly in 2002, the concept of a **fusion center** blended the power of information technology with terrorism prevention and crime fighting. With a price tag exceeding $11 million, the Real Time Crime Center (RTCC) in New York City combs through tens of millions of criminal complaints, arrest and parole records, and 911 call records dating back a decade in an effort to provide NYPD officers with the information tools necessary to stop a terrorist event.[66] Fusion centers serve the function of distributing relevant, actionable, and timely information and intelligence incorporating a simultaneous vertical (i.e., federal, state, and local) and horizontal (i.e., within the agency, with other local agencies, and across disciplines such as fire, EMS, public works, private partners) approach in a timely and efficient manner within a given jurisdiction.

Fusion centers are composed of talented and trained individuals using sophisticated application software in crime analysis and mapping to manage and manipulate information and intelligence into a usable product. The resulting analysis acts as a basis for the deployment of police resources and directed operations in a real-time format, that is, almost immediately. The fusion center not only acts as a centralized host for intelligence information and analysis, but also serves as a conduit for passing critical information out to other regional, state, and national authorities. This is a particularly important point that fulfills the National Criminal Intelligence Sharing Plan in protecting the homeland.

Almost every state and several large metropolitan cities have undertaken the development of fusion centers with significant funding assistance from the Department of Homeland Security, Office of Intelligence and Analysis. For instance, the Chicago Police Department Deployment Operations Center (DOC) was one of the first centers to combine real-time intelligence analysis with the deployment of officers and other resources. In Los Angeles, both the city and county have well-developed fusion centers, and in Dallas, Texas, the Metropolitan Operations and Analytical Intelligence Center (MOSAIC) provides real-time, tactical information to officers on the street 24/7.

The goals of a fusion center are fourfold:

1) Fusion centers support the broad range of activities undertaken by a police department relating to the detection, examination, and investigation of a potential terrorist attack and/or criminal activity. Similar to the NCTC, local and state fusion centers serve as a hubs of anti-terrorist and anti-crime operations in a specific region focusing on the recognition of patterns, indications and warnings, source development, interdiction, and coordination of critical criminal justice resources. These are critical activities for any police agency attempting to be proactive and intelligence-led to be successful in deterring, detecting, disrupting, investigating, and apprehending suspects involved in terrorist activity.

2) Fusion centers provide support for operations that protect critical infrastructure and key resources (CI/KRs) in a given region, support major incident operations, support specialized units charged with interdiction and investigative operations, and assist in emergency operations and planning. See Chapter 11 for discussion on protecting America's infrastructure.

3) Fusion centers often maintain public "tip lines" or the capability to promote more public involvement/awareness to terrorist threats. The goal is to identify and recognize warnings signs and potential threats in a timely manner in order to preempt potential terrorist attacks. Fusion centers accomplish this task on a daily basis, focusing on the analysis of crimes that are often linked to terrorist cells and activity for funding, such as narcotics trafficking, credit card abuse, armament and gun theft, prostitution, and human trafficking by distributing information relating to these linkages to all agencies within a given region. The timeliness of gathering, analyzing, and disseminating information is vital to successfully preventing acts of violence and threats to Homeland Security.

4) Fusion centers assist police executives in making better-informed decisions, especially during emergencies or critical incidents. Fusion centers serve as an ongoing deployment operations center with the real-time ability to monitor critical resources. This includes real-time status monitoring of major events, communicating with area medical facilities and trauma units, coordinating the allocation and deployment of multi-agency personnel resources (including military reserve units), monitoring changing weather conditions, and directing all support services through a centralized operations center.[67]

U.S. Department of Homeland Security and Fusion Centers

The U.S. Department of Homeland Security (DHS) has played an integral role in the development and implementation of fusion centers as part of the intelligence-led policing paradigm. The primary goal of DHS in this area has been to promote a strong relationship between state/local and federal law enforcement agencies through financial grants. Many states and larger cities have created fusion centers to share information and intelligence within their jurisdictions as well as with the federal government funded through DHS grants. The Office of Intelligence and Analysis within DHS provides support personnel with operational and intelligence skills to fusion centers when requested. This support is tailored to the unique needs of the locality and serves to help the classified and unclassified information flow, provide analysis expertise, coordinate with local law enforcement and other agencies, and provide local awareness and access to sensitive data (Department of Homeland Security, 2008).

As of 2014, there were 77 state and major urban fusion centers within the United States.[68] Almost every state has a statewide fusion center, as well as most major urban areas (see Figure 9–11). The **National Fusion Center Association (NFCA)** is a formal group that represents the interests of state and major urban area fusion centers nationally. In addition, the NFCA promotes the development and sustainment of fusion center to enhance public safety, and the ethical and lawful collection of intelligence gathering, analysis, and dissemination.[69] Like many federal agencies and individual fusion centers, the goal of the NFCA is to prevent the next terrorist attack on the homeland. The **Homeland Security Data Network (HSDN)**, which allows the federal government to move information and intelligence to the states at the "secret" level, is deployed at most fusion centers. Through HSDN, fusion center staff can access the National Counterterrorism Center (NCTC) via a secure and classified portal to the most current terrorism-related information. Certainly, we have witnessed an unprecedented movement on the part of the federal government to employ local and state police agencies into the anti-terrorism mission.

National Fusion Center Association (NFCA)
A formal group that represents the interests of state and major urban area fusion centers nationally.

Homeland Security Data Network (HSDN)
A classified information network that allows the federal government to move information and intelligence to state and local jurisdictions at the "secret" level.

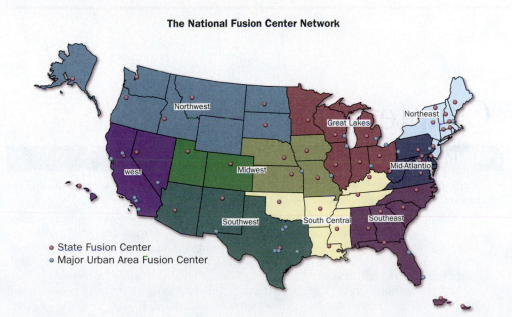

The National Fusion Center Network

• State Fusion Center
• Major Urban Area Fusion Center

FIGURE 9–11
Locations of the 77 recognized U.S. Department of Homeland Security (DHS) fusion centers.
Source: DHS and NFCA 2014, www.dhs.gov/fusion-center-locations-and-contact-information.

Primary Fusion Centers

- Alabama Fusion Center
- Alaska Information and Analysis Center
- Arizona Counter Terrorism Information Center
- Arkansas State Fusion Center
- California State Threat Assessment Center
- Colorado Information Analysis Center
- Connecticut Intelligence Center
- Delaware Information and Analysis Center
- Florida Fusion Center
- Georgia Information Sharing and Analysis Center
- Hawaii Fusion Center
- Idaho Criminal Intelligence Center
- Illinois Statewide Terrorism and Intelligence Center
- Indiana Intelligence Fusion Center
- Iowa Intelligence Fusion Center
- Kansas Intelligence Fusion Center
- Kentucky Intelligence Fusion Center
- Louisiana State Analytical & Fusion Exchange
- Maine Information and Analysis Center
- Mariana Regional Fusion Center (Guam)
- Maryland Coordination and Analysis Center
- Massachusetts Commonwealth Fusion Center
- Michigan Intelligence Operations Center
- Minnesota Fusion Center
- Mississippi Analysis and Information Center
- Missouri Information Analysis Center
- Montana All-Threat Intelligence Center
- Nebraska Information Analysis Center
- New Hampshire Information and Analysis Center
- New Jersey Regional Operations Intelligence Center
- New Mexico All Source Intelligence Center
- New York State Intelligence Center
- North Carolina Information Sharing and Analysis Center
- North Dakota State and Local Intelligence Center
- Ohio Strategic Analysis and Information Center
- Oklahoma Information Fusion Center
- Oregon Terrorism Information Threat Assessment Network
- Pennsylvania Criminal Intelligence Center
- Puerto Rico National Security State Information Center
- Rhode Island State Fusion Center
- South Carolina Information and Intelligence Center
- South Dakota Fusion Center

- Southern Nevada Counter-Terrorism Center (Las Vegas, Nevada)
- Tennessee Fusion Center
- Texas Joint Crime Information Center
- U.S. Virgin Islands Fusion Center
- Utah Statewide Information and Analysis Center
- Vermont Intelligence Center
- Virginia Fusion Center
- Washington Regional Threat and Analysis Center (Washington, D.C.)
- Washington State Fusion Center
- West Virginia Intelligence Fusion Center
- Wisconsin Statewide Information Center

Recognized Fusion Centers

- Austin Regional Intelligence Center; Austin, TX
- Boston Regional Intelligence Center; Boston, MA
- Central California Intelligence Center; Sacramento, CA
- Central Florida Intelligence Exchange; Orlando, FL
- Chicago Crime Prevention and Information Center; Chicago, IL
- Cincinnati/Hamilton County Regional Terrorism Early Warning Group; Cincinnati, OH
- Dallas Fusion Center; Dallas, TX
- Delaware Valley Intelligence Center; Philadelphia, PA
- Detroit and Southeast Michigan Information and Intelligence Center; Detroit, MI
- El Paso Multi-Agency Tactical Response Information eXchange (MATRIX); El Paso, TX
- Houston Regional Intelligence Service Center; Houston, TX
- Kansas City Terrorism Early Warning Fusion Center; Kansas City, MO
- Los Angeles Joint Regional Intelligence Center; Los Angeles, CA
- Nevada Threat Analysis Center; Carson City, NV
- North Central Texas Fusion Center; McKinney, TX
- Northeast Ohio Regional Fusion Center; Cleveland, OH
- Northern California Regional Intelligence Center; San Francisco, CA
- Northern Virginia Regional Intelligence Center; Fairfax, VA
- Orange County Intelligence Assessment Center; Orange County, CA
- San Diego Law Enforcement Coordination Center; San Diego, CA
- Southeast Florida Fusion Center; Miami, FL
- Southeastern Wisconsin Threat Analysis Center; Milwaukee, WI
- Southwest Texas Fusion Center; San Antonio, TX
- Southwestern PA Region 13 Fusion Center; Pittsburgh, PA
- St. Louis Fusion Center; St. Louis, MO

FIGURE 9–11 (CONTINUED)

Chapter Summary

SUMMARY BY LEARNING OBJECTIVE

1. **Explain the impact of the Gilmore Commission and provide a brief statement regarding its major findings.**

   The Gilmore Commission was an important inquiry into the federal government's response to terrorism after the attacks of 9/11. The Commission is named after its chairperson, Virginia Governor Jim Gilmore, and identified five important issues relating to the intelligence function in the United States: (1) failure to emphasize traditional human intelligence (HUMINT) gathering and analysis in favor of an overreliance on technology tools such as spy satellites and computer programs; (2) failure to provide timely, accurate, and specific intelligence information to law enforcement agencies; (3) an overly bureaucratic and decentralized structure (particularly within the FBI) that hindered counter terrorism efforts; (4) outdated and obsolete computer systems that prevented the timely sharing of critical information among the different branches of law enforcement; and (5) overly restrictive guidelines and laws that hindered the effective use of informants and intelligence gathering relating to terrorists.

2. **Define intelligence and counterintelligence.**

    Intelligence is an information process and product derived from systematic and thoughtful examination (analysis), placed in context and provided to governmental executives and military leaders with facts and alternatives than can inform critical decisions, particularly those involving the deployment of critical resources. Counterintelligence, on the other hand, is a myriad of activities intended to prevent adversaries from acquiring accurate information about an organization's capabilities, actions, personnel, and/or plans.

3. **Provide a brief overview of the U.S. Intelligence Community and discuss the role of the Office of the Director of National Intelligence.**

    The current U.S. Intelligence Community (IC) was established in 2004 in response to the Gilmore Commission. Sixteen different government agencies (including the CIA, FBI, and NSA) answer to the Office of the Director of National Intelligence (ODNI). The primary role of the ODNI is to coordinate, integrate, and manage the collection, analysis, and dissemination of intelligence information, including the intelligence that relates directly to international and domestic threats posed by terrorist organizations. The ODNI also administers the National Intelligence Program (NIP) representing the estimated $60 billion annual budget designed to strengthen the nation's intelligence capabilities.

4. **Describe the National Counterterrorism Center (NCTC).**

    The National Counterterrorism Center (NCTC), located in Washington, D.C., acts as the nation's centralized fusion center, integrating and analyzing threat information from various sources and then disseminating that intelligence to the other members of the intelligence community as well as state and local agencies.

5. **Explain the differences between the CIA and the FBI relating to terrorism and intelligence.**

    The Central Intelligence Agency (CIA) collects and analyzes information regarding national security issues, including potential strikes against the U.S. homeland and interest abroad. Its role is intelligence related and is relegated to working primarily outside the United States. It has no arrest powers within the United States; however, it conducts clandestine operations to thwart terrorist groups and potential attacks. In contrast, the FBI is the primary criminal investigative body on any terrorist attack against the United States both domestically and internationally; and is responsible for collecting, analyzing, and disseminating all domestic intelligence information relating to terrorist attacks or threats.

6. **Discuss the differences between investigation and intelligence.**

    Investigations are reactive in nature (a crime has already occurred), reports and sources are generally open, and the goal is to make an arrest based on evidence and facts (probable cause). On the other hand, intelligence is usually proactive (before an event occurs), reports and sources are almost always closed and confidential, and arrests are rarely made.

7. **Define JTTFs and discuss the importance of their role and mission.**

    Joint Terrorism Task Forces (JTTFs) is a group of highly trained federal, state, and local law enforcement officers and agents committed to gathering intelligence relating to potential terrorist activities, investigating specific terrorist-related crimes, making arrests, and responding to threats at a moment's notice. The task forces are managed and directed by the FBI and are based in 102 cities nationwide, including one in each of the 56 FBI field offices.

8. **Discuss the role of the National Security Agency as an intelligence agency.**

    The NSA is primarily responsible for designing and maintaining computerized coding systems designed to protect the integrity of U.S. information systems. It has also become the lead agency responsible for monitoring and protecting all of the federal government's computer networks from acts of cyberterrorism. In direct relation to these responsibilities, NSA agents are also responsible for detecting and exploiting weaknesses in an adversarial country's computerized secret coding systems. The NSA's role in providing information system security and information assurance has expanded with the parallel growth in computerized communications technology. The NSA also has an active role in providing information security training to both government and private entities. Additionally, the NSA works to provide information security through security tools, security products, threat warnings, analysis of potential attacks by terrorists, and security bulletins.

9. **Define the concept of "cyberterrorism" or "digital terrorism."**

Cyberterrorism or digital terrorism is the premeditated, politically or ideologically motivated attack against information networks, computer systems, computer programs, and/or data that can result in violence against civilian targets.

10. **List the other agencies within the intelligence community.**

There are 16 separate agencies reporting to the Office of the Director of National Intelligence (ODNI). Although the Central Intelligence Agency, the Federal Bureau of Investigation, and the National Security Agency remain the largest and most well-known of these agencies, there are a number of lesser known agencies that collect, analyze and disseminate intelligence related to potential terrorist activities. These include the Department of Defense Intelligence Agency, the National Geospatial Agency, the National Reconnaissance Office, the Department of State Bureau of Intelligence and Research, and the Department of Homeland Security Office of Intelligence and Analysis. Other members of the intelligence community include smaller units within various governmental departments and agencies such as the Drug Enforcement Administration Office of National Security Intelligence, the Department of Energy Office of Intelligence and Counterintelligence, the Department of Treasury Office of Intelligence and Research, and the intelligence services within each branch of the military: Air Force, Army, Coast Guard, Marine Corps, and Navy.

11. **Describe the intelligence cycle.**

The intelligence cycle is an important effort to bring varied pieces of information together in an effort to draw logical conclusions from a thorough and systematic process, yet protect the civil liberties of all individuals within the United States. It is an important process for analyzing intelligence presented by the FBI, with the goal of developing a universal process that attempts to integrate both law enforcement and national security intelligence agendas.

12. **Define and describe the four goals of a fusion center.**

A fusion center is "clearinghouse" or information "hub" that blends the power of information technology with terrorism prevention and crime fighting. Fusion centers are located throughout the United States and have four goals: (1) Support the broad range of activities undertaken by a police department relating to the detection, examination, and investigation of a potential terrorist attack and/or criminal activity; (2) provide support for operations that protect critical infrastructure and key resources (CI/KRs) in a given region, support major incident operations, support specialized units charged with interdiction and investigative operations, and assist in emergency operations and planning; (3) maintain public "tip lines" or the capability to promote more public involvement/awareness in an effort to identify and recognize warnings signs and potential terrorist threats or attacks; and (4) assist police executives in making better-informed decisions, especially during emergencies or critical incidents like a terrorist attack, a major criminal activity, or a natural disaster.

REVIEW QUESTIONS

1. Discuss the Gilmore Commission. What were the Commission's major findings?
2. Define the terms "intelligence" and "counterintelligence"
3. Discuss the structure of the U.S. intelligence community (IC) and identify several of its key component agencies.
4. What is the National Counterterrorism Center (NCTC) and what is its primary role and mission?
5. Discuss the differences between the CIA and the FBI. Discuss the role of each agency and the ways they may accomplish their respective missions.
6. What is a JTTF? What are the primary missions of these entities?
7. Discuss the differences between investigation and intelligence.
8. Discuss the primary role of the NSA.

9. Discuss the concepts of "cyberterrorism" or "digital terrorism." How vulnerable is the United States to such attacks?
10. Discuss the purpose of the intelligence cycle. Why is it important?
11. What are fusion centers? Discuss their four primary goals.

CRITICAL THINKING EXERCISES

1. **Research Intelligence on Terrorist Organizations and Groups Globally.** Visit and preview the Terrorism Research and Analysis Consortium (TRAC), created by the Beacham Group, LLC on the Internet at www.terrorismresearch.org. Watch the preview and explore the site. TRAC is one of the most comprehensive terrorism research sites on the Internet and provides an efficient series of filters in which to study various types of terrorist targets, tactics, and groups. Play with the filters, watch some of the posted videos, read some of the articles on ideology, and read the intelligence reports about the latest information on active groups in any area of your choosing. Consider subscribing or having your university or college subscribe to the site. TRAC was specifically designed to fulfill the research and intelligence needs of faculty, scholars, students, and government and defense professionals studying terrorism.
2. **The National Counterterrorism Center (NCTC).** The Office of the Director of National Intelligence houses the National Counterterrorism Center (NCTC). The two core missions of the NCTC are to serve as the primary organization in the United States for the analysis and integration of terrorism intelligence, and the second mission is to conduct strategic operational planning for counterterrorism activities. Visit the NCTC website at www.nctc.gov. Name the key partners associated with the NCTC and view the Counterterrorism Calendar. Now explore career possibilities within the intelligence field. What types of career opportunities exist within the intelligence community at the federal level? As important, what are the knowledge, skills, and abilities required to fulfill these types of positions and are you qualified? Develop an action plan for yourself to accomplish education and training goals that would qualify you for an intelligence analyst position within the National Counterterrorism Center.

NOTES

1. D. Priest and W. Arkin, "Top-Secret America," *Dallas Morning News*, July 25, 2010, p. 26A.
2. A.L. Jackson and M. Brown, "Ensuring Efficiency, Interagency Cooperation, and Protection of Civil Liberties: Shifting from a Traditional Model of Policing to an Intelligence-Led Policing (ILP) Paradigm," *Criminal Justice Studies*, Vol. 20, pp. 111–129.
3. *The 9/11 Commission Report* (Washington, D.C.: UGPO, July 22, 2004), see www.gpo.gov/fdsys/pkg/GPO-911REPORT/pdf/GPO-911REPORT.pdf.
4. See K. Riley, G. Teverton, J. Wilson, and L. Davis, *State and Local Intelligence in the War on Terrorism, Volumes 1-5* (Washington, D.C.: RAND Corporation, 2005). These volumes are commonly referred to as the Gilmore Commission Reports, named after Virginia Governor Jim Gilmore, chair of the congressionally mandated commission to assess the domestic response capability against terrorism between 1999 and 2003.
5. Summary of Classified Report to the U.S. Congress, House of Representatives Intelligence Subcommittee, *Report on Intelligence Gathering and Analysis pre September 11, 2001*, July 16, 2002.
6. Ibid.
7. Marilyn Peterson, *Intelligence-Led Policing: The New Intelligence Architecture* (Washington, D.C.: The RAND Corporation, 2005).
8. Richard J. Hughbank and Don Githens, "Intelligence and Its Role in Protecting Against Terrorism," *Journal of Strategic Security*, Vol. 3, No. 1, March 2010, p. 31.
9. Blake W. Mobley, *Terrorism and Counter-Intelligence: How Terrorist Groups Escape Detection* (New York: Columbia University Press, 2012), p. 8.

10. Ben Brandt, "The Taliban's Conduct of Intelligence and Counter-Intelligence," *CTS Sentinel*, Vol. 4, Issue 6, June 2011, p. 20.

11. Loc. cit.

12. Ibid., p. 22

13. Loc. cit.

14. Mobley, *Terrorism and Counter-Intelligence*, p. 8.

15. Ibid., p.40.

16. Ibid., p. 41.

17. Ibid., p. 38.

18. Ibid., p. 40.

19. Ibid., p. 55.

20. See www.whitehouse.gov/omb/factsheet_department_intelligence.

21. See a description of the National Counterterrorism Center at www.nctc.gov.

22. Ibid.

23. See www.nctc.gov/calendar.html.

24. *Joint Counterterrorism Assessment Team (JCAT)*, Vol. 1, Issue 4, 2013, p. 4.

25. J. Deutsch and J.H. Smith, "Smarter Intelligence," *Foreign Policy*, 128 (2002), pp. 64–69.

26. This account is drawn from S. D. Murphy, "Steganography—The New Intelligence Threat" (Quantico, Virginia: Maine Corps War College, Research paper, 2005), p. 2.

27. See Jennifer Wilcox, "Revolutionary Secrets: The Secret Communications of the American Revolution" (Washington, D.C.: National Security Agency, undated paper), www.nsa.gov/about/_files/cryptologic_heritage/publications/prewil/revolutionary_secrets.pdf.

28. Loc. cit.

29. This synopsis is taken from Paul Stillwell, "The Lead Code-Breaker of Midway," (Annapolis, Maryland: U.S. Naval Institute, Proceedings 0041798X), Vol. 138, Issue 6, June 2012, pp. 62–65.

30. Loc. cit.

31. Restated from Nic Robertson, Paul Cruichshank, and Tim Lister, "Documents Reveal Al Qaeda's Plans for Seizing Cruise Ships, Carnage in Europe," *CNN World*, May 1, 2012, www.cnn.com/2012/04/30/world/al-qaeda-documents-future

32. Barton Gellman and Ellen Nakashima, "U.S. Spy Agencies Mounted 231 Offensive Cyber Operations in 2011, Documents Show," *The Washington Post*, August 30, 2013, www.washingtonpost.com/world/national-security/us-spy-agencies-mounted-231-offensive-cyber-operations-in-2011-documents-show/2013/08/30/d090a6ae-119e-11e3-b4cb-fd7ce041d814_story_3.html

33. See www.fbi.gov/about-us/intelligence/intel-driven

34. See www.fbi.gov/about-us/investigate/terrorism/terrorism_jttfs

35. The USA PATRIOT Act of 2001 was quickly rushed into law after the 9/11 attacks and signed by President George W. Bush on October 26, 2001. It was a rushed piece of legislation, without normal review and skirting traditional Congressional processes. The act changed 15 separate federal statutes, and has been attacked in court on various constitutional issues. Over the last decade, the Appellate Courts have struck down many parts of the act as challenges continue to be filed.

36. See Attorney General Edward Levi, *Guidelines for Domestic Security Investigations* (April 4, 1976), Attorney General William French Smith, *Guidelines on General Crimes, Racketeering Enterprise and Domestic Security/Terrorism Investigations* (1983), and Attorney General Dick Thornburgh, *Guidelines on General Crimes, Racketeering, Enterprise and Domestic Security/Terrorism Investigations* (March 21, 1989).

37. The constitutional and human rights violations of the turbulent 1960s were not just within the purview of the FBI. Several highlighted abuses by local police departments in Chicago, Los Angeles, and New York have also been detailed. See ACLU, *The Dangers of Domestic Spying by Federal Law Enforcement: A Case Study on FBI Surveillance of Dr. Martin Luther King* (January 2002); ACLU, *History Repeated: The Dangers of Domestic Spying by Federal Law Enforcement* (May 29, 2007); and W. Churchill and J. V. Wall, *The COINTELPRO Papers: Documents from the FBI's Secret Wars Against Dissent in the United States* (Cambridge, MA: South End Press, 1990).

38. J. B. Motley, *U.S. Strategy to Counter Domestic Political Terrorism* (Washington, D.C.: National Security Affairs) Monograph Series, 2 (1983), pp. 62–70.

39. www.nsa.gov.

40. Ellen Nakashima, "Bush Order Expands Network Monitoring: Intelligence Agencies to Track Institutions," *The Washington Post,* January 1, 2008, www.washingtonpost.com/wp-dyn/content/article/2008/01/25/AR2008012503261_pf.html

41. Ibid., p. 28.

42. Ibid.

43. Ibid.

44. www.nsa.gov/ia/ia_at_nsa/index.shtml

45. Glenn Greenwald, Ewen MacAskill, and Laura Poitras, "Edward Snowden: The Whistle Blower Behind the NSA Surveillance Revelations," *The Guardian* (London), June 10, 2013.

46. Mark Pollit, "Cyberterrorism—Fact or Fancy?" *Proceedings of the 20th National Information Systems Security Conference*, October 25, 1977, pp. 285–289.

47. M. Grossman, "Cyberterrorism," February 15, 1999, http://www.mgrossmanlaw.com/articles/1999.cyberterrorism.htm

48. Ibid., p. 4.

49. Dorothy E. Denning, "Cyberterrorism," www.cs.georgetown.edu/~denning/infosec/cyberterror-GD.doc

50. For a more advanced discussion of cyberterrorism, refer to Robert W. Taylor, Eric J. Fritsch, and John Liederback, *Digital Crime and Digital Terrorism,* 3rd edition (Upper Saddle River, NJ: Pearson, 2015), Chapter 2.

51. "Al Qaeda Poses Threat to the Net," *Computerworld,* November 25, 2002.

52. "Cyber-Attacks by Al Qaeda Feared," *Washington Post,* June 27, 2002.

53. Ibid.

54. Summarized from Public Broadcasting Station interviews, April 24, 2013, see www.pbs.org/wgbh/pages/frontline/shows/cyberwar/interviews/

55. Ibid.

56. The box adapted from Taylor, Fritsch, and Liederbach, *Digital Crime and Digital Terrorism.*

57. See www.dia.mil/Home.aspx

58. Geographic information systems (GIS) are an integration of computer hardware, software, and data for capturing, managing, analyzing, and displaying all forms of geographic data from simple maps to complex remote sensing operations.

59. See www.nga.mil/

60. See www.nro.gov/about/index.html

61. See www.state.gov/s/inr/

62. See www.dhs.gov/about-office-intelligence-and-analysis

63. Jerry H. Ratcliffe and Ray Guidetti, "State Police Investigative Structure and the Adoption of Intelligence-Led Policing," *Policing: An International Journal of Police Strategies and Management,* Vol. 31, 2008, pp. 109–128.

64. This material on the intelligence cycle was taken from the FBI website at www.fbi.gov/about-us/intelligence/intelligence-cycle.

65. Kevin Riley, G. Teverton, J. Wilson, and L. Davis, *State and Local Intelligence in the War on Terrorism* (Washington, D.C.: RAND Corporation, 2005).

66. Joseph D'Amico, "Stopping Crime in Real Time," *The Police Chief* (September 2006), pp. 20–24.

67. This section on fusion centers was adapted from Charles R. Swanson, Leonard Territo, and Robert W. Taylor, *Police Administration: Structures, Processes and Behavior,* 8th edition (Upper Saddle River, NJ: Pearson, 2012), pp. 90–93; and Robert W. Taylor and Jennifer Elaine Davis, "Intelligence-Led Policing and Fusion Centers," in Roger G. Dunham and Geoffrey P Alpert, *Critical Issues in Policing,* 6th edition (Long Grove, IL: Waveland Press, 2010), pp. 224–245.

68. U.S. Department of Homeland Security, "Fusion Center Locations and Contact Information," www.dhs.gov/files/programs/gc_1301685827335.shtm

69. See https://nfcausa.org/

Intelligence, Terrorism and the U.S. Constitution

Learning Objectives

After completing this chapter, you should be able to:

1. Summarize the genesis of the PATRIOT Act and its subsequent amendments.

2. Discuss the conflicts between the PATRIOT Act and the First, Fourth, Fifth, and Sixth Amendments.

3. Articulate how the New York Police Department has instituted its own domestic intelligence program and discuss the implications of that on law enforcement agencies nationwide.

4. Explain the concept of *posse comitatus* and how our military might be called to supplement civilian policing functions.

5. Describe how drones are used both domestically and abroad for intelligence purposes and state the Constitutional issues that arise with each type of use.

6. Discuss the use of torture in intelligence functions in the United States and describe the constitutional issues involved.

7. Outline the events surrounding the Chelsea Manning case, the Wikileaks scandal, and the Edward Snowden intelligence leaks.

The Naval Station Guantanamo Bay, Cuba, is the United States' frontline facility for security in the Caribbean region. Enemy combatants suspected of terrorism are also housed there. Two guards escort a detainee to the recreation area. Methods used to obtain information from detainees has been described by the government as "enhanced interrogation techniques"; other sources describe the methods as torture.

(© Michael Billings/Zuma Press/Newscom)

Introduction

After September 11, 2001, the intelligence shortcomings that allowed al-Qaeda operatives to carry out the terrorist attacks were highlighted, debated, discussed, and promoted as an example of a post–Cold War mentality that cost nearly 3,000 American lives. Government agencies responsible for intelligence gathering were denounced for failing to think beyond threats from nations-states (such as Iran, Libya, or even China), for failing to link together key pieces of intelligence information about terrorist groups, and furthermore, for failing to share those pieces of information with other agencies. This created an environment obviously ripe for communications and intelligence reform, and in the decade that has followed the attacks of 9/11, a number of such reforms have been enacted.

Some civil libertarians have raised alarms that new and sweeping intelligence powers and swift changes to the culture of American law enforcement and intelligence agencies—particularly as detailed in the USA PATRIOT Act—were pushed through opportunistically, at a time when the public was reeling from the horror of the attacks and unlikely to fight anything that potentially could prevent future occurrences of terror on American soil. There was controversy associated with the passage of many of these reforms; however, Americans would wrestle with the balancing of civil rights and individual freedoms with national security and safety. Increased and more coordinated intelligence efforts on the part of the military, the police, and the national intelligence agencies raises a host of questions related to the balance between liberty and public safety; for example, can there be Fourth Amendment guarantees related to the expectation of privacy when the government has a host of tools at its disposal for large-scale data exploration? What governmental body does an individual hold accountable if there are breaches in personal security in the name of national security? Where is the bright line between intelligence agencies and police departments … and should this line ever be crossed? In this chapter, these questions will be explored, as will other issues related to the intersection of terrorism and the constitutional rights guaranteed to all American citizens. Most dear of these rights are held in the Fourth Amendment guarantee against unreasonable searches and seizures; however, the First Amendment right to free speech and freedom of religion, Fifth Amendment protections related to due process, and the Eighth Amendment guarantees against cruel and unusual punishment all relate to the new "war on terrorism." This may be particularly true when the methods used by the United States to gather intelligence about terrorism is scrutinized.

The USA PATRIOT Act

In an effort to improve the collection of intelligence information by federal agencies after 9/11 and provide sweeping new powers to both domestic law enforcement and traditional intelligence agencies, President George W. Bush signed into law the **USA PATRIOT Act** on October 26, 2001. The USA PATRIOT Act (**P**rovide **A**ppropriate **T**ools **R**equired to **I**ntercept and **O**bstruct **T**errorism) changed over 15 different statutes with little or no external review—in fact, many members of Congress themselves reported that they themselves had not read the entire act all the way through.[1] The law addressed not only terrorism and intelligence issues but also focused on more traditional money laundering, computer abuse and crime, immigration processes, and fraud. However, the most substantial part of the act is that it expanded traditional tools of surveillance used by law enforcement and intelligence agencies with significantly reduced checks and balances.

- *Records Searches:* Records kept on an individual's activity being held by third parties—including doctors, libraries, and Internet Service Providers (ISPs).

- *Wiretaps:* The surreptitious eavesdropping on a third-party conversation by wire, oral, or electronic communication. Usually conducted with a microphone receiver ("bug") on a telephone device; requires both a search warrant and a court order.

- *Search warrants:* A **search warrant** is a legal document signed by a judge directing police officers to search a specific area for a specific person or item of evidence/contraband. The document must be based on probable cause, but the PATRIOT Act

USA PATRIOT Act
Act of Congress that was signed into law by President George W. Bush on October 26, 2001. The title stands for Uniting and Strengthening America by Providing Appropriate Tools Required to Intercept and Obstruct Terrorism Act.

Search Warrant
Legal document that authorizes police to search a specific area for a specific person or item of interest. Must be based on probable cause and signed by a judge.

allowed search warrants to occur without the "knock and announce" requirement outlined in the Fourth Amendment.

- *Pen/trap and trace orders:* Telephone call set-up information only is intercepted without individual communications. A "**pen register**" provides the law enforcement agency access to the numbers dialed from a subject's phone, whereas a **trap and trace** provides the incoming numbers to the subject's phone (like caller ID).

- *Court orders and subpoenas:* A court document signed by a judge that instructs the police to perform a specific task. A subpoena is a court order that commands a person to appear in court at a specified date and time to testify.

Law enforcement and intelligence agencies can now easily and more surreptitiously monitor Web surfing and communication of individuals using the Internet, conduct nationwide roving wiretaps on cell and line telephones, and build profiles on the reading habits of people visiting public libraries. Under the act, police or government officials can force **Internet Service Providers (ISPs)** to "voluntarily" hand over information on customer profiles and Web-surfing habits *without* a warrant or court order.

Pen register
Provides law enforcement agency access to the numbers dialed from a subject's phone.

Trap and trace
Provides law enforcement agency access to incoming numbers on a subject's phone.

Internet Service Providers (ISPs)
An organization or private corporation that provides services for accessing, using, or participating on the Internet (e.g., AOL, NetZero, Comcast, Microsoft Network, EarthLink, Verizon, Google Prodigy, Sprint, and local telephone companies).

The Reauthorized PATRIOT Act—2006

In 2005, provisions of the USA PATRIOT Act were to sunset, and Congress acted to review, reauthorize, and pass this bill. The revisions were passed into law by President George W. Bush in March 2006. The roving wiretap provisions were maintained, though greater oversight was added to ensure that these powers would not be abused. The changes include judicial review and approval by the Director of the Federal Bureau of Investigation (FBI) or the National Security Administrations (NSA), along with a more detailed application process to specify targets and actions. The provision that allowed library records to be subpoenaed was also removed to protect citizens from unwarranted search, with the exception of monitoring electronic communications through a library. The original USA PATRIOT Act also allowed law enforcement agencies to conduct covert, or "sneak and peek," searches in the homes of potential suspects without their knowledge or authorization. Since this was considered by some to be too extreme, the reauthorization act changed this portion of the law to limit the time when such a search could be conducted so as not to give unreasonable power to law enforcement. However, the ability to conduct surveillance against what are defined as "lone wolf terrorists" or individuals that seemingly act alone and without direction was increased to provide greater time to monitor a specific target. (Refer to Chapter 5 for more information on lone wolf terrorists.) The definition of terrorism was also expanded with several provisions: (1) to include receiving military-type training from a foreign terrorist organization; (2) engaging in narco-terrorism; and (3) criminalizing the act of planning a terror attack specifically against a mass transit entity or system (e.g., bus stations, airliners, GPS, and other navigation or communication systems).

Information Link
For more information regarding the USA PATRIOT Act, visit the website hosted by the U.S. Department of Justice at www.justice.gov/archive/ll/highlights.htm.

The Reauthorized PATRIOT Act—2011

Provisions of the USA PATRIOT Act were once again set to sunset in 2011 and Congress acted to review, amend, and reauthorize it. First, roving wiretaps in relation to foreign intelligence collection were reauthorized and allowed electronic surveillance of a person, without specifying the phone or computer, if that person demonstrates an intent to evade surveillance by, for example, switching cell phones on a regular basis. In short, the government may obtain an order to conduct surveillance that specifies a target but not a specific device (e.g., cell phone, home phone, Internet connection, specific website) to tap. Second, the reauthorization extended access to business records and other tangible evidence. The USA PATRIOT Act allowed the government to seek court-ordered production of "any tangible thing," including business records, in intelligence investigations. The new provision to the USA PATRIOT Act both expanded the scope of materials that may be sought and lowered the standard for a court to issue an order compelling their production. Third, the "lone wolf" provision was extended, which permits surveillance against a non-U.S. person engaged in international terrorism for which the government does not have evidence of ties to a specific foreign terrorist group.

Quick Facts
The USA PATRIOT Act

On October 26, 2001, just 35 days after the 9/11 terrorist attacks, then-President George W. Bush signed into law the USA PATRIOT ACT (see Figure 10–1). The legislation was expansive, and changed over 15 different statutes with little or no eternal review. Several members of Congress admitted that they did not read the legislation before they voted affirmatively for it. Since its passage, 8 states and over 400 local cities and counties have passed resolutions against the act, characterizing it as a federal attack on fundamental rights and liberties guaranteed by the U.S. Constitution and its Amendments. Still, the USA PATRIOT Act was soundly re-authorized by Congress in 2006 and extended for another four years by President Barak Obama in 2011.

Constitutional Rights and the USA PATRIOT Act

The expanded scope and breadth of the act has raised concerns from a variety of sources.[2] Most agree that intelligence gathering and analysis had to improve (especially since 2001) in order to prevent future domestic and international terrorist attacks. However, some argue that the USA PATRIOT Act may have gone too far. One group that has done so is the **American Civil Liberties Union (ACLU)**, a national organization composed primarily of attorneys that defends and preserves the individual rights and liberties that are secured within the U.S. Constitution. The first ten Amendments to the U.S. Constitution are commonly called the **Bill of Rights** (see Figure 10–2). The ACLU works to extend these freedoms to segments of the population that have traditionally been denied their rights. Historically, this includes people of color, women, lesbians, gay men, bisexuals and transgender people, prisoners, and people with disabilities.[3] Subsequently, the ACLU is often pitted against agencies of the federal government over constitutional issues surrounding arrest, search and seizure, and the imprisonment of individuals. Relating to intelligence collection and gathering on potential terrorists as well as the investigation of individual terrorist groups, the First, Fourth, and Fifth Amendments to the U.S. Constitution are most often tested.

FIGURE 10–1
President George W. Bush signed the USA PATRIOT Act on October 26, 2001.
(Bush-Cheney 2004/AP Images)

Informational Link
To see all of the changes proposed by the Senate visit www.archives.gov/legislative/features/bor/.

The First Amendment

The First Amendment of the United States Constitution:

> Congress shall make no law respecting an establishment of religion, or prohibiting the free exercise thereof; or abridging the freedom of speech, or of the press; or the right of the people peaceably to assemble, and to petition the Government for a redress of grievances.

Civil libertarians argue that the USA PATRIOT Act has a "chilling effect on free speech," and, in fact, some of its provisions have stirred controversy in this area. The most high-profile of these First Amendment challenges can be observed in a 2010 Supreme Court decision, *Holder v. Humanitarian Law Project (HLP)*.[4] In this case, the government asserted that members of a charity group, The Humanitarian Law Project, were in violation of the "**material support**" clause of the USA PATRIOT Act, and formal charges were brought to bear. The clause prohibits supporting any designated terrorist group via "any property, tangible or intangible, or service, including currency or monetary instruments … expert advice or assistance … weapons, lethal substances, explosives, personnel … except medicine or religious materials."[5] In this case, the HLP—a group of human rights and peace activists—worked to "advise" the Workers' Party of Kurdistan (PKK)—a designated terrorist group by the United States—on how to file human rights violations with the United Nations. Further, the HLP was actively advising the PKK on the peace

American Civil Liberties Union (ACLU)
A national organization (primarily composed of attorneys and legal scholars) focused on defending and preserving the rights and liberties guaranteed to individuals within the United States Constitution.

Bill of Rights
The collective name for the first ten amendments of the U.S. Constitution, explicitly enumerating such freedoms of religion, speech, a free press, freedom to assemble, the right to bear arms, freedom from unreasonable searches and seizures, security and privacy of personal effects, freedom from warrantless searches not based on probable cause, guarantee of a speedy trial and judgment by an impartial jury, prohibition of cruel and unusual punishments including torture, prohibition of double jeopardy, and the guarantee to live without unnecessary governmental intrusion.

FIGURE 10–2
In 1789, at the First Continental Congress, James Madison introduced a series of amendments to the newly ratified U.S. Constitution. The House of Representatives sent 17 of them to the Senate, which consolidated the amendments into 12. The 12 proposed amendments were sent to the respective states for ratification, which ratified proposed amendments 3–12. These became the Bill of Rights. The image is the Senate's changes to the first page of the House of Representatives' amendments.

(Courtesy National Archives and Records Administration)

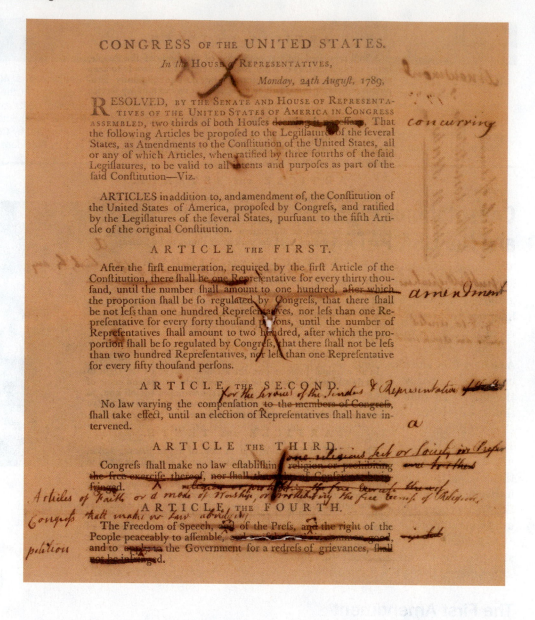

Material support
Defined by the PATRIOT Act as "training," "expert advice or assistance," "service," and "personnel" given to terrorist organizations.

negotiation process with the country of Turkey. The group challenged the "material support" on the grounds that peace negotiations were not a terrorist endeavor, and that the clause infringed on their ability to associate with a group for these purposes, thereby impinging on their First Amendment rights. The Supreme Court did not agree, stating that the HLP's services did indeed qualify as material aid under the "service," "expert advice or assistance," and "personnel" clause of the act. The government argued successfully that the PKK benefited from the assistance rendered by the HLP. The services and expert assistance could potentially benefit the terror group by legitimizing its interests, thereby potentially helping the terror group conserve resources.[6] The decision was quickly followed by a series of FBI raids on other peace activists' homes in Minneapolis and St. Paul, further bolstering the government's assertion that material support would be investigated and prosecuted.[7]

In yet another case, Tarek Mehanna, an American pharmacist, was convicted of providing material support, conspiring to kill American soldiers in a foreign country, and lying to authorities in a terrorism investigation in Boston in late 2011. Mehanna travelled to Yemen in 2004 and joined a terrorist training camp. His plan was to attack American soldiers in Iraq; however, his plan failed. When he returned to the United States, he began translating Arabic material into English and posting it online in promotion and support of al-Qaeda and radical Islamic fundamentalism. He inspired others to engage in violent jihad against the West and the United States by posting Jihadist Salafist material online. He was successfully prosecuted under the "material support" clause of the USA PATRIOT Act, and is currently serving a 17-year sentence in federal prison.[8] Unconvincingly, the ACLU argued that, "...*under the government's theory of the case, ordinary people—including writers and journalists, academic researchers, translators, and even ordinary web surfers—could be prosecuted for researching or translating controversial and unpopular ideas ... the First Amendment [is] seriously compromised.*"[9] Again, appellate courts disagreed, indicating that Mehanna went well beyond the scope of just translating documents, he did indeed "go down a treacherous path" that not only provided material support to al-Qaeda, but jeopardized the safety and security of American soldiers in Iraq.[10] While appeals continue in the Mehanna case, it is clear that the current Supreme Court views terrorist activities and groups significantly different than international criminal organizations or enterprises. Like so many other areas of criminal law, cases involving the USA PATRIOT Act are often reviewed on a case-by-case basis—trying to balance individual freedoms with national security.

Interestingly, the freedom of religion clause within the First Amendment has also been tested under the USA PATRIOT Act. The American Civil Liberties Union asserts that the government's use of religious profiling to target Muslims for investigation infringes on their constitutional right to practice religion. For example, in the months leading up to the November 2004 elections, the FBI engaged in large-scale surveillance or "fishing expeditions" on American Muslims in large cities. FBI agents visited mosques and questioned attendees in an attempt to identify suspected terrorist (al-Qaeda) sympathizers. Known as the "October Plan," the coordinated effort between the FBI and Immigrations and Customs Enforcement (ICE) outraged the Muslim-American community. Legal challenges against the huge intelligence gathering and investigative practices were defeated and subsequently allowed under the auspices of the amended USA PATRIOT Act.[11] Clearly, the Court sees non-specific intelligence gathering of a wide audience in an attempt to uncover an act of terrorism significantly different than a targeted investigation of a specific individual leading to an arrest.

The Fourth Amendment

The Fourth Amendment of the United States Constitution:

> The right of the people to be secure in their persons, houses, papers and effects, against unreasonable searches and seizures, shall not be violated, and no Warrants shall issue, but upon probable cause, supported by Oath or affirmation, and particularly describing the place to be searched and the persons or things to be seized.

On cursory examination, this passage of the U.S. Constitution is particularly relevant to the USA PATRIOT Act and its subsequent reauthorizations. There certainly appears to be contraction. For example, under the PATRIOT Act the government does not have to show probable cause, or even reasonable suspicion, to obtain third-party records, or conduct searches or wiretaps, as long as the government asserts a request for such records is related to an ongoing terrorism or foreign intelligence operation—or has a significant foreign intelligence purpose.[12] Essentially, the USA PATRIOT Act amends another important law—the **Foreign Intelligence Surveillance Act of 1978 (FISA)**, which is widely used in foreign espionage and spying cases.

FISA was initially developed and passed in Congress in 1978 to address a difficult history of abuse by federal agencies using **wiretaps** and other forms of electronic eavesdropping during the 1960s and 70s. Law enforcement agencies were not required to gain a warrant in a criminal case until the passage of the Wiretap Act in 1968. However, the legality of warrantless searches and seizures, and the use of wiretaps and other electronic eavesdropping methods during intelligence and/or national security operations, was not settled until 1972. The Supreme Court unanimously held, in their landmark case *United State v. U.S. District* (known as the "Keith case"), that the federal government did not have unlimited power to conduct wiretaps and electronic surveillance without the approval of a neutral magistrate just by claiming that the act was for national security—warrantless wiretapping of U.S. citizens was found unconstitutional.[13] Indeed, the court recognized that a history of abuse (unauthorized governmental spying on U.S. citizens "suspected" of unnamed national security

Foreign Intelligence Surveillance Act of 1978 (FISA)
Passed by Congress in 1978, the law was intended to increase counterintelligence capabilities and established procedures for the judicial authorization of foreign intelligence surveillance and established the Foreign Intelligence Surveillance Court.

Wiretaps
Surreptitious eavesdropping on a third-party conversation by wire, oral, or electronic communication.

Quick Facts
FISC—The Foreign Intelligence Surveillance Court

The Foreign Intelligence Surveillance Court meets in a high security area of the E. Barrett Prettyman United States Courthouse in Washington, D.C. All proceedings are secret, and there are two separate parts of the court: One is a full lower court panel and the other is a "Court of Review." The lower court has a rotating panel of 11 Federal District Court judges, three of whom must reside within 20 miles of the Washington, D.C. The Court of Review is comprised of three judges. All judges on the FISC are appointed by the Chief Justice of the United States.

Information Link
For more information on FISA and FSIC, visit the website hosted by the Federal Judicial Center at www.fjc.gov/history/home.nsf/page/courts_special_fisc.html.

Foreign Intelligence Surveillance Court (FISC)
Secret federal court created by the Foreign Intelligence Surveillance Act in 1978. The court authorizes wiretaps and other forms of electronic surveillance and authorizes searches involving suspected terrorists and spies by U.S. intelligence agencies.

violations) had occurred during the turbulent 1960s and 70s Civil Rights/Vietnam War era. The Foreign Intelligence Surveillance Act of 1978 created a procedure, similar to the procedure for any governmental or law enforcement agency pursuing a criminal case, to present evidence to a judge (or court) and procure a warrant. Essentially, FISA severely limited unauthorized spying and provided a procedure for judicial oversight in cases involving foreign intelligence surveillance and investigation.

FISA is significantly different than law enforcement processes enacted to gain a warrant. First, it authorized the FBI to conduct surveillance on identified foreign intelligence agents operating in the United States because these actions are inherently different than a criminal investigation conducted by a law enforcement agency. FISA was justified at its inception because it was asserted that its authority could *not* be used for the purpose of investigating a crime against an American citizen. Hence, a FISA warrant could be obtained only if the primary purpose of the investigation was directly related to the collection of foreign intelligence by either surveilling a place or a specific person. However, the USA PATRIOT Act, as reauthorized in 2011, eliminated that primary purpose clause within FISA, allowing warrants to proceed without probable cause if the government intrusion had a "significant purpose" for collecting foreign intelligence.[14] Second, because of the secretive nature of the Foreign Intelligence Surveillance Act (FISA), individual and specific cases are presented to a special court, known as the **Foreign Intelligence Surveillance Court (FISC)**. This court serves to hear evidence and justification presented by government agencies relating to the securing of a warrant to eavesdrop or wiretap. Indeed, the FISC initially served to approve wiretapping orders. However, under the new PATRIOT Act, the secret FISA court functions only as the main arbiter of surveillance issues.

The Fourth Amendment also guarantees an ancient common-law principle called "knock and announce" under its protections against unreasonable searches and seizures. This principle requires that law enforcement give notice of their authority and purpose to those occupants of a place or home about to be searched. The rule serves three important purposes: First, it reduces the risk of violence during a police entry by informing the person whose property is to be searched that it is indeed the police, as opposed to a criminal breaking and entering. Secondly, it allows the inhabitant to ensure that their privacy is indeed maintained, particularly when it involves activities not subject to the warrant. Finally, it protects a citizen's individual property interests.[15]

The PATRIOT Act expands the ability of the government to search places and homes *without* providing notice at the time of the search. In other words, a governmental intelligence agency (like the FBI) can enter a person's home, search through their belongings and gather evidence, and not inform the individual that a governmental agency was there for a "reasonable period thereafter." Before the passage of the PATRIOT Act, this activity could only occur under extreme circumstances, such as when a life was in danger or when evidence was likely to be destroyed. However, under the current PATRIOT Act it occurs any time such notice would "seriously jeopardize" an investigation. More importantly, notifications to the searched individual are routinely *not* made less than 30 to 90 days after the intrusion, and extension to this timeframe are possible (and often probable).[16]

This provision of the USA PATRIOT Act was tested in the case of Brandon Mayfield, a Portland, Oregon, attorney who had converted to Islam in the late 1980s after meeting his future wife, who was a practicing Muslim. Mayfield was linked, erroneously and through

FIGURE 10–3
Brandon Mayfield a press conference moments after being released in 2005. He was erroneously charged with being a terrorist because of a mistake in analyzing a fingerprint left at the scene of a bombing of a train in Madrid, Spain, in 2004. The case rocked the forensics world as the veracity of fingerprints as unique human identifiers was initially challenged. The FBI eventually apologized, blaming the mistake on faulty supercomputer software and compounded by human error during the initial fingerprint analysis.
(© Ross William Hamilton/The Oregonian/EPA/Newscom)

a litany of spectacular coincidences, to the 2004 train bombings in Madrid carried out by terrorists thought to be inspired by al-Qaeda. The FBI asserted that fingerprints on detonating devices found at the scene were identified as belonging to Brandon Mayfield. The FBI continued its investigation, offering completely false and ambiguous statements to a judge in order to procure a warrant for Mayfield's home. A warrant was issued, and Mayfield's home was searched and electronically surveilled ("bugged"), including a wiretap on his telephone. In reality, Brandon Mayfield had absolutely no involvement in the attacks and the FBI subsequently recanted that the fingerprints found on the scene were not Mayfield's (see Figure 10–3). Mayfield sued the FBI in 2005, asserting that the search and seizure under the USA PATRIOT Act were unlawful. The federal government settled the case with Mayfield for a reported $2 million; however, he continued to challenge the constitutionality of the USA PATRIOT Act. In an initial ruling, a U.S. District Court judge asserted that the provisions of the Fourth Amendment, particularly those related to the probable cause requirement and the lack of "knock and announce," were unconstitutional.[17] However, the ruling was overturned in a 9th Circuit Court of Appeals decision in 2009, and the USA PATRIOT Act remains as amended.

The Fifth and Sixth Amendments

The Fifth Amendment of the U.S. Constitution:

> "No person shall be held to answer for a capital, or otherwise infamous crime, unless on a presentment or indictment of a grand jury, except in cases arising in the land or naval forces, or in the militia, when in actual service in time of war or public danger; nor shall any person be subject for the same offense to be twice put in jeopardy of life or limb; nor shall be compelled in any criminal case to be a witness against himself, nor be deprived of life, liberty, or property, without due process of law; nor shall private property be taken for public use, without just compensation."

The Sixth Amendment of the U.S. Constitution:

> "In all criminal prosecutions, the accused shall enjoy the right to a speedy and public trial, by an impartial jury of the State and district wherein the crime shall have been committed, which district shall have been previously ascertained by law, and to be informed of the nature and cause of the accusation; to be confronted with the witnesses against him; to have compulsory process for obtaining witnesses in his favor, and to have the Assistance of Counsel for his defense."

Box 10-1
The Snowden Leak

In 2013, a classified intelligence leak from former defense contractor Edward Snowden revealed that the FISA court had authorized the collection of *all* phone-tracing **metadata** from *all* Verizon digital telephone communications under the PATRIOT Act. The FISC required the company to produce on an:

...ongoing, daily basis all call detail or telephony metadata created by Verizon for communications (i) between the United States and abroad; or (ii) wholly within the United States, including local telephone calls. Telephony metadata includes comprehensive communications routing information, including but not limited to session identifying information (e.g., originating and terminating telephone number, International Mobile Subscriber Identity (ISMI) number, International Mobile station Equipment Identity (IMEI) number, etc.), trunk identifier, telephone calling card numbers, and time and duration of call. Telephony metadata does not include the substantive content of any communication, as defined by 18 U.S.C. § 2510(8), or the name, address, or financial information of a subscriber or custom.[18]

The revelation from Snowden's leak made is clear that at least some intelligence agencies were overstepping their power under FISA and the new USA PATRIOT Act. What also became clear after significant internal investigation was that most of the actual content of the calls was not being gathered. In other words, the most important and salient parts of the conversations were never being analyzed. The primary intelligence agency involved in the case, the NSA, appeared to be not only overstepping its bounds, but also inept in actually collecting the very information that may be used to thwart a terrorist attack or identify a specific terrorist individual. The actions by NSA continue to be a subject of much debate. Phone records can reveal a number of important personal items about individuals on their own, including the people that they communicate and associate with on a regular basis.

The collection of phone numbers alone may also conflict with Fourth Amendment protections against unreasonable searches and seizures, as a search generally must be based on individualized suspicion of wrongdoing to be considered "reasonable." Obviously, such a broad search cannot be individualized or based on any suspicion, and a "special needs" exception to this rule is problematic. At least one jurist has expressed a strong opinion relating to this issue: "*To my knowledge, no court has ever recognized a special need sufficient to justify continuous, daily searches of virtually every American citizen without any particularized suspicion.* In November 2014, in the wake of the Snowden leaks and a new civil suit filed by *Twitter* requiring the NSA to publish a full transparency report on its surveillance activities, the Senate failed to block the agency from continuing to collect individual phone records and other metadata from social media and Internet companies. In response, *Apple* and *Google*, as well as other companies, began offering an encryption program to secure private data and text messages on cell phones. The encryption program renders a locked cell phone impervious to external intrusion without a key, held only by the owner of the phone. These actions continued to fuel the push back against governmental snooping."[19]

Do you think that the actions of the NSA are reasonable in weighing the impact of safety and security with personal liberties and privacy?

Alien
A foreign national living in the United States.

Metadata
Data that describes other data; for example, telephone metadata records the number called, what time the call was made, and how long it lasted.

Extraordinary rendition
The apprehension, detention and extrajudicial transfer of a person from one country to another, outside the confinements and jurisdiction of the United States.

One of the most controversial challenges to the Bill of Rights by the USA PATRIOT Act is the power to arrest and hold any **alien** (or foreign national) "certified" by the Attorney General as a "suspected terrorist" *without* any initial charge for up to seven days. The Attorney General must either place the alien in removal proceedings from the United States, or charge the alien with a criminal offense. At first glance, this power appears to be a blatant violation of the due process clause of the Fifth Amendment, and the speedy and fair trial concepts of the Sixth Amendment. The government only has to show "reasonable grounds" to believe that a foreign national has committed any of a wide range of violations related specifically to terrorism, or is engaged in any other activity that endangers the national security of the United States. The practice is not widely used, and is specifically aimed at highly suspected "foreign nationals" that pose an immediate threat to the national security of the United States. So far, the clause has not been tested at the Supreme Court level for foreign nationals residing inside the United States. However, similar activities relating to the detention of foreign nationals from foreign lands has been the subject of much controversy.

The practice known as **extraordinary rendition** was started after 9/11 by the Central Intelligence Agency. It involves the detention and interrogation of foreign suspects without bringing them to the United States. The program allows the CIA to essentially apprehend and interrogate individuals from one country and place them into a jail or prison in another country without ever charging them with a crime in the United States. The extrajudicial transfer of these terrorism suspects became infamous when it became widely known that they were often tortured in the host countries. Individuals under the extraordinary rendition program were not labeled as "enemy combatant," which will be discussed later in this chapter. Although the practice of extraordinary rendition has not been heard at the Supreme Court, several lower appellate courts have ruled that former prisoners of the program could not sue over their alleged torture in overseas prisons because such a suit may expose the classified information related to the government's fight against terrorism. Torture of prisoners is addressed later in this chapter. The courts have been reluctant to challenge the presidential privilege of executive secrets, a judicially created doctrine that shields the government from judicial review related to national security protections and measures.[20] The privilege has been successfully used by both Presidents Bush and Obama; however, recent leaks by Edward Snowden (see Box 10–1) have presented new challenges to the states-secret doctrine.[21]

Balancing Acts: Issues for Modern Intelligence

The events of the last decade have pounded into the American psyche one important message: We are not safe from domestic nor foreign threats. Remembering some of the consequences of such attacks as discussed in previous chapters, the primary goal of terrorism is to replace trust and social cohesiveness with distrust and insecurity. Terrorism plays to emotion rather than intellect. Clearly, America wrestles with this complex and difficult perspective. Random yet relatively consistent acts of violence and terrorism over a short 10-year period of time reinforce the concept that the United States (and its people) is vulnerable. As a reaction, the U.S. government has instituted a variety of new law enforcement, military, and intelligence operations that are designed to prevent acts of terrorism. Many of these measures have proven crucial to the government's ability to combat terrorism. However, the effort to provide these tools often conflicts with the need to protect constitutional rights to privacy and due process—in essence, to ensure and secure not only our physical homeland, but also our way of life. This is an important balance to keep in mind while addressing the following issues.

NYPD and Intelligence

Increasingly, after the events of 9/11, local law enforcement agencies have taken on greater roles in domestic anti-terrorism. As discussed in Chapter 9, fusion centers have become the norm in large cities, and joint task forces composed of local, state, and federal law enforcement officers regularly work to identify and arrest terror suspects. Nowhere, however, has local law enforcement been more active in preventing terrorism than in New York City. The city bore the brunt of the 9/11 attacks, and remains a place of huge symbolic importance in the American psyche. As such, the city has confronted its vulnerability to terror attacks by preparing an unprecedented response in the form of proactive and intelligence-led policing that yields a specific police counterterrorism unit within the New York City Police Department. It is a sophisticated unit that can respond by land, sea, or air in New York City, and was founded in 2002 by then-Mayor Michael Bloomberg and Police Commissioner Ray Kelly. It is considered by the city to be the first line of defense against terrorism, asserting that the failures of federal agencies like the FBI and the CIA to protect against the 9/11 attacks means that New York City will no longer rely on those federal agencies alone to identify and disrupt potential terror attacks in their city (see Figure 10–4).

The unit is a well-funded and highly organized endeavor; it is, however, not without its problems. For example, there is no external (federal or state) oversight of the bureau—it functions largely at the discretion of the Police Commissioner and the Mayor

FIGURE 10–4
A member of the NYPD's Counter-Terrorism unit rides the M Train from Herald Square to Times Square, alert for indicators of a terrorist incident. CT officers are considered the first line of defense against terrorist attacks.

(© Nicholas Jason/SIPA/Newscom)

of New York City. In addition, the unit deploys local NYPD police personnel overseas, to foreign countries, without the formal sanctions of diplomatic recognition through the U.S. Department of State. NYPD officers are commonly observed at the scene of terrorist strikes throughout the United States and around the world, collecting information and providing relevant intelligence back to NYPD commanders. As such, NYPD's counterterrorism unit has been accused of violating the Constitution and overstepping its bounds on more than one occasion.

For example, it was revealed in 2011 that the unit had been secretly monitoring the Muslim community extensively over a decade—conducting surveillance in mosques, and even sending out officers to act as "rakers" or "crawlers" within the Muslim community, essentially serving as part of a "human mapping program" within not only New York City, but also the entire United States.[23] Clearly, NYPD officers are out of their jurisdiction when operating outside the confines of New York City. The NYPD used its diverse force of officers to infiltrate ethnic neighborhoods in a number of other east coast cities, going undercover to monitor individuals at bookstores, markets, restaurants, and religious centers. There was no criminal predicate and the only variable for being the target of surveillance was being Muslim. The unit also developed a team of informants, known as "mosque crawlers," who reported to their NYPD handlers on routine religious activities—an undertaking that would blatantly violate constitutional and other legal protections against collecting intelligence on purely First Amendment activities had a federal agency been involved.[24]

In fact, a federal agency (Central Intelligence Agency) *was* involved in the original development of the unit. NYPD Intelligence Division & Counter-Terrorism Bureau officers were sent to CIA training academies, essentially equipping them with the skills needed for foreign intelligence operations. Unfortunately, these skills were then used in a domestic setting against U.S. citizens. Active CIA operatives were also sent on special assignment to assist the unit in undercover operations, further drawing criticism from civil liberties groups and the local Islamic population, which was the target of the unit's activities.[25]

The "New York Model" of post-9/11 policing with the development of the Intelligence Division & Counter-Terrorism Bureau has influenced police departments around the nation; several of their deployment models have been adapted by other law enforcement agencies. However, few police departments have the resources to develop their own intelligence and counterterrorism unit: NYPD has a massive budget—the 2014 proposed budget was $4.678 billion dollars[26]—and deep ties to the CIA, both of which are unique to the organization. It is also unique in that its citizens are tolerant of the sometimes questionable activities that the unit undertakes where civil liberties are concerned. For instance, a move to develop a similar unit in Los Angeles was scrapped due to protests from local immigrant communities. It is likely that NYPD's unit thrives because the citizenry still bears deep scars from 9/11, and as former CIA officer and NYPD advisor Larry Sanchez testified on Capitol Hill, "We've been given the public tolerance and luxury to be very aggressive on this topic."[27]

Interestingly, there is little data that indicates that NYPD's counterterrorism program is effective. Though New York City officials claim that the unit has thwarted at least 14 terror plots (from 2001 to 2012), only three can actually be confirmed. The rest were predicated on such heavy-handed enabling by informants that federal officials declined to bring charges or were never brought anywhere close to fruition. In addition, the three terror plots claimed by NYPD were not actually disrupted by the Intelligence Division & Counter-Terrorism Bureau; in one case, a bomb was discovered in Times Square by street vendors, and in the other two cases, the plots were disrupted by agencies other than the NYPD.[28] Balancing security and safety with individual freedoms and constitutional rights is a difficult task. There are those that argue that such aggressive tactics as described by the NYPD's Intelligence Division & Counter-Terrorism Bureau are actually counterproductive by eroding trust and driving those who might potentially be a good source of information on terror plots into silence. Muslim-Americans who may have otherwise been forthcoming about signs of jihadist radicalization in their community may fear that approaching law

Box 10-2
NYPD Intelligence Unit Infiltrated Activist Group

Although many in New York are supportive of the NYPD's efforts to prevent a terror attack like the one that happened on September 11, 2001, a report that surfaced in 2012 brought up questions about the Intelligence & Counter-Terrorism Bureau's focus—and its seeming overreach that skirts First and Fourth Amendment protections. Case in point: Undercover officers with the unit attended meetings of liberal political groups, keeping intelligence files on activists engaged in legal protests throughout the country.

NYPD asserts that they have good reason to go undercover in such organizations. Protests have turned into riots in other cities, such as Seattle in 1999, and police like to be prepared for elements within an organization that may cause a disturbance to the peace. In a lawsuit related to similar surveillance before the Republican National Convention in 2004, former Intelligence Division Director David Cohen stated "There was no political surveillance; this was a program designed to determine in advance the likelihood of unlawful activity or acts of violence." However, the activists were catalogued in intelligence reports not for violent acts or unlawful activity—but merely for being present at a meeting and associating with other group members.[29]

Do you think asking local police agencies to infiltrate political and religious groups blurs the line between policing and intelligence gathering? Should the police be involved in such activities?

enforcement would only further invite intrusive and unconstitutional policing tactics into their neighborhoods and mosques.[30]

The NYPD Intelligence Unit & Counter-Terrorism Bureau represents one local agency's unique methodology to gain advantage over those that employ terrorism against the United States. In Chapter 14, other agencies are presented that have recognized counterterrorism missions.

The Military and Policing Functions: Posse Comitatus

Local and state police departments are not the only entities that have found it difficult to balance their activities in the wake of 9/11. Similar to law enforcement, U.S. military forces have increasingly found themselves participating in *domestic* intelligence and security operations—a role that has been historically illegal.

The Posse Comitatus Act was passed by Congress in 1878, as a reaction to the events that took place during the post–Civil War, Reconstruction era. (Please note that the Posse Comitatus Act is *not* to be confused with early right-wing terrorist group "Posse Comitatus" discussed in Chapter 8.) In one of the most hotly contested elections in national history (1876) between Democrat Samuel Tilden and Republican Rutherford B. Hayes, southern Democrats claimed that military officers who had been assigned to monitor voting stations had prohibited newly freed black men from casting ballots, resulting in the loss of the election. After much debate, a Congressional commission awarded Hayes 20 electoral votes and he was inaugurated the following year in 1877 as the 19th President of the United States. The Great Compromise of 1877 provided the needed electoral votes for Hayes, but also ended all federal military (army) interventions in the Southern states. The Posse Comitatus Act became law, and set forth the provision that federal troops could not be used in a policing action within a State, no branch of the military could be used "*as a posse comitatus or otherwise to execute the laws of a State, except in cases and under circumstances expressly authorized by the Constitution or Act of Congress.*"[31]

Source: Expert from "War on Terrorism Will Compel Revisions to Posse Comitatus" by Juliette N. Kayyem, Steven E. Roberts. Published by National Defense Industrial Association, © 2002.

The term **posse comitatus** translates from Latin into "power of the county," and hails from common law. It refers to a practice dating from England in the 1400s where a posse composed of ordinary citizens could be assembled by a local sheriff in order to enforce certain laws or quell certain disturbances. Because the military was once composed of average citizens, as opposed to professional soldiers, the term has evolved in the United States to refer to the use of the federal military to enforce state or civilian laws. The USA PATRIOT Act expanded the ability of the military to *assist* with domestic intelligence and security after 9/11, and thereby challenged the validity of the Posse Comitatus Act in modern

Posse comitatus
Common law term meaning literally "power of the county"; refers to the military's role in enforcing state or civilian law.

history. Further the USA PATRIOT Act created the new U.S. Department of Homeland Security (see Chapters 12 and 13) and the new U.S. Northern Command (NORTHCOM). NORTHCOM is a military command responsible for the entire Northern American continent, plus the Caribbean basin. It also is responsible for protecting all U.S. borders and U.S. coastal waters up to 500 nautical miles from land. NORTHCOM's purpose is to support local and state authorities in the case of a domestic terror attack or natural catastrophe; it also is tasked with prevention, deterrence, and response to external threats to the security of the United States. Although this doesn't sound terribly intrusive on its face, the problem—as with many of the issues discussed so far—is that the word "support" often becomes broadly defined and blurs the line between military and local police separation. For example, the presence of government troops at large sporting events like the Super Bowl or the Olympics is justified because of their "support" to federal, state, or local law enforcement entities. The military involvement in anti-narcotics and border control functions has also been authorized, and the military was also greatly involved in supportive operations after Hurricane Katrina. However, formally staffing local fusion centers with military personnel who have access to intelligence systems used to help establish criminal cases against individuals citizens has been severely questioned and abandoned. Similarly, using military officers as "partners" with state and local officers to routinely patrol parts of a city or the southern border with Mexico have also been met with significant resistance, as these types of initiatives "push the envelope" in violating the Posse Comitatus Act.

> **Information Link**
> For more information on The Posse Comitatus Act, visit the website hosted by the U.S. Northern Command (NORTHCOM) at www.northcom.mil/Newsroom/FactSheets/ArticleView/tabid/3999/Article/1888/the-posse-comitatus-act.aspx.

So far, the use of the military in post-9/11 domestic operations has indeed been rather ad hoc, and limited to a supplemental and supportive status. Many legal scholars have advocated that the Posse Comitatus Act be revisited as a means to clarify the role of the military during a national crisis, such as during another major terrorist strike on the order of 9/11.[32] Certainly, defining the role of the military, and specifically NORTHCOM, before such an emergency would greatly enhance the government's ability to effectively respond to such a crisis.

The Use of Domestic Drones

Drones
Unmanned aircraft that can navigate autonomously.

The use of domestic drones as a means to collect intelligence information is a hot-button topic in the United States. This is especially true considering that the use of domestic drones by law enforcement is posed to dramatically increase. **Drones** are unmanned aerial vehicles that are widely used for the purposes of both commercial and governmental endeavors, including the monitoring and/or surveying of commercial property, the scientific and academic research of geography and space, the surveillance of private and public transportation systems, and a host of intelligence gathering operations from crowd monitoring to border enforcement to routine law enforcement and security monitoring. For example, a drone was recently used in a 2013 hostage situation in Midland County, Alabama.[33] Police and FBI agents deployed a drone with a camera to monitor the health and well-being of a 5-year-old autistic boy being held captive by a 65-year-old Vietnam War-era veteran. The drone also provided critical intelligence information regarding potential access into the underground bunker that was being secured by the suspect. Police officers used this information to breach the location and rescue the boy.[34]

The technology used in drones is evolving rapidly; one manufacturer has produced a device equipped with a 1.8 gigapixel resolution camera that is capable of the high-resolution monitoring and recording of entire cities. Pictures of individuals can then be analyzed by computer systems using high speed visual recognition software and databases of known terror suspects and wanted persons. Additionally, the listening capability of drones has also dramatically improved. It is now possible to listen and record normal conversations between individuals within a house, building, or office simply by having a drone hover nearby.

Similar to the discussion regarding the use of the military in supporting law enforcement, drones have only been allowed on an ad hoc, case-by-case basis in the United States. However, the proposed opening of U.S. airspace in 2015 to wider drone activity has created a general uneasiness among the American public and civil liberties advocates who fear the potential for wide-scale surveillance and invasions of privacy. Truly, the potential for "big brother" to spy form the sky has now become a reality.

Drones are becoming more and more popular among domestic law enforcement agencies. Police use drones to assist in locating bombs, finding lost children, monitoring weather, traffic, and wildlife patterns, and rescuing people during natural disasters. Most agencies also use the drones to assist in deploying personnel during emergencies as well as assist in monitoring existing problems or critical incidents. For the most part, drones are not practical for large-scale surveillance operations.[35] In 2013, Congress attempted to set limits on the use of drones during such type of non-specific endeavors by federal law enforcement agencies. Further, several states, including Virginia, Florida, and Idaho, enacted specific limits on the ways that drones might be used by police agencies.[36] A recent survey showed that one-third of Americans fear the potential of domestic drones to spy on their daily activities.[37] In response, the ACLU has recommended that drone usage be subject to the following safeguards:

- *USAGE LIMITS:* Drones should be deployed by law enforcement only with a warrant, in an emergency, or when there are specific and articulable grounds to believe that the drone will collect evidence relating to a specific criminal act.

- *DATA RETENTION:* Images should be retained only when there is reasonable suspicion that they contain evidence of a crime or are relevant to an ongoing investigation or trial.

- *POLICY:* Usage policy on domestic drones should be decided by the public's representatives, not by police departments, and the policies should be clear, written, and open to the public.

- *ABUSE PREVENTION & ACCOUNTABILITY:* Use of domestic drones should be subject to open audits and proper oversight to prevent misuse.

- *WEAPONS:* Domestic drones should not be equipped with lethal or non-lethal weapons.[38]

Source: Excerpt from Domestic Drones by American Civil Liberties Union. Copyright © by American Civil Liberties Union. Used by permission of American Civil Liberties Union.

Finally, there has also been much controversy about the use of drones to carry out "military-type strikes" against combatants on foreign soil. Drones have been a key weapon in the fight against al-Qaeda in Pakistan, Yemen, Iraq, Afghanistan, and Somalia. These drones differ greatly from the ones previously discussed relating to domestic law enforcement use. These are militarized or "weaponized" drones, capable of firing missiles at targets or crashing into their targets with bombs, and are discussed more thoroughly in Chapter 14 as a counterterrorism tactic. Not all use of technology is used for apprehension. In Figure 10–5, rescue units are being readied to deploy in the desert.

FIGURE 10–5
In 2014, with the assistance of the Arizona National Guard, the Border Patrol assembles and distributes rescue beacons across the remote desert area between Mexico and the United States. Illegal "crossers" often get in physical danger and some die in the rugged country through which they walk. The beacons are solar powered with metal panels that reflect sunlight in day and emit a blinking blue light that can be seen from 10 miles at night. Instructions about the operation of the beacon is written in several languages and is supplemented with a drawing for those who may not be able to read in order to lower the number of deaths of those making the dangerous journey from Mexico to the United States.
(Courtesy U.S. Customs and Border Protection)

Box 10–3
Domestic Drones and Crime Fighting

In 2015, the Federal Aviation Administration will open U.S. airspace for drone flights; in the years leading up to that date, though, several dozen law enforcement agencies throughout the country have already begun utilizing drones for law enforcement efforts.

One such agency is the Mesa County Sheriff's Department in rural Colorado, which flew more than 40 missions with their approved device in a three-year period. Armed with a GPS-enabled Draganflyer X6, weighing just 3.5 pounds, the agency utilized the device extensively for 3-D reconstruction of accident and crime scenes—the drone photographs the areas involved and downloads the pictures into an imaging program which then creates a virtual recreation of the site. Deputy Ben Miller, who wrote the protocols for the agency's drone use and training, says that the device can revolutionize accident reconstruction, eliminating the need to shut down highways and other roadways after incidents. He also estimates that the device costs about $25 an hour to operate; most drones of this size and capability run about $10,000 to $20,000.

Drone use is also employed for searches that aid first responders in finding missing persons: The Royal Canadian Mounted Police have utilized them extensively when equipped with infrared cameras. One successful mission located an injured person in snowy conditions when his car flipped over. They've also been used after catastrophic floods to survey conditions, and to assist fire departments in assessing structure blazes from above. Though much of the worry related to domestic drone use centers on surveillance and Fourth Amendment overreaches, law enforcement agencies see much of the value in the devices outside of such purposes. As of early 2014, many states were considering limiting drone use for law enforcement purposes to situations where warrants had been obtained; however, many of those had clauses for exceptions due to emergency situations or activities not related to crime-fighting. This may be a fair compromise for many agencies. Miller states that tactical missions are few and far between anyway, and that no surveillance missions had been flown during the years that the program was in place.[39]

Do you think that domestic police agencies should be able to routinely use drones, or should their use be restricted to specific conditions?

Intelligence and Torture

The 9/11 attacks produced a series of unforeseeable events. The desire to strike back at terrorists was predictable, but the authorization of a new set of "harsh" or "enhanced interrogation techniques" (EITs) was not. The new methods were at odds with American values, our Constitution and case law, and the Third Geneva Convention (1949) that, in part, requires prisoners of war to be humanely treated and protected, particularly against acts of violence, intimidation, and insults. Enhanced interrogation techniques were also contrary to a 1994 United Nations international agreement signed by the United States that prohibited, as a matter of human rights, torture, and other cruel, inhumane, or degrading treatment or punishment.[40] However, all of these authorities were brushed aside in the pursuit of terrorists. Illustratively, in 2002, our government concluded that captured terrorists were not entitled to the protection of being prisoners of war (POWs) because they were "enemy combatants."[41] Part of the underlying logic was that because there was no declared war, there could be no POWs.

The use of EITs is not simply a case of a few agents "going rogue." EITs were used globally. The American governmental apparatus was substantially involved in approving these new methods and their use was not just for a handful of isolated cases. A small bipartisan group of Congressional members were briefed on EITs by the CIA, with no dissent about the methods.[42] The U.S. Attorney General's Office approved them, as did the Secretary of Defense. Moreover, it is also clear that the White House supported these new measures or they could not have been implemented.

In retrospectively looking at the record, it is arguably true that on the issue of intelligence and torture that for a time America lost its way. Some people, groups, and institutions may readily endorse this conclusion while others may say that is naïve and doesn't give sufficient weight to the urgent necessity of gathering potentially life-saving intelligence. The latter view does give rise to larger questions, such as "Do the ends justify the means? "Even if an action is legal, must it also be moral?"[43] "How reliable is 'evidence' obtained by coercion?"[44] "Is there a natural and unavoidable clash between individual rights and protection of the homeland?"

It is essential to note that many of the activities now labeled as "torture" were EITs previously approved by our government as "counter resistance measures" and legally permissible under existing guidelines. A partial list of EITs approved in 2002 includes:

Information Link
Visit the National Security Archives at www2.gwu.edu/~nsarchiv/NSAEBB/NSAEBB127 to view documents relating to the use of enhanced interrogation techniques and U.S. policy.

Quick Facts
The Lingering Results of Enhanced Interrogation Techniques (EITs)

Beginning with the Lieber Code during the American Civil War, the U.S. Military championed the humane and responsible handling of combatants and civilians."[45] EITs, which seemed so necessary in 2002 are now regarded as a national mistake by human rights, the courts, think tanks, and studies. Many known and suspected terrorists were confined at the United States facility at Guantanamo Bay, Cuba and subjected to EITs. Other detainees were held abroad in facilities in foreign countries. In December 2014, the U.S. Senate Select Committee on Intelligence released a declassified study on the Central Intelligence Agency's Detection and Interrogation Program.[46] Although highly controversial upon its release, the report concluded that CIA personnel, aided by two outside contractors initiated a program of indefinite secret detention and the use of brutal interrogation techniques in violation of U.S. law, treaty obligations and American values.[47]

More than 500 "Guantanamo veterans," have been released. Most, if not all of them, were held without charges, access to legal counsel, or trial. They live in some 30 countries and have distinctly negative views of the United States. Many have lost their homes, businesses, and assets. Some are thought to be American spies and are shunned. Two-thirds have emotional problems and only six have regular jobs. As of October 2008, of the 770 Guantanamo detainees only 23 have been charged with war crimes.

1. *Category I Techniques:* During the initial interrogation the detainee should be provided a chair in a generally comfortable environment. If cooperative, give cookies or cigarettes. If uncooperative, authorized techniques include yelling at the detainee, use of deception, multiple interrogator techniques, and leading the detainee to believe the interrogator is from a country with a reputation for harsh treatment of detainees.

2. *Category II Techniques:* The use of stress positions, such as standing for four hours, the use of falsified documents or reports, isolation for up to 30 days, use of other than standard interrogation techniques, use of hoods over heads while being transported and interrogated, 20-hour interrogations, removal of all comfort items, including religious items, reducing rations to standard military Meals Ready-to-Eat (MREs), removal of clothing, forced grooming (shaving of facial hair) and using detainee phobias to induce stress, such as claustrophobia, and fear of dogs and snakes. See Figure 10–6.

> **Information Link**
> The full Taguba Report with Annexes (AR 15 - 16 Investigation of the 800th Military Police Brigade) can be found at www.dod.mil/pubs/foi/operation_and_plans/Detainee/taguba.

3. *Category III Techniques:* Within the military, prior approval by a General grade officer was required to use Category III Techniques. Such techniques include the use of scenarios to convince the detainee that death or severely painful consequences were imminent for the detainee or his family, exposure to cold weather or water with appropriate medical monitoring, use of waterboarding (although not actually referred to as such) to induce the misperception of suffocation, use of mild, non-injurious physical contact such as grabbing, poking in the chest with the finger, and light pushing.[48]

It is easy to conclude that criticisms of EITs emerged only after the emergency climate created by 9/11 faded. However, it is more likely that as the secrecy surrounding EITs was peeled away and repugnant actions reported, opposition to them emerged. In 2004, the United States Army released the "Taguba Report,"[49] an investigation of alleged abuses and accountability lapses at the Abu Ghraib Prison in Iraq. It found that "numerous incidents of sadistic, blatant, and wanton criminal abuses were inflicted on several detainees."[50] This conclusion was supported by witness statements and photographic evidence. Among the abuses were a male military policeman having sex with a female detainee and a detainee who was sodomized with a chemical light.

The Constitution Project formed an independent, bipartisan, blue ribbon group to examine the capture, detention, and treatment of suspected terrorists during the presidential administrations of Clinton, Bush, and Obama, called the Task Force on Detainee Treatment (TFODT).[51] In 2013, the Task Force released its report, which found that the U.S. government had engaged in the widespread use of sanctioned torture of detainees

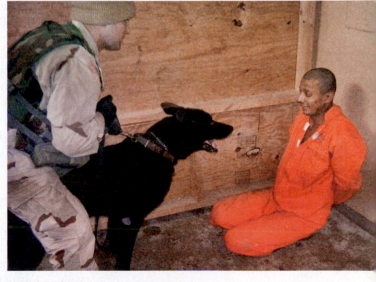

FIGURE 10–6

An enemy combatant detainee undergoes "enhanced interrogation" methods at an unknown location at the hands of CIA and U.S. military personnel.

(Courtesy Washington Post/Getty Images)

and suspected terrorists after 9/11, including some American citizens. The report describes interrogations of prisoners at Guantanamo Bay and other detention facilities controlled by the CIA, which included extreme sleep deprivation, waterboarding, chaining of prisoners to walls in painful positions, slamming prisoners into walls and floors, beating prisoners, extending long periods of nudity and humiliation, and a variety of psychological torture techniques.

In 2014, a report by the U.S. Senate Intelligence Commission concluded that the CIA had intentionally misled Congress and the public about the success of the brutal interrogation program.[52] The CIA had described the program to both the U.S. Department of Justice as well as to Congress as retrieving unique and otherwise unobtainable intelligence that helped disrupt terrorist plots and saved thousands of American lives both domestically and in combat throughout the Middle East (Yemen, Somalia, Iraq, and Afghanistan).[53] This representation may not be accurate. There are consistent findings that the information gained from torture is often unreliable, despite such claims, popular belief, and media representations to the contrary.[54] The report also documented a sprawling network of secret detention sites where some detainees were tortured. These secret detention sites were finally dismantled by President Obama in late 2009.

The use of torture is abhorrent to most Americans and most of the international community. Although mention has been made of the authorities violated by using torture, a closer examination of how it violates key constitutional provisions is warranted. The Fifth Amendment guarantees the right to a grand jury, protects against self-incrimination, guarantees due process, and precludes double jeopardy for the same offense. The Eighth Amendment prohibits cruel and unusual punishment, including torture, as well as excessive fines and bail. The USA PATRIOT Act of 2001 and the **Military Commissions Act of 2006 (MCA)** combine to provide exceptions to granting detainees Constitutional protections.

The MCA allowed the president to determine who is an "**enemy combatant.**" Being labeled as such dispenses with the U.S. government's obligation to provide the protections of the Fifth and Eighth Amendments. Therefore, an enemy combatant "detainee" can be held indefinitely without being charged. The MCA also allows enemy combatant to be subjected to extraordinary interrogation methods. The U.S. Department of Justice has ruled that the Fifth and Eighth Amendments do not apply to foreign enemy combatants held abroad[55] and that even U.S. citizens are subject to the designation of "enemy combatant" when captured abroad.

The case of Jose Padilla clearly illustrates the excesses that can be inflicted on a person labeled an "enemy combatant." Padilla was born in Brooklyn, New York, in 1970. He was arrested in Chicago in 2002, after returning from a trip to Egypt, Saudi Arabia, Afghanistan, Pakistan, and Iraq. Padilla was suspected of plotting to detonate a "dirty bomb" (radiological bomb) somewhere in the United States. Then-President George W. Bush ordered him held as an "enemy combatant" and authorized "enhanced interrogation techniques," including extended solitary confinement and sensory deprivation, administration of psychotropic substances, and sleep deprivation. Padilla was not charged with a crime for nearly five years. He was never charged for conspiring to detonate a bomb within the United States, but for a much less grievous charge of conspiring with and supporting terrorist overseas. He was found guilty in 2007 and sentenced to 17 years in prison.

In a subsequent civil suit that reached the Ninth Circuit Court of Appeals in 2012, Padilla claimed he was entitled to a settlement from the U.S. government in light of the torture that he experienced during his detainment. The court, however, disagreed, stating that at the time, the things that Padilla experienced (shackling, stress positions, extreme sleep deprivation) were not considered torture and so the government could not be held responsible.[56] Furthermore, in 2012, the Seventh Circuit Court of Appeals ruled in *Vance and Ertel vs. Rumsfield* that U.S. citizens labeled "enemy combatants" could not recover damages from military personnel and their commanding government officials for torture, leaving U.S. citizens without remedy against government officials who authorized or participated in their torture.[57]

The Padilla case is an example of a government gone awry post-9/11 and brings into clear relief the difficulty of finding an equitable and constitutional balancing of homeland security and individual rights.

Military Commissions Act of 2006 (MCA)
An act of Congress signed by President George W. Bush in 2006 to authorize trial by military commission for violations of the law of war and for other purposes. It prohibited detainees who had been classified as enemy combatants or were awaiting hearings on their status from using "Habeas corpus" to petition federal courts in challenges to their detention.

Enemy combatant
A special designation of an individual as engaged in hostilities against the United States or its coalition partners.

"Outing" Intelligence: Leaks and Insecurity

Beginning in 2010, a series of intelligence leaks by U.S. military personnel and contractors rocked American perceptions of intelligence and privacy, and laid bare shocking details related to nearly every facet of American intelligence gathering. Intelligence leaks have occurred throughout history—but in the past several years, it has become obvious that technology now enables those inclined to gather and leak classified materials to do so in large quantities and to gain widespread exposure and attention to their materials. The use of flash drives/thumb drives allows would-be spies to quickly and surreptitiously copy massive amounts of information; in the past, such gathering of mass data would have been cumbersome and extremely obvious to others. However, in the cases of Bradley Manning and Edward Snowden, nobody was even aware of their access and copying of mass information related to national security until it was headline news around the world.

The case of Bradley Manning was the first major exposure of United States intelligence secrets and wartime tactics since World War II. The Army private was deployed to Iraq in 2009, and by 2010 he had surreptitiously downloaded hundreds of thousands of classified military documents onto a CD while passing the media off as a Lady Gaga record. Those documents were passed on to **Wikileaks**, a non-profit international organization claiming to be dedicated to publishing classified documents in the name of transparency. The classified items that Manning stole and subsequently leaked include the following:

Wikileaks
A non-profit international organization dedicated to publishing classified documents in the name of transparency.

- *Video:* Manning procured video documentation of an air strike that showed Apache helicopter pilots firing on a group on people in Iraq that included civilians, two of whom were Reuter's photographers. Those coming to the aid of the photographers were also fired on. The video was edited by Wikileaks personnel, and showcased callous dialogue from the helicopter pilots as they killed innocent civilians on the ground.

- *"War Logs":* This included thousands of incident reports from the combat engagements in both Afghanistan and Iraq.

- *State Department Diplomatic Cables:* A large number of diplomatic communications that revealed—among other things—that the U.S. government was secretly cooperating with several oppressive Arab regimes in the Middle East. The cables revealed the collusion of military and intelligence activities with governments, in stark opposition to U.S. Department of State public and policy positions.

- *Guantanamo Documents:* These documents were less shocking in nature, primarily because the reports on the prisoners and their detention, abuse, and torture had already been made public by the U.S. government.[58]

The effects of Manning's leaks were wide-ranging from a number of different perspectives. First, U.S. officials blamed him for putting a number of diplomatic relationships on ice, particularly those involving the governments of Syria, Egypt, Saudi Arabia, and Yemen. Second, government officials who testified against him in 2013 blamed the leaks for harming military relationships with Afghan villagers and for straining operational relationships with the Pakistan and Afghan governments. Accordingly, these "strained operational relationships" endangered the lives of foreign citizens who worked with U.S. diplomats and for hampering efforts of the U.S. Department of State to work with human rights groups overseas.[59] The United States also claimed that the leaks put the lives of U.S. soldiers and citizens at risk as it inflamed terrorist rhetoric. However, there is little to no evidence to support this contention.[60] Regardless, Bradley Manning was charged with 22 offenses related to the leaked documents. He pled guilty to 10 of those 22 offenses and was found guilty in a military court of all but one of the remaining charges. He was sentenced to 35 years confinement in a maximum security federal prison in Leavenworth, Kansas. He was, however, acquitted of the charge of "aiding the enemy," which could have carried the death sentence. Finally, and adding to the controversy of the case, after his conviction Bradley Manning his desire to undergo transgender treatment and live as a woman (see Figure 10–7). He subsequently changed his name to "Chelsea" Manning and received sex change treatment, including hormone therapy and psychological counselling, while in prison. The procedures were approved by the U.S.

FIGURE 10–7
Bradley/Chelsea Manning's transgender status added to the controversial issues surrounding his leaking of classified documents to Wikileaks in 2010.

(Saul Loeb/AFP/Newscom)

(Courtesy Gail Orenstein/Zuma Press/Newscom)

Department of Defense Secretary, Chuck Hagel, and raised question as to whether Manning would be transferred to a female prison. The prison at Leavenworth, Kansas, is all-male. Some have argued that being transgender as a woman and living as man in an all-male prison could constitute "cruel and unusual punishment.[61] The reputation of Julian Assange, the founder of Wikileaks, was also questioned during this same time period after being indicted by the Swedish Prosecution Authority for multiple counts of sexual molestation and one count of rape. While denying the allegations and contending that the charges were brought in retaliation to the Manning case, Assange fled to the Ecuadorian Embassy in London, England, and subsequently was given political asylum by Ecuador.[62] With Metropolitan Police stationed outside the embassy in London, Assange remains confined to the Ecuadorian Embassy building.

Manning's legacy is mixed: Some see him as nothing more than a traitor to his nation, while others point to his gender identity issues as proof that U.S. servicemen and women who are gay or transsexual are not fit for military service. Others credit him with being a whistleblower who uncovered a series of injustices by the U.S. government in the Middle East. He may have even been a catalyst for the Arab Spring, in which indigenous populations rose up against the corruption detailed in some of the diplomatic materials leaked by Manning. The Manning case also served to legitimize Wikileaks as a news source, bringing it to the forefront of journalistic source material.[63]

The legacy of Edward Snowden will likely be similarly mixed. Beginning in June of 2013, a series of leaks to news organizations (including British newspaper *The Guardian* and *The Washington Post*) began to surface that detailed orders from the Foreign Intelligence Surveillance Court (FISC) discussed earlier in this chapter. The court order required Verizon to hand over telephone metadata to the National Security Agency (NSA). Under a secret program, entitled PRISM, the leaks revealed that a total of nine Internet service companies were being forced to give the NSA broad access to audio and video chats, photographs, emails, documents, and connection logs of "suspected foreign terror targets."[64] This information allowed the NSA to document, trace, and conduct further surveillance on these individuals. One day after the initial leaks, it was further revealed that the U.S. government had developed a specific program (Boundless Informant) that listed these individuals as well as other targets for offensive cyber-attack. **Boundless Informant** is/was a real-time global surveillance tracker that details and maps, by country, the metadata it receives from computer and phone networks. The leaked information about Boundless Informant revealed a surprising statistic: The NSA had collected 3 billion pieces of information in just one 30-day period (March 2013) from U.S. citizens alone, and 97 billion records from individuals worldwide![65] This was a surprising development, particularly since the NSA had long maintained—to Congress and the American public—that

Boundless Informant
A real-time global surveillance software tracker used by the NSA that details and maps the metadata it received from computers, phone systems and the Internet.

Quick Facts
PRISM

The NSA program revealed by Edward Snowden in June of 2013 known as PRISM allowed U.S. intelligence agencies to tap into the servers of nine internet companies, including Microsoft, Google, Yahoo!, Facebook, PalTalk, YouTube, Skype, AOL, and Apple. Materials collected include email content, chats, videos, photographs, stored data, VOIP (Voice Over Internet Protocol, or Internet phone calls), file transfers, videoconferencing, social networking details, and notifications of targeted activity (such as log-ins). The program had been operational since 2007.

Dates When PRISM Collection Began for Each Provider

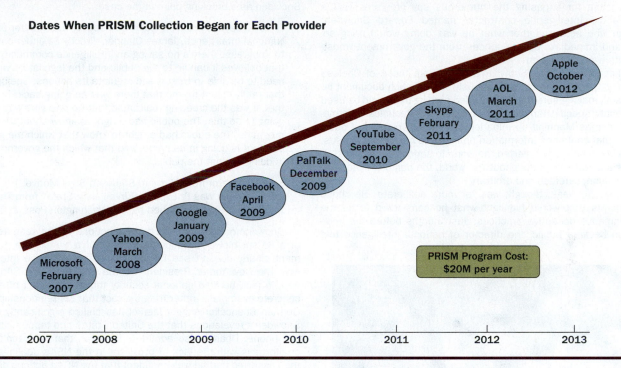

PRISM Program Cost: $20M per year

it was technologically not feasible to track, record, or analyze such abstract intelligence data and that such programs did not exist within the agency. To cap off the series of leaks (June 2013), the identity of the "leaker" was self-revealed as a 29-year-old former NSA and CIA information technology security contractor, Edward Snowden. Comments about his leaks indicated that he was well-aware of the consequence of his actions: "*I understand that I will be made to suffer for my actions ... but ... I will be satisfied if the federation of secret law, unequal pardon and irresistible executive powers that rule the world that I love are revealed even for an instant.*"[66] Snowden also asserted that his case was different than that of Chelsea Manning. According to him, he "carefully evaluated" every single document disclosed to ensure that each was legitimately in the public interest, and that there were many other documents that he could have leaked but chose not to do so. In his words, his intention was not to "harm people" but rather to provide "transparency" to the U.S. government.[67]

The leaks didn't stop with the revelation that Snowden was the source. Information that the United States had spied on hundreds of Chinese and Hong Kong citizens and foreign diplomats, including the Chancellor of Germany, Angela Merkel, were also made public. Further, documents that illustrated a complete lack of judicial oversight on the part of the FISA court became accessible, as were NSA documents that detailed the technology used in gathering and analyzing domestic information used to track a billion cell phone calls a day. Snowden also released a list of over 500 servers used by the NSA to "capture nearly everything a user does on the Internet and store it in databases searchable by name, email, IP address, region and language," and it was revealed that the NSA has cracked the common encryptions used to secure email, commerce, and financial transactions domestically and worldwide.[68] Furthermore, the NSA's ability to peer into smartphones was revealed, as was its ability to trace social connections of

Box 10-4
Reflections on Edward Snowden

For a time in June of 2013, every day brought a new and stunning revelation about the depth of U.S. intrusion into everyday communications. The world learned that the NSA could read its emails, intrude into its social networks, and learn intimate details based on phone records. It also learned that the man responsible for exposing the numerous spy programs was a 29-year-old intelligence contractor named Edward Snowden; a man who accepted that what he was doing would bring severe and immediate consequences from the government whose secrets were uncovered.

What differentiates Snowden's leaks from those of Chelsea Manning is that Snowden meticulously studied each document he released, making sure that he revealed nothing that could be used to identify specific targets, secret agents, or technical information, whereas Manning downloaded an unwieldy number of documents that contained information unknown to her, in many cases. While Manning's leaks alerted the world to serious abuses of U.S. power and authority throughout the world, the dump of data was, by definition, careless and arbitrary.

Snowden's leak, though, was far more deliberate. He chose documents that would highlight what he considered to be the government's deceptive practices: Just months before the information became public, the director of national intelligence told

Congress that the NSA did not engage in widespread data mining that affected American people.

Similarly, General Keith Alexander, then-director of the NSA, denied that the agency had the technology to capture emails and other online communications. This testimony was cited by Snowden as a breaking point in the case:

"I would say the breaking point was seeing the Director of National Intelligence, James Clapper, directly lie under oath to Congress. There's no saving an intelligence community that believes it can lie to the public and the legislators who need to be able to trust it and regulate its actions. Seeing that really meant for me that there was no going back. Beyond that, it was the creeping realization that no one else was going to do this. The public had a right to know about these programs. The public had a right to know that which the government is doing in its name, and that which the government is doing against the public."

Source: Excerpt from "Edward Snowden Says Motive Behind Leaks Was to Expose Surveillance State" from The Washington Post. Published by The Washington Post, © 2013.

Snowden obviously hopes that his actions will be seen as that of a whistle-blower as opposed to that of a traitor; the government clearly doesn't see it that way. In an extensive interview with The New Yorker, President Obama reiterated that Snowden had, in fact, harmed national security though he didn't offer any concrete examples—other than the fact that his relationship with German Chancellor Angela Merkel had chilled significantly since Snowden's revelations that the United States had tapped into her cell phone. Obama also admitted, however, that he wasn't fully comfortable with the lack of oversight in the NSA's dealings, but then asserted that he was confident that the NSA's actions did not threaten the privacy and constitutional rights of Americans. This viewpoint could be bad news for Snowden, who has expressed hopes that he will be granted clemency by the government.

For now, as he resides in Russia on political asylum, Snowden's status as a hero is not solidified: In some circles, the pale computer geek is indeed a champion of civil liberties. In others, however, he is a man who betrayed the trust that his position granted—and gave terrorists information that allowed them to burrow even further into communication rabbit holes—and even further out of our grasp.[69]

▲ During a demonstration in Washington, D.C., in 2014, a protestor holds up a placard supporting Edward Snowden. Many people believe he is a traitor, whereas others see him as a patriot.

(© Miguel Juarez Lugo/Newscom)

What do you think—is Edward Snowden a criminal or a patriot?

Americans through phone and email metadata, social networking site information, and email contact lists or electronic address books. Snowden revealed how drone strikes in the Middle East had been informed by NSA data collection via cyber-espionage, how the agency had intentionally propagated malicious surveillance software, how massive numbers of cell phone location records were archived in a NSA database, how U.S. intelligence agencies monitored online game playing such as World of Warcraft and Second Life, how the NSA cracked a common cellphone encryption methodology and captures every SMS text messages, how the NSA can access data from any smartphone app, and most importantly, that the NSA maintains and stores this data for years on end without probable cause, warrant, or court oversight.[70]

Immediately after the leaks, Edward Snowden was charged with three felony counts of espionage by the U.S. government. He initially fled to Hong Kong, and then, with the help of Wikileaks, to Russia, where he has been granted asylum. The United States has agreed not to seek the death penalty in his case; however, requests to pardon Snowden as a whistleblower have been strongly rejected by the U.S. government. Edward Snowden remains a wanted man. He remains something of a folk hero to U.S. civil rights advocates who assert that because of Snowden's actions, the American people are now aware of the "surveillance state" that undermines their guaranteed constitutional right to privacy and freedom from unwarranted governmental intrusion. To others, he is a traitor to his government and a person that has made the country more vulnerable to foreign as well as terrorist attack. According to the director of the NSA, General Keith Alexander, Snowden's leaks caused "irreversible and significant damage" to terrorist surveillance programs.[71] The government has also claimed that it caused unnecessary and difficult rifts between the United States and foreign allies (like Germany) who were spied on. It may take years to evaluate and assess the full effects of Snowden's actions: What is clear, however, is that his actions dramatically changed the perception of domestic intelligence in this country, laying bare a litany of constitutional breaches by the U.S. government, and drastically skewing the perceived balance between liberty and security.

Chapter Summary

SUMMARY BY LEARNING OBJECTIVE

1. **Summarize the genesis of the PATRIOT Act and its subsequent amendments.**

   THE USA PATRIOT Act was authorized after the 9/11 attacks and addressed not only terrorism and intelligence issues but also focused on more traditional money laundering, computer abuse and crime, immigration processes, and fraud. However, the most substantial part of the act is that it expanded traditional tools of surveillance used by law enforcement and intelligence agencies with significantly reduced checks and balances. It was reauthorized in 2006 and 2011 for the purposes of revision, clarification, and in some cases, expansion of powers set forth in the original document.

2. **Discuss the conflicts between the PATRIOT Act and the First, Fourth, Fifth, and Sixth Amendments.**

   Provisions of the PATRIOT Act seemingly clash with First Amendment protections related to freedom of association because of the broadness of the "material support" clause in the Act. It also challenges freedom of religion as a result of religious profiling authorized under its authority, and freedom of speech by allowing the prosecution of those who advocate jihadist material. The PATRIOT Act conflicts with Fourth Amendment rights against unreasonable searches and seizures by skirting the probable cause requirement, allowing broad searches instead of ones based on individualized suspicion, and allowing intrusion into homes without a "knock and announce" warning.

3. **Articulate how the New York Police Department has instituted its own domestic intelligence program and discuss the implications of that on law enforcement agencies nationwide.**

   NYPD has developed a domestic intelligence program that sprang from the citizens' desire to not rely on the federal government to prevent and disrupt future terror attacks after the events of 9/11. It's a large unit within the NYPD, with a host of deployments at its disposal and the ability to take to land, air, or sea. Many law enforcement agencies across the country have emulated pieces of the NYPD unit; however, funding, the deep-rooted CIA involvement, and a permissible public sentiment that make the unit's activities possible are not available in any other American city.

4. **Explain the concept of *posse comitatus* and how our military might be called to supplement civilian policing functions.**

   Posse comitatus is a common law concept that asserts that military forces may not take on domestic law enforcement functions. However, the PATRIOT Act expanded the ability of our military to supplement civilian functions during major national security events, terror attacks, and natural catastrophes.

5. **Describe how drones are used both domestically and abroad for intelligence purposes and state the constitutional issues that arise with each type of use.**

Domestically, drones are used for a variety of functions from commercial land surveys to law enforcement surveillance and border patrol. The use of these types of drones are increasing with the approach of open air space provisions to be set into place in 2015, and constitutional scholars are concerned about their impact on protections against unlawful searches and broad surveillance. Drones on foreign soil have been militarized and "weaponized," sometimes employed for the purposes of killing American terrorists. This is a direct conflict with protections found in the Fifth Amendment that guarantee of due process of law.

6. **Discuss the use of torture in intelligence functions in the United States and describe the constitutional issues involved.**

Torture and intelligence have an uncomfortable association; recent reports prove that it was used extensively and authorized by the very highest levels of U.S. government to interrogate those suspected of involvement with al-Qaeda and other radical terror groups. Torture is specifically prohibited in the Eighth Amendment; however, courts have repeatedly denied relief to both foreign and domestic detainees under these protections.

7. **Outline the events surrounding the Chelsea Manning case, Wikileaks scandal, and the Edward Snowden intelligence leaks.**

Private Chelsea Manning downloaded hundreds of thousands of documents she had access to in her classified Army position and made them available to the Wikileaks organization in 2010. As a result, videos of U.S. military strikes against civilians were made publicly available, as were incident reports from Iraq and Afghanistan, diplomatic cables that showed a disconnect between what the U.S. government reported publicly and how it conducted itself in communications with nations perceived to have oppressive regimes, and documents about the treatment of detainees in Guantanamo. The releases strained diplomatic relations and may, according to some, have further inflamed the hatred of America by extremist groups.

The Edward Snowden leaks exposed the previously unknown techniques and tools that the NSA uses to spy on domestic cell phone, Internet, social network, and smartphone use, as well as those used to spy on foreign diplomats. The massive leak, enabled by Snowden's access to NSA files via his job as a contractor with the agency, made obvious that the intrusion of the intelligence community into everyday domestic communications is far broader than the average American ever thought.

REVIEW QUESTIONS

1. Discuss the PATRIOT Act. What reasons might the U.S. government have had to pass it so quickly after the events of 9/11?
2. How does the U.S. government determine what the balance should be between civil liberties and the protections against terrorist acts that the PATRIOT Act offers?
3. Which traditional tools of surveillance did the PATRIOT Act expand upon and why?
4. Has the PATRIOT Act had a chilling effect on First Amendment rights among certain populations? Why?
5. Describe the ways in which the PATRIOT Act defies the due process clause.
6. Give examples of searches under the PATRIOT Act that might otherwise be considered unreasonable.
7. Would the NYPD counterterrorism model work in other cities? Why or why not?
8. What should be the military's role in a domestic terror incident?
9. Why are civil liberties advocates concerned about drone use, both domestically and on foreign soil?
10. Is the torture of terrorist detainees ever justified? Why or why not?
11. What are the long-term implications on U.S. intelligence gathering as a result of the Manning and Snowden leaks?
12. Are Chelsea Manning and Edward Snowden whistle-blowers or traitors? Why?

CRITICAL THINKING EXERCISES

1. **Is the U.S. Constitution Out of Date?** The first ten amendments to the United States Constitution are more commonly known as the "Bill of Rights" and were ratified by Congress in 1791. The Bill of Rights and the U.S. Constitution have survived for nearly 225 years of history. However, the founding fathers never imagined a technological world marked by amazing global communication through computers and the Internet at the current scale, nor a lifestyle that often hinges on personal telephone usage, texting, gaming, and access to online and social media sites. Should the Constitution be updated and rewritten to address such changes in our society? Why or why not?

2. **Torture and the U.S. Government.** Search the Internet on the subject of "torture by the U.S. government" and read the accounts of such activity by members of the CIA and the military over the last decade. Now, search the Internet under *Human Rights Watch* and *Amnesty International* to gain a different perspective. Do you think that torture should be used to illicit information from suspects? How reliable is information obtained from torture? Are you willing to allow torture of some suspects in order to potentially prevent another terrorist attack on the homeland on the scale of 9/11?

NOTES

1. M. Moore, *Farenheit 9/11* (documentary). Timestamp: 01:01:39-01:01:47.
2. Electronic Frontier Foundation, "EFF Analysis of the Provisions of the USA PATRIOT Act," October 31, 2001, www.eff.org/Privacy/Surveillance/Terrorism_militias/20011031_eff_usa_patriot_analysis.html
3. See: "About the ACLU" at the American Civil Liberties Union website at www.aclu.org/about-aclu-0
4. See *Holder v. Humanitarian Law Project*, 561 U.S. 1 (2010), 130 S.Ct. 2705.
5. 18 U.S. Code § 2339A - Providing material support to terrorists, www.law.cornell.edu/uscode/text/18/2339A
6. "The Supreme Court goes too far in the name of fighting terrorism," Editorial, *Washington Post* (Washington, D.C.), June 22, 2010, www.washingtonpost.com/wp-dyn/content/article/2010/06/21/AR2010062104267.html
7. Sheila Reagan. "FBI raids activist homes in Minneapolis, Chicago," *Twin Cities Daily Planet* (Minneapolis, MN), Sept. 24, 2010, www.tcdailyplanet.net/news/2010/09/24/fbi-raids-activist-homes-minneapolis-chicago
8. Travis Anderson, "Federal Appeals Court Upholds Tarek Mehanna Terror Convictions." *The Boston Globe*, November 13, 2013.
9. American Civil Liberties Union, "Mehanna Verdict Compromises First Amendment, Undermines National Security," December 20, 2011, www.aclu.org/free-speech/mehanna-verdict-compromises-first-amendment-undermines-national-security
10. Ibid., see also *United States v. Mehanna* 735 F. 3rd 32, 2011.
11. American Civil Liberties Union, "FBI's New Surveillance Plan Chills Religious and Political Activity, Bay Area Civil Rights Groups Warn," October 5, 2004, www.aclu.org/national-security/fbis-new-surveillance-plan-chills-religious-and-political-activity-bay-area-civil-
12. ACLU: Surveillance Under the USA Patriot Act, www.aclu.org/national-security/surveillance-under-usa-patriot-act
13. See *United States v. U.S. District Court*, 407 U.S. 297 (1972) – The "Keith Case."
14. David Cole and James X. Dempsey, *Terrorism and the Constitution: Sacrificing Civil Liberties In the Name of National Security*, Third Edition (New York: The New Press, 2013).
15. M. Josephson. "Fourth Amendment: Must Police Knock and Announce Themselves Before Kicking in the Door of a House?" *Journal of Criminal Law and Criminology* Vol. 86, Issue 4, 1996.

16. David Cole and James X. Dempsey, *Terrorism and the Constitution*.

17. S. Herman, *Taking Liberties: The War on Terror and the Erosion of American Democracy* (New York: Oxford University Press, 2011).

18. Judge Roger Vinson, "In re Application of the Federal Bureau of Investigation for an Order Requiring the Production of Tangible Things from Verizon Business Network Services, Inc. on Behalf of the MCI Communication Services, Inc. d/b/a Verizon Business Services," *Top Secret order of the Foreign Intelligence Surveillance Court,* http://epic.org/privacy/nsa/Section-215-Order-to-Verizon.pdf

19. Marjorie Cohn, "The Surveillance State: NSA Telephony Metadata Collection: Fourth Amendment Violation," January 16, 2014, http://jurist.org/forum/2014/01/marjorie-cohn-nsa-metadata.php

20. See Adam Liptak, "Obama Administration Weighs in on State Secrets, Raising Concern on the Left," *The New York Times*, August 4, 2009.

21. See Charlie Savage and David E. Sanger, "White House Tries to Prevent Judge from Ruling on Surveillance Efforts," *The New York Times*, December 21, 2013.

22. "NYPD Counterterrorism Units," www.nyc.gov/html/nypd/html/administration/counterterrorism_units.shtml

23. Matt Apuzzo and Adam Goldman, "With CIA Help, NYPD Moves Covertly in Muslim Areas," *Associated Press*, August 23, 2011, www.ap.org/Content/AP-in-the-News/2011/With-CIA-help-NYPD-moves-covertly-in-Muslim-areas

24. Diala Shamas and Nermeen Arastu, "Mapping Muslims: NYPD Spying and Its Impact on American Muslims," The Creating Law Enforcement Accountability & Responsibility (CLEAR) Project, City University of New York School of Law, 2012, www.law.cuny.edu/academics/clinics/immigration/clear/Mapping-Muslims.pdf

25. Ibid.

26. "Hearing on the Fiscal Year 2014 Executive Budget for the Police Department," May 23, 2013, http://council.nyc.gov/downloads/pdf/budget/2014/execbudget/2police.pdf

27. Apuzzo and Goldman, "With CIA Help, NYPD Moves Covertly in Muslim Areas."

28. Justin Elliot. "Fact-Check: How the NYPD Overstated Its Counterterrorism Record," *ProPublica*, July 10, 2010, www.propublica.org/article/fact-check-how-the-nypd-overstated-its-counterterrorism-record

29. Sources for this box item are Matt Apuzzo and Adam Goldman, "NYPD Infiltrated Liberal Political Groups, According to New Documents," *Associated Press*, www.huffingtonpost.com/2012/03/23/nypd-infiltrated-liberal-political-groups_n_1374823.html, and the website of the NYPD Intelligence & Counter-Terrorism Bureau at www.nyc.gov/html/nypd/html/administration/counterterrorism_units.shtml

30. Ben White, "NYPD Counterterror Investigations," *Harvard National Security Journal*, April 10, 2012, http://harvardnsj.org/2012/04/nypd-counterterror-investigations/.

31. J. Kayyem and S. Roberts, "War on Terrorism Will Compel Revisions to Posse Comitatus," *National Defense Magazine,* December 2002.

32. Ibid.

33. ABCNews, *20/20*, "The Bunker Tapes: Alabama Hostage Standoff," May 31, 2013, http://abcnews.go.com/2020/video/bunker-tapes-alabama-hostage-standoff-19302211.

34. Ibid.

35. Somini Sengupta, "Rise of Drones in US Spurs Efforts to Limit Uses," *New York Times*, February 15, 2013, www.nytimes.com/2013/02/16/technology/rise-of-drones-in-us-spurs-efforts-to-limit-uses.html?_r=0.

36. Ben Wolfgang, "Congress Seeks to Regulate Drone Use, Looks for Bipartisan Ground," *Washington Times*, May 17, 2013, www.washingtontimes.com/news/2013/may/17/congress-seeks-regulate-drone-use/

37. Joan Lowy, "AP-NCC Poll: A Third of the Public Fears Police Use of Drones for Surveillance Will Erode Their Privacy," *Associated Press*, September 27, 2013, http://ap-gfkpoll.com/uncategorized/our-latest-poll-findings-13

38. American Civil Liberties Union, "Domestic Drones," www.aclu.org/blog/tag/domestic-drones.

39. For more information regarding this subject, see the sources used for this box item: Chris Francescani. "Domestic Drones Are Already Reshaping U.S. Crime-fighting," *Reuters*,

March 3, 2013, www.reuters.com/article/2013/03/03/us-usa-drones-lawenforcement-idUS-BRE92208W20130303 and Nidhi Subbaraman, "Swarms of Drones Could Be Next Frontier in Emergency Response," *NBC News*, January 25, 2014, www.nbcnews.com/technology/swarms-drones-could-be-next-frontier-emergency-response-2D11988741

40. *International Convention Against Torture and Other Cruel, Inhumane and Degrading Treatment or Punishment* (1994). See United Nations, Treaty Series, Vol. 1465, p. 85.

41. Karen De Young, "Bush Approves New CIA Methods," *The Washington Post*, July 21, 2007, www.washingtonpost.com/wp-dyn/content/article/2007/07/20/AR2007072001264.html. This article covers both the 2002 guidelines and the 2007 ones approved by "the second Bush."

42. Jody Warrick and Dan Eggen, "Hill Briefed on Waterboarding in 2002," *Washington Post*, December 9, 2007, www.washingtonpost.com/wp-dyn/content/article/2007/12/08/AR2007120801664.html

43. Adolph Eichmann, one of the major architects of the Nazi Holocaust, defended himself at trial in Jerusalem by asserting he was "only following orders." In fact, Eichmann was acting on orders that were legal, but not moral. For more information on this issue, see Hannah Arendt, *Eichmann in Jerusalem: A Report on the Banality of Evil* (New York: Penguin Books, 1963).

44. John Clooman, Testimony Before the U.S. Senate of the Judiciary, Washington, D.C., "Coercive Interrogation Techniques: Do They Work, Are They Reliable, and What Did the FBI Know About Them?" June 10, 2008, www.loc.gov/rr/frd/Military_Law/pdf/Senate-Judiciary-Hearing-June-10-2008.pdf. Clooman, an FBI agent, took issue with the use of EITs.

45. The Honorable Patricia M. Wald, "Forward" in Laurel E. Fletcher, et. al, "Guantanamo and Its Aftermath," (Berkeley, CA: The Human Rights Center, International Human Rights Clinic in partnership with the Center for Human Rights, University of California, November 2008), pp. Vii–Viii, and p. 2, https://www.law.berkeley.edu/files/IHRLC/Guantanamo_and_Its_Aftermath.pdf.

46. Senate Select Committee on Intelligence, *Committee Study on the Central Intelligence Agency's Detention and Interrogation Program*, (Washington, D.C: USGPO, declassified December 3, 2014).

47. Ibid., *Executive Summary*, p. 2.

48. These EITs are taken from a Memorandum from the Commander of Joint Task Force 170, Subject: Request for Approval of Counter-Resistance Strategies, 11 October 2002, which were approved by the Secretary of Defense on December 2, 2002. These documents can be located as described in the "Informational Link" in this chapter.

49. This common name for the report is derived from Major General Taguba, who directed the military investigation. It is formerly identified as "Article 15-5 Investigation of the 800th Military Police Brigade."

50. "Article 15-5 Investigation of the 800th Military Police Brigade," United States Army, 2004, p. 17.

51. "The Constitutional Project's Task Force on Detainee Treatment, 2013, p. 1, http://detaineetaskforce.org

52. Greg Miller, Adam Goldman, and Ellen Nakashima, "Report Finds that the CIA Misled on Interrogation," The Washington Post, April 1, 2014.

53. Ibid.

54. John W. Schiemann, "Interrogational Torture: Or How Good Guys Get Bad Information with Ugly Methods," *Political Research Quarterly*, Volume 65, Issue 1, March 28, 2012, p. 3, DOI: 10.1177/1065912911430670

55. U.S. Department of Justice, Office of Legal Council, "Memorandum for William J. Haynes II, re: Military Interrogation of Alien Unlawful Combatants Held Outside the United States." March 14, 2003, www.justice.gov/olc/docs/memo-combatantsoutsideunitedstates.pdf

56. Andrew Rosenthal, "Tortured Logic," *New York Times Taking Note Blog*, May 3, 2012, http://takingnote.blogs.nytimes.com/2012/05/03/tortured-logic/

57. "Getting Away with Torture," *New York Times Editorial*, November 14, 2012, www.nytimes.com/2012/11/14/opinion/getting-away-with-torture.html

58. Julian Barnes, "What Bradely Manning Leaked," *Wall Street Journal Washington Wire Blog*, August 21, 2013, http://blogs.wsj.com/washwire/2013/08/21/what-bradley-manning-leaked/

59. Associated Press, "Bradley Manning Leak Has Had Chilling Effect on US Foreign Policy, Court Hears," *The Guardian* (London), August 5, 2013, www.theguardian.com/world/2013/aug/05/bradley-manning-leak-foreign-policy-sentencing

60. Abby Ohlheiser, "The U.S. Can't Connect a Single Death to Bradley Manning's Leaks," *The Wire*, July 31, 2013, www.thewire.com/national/2013/07/us-cant-connect-single-death-bradley-mannings-leaks/67851/

61. See Philip Caulfield, "Chelsea Manning to Get Sex Change Treatments at Military Lockup, not Civilian Prison," *New York Daily News,* July 18, 2014 and Pauline Jelinek and Lollita C. Baldor, "Pentagon OKs Manning Treatment for Transgender," *AP Big Story*, May 14, 2014.

62. See Andrew Hough, "Julian Assange: Wikileaks Founders Seeks Political Asylum from Ecuador," *The Daily Telegraph*, June 19, 2012 and Nick Davies, "10 Days in Sweden: The Full Allegations against Julian Assange," *The Guardian*, December 17, 2010.

63. Joshua Keating, "According to Wikileaks: The Journalistic Legacy of Bradley Manning," *Foreign Policy*, March 1, 2013, http://blog.foreignpolicy.com/posts/2013/03/01/according_to_wikileaks_the_journalistic_legacy_of_bradley_manning

64. Barton Gellman and Laura Poitras, "US Intelligence Mining Data From Nine US Internet Companies in Broad Secret Program," *Washington Post*, June 6, 2013, www.washington-post.com/investigations/us-intelligence-mining-data-from-nine-us-internet-companies-in-broad-secret-program/2013/06/06/3a0c0da8-cebf-11e2-8845-d970ccb04497_story.html

65. Glenn Greenwald and Ewen MacAskill, "Boundless Informant: The NSA's Secret Tool to Track Global Surveillance Data," *The Guardian* (London), June 8, 2013, www.theguardian.com/world/2013/jun/08/nsa-boundless-informant-global-datamining

66. Barton Gellman and Jerry Markon, "Edward Snowden Says Motive Behind Leaks Was to Expose Surveillance State," *Washington Post*, June 9, 2013,www.washingtonpost.com/politics/edward-snowden-says-motive-behind-leaks-was-to-expose-surveillance-state/2013/06/09/aa3f0804-d13b-11e2-a73e-826d299ff459_story.html

67. Ibid.

68. Ibid.

69. For more information about Edward Snowden, refer to John Cassidy, "Why Edward Snowden Is a Hero," *The New Yorker,* June 10, 2013, www.newyorker.com/online/blogs/johncassidy/2013/06/why-edward-snowden-is-a-hero.html; Conor Friedersdorf, "What James Clapper Doesn't Understand About Edward Snowden," *The Atlantic* February 24, 2014, www.theatlantic.com/politics/archive/2014/02/what-james-clapper-doesnt-understand-about-edward-snowden/284032/; David Remick, "Going the Distance: On and Off the Road with Barack Obama," *The New Yorker*, January 27, 2014, www.newyorker.com/reporting/2014/01/27/140127fa_fact_remnick?currentPage=all

70. Much of the information in this paragraph was adapted from a timeline of Edward Snowden's revelations. See http://america.aljazeera.com/articles/multimedia/timeline-edward-snowden-revelations.html

71. Tom Gjelten, "The Effects of the Snowden Leaks Aren't What He Intended," *National Public Radio*, September 20, 2013, www.npr.org/2013/09/20/224423159/the-effects-of-the-snowden-leaks-arent-what-he-intended

Homeland Security

Customs and Border Protection (CBP) is a component of the Department of Homeland Security (DHS). Border Patrol agents assigned to patrol remote areas of America's borders must be competent trackers. The CBP's elite tracking unit is referred to as the "Shadow Wolves." Membership in the unit is drawn from the Navajo, Lakota, and Blackfeet Native American tribes. The Shadow Wolves rely on traditional tracking techniques and are often used to track illegal migrants and smugglers moving through a wilderness area.

(© CBP/Alamy)

Learning Objectives

After completing this chapter, you should be able to:

1. Briefly describe the formation of the Department of Homeland Security (DHS).
2. Identify the five DHS security missions.
3. State the broad purpose of Customs and Border Protection.
4. Identify the "three wars" being fought on America's southern border.
5. Distinguish between a "major disaster" and an "emergency."
6. Identify the U.S. Coast Guard's five homeland security missions.
7. State the Transportation Security Administration's four specific responsibilities.
8. State the primary mission of the Secret Service.
9. Identify the priorities of Enforcement Removal Operations.
10. Explain the services provided by the Forensic Laboratory and the Law Enforcement Support Center.

Introduction

This chapter focuses on the U.S. Department of Homeland Security (DHS) and its responsibilities, as well as key agencies within it. The reason to study DHS is its mission: To lead the unified national effort to protect America by deterring terrorist attacks and protecting against and responding to threats and hazards to the nation. DHS protects our national borders while welcoming lawful immigrants, visitors, and trade.[1] Understanding the organization and function of DHS is a civic responsibility. Those who protect us must be scrutinized so that in their zeal to accomplish their mission they do not also infringe upon on our rights as citizens.

The United States neither detected the oncoming 9/11 attacks nor was it prepared to deal effectively with their aftermath. To illustrate, President Bush's national security leadership met 100 times in the months before the attacks, yet terrorism was only a topic of discussion in two of those meetings.[2] Arguably, if some of the parcels of data relating to 9/11 which were "stove piped" or isolated in various agencies, had been shared and analyzed, the loss of life and destruction of property may have been mitigated to some degree or avoided altogether. As a matter of conjecture a single key arrest may have caused the attacks to be delayed, providing further opportunity to derail them, or even aborted by the terrorists.

The 9/11 attacks inflicted terrible human losses and produced psychological wounds as well.[3] Nearly 3,000 people died, more deaths than were inflicted by the December 7, 1941, surprise attack on Pearl Harbor. Families lost loved ones in the attacks and rescuers died in desperate attempts to save trapped people. Families were left to cope with their bereavement and uncertain futures. Survivors who worked at or were visiting the Twin Towers, as well as firefighters, police officers, and utility workers, experienced high levels of continuing health problems, including alcoholism, acid reflux, sleep disturbance, and respiratory illnesses.[4] Similar results are reported for survivors and rescuers from the Pentagon on 9/11.[5]

United Flight 93 was among the four hijacked planes on 9/11. Determined not to let it be used as a flying bomb, heroic passengers called loved ones on their cell phones and told them of their plans to take back control of the plane. Flight 93 crashed in Shanksville, Pennsylvania, killing all aboard. It is speculated that the White House or the U.S. Capitol building (offices for members of Congress) was the terrorists' intended target for Flight 93. As did the people trapped in the Twin Towers, some passengers on the planes had brief conversations or left messages for loved ones as they lived out what little time they had left.[6]

As discussed earlier,, Americans were anxious about their safety and security after 9/11, fearing more attacks. Many people experienced **Post-Traumatic Stress Disorder** (PTSD) while others struggled with panic attacks and other disorders. Stock markets closed for four days, and when they reopened there were significant declines. There was a precipitous drop in flights from overseas and fewer people took domestic flights.[7] Some people didn't pick up luggage that had been lost and then found, fearing it may have been booby-trapped.[8] Security screening intensified at sporting events, governmental building, and airports. Between 2001 and 2003, Trans World Airlines, U.S. Airways, United Airlines, and Air Canada all declared bankruptcy. For the first time in its history, America was fighting a non-state enemy on two fronts, Iraq and Afghanistan, which later resulted in a massive National Guard and Reserve Unit call up to active duty,[9] which further impacted American lives. What rights to extend to captured terrorists or "enemy combatants" and where they would be housed provoked important national conversations.[10] Human rights advocates unsuccessfully opposed America's use of extraordinary **rendition**—transferring captured terrorists to countries where harsh interrogation methods could be used. This may have involved over 130 prisoners sent to some 54 countries.[11]

Eleven days after the 9/11 attacks, Pennsylvania Governor Tom Ridge was appointed as the first director of the Office of Homeland Security in the White House. His job was to develop, oversee, and coordinate a comprehensive national strategy to safeguard the country against terrorism and respond to any future attacks. Over a year later, on November 25, 2002, Public Law 107-296 created the new **U.S. Department of Homeland Security (DHS)** as a stand-alone agency, headed by a secretary who was to be a member of the President's Cabinet.

Post-Traumatic Stress Disorder
Classically, some people involved in a terrifying, life-threatening event develop the anxiety disorder PTSD. They may relive the event frequently, have angry outbursts, dramatic bad dreams and frightening thoughts, be easily startled, or constantly seem "on edge."

Rendition
The "handing over" or transfer of a person from one legal jurisdiction to another. Some apprehended terrorists have immediately been handed over to foreign countries to avoid providing them with the full range of American legal rights and to be able to use more harsh interrogation methods.

U.S. Department of Homeland Security (DHS)
The largest civilian federal agency in the United States with over 240,000 employees focused on securing the border and safety of the United States.

Quick Facts
President Bush Learns of the 9/11 Attacks

On September 11, 2001, as he was en route to Booker Elementary School in Sarasota, Florida, President Bush learned that a plane had hit one of the Twin Towers in New York City. Earlier he had been briefed of a non-specific threat of a terrorist attack, but the connection of terrorism to this first plane was not immediately made. Later, while President Bush was reading to Booker students, Andrew Card whispered in his ear that a second plane struck the Twin Towers. At that point a terrorist attack was abundantly clear (see Figure 11–1). The President continued reading for perhaps another eight or nine minutes and left after commending the students for their reading ability. Although there was some discussion about President Bush not returning to the Capitol, he did so later in the day.[12]

That evening President Bush addressed the nation and vowed, "The search is underway for those who are behind these evil acts. I've directed the full resources of our intelligence and law enforcement communities to find those responsible and to bring them to justice. We will make no distinction between the terrorists who committed these acts and those who harbor them."[13]

Overview of the U.S. Department of Homeland Security (DHS)

On March 1, 2003,* the U.S. Department of Homeland Department Of Homeland Security Security (DHS) became operational with parts or all of 22 different pre-existing federal agencies (see Table 11–1). It was the largest reorganization of the federal bureaucracy since the **National Security Act of 1947**.[14] Some of the agencies assigned to DHS remained intact, such as the U.S. Coast Guard (USCG). Others, such as the Immigration and Naturalization Service (INS), had various units parceled out to three separate DHS organizations: U.S. Citizenship and Immigration Services (USCIS), Immigration and Customs Enforcement (ICE), and Customs and Border Protection (CBP).[15] Figure 11–2 depicts the formation of DHS and the accompanying Quick Facts box shows the five missions of DHS.

The question has been raised that inasmuch as it was intelligence coordination failures that had some culpability for the 9/11 attacks, why wasn't there a major federal effort to reform America's intelligence apparatus,[16] as opposed to creating a sprawling new federal

National Security Act of 1947
The Act reorganized the military and foreign policy elements of the federal government, including the creation of the Central Intelligence Agency (CIA). Illustratively, it also combined the War and Navy departments into the Department of Defense.

FIGURE 11–1
White House Chief of Staff Andrew Card interrupts President Bush to inform him of the terrorist attack on the Trade Center's Twin Towers.

(© Win McNamee/Corbis)

---

*Public Law 107-296, enacted November 25, 2002, created DHS, mandating it to take effect in 60 days (by January 24, 2003). However, March 1, 2003, is conventionally given as DHS's "inception date" and it is used here.

TABLE 11–1
Movement of Agencies into the Department of Homeland Security (DHS)

Prior to 9/11, Before DHS Existed	Now Within DHS
The U.S. Customs Service (Treasury)	U.S. Customs and Border Protection – inspection, border, and ports of entry responsibilities
	U.S. Immigration and Customs Enforcement – customs law enforcement responsibilities
The Immigration and Naturalization Service (Justice)	U.S. Customs and Border Protection – inspection functions and the U.S. Border Patrol
	U.S. Immigration and Customs Enforcement – immigration law enforcement: detention and removal, intelligence, and investigations
	U.S. Citizenship and Immigration Services – adjudications and benefits programs
The Federal Protective Service	U.S. Immigration and Customs Enforcement (until 2009), currently resides within the National Protection and Programs Directorate
The Transportation Security Administration (Transportation)	Transportation Security Administration
Federal Law Enforcement Training Center (Treasury)	Federal Law Enforcement Training Center
Animal and Plant Health Inspection Service (part) (Agriculture)	U.S. Customs and Border Protection – agricultural imports and entry inspections
Office for Domestic Preparedness (Justice)	Responsibilities distributed within FEMA
The Federal Emergency Management Agency (FEMA)	Federal Emergency Management Agency
Strategic National Stockpile and the National Disaster Medical System (HHS)	Returned to Health and Human Services, July 2004
Nuclear Incident Response Team (Energy)	Responsibilities distributed within FEMA
Domestic Emergency Support Teams (Justice)	Responsibilities distributed within FEMA
National Domestic Preparedness Office (FBI)	Responsibilities distributed within FEMA
CBRN Countermeasures Programs (Energy)	Science & Technology Directorate
Environmental Measurements Laboratory (Energy)	Science & Technology Directorate
National BW Defense Analysis Center (Defense)	Science & Technology Directorate
Plum Island Animal Disease Center (Agriculture)	Science & Technology Directorate
Federal Computer Incident Response Center (GSA)	US-CERT, Office of Cyber Security and Communications in the National Protection and Programs Directorate
National Communications System (Defense)	Office of Cyber Security and Communications in the National Protection and Programs Directorate
National Infrastructure Protection Center (FBI)	Dispersed throughout the Department, including Office of Operations Coordination and Office of Infrastructure Protection
Energy Security and Assurance Program (Energy)	Integrated into the Office of Infrastructure Protection
U.S. Coast Guard	U.S. Coast Guard
U.S. Secret Service	U.S. Secret Service

Information Link
To further understand the five DHS missions, visit www.dhs.gov/publication/2014-quadrennial-homeland-security-review-qhsr. Under each of the five missions are the goals and their subordinate objectives that must be achieved to support each mission.

bureaucracy (DHS) with some 178,000 employees and an appropriated budget of $29.28 billion?[17] Clark concluded that the real agenda was not solving a problem. Instead, politicians wanted to have the appearance of having taken swift and decisively action in light of the 9/11 catastrophes.[18]

The creation of DHS created bureaucratic wrangling from individuals and agencies seeking to be prominently placed in it, as well as some Congressional political discontent, because of lost influence. For instance, one senator, furious about the changes, bluntly said, "Hell hath no fury like a committee chair whose jurisdiction has been taken away."[19] The numbers suggest, however, that Congressional committee chairs may have not lost any jurisdiction. More than 100 committees and subcommittees of the 112th Session of Congress (2011–2013) asserted some jurisdiction over DHS. There were 289 formal House and Senate hearings and another 28 before caucuses and commissions.

Quick Facts
The Five Missions of the U.S. Department of Homeland Security (DHS)

MISSION 1: STOPPING TERRORISM AND ENHANCING SECURITY

Preventing a terrorist attack in the United States remains the cornerstone of the Department of Homeland Security (DHS). Its vision is a secure and resilient Nation that effectively prevents terrorism in ways that preserve our freedom and prosperity. Achieving this vision requires us to focus on the core goal of preventing terrorist attacks, highlighting the challenges of preventing attacks using chemical, biological, radiological, and nuclear (CBRN) weapons and managing risks to critical infrastructure.

MISSION 2: SECURING AND MANAGING OUR BOARDERS

A safe and secure homeland requires that DHS maintain effective control of our air, land, and sea borders. Secure, well-managed borders must not only protect the United States against threats from abroad; they must also expedite the safe flow of lawful travel and commerce.

MISSION 3: ENFORCING AND ADMINISTERING OUR IMMIGRATION LAW

Virtually all Americans are affected by out immigration system. A fair and effective immigration system enriches American society, unifies families, and promotes our security. Conversely, persistent problems in immigration policy can consume valuable resources needed to advance other security objectives, undermine confidence in the rule of law, and make it harder to focus on the most dangerous threats facing our country.

MISSION 4: SAFEGUARDING AND SECURING CYBERSPACE

Our economic vitality and national security depend today on a vast array of interdependent and critical networks, systems, services, and resources. We know this interconnected world as *cyberspace*, and without it we cannot communicate, travel, power our homes, run our economy, or obtain government services. Its benefits are enormous.

MISSION 5: ENSURING RESILIENCE TO DISASTERS

Despite ongoing vigilance and efforts to protect this country and its citizens, major accidents and disasters, as well as deliberate attacks, will occur. The challenge is to build the capacity of American society to be resilient in the face of disruptions, disasters, and other crises. Our vision is a Nation that understands the hazards and risks we face; is prepared for disasters; can withstand the disruptions disasters may cause; can sustain social trust, economic, and other functions under adverse conditions; can manage itself effectively during a crisis; can recover quickly and effectively; and can adapt to conditions that have changed as a result of the event.[20]

Altogether these events required 400 DHS witnesses. Congress made 4,300 inquiries or other engagements of DHS, the response to which involved 66 work years of effort at a cost of $10 million.[21]

Grossman noted that Americans have proven supremely adept at war fighting, but not at creating long-term security bureaucracies.[22] The history of the DHS confirms the validity of this observation:

1. The enormity of the challenge to DHS for transforming its 22 constituent agencies and bureaus into a single agency was overwhelming. At the heart of this challenge was creating one dominant culture from 22 different cultures. In 2003, the **U.S. Government Accountability Office** (GAO) described this transformation as a "high risk" proposition.[23] In GAO's view, this transformation was expected to take 5 to 7 years.[24] The challenge was twofold: build an effective agency and get it "up and running" quickly. Seemingly, efforts expended on one of these challenges detracted from accomplishing the other.

U.S. Government Accountability Office

The U.S. "Government" Accountability Office (GAO) is an independent, nonpartisan agency that works for Congress. Often called the "Congressional watchdog," the GAO investigates matters of concern to the Congress.

FIGURE 11–2
The Evolution of Homeland Security

Source: Quadrennial Homeland Security Report (Washington, D.C.: Department of Homeland Security, February 2010), Figure 1, p. 14.

Traditional Responsibilities

Maritime Security
Foreign Agricultural Threats
Aviation Security
Land Border Security
Transportation Security
Leadership Protection

Financial System Security
Trade Facilitation
Migration Security
Emergency Management
Immigration Administration and Enforcement
Intelligence and Law Enforcement

New Threats and Evolving Hazards

Weapons of Mass Destruction
Global Terrorism
Cyber Attacks
Pandemics and Natural Disasters
Illegal Trafficking and Related Transnational Crime
Smaller Scale Terrorism

Core Homeland Security Mission Areas
Preventing Terrorism and Enhancing Security
Securing and Managing Our Borders
Enforcing and Administering Our Immigration Laws
Safeguarding and Securing Cyberspace
Ensuring Resilience to Disasters

FIGURE 11–3
In 2005, Hurricane Katrina caused levees, which had long protected New Orleans, to fail, producing catastrophic flooding. Some people waited too long to evacuate and retreated to their rooftops. There they waited to be rescued, attracting attention by making signs or waving to attract rescuers. As houses were cleared, their roofs were spray painted with USR (Urban Search and Rescue) to avoid wasted effort in repeatedly visiting that home to check for survivors.

(Courtesy Federal Emergency Management Agency, photograph by Mary Bahamonde)

DHS Inspector General (IG)
The DHS IG was created by Congress to ensure integrity and efficiency in the DHS. The office conducts or supervises studies and research to improve DHS administration and operations.

2. In 2002, 300 applications for aid relating to the 9/11 attacks were sent to the Federal Emergency Management Agency (FEMA), a new agency within DHS. They were sent back to the applicants stamped "Return to Sender." FEMA had forgotten to pay the rental fees for a Post Office box, adding to its reputation of failing to get things right.[25]

3. To make matters worse and add to the confusion, in 2005, a major hurricane devastated parts of the Gulf Coast and particularly New Orleans—Hurricane Katrina (see Figure 11–3). The Department of Homeland Security and FEMA specifically had substantial responsibilities with respect to responding to the needs created by Hurricane Katrina. FEMA responded so slowly and performed so poorly that both DHS and FEMA came under scathing criticisms. In 2006, the **DHS Inspector General (IG)** wrote a hefty 216-page report of FEMA's performance in the aftermath of Hurricane Katrina, confirming most of the criticisms including that it took three days before FEMA understood the magnitude of the disaster, it was ill-equipped to conduct massive search and rescue operations, and FEMA workers had to order twice as many supplies as they needed because they had no confidence in their delivery system.[26] Another report concluded that state and local first responders were not adequately trained to handle large-scale disasters because FEMA had awarded 75 percent of its grant money for terrorist training.[27]

4. Senator Dayton (D-MN) claimed that the performance of FEMA before and after Katrina was "so dysfunctional or non-productive it was frightening."[28] His observation underscored just how much of a high risk transforming DHS with new agencies like FEMA would be. Following the Katrina debacle, there was some Congressional sentiment to disband FEMA or remove it from DHS.[29] In the end FEMA remained in DHS.

5. As Hurricane Sandy plowed through the Atlantic Ocean toward the upper East coast (see Figure 11–4), President Obama, in anticipation of vast destruction, issued emergency declarations for a number of states on October 28, 2012. It was a chance for FEMA to redeem its image and demonstrate its nimbleness. Initially, FEMA received high marks for its efforts, but as time wore on complaints became more common and familiar. Unfair comparisons were made to Hurricane Katrina in New Orleans. The reality is that FEMA has significantly improved since then. In mass catastrophes enviably there will be some mistakes because of the sheer volume of work that has to be done perfectly every time in an emotionally charged atmosphere.[†]

6. Agencies were included in DHS whether or not it made sense—for example, the Secret Service, with a primary mission of protecting the president, became part of DHS whereas more security-related agencies, such as the FBI and Central Intelligence Agency (CIA), "stayed outside."[30]

7. DHS grants to state and local governments were distributed without any analysis of whether the jurisdiction was rationally "at risk." One example of this is a small Vermont town of 18,000 that got a truck capable of boring through concrete to find survivors. Some grant funds were diverted by recipients to non-terrorism programs, such as a popular mayor's summer intern program and a computerized

car-towing program to prevent fraud from private towing companies.[31] There is, however, no record of systematic fraud.

8. Many DHS agencies had never worked closely with their new "brothers and sisters" and numerous new routines had to be created, as well as clarifying the mission of each agency to eliminate competition and duplication of effort. They also had to agree upon how various terms would be defined so they could "speak the same language."

9. The 22 agencies DHS "inherited" had different operational and management systems that conflicted with or duplicated other capabilities. Across these agencies there were numerous areas that needed consolidation, which was time consuming. To illustrate, in the beginning there were 19 different financial centers, 22 human resource offices, and 27 different bankcard programs. In the absence of a single and mature procurement system some misconduct occurred. One program official bought $500,000 in art and silk plants from a tool company that had never previously sold such merchandise.

10. DHS funding was not sufficient to perform all functions. For example, it could not take the lead in consolidating terrorist watch list information.[32] The imperative of making rapid progress meant, in retrospect, some decisions were made too quickly or initially overlooked entirely. Too often, the focus was overwhelmingly on protecting the homeland from terrorist attacks to the neglect of other responsibilities, such as the previously mentioned lack of training for state and local first responders for natural disasters.

11. The ability of DHS's human capital to lead the transformation was suspect. Only 93 of 175 program managers were certified (53 percent) to perform those duties. Although political appointees proliferate in bureaucracies, DHS accumulated "political hacks" far beyond what had been seen in any federal agency.[33]

12. In 2005, there was still no DHS unit tasked with the responsibility of establishing policies and procedures for program management.[34]

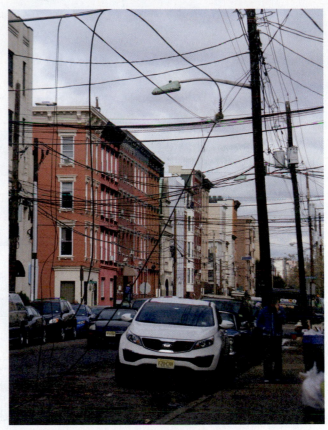

FIGURE 11–4
Hurricane Sandy's storm surge tossed cars about and its high winds ripped down power lines. Among FEMA's responses was setting up charging stations so people could charge their cell phones and other critical equipment.

(Courtesy Federal Emergency Management Agency, photograph by Liz Rol)

Today, the DHS is a maturing organization that has overcome the initial hurdles it faced, although like all other organizations DHS will always have challenges. To execute its five missions, DHS also relies upon hundreds of thousands of people across federal, state, local, tribal, and territorial governments and some nongovernmental organizations. The organizational chart in Figure 11–5 reveals the complexity of DHS. Although both the DHS's Office of Inspector General and the federal government's GAO continue to make recommendations for strengthening DHS, it is well-past its "high risk" stage.

Information Link
For more information relating to the history and agencies within the U.S. Department of Homeland Security, visit the homepage at www.dhs.gov/.

A budget is a plan; it is also an agreement between those who appropriate the funds and those who receive them. Appropriators have the reasonable expectation that if DHS requests funds to do certain things, such as hire and train 1,000 new Border Patrol Agents, it will in fact do so if the request is approved. In Fiscal Year 2014 (FY 2014, July 1, 2013–June 30, 2014) DHS's total budget authority was $59,959,337,000 with 240,000 employees deployed to every state and 75 foreign countries (see Figure 11–6 and Table 11–2).[35] A budget also reveals the priorities of an organization. In FY 2014 just five agencies—CBP, the Federal Emergency Management Agency/FEMA, the U.S. Coast Guard/USCG, the Transportation Security Administration/TSA, and Immigration and Customs Enforcement/ICE—accounted for 81 percent of the budget.

U.S Department of Homeland Security

FIGURE 11–5
Organizational Chart for the Department of Homeland Security

Source: DHS Organizational Chart, April 10, 2013, www.dhs.gov/organizational-chart.

Components of the U.S. Department of Homeland Security (DHS)

The major operational DHS components identified in Figure 11–7 are discussed in this section; however, support and administrative units are not. The units discussed include the (1) U.S. Customs and Border Protection, (2) Federal Emergency Management Agency, (3) U.S. Coast Guard, (4) Transportation Security Administration, (5) U.S. Secret Service, (6) Immigration and Customs Enforcement, and (7) U.S. Citizenship and Immigration Services.

TABLE 11–2
DHS Acronyms

Acronyms	DHS Budget Unit
A&O	Analysis and Operations
CBP	Customs and Border Protection
Depart. Ops	Departmental Operations
DNDO	Domestic Nuclear Detection Office
FEMA	Federal Emergency Management Agency
FLETC	Federal Law Enforcement Training Center
ICE	Immigration and Customs Enforcement
NPPD	National Protection and Programs Directorate
OHA	Office of Health Affairs
OIG	Office of Inspector General
S&T	Science and Technology Directorate
TSA	Transportation Security Administration
USCIS	U.S. Citizenship and Immigration Services
USCG	U.S. Coast Guard
USSS	U.S. Secret Service

FIGURE 11–6
DHS total budget authority by component in FY 2014.

Source: "Budget in Brief: Fiscal Year 2014" (Washington, D.C.: Department of Homeland Security, 2014), p. 5.

The largest industry and employer in the United States is agriculture with more than $1 trillion in annual economic activity.[36] Nearly one in six jobs is linked to it.[37] Invasive species that slip into America cause an annual loss of $136 billion.[38] Agriculture is also a potential target for **agro-terrorism** because of its vulnerability: It is the least protected potential target.[39] Agro-terrorism is not new; the ancient Assyrians poisoned enemy wells and during World War I, German agents in the United States infected horses and cattle bound for the war effort in France.[40] CBP employs 2,300 agricultural agents to counter both the general and terrorist threats to America's agricultural industry.[41]

Based on prior seizures, drug cartels know that all imported flowers and other plants are carefully inspected. Yet episodically they still try to use this method of smuggling drugs into the United States. Why do you think the cartels still try to use this method?

Customs and Border Protection (CBP)

Broadly, the purpose of CBP is to prevent harmful individuals and substances from entering the Unites States (see Figure 11–7). This includes terrorists, criminals, illegal immigrants and drugs, weapons, and other contraband, as well as harmful pests and diseases.

A major CBP responsibility is regulating international trade, collecting import duties, enforcing trade laws, and protecting U.S. businesses from counterfeit goods and the theft of intellectual property,[42] such as software. CBP also works to prevent and intercept the illegal export of U.S. currency and other monetary instruments, stolen goods, and strategically sensitive technologies,[43] such as advanced radar. CBP began as a legal entity on March 1, 2003, by transfers into it from:

1. The U.S. Border Patrol and the Inspections Program (IP), both of which had been in the Immigration and Naturalization Services (INS), a unit in the Department of Justice. IP inspectors determine whether people seeking to enter the United States through a point-of-entry are entitled to do so;

2. The Animal and Plant Health Inspection Service (APHIS) in the Department of Agriculture, plant protection quarantine inspectors (see Box 11–1 and Figure 11–8); and

3. Approximately 2,500 people "came over" to DHS from the U.S. Customs Service in the Department of Treasury. Their role in CBP was to collect entry duties, tariffs, and to prevent fraud. Investigators from the U.S. Customs Service became part of DHS's U.S. Immigration and Customs Enforcement (ICE) unit.

Customs and Border Protection: Legacy Agencies

Agencies that existed prior to the formation of DHS and "came over" to it, in part or whole, are called "legacy agencies." The two largest legacy agencies for CBP were U.S. Customs and the Border Patrol. Because of their sheer size a brief, pre-DHS history of them is warranted.

The U.S. Customs Service (USCS) was created in 1789 by the First Congress, making it the oldest federal agency.[44] The United States was in dire financial straits and on the brink of bankruptcy.[45] Six days after becoming operational, Customs collected its first duty,‡ $774 on a cargo of miscellaneous goods from Italy; in its first year it collected approximately $2 million, a substantial boost for the cash-strapped government.[46] The customs service assesses and collects duties and taxes on imported goods, controls carriers of imports and exports, and combats smuggling and revenue fraud.[47]

FIGURE 11–7
Motorists lined up at the border crossing in San Ysidro, California. It is the busiest land border crossing point in the world. Daily, 90,000 people pass through it.

(Courtesy U.S. General Services Administration)

Agro-terrorism
Malicious acts directed at the agricultural or food supply system in the United States.

Point of entry (POE)
A specific location where one may lawfully enter the United States; typically where passports and visa are inspected (e.g., international airports, seaports).

Speakeasies
Illegal bars operating during the prohibition era gained the name of speakeasies because patrons desiring to enter were allegedly told to knock and softly (speak easy) say the password.

---

‡ A duty is a tax on imported goods and some goods purchased abroad.

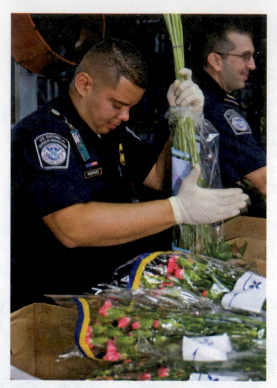

FIGURE 11–8

A CBP agricultural inspection officer checks cut flowers for pests and drugs. Ninety percent of Valentine Day gifts of flowers are imported, the vast majority from Columbia and Ecuador. England, Spain, and the United States are among the nations that have found drugs hidden in imported flowers. One technique is to cut a stem, insert drugs, and glue the stem back together.

(Courtesy U.S. Customs and Border Protection)

Texas Rangers

In 1823, when Texas was still part of Mexico, Stephen Austin gained permission to employ 10 men to range over the territory and scout for Indian threats. These men were the first of the Texas Rangers.

Blind pigs

In modern use, unlicensed bars that sell alcohol to patrons after legal bars have closed. Gambling may also be conducted in some blind pigs.

FIGURE 11–9

Border Patrol Agents check a sophisticated cross-border tunnel. In 2010, most of the tunnels discovered were in California and Arizona.

Source: "CBP's Strategy to Address Cross Border Tunnels" (Washington, D.C.: Office of the Inspector General, Department of Homeland Security, September 2012), p. 3.

(© Will Seberger/ZUMA Press/Corbis)

As early as 1904 "Mounted Guards," which were part of the U.S. Immigration Service, patrolled the border from Texas to California.[48] Never numbering more than 75 people, the patrolling was secondary to their immigration duties and therefore the border was only protected on an irregular basis.[49] The Army and the **Texas Rangers** also patrolled the border episodically during this period.[50] The Immigration Act of 1907 required all immigrants entering the United States to pass through an official **port of entry (POE)**, submit themselves for inspection, and receive official authorization to legally enter the United States.[51]

The 18th Amendment to the U.S. Constitution, which went into effect in 1920, prohibited the importation, transportation, manufacture, or sale of alcoholic beverages.

"Rum runners" brought "booze" in by sea while bootleggers smuggled it into the United States by land or transported it from illegal distilleries in America to "**speakeasies**" or "**blind pigs**," where it was illegally sold to drinkers. To no small degree, the 18th Amendment was an impetus to the creation of the U.S. Border Patrol in 1924[§] and expansion of its jurisdiction to the sea the following year. Ten years after its formation, the first Border Patrol Academy was held in Camp Chigas, El Paso, with an emphasis on horsemanship and marksmanship.[52] The role of the Border Patrol has been securing the border between POE inspection stations, particularly along America's southern border with Mexico.[53] Although Border Patrol Officers "patrolled the line"—the border with Mexico—they were also involved with liquor law violations, smuggling, and other violations of the law during prohibition. Away from the border during those early years, they used a "Mexican appearance" as a surrogate for an illegal border crosser,[54] a tactic referred to today as racial profiling.

Customs and Border Protection Activities

CBP has responsibility for approximately 5,000 miles of border with Canada, 1,900 miles with Mexico, and 95,000 miles of shoreline.[55] Watching for illegal land crossings is not sufficient: On average, CBP discovers seven tunnels a year, some of which stretch from Mexico 2,000 feet across the border into residences and warehouses. Some tunnels are sophisticated, with electricity, ventilation, and rail systems, and they may connect to other tunnels. The tunnels are a potential means by which terrorists with weapons of mass destruction (WMD) can reach the United States surreptitiously (see Figure 11–9).

[§]An excellent history of the Border Patrol is Kelly Lytle Hernandez, *Migra!* (Berkeley, California: University of California Press, 2010). The National Border Patrol Museum is located in El Paso, Texas.

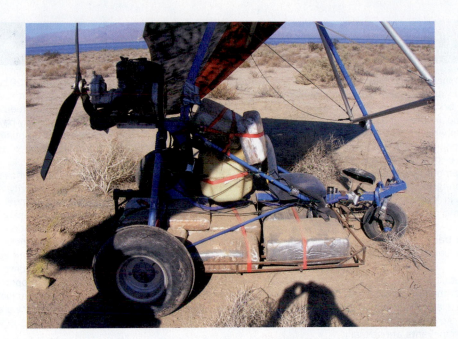

FIGURE 11–10
An ultralight seized by U.S. Border Patrol Agents. The aircraft was loaded with 189 pounds of marijuana and 12 pounds of methamphetamine, together worth $557,650.

(Courtesy U.S. Customs and Border Protection)

Ultralights
Powered ultralights are regulated by the FAA and are single-seat aircraft flown for recreation or sport.

Hang glider
A light-weight, single occupant, unpowered flight apparatus whose "pilot" controls its movement by shifting his/her body, which is suspended under a large delta-shaped wing. The Federal Aviation Administration (FAA) regulates hang gliders.

In the air, drugs are being smuggled by **ultralights** (see Figure 11–10) and **hang gliders**. The ultralights may land or make a drop from the air to waiting confederates.

Customs and Border Protection (CBP) officers, who number 25,252,[56] are law enforcement personnel that work at POEs (e.g., international airports, seaports, and land crossings), performing physical checks of travelers, luggage, cargo, containers, ships, and commercial and passenger vehicles. Annually, CBP officers process 350 million travelers a year at POEs and 30.4 million trade entries.[57] In contrast, 21,370 U.S. Border Patrol agents,[58] who also have law enforcement status, retain their customary role of protecting the areas between POEs (see Figure 11–11). It has been estimated that presently there are 10 to 12 million undocumented migrants living in the United States.[59] Other resources of the CBP are 766 Air Interdiction Agents/Pilots, 343 Marine Interdiction Officers, and 2,382 agricultural specialists.[60] Daily, CBP deploys 1,500 canine teams, 250 horse patrols, and flies 169 hours of law enforcement missions.[61]

On any given day, CBP will apprehend 1,153 persons between POEs, process 269,753 incoming privately owned vehicles, refuse entry to 366 inadmissible persons at POEs, arrest 22 wanted persons, seize 11,945 pounds of drugs and $291,039 in undeclared or illicit currency, and $4.7 million dollars worth of products that violate Intellectual Property Rights.[62] CBP also daily identifies 137 persons that are of concern to our national security.

Customs and Border Protection also makes effective use of technologies. It deploys unmanned aircraft systems/drones, radiation screening, unattended ground guard sensors (UGS) with infrared and other sensors, and at 290 border sites, remote video surveillance system cameras with color/daytime and thermal/night imaging capabilities.[63] Despite its various missions, protecting the United States from terrorism is CBP'S core responsibility.

Federal Emergency Management Agency (FEMA)

The first piece of federal disaster legislation was in 1803, when Congress voted relief funds for a town in New Hampshire ravaged by a fire.[64] Over the next century such federal **ad hoc** legislation was passed more than 100 times.[65] During the 1930s some federal agencies were empowered to make loans to repair public buildings damaged by

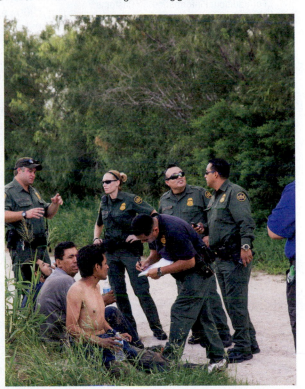

FIGURE 11–11
Border Patrol agents question undocumented immigrants from Central America after the van transporting them crashed on a Texas Highway.

(© Jim West/Alamy)

Box 11-2
Cartels, Coyotes, Rape Trees, and Homeland Security

In the Pima County, Arizona, Medical Examiner's Office there are 774 sets of unidentified remains of illegal immigrants who died trying to cross the United States-Mexico border.[66] Since 2001, more than 2,100 migrants have ended up in the Pima County Medical Examiner's Office.[67] Migrant apprehensions are down in recent years, suggesting the CPD's strategies are working, but more immigrants are dying. As security has become more stringent, border-crossers are trying more remote and dangerous routes.[68] Coyotes are paid guides who bring illegal immigrants into the United States from staging areas in Mexico. Immigrants who are unable to keep up with their coyote are left behind and many die in the desert. Some Americans trespass on ranch land and place water and food on coyote trails to prevent such deaths.[69] Many ranchers complain about crimes committed by coyotes and immigrants.

The Mexican cartels, known for their brutality, control most coyotes. Although some guides are strict about their behavior, others victimize immigrants. Girls as young as 12 are raped and their underclothes thrown onto "rape trees."[70] According to Amnesty International 60 percent of these female immigrants are sexually assaulted.[71] Immigrants may also be robbed of any money they have, and some are taken to "stash houses" where they are held prisoner until a relative comes and pays an additional fee. Once "established," border crossers hope to send for family members.

Fees vary from a thousand to several thousand dollars. A 2012 immigrant reported that he paid $500 at the beginning of the trip and another $1,600 after crossing.[72] Immigrants save the fee or borrow money from friends and family with the hope of quickly paying it back from a good earning job. The cartels charge substantially more to help people from Pakistan, Iran, and China, as much as $50,000–$100,000.[73]

Payan maintains three wars are being waged along America's southern border: drugs, immigration, and homeland security.[74] Even a handful of enemies gaining illegal entry can potentially commit acts that produce mass casualties. Iran is an implacable enemy of the United States and there is substantial international concern about it developing a nuclear weapons capability, including small "backpack" devices. Radical Islamic groups want to have such a capability and while waiting for them to be developed and acquired could use coyotes to move a handful of operatives into the United States to form sleeper cells or to conduct reconnaissance tasks. Border Security and homeland security are closely linked.

Because some illegal immigrants commit crimes on remote U.S. border ranches, should ranchers and their "hands" be authorized to arrest and hold them for the Border Patrol when the illegals are on their ranch property? What are the dangers and advantages of such authorizations?

Information Link
For additional information on Customs and Border Protection, visit the website at www.cbp.gov/.

Ad hoc
A Latin phrase meaning "for this." Ad hoc generally means a process, decision, or solution that applies only to "this" particular situation and does not have a wider/general application.

Category 4 hurricane
Hurricanes are characterized as being one of five categories. Category 1 is the least severe and has winds from 74–95 MPH and other descriptors also apply, such as damage to unanchored mobile homes. The most severe hurricane is Category 5, with winds of 156 MPH or greater and descriptors such as complete roof failures of many buildings and massive evacuations may be required.

earthquakes, later expanded to include other types of disasters, and to repair roads and bridges damaged by natural disasters. Similar legislation was passed during the 1960s and 1970s.[75] For several years Governors claimed they had to go "hat in hand" to too many federal agencies when disasters struck. In 1979, by Executive Order 12127, President Jimmy Carter created the Federal Emergency Management Agency, which centralized a number of pre-existing programs. To some degree, FEMA faced changes similar to DHS in terms of trying to build an effective organization quickly. FEMA has been periodically criticized for being too large, too bureaucratic, too ponderous, and too slow to react to large-scale disasters.

With winds gusting to 137 miles per hour Hugo plowed into South Carolina in 1989 as a **Category 4 hurricane**. It was on a course that had already done $9 billion of dollars in damages in Puerto Rico. Hugo was the strongest hurricane to strike the United States in 30 years. It made landfall just north of Charleston, South Carolina. Despite advance knowledge of the ferocity of the storm FEMA didn't open its first temporary disaster center in South Carolina until seven days later.[76] United States Senator Fritz Hollings (D –SC) related a conversation with a FEMA administrator who said before they could deliver any supplies they had to advertise in state newspapers for two weeks.[77] Senator Hollings concluded FEMA officials were "a bunch of bureaucratic jackasses"**

FEMA's Role in DHS

FEMA was adsorbed by DHS on March 1, 2003. FEMA has a headquarters in Washington, D.C., ten regional officers, three area offices, and as many temporary disaster-related sites as are needed to accomplish its mission, as well as 12,170 employees.[78] FEMA's mission can be summarized as supporting our citizens and emergency first responders to ensure that the country can work together to build, sustain, and improve the capability to prepare for, protect against, respond to, recover from, and mitigate all hazards, including terrorist attacks.

**There are two versions to Senator Hollings' characterization of FEMA officials, the one above and "the *sorriest* bunch of bureaucratic jackasses."

One of the most familiar artifacts of early homeland security efforts was the color-coded Homeland Security Advisory System (HSAS). Its replacement, the National Terrorism Advisory System (NTAS), is issued as a bulletin and distributed widely through the news media, DHS websites, Facebook, Twitter, and email by free subscription. NTAS has two levels of warning: (1) Imminent Threat Alert, meaning a credible, specific, and impending terrorist threat has been made against the United States and (2) Elevated Threat Alert, which denotes a credible terrorist threat has been made against the United States.

The Robert T. Stafford Disaster Relief and Emergency Assistance Act of 1988,[††] as amended, is the statutory authority for most federal disaster response activities, especially as applied to FEMA and its activities. The president is authorized by the Stafford Act to issue emergency and fire management declarations, which enables federal agencies to provide assistance to state and local units of government overwhelmed by catastrophes.[79] The statute also authorizes the president to determine what types of assistance can be provided and the conditions under which aid is distributed.[80] A variety of assistance may be provided to qualified individuals with special needs (e.g., handicapped), including durable medical equipment, as well as to qualified persons or families needing such things as transportation, temporary housing, emergency food, consumables, unemployment assistance, crisis counseling, home repair grants, and financial assistance for uninsured expenses including medical, dental, funeral, personal property, and other expenses. Nonprofit organizations, such as private museums, may also be eligible for assistance. The Stafford Act amended the Disaster Relief Act (1974), and since 1988 the Stafford Act has since been amended several times.

The definition of a *major disaster* is relatively restrictive and covers any natural catastrophe from storms, earth movements, and high water.[81] "Major disaster" declarations may be issued for a hurricane, tornado, storm, high water, tidal wave, tsunami, earthquake, volcanic eruption, landslide, mudslide, snowstorm, drought, or regardless of cause, after a fire, flood, or explosion.[82] In contrast, an *emergency* is a non-specific word allowing the president to determine "any occasion or instance" in which assistance can be provided.[83] Between 1953 and 2011, annual major disaster declarations averaged approximately 35 while there was an annual average of 8.4 emergency declarations.[84] However, during 2000–2009, emergency declarations jumped to an annual average of 15.[85] Requests for declarations come from governors. During the 2000s presidents denied 11 such requests, referred to as turndowns."[86] Presidential turndowns drop to 1.75 in election years,[87] and during presidential election years emergency declarations shift upward from an average of 2.6 to 5.6 per year,[88] suggesting a political motivation in some instances, although the data is not sufficient to make a definitive conclusion.

Presidential Policy Directive 8: National Preparedness (PPD-8) describes the nation's approach to preparing for threats and hazards that pose the greatest risk to the security of the United States. FEMA intends to achieve its National Preparedness Goal by the following activities:

1. Preventing, avoiding, or stopping a threatened or an actual act of terrorism.

2. Protecting our citizens, residents, visitors, and assets against the greatest threats and hazards in a manner that allows our interests, aspirations, and way of life to thrive.

3. Mitigating the loss of life and property by lessening the impact of future disasters.

4. Responding quickly to save lives, protect property and the environment, and meet basic human needs in the aftermath of a catastrophic incident.

Quick Facts
The Twin Fire Disasters of 1871

In legend, the Great Chicago fire of 1871 was caused when a cow owned by Patrick and Catherine O'Leary kicked a lantern over. Skarbek notes The Great Chicago fire resulted in 300 deaths, 300,000 people left homeless, and the loss of approximately 17,420 buildings.[89] The federal response was initially limited to sending troops to maintain order. Foreign governments, American cities, and wealthy Chicago citizens quickly donated approximately $4.8 million to help survivors. In 1872, Congress gave some relief to those caught up in the Chicago Fire. Individuals received tax relief and the duties on goods shipped to Chicago for the relief of sufferers was dismissed.

Ironically, at the same time as the Chicago fire, another one was raging just a few hundred miles away in Wisconsin. The Peshtigo Fire caused 1.5 million acres of forestland to burn to the ground, 2,400 deaths, and the destruction of 17 towns. It remains America's most deadly and least-known fire. Because all telegram stations in the burned area were destroyed, the world did not learn of the disaster for several days. There does not appear to be any federal relief for the Peshtigo Fire.

▲ A stereoscopic card depicting a horse-drawn carriage leaving a scene of ruins at the Great Chicago Fire of 1871.
(Courtesy Library of Congress)

5. Recovering through a focus on the timely restoration, strengthening, and revitalization of infrastructure, housing, and a sustainable economy, as well as the health, social, cultural, historic, and environmental fabric of communities affected by a catastrophic incident.

FEMA deals with potential catastrophes, including terrorist attacks, by a variety of activities (see Quick Facts: Examples of Extreme Mass Casualties). For example, a catastrophe or terrorist attack that produces mass casualties will overwhelm the capacity of morgues, funeral homes, and cemeteries to handle the dead. FEMA develops contingency plans to deal with that possibility, which includes Disaster Mortuary Response Teams (DMORTs) comprised of citizens with, hopefully, some applicable background, such as a forensic anthropology. DMORTs become temporary federal employees.

FEMA also prepares states, tribes, and local communities by providing technical assistance, conducting residential and online training, as well as offering courses on-site supporting the continuous development of the emergency management profession, conducting exercises to identify areas that need corrective attention, and providing grants to acquire equipment and otherwise strengthen capabilities. Preparedness is not a destination; it's a continuous process. Mitigation is FEMA's strategy to reduce or eliminate long-term risks, such as flooding, by building dams and levees, which are man-made structures that restrain floodwaters or the direction in which they move. The Disaster Mitigation Act of 2000 allows additional funding to states, tribes, and local governments that take a comprehensive approach to mitigating the risks posed by natural hazards.

U.S. Coast Guard (USCG)

The United States Coast Guard is the descendent of the Department of Treasury's Revenue Cutter Service established in 1790 with ten ships to collect tariffs and enforce import laws.[90] This role was important to a new nation strapped for cash. In its long and distinguished history the USCG also fought pirates, smugglers, and the British during the War of 1812. Today's USCG was created in 1915. At the same time the U.S. Lifesaving Service was "folded" into it. Subsequent additions to the Coast Guard were the U.S. Lighthouse Service (1939) and the Bureau of Marine Inspections and Navigation (1942).[91] In both the European and Pacific theaters during World War II the USCG was involved in combat operations against the Axis Powers and Japan. The Magnuson Act (1950) solidified the USCG's responsibility for the security of America's harbors and ports.[92] The Coast Guard returned to combat duties during the Vietnam War (1965–1975),[93] conducting "blue water" (open seas) and "brown water" (inland waterways) patrol and surveillance duties. Similar duties were performed in the Arabian Gulf in support of Operation Iraqi Freedom (2003).[94]

The US Coast Guard is one of five U.S. armed services and the only one not "housed" in the Department of Defense.[95] Following its placement in the Department of Transportation (1967) the USCG was transferred to DHS in 2003.

The U.S. Coast Guard's Homeland Security Mission

In DHS the Coast Guard's overarching mission is to protect the public, the environment, and U.S. economic interests—in the nation's ports and waterways, along the coast, on international waters, or in any maritime region as required to support national security (see Figure 11–12). More specifically, the USCG retained traditional missions and assumed additional homeland security missions. It is responsible for executing both types of missions along 95,000 miles of coastline[96] and 4.5 million square miles of the sea, including the maritime Exclusive Economic Zone (EEZ), which typically extends 200 miles from a country's shoreline.[97]

Forty-eight percent of the Coast Guard's annual budget goes for its traditional missions, protecting marine natural resources; preventing marine related injuries, deaths, and property losses; protecting the environment from oil and hazardous substances; maintaining navigational aides; and ice breaking internationally and on the Great Lakes. Fifty-two percent of the USCG's annual budget is expended on the homeland security missions identified in Table 11–3.

FIGURE 11–12
The USCG patrols under the San Francisco-Oakland Bay Bridge in 2001 after a "credible threat" was made that California's four main bridges would be attacked.

(© Christina Koci Hernandez/San Francisco Chronicle/Corbis)

Coast Guard Activities

In Fiscal Year (FY) 2014, the USCG had a budget of $9.9 billion, which represents 17 percent of the total DHS FY 2014 budget authority.[98] During that same year, the USCG had

TABLE 11–3
USCG Homeland Security Missions

Ports, Waterways, and Coastal Security: The USCG's mission is to deny the use or exploitation of these venues to terrorists seeking to attack U.S. territories.

Drug Interdiction: This mission supports national strategies to disrupt illegal drug markets and prevent transnational threats from reaching U.S. territories. The connection between some terrorist groups and certain transnational criminal organizations is well established. The USCG is the lead agency for drug interdiction on U.S. territorial seas, a role that is shared with DHS's Customs and Border Patrol.

Migrant Interdiction: The three prongs to this mission are to (1) deter undocumented migrants and human smugglers from entering the United States, (2) detect and deter undocumented migrants far from U.S. borders, and (3) expand participation in multi-agency and bi-national border security initiatives.

Defense Readiness: This mission requires USCG to establish and maintain readiness and training for immediate integration with the Department of Defense in peacetime operations or times of war.

Other Law Enforcement Activities: This mission focuses on enforcement of regulations on foreign fishing vessels to protect our renewable maritime natural resources and promote compliance with international agreements.

FIGURE 11–13

A USCG C-130 aircraft was on maritime patrol when it spotted drugs on the deck of the Gatun, a Panamanian ship. The USCG cutters *Hamilton* and *Sherman* were notified and stopped the vessel, seized the drugs, and arrested 15 crew members.

(Courtesy Drug Enforcement Agency)

42,000 personnel and operated 211 aircraft and 1,260 vessels in two classes: (1) those ranging in length from 12 to 64 feet, which are designated as "boats" and (2) those exceeding 65 feet in length referred to as "cutters," three of which are ice breakers.[99] Illustrations of its non-DHS mission accomplishments include 19,790 search and rescue missions and saving 3,560 lives or roughly 10 every day throughout the year. In fulfilling its homeland security missions, the USCG conducts a variety of programs, including training foreign governments in port security; maritime operations against pirate groups, some of whom are closely tied to terrorist groups; and anti-smuggling techniques.

The USCG's Law Enforcement Detachments (LeDets) accompany foreign governments on actual operations to evaluate their capability and training needs.[100] These and other anti-terrorism efforts supporting foreign governments contribute to the expansion of governed space, which deprives terrorists of some safe havens. In another homeland security mission, The USCG made the largest cocaine drug interdiction in American history when two of its cutters stopped the Gatun, a Panamanian flagged ship, and seized 42,845 pounds of cocaine—nearly 20 tons—with a street value of $600 million[101] (see Figure 11–13). The seizure prevented substantial funds flowing to transnational criminal organizations and perhaps some portion of it to support a terrorist movement. Peru's Sendero Luminoso (Shining Path) is described both as a communist/socialist movement as well as being designated as a foreign terrorist organization (FTO).[102] It has played a large role in Peru's cultivation of the coca leaf, from which cocaine is made. By 2013, Peru was the world leader in coca production.[103]

Transportation Security Administration (TSA)

The first American airliner was hijacked in 1961, when a passenger demanded that a National Airlines plane take him to Cuba. Following three more hijacking of U.S. flights over the next three months President Kennedy ordered the creation of armed "sky marshals" to thwart hijackings. Initially there were 18 of them, all U.S. Border Patrol agents. By 9/11 there were only 33 sky marshals and none of those were on hijacked

Information Link

For more information regarding the U.S. Coast Guard, visit the website at www.gocoastguard.com/.

Quick Facts
Three Cases on the Road to Airport Security

In 1955, John G. "Jack" Graham put a bomb in his mother's luggage. She was flying on United Airlines from Denver to Portland, Oregon. Eleven minutes after takeoff the bomb exploded, killing 39 passengers and a crew of 11. Graham, after an exhaustive FBI investigation, was arrested, convicted, and executed two years later. His motive for the bombing was to collect a $37,500 insurance policy on his mother's life.

A man using the name of "Dan Cooper," who has been misidentified in the news media as "D. B. Cooper," hijacked a Northwest Orient Airliner in 1971. It landed in Seattle where he demanded $200,000 in ransom. After receiving the money, Cooper allowed the passengers and some crew members to leave the plane in Seattle and ordered it to take off again. During that night flight he parachuted into the lower Cascade Mountains. The case was never officially cleared, although a deceased man identified years latter is thought to have been the mysterious Cooper.

A Dan Cooper "copycat" hijacking occurred in 1972. A man rode his bicycle onto the airport tarmac in Reno, laid his bike down at the foot of the portable stairs leading to a United Airlines plane, climbed up the stairs, and entered the plane. In preparation for their flight the attendants and pilots were already on board. The man put a gun to the head of a flight attendant, and demanded $200,000.[104] It was a Friday evening and the banks were closed. The ransom money was gathered from two casinos, receipted by a note on a cocktail napkin, and rushed to the airport. The plane took off on a heading given by the hijacker. Like Dan Cooper, the hijacker put on a parachute and jumped from the lowered tail stairs. The pilot immediately radioed the plane's position and law enforcement officers rushed to that area. They found a car parked in some trees with a license plate reading "Parachute." Thirty minutes later a limping man walked up to the car carrying the ransom money and was arrested.

planes that day because they were not being assigned to domestic flights. The number of air marshals is not publicized, but has varied widely. The "descendants" of the sky marshals are now designated as the Federal Air Marshal Service (FAMS) and are part of TSA.

Few hijackings of U.S. airliners have occurred in recent years, 9/11 providing a grotesque exception to this statement. The general absence of hijackings may be due to several factors: (1) a lack of intent or capability by terrorists, (2) marshals may be providing a deterrent, or (3) a shift in tactics by terrorist groups. For example, recent terrorist attacks in Europe suggest a preference for attacks on mass transit systems. On average, attacks against mass transit systems create more than two and a half times the casualties per incident as attacks on aviation targets.[105]

In 1972, a Trans World Airlines Flight 7 (TWA) jet departed from JFK International Airport in New York bound for Los Angeles.[106] Minutes later an anonymous caller identified only as "Gomez" said there was a bomb on board Flight 7 and it returned to JFK where the passengers were evacuated. Brandy, a bomb-sniffing dog, found the bomb 12 minutes before it exploded. That same day, then-President Richard Nixon ordered the Secretary of Transportation to develop a plan to combat problems cropping up in civil aviation. One result was the Federal Aviation Authority's (FAAs) Explosives Detection Canine Team program that placed such units at many airports across the country.

The Airport Transportation Security Act (ATSA) of 1974 required U.S. airport operators to establishing weapons-detecting screening of all passengers and carry-on luggage. Many airports elected to contract with private security firms for these tasks. Following the 9/11 attacks, federal legislation in 2001 established the Transportation Security Administration (TSA) and transferred responsibility for civil aviation security from the Federal Aviation Administration (FAA) to TSA. In 2002, the Homeland Security Act (HSA) moved TSA into the Department of Homeland Security (DHS).

FIGURE 11–14
Port Authority Police officers search the bags of riders at the Hoboken PATH station in Hoboken on July 25, 2005. New Jersey transportation agencies started searching the bags of some passengers today.
(Courtesy © Noah Addis/Star Ledger/ Corbis)

TSA Responsibilities

In FY 2014, TSA had 55,608 employees and a budget of approximately $7.4 billion.[107] Its mission is to maximize transportation security in response to evolving threats while protecting passengers' privacy and facilitating the flow of legal commerce. Although the mere mention of TSA is likely to invoke the image of long screening lines at airports (see Figure 11–14), its

Quick Facts
What the TSA Protects and Checks Annually

- ✓ 751 million bus passengers
- ✓ 9 billion mass transit passengers
- ✓ 640 million domestic and international flights
- ✓ 140,000 miles of railroads
- ✓ 582,000 bridges over 20' long
- ✓ 366 highway tunnels longer than 100 meters
- ✓ 2.5 million miles of pipelines

- ✓ 800,000 hazardous waste shipments
- ✓ 629 million pounds of cargo using canine teams
- ✓ 425 million bags
- ✓ 2 billion items at checkpoints
- ✓ Over 117,000 dangerous items, including guns and explosives, from reaching carriers[108]

responsibilities are much broader than airports and include rail, bus, mass transit, pipelines, highways, and port systems. TSA has four specific responsibilities:

1. Ensuring effective and efficient screening of all air passengers, baggage, and cargo on passenger planes;

2. Deploying federal air marshals internationally and domestically to detect, deter, and defeat hostile acts targeting air carriers, airports, passengers, and crews;

3. Managing security risks of the surface transportation systems by working with stakeholders, providing support and program direction, and conducting on-site inspections; and

4. Developing and implementing more efficient, reliable, integrated, and cost-effective screening programs.

TSA employs a strategy of focusing resources on known and emerging risks/threats. A key component of this strategy to protect U.S. aviation is using layers of security as shown in Figure 11–15. The TSA deploys Behavioral Detection Officers (BDOs) to detect potential terrorists using 94 different factors in its Screening Passengers by Observation Techniques (SPOT) program. A Government Accountability Office study concluded that although TSA spent $900 million on the program there is no evidence that it works and urged Congress to cut funding.[109] Only 0.59 percent of all passengers screened were arrested and none were charged with terrorism.[110] The ability of SPOT to detect potential threats is only slightly better than random chance.[111] TSA has also had difficulties with the performance of airport TSA members. During 2010–2012, employee violations increased from 2,691 to 4,408; 55 percent of the cases were accounted for by a handful of charges: screening and security lapses, failure to follow instructions, inappropriate conduct or comments, drug and alcohol violations, and neglect of duty.[112]

Despite some problems, TSA has done an excellent job of executing its homeland security mission. A recent innovation that has been well-received by the flying public is the "TSA Pre✓™" program, which is based on intelligence and risks. Rather than clinging to a single model of screening aviation passengers, the TSA Pre✓ program ("Pre-Checked") provides expedited screening for low-risk passengers, such as military personnel and trusted traveler protection program who are part of the "trusted Traveler" program, and frequent travelers nominated by airlines.

Information Link
To read about TSA Prohibited Items on commercial airlines (No-Fly Items), visit the website at /www.tsa.gov/traveler-information/prohibited-items.

U.S. Secret Service (USSS)

Counterfeiting has a long history. During the American Revolution the British counterfeited Continental currency in such large quantities that it became worthless.[113] During the American Civil War, one-third to one-half of the currency was counterfeit, leading to the establishment in 1865 of the Secret Service to fight this problem.[114] As time passed, the jurisdiction of the Secret Service included other responsibilities.

The U.S. Secret Service has a unique dual mission of protection and investigation.[115] The primary mission of the Secret Service is to protect the President of the United States

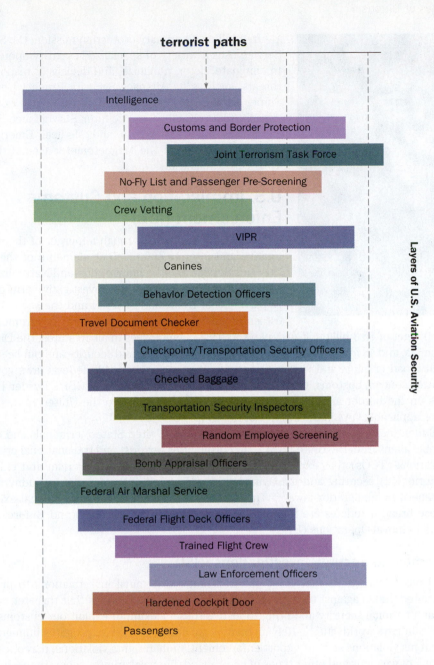

terrorist paths

Intelligence

Customs and Border Protection

Joint Terrorism Task Force

No-Fly List and Passenger Pre-Screening

Crew Vetting

VIPR

Canines

Behavior Detection Officers

Travel Document Checker

Checkpoint/Transportation Security Officers

Checked Baggage

Transportation Security Inspectors

Random Employee Screening

Bomb Appraisal Officers

Federal Air Marshal Service

Federal Flight Deck Officers

Trained Flight Crew

Law Enforcement Officers

Hardened Cockpit Door

Passengers

Layers of U.S. Aviation Security

FIGURE 11–15
Layers of Security
Source: "Layers of Security"
(Washington, D.C.: Transportation
Security Administration, January 14,
2014), p. 1, www.tsa.gov/about-tsa/
layers-security.

(see Figure 11–16), the Vice President, other visiting heads of state and government, and any **National Special Security Events (NSSEs)**. A NSSE is any national or international meeting deemed by DHS as a potential target for terrorism or other criminal activity, such as a specific summit of world leaders (e.g., World Trade Organization—WTO Conference) or any other meeting of foreign leaders in the United States. Further, the Secret Service safeguards the nation's financial infrastructure and payment systems to preserve the integrity of the economy, investigates cyber/electronic crimes, and protects the White House and other designated buildings within the Washington, D.C. area. To meet its responsibilities, the Secret Service has an annual budget of $1.8 billion, 6,705 employees, and operates 114 domestic and 24 foreign investigative offices.[116]

The investigative responsibility of the Secret Service is broad and include thefts and frauds involving ATMs, debit cards, identity theft, credit cards, computers, passwords, and financial deposits.[117] Secret Service Electronic Crimes Task Force (ECTF) units are spread around the country and protect the integrity of America's financial systems. In a single year (1) ECTFs prevented $1.2 billion in potential losses and arrested 1,383 persons;[118] (2) The Secret Service's shut down 250 plants counterfeiting U.S. currency;[119] and (3) while screening people seeking to enter protected venues, such as the White House complex, seized 3,300 weapons.[120]

National Special Security Events (NSSE)

Any national or international meeting deemed by DHS as a potential target for terrorism or other criminal activity.

FIGURE 11–16
Secret Service agents rush a lone assassin who fired six shots, wounding President Ronald Reagan and two other men on March 31, 1981, outside of the Washington Hilton Hotel in Washington, D.C. Ronald Reagan had been president for only 69 days at the time of this attempt on his life.

(© Michael Evans/Bettmann/Corbis)

Information Link
For more information regarding the role and responsibilities of the U.S. Secret Service, visit the website at www.secretservice.gov/.

Detainer
An immigration detainer or "hold" is sent to local and state jails to keep a person of interest in custody 48 hours beyond the time they would otherwise be released. This gives ICE time to investigate the subject's immigration status and assume custody if appropriate.

In fulfilling its primary protection mission, the Secret Service uses a variety of specialized security operations to eliminate, deter, minimize, and decisively respond to threats, such as its Airspace Security Branch, Counter Sniper Team, Emergency Response Team, Counter Assault Team—CAT Team, Counter Surveillance Team, Hazardous Agent Mitigation and Medical Emergency Response Team, and the Magnetometer (metal detection) Operations Unit.[121]

U.S. Immigration and Customs Enforcement (ICE)

ICE was formed in 2003 through a merger of the investigative and interior enforcement elements of the U.S. Customs Service and the Immigration and Naturalization Service.[122] ICE is the principal investigative arm of the Department of Homeland Security and the second largest enforcement agency in the federal government.[123] With a budget of $5.3 billion, ICE deploys its 19,332 employees in all 50 states, the District of Columbia, and 48 foreign countries.[124] ICE promotes homeland security and public safety through broad criminal and civil enforcement of approximately 400 federal laws governing border control, customs, trade, and immigration.[125] Whereas the CBP's Border Patrol focuses on the border areas between ports of entry (POEs) into the United States, ICE enforces applicable laws in the interior of the United States.

ICE identifies, apprehends, and removes (from the United States) criminals and other removable aliens from the United States and dismantles terrorist and transnational criminal organizations (TCOs) that exploit our borders by (1) preventing terrorism and enhancing security, (2) securing and managing our borders, and (3) enforcing and administering American immigration laws.[126] The two principal operating components that execute these broad mandates are Homeland Security Investigations (HSI) and Enforcement and Removal Operations (ERO).

Homeland Security Investigations (HSI)

HSI has 6,500 agents that carry out transnational criminal investigations to protect the United States against terrorist and other criminal organizations that threaten public safety and national security and bring to justice those seeking to exploit our customs and immigration laws worldwide.[127] Relying on its legal authority, HSI investigates immigration and customs violations such as export enforcement, human rights violations, narcotics, the smuggling of weapons and other types of contraband, financial crimes, cybercrimes, human trafficking and smuggling, child exploitation, commercial fraud, such as intellectual property violations, transnational gangs, and identity and immigration benefit fraud.[128]

In 2012, the federal Jaime Zapata Border Enforcement Security Task Force (BEST) Act became law. It fields BEST teams to work jointly with federal, state, local, and foreign law enforcement agencies along America's northern and southern borders, and at major seaports to identify, disrupt, and dismantle criminal organizations that pose significant threats to border security.[129] In FY 2012, BEST units made 2,775 criminal arrests, seized 289,000 pounds of narcotics and other dangerous drugs, took 7,950 weapons out of circulation, and impounded $19.6 million in U.S. currency and monetary instruments.

Two important organizational units within the Homeland Security Investigations Division of ICE are the Forensic Laboratory (FL), which has great expertise in several forensic sciences, including questioned document examination, which determines the authenticity of identity, travel, and other documents; and the Law Enforcement Support Center (LESC), which is a single national point of information that provides timely data about immigration status, identity information, and real-time assistance to local, state, and federal law enforcement agencies on aliens suspected, arrested, or convicted of criminal activity.[130] During FY 2012 LESC placed **detainers** on 17,890 aliens suspected of immigration violations.[131]

Enforcement and Removal Operations (ERO)

The Enforcement and Removal Operations Division of ICE identifies and apprehends removable aliens, detains them when necessary, and removes them from the United States.[133] ERO's removal priorities are convicted criminals, those who are a threat to national security, fugitives, and recent border crossers. ERO also transports removable aliens from one point to another, manages aliens in custody, and provides aliens with access to legal resources and representatives of advocacy groups. In FY 2013, ERO removed 368,644 people.[134] Their four most common countries of origin were Mexico (241,493), Guatemala (47,769), Honduras (37,049), and El Salvador (21,602), representing 94 percent of all removals.

In addition to these extensive programs, ICE maintains a Counterterrorism and Criminal Exploitation Unit, a Firearms and Explosives Smuggling Unit, a Visa Security Unit, and a National Security Division that concentrates efforts against potential terrorists and assists the FBI in complex terrorist investigations. As important, ICE also maintains a Human Rights Violators and War Crimes Center that actively pursues war criminals from foreign lands, including past dictators and individuals guilty of state terrorism and genocide. For instance, the center has been involved in arresting and deporting former military officers in Central America (e.g., Guatemala, El Salvador) involved in past massacres in their home countries. The Human Rights Violators and War Crimes Center has been in existence for over 10 years and marks one of the most important coordination, liaison, and extradition programs in the country. Its work has been instrumental in bringing those that would hide behind the cloak of government to torture and kill their own people to justice in such war-torn areas as Bosnia-Herzegovina, Rwanda, Burma, Guatemala, and El Salvador.

Information Link
For more information on Immigration and Custom Enforcement (ICE), visit the website at www.ice.gov/index.htm.

U.S. Citizenship and Immigration Services (USCIS)

The U.S. Citizenship and Immigration Services (USCIS) has an annual budget of $3.3 billion and 13,151 employees distributed across 240 domestic and foreign offices.[135] In light of the fact that some of the 9/11 attackers entered the United States several times and received flight training here, the work of this agency has become a critical part of preventing future terrorist attacks.

In a single year USCIS (1) processed 36,000 political asylum applications; (2) and received 21 million E-Verify inquiries.[136] The E-Verify Program requires employers to fill out Form 1-9 on citizen and non-citizens for all potential hires.[137] The Internet-based system returns a confirmation of eligibility or non-eligibility within 3–5 seconds by reviewing select federal records; (3) naturalized 763,690 new citizens, some 9,000 of whom qualified by military service while a non-citizen immigrant.[138] When their enlistment period is over the veterans and qualified members of their families can apply to become citizens. If killed in action, the deceased's immediate family, spouse, children, and parents get special preference for immigration.[139] Hurdles to non-citizens seeking to enlist include no high school degree, a lack of English proficiency, and an inability to get a security clearance;[140] and (4) interviewed more than 76,750 refugees[141] in 60 countries.[142]

The USCIS is responsible for the delivery of information on citizenship and immigration benefits to applicants in a timely, accurate, consistent, courteous, and professional manner, while also safeguarding our national security.[143] All cases are unique and require attention from experienced USCIS immigration officers. The USCIS is also responsible for enhancing the integrity of America's legal immigration system by deterring, detecting, and pursuing immigration related fraud.

Quick Facts
The Mission of the Minnesota Homeland Security and Emergency Management (HSEM)

HSEM's mission is to help Minnesota prevent, prepare for, respond to, and recover from natural and human-caused disasters. The primary purpose of the program is to build communities that are prepared to respond to emergencies and have the resilience to quickly recovery from the effects of disaster.[144]

DHS and Other Homeland Security Units

In support of the U.S. Department of Homeland Security (DHS), there are many homeland security units in state, local, tribal, and territorial governments (SLTT). Forty-nine states, the District of Columbia, and five territories/possessions[‡‡] have their own homeland security organizations. State level homeland security units are often co-located with fusion centers within the same organizational structure, which may also have an emergency function. Such arrangements end up with a title such as "Department of Homeland Security and Emergency Management," as in the case of Iowa, Alaska, Minnesota, West Virginia, and New Mexico. In other states, the fusion center, emergency management, and homeland security end up in a unit whose title does not include the homeland security tag. Connecticut's Division of Emergency Services and Public Protection illustrates this situation. A common organizational arrangement is to place state homeland security units within a state police, state investigative agency, or a state department of public safety. Additionally, local governments have their own homeland security units.

DHS provides training, guidance, and other resources, including further grants to enhance existing capabilities or add new ones to state, local, tribal, and territorial governments. SLTT and fusion centers excel in gathering human intelligence (HUMINT)[145] because their law enforcement agencies are out in the community and across the state 24/7, giving them many opportunities to see and learn things. Similarly, local fire departments responding to a fire may stumble across bomb making activity. SLTT programs are also effective at engaging the public and recruiting private sector partners, for example, local aviation. DHS has put $37 billion[146] into creating, staffing, and equipping state, local, tribal, and territorial homeland security units.[147]

[‡‡] These five territories or possessions of the United States are the Commonwealth of Puerto Rico, Guam, American Samoa, U.S. Virgin Islands, and the Commonwealth of the Northern Mariana Islands. There are also eight largely uninhabited islands that are possessions: Baker, Howland, Kingman Reef, Jarvis, Johnson, Midway, Palmyra, and Wake.

Chapter Summary

SUMMARY BY LEARNING OBJECTIVE

1. **Briefly describe the formation of the Department of Homeland Security (DHS).**

   DHS was created on November 25, 2002, and it became operational or "opened its doors" March 1, 2003. All or parts of 22 existing federal agencies became part of DHS.

2. **Identify the five DHS security missions.**

   The five security missions are (1) stopping terrorism and enhancing security, (2) securing and managing our borders, (3) enforcing and administering our immigration laws, (4) safeguarding and securing our cyberspace, and (5) ensuring resilience to disasters.

3. **State the broad purpose of Customs and Border Protection.**

   Broadly, the purpose of CBP is to prevent harmful individuals and substances from entering the Unites States. This includes terrorists, criminals, and illegal immigrants.

4. **Identify the "three wars" being fought on America's southern border.**

Payan maintains there are three wars being waged along America's southern border with Mexico. They are the drug war, the immigration war, and the homeland security war.

5. **Distinguish between a "major disaster" and an "emergency."**

A *major disaster* is a restrictive term and covers any natural catastrophe from storms, earth movements, and high water.[148] "Major disaster" declarations may be issued for a hurricane, tornado, storm, high water, tidal wave, tsunami, earthquake, volcanic eruption, landslide, mudslide, snowstorm, drought, or regardless of cause, after a fire, flood, or explosion. In contrast, an *emergency* is a non-specific word allowing the president to determine "any occasion or instance" in which assistance can be provided.

6. **Identify the U.S. Coast Guard's five homeland security missions.**

These missions are (1) security of ports, waterways, and coastal security; (2) drug interdiction; (3) illegal migrant interdiction; (4) defense readiness; and (5) other law enforcement activities.

7. **State the Transportation Security Administration's four specific responsibilities.**

These responsibilities are (1) ensuring effective and efficient screening of all air passengers, baggage, and cargo on passenger planes; (2) deploying federal air marshals internationally and domestically to detect, deter, and defeat hostile acts targeting air carriers, airports, passengers, and crews; (3) managing security risks of the surface transportation systems by working with stakeholders, providing support and program direction, and conducting on-site inspections; and (4) developing and implementing more efficient, reliable, integrated, and cost-effective screening programs.

8. **State the primary mission of the U.S. Secret Service.**

The primary mission of the Secret Service is to protect the President of the United States the Vice President, other visiting heads of state and government, and any National Special Security Events (NSSEs). A NSSE is any national or international meeting deemed by DHS as a potential target for terrorism or other criminal activity, such as a specific summit of world leaders (e.g., World Trade Organization—WTO Conference) or any other meeting of foreign leaders in the United States.

9. **Identify the priorities of Enforcement Removal Operations.**

ERO's removal priorities are convicted criminals, those who are a threat to national security, fugitives, and recent border crossers. ERO also transports removable aliens from one point to another, manages aliens in custody, and provides aliens with access to legal resources and representatives of advocacy groups.

10. **Explain the services provided by the Forensic Laboratory and the Law Enforcement Support Center.**

The Forensic Laboratory (FL) has great expertise in several forensic sciences, including questioned document examination, which determines the authenticity of identity, travel, and other documents. The Law Enforcement Support Center (LESC) is a single national point of information that provides timely data about immigration status, identity information, and real-time assistance to local, state, federal, law enforcement agencies on aliens suspected, arrested, or convicted of criminal activity.

REVIEW QUESTIONS

1. If the success of the 9/11 attacks was in part an intelligence failure, why weren't any major intelligence agencies transferred to DHS?
2. Following 9/11 DHS grants were made to states and local jurisdictions without any need analysis being done. Why did this happen?
3. What twofold challenges faced DHS as it attempted to create a single organizational culture among personnel from 22 different agencies?
4. Why did some people believe that DHS managers were not up to the task of transforming it?
5. What are legacy agencies?
6. How does the role of the Border Patrol and Homeland Security Investigations differ?
7. What criticisms have been made of the SPOT Program?
8. What is the purpose of BEST Teams?

CRITICAL THINKING EXERCISES

1. **The Texas-Mexican Border.** Texas has a 1,200-mile border with Mexico that creates unique problems for that state's homeland security effort. Visit the website of the Texas Governor at www.governor.state.tx.us. Search for "Homeland Security Strategic Plan 2010–2015" or its successor. Read about Mexican cartels, transnational gangs, illegal entry, and public health threats on the Texas-Mexico Border. As a class, choose one of these topics and develop a plan to diminish the threat posed by one of these issues. Do you think we can totally secure our border with Mexico? Do you think we should use the military to patrol the border? What will be the impact of a secure border to the social and economic systems of both Mexico and the United States?

2. **Learn about Human Trafficking.** As a class, learn more about the crime of human trafficking. Human trafficking is a major crime investigated by ICE. It is hard to know the exact scope of the problem, as human trafficking is often clouded in an underground activity that thrives on secrecy, seclusion, and fear, and often begins in foreign countries. The victims are usually illegally transported to large cities and/or vacation and tourist areas, for the purposes of prostitution and child sex slavery. Visit the following webpages:

   U.S. Department of State, Diplomacy in Action website at www.state.gov/j/tip/laws.
   The United Nations Office of Drugs and Crime website at www.unodc.org/unodc/en/human-trafficking/what-is-human-trafficking.html?ref=menuside.
   The International Justice Mission website at www.ijm.org.

   As a class, discuss the following questions:

   1. What is the Trafficking and Victim's Protection Act (TVPA)?
   2. What is the Protocol to Prevent, Suppress and Punish Trafficking in Persons, Especially Women and Children?
   3. What is bonded and forced labor?
   4. Why is human trafficking considered "modern-day slavery?"
   5. What do you think of the solution proposed by the International Justice Mission?
   6. What do you think we could do to prevent human trafficking, especially in the United States?

NOTES

1. *One Team, One Response, Securing Our Homeland, U.S. Department of Homeland Security, Strategic Plan Fiscal* (Washington, D.C.: Department of Homeland Security, 2008), p. 3.
2. Charles Perrow, "The Disaster After 9/11: The Department of Homeland Security and the Intelligence Reorganization," *Homeland Security Affairs*, VII, No. 1, April 2006, p. 4, www.hsaj.org/?fullarticle=2.1.3.
3. See Christine A. Henriksen, James M. Bolton, and Jitender Sareen, "The Psychological Impact of Terrorist Attacks: Examining a Dose-Response Relationship Between Exposure to 9/11 and Axis I Mental Disorders," *Depression and Anxiety*, Vol. 27, Issue 11, November 2010, pp. 993–1000.
4. Data on these problems is available at *9/11 Health: What We Know From the Research*, City of New York, www.nyc.gov/html/doh/wtc/html/rescue/know.shtml. This source is undated, but its most recent citation is 2013.
5. See Monica L. P. Robbers and Jonathan Mark Jenkins, "Symptomology of Post-Traumatic Stress Disorder Among First Responders to the Pentagon on 9/11: A Preliminary Analysis of Arlington County Police First Responders," *Police Practice and Research*, Vol. 6, Issue 3, July 2005, pp. 235–249. A 2002 survey of New Yorkers reported 47.5 percent of respondents feared another terrorist attack. See Joseph A. Boscarino, Charles R. Figley, and Richard E. Adams, "Fear of Terrorism in New York After the 9/11 Terrorist Attacks: Implications for Emergency Mental Health and Preparedness," *International Journal*

of Mental Health, Volume 5, Issue 4, 2003, p. 4, www.ncbi.nim.nih.gov/pmc/articles/pmc/articles/pmc26975671.

6. Angie Cannon et al., "Final Words from Flight 93," *U.S. News and World Report*, Vol. 131, Issue 18, October 29, 2001.

7. Derekh Cornwell and Bryan Roberts, "The 9/11 Terrorist Attack and Overseas Travel to the United States: Initial Impacts and Longer-Run Recovery," Department of Homeland Security, Working Paper, March 2010, p. 1.

8. Dov S. Zakheim, "What 9/11 Has Wrought," *Middle East Quarterly,* Vol. 18, Issue 4, Fall 2011, pp. 3–4.

9. Defense Science Board Task Force, "Deployment of Members of the National Guard and Reserve in the Global War on Terrorism," Office of the Under Secretary for Acquisition, Technology, and Logistics, Washington, D.C., September 2007.

10. Zakheim, "What 9/11 Has Wrought," pp. 3–4.

11. Matthew DeLuca, "Report Pulls Back Veil on CIA'S Rendition Program," *NBC News*, February 5, 2013, pp. 1–2, www.usnews.nbcnews.com/_news/2013/02/05/16853156-report-pulls-back-veil-on-cias-rendition-program.

12. This paragraph was prepared from Thomas H. Kean, Chair, The 9/11 Commission Report (Washington, D.C., July 22, 2004), pp. 38–39 and "Bush Learns of Attacks on World Trade Center," *This Day in History*, www.history-com/this-day-in-history/bush-learns-of-attack-on-world-trade-center, undated.

13. George W. Bush, Address to the Nation on the Terrorist Attacks on September 11, 2001 (University of California, Santa Barbara, The Presidency Project), www.presidency.ucsb.edu/ws/?pid=58057, undated.

14. Darcy Noricks, "Less Than the Sum of Its Parts: Institutional Change, Policy Entrepreneurs, and the Development of the Department of Homeland Security," International Studies Association Annual Meeting, Chicago, Illinois, February 28–March 3, 2007, p. 1.

15. David Wolfe, "Transforming the U.S. Immigration Service After 9/11: The Impact of Organizational Change and Collaboration in the Context of Homeland Security" (Monterey, CA: Masters Thesis, Naval Postgraduate School, December 2008), p. 1.

16. Noricks, "Less Than the Sum of Its Parts," p. 1.

17. The budget figure does not include any funds appropriated in supplemental budgets. See Chad C. Haddal, Homeland Security Department: FY 2011 Appropriations (Washington, D.C. Congressional Research Service, August 27, 2010), p. 29.

18. Richard A. Clark, *Your Government Failed You: Breaking the Cycle of National Security Disasters* (New York: HarperCollins Publishing, 2008), p. 204.

19. Perrow, "The Disaster After 9/11," p. 6.

20. Source: Quadrennial Homeland Security Report (Washington, D.C.: Department of Homeland Security, February 2010), pp. 21–34.

21. "Task Force Report on Streamlining and Consolidating Congressional Oversight of the U.S. Department of Homeland Security" (Aspen, Colorado: Aspen Institute for Justice and Society Program, September 2013), p. 10.

22. Andrew D. Grossman, "So Dysfunctional ... It's Frightening: The Department of Homeland Security and Public Policy in the Car Bomb Age," American Political Science Association Annual Meeting, Chicago, Illinois, August 30–September 2, 2007.

23. U.S. General Accountability Office, "Homeland Security: Overview of the Department of Homeland Security Management Challenges," April 20, 2005, www.gpo.gov/fdsys/pkg/gaoreports.gao-05-573t/html/gaoreports-gao-05-573t.htm.

24. Loc. cit.

25. David W. Chen, "9/11 Aid Requests Returned: FEMA Didn't Pay for P.O. Box," *The New York Times*, Vol. 152, November 27, 2002.

26. Mike M. Ahlers, "Report: Criticism of FEMA's Katrina Response Deserved," *CNN.com*, April 14, 2006, p. 1, www.cnn.com/2006/politics/04/14/fema.ig.

27. Anna Shoup, "FEMA Faces Intense Scrutiny," *Public Broadcasting System*, September 5, 2005, p. 6, www.pbs.org/newshour/updates/government_programs-july-dec05-fema_09-09.

28. Grossman, "So Dysfunctional ... It's Frightening," p. 13. Also see "Chertoff Says He'd Do Things Differently," *USA Today*, February 15, 2006.

29. See, for example, Jena Baker McNeill and Jessica Zuckerman, "Five Reasons Why FEMA Should Stay at DHS," The Heritage Foundation, December 15, 2009, www.heritage.org/research/reports/2009/12/five-reasons-why-fema-should-stay-at-dhs.

30. Veronique de Rugy, "Are We Ready for the Next 9/11?" *Reason*, Vol. 37, Issue 10, March 2006, p. 1.

31. Ibid., pp. 2–3.

32. Office of the Inspector General, "Department of Homeland Security Challenges in Consolidating Terrorist Watch List Information," Department of Homeland Security, August 2004, pp. 3–4.

33. Clark, *Your Government Failed You*, p. 204.

34. Office of the Inspector General, "Department of Homeland Security Challenges in Consolidating Terrorist Watch List Information," pp. 3–4.

35. "Budget in Brief Fiscal Year 2014, Homeland Security" (Washington, D.C.: Department of Homeland Security, 2014), p. 5.

36. "Agricultural Fact Sheet," U.S. Customs and Border Patrol, undated, p. 1, www.cbp.gov/linkhandler/cgov/trade/trade_programs/agriculture/agriculture_factsheet.ctt/agriculture_factsheet.pdf.

37. Dean Olson, "Agroterrorism," *FBI Law Enforcement Bulletin*, Vol. 81, Number 2, p. 1.

38. "Agricultural Fact Sheet," p. 1.

39. Olson, "Agroterrorism," p. 1.

40. Loc. cit.

41. "Agricultural Fact Sheet," p. 1.

42. Nadav Morag, "Customs and Border Patrol Protection: Rooted in Nation's First Congress," Colorado Technical University, p. 1, September 17, 2013, www.coloradotech.edu/resources/blogs/september-2013/customs-border-protection.

43. "Budget in Brief Fiscal Year 2014," p. 110.

44. "Alexander Hamilton U.S. Custom House, New York, NY" (Washington, D.C.: U.S. General Services Administration, no date), p. 1, www.gsa.gov/portal/ext/html/site/hb/category/25431/actionparameter/explorebybuilding/buildingld/644.

45. "DHS at Work: History of the U.S. Customs Service," undated, p. 1, http://trac.syr.edu/tracus/findings/aboutcus/cushistory.html.

46. "DHS at Work: History of the U.S. Customs Service," p. 1.

47. "Alexander Hamilton U.S. Custom House, New York, NY," p. 1.

48. "Border Patrol History," undated, p. 1, www.cbp.gov/xp/cgov/border-security/border_patrol/border_patrol_ohs/history/history.xml.

49. Loc. cit.

50. Loc. cit.

51. Loc. cit.

52. Ibid., p. 2.

53. Kelly Lytle Hernandez, *Migra!* (Berkeley, California: University of California Press, 2010), p. 2.

54. Ibid., p. 47.

55. "Budget-in-Brief: Fiscal Year 2014, Homeland Security" (Washington, D.C.: Department of Homeland Security, February 2012), p. 109.

56. Ibid., p. 115.

57. Ibid., p. 109.

58. Ibid., p. 115.

59. Justin A. McCarty, "The Volunteer Border Patrol: The Inevitable Disaster of the Minuteman Project," *Iowa Law Review*, Vol. 92, Issue 4, May 1, 2007, p. 1461.

60. "Snapshots: A Summary of CBP Facts and Figures," Department of Homeland Security, p. 1, based on FY 2012 data, www.cbp.gov.

61. Loc. cit.

62. Loc. cit.

63. Tiffany Williams, "U.S. Customs and Border Patrol Protection Use of Technology to Better Secure U.S. Borders," *The Police Chief*, Vol. LXXVI, No. 9, September 2009, p. 1.

64. "History of Federal Disaster Mitigation," *Congressional Digest*, Vol. 84, Issue 9, November 2005, p. 258.

65. Loc. cit.
66. Fernanda Santos and Rebekah Zemansky, "Arizona Desert Swallows Up Migrants on Riskier Paths," *The New York Times*, May 20, 2013.
67. Loc. cit.
68. Loc. cit.
69. Peter Sieven, "In Arizona, 'Los Samaritanos' Leave Water and Food on Trails Used by Immigrants," *The Washington Post*, June 6, 2010.
70. Emilie Eaton, "Crimes of the Coyotes," *The State Press* (Arizona), October 11, 2010, www.statepress.com/2010/10/11/crimes-of-the-coyotes.
71. Loc. cit.
72. No author, "Deadly Crossing: Death Toll Rises Among Those Desperate for the American Dream, *NBC News*, October 9, 2012, p. 8, http://investigations.nbcnews.com/_news/2012/10/09/14300178-deadly-sing-death-toll-rises-among-those-desperate-for-the-american-dream.
73. Loc. cit.
74. See Tony Payan, *The Three U.S.-Mexico Border Wars* (Westport, CT: Praeger International Press, 2006, revised 2010).
75. Loc. cit.
76. Schuyler Kropf, "Angry Words for FEMA," *The (Charleston) Post and Courier*, March 22, 2012, p. 1, www.postandcourier.com/article/20090921/pc1602/309219933.
77. Loc. cit.
78. "Budget-in-Brief: Fiscal Year 2014, Department of Homeland Security," p. 171.
79. Francis X. McCarthy, "Federal Stafford Act Disaster Assistance: Presidential Declarations, Eligible Activities, and Funding" (Washington, D.C.: Congressional Research Service, June 7, 2011), p. 1.
80. Loc. cit.
81. Loc. cit.
82. Ibid., p. 10.
83. Ibid., pp. 1–2.
84. Bruce R. Lindsay, "Stafford Act Declarations 1953–2011: Trends and Analyses, and Implications for Congress" (Washington, D.C.: Congressional Research Service, August 31, 2012), p. 1 of unnumbered Summary Section.
85. Loc. cit.
86. Ibid., pp. 2 and 9.
87. Ibid., p. 6.
88. Ibid., p. 17.
89. Email, March 17, 2014, from Emily Skarbek to Charles Swanson, "The Chicago Fire of 1871: A Bottom-Up Approach to Disaster Relief," *Public Choice*, forthcoming.
90. "U.S. Coast Guard Organization and Missions," *Sea Power*, Vol. 55, Issue 1, January 2012, p. 131.
91. Loc. cit.
92. Loc. cit.
93. The 1965–1975 period reflects when the Unites States had substantial forces in South Vietnam, although advisors were deployed as early as 1954, and other authorities use 1956.
94. See Robert T. Hanley, "Keep the Coast Guard Expeditionary," *U.S. Naval Institute Proceedings*, Vol. 130, Issue 11, November 2004, pp. 64–67.
95. "U.S. Coast Guard Organization and Missions," p. 129.
96. Most sources state the United States has 12,383 miles of coastline. However, "The Coast Guard and Homeland Security," www.uscg.mil/history/uscghist/homeland_security.asp, states USCG patrols 95,000 miles of coastline.
97. "DHS at 10: The U.S. Coast Guard," www.dhs.gov/blog/2013/04/04/dhs-10-us-coast-guard.
98. "Budget in Brief Fiscal Year 2014," p. 5.
99. Memo of February 22, 2013, from the Staff of the Subcommittee on Coast Guard and Maritime Transportation to the members of that committee, pp. 1–2.
100. Gary R. Bowen, "Coast Guard Law Enforcement Detachments in the War on Terrorism," a monograph submitted to the School of Advanced Military Studies, United States Command and General Staff College, Fort Leavenworth, May 26, 2006, p. 28.

101. Theresa Cook, "U.S. Coast Guard Makes Biggest Cocaine Bust in U.S. History," *ABC News,* www.abcnews.go.com/us/story?id=2799.

102. "Terrorist Organization Profile: Shining Path," National Consortium for the Study of Terrorism and Responses to Terrorism, undated, accessed January 19, 2014. The National Counter Terrorism Center lists it as an FTO by the U.S. Department of State as of January 14, 2014, see "Foreign Terrorist Organizations," www.nctc.gov/site/other/fto.html.

103. "U.S. Ups Anti-Drug Aid as Peru Becomes World Leader in Coca Production," *Fox News Latino,* September 25, 2013, www.latino.foxnews.com/latino/news/2013/09/25/us-ups-anti-drug-aid-as-peru-becomes-world-leader-in-coca-production.

104. This account is drawn, with restatement and additions, from Howard Putnam, "Through Turbulent Times: The Days of NO Airport Security," undated, www.howardputnam.com/security.php.

105. Daniel B. Prieto, "Written Testimony of Daniel B. Prieto before the Massachusetts Joint Committee on Public Safety and Homeland Security," August 4, 2005, p. 2.

106. "Program History," *Transportation Security Administration,* revised December 16, 2012, www.tsa.gov/about-tsa/program-history.

107. "Budget in Brief Fiscal Year 2014, Homeland Security" (Washington, D.C.: Department of Homeland Security, 2014), p. 131.

108. Ibid., pp. 132–133.

109. Stephen M. Lord, "Airport Security: TSA Should Limit Future Funding for Behavioral Detection Activities" (General Accountability Office, Washington, D.C.: November 14, 2013), p. 1.

110. Michael W. Chapman, "TSA Spent $900 Million on Behavior Detection Officers Who Detected 0 Terrorists." *CNSN News,* November 25, 2013, p. 1, www.cnsn.com/news/article/michael-w-chapman/tsa-spent-900-million-behavior-detection-officers-who-detected-0.

111. Lord, "Airport Security," p. 1.

112. "Transportation Security, TSA Could Strengthen Monitoring of Allegations of Employee Misconduct" (Washington, D.C.: General Accountability Office, July 2013), p. 12.

113. "United States Secret Service, Criminal Investigations," p. 1, undated, but with a 2014 copyright, www.secretservice.gov/criminal.shtml.

114. Loc. cit.

115. The information in this paragraph is taken from "Budget in Brief Fiscal Year 2014, Homeland Security," p. 151.

116. Ibid., pp. 150 and 152.

117. "United States Secret Service, Criminal Investigations," p. 1.

118. "Budget in Brief Fiscal Year 2014, Homeland Security," p. 153.

119. Loc. cit.

120. Loc. cit.

121. Ibid., p. 152.

122. "ICE Overview," undated, p. 1, http://www.ice.gov/about/overview.

123. "Budget in Brief Fiscal Year 2014, Homeland Security," p. 121.

124. Loc. cit.

125. Loc. cit. and "Written Testimony of ICE Deputy Director Daniel Ragsdale for a House Committee on Appropriations Subcommittee on Homeland Security on ICE's FY 2015 Budget Request," March 13, 2014, p. 1, www.dhs.gov/news/2014/03/13/written-testimony-ice-house-appropriations-subcommittee-homeland-security-hearing.

126. "Budget in Brief Fiscal Year 2014, Homeland Security," p. 121.

127. Loc. cit.

128. Loc. cit.

129. Ibid., p. 123.

130. "Law Enforcement Support Center" (Washington, D.C.: Immigration and Customs Enforcement, undated), p. 1, www.ice.gov/lesc.

131. Loc. cit.

132. Alberto Cuadra, Laris Karkis, and Bill Webster, "The Killing of Special Agent Jaime Zapata," *The Washington Post,* February 15, 2012, www.washingtonpost.com/world/the-killing-of-special-agent-jaime-zapata/2012/02/14/glqalu8qfr_graphic.html.

133. Except as otherwise footnoted, the information in this paragraph is paraphrased from "Enforcement and Removal Operations" (Washington, D.C.: Immigration and Customs Enforcement, undated), p. 1, www.ice.gov/about/offices/enforcement-removal-operations.

134. "FY 2013 ICE Immigration Removals" (Washington, D.C.: Immigration and Customs Enforcement, undated), pp. 1 and 4. Although undated, FY 13 ended on June 30, 2013, so the publication date of this document is almost certainly within a few months after that.

135. "Budget in Brief Fiscal Year 2014, Homeland Security," p. 183.

136. Loc. cit.

137. "What is E-Verify?" U.S. Citizenship and Immigration Services, undated, www.uscis.gov/e-verify/what-e-verify.

138. "Budget in Brief Fiscal Year 2014, Homeland Security," p. 183.

139. Anita U. Hattiangadi et al., "Non-Citizens in Todays Military Research Brief," *CNA*, www.cna.org/centers/marine-corps/selectedc-studies/non-citizens-brief.

140. Ibid., pp. 1 and 5.

141. "Budget in Brief Fiscal Year 2014, Homeland Security," p. 183.

142. Ibid., p. 184.

143. Ibid., p. 183.

144. "Minnesota Homeland Security and Emergency Management FY 2013 Annual Report", www.dps.mn.gov/divisions/hsem/about/documents/2013-hsem-annual-report.pdf.

145. James E. Steiner, "Needed: State Level Integrated Intelligence Enterprises," *Studies in Intelligence*, Vol. 53, No. 3, September 2009, pp. 1–2.

146. "Homeland Security/Law Enforcement: Homeland Security Grants" (Washington, D.C.: Government Accountability Office, undated), p. 1. The data is for fiscal years 2002–2011, www.gao.gov/modules/ereport/handler.php?1=1&path=/ereport/G...er/homeland_security-law_enforcement/17._homeland_security_grants.

147. There has been some debate about whether DHS grants have been allocated to the states on the basis of risk/need or "pork barrel politics." On this subject see Holly Goerdel, "Managing Homeland Security in American States: Politics Versus Risk in State Allocations of Federal Security Grants," Conference Paper, 2009 Annual Meeting of the Midwestern Political Science Association, 2009, Toronto, Canada.

148. Loc. cit.

America's Vulnerability to Terrorism

CHAPTER

12

Learning Objectives

After completing this chapter, you should be able to:

1. Define critical infrastructure in the United States and provide a brief description of how this infrastructure impacts daily life.

2. Explain the all-hazards model in planning for critical infrastructure protection.

3. Describe the role of the Federal Bureau of Investigation (FBI) relating to terrorism.

4. Describe the role of the Federal Emergency Management Agency (FEMA) relating to terrorism.

5. Discuss the National Infrastructure Protection Plan (NIPP) and list the critical infrastructure sectors that make up the plan.

6. Describe why the Information Technology (IT) Sector is so important to secure in the United States and discuss some of the current threats to this sector.

The Three Mile Island nuclear generating station is in Middletown, Pennsylvania. A government study assigns a low probability as to the success of a 9/11-style attack using airplanes to damage the reactor core and causing radioactivity to be release. The study also assigned a low probability that such an attack could cause the release of sufficient radioactivity to harm the public's safety and health.

(© Laurence Kesterson/KRT/Newscom)

Introduction

Awake to the startling sounds of the newest Bruno Mars song as you roll over and hit the "snooze" button. You desperately try to get a few more winks of sleep, but the new song reminds you of last night's gathering at the local pub. As you embrace yet another day, the shrill siren of an ambulance whizzes by on the busy street below your apartment. You stumble from the bed to turn on the lights and move toward the bathroom, a hot shower and a little dental hygiene to start the new day. Hmmm, that throat is still a little sore and a cough lingers, probably need to get that checked out at the health clinic today. A bowl of cereal, some fruit …. and the sound of a familiar beep… a text message from the bank indicating that funds are getting low. Classes start in an hour, just enough time to swing by the ATM and remedy that situation. On the way out the door, send a quick email to mom and wish her a happy birthday. Hop in the car and hope the traffic isn't too bad before your morning meeting with fellow students at the chemistry lab. It's just another day like any other.

This may be a typical day across America for many students. It also is an excellent example of critical infrastructure at work, and the benign attitude that everyday people have regarding the services they receive on a daily basis. Let's take another perspective. Each of the daily activities mentioned above requires critical infrastructure within the country that is generally taken for granted by most people. **Critical infrastructure** is defined as those systems and assets, whether physical or virtual, so vital to the United States that the incapacity or destruction of such systems and assets would have a debilitating impact on national security, national economic security, national public health or safety, or any combination of these matters.[1] Each of the above daily activities requires a properly functioning critical infrastructure at federal as well as local levels. This everyday scenario touches several critical infrastructure sectors. The song on the radio had to travel over the airwaves using equipment from the Communications Sector, the electricity for the lights was carried by transmission lines from the Energy Sector, and the power was most likely generated by the Nuclear Sector or the Dams Sector. The shower water came and went as part of the Water and Wastewater Systems Sector. The soap and shampoo used in the shower contained ingredients created by the Chemical Sector. The original concert where Bruno Mars performed his number one hit was recorded at a New York stadium protected by the Commercial Facilities Sector. And the ambulance racing down the street heading for a nearby health clinic where you need to get your throat and cough "checked out" are all part of the Healthcare and Public Health Sector. Milk, cereal, and fruit fall into the Food and Agriculture Sector and that low bank account balance is tightly controlled by the Banking and Finance Sector. The car you drove to school was built by the Critical Manufacturing Sector, the fuel used was provided by the Energy Sector, your auto insurance was again, part of the Banking and Finance Sector as well as the ATM you stopped by on your way to school. The freeways you crossed while travelling as well as the roads and bridges you crossed and the traffic lights you stopped at were all part of the Transportation Sector. And, of course, that email you sent to mom as well as all of the other sectors used within this short period of time all relied on the Information Technology Sector.

The loss or disruption of all or part of one of these critical infrastructure sectors would have a devastating impact on this country. The simple fact of the matter is that as our society becomes more advanced and complex, the more we rely on critical infrastructure to support our lifestyle and existence. The simple activities we undertake each day could be interrupted, potentially for an extended period of time, wreaking havoc on our nation. Each critical infrastructure sector relies on the others, just like the example described earlier. A failure in one sector could lead to a cascading failure in others, creating an even bigger problem. Witness the recent impact of winter storms on the nation as houses lost power, roads and freeways were impassable due to ice, airlines were grounded, Internet providers failed, and, essentially, the nation's economic engine ground to a crawl as people could simply not get to work!

Critical infrastructure
Those systems and assets, whether physical or virtual, so vital to the United States that the incapacity or destruction of such systems and assets would have a debilitating impact on national security.

Information Link
For more information on critical infrastructure, see the definition presented by the U.S. Department of Homeland Security at www.dhs.gov/what-critical-infrastructure.

FIGURE 12–1
On 9/11, the role of police changed forever. In addition to keeping our citizenry safe from crime and maintaining order, police officers must now defend and secure infrastructure resources in the homeland. Members of the Orange County (California) Counter Terrorism Team protect the transportation infrastructure by using a canine to search for bombs.

(© Jebb Harris/Zuma Press/Newscom)

The 9/11 terrorist attacks also highlighted the threat and vulnerability to critical infrastructure. Federal, state, and local government agencies have recognized this vulnerability and the impending threats posed by terrorist organizations, and have taken a number of steps to ensure that a catastrophe of this magnitude is reduced. These measures are known as critical infrastructure protection and were a major part of the USA PATRIOT Act, signed by then-President George W. Bush in 2001.[2]

The Impact of 9/11 and the USA Patriot Act

Clearly, the attacks on the World Trade Center and the Pentagon on 9/11and the ensuing passage of the USA PATRIOT Act in 2001 changed our country forever. The attacks set in motion the development of new roles for federal agencies as well as a national commitment to the prevention of terrorism. Indeed, the role of law enforcement changed dramatically from not only thwarting crime, but also preventing, deterring, and investigating potential acts of terrorism. Nowhere is the nation's commitment to preventing terrorism on the homeland more evident than in the *National Strategy for Counterterrorism* reaffirmed in 2011.[3] Although the focus of the document was on dismantling the al-Qaeda network, the far-reaching plan clearly articulates the United States' broad, sustained, and integrated plan to safeguard the homeland[4] (see Figure 12–1). Combined with the USA PATRIOT Act, these two documents not only defined the concept of critical infrastructure and the development of specific critical infrastructure plans, but also set forth specific roles and duties for federal agencies before and during a potential disaster, particularly those that may be caused by man-made or terrorist activities.

The All-Hazards Model

Catastrophe can occur as a result of a natural disaster (e.g., hurricane, flood, earthquake, or tornado) or from a man-made act such as those stemming from a terrorist bombing or intentional forest fire. The coordinated plans and efforts designed to protect critical infrastructure and/or coordinate and manage resources during an emergency are often similar. For instance, target hardening a building or dam assists in deterring a terrorist attack as well as strengthens the physical structure from potential natural disasters. Techniques for safeguarding the general population from disease and dangers stemming from a major earthquake may be similar to those that are undertaken after a significant bombing. Hence, the "all-hazards model" recognizes that there are aspects of planning and response that are common in many kinds of catastrophes and disasters regardless of causation. The activities are similar; however, they not identical. Actual disaster response by federal agencies to acts of terrorism is divided into two distinct responsibilities: crisis management and consequence management.

All-Hazards model
The concept that there are similar aspects to planning and responding to a catastrophe or emergency event cause by either natural or man-made origins.

The Role of the Federal Bureau of Investigation (FBI)

Crisis management is handled by law enforcement, principally the Federal Bureau of Investigation (FBI). This includes developing, coordinating, and managing a response to major terrorist events that threaten to harm the national security of the United States. The FBI is also the primary federal agency responsible for investigating crimes conducted by terrorist organizations, and includes investigating the crime (terrorism), evidence collection, scene security, and other law enforcement activities.

Working closely with a variety of federal, state, and local law enforcement partners, the FBI is the primary agency responsible for protecting the United States from terrorist

Crisis management
Developing, coordinating, and managing an effective response to a major emergency event.

attacks[5] (see Figure 12–2). In addition to the Joint Terrorism Task Forces discussed in Chapter 9, the FBI manages the nation's domestic effort to detect, investigate, and prevent terrorist strikes through a variety of major programs:

- *National Counterterrorism Center and the Public Internet Tip Line.* As discussed in Chapter 9, the FBI is a major partner in the nation's effort to thwart terrorism through the analysis and sharing of intelligence information.

- *Strategic Information and Operations Center (SIOC).* The SIOC is a state-of-the-art national fusion center located at the FBI Headquarters in Washington, D.C. It acts as a national-level clearinghouse to collect, process, and disseminate intelligence information about terrorist threats and incidents. It provides real-time information to the active JTTFs across the nation. The SIOC also serves as the primary national operations, coordination, and command center dedicated to assisting law enforcement personnel during a national or global crisis or major investigation.[6]

- *The Counterterrorism Fly Team.* The FBI maintains a small, highly trained cadre of terrorism first responders—including field agents, SWAT personnel, intelligence analysts, Middle East experts, bomb technicians, and HAZMAT personnel—readily available to respond to any terrorist incident worldwide.[7] Although their primary mission is to quickly respond to domestic emergencies, most of their deployments have been overseas during the last several years.

- *The Most Wanted Terrorist List.* Historically derived from the FBI's 10 Most Wanted Fugitives, the Most Wanted Terrorist List highlights the 10 most wanted terrorists. All individuals on the list have been indicted and/or are wanted on a terrorism-related crime stemming from an international or domestic terrorist event.[8] Usama bin Laden, as well as other al-Qaeda leadership members, have been or were members of this infamous group.

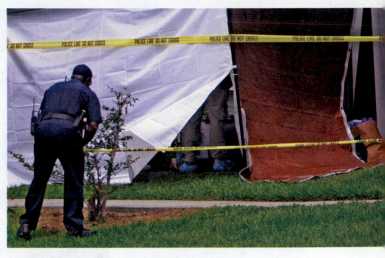

FIGURE 12–2
As part of the FBI's investigation following the Boston Marathon bombing in 2013, agents interviewed Ibragim Todashev in Orlando because he was believed to be associated with the brothers who were suspects in that crime. The interview suddenly became violent, and Todashev was shot and killed by the FBI. An Orlando officer surrounds the scene with yellow barrier tape. The blue evidence booties of a member of the FBI's Evidence Response Team are seen at the corner of the tent.
(© Brian Blanco/EPANewscom)

The Role of the Federal Emergency Management Agency (FEMA)

On the other hand, **consequence management** is managed by the Federal Emergency Management Agency (FEMA), and includes search and rescue operations, sheltering and caring for affected persons, debris removal, and mitigating damages *after* an event. **Mitigation** is an effort to reduce loss of life and property by lessening the impact of a terrorist attack or natural disaster. However, according to the Department of Homeland Security, it includes taking action *now*—before the incident—to reduce human and financial consequences later as well responding effectively after the event.[9] Although FEMA is the key federal agency for the emergency management of a terrorist attack or natural disaster site after the event (see Chapter 13), a myriad of other agencies have specific roles in responding to and recovering from a disaster. For instance, the coordination of local relief agencies, food banks, shelters, and the like fall within the FEMA management guideline, while specific responses to public health issues from open sewage lines, biological agents, or even radiation may be more appropriately handled by another agency such as the Center for Disease Control (CDC), the Environmental Protection Agency (EPA), or the Nuclear Regulatory Commission (NRC).

The Federal Emergency Management Agency (FEMA) was created in response to a series of domestic natural disasters in the 1960s and 1970s, and a number of international events in the 1980s.[10] In 1970, then-President Jimmy Carter signed into law Executive Order 12148, charging FEMA with handling "civil emergencies," which included acts of terrorism. In 1988, President Ronald Reagan assigned further responsibility to FEMA to protect "essential resources and facilities" to national security and national welfare at various

Consequence management
Developing, coordinating, and managing mitigation after an emergency event.

Mitigation
An effort to reduce loss of life and property by lessening the impact of a terrorist attack or natural disaster.

The National Infrastructure Protection Plan (NIPP) is an actual document produced by the U.S. Department of Homeland Security. The plan is reviewed and updated every year through a collaborative process involving private sector partners; local, state, and tribal governments; and federal agencies working together to identify weaknesses and continually strengthen those assets, systems, and networks that underpin American society. The plan can be purchased on Amazon for $9.95.

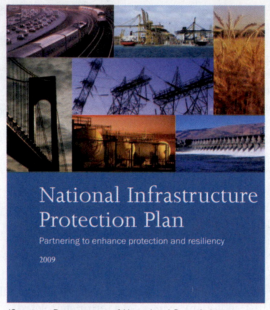

(Courtesy Department of Homeland Security)

federal, state, and local levels.[11] Today it is the responsibility of FEMA to protect these "essential resources and facilities" through a systematic plan of identifying, vulnerability assessment, and security preparedness.

The National Infrastructure Protection Plan (NIPP)

In 2003, then-President Bush signed Homeland Security Presidential Directive 7, defining a framework for a coordinated approach to identifying and protecting critical infrastructure in the United States.[12] Known as the **National Infrastructure Protection Plan (NIPP)**, the directive originally established 13 critical infrastructure sectors and added a number of key resources that were identified as potential targets from terrorist activities. This included adding agriculture as a critical sector, highlighting dams and nuclear facilities as potential targets, and identifying a number of private commercial facilities (e.g., sports stadiums, entertainment districts like downtown Las Vegas and Disney World, museums, and monuments). The directive also established reference to critical infrastructure and key resources as the acronym **CI/KRs**.

In February 2013, President Barack Obama further extended the NIPP by signing Presidential Policy Directive 21—The Critical Infrastructure and Resilience Directive.[13] This directive consolidated the key resources category into sectors of their own, and produced a total of 16 current critical infrastructure sectors:[14]

- Communications Sector
- Emergency Services Sectors
- Energy Sector
- Dams Sector
- Nuclear Sector

National Infrastructure Protection Plan (NIPP)

A formal directive that defines critical infrastructure within the United States and identifies 16 critical infrastructure sectors for protection against man-made (e.g., bombing, terrorist strike, information warfare) as well as natural (e.g., hurricane, flood, tornado, earthquake) disasters.

CI/KRs

Acronym in reference to Critical Infrastructure and Key Resource(s) identified within the National Infrastructure Protection Plan (NIPP).

- Water Sector
- Chemical Sector
- Commercial Facilities Sector
- Healthcare and Public Health Sector
- Food and Agriculture Sector
- Critical Manufacturing Sector
- Transportation Sector
- Government Facilities Sector
- Banking and Finance Sector
- Defense Industrial Base Sector
- Information Technology Sector

Each of these sectors has a designated federal agency (or list of related agencies) that serves as the Sector Specific Agency (SSA) and is charged with coordinating all federal, state, and local entities, both public and private, that ensures that each sector CI/KR is identified, secured, and resilient to a terrorist attack or natural disaster. For instance, the Environmental Protection Agency (EPA) is the SSA for the Chemical Sector. The sector is primarily composed of private chemical companies located throughout the United States, with storage facilities often near major water transportation routes and large urban centers. In addition, each state has an agency with similar duties and functions of the EPA. The National Infrastructure Protection Plan (NIPP) requires the EPA to develop a coordinated plan that identifies potential vulnerabilities within the sector and develop responses to various threat scenarios, coordinating public and private entities at all levels of government. The formalized plan for each of the 16 sectors is then annexed to the NIPP. This is a monumental task that takes considerable resources because the development of these plans is constantly ongoing … new entities are being built, state and local governmental units change, new threats emerge, and new vulnerabilities are discovered.

Communications Sector

Telecommunications was the first infrastructure to be identified as critical. During the Cuban Missile Crisis, President John F. Kennedy and Soviet Premier Nikita Khrushchev were unable to negotiate directly, and were forced to communicate through written letters. Fax, email, and secure telephones did not exist at the time. As a result, the National Communications System (NCS) was created in 1963 as a planning forum composed of six federal agencies.[15] In 1982, the National Security Telecommunications Advisory Committee (NSTAC), composed of the chief executives of the major telecommunications companies, was established by Executive Order 12382 to advise the president on critical infrastructure protection. The NSTAC was limited to 30 representatives and included companies such as AT&T Communications, General Electric Company, Edison-Bell Telephone Company, American Broadcasting Company-ABC, and the National Broadcasting Company-NBC. In 1984, then-President Ronald Reagan signed Executive Order 12472, which formally made the NCS responsible for the telecommunications infrastructure sector. Today, the NSTAC includes 23 member organizations that ensure national security and emergency preparedness telecommunications. The NCTAC represents companies from traditional telephone and broadcasting companies, but also those that are more active in the Internet, cellular telephone, computer, and satellite communication technologies as well, such as Symantec, Microsoft, Intel, Neustar, and Vonage Corporation.[16]

Today the Communications Sector consists of complex systems that incorporate multiple technologies and services, including wireline, wireless, satellite, cable, and broadcasting capabilities, and includes the distribution networks for the Internet and other critical information systems. This sector includes cable, commercial and public broadcasters, information service providers, satellite, undersea cable, telecommunications utility providers, service integrators, equipment vendors, wireless and wireline owners and operators, and the members' respective trade associations. Federal agencies primarily tasked with protecting

Quick Facts
The Massive Impact of Hurricane Katrina

Hurricane Katrina made landfall on the Gulf Coast (see Figure 12–3) and caused tremendous damage to all Critical Infrastructure Sectors, as wells as homes, docks, and other areas (see Figure 12–4). According to Paul McHale, then-Assistant Secretary of Defense, "the magnitude of the storm was such that the local communications system wasn't simply degraded; it was, at least for a period of time, destroyed." In the aftermath of Hurricane Katrina, an estimated 100 commercial radio stations were unable to broadcast, at least 2,000 cell phone towers were out of service, first responder communications were severely degraded, and 911 dispatch centers were damaged. Those 911 dispatch centers (Emergency Services Sector) that were able to remain online were quickly overwhelmed by the sheer volume of calls for assistance. Wireless communications were wiped out, as was the wired telephone system. Even the communications nodes with backup power supplies quickly failed without the ability to resupply fuel for generators in a timely manner, proving once again the impact on multiple sectors during an emergency event.[17]

FIGURE 12–3
In 2005, Hurricane Katrina's eye (the roughly round black area at the center of the radar screen) approaches Louisiana's coast.

(Courtesy National Oceanic and Atmospheric Administration)

the Communications Sector include the Department of Commerce, the Federal Communications Commission, and Department of Justice. These agencies have established information-sharing relationships with state and local jurisdictions and conducted vulnerability assessments of their communications networks. State and local agencies are also involved in Communications Sector protection through state public utility commissions (PUCs), state and local emergency operation centers, and emergency response activities, including first responders and 911 emergency services centers.[18] Unfortunately, even with necessary planning and preparation, communication can be disrupted by violent natural disasters.

Emergency Services Sector

The Emergency Services Sector is the first line of defense in the prevention and mitigation of risk from terrorist attacks, man-made incidents, and natural disasters. This sector includes state and local first responders, composed of law enforcement, fire and emergency services, emergency management agencies, emergency medical services, and public works and utility companies. The Emergency Services Sector represents the primary emergency management agencies and includes a variety of specialized teams, such as Hazardous Materials (HAZMAT), Search and Rescue (SAR), Explosive Ordnance Disposal (EOD), Special Weapons and Tactics and Tactical

FIGURE 12–4
In Venice, Louisiana, Hurricane Katrina littered a beach with boats and other debris.

(Courtesy National Oceanic and Atmospheric Administration NOAA)

Quick Facts
Blackout

In July 1977, New York City suffered the longest blackout in history when a simple lightning strike took out two major transmission lines. New York City was without power for nearly two days. Looting, vandalism, and rioting were widespread, in contrast to shorter blackouts suffered in New York in 2003 and 2011.

Operations (SWAT), helicopter and other aviation capabilities, and 911 dispatch centers.[19] Chapter 13 discusses the emergency management function of many of these special units. Unfortunately, as a result of their key role in responding to emergency incidents, terrorists have often targeted first responders by setting secondary explosive devices. For instance, after a bombing, active shooting event, or other criminal act is conducted, **secondary bombs** are hidden and set to detonate when the first responders arrive. The Olympic Park bombing that was perpetrated by Eric Robert Rudolph (July 27, 1996) was the first example of the use of secondary explosive devices in the United States. Rudolph, an active member of the "Army of God," a right-wing, Christian Identity movement, set secondary explosive devises aimed at killing or maiming emergency personnel first arriving at the scene.[20] The phenomenon has also occurred outside the United States in Israel and other countries plagued by terrorist bombings.

Secondary bombs
Hidden bombs often set by terrorists targeting first responders to an emergency event.

Energy Sector

The Energy Sector is divided into three subsectors: Electricity, Petroleum, and Natural Gas. According to the U.S. Department of Homeland Security, the electrical subsector is huge and vast, containing more than 6,413 power plants producing over 1,075 gigawatts of installed generation per day. This electricity is carried by over 200,000 miles of high-voltage transmission lines and delivered to nearly 200 million customers over an innumerable amount of above and underground lower voltage lines.[21] The electrical subsector is monstrously large and poses a significant vulnerability to the homeland. The system is interconnected and managed by several **electrical power grids**. Each grid serves a specific region of the United States with a secondary grid responsible as a primary or redundant backup. When electric power is interrupted or stopped to a specific area, a **blackout** occurs, and the redundant source immediately transmits power to that area; however, that transmission is often over very long distance lines. The excessive demand on the redundant grid can be enormous, resulting in a lower transmission to both regional areas that causes a **brownout**, or a drop in voltage to a specific power grid limiting electrical use and causing lights to glow much dimmer due to the sag in power. The reduction may last for minutes or days, dependent upon restoration of full power to the affected area. Blackouts and brownouts can be the result of a natural disaster, a terrorist attack, or even simple overuse as observed during extreme temperature dips and spikes. New York City has experienced brownouts due to summer heat waves for the past three years, and more are expected as electrical demand for air conditioners often exceeds supply.

Electrical power grid
A system of interconnected electrical processes serving regional areas within the United States.

Blackout
The loss of electrical power in a specific area.

Brownout
A drop in electrical voltage to a specific area.

The petroleum subsector of the Energy Sector includes the entire lifecycle of oil from exploration and discovery, extraction from the ground, storage and transportation, to refinement and transmission. It also includes the transmission lines, facilities, and docks used to import foreign crude oil to the country. Today there are more than 525,000 crude oil-producing wells, 30,000 miles of gathering pipeline, and over 51,000 miles of crude oil transmission pipelines in the United States. In addition, there are 150 refineries in operation, 116,000 miles of product pipeline, and 1,400 petroleum terminals.[22] Natural gas is also part of the Energy Sector and is produced from more than nearly 500,000 gas wells and gathered in over 20,000 miles of pipeline. There are more than 500 gas-processing plants and about 320,000 miles of natural gas pipeline throughout the country. Natural gas is stored in over 400 underground storage fields and nearly 110 liquid natural gas (LNG) facilities.[23] Any threat to the Energy Sector not only impacts the physical security of the United States, but also impacts the price of oil on the worldwide market. Threats to

Box 12-1
Asymetrical Attacks on the Energy Sector

In 2004, Usama bin Laden stated in an audio recording that "oil prices should be at least $100 a barrel," and called upon radical Islamic groups worldwide to attack oil facilities and pipelines. This was the first documented statement hinting at al-Qaeda's strategy to negatively impact Western economies by disrupting oil supplies and transmission routes. As a result of this threat alone, the price of a barrel of oil skyrocketed by 5% the next day. However, bin Laden's strategy was not implemented until spring 2006 when the Abqaiq Oil Refinery in Saudi Arabia was attacked by a suicide truck bomber. The Abqaiq field is one of the largest oil-producing areas in the world and has over 17 billion barrels of oil reserves. In comparison, the entire country of Mexico has only 14.8 billion barrels of reserve; Canada has an estimated 16.8 billion barrels of reserve. Although the attack was averted, the threat was enough to shock the world's oil prices. In just one day, the price of oil

increased $3.00, nearly 7 percent per barrel in one day. Just a few short months later in 2007, in an operation known as *Operation Bin Laden Conquest*, an Islamic rebel group based in Nigeria and known as MEND attacked an oil port and pipeline in that nation. These were simultaneous attacks again, aimed at impacting the price of oil on the world economic stage. Bin Laden's statements following these attacks made it clear that al-Qaeda was carrying out attacks against the Western "crusaders and Jews to stop their plundering of Muslim wealth."[24]

How reliant is the American economy on foreign oil? In 2012, 40 percent of the petroleum consumed by the United States was imported from foreign counties. How vulnerable is the Energy Sector to terrorism, both domestically and internationally?

---

this sector can also occur outside the United States in OPEC (Organization of Petroleum Exporting Countries), countries such as Saudi Arabia, Iraq, Venezuela, and Nigeria.

Dams Sector

Levees and dams
A dyke, embankment, or wall specifically constructed to regulate water.

Dams in the United States are included in the National Inventory of Dams (NID), maintained by the United States Army Corps of Engineers. Historically, **levees and dams** in the United States were built to protect agricultural operations. Many of these structures are old and were built at a time when good engineering practices were not mandatory. Congress enacted Flood Control Acts in 1928 and 1936 after flooding on the Mississippi and Ohio Rivers. Unlike the National Inventory of Dams, there is not a comprehensive list of levees in the United States, although up to 100,000 miles of levees are

> **Information Link**
> For more information on dams in the United States, refer to the website by the U.S. Department of the Interior, Bureau of Reclamation at www.usbr.gov/.

estimated. Hurricanes Katrina and Rita, and the resulting flooding throughout the Gulf Coast (Louisiana, Mississippi, Texas, Alabama and Florida) stemming from the failure of decaying levees and damns, prompted the National Levee Safety Act of 2007, which required significant remediation of existing levees and damns throughout the United States.[25]

The Department of Homeland Security, Office of Infrastructure Protection is the Sector Specific Agency responsible for the Dams Sector. Other DHS agencies involved in the Dam Sector include the Federal Emergency Management Agency, U.S. Coast Guard, U.S. Army Corps of Engineers, and the Environmental Protection Agency. Like most critical infrastructure, the majority of dams are privately owned. Private-sector organizations, including the Association of State Dam Safety Officials (ASDSO) and the National Mining Association, among others, are also important partners in securing the Dams Sector.[26] The Dams Sector is also regulated by state, tribal, and territorial governments. Each state has a dam safety regulatory program responsible for the more

FIGURE 12-5
Hoover Dam on the Lower Colorado River near Las Vegas, Nevada, is one of the largest concrete structures built in North America. It also is one of the largest electric power-generating facilities in the United States. Being in a remote area makes the dam more vulnerable to terrorist attack.

(Courtesy U.S, Department of the Interior, Bureau of Reclamation)

that 70,000 dams across the United States. Although the Dams Sector is most vulnerable to natural disasters (hurricanes, tornados, earthquakes), there are an increasing number of terrorist threats made against such structures as well (see Figure 12–5).

Nuclear Sector

Nuclear power provides approximately 20 percent of the electricity in the United States. This electricity is produced by 104 commercial nuclear reactors located at 65 nuclear power plants. The Nuclear Sector incorporates a variety of related assets aside from

Quick Facts
Terrorists Are Not the Only Threat to the Dams Sector

In 2010, the Los Zetas Drug Cartel in Mexico threatened to blow up the 5-mile-long Falcon Lake Dam on the Rio Grande River (near Laredo, Texas), causing significant danger to the more than 4 million people that lived downriver from the dam; an area claimed as "turf" by the rival Gulf Cartel. The cartel had stolen a significant amount of explosives in the past and was clearly capable of carrying out such a threat. Combined with known intelligence that hackers had illegally accessed the *National Inventory of Dams* escalated the threat; revealing that terrorist organizations are not the only threat to critical infrastructure. Fortunately, the plot never came to pass.[27]

the power plants, including non-power nuclear reactors used for research, testing, and training; manufacturers of nuclear reactors or components; radioactive materials used primarily in medical, industrial, and academic settings; nuclear fuel cycle facilities; decommissioned nuclear power reactors; and the transportation, storage, and disposal of nuclear and radioactive waste.[28]

Water Sector

Drinking water and wastewater utilities are included in the Water Sector. Approximately 84 percent of the U.S. population is supplied by 160,000 public drinking water systems and there are more than 16,000 public wastewater treatment systems. More than three-quarters of the country's population has their sewerage treated by these wastewater treatment systems.[29] Bioterrorism or chemical attacks using relatively small quantities of toxic chemicals or biological agents could cause massive contamination, threatening the public health of millions of people in the United States.[30]

Chemical Sector

The Chemical Sector is a major portion of the economy of the United States. There are several hundred thousand facilities that use, store, manufacture, transport, or deliver chemicals throughout the country. The Chemical Sector is a vast industry that employees over a million people which generates nearly $700 billion in revenue, and can be divided into five main segments, based on the end product produced: basic chemicals, specialty chemicals, agricultural chemicals, pharmaceuticals, and consumer products. Like other sectors, the majority of the Chemical Sector is privately owned and includes several functional areas such as manufacturing plants, transport systems, warehouses and storage facilities, and end users.[31]

> **Information Link**
> For more information about the U.S. Department of Homeland Security, Office of Infrastructure Protection, see the website at www.dhs.gov/office-infrastructure-protection.

By its very nature, the Chemical Sector evokes environmental regulation and concern, hence, the primary agency for this sector is the Environmental Protection Agency. The EPA maintains a well-trained and well-equipped **Hazardous Materials (HAZMAT)** team dedicated as a first response to major incidents involving the Chemical Sector (see Chapter 13 on Emergency Management). Individual states, tribal governments, and territories also have occupational safety and health units that may be involved in responding to threats and incidents involving the Chemical Sector.

Hazardous Materials (HAZMAT)
Substances (solid, liquid, or gas) that are dangerous to people, other living organisms, or the environment.

Commercial Facilities Sector

The Commercial Facilities Sector includes large retail centers, hotels, casinos, theme parks, motion picture production studios, office and apartment buildings, convention centers, and sports stadiums. It also includes other sites where large numbers of people congregate to pursue business activities, conduct personal commercial transactions, or enjoy recreational pastimes.[32]

There are eight subsectors in this sector. The Entertainment and Media Subsector includes television and movie media production facilities, print media companies, and broadcast companies. The Gaming Facilities Subsector includes casinos and their accompanying hotels, conference centers, arenas, and shopping centers. The Lodging Subsector consists of non-gaming resorts, hotels and motels, hotel-based conference centers, and bed-and-breakfast establishments. The Outdoor Events Subsector includes amusement

Box 12–2
The First World Trade Center Terrorist Attack in 1993: Bomb-Making Material Came from Local Chemical Plant

Nidal Ayyad, a naturalized Palestinian, was a distinguished student at Rutgers University who studied chemical engineering and eventually gained a good job at a nearby Morristown, New Jersey, chemical plant. He was well-mannered, quiet, married, and expecting his first child when he first heard a sermon by the radical Islamic cleric, Sheik Omar Abdul Rahman, at his local mosque. Rahman was fighting extradition to Egypt, where he was linked to the political assassination of Anwar Sadat and a variety of terrorist attacks. Rahman expressed rage toward the United States and called on all Muslims to help destroy the American economy. Ayyad became a follower and over the course of his employment stole the chemicals necessary to make the vehicle bomb that was detonated in the first attack of the World Trade Center in 1993. The attack was devastating, causing widespread injury, loss of life, and millions of dollars in damage. It was the worst terrorist attack on American soil to that date. During his trial, information was released that indicated another plan—to use cyanide in combination with the explosives used at the World Trade Center or release massive quantities of cyanide in the ventilation systems of office buildings throughout New York City and Washington, D.C. The cyanide was to be stolen from Ayyad's workplace. The Chemical Sector employs over a million people and the potential threat posed by such workers crosses many critical infrastructure sectors.[33]

▲ This massive crater under the World Trade Center is part of the damage caused by the first attack.

(© Mike Segar/Reuters/Corbis)

How would you secure the Chemical Sector in the United States? How would you go about securing private corporations that conduct open commerce of explosives and other dangerous chemicals as part of their business venture?

Quick Facts
The Commercial Facilities Sector

The Commercial Facilities Sector is a huge part of the U.S. economy. In 2012, the retail industry alone accounted for $2.5 trillion in annual GDP, included over 3.6 million establishments, and employed more that 42 million people.[34]

parks, fairs, exhibitions, parks, and other outdoor venues. The Public Assembly Subsector encompasses convention centers, auditoriums, stadiums, arenas, movie theaters, cultural properties, and other assets where large numbers of people congregate. The Real Estate Subsector includes office buildings and office parks, apartment buildings, multi-family towers and condominiums, self-storage facilities, and property management companies. The Retail Subsector consists of enclosed malls, shopping centers, strip malls, and freestanding retail establishments. The Sports Leagues Subsector represents the major sports leagues and federations and the ESPN sports broadcasting company[35] (see Figure 12–6).

Healthcare and Public Health Sector

Seventeen percent of the U.S. economy is produced by the Healthcare and Public Health Sector, and like many of the other sectors discussed, most of it is privately owned and operated. It consists of hospitals, clinics, and medical research centers located throughout the United States.[36] Aside from the sheer size and economic importance of the sector, it also has a significant role in response, mitigation, and recovery during natural disasters or terrorist events. For instance, during the **anthrax** attack in 2001, following 9/11, five people died and 17 others were sickened. Anthrax is a spore-forming bacterium that is naturally occurring in the United States. Letters containing anthrax spores were mailed to media outlets, news commentators, and government officials. The anthrax contained in these letters was "weaponized," or genetically altered to make it much more deadly. The Healthcare and Public Health Sector quickly responded with plans to distribute antibiotics to a major portion of the population of the United States in the event of a large scale anthrax attack. In 2013, a similar biological attack occurred when letters containing **ricin** were sent to President Obama

Anthrax
Spore-forming bacterium that is often "weaponized" or genetically altered to be more deadly.

Ricin
An easily made and highly toxic poison refined from castor beans.

and members of Congress. Ricin is an easily made and very potent toxin that is refined from castor beans. It was popularized in the hit TV show *Breaking Bad*, as Mr. White conjured up the white powder to take care of troublesome business associates. In reality, a lethal dose of ricin for humans is very small, about the size of a grain of salt either injected or inhaled. Although no one was injured during these mail attacks, the Healthcare and Public Health Sector was again available with mobile treatment facilities to assist potential victims from a large scale attack.[37] Unfortunately, there is no known antidote for ricin.

Food and Agriculture Sector

The Food and Agriculture Sector includes the farming, breeding, production, processing, and delivery systems associated with agricultural and livestock food in the United States. The Sector includes various industry and trade associations, including the American Farm Bureau Federation, National Cattlemen's Beef Association, National Milk Producers Federation, and the National Restaurant Association, among others. The Sector accounts for roughly one-fifth of the economic engine of the United States, with about one-fifth of this production exported to foreign countries. Crop production in the United States alone accounts for nearly $200 billion of **gross domestic product (GDP)**.[38]

Critical Manufacturing Sector

The Critical Manufacturing Sector is another major part of the economic engine of the United States. This sector provides 13 percent of the gross domestic product (GDP) of the United States and employs an estimated 11.7 million people.[39] Primary metal manufacturing, machinery manufacturing, electrical equipment manufacturing (which provides the components that "turn the lights on"), transportation equipment manufacturing, and railroad rolling stock manufacturing are considered major subsectors of the Critical Manufacturing Sector. Any direct attack or disruption of certain elements of the manufacturing industry could easily disrupt essential functions at the national level and across multiple critical infrastructure sectors.[40] A terrorist attack in any of these subsectors with the Critical Manufacturing Sector could have a cascading effect that would limit the ability to move goods, restore electricity, and keep America working.

Transportation Sector

People and goods move across the country as part of the Transportation Sector. There are six subsectors of the Transportation Sector: Aviation, Highway, Maritime, Mass Transit, Pipeline Transmission, and Rail. The transportation of people and goods is an essential service to maintain the economic efficiency of the country. Most of the raw materials and manufactured products in the United States are transported over the 4 million miles of freeways and highways that interconnect almost every community in the country. The other primary mode of transporting goods is accomplished by the nearly 1.3 million freight cars that run over nearly 150,000 miles of track.[41] Most of the track is highly vulnerable to terrorist activity. Derailment (either intentionally or by accident) of tank cars commonly transporting chemicals could cause significant harm to populated areas. For instance, in Willard, Ohio, in 2013, the accidental derailment of a tank car carrying styrene monomer, a highly flammable and toxic substance, resulted in over 400 residents being evacuated. Although no deaths or serious injuries occurred, the incident highlighted the vulnerability of dangerous chemicals commonly being transported by both rail and river barges across America every day.

However, when one talks about the Transportation Sector and terrorism, it is the aviation subsector that immediately comes to mind. The skyjacking of five commercial flights and the subsequent use of those fully loaded aircraft as weapons against the World Trade

FIGURE 12–6
The 2014 Super Bowl was held at MetLife Stadium in New Jersey's Meadowlands. Nearly 80,000 people attended the game. Protecting sports venues where large numbers of people congregate is a major part of securing America's Homeland.
(Courtesy Kevin P. Coughlin/Flying Dog Photos/Newscom)

Gross domestic product (GDP)
The total value of goods and services produced by a nation during one year.

Box 12–3
The 2013 Boston Marathon Bombing

On April 15, 2013, two bombs exploded during the Boston Marathon, killing three people and wounding another 250 spectators and runners. The bombs were crudely constructed using ordinary pressure cookers as an improvised explosive device (IED) stuffed with explosive material (black powder) and scrap metal (e.g., BBs, nuts, and bolts). A blasting cap was then placed through the cooker cover and attached to a simple timing device or cell phone.

Within two hours after the bombing, a police officer for Massachusetts Institute of Technology (MIT) was killed while confronting two potential suspects, and an ensuing gun battle with police in Watertown, Massachusetts, ensued. On suspect, 27 year old Tamerlan Tsarnaev was shot and killed during the incident. The other suspect (Tamerlan's brother), 20-year-old Dzhokhar Tsarnaev, was arrested after he was found hiding in a boat parked in the backyard of a Watertown resident later that same night. During the initial investigation, Dzhokhar alleged that Tamerlan was the mastermind of the entire bombing and that they had learned how to build the bombs from online instructions hosted by an al-Qaeda affiliate in Yemen. Both Tsarnaev brothers were born in remote areas of the former Soviet Union, near Chechnya, and grew up in Kyrgyzstan. Both were Muslims who became increasingly radicalized by watching Anwar al-Awlaki lectures and other jihadist speakers on the Internet. Dzhokhar Tsarnaev is currently awaiting trial on 30 felony counts including using and conspiring to use a weapon of mass destruction resulting in death.

How vulnerable are we to such attacks? How can the safety and security of players (runners) be improved while still maintaining access for spectators and media? What would you do to improve the security at such events?

A pressure cooker bomb

Investigators say the bombs detonated at the Boston Marathon were made using a pressure cooker; how a common kitchen utensil becomes deadly:

How a pressure cooker works

Sealing lid | Pressure valve

Steam

Food

Locking handle

- Cooker uses pressure and steam to cook food faster at a higher temperature
- Air-tight lid keeps steam in pot
- Pressure builds in pot allowing temperature to rise above boiling point of **212 F (100 C)**
- Pressure pushes hot steam into food

Building a bomb
- TNT or other explosives put in 6.3- qt. (6-liter) pressure cooker along with metal shards, nails ball bearings to inflict maximum injury

- Blasting cap attached to top of Cooker

- Can be detonated with digital watch, cell phone, garage door opener

Heat from explosion causes fire

1 When primary charge explodes, gases heat up, expand rapidly under pressure

2 Expansion creates shock waves travelling outward

3 Blast fragments cooker, sends pieces of shrapnel outward at high speeds

Why bombs like this can maim
- Police say explosives used in Boston traveled under 3,300 feet per second (1,005 meters per second), but fast enough to propel shrapnel a long distance

- Shrapnel, debris can cause penetrating wounds, blunt injury

- Force of blast can knock people down, throw them in the air, break bones, amputate limbs, cause brain trauma

Earlier uses
- Pressure cooker bombs used in India, Afghanistan, Pakistan, Nepal and 2010 Times Square bombing attempt

---

Skyjacking

The diversion of a commercial airline flight away from its scheduled flight plan, usually by violence or threat of violence against passengers and/or crew.

Center and the Pentagon emphasizes the impact of terrorism on both the Transportation and Government Facilities Sector. **Skyjacking** is the diversion of a commercial airline flight away from its scheduled flight plan, usually involving violence or the threat of violence against the passengers and/or crew of the aircraft. The events of 9/11 greatly impacted world air travel—from pre-flight records checks to submission of individual persons for physical screening and pat downs, to the target hardening of flight cockpits—air passengers are ever minded of the potential for terrorism. Anyone who has travelled by air in the last decade has certainly been impacted by these changes.

Government Facilities Sector

A wide variety of buildings and structures are owned by federal, state, local, tribal, and territorial governments. For instance, there are nearly 40,000 post offices alone, with a myriad of federal and state buildings, and monuments. Securing these facilities is a huge challenge. Federal facilities alone cover more than 3 billion square feet and there are another 90,000 municipal governments that maintain their own facilities.[43] Individual government facilities are attractive and strategically important targets for terrorists due to their symbolic value. In 1995, the Alfred P. Murrah Federal Building in Oklahoma City was targeted by two home-grown terrorists (Timothy McVeigh and Terry Nichols). The suspects used a Ryder rental truck loaded with approximately 7,000 pounds of explosives and detonated it in front of the building. The attack killed 168 people; many were the children of federal workers attending day care in the building. The General Services Administration provides physical security for most federal facilities, which has been significantly upgraded since the attack on the Murrah Building.

Banking and Finance Sector

The U.S. Department of Treasury is the Sector Specific Agency for the Banking and Finance Sector. Federal financial regulators, such as the Board of Governors of the Federal Reserve System (FRB), Federal Deposit Insurance Corporation (FDIC), Federal Housing Finance Agency (FHFA), and Securities and Exchange Commission (SEC) are also heavily involved in this sector. Exchanges, such as the Chicago Mercantile Exchange (CME) and the New York Stock Exchange (NYSE) also play an important role in this sector.

The Banking and Finance Sector is regulated (and categorized) by the various products provided by the sector. These include deposit and payment systems, credit and liquidity products, investment products, and risk transfer documents such as insurance and annuity products. The Banking and Finance Sector accounts for all monetary and fiscal assets of both the government and private enterprise within the country. There are more than 18,800 federally insured depository institutions, thousands of investment product providers, including 18,440 broker-dealers, investment advisers, and investment companies, and millions of risk transfer documents stemming from nearly 10,000 domestic insurers in the United States.[44] It is, by far, the most "valuable" of all sectors within the United States.

Defense Industrial Base Sector

The Department of Defense is the Sector Specific Agency for the Defense Industrial Base Sector. The sector consists of the various public- and private-sector industrial complexes that support military operations directly, conduct research and development, including the design, production, delivery, and maintenance of military weapons systems, subsystems, and components or parts for the United States military.[45] The private component of this sector is huge and includes hundreds of thousands of domestic and foreign companies, including their manufacturing supply chains.

Information Technology (IT) Sector

As previously mentioned, each of the critical infrastructure sectors are interconnected and rely on one another for functionality, effectiveness, and efficiency. Nowhere is this interdependence more evident than within the Information Technology (IT) Sector. Indeed, all

Quick Facts
Russian Hacking Data Breach Case Is Largest in History

In July 2013, federal prosecutors brought charges against four Russian nationals and one Ukrainian suspect charged with running an organization that hacked the computer networks of more than a dozen corporations, stealing and selling at least 160 million credit and debit card numbers. The scheme had run since 2005 and included, among others, some of the largest credit card corporations, including VISA, Heartland Payment Systems, and J.C. Penney.

A separate case involving the NASDAQ stock exchange was also filed against one of the suspect. This "hack" represented the cutting edge of financial fraud and highlights the broader threat that cybercrime poses to a financial system that is almost entirely reliant on networked communications and systems. **Hacking** is the illegal intrusion into a secure data or computer system. The losses from this case alone are staggering, and run in the billions of dollars.[46]

Box 12–4
Foreign Cyber Threats: Information Warfare as a Threat to Critical U.S. Infrastructure

In early 2013, one of the most significant and controversial security reports regarding cyber threats to U.S. infrastructure emerged from Mandiant, a computer security consulting corporation. The report documented thousands of cyber-attacks aimed primarily against public and corporate entities within the United States since 2006 from China, and identified a group known as Advanced Persistent Threat One (APT1) as the primary culprit. APT1 is a single organization of individual operators working within China that have conducted one of the most aggressive and sophisticated cyber espionage campaigns ever uncovered. The sheer amount of activity along with the discovery of various sophisticated tools and tactics used by APT1 led Mandiant to conclude that APT1 is likely a Chinese government-sponsored group with direct ties to the People's Liberation Army (PLA), Unit 61398. Both groups have similar missions, capabilities, and resources and are located in precisely the same building in Shanghai, China.

Mandiant believes that indeed APT1 *is* PLA Unit 61398. APT1's cyber-attack information technology is composed of over 1,000 servers within a large organization staffed by hundreds of human operators with direct access to Shanghai communication systems and capabilities. The conclusion that the Chinese government was not only aware of APT1, but now actively involved in the direction and management of a group designed primarily to steal digital information and attack Western enterprises, sent shockwaves through the international community. The Mandiant report represents the first conclusive evidence that foreign governments do indeed sponsor military-based, cyber activity designed specifically to steal information and disrupt American critical infrastructure. The Mandiant Report indicates that APT1 poses the single largest threat to American cybersecurity. Since 2006, APT1 has successfully attacked 115 governmental and private-sector infrastructure, some of which represent America's largest banks, corporate and manufacturing entities, defense contractors, and national security agencies. Awareness of this type of threat has provided the stimulus for billions of dollars dedicated to retaining cutting-edge capability in defending infrastructure within the Information Technology Sector.[47]

Information warfare and terrorist attacks sponsored by a nation-state may rise to the level of open conflict and war. How do you think the United States should respond to such attacks? Do you think the United States should also conduct information warfare attacks on other countries, like China, Russia, North Korea and Iran, in retaliation?

Hacking
The illegal intrusion into a secure data or computer system.

Information warfare (IW)
The concept of using information technology to gain tactical or strategic advantage over an opponent.

Information Link
For more information on the potential for a major cyber-attack on our critical infrastructure, and the use of information warfare as both a defensive and offensive weapon of the future, see the U.S. Army Cyber Command (CYBERCOM) website at www.arcyber.army.mil/org-uscc.html.

other critical infrastructure and key resources (CI/KRs) are reliant upon the IT Sector to provide data, coordination, and communication during a natural disaster or terrorist event. The IT Sector is basically the "tie that binds" many other assets within critical infrastructure together. As such, it is often the target of terrorists, hackers, social activists, criminals, international organized cartels (see Box 12–4), and state-supported intelligence services that engage in information warfare.

Information warfare (IW) is the concept of using information technology to gain tactical or strategic advantage over an opponent during a conflict. This can be intelligence in the sense of knowing the enemy's capabilities, intentions and dispositions (deployment), or undermining their capabilities and will to fight. Propaganda, disinformation, counterintelligence, deception, and the disruption of critic infrastructure are all aspects of information warfare.[48] The IT Sector includes physical assets, as well as virtual systems and networks, across the public and private arenas within the United States. Federal agencies involved in the IT Sector include the U.S. Departments of Homeland Security, Commerce, Energy, and Defense; the National Institute of Standards and Technology; and the General Services Administration. Private partners include easily recognizable IT companies, defense contractors, and fiscal entities, such as Apple, Boeing, JP Morgan-Chase, Google, eBay, Raytheon, Cisco, Citibank, Intel, Microsoft, Bank of America, and Lockheed Martin.[49] State and local governments, as well as international partners, are also involved in securing the IT Sector.

Chapter Summary

1. **Define critical infrastructure in the United States and provide a brief description of how this infrastructure impacts daily life.**

   Critical infrastructure is the systems and assets so vital to the United States that the incapacity or destruction of these systems and assets would have a debilitating impact on national security, national economic security, national public health, or any combination of these matters. As individuals, we rarely think of the importance of critical infrastructure in our country. However, almost every aspect of life in the United States is dependent upon a critical infrastructure sector. From the clean air, water, and food that sustains life to the variety of physical and virtual systems that allows us to share our lives with one another to the jobs and recreation we enjoy, the amenities of daily life in the United States is dependent upon a well-functioning, coordinated, and efficient infrastructure.

2. **Explain the all-hazards model in planning for critical infrastructure protection.**

   The all-hazards model recognizes that there are aspects of planning and response that are common in many kinds of catastrophes and disasters regardless of causation. Therefore, protecting critical infrastructure and responding to and mitigating emergency events are similar in both natural as well as man-made catastrophes.

3. **Describe the role of the Federal Bureau of Investigation (FBI) relating to terrorism.**

   The FBI is the primary agency responsible for crisis management during a terrorist event. The FBI is responsible for developing, coordinating, and managing a response to terrorism as well as conducting and coordinating all aspects of an investigation involving a terrorist event (e.g., crime scene security, interviewing witnesses and victims, collecting evidence, arresting suspects). The FBI works closely with state and local law enforcement agencies and hosts a variety of programs aimed at coordinating investigations and preventing future terrorist strikes. These include the management of the Joint Terrorism Task Forces, the National Counterterrorism Center and the Public Internet Tip Line, the Counterterrorism Fly Team, and the Ten Most Wanted Terrorist List.

4. **Describe the role of the Federal Emergency Management Agency (FEMA) relating to terrorism.**

   The role of FEMA during a terrorist event is consequence management. That is, FEMA is responsible for the emergency management of a major event such as a natural disaster or a terrorist strike. This includes mitigation, or the effort to reduce loss of life and property by lessening the impact of the event. Some of the duties of FEMA at a catastrophe include search and rescue, sheltering and caring for affected persons, managing debris removal, and maintaining safeguards for the general public.

5. **Discuss the National Infrastructure Protection Plan (NIPP) and list the critical infrastructure sectors that make up the plan.**

   The National Infrastructure Protection Plan (NIPP) was developed under President George W. Bush in 2003. It is a formal document that provides a framework for a coordinated approach to identifying and protecting critical infrastructure in the United States. The NIPP establishes an acronym (CI/KR) to refer to critical infrastructure and key resources that are imperative for the broad national security of the United States. The NIPP recognizes 16 critical infrastructure sectors: Communications, Emergency Services, Energy, Dams, Nuclear, Water, Chemical, Commercial Facilities, Healthcare and Public Health, Food and Agriculture, Critical Manufacturing, Transportation, Government Facilities, Banking and Finance, Defense Industrial Base, and Information Technology (IT).

6. **Describe why the Information Technology (IT) Sector is so important to secure in the United States and discuss some of the current threats to this sector.**

   The Information Technology (IT) Sector includes the physical and virtual systems and networks that allow all other sectors to coordinate efforts and effectively function both independently and jointly. The IT Sector is, quite literally, the "tie that binds" all other critical infrastructure sectors together. As such, it may be the "most critical" of the critical infrastructure sectors as it confronts an evolving set of physical as well as cyber-based threats from terrorists, hackers, social activists, criminals, international organized cartels, and state-supported intelligence services. Some of the most significant threats to the IT Sector stem from sophistical criminal cartels originating in Russia and information warfare practices stemming from China. For instance, in 2013, the Mandiant Corporation identified China's Advanced Persistent Threat 1 (APT 1) as being an entire intelligence effort aimed at attacking the virtual world of governmental and private-sector critical infrastructure (e.g., defense agencies and contractors, banks, transportation entities, IT corporations). APT 1 represents a current and significant threat to the critical infrastructure of the United States.

REVIEW QUESTIONS

1. What is critical infrastructure, and how does it impact people living in the United States?
2. What is the role of the FBI and FEMA during a terrorist event in the United States?
3. Discuss some of the major programs managed by the FBI to detect, investigate, and prevent terrorist strikes on the homeland.
4. Define the all-hazards model.
5. What is the National Infrastructure Protection Plan (NIPP)? Name some of the identified critical infrastructure sectors identified in the plan.
6. How did Hurricane Katrina impact critical infrastructure in the United States?
7. What are anthrax and ricin?
8. Define the term "skyjacking."
9. Relate the activities of hacking and information warfare to threats against the IT Sector.
10. What is APT1?

CRITICAL THINKING EXERCISES

1. **The Mandiant Group.** Visit the Mandiant Group website at www.mandiant.com/. Check out the "Threat Landscape" and learn about the use of malware, social engineering, and other tactics and strategies often employed by people attempting to gain illegal access to computer systems. Watch the video entitled, "Anatomy of an Attack." Now, read the M-Trends Report for the year. What new threats lurk in the cyberworld to our infrastructure? Discuss as a class the huge issue of cybersecurity and information warfare as a major threat to our infrastructure. Can you think of additional ways to make our country less vulnerable from these types of attack? Think outside the box!

2. **Preparing for Security at this Year's Super Bowl.** Explore the Internet and find articles focused on preparing for this year's Super Bowl. Read the U.S. Department of Justice COPS paper entitled "Planning and Managing Security for Major Special Events" at www.cops.usdoj.gov/Publications/e07071299_web.pdf. Read also the U.S. Department of Justice BJA booklet entitled "Managing Large-Scale Security Events: A Planning Primer for Local Law Enforcement Agencies" at www.bja.gov/Publications/ LSSE-planning-Primer.pdf. Now, think about the difficulties in planning for security at the Super Bowl. Where will the event be held? What new arsenal of security initiatives should be enacted for the event? How will parking and public access to the stadium be limited? What agencies will be primarily involved in the security of the event, and more importantly, what will be the role of those agencies? Identify other areas of the city where the Super Bowl is being held that will also be "on alert." Imagine how much time, energy, and money goes into preparing for and providing the security for such an event. Who do you think should pay for the security at the Super Bowl? The host city? The NFL? The people attending the big game? The media networks broadcasting the game? The general public? Now, try to find out by scouring the web. It won't be easy … try to find out how much security cost for the last Super Bowl.

NOTES

1. The National Infrastructure Protection Plan as defined by the *Critical Infrastructures Protection Act of 2001*, Title 42 USC, Chapter 68, Subchapter IV-B, Subsection 5195c. See also William J. Clinton, Presidential Decision Directive, Critical Infrastructure Protection, May 22, 1998, www.fas.org/irp/offdocs/pdd/pdd-63.pdf.

2. USA PATRIOT ACT, signed on October 26, 2001.

3. See www.whitehouse.gov/blog/2011/06/29/national-strategy-counterterrorism.

4. Ibid.

5. See www.fbi.gov/about-us/investigate/terrorism.

6. See www.fbi.gov/about-us/cirg/sioc.

7. See www.fbi.gov/news/stories/2005/march/flyteam_033005.

8. See www.fbi.gov/wanted/wanted_terrorists.

9. See www.fema.gov/what-mitigation.

10. Federal Emergency Management Agency "About the Agency," July 22, 2013, www.fema.gov/about-agency.

11. Ted G. Lewis, *Critical Infrastructure Protection in Homeland Security: Defending a Networked Nation* (Hoboken, NJ: Wiley Inter Science, 2006).

12. George W. Bush, Homeland Security Presidential Directive 7, Critical Infrastructure Identification, Prioritization, and Protection. *Code of Federal Regulations.* Title 3, Volume 39, Issue 51 (December 22, 2003) § 1816–1822, www.dhs.gov/homeland-security-presidential-directive-7#1.

13. Barack Obama, Presidential Policy Directive 21, Critical Infrastructure Security and Resilience, February 12, 2013, www.whitehouse.gov/the-press-office/2013/02/12/presidential-policy-directive-critical-infrastructure-security-and-resil.

14. U.S. Department of Homeland Security, "Critical Infrastructure Sectors," no date, www.dhs.gov/critical-infrastructure-sectors.

15. Ted G. Lewis, *Critical Infrastructure Protection in Homeland Security: Defending a Networked Nation* (Hoboken, NJ: Wiley Inter Science, 2006).

16. Refer to membership of the National Security Telecommunications Advisory Committee (NSTAC), as of November 12, 2013, www.dhs.gov/nstac-members.

17. See Robert Miller, "Hurricane Katrina: Communications & Infrastructure Impacts." *National Defense University*, June 2006, www.carlisle.army.mil/DIME/documents/Hurricane%20Katrina%20Communications%20&%20Infrastructure%20Impacts.pdf.

18. U.S. Department of Homeland Security, *Communications Sector-Specific Plan: An Annex to the National Infrastructure Plan*, 2010, www.dhs.gov/xlibrary/assets/nipp-ssp-communications-2010.pdf.

19. U.S. Department of Homeland Security, *Emergency Services Sector-Specific Plan: An Annex to the National Infrastructure Plan*, 2010, www.dhs.gov/xlibrary/assets/nipp-ssp-emergency-services.pdf.

20. U.S. Department of Justice, "Eric Rudolph Charged in Centennial Olympic Park Bombing." *FBI News Release,* October 14, 1998. See also additional information on secondary explosive devices, "FBI Again Warns of Secondary Explosive Devices, Cautions Officer to Watch Surroundings," May 17, 2004, www.policeone.com/terrorism/articles/86852-FBI-Again-Warns-of-Secondary-Explosive-Devices-Cautions-Officers-To-Watch-Surroundings/.

21. U.S. Department of Homeland Security, *Energy Sector-Specific Plan: An Annex to the National Infrastructure Plan*, 2010, www.dhs.gov/xlibrary/assets/nipp-ssp-energy-2010.pdf.

22. Ibid.

23. Ibid.

24. For more information on this subject, refer to the sources for this box item: Mordechai Abir, "The Al-Qaeda Threat to Saudi Arabia's Oil Sector," *Journal of Jerusalem Center for Public Affairs*, Vol. 4, No. 13, 28. December 2004; and Khalid R. Al-Rodham, "The Impact of the Abqaiq Attack on Saudi Energy Security," *Center for Strategic and International Studies*, February 27, 2006.

25. U.S. Department of Homeland Security. *Dams Sector-Specific Plan: An Annex to the National Infrastructure Plan*, 2010, www.hsdl.org/?view&did=7980.

26. Ibid.

27. For more information, see the source for this box item: Dane Schiller and James Pinkerton, "Agents Feared Mexican Drug Cartel Attack on Border Damn," *Houston Chronicle*, June 2, 2010.

28. U.S. Department of Homeland Security, *Nuclear Reactors, Materials, and Waste Sector-Specific Plan: An Annex to the National Infrastructure Plan*, 2010, www.dhs.gov/xlibrary/assets/nipp-ssp-nuclear-2010.pdf; and U.S. Department of Homeland Security, *Nuclear Sector Snapshot*, 2011, www.dhs.gov/xlibrary/assets/nppd/nppd-ip-nuclear-sector-snapshot-2011.pdf

29. U.S. Department of Homeland Security, *Water Sector-Specific Plan: An Annex to the National Infrastructure Plan*, 2010, www.dhs.gov/xlibrary/assets/nipp-ssp-water-2010.pdf.

30. Claudia Copeland and Betsy Cody, "Terrorism and Security Issues Facing the Water Infrastructure Sector," May 21, 2003, Congressional Research Service. www.cfr.org/targets-for-terrorists/crs-report-terrorism-security-issues-facing-water-infrastructure-sector/p9974.

31. U.S. Department of Homeland Security, *Chemical Sector-Specific Plan: An Annex to the National Infrastructure Plan*, 2010, www.dhs.gov/xlibrary/assets/nppd/nppd-ip-chemical-sector-snapshot-2011.pdf; U.S. Department of Homeland Security, *Chemical Sector Snapshot*, 2011, www.dhs.gov/xlibrary/assets/nppd/nppd-ip-chemical-sector-snapshot-2011.pdf; and U.S. Department of Homeland Security, *Chemical Stockpile Emergency Preparedness Program*, September 30, 2013, www.fema.gov/technological-hazards-division-0/chemical-stockpile-emergency-preparedness-program.

32. U.S. Department of Homeland Security, *Commercial Facilities Sector-Specific Plan: An Annex to the National Infrastructure Plan*, 2010, www.dhs.gov/xlibrary/assets/nipp-ssp-commercial-facilities-2010.pdf.

33. For more information, see the references for this box item: (1) Gebe Martinez and William C. Rempel, "Bombing Suspects: Ties that Bind a Seemingly Odd Pair," *Los Angeles Times*, March 11, 1993; (2) U.S. Congress, Senatorial Records 332-335. See U.S. Congressional Serial Set, Serial No. 15016. 2006; and (3) Eben Kaplan, Council on Foreign Relations. "Targets for Terrorists: Chemical Facilities," December 11, 2006, www.cfr.org/united-states/targets-terrorists-chemical-facilities/p12207#p8.

34. See Kathy Grannis, "NRF Forecasts Retail Industry Sales Growth of 3.4 percent in 2012," *National Retail Federation*, January 16, 2012.

35. Ibid.

36. U.S. Department of Homeland Security, *Healthcare and Public Health Sector-SpecificPlan: An Annex to the National Infrastructure Plan*, 2010, www.dhs.gov/xlibrary/assets/nipp-ssp-healthcare-and-public-health-2010.pdf.

37. Brad Bell, "Ricin Scares Reminiscent of Anthrax Attacks for Mail Handlers," *ABC News*, 2013, www.wjla.com/articles/2013/04/ricin-scares-reminiscent-of-anthrax-attacks-for-mail-handlers-87655.html. For more information on the anthrax attacks in 2001, see Council on Foreign Relations, "The Anthrax Letters," January 2006, www.cfr.org/weapons-of-mass-destruction/anthrax-letters/p9555.

38. U.S. Department of Homeland Security, *Food and Agriculture Sector-Specific Plan: An Annex to the National Infrastructure Plan*, 2010, www.dhs.gov/xlibrary/assets/nipp-ssp-food-ag-2010.pdf.

39. U.S. Department of Homeland Security, *Critical Manufacturing Snapshot*, 2011, www.dhs.gov/xlibrary/assets/nppd/nppd-ip-critical-manufacturing-snapshot-2011.pdf.

40. U.S. Department of Homeland Security, *Critical Manufacturing Sector-Specific Plan: An Annex to the National Infrastructure Plan*, 2010, www.dhs.gov/sites/default/files/publications/nipp-ssp-critical-manufacturing-2010.pdf.

41. U.S. Department of Homeland Security, *Transportation Systems Sector-Specific Plan: An Annex to the National Infrastructure Plan*, 2010, www.dhs.gov/xlibrary/assets/nipp-ssp-transportation-systems-2010.pdf.

42. See Brendan I. Koerner, *The Skies Belong to Us: Love and Terror in the Golden Age of Hijacking* (New York: Random House, 2013).

43. U.S. Department of Homeland Security, *Government Facilities Sector Snapshot*, www.dhs.gov/xlibrary/assets/nipp-ssp-chemical-2010.pdf.

44. U.S. Department of Homeland Security, *Banking and Finance Sector-Specific Plan: An Annex to the National Infrastructure Plan*, 2010, www.dhs.gov/sites/default/files/publications/nipp-ssp-banking-and-finance-2010.pdf.

45. U.S. Department of Homeland Security, *Defense Industrial Base Sector-Specific Plan: An Annex to the National Infrastructure Plan*, 2010, www.dhs.gov/xlibrary/assets/nipp-ssp-defense-industrial-base-2010.pdf.

46. See Nathaniel Popper and Somini Sengupta, "U.S. Says Ring Stole 160 Million Credit Card Numbers," *New York Times-DealBook*, July 25, 2013, http://dealbook.nytimes.com/2013/07/25/arrests-planned-in-hacking-of-financial-companies/.

47. For more information on this subject, refer to the sources for this box item: Mandiant Corporation, *APT1: Exposing One of China's Cyber Espionage Units* (Alexandria, VA: Mandiant, 2013). For more information regarding Mandiant, refer to its website at www.mandiant.com; and Robert W. Taylor, Eric J. Fritsch, and John Liederbach, *Digital Crime and Digital Terrorism,* 3rd edition (Upper Saddle River, NJ: Pearson, 2014).

48. Robert W. Taylor, Eric J. Fritsch, and John Liederbach, *Digital Crime and Digital Terrorism*, 3rd edition (Upper Saddle River, NJ: Pearson, 2014).

49. U.S. Department of Homeland Security, *Information Technology Sector-Specific Plan: An Annex to the National Infrastructure Plan*, 2010, www.dhs.gov/sites/default/files/publications/IT%20Sector%20Specific%20Plan%202010.pdf.

Emergency Management

A trainer preparing a canine for urban search and rescue directs a dog through heavy rubble.
(Courtesy © blickwinkel/Alamy)

Learning Objectives

After completing this chapter, you should be able to:

1. Describe and give examples of the three major categories of threats or hazards.

2. Summarize the severity continuum.

3. Explain how the New Deal Programs of the 1930s altered the federal government's long-standing position that relief assistance was a local government issue.

4. Discuss the impact of World War II and the development of the Federal Civil Defense Administration on emergency management.

5. Explain the rise and role of FEMA.

6. Describe the acronyms WMD, CBRNE, and CDC.

7. Describe and briefly explain the National Incident Management System (NIMS) and the Incident Command System (ICS).

8. State the National Preparedness Goal and define the concept of "whole community."

9. Explain the National Preparedness Report and identify the areas of national strength and weakness noted in the 2013 NPR.

Introduction

Historically, disaster relief has suffered from several major issues: (1) The movement toward relief generally was retarded by early American beliefs that were commonly held in colonial times and beyond. Individualism, self-reliance, and the tenets of the Protestant ethic—meaning people should work hard, have self-discipline, and be thrifty with what they earned or produced—greatly impacted the idea of giving aid to others, even during an emergency. Many people thought that any kind of aid, even in limited quantities would make people dependent and was therefore counterproductive. (2) For nearly 130 years, the federal government insisted that local government was the appropriate responder to disasters and gave it little or no assistance. (3) Once established, civil defense had substantial value to the federal government primarily because one of its missions was supporting and protecting the country from foreign enemies by mobilizing public support. However, civil defense had little regard for providing aid and relief. (4) As it emerged, emergency management (EM) as a whole did not speak the same "language." The definitions of terms and concepts varied widely from one state to another as well as from one community to another. (5) Until emergency management achieved some standardization of language, approaches, equipment, and capabilities it had difficulty communicating and operating in a multi-agency environment, which often caused confusion during responses. This chapter explores how these and other related issues changed over time, and describes the new emergency management practices that are now at the forefront of hazard and disaster mitigation.

Emergency management (EM) is the managerial function that creates the framework within which communities reduce their vulnerability to hazards and cope with incidents and disasters.[1] The goals of emergency management are to (1) save lives, (2) prevent injuries, and (3) protect property and the environment.[2] All communities face a variety of threats/hazards, which endanger people, property, and other assets.[3]

There are three categories of threats/hazards (Also see Figure 13–1):

1. Natural, which include weather conditions as well as animal and human diseases. These threats/hazards are relatively well understood because we learn about many of them from weather and news reports. Examples include tornados, hurricanes, Mad Cow disease, and Ebola. In late 2014, there were several cases of Ebola Virus Disease (EVD, "Ebola") in the United States, creating fears of an epidemic. These fears were compounded when the Centers for Disease Control changed its guidelines for handling Ebola cases, suggesting we were not as well prepared as initially thought. The first American Ebola case resulted from a man being exposed to the disease in a West Africa nation and traveling to Dallas, Texas, where the symptoms manifested. A health care worker taking care of the man contracted Ebola, but was quickly treated and recovered. There have also been several other Ebola cases in the United States. Based on what little data we have, the pattern is a health professional or a person visiting a West Africa nation is exposed to Ebola. Subsequently, the person returns to the United States and at some point is diagnosed as having Ebola. A limited number of health professionals have contracted Ebola treating such patients. The fear of Ebola is so great that staff members at a New York City hospital reportedly took sick days rather than treat the hospital's first Ebola patient.[4] Flooding is the most common type of disaster in the United States.[5]

2. Technological and accidental, created by (1) technological failures, such as a collapsed building or a failed dam that causes flooding, and (2) accidents, such as the unintended release of hazardous materials into the environment.

3. Terrorist and human, which arise from intentional acts intended to disrupt systems, destroy property, and/or kill people. To illustrate, **sarin** is a nerve agent (loosely, a "poison gas") that acts quickly and causes the nervous system not to function properly. In 1995, five two-man teams entered the Tokyo subway system and released sarin. The attackers from the **Aum Shinrikyo** group quickly took an antidote

Sarin
A man-made chemical gas that is extremely poisonous; used in a terrorist attack by the Aum Shinrikyo group in the subways of Tokyo, Japan in 1995.

Aum Shinrikyo
An apocalyptic Christian group in Japan that became the first terrorist organization to use chemical warfare. In 1995, five two-man teams released sarin, a quick-acting nerve agent, in a Tokyo subway system.

Quick Facts
Saddam's Use of "Poison Gas"

In 1983, Iraqi dictator Saddam Hussein used mustard gas against Iranian troops during Iraq's war against them,[6] which constituted a war crime. Mustard gas is a blistering agent/vesicant that severely blisters the eyes, respiratory tract, and skin on contact. Five years later, Hussein used Tabun against Iranian troops. Tabun is a highly poisonous chemical nerve agent that prevents the nervous system from functioning properly.

Starting in 1987, Hussein sought revenge against the Kurds in northern Iraq, some of whom had allied themselves with Iran. He used sarin, mustard gas, and Tabun indiscriminately against the Kurds generally. It is estimated that between 53,000 to 105,000 Kurds were killed. Hundreds of villages were decimated or abandoned.

FIGURE 13–1

Examples of the Three Major Categories of Threats/Hazards[9]

Source: Drawn with some additions from *Resolve to Be Ready in 2014* (Washington, D.C.: Federal Emergency Management Agency, December 24, 2013), www.ready.gov/prepared2014.

Natural	Technological and Accidental	Terrorist/Human Caused
• Animal Disease Breakout	• Aircraft Crash	• Biological
• Avalanche	• Bridge Failure	• Chemical
• Drought	• Building Collapse	• Cyber
• Earthquake	• Dam Failure	• Explosion
• Epidemic/Pandemic	• Hazardous Materials Release/Spill	• Nuclear
• Flood	• Levee Failure	• Radiological Dispersion Device (RDD)
• Hurricane/Cyclone	• Maritime Accident	• Sabotage
• Landslide/Rock Fall	• Mine Accident	
• Lightening	• Power Failure/Blackouts	
• Tornado	• Radiological Release	
• Tropical Storm	• Train Derailment	
• Tsunami	• Urban Fires	
• Volcanic Eruption	• Vehicle Crash	
• Wildfire		
• Winter Storm		

Note: The threats/hazards listed under terrorist/human caused are the means. The *targets* or *settings* at which they are directed may be schools, government buildings, national monuments, resorts, mass transit systems, and similar entities. In late 2014, a lone wolf terrorist, a recent convert to Islam, shot his way into Canada's Parliament before he was killed, an example of a terrorist/human caused event.

and fled. Twelve people were killed and 5,500 injured. It was the first instance of a terrorist group using chemical warfare. Except for a mistake by the group in making the sarin and not using a more effective way of distributing it, fatalities would have been much higher. Although some early arrests were made quickly, it was not until 2012 that the last three attackers were finally brought to justice.[7] Parenthetically, Saddam Hussein's use of poison gas on Kurds living in the north of Iraq beginning in1987 constituted state terrorism. However, it was undertaken by a government and not a "terrorist group." Therefore, the Aum Shinrikyo action in the Tokyo subway is the first terrorist group attack using "poison gas."

The Severity Continuum

There are many ways to gauge the severity of an incident. Examples of these measures include the number of (1) deaths and injuries, (2) people displaced and evacuated, (3) homes and business that have major damage or are destroyed, and (4) financial indicators such as dollar loss and assistance expenditures. In an unusual development, the Federal Emergency Management Agency (FEMA) came up with the idea of the "Waffle House Index" as a measure to gauge severity. FEMA's Waffle House Index is an informal measure. If a Waffle House is up and running, the disaster is green; if it is operating with a backup generator and offering only a limited menu, the disaster is yellow; and if closed, badly damaged, or destroyed, as many were during Hurricane Katrina, the disaster is red.[8]

In contrast, the severity continuum (see Figure 13–2) is a quick "front end" tool that allows officials to quickly gauge the preliminary answer to the question "How hard did we get hit?"

Emergency

A condition of actual danger to the lives of persons and/or the safety of property that requires a response. Emergencies ordinarily are handled locally.

Quick Facts
America's Grain Elevators and Bins

In America's Wheat Belt, which includes such states as Kansas, Iowa, Nebraska, and Oklahoma, grain is often stored in great bins, each of which may hold a million or more bushels. In the process of milling and moving the grain on belts, small particles of grain may begin to float around, suspended in the air. If these particles are coupled with oxygen and an ignition source, small to devastating explosions can occur. Between 1976 and 2011, there were 50 grain elevator explosions with 677 injuries and 188 fatalities.[10]

The Severity Continuum

Lowest Severity → Highest Severity

Emergency — Disaster — Catastrophe — Extinction Event

FIGURE 13–2
The Severity Continuum

Disaster
A "disaster" is more severe than an emergency because it causes a serious disruption of the functioning of an entity, such as a community, and produces widespread human, material, economic, and/or environmental losses that exceed the ability of a community to cope with it using just its own resources.

Mutual aid agreement
Mutual aid agreements are agreements between agencies, organizations, and jurisdictions that provide a mechanism to quickly obtain emergency assistance in the form of personnel, equipment, materials, and other associated services. The primary objective is to facilitate rapid, short-term deployment of emergency support prior to, during, and after an incident.

Figure 13–3 is the severity continuum. To be useful, the points on a scale must have meaningful definitions so important distinctions can be made. The points on the severity continuum are defined below Figure 13–3.

1. An "**emergency**" is a condition of actual danger to the lives of persons and/or the safety of property that requires a response. Emergencies ordinarily are handled locally. One example of a locally handled disaster is a small city in which floodwaters crossed a section of a road and washed it away. The city rebuilt the road at its own expense. However, some emergencies may require limited outside assistance, such as ambulances from a neighboring jurisdiction. There is an exception to this general description: When an emergency involves federal property it automatically triggers a federal response, or when an emergency requires specialized groups available from FEMA, such as search and rescue teams.

2. A "**disaster**" is more severe than an emergency because it causes a serious disruption of the functioning of an entity, such as a community, and produces widespread human, material, economic, and/or environmental losses that exceed the ability of a community to cope with it using just its own resources.[11] For example, hospitals may have been severely damaged by tornados, clean drinking water cannot be provided, temporary housing for displaced persons is inadequate, power has been knocked out, there are pockets of looting, food supplies urgently need replacement, and few business have continuity of operation.

   As a community quickly uses its own resources to respond to a disaster, it will reach a tipping point. Its diminishing resources are no longer sufficient to handle increasing demands and assistance from others becomes essential. The sooner that decision can reliably be made, the faster people in need can be helped (e.g., quickly bringing in temporary housing for displaced people). Under a **mutual aid agreement**, a disaster-stricken community can receive significant assistance from neighboring local governments, and state and federal assistance may be needed as well. If there has been a geographically widespread disaster, for example, from a cluster of tornados or wildfires, neighboring jurisdictions may have their own incidents with which to deal, and mutual aid assistance agreements will be impossible to honor. It is a long-standing principal that federal assistance is intended to supplement state, local, and private assistance, but not to be a substitute for it.[12]

FIGURE 13–3
Substanial rainfall from a weather system that stalled over parts of Colorado produced extensive flooding, a natural disaster. Disaster response groups Hands.org and AmeriCorps joined forces to help muck out homes in Evans.
(*Courtesy Federal Emergency Management Agency, photograph by Michael Rieger*)

Box 13-1
Mutual Aid Agreements

Mutual aid agreements are agreements between agencies, organizations, and jurisdictions that provide a mechanism to quickly obtain emergency assistance in the form of personnel, equipment, materials, and other associated services.[13] The primary objective is to facilitate rapid, short-term deployment of emergency support prior to, during, and after an incident.[14]

Emergency Management Assistance Compact (EMAC): The Emergency Management Assistance Compact is an interstate mutual aid agreement that allows states to assist one another in responding to all kinds of natural and manmade disasters. It is administered by the National Emergency Management Association (NEMA). EMAC is the law in 50 states, Puerto Rico, Guam, U.S. Virgin Islands, and the District of Columbia.[15]

Model Intrastate Mutual Aid Legislation: This legislation was produced by NEMA in concert with DHS/FEMA and a cross-section of emergency response disciplines to facilitate intrastate mutual aid among participating political subdivisions in a state. The document also contains a list of states that have passed intrastate agreements with links to their legislation, as reference.

Model State-County Mutual Aid Deployment Contract: This is a model intergovernmental contract that allows for the deployment of local emergency responders under the auspices of EMAC.

How useful are these types of agreements are during an emergency, disaster or catastrophe?

Information Link
For more information on FEMA Urban Search and Rescue Task Forces, visit the website at www.fema.gov/urban-search-rescue.

Catastrophe
A catastrophe is an incident that directly or indirectly affects large portions or all of a country and requires national and sometimes international responses.

An example of a disaster occurred in the city of West, Texas, in 2013 (see Figure 13–4). A fertilizer plant inexplicably exploded and devastated the town, killing 15 people and injuring hundreds more. Aid rushed to the city from nearby communities and the rest of the state of Texas. Previously developed mutual aid agreements allowed neighboring police, fire, and emergency services to work in the city of West. In such disasters, coordination and cooperation are necessary ingredients to mitigate the damages. For instance, in such types of large explosions, there may be missing persons that require the expertise of specially trained search and rescue teams. FEMA's Urban Search and Rescue Task Forces are often combined teams of individuals from local and state agencies, trained together as a federal unit to respond to emergencies anywhere in the United States, as they did in West, Texas, in 2013.

3. A **catastrophe** is an incident that directly or indirectly affects large portions or all of a country and requires national and sometimes international responses. Early in 2010, a major earthquake struck one of the most impoverished countries in the Western Hemisphere, Haiti, killing 200,000 people and leaving 2.3 million Haitians homeless (see Figure 13–5).[16] Despite massive assistance from the United Nations and a number of countries, Haitian refugees living in temporary camps suffered from deadly outbreaks of cholera later in the year.[17] In the fall, Hurricane Tomas lashed Haiti, creating more misery and deaths.

FIGURE 13–4
Local and FEMA officials walk through West, Texas, discussing the destruction caused by the explosion of the fertilizer plant. In addition to the dead and injured, jobs were lost, and 350 homes damaged. FEMA relief mitigated some of that. However, nothing ever replaces the loss of loved ones, homes, and jobs.

(Courtesy Federal Emergency Management Agency, photograph by Earl Armstrong)

4. An **extinction event** could result or results in the loss of all human life on the planet. In the extreme, there is no effective emergency response to an extinction event. Although these types of apocalyptic events have been historically portrayed in the popular media [e.g., *Planet of the Apes* (1968), *The Last Wave* (1977), *Armageddon* (1998), *Sharing a Friend for the End of the World* (2012), and *Transformers: The Age of Extinction* (2013)], the probability of a human extinction event is presently statistically slight. Nonetheless, it is a possibility.

The Evolution of Emergency Management

In colonial America there was an ingrained belief that people should be **self-reliant** and responsible for their own lot in life.[18] For more catastrophic events, people helped each other.[19] If a barn burned down, neighbors pitched in to "raise" (build) a new one; when crop fields were washed away, others shared their bounty. To some degree, that tradition also later translated to towns and cities—for example, volunteers serving as fire fighters. A corollary of this tradition was that if people were given too much help it would ultimately make them dependent. American philosophers also praised self-reliance, as did Ralph Waldo Emerson (1803–1882) in an 1841 essay.[20] For these reasons there was donated money that was not distributed to otherwise worthy recipients after the Great Chicago Fire of 1871.

As cities grew, private **mutual aid societies** provided some assistance "to their own" when disasters struck. These societies were often based on country of origin, religion, or ethnicity, and their other purposes included helping immigrants make the transition to living in America and preserving cultural heritage. In 1910, there were reportedly 400 Italian mutual aid associations in Chicago.[21] As the United States developed economically, insurance became more available, but many people either didn't know about it or simply could not afford it.[22]

Except for the ad hoc disaster assistance Congress provided starting in 1803, there was little interest in federal or state governments doing more for roughly 130 years. As an example, federal troops were dispatched to the Chicago Fire of 1871 ready to intervene if riots or looting broke out. However, Chicago leaders were annoyed because they neither asked for nor wanted them. They felt like it was their responsibility to deal with the consequences of the fire.

Founded in 1881, the **American Red Cross** has provided domestic and international relief, although there was often not much to distribute. In 1900, the American Red Cross was given a Congressional charter, giving it the legal status of "a federal instrumentality." The charter recognized the exceptional work of the Red Cross and tasked it to continue its relief work. No other similar American organization has attained this recognition.

Despite various piecemeal efforts, the federal government's central position for many decades was that disaster relief was the purview of state and local governments,[23] which should not surprise us. The pervasive ethos of individualism, self-reliance, and the tenets of the Protestant work ethic often got in the way of relief. These views help explain why unemployment compensation did not exist in American states until 1932, when Wisconsin became the first state to enact such assistance.

World War I to the 1930s

During World War I (1914–1918) the Germans bombed English cities. Anticipating America's entry into the war, the Council of National Defense (CND) was formed in 1916. German air attacks on the United States were considered unlikely because of the limited abilities of air warfare at that time.[24] Therefore, national defense focused on coordinating war resources, such as manpower, and maintaining high morale among the civilian population.[25] A key tactic in maintaining morale was keeping the public involved. As America

FIGURE 13–5
A portion of the damage caused by the 2010 earthquake damage in Port-au-Prince. More than 250,000 homes and 30,000 businesses were damaged or totally destroyed. In 2014, many of these structures had still not been rebuilt.
(© Stocktrek Images, Inc./Alamy).

Extinction event
An extinction event could result or results in the loss of all human life. In the extreme, there is no effective emergency response to an extinction event.

Self-reliant
In colonial America there was already an ingrained belief that people should be self-reliant and responsible for their own lot in life. A corollary of this tradition was that if people were given too much help it would ultimately make them dependent.

Mutual aid societies
Developed in America during the 1800s and were often faith, country of origin, or ethnicity based. They had several purposes, such as preserving cultural heritage and helping immigrants newly arrived in America to adjust.

American Red Cross
Humanitarian organization originally developed in 1881 by Clara Barton; modeled after the International Red Cross in Europe to provide aid to civilians during emergencies and disasters.

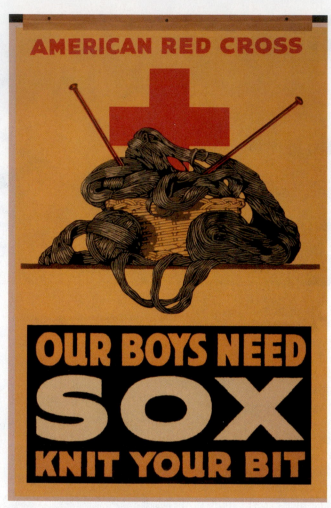

FIGURE 13–6
A 1917 American Red Cross poster exhorting women to support the troops by knitting. Such a program now seems unimaginable.

(© Library of Congress)

fought against Germany in World War I (1917–1918), the CND's Women's Committee had its constituents rolling bandages, selling war bonds, planting Victory Gardens for personal consumption to preserve other food for the war effort, and knitting socks and sweaters for the troops to wear.[26] Nationally, much of the knitting was done under the auspices of the American Red Cross (see Figure 13–6). Following the end of the war, the Council for National Defense was abolished in 1921.

From a national perspective, emergency management ultimately grew out of World War I's modest efforts in civil defense.[27] As civil defense evolved, it ultimately took on a few emergency management–type tasks. However, civil defense had a "dual use" character for most of its existence.[28] On the one hand, it was a part of the national security effort to protect citizens and much later it responded to natural disasters.[29]

Two events shaped the 1930s: (1) the crash of the stock market in 1929, which produced a loss of $75 billion[30] and ushered in the Great Depression (see Figure 13–7), the effects of which lasted until roughly 1940 when the economy turned upward as World War II approached; and 2) a drought so severe that it drove many farmers off their land in the heartland of the United States. For instance, in Mississippi alone, 40 percent of the farms went to the auction block.[31] Thirty-seven percent of non-farm workers lost their jobs and most of them their homes.[32] Many Americans left their familiar surroundings in search of a better life. The combination of these events resulted in some cities developing "bum blockades" so unemployed outsiders couldn't come into their communities and use their already strained resources.

Within 100 days of taking office, President Roosevelt and Congress collaborated to produce 15 "New Deal Programs," many of which focused on employment. Most importantly, the New Deal Programs reflected a policy shift away from the federal government's long-standing attachment to the self-reliant philosophy. It was finally recognized that some problems are just too big for communities and states to address, although emergency management still took a long time to emerge.

The Federal Emergency Relief Act of 1933 provided assistance for the unemployed. Illustratively, the Civilian Conservation Corps (CCC) began operation in 1933. It was a public work program that enrolled 2.5 million unmarried men.

FIGURE 13–7
The stock market began its crash on "Black Tuesday," October 29, 1929. In the Great Depression that followed many companies and banks failed as well. A bankrupted investor tries to sell his car as quickly as possible, while some people still had money.

(© Scherl/SZ Photo/DIZ Muenchen GmbH, Sueddeutsche Zeitung Photo/ Alamy)

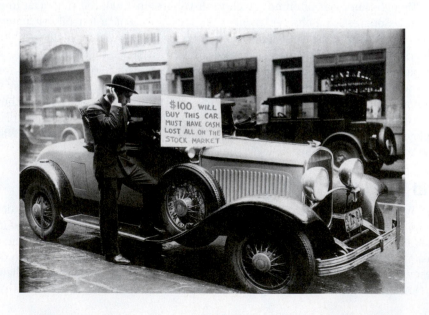

Clara Barton (1821–1912) was an independent nurse during America's Civil War. She also saw suffering firsthand while working with the International Red Cross in Europe during the Franco-Prussian War in 1869. Out of the experience she founded the American Red Cross and was its first president. Barton often took personal charge of major relief efforts such as the Great Fire of 1881 and the Johnstown, Pennsylvania, flood in 1889. Starting with President Woodrow Wilson in 1913, American presidents have served as honorary presidents of the American Red Cross.

CLARA BARTON
From portrait taken in Civil War and authorized
by her as the one she wished to be remembered by

▲ Clara Barton *(Courtesy Library of Congress)*

The New Deal programs established a major precedent for the federal government to provide assistance to people in distress. Despite the New Deal Programs, millions of other people in great need still received no governmental relief (see Figure 13–8).

The Impact of World War II

The successful Japanese attack on Pearl Harbor in 1941 propelled the United States into World War II (1941–1945). It also raised significant fear of attacks on the mainland. In 1941, the newly created Office of Civilian Defense (OCD) coordinated federal, state, and local defense programs for the protection of civilians during air raids and other emergencies, as well as facilitating civilian participation in war programs.[33] One of these was the volunteer Air Raid Warden Program.[34] The wardens made sure that cities were "blacked out," meaning no lights showed at night so as to deny their use as navigational aids by possible attackers.[35] Civilian volunteers were also trained to be "spotters" and recognize different types of enemy planes and the presence of enemy submarines.

Victory in Europe (V-E Day) was declared on May 8, 1945, and attention turned to ending the war in the Pacific. Following America's dropping of atomic bombs on Hiroshima and Nagasaki, the surrender of the Japanese was announced on Victory over Japan Day (V-J Day) on August 9, 1945. Almost immediately after World War II, Russia began working on a nuclear bomb and successfully tested such a device in 1949. The United States and the American public had a new worry … the Cold War with Russia and the potential for nuclear exchange.

FIGURE 13–8
Migrant workers came to work at a pea picking camp in California during 1936. The crop failed and the camp broke apart as workers left to find other work. The wife of a picker looks out from under the tent she and her husband just sold to get food for the children. Although only 32 years old, worry is etched in her face.

(Courtesy Library of Congress, photograph by Dorothea Lang)

The 1950s and 1960s

The Korean War (1950–1953) heightened the public's anxiety about nuclear war, some of which turned to outright fear. In late 1950, Congress passed a bill creating the Federal Civil Defense Administration (FCDA). Congress had abolished the Office of Civil Defense at the end of World War II, and the creation of the FCDA tacitly acknowledged the public's mood and created a nationwide system of civil defense agencies. Interestingly, most of the responsibility for civil defense was placed on state and local governments with limited

Box 13–2
The Civilian Conservation Corps (CCC)

The primary enrollees in the **Civilian Conservation Corps** were 18- to 25-year-old unmarried men. The CCC planted over three billion trees, built 800 parks, dug canals, stocked fish, and otherwise worked hard. Crime was rampant during the 1930s and the CCC kept its enrollees out of trouble.[36] Most members lived in tents and under a military-style discipline. They were paid $30 monthly, $25 of which they were required to send home.[37] Free evening classes were available and 40,000 young men were given their first opportunities to learn how to read and write.[38] An ancillary organization, the **Works Progress Administration (WPA)**, employed 8.5 million people to build bridges, public buildings, and airports. Even today, you can still occasionally find municipal buildings with a bronze placard on them commemorating their construction by the WPA. The CCC and WPA are what today is called "workfare." Instead of simply receiving benefits, people receive money in exchange for their work efforts on public projects.

As unemployment rises in some of our cities, do you think that a similar program might work today?

▲ A CCC member stands on a scaffold as he helps construct a building to be used as a camp work shop.

(Courtesy Library of Congress)

Civilian Conservation Corps
A federal program during the 1930s that employed young men in a military-style manner to plant trees and build parks, canals, and other recreational sites throughout America's forests and governmental land.

Works Progress Administration (WPA)
An ancillary organization to the Civilian Conservation Corps during the 1930s; employed over 8.5 million people involved in building bridges, public buildings, and airports throughout the country.

Information Link
For more information about the Civilian Conservation Corps, refer to the website hosted by the National Park Service at www.nps.gov/history/history/online_books/ccc/ccct.htm.

federal assistance. One of the Federal Civil Defense Administration's most immediate tasks was developing a national policy to guide state and local civil defense efforts.[39] The FCDA led bomb shelter–building programs, worked to achieve better coordination between federal and state governments, established an attack warning system, and stockpiled supplies.[40] It also conducted thousands of civil defense exercises, sent "Alert America" conveys to 83 cities educating over a million people about civil defense, established emergency communication facilities and emergency radio broadcasting capabilities, and educated children in schools.[41]

As far-fetched as it now appears, "Bert the Turtle" was a cartoon character developed by the FCDA to encourage children to "duck and cover" when there was a "bright light" from a nearby nuclear explosion. Teachers actually ran drills, training children to drop under their school desks for cover in the event of a nuclear attack. Some schools even distributed military-style metal "dog tags" so students could be identified after such an attack.[42]

In many regards the FCDA shaped the practice of civil defense for a decade or more. The Disaster Relief Act of 1950 gave the president the authority to issue disaster declarations and authorized federal agencies to provide limited direct assistance to state and local governments in the event of a disaster.

The FCDA's strategy vacillated between planning to evacuate people in the event of nuclear attacks and urging them to stay in place in their personally constructed backyard or public bomb shelters (see Figure 13–9). This vacillation was a reflection of views expressed by the Congress and various federal leaders. Ultimately, the federal government concluded that given the short warning it might be able to give there would inevitably be enormous civilian casualties.

In 1958, FCDA was merged with the Office of Defense Mobilization (ODM), which had been a powerful independent agency responsible for planning, coordinating, and controlling the mobilization of federal wartime assets, including manpower.[43] The new organization was placed in the Executive Office of the President as the Office of Civil and Defense Mobilization (OCDM).[44]

Throughout the many organizational changes, natural disasters continued to command attention despite the federal government's focus on preparation for war and

Doomsday "**preppers**" believe that a collapse of society is approaching and they are preparing for it. There are numerous reasons given for the impending doom, including asteroids hitting the earth, worldwide epidemics, a biological terrorist attack, hyperinflation, and even the rise of zombies. "Preppers" stock up on all sorts of weapons and supplies in an effort to survive the impending doom: guns and ammunition, cross and traditional bows, grains, foodstuffs, medical supplies, fuel, communications gear, clothing, seeds, and other necessities. They may buy tracts of land as a retreat and recruit former military and medical practitioners, such as surgeons and nurses, to join their group. Although once considered a fringe movement, a recent National Geographic poll revealed 28 percent of respondents knew at least one "prepper."[45]

One of the proponents of prepping is James Wesley Rawles, a retired military intelligence officer. He is the author of several novels, including *Survivors: A Novel of the Coming Collapse*, which examines the decisions people make and what happens to them in a collapsed society. Rawls's Internet site can be located at www.survivalblog.com. In early 2014, the site was receiving 320,000 individual visits weekly.

Why do you think "prepping" has become a movement in the United States? What factors are related to the "prepper" movement?

national security during peacetime. Illustratively, in 1953, a tornado hit Beecher, Michigan, with winds of 261–318 mph, killing hundreds.[46] A powerful earthquake pummeled Alaska in 1964. Hurricane Betsy obliterated eight offshore platforms, hammered New Orleans, and caused 76 deaths in 1965.[47] The Army Corps of Engineers was ordered to build flood protection for New Orleans in 1965, only to see it obliterated by Hurricane Katrina in 2005.

In 1961, President Kennedy changed the federal approach to disasters, dividing the Office of Civil Defense and Mobilization (OCDM) into two entities: the Office of Emergency Preparedness (OEP) was created in the Executive Office of the President to respond to natural disasters, and civil defense responsibilities were housed in the Department of Defense.

"Prepper"
Slang word to describe those individuals who are preparing for major apocalyptic events in the future.

The 1970s and the Emergence of FEMA

Building on the federal National Flood Insurance Act of 1968 that encouraged taking mitigation steps to reduce the impact of a disaster, Congress passed the Disaster Relief Act of 1970, setting forth the first major attempt by the federal government to emphasize hazard mitigation as a priority to reduce the impact of future disasters.[48] Further, the Disaster Relief Act of 1974 gave presidents additional authority to declare emergencies and disasters offering federal funding and assistance. Other federal disaster legislation included the Earthquake Reduction Act of 1977 that was later amended by The National Earthquake Hazards Reduction Program Reauthorization Act of 2004. The later act provided for

FIGURE 13-9
One of several models of family-sized underground bunkers designed to protect against nuclear blasts. Notice the lack of a kitchen and a restroom. Homeowners were urged to have two weeks of survival supplies and local and state governments needed to be able to supply such for another four weeks.

Source: "Annual Report of the Office of Civil and Defense Mobilization for Fiscal Year 1959," p. 14a.

specific public earthquake education, changes in building codes that called for more earthquake-resistant construction, and development, as far as was practical, of a system to predict earthquakes.

By 1975, nearly 100 federal agencies had some aspect of disaster assistance.[49] Frustrated with this fragmentation, the National Governors Association (NGA) pushed for a single agency to have jurisdiction over natural and environmental disasters.[50] In 1978, President Jimmy Carter responded by issuing Executive Order 12127 creating the **Federal Emergency Management Agency (FEMA)**.[51] Finally, after many historical, legislative, and bureaucratic twists and turns, the apex of modern emergency management arrived.

The 1980s to Present

Only three hurricanes hit the United States between 1980 and 1984, but the new agency (FEMA) had to deal with a variety of other incidents in its early years. As an example, local residents along the Love Canal area located in Niagara Falls (New York) began suffering from high incidents of cancer, birth defects, and other health problems. According to the Environmental Protection Agency (EPA), the problem was caused by human poisoning from toxic waste dumping in the canal and resulted in over 200 homes being demolished. The EPA was responsible for cleaning the site and FEMA was ordered to assist with residential relocation.

Also in 1980, the eruption of Mount St. Helens in the State of Washington, near Portland, Oregon, marked the first major natural disaster that introduced FEMA as the primary emergency management agency in the United States. The Mount St. Helens eruption was a significant event that was preceded by a series of earthquakes and landslides affecting the area. On May 18, 1980, the entire north face of the mountain suddenly exploded, spewing molten lava and steam down its side, as well as expelling gas and ash 80,000 feet into the air.[52] The resulting eruption killed 57 people and caused over $2.8 billion in damages. The impacted area was huge, covering most of the Pacific Northwest and at least 11 other U.S. states that received significant deposits of ash from the eruption. Spokane, Washington, which is located 250 miles due east of Mount St. Helens, was plunged into darkness for several days.

FEMA's response was lauded as it provided federal funding for cleanup of impacted cities as well as directed the states of Oregon and Washington in a massive reforestation project that continues today. The McKinney-Vento Homeless Assistance Act of 1987 authorized FEMA to help the homeless through the Emergency Food and Shelter Program, adding a new clientele to everyday operations of the agency. Other important challenges also occurred during the late 1980s as Hurricane Hugo slammed into the coast of South Carolina. FEMA's poor performance in responding to Hurricane Hugo resulted in the first major Congressional interest in disbanding FEMA. However, the discussion was abandoned early on, and in 1993, FEMA re-emerged with significant reforms. One of the more crucial changes made it easier for FEMA to redirect civil defense resources made available by the end of the Cold War.[53]

The bombing of Oklahoma City's Alfred P. Murrah Federal Building in 1995 by Timothy McVeigh and his co-conspirators elevated America's awareness about terrorism.[54] The Antiterrorism and Effective Death Penalty Act of 1996 required the Department of Justice (DOJ) and FEMA to train metropolitan firefighters in responding to events caused by weapons of mass destruction. Three years later, the Defense Against Weapons of Mass Destruction Act required training state and local first responders on handling threats and actual weapons of mass destruction incidents. FEMA supported Pennsylvania, Virginia, and New York in responding to the 9/11 attacks in 2001 with thousands of staff and mobile communications gear. In 2003, FEMA was officially moved to the Department of Homeland Security, where it remains today.[55]

In 2005, after severe criticism of FEMA's performance during Hurricane Katrina, the fourth most powerful Gulf of Mexico hurricane ever recorded, Congress passed the Post-Katrina Emergency Management Reform Act of 2006. Among the most important changes developed by the act were (1) FEMA remained a stand-alone agency within the Department of Homeland Security; (2) FEMA was given control over more emergency

Federal Emergency Management Agency (FEMA)
Originally developed by Presidential Order in 1978 by President Jimmy Carter, FEMA is the primary federal agency responsible for responding to and mitigating a major disaster within the United States.

Weapons of mass destruction (WMD)
Weapons designed to cause significant devastation to a population; involves the release of a CBRNE agent.

resources and designated as the primary agency responsible for disaster relief and mitigation; and (3) FEMA's top official became the president's principal advisor on emergencies and disasters regardless of causation.[56] In addition to the laws applicable to FEMA, Presidential Policy Directives (PPDs) have also played a large role in shaping the role of FEMA.

Weapons of Mass Destruction and CBRNE Attacks

Following the 1995 bombing of the Murrah Federal Building in Oklahoma City, President Clinton issued Presidential Decision Directive 39 (PDD-39), "U.S. Policy on Counterterrorism."[57] It required: (1) all federal government units to take actions to reduce vulnerabilities to terrorism at home and abroad and (2) that terrorists and their sponsors would be dealt with vigorously and their actions would not alter American policies. Among other provisions, FEMA became responsible for the development of federal and state response plans associated with a terrorist strike directed at large U.S. populations, especially those utilizing **weapons of mass destruction (WMD)**.

This directive coincided with previous legislation that established FEMA's **Center for Domestic Preparedness (CDP)** in Anniston, Alabama. The CDP is the only federal chartered center responsible for training state and local agencies on WMD and is the nation's premier **all-hazards** training center that prepares individual agencies to respond to major catastrophic events, often addressing real-world scenarios. In addition, in May 2011, the White House initiated the National Strategy for CBRNE to address attacks that were WMD in nature.[58] The acronym **CBRNE** became the standard to describe these types of attacks:

Chemical
Biological
Radiological
Nuclear
Explosive

The Center for Domestic Preparedness carries out large, multi-agency and whole community simulations in an effort to prepare for large-scale events (see Figure 13–10). Much of its training focuses on conditions requiring a **HAZMAT** response, which requires first responders to wear **personal protection equipment (PPE)** or a personal protection suit in order to address the event. In real situations, these types of incidents almost always involve a CBRNE release and are very dangerous for first responders. The CDP provides training for state and local police, as well as fire and medical personnel, that may respond to such incidents. In addition, every FEMA region, as well as most large metropolitan cities, has specially trained units that can respond to HAZMAT events. In most cases, these types of incidents involve overturned trucks carrying chemicals that might spill on the roadway, or accidents that involve train cargo containers that have ruptured and endanger the immediate environment. Remediation and cleanup are key concerns during these types of incidents. However, the use of CBRNE agents during a terrorist attack is one of the most frightening of all scenarios, and one which most endangers first responders.

The U.S. Military and CBRNE Attacks

In addition to the responsibilities assumed by the U.S. Department of Homeland Security and the Federal Emergency Management Agency, several other agencies have a primary or supportive role in case of a CBRNE attack. The U.S. Department of Defense maintains a highly trained, CBRNE rapid response team, using various specialists from all branches

Center for Domestic Preparedness (CDP)

The primary training facilities in Anniston, Alabama, operated by FEMA to train members of federal, state, and local agencies on all aspects of domestic preparedness; focuses on response training during WMD and CBRNE events.

All-hazards

National preparedness is based on the all-hazards approach. This approach uses a capabilities-based preparedness to prevent, protect against, respond to, and recover from terrorist attacks, major disasters (natural, technological, or human caused), and all other emergencies.

CBRNE

Acronym for Chemical, Biological, Radiological, Nuclear, and Explosive, used to define types of mass destruction attacks.

HAZMAT

Acronym for hazardous and dangerous materials.

Personal protection equipment (PPE)

Used by first responders to protect them against CBRNE agents.

Information Link
For more information on the Center for Domestic Preparedness (CDP), visit the website at https://cdp.dhs.gov/.

FIGURE 13–10
First responders train at the Center for Domestic Preparedness to be mission ready for actual CBRNE search and rescue operations.
(Courtesy Center for Domestic Preparedness, Federal Emergency Management Agency)

of the military.[59] In addition, the U.S. Army, 20th Support Command (CBRNE) integrates, coordinates, deploys, and provides trained and ready CBRNE forces capable of addressing any CBRNE contingency globally. The 20th Support Command (CBRNE) has some 5,000 employees spread over 19 installations in 16 states. Although their primary purpose is in support of warfighting operations, the unit also supports federal, state, and local CBRNE assets in support of homeland defense. The concept is that state and local personnel may be overwhelmed should an actual, large-scale CBRNE terrorist attack occur on the homeland. In addition to the 20th support command (CBRNE), specific National Guard units have been CBRNE trained and are located in and support each of the ten regional districts of FEMA.

The Centers for Disease Control and Prevention (CDC)

The Centers for Disease Control and Prevention (CDC) located in Atlanta, Georgia, has a very unique and specific role in securing the country from and during a potential CBRNE attack. The CDC not only responds directly to such attacks, but also prepares first responders and community leaders for these potential hazards. The CDC provides assistance in the design and development of protective gear for first responders as well as information relating to mitigation after an incident, such as cleanup protocols and best practices.

Clearly, the role of the CDC is much more pronounced during real or suspected biologic, nuclear, and radiologic type attacks than during more traditional bombings and shootings that have been the hallmark of terrorist organizations in the past. However, with the higher potential for a CBRNE attack from a sophisticated terrorist group, the CDC's mission has escalated over the last decade. In addition, the 2012 popular hit movie, *Contagion*, highlighted the possibility of a lethal airborne virus that kills within a few days of exposure and sweeps across the globe in a highly connected world. Although not at the same lethality level, we have already witnessed such a **pandemic** (an epidemic of an infectious disease that involves a large area, usually one that has crossed international boundaries and involves multiple continents) in modern history. The SARS (Severe Acute Respiratory Syndrome) in 2003 and the H1N1 flu pandemic in 2009 spread globally within just a few weeks, and the CDC was instrumental in tracking down the source of the outbreaks and the development of remedial therapies and vaccines used to combat the diseases.

Although the likelihood of a terrorist using a biologic agent is relatively remote because the germ would have to be "weaponized"—meaning highly refined and concentrated, developed under very precise and consistent environmental conditions, and then released over a period of time—such an attack is possible. More likely, any future pandemic would involve accidental human exposure to the myriad of diseases shared with animals. For instance, SARS, HIV, Ebola, Nipah, and various strains of the influenza virus (flu) are just a few of the many diseases humans share with animals. Hence, food markets and food preparation sites are often the pathways for the spread of diseases to humans.

The National Incident Management System

In 2003, President George W. Bush issued Homeland Security Presidential Directive-5 (HSPD-5). The purpose of HSPD-5 was to increase the ability of the United States to respond to domestic emergencies[60] by a system that would prevent, prepare for, respond to, and recover from terrorist attacks, major disasters, and other emergencies. HSPD-5 required DHS to coordinate with other federal departments and agencies and state, local, and tribal governments to establish a single, comprehensive **National Incident Management System (NIMS)**.

The National Incident Management Systems is FEMA's template of best all-hazards incident management practices from which local, state, tribal, and federal governments, nongovernmental organizations, volunteer organizations, and the private sector can select best practices that are most useful in developing emergency plans to respond to their anticipated and most likely incidents.

The all-hazards template approach reveals two major strengths of NIMS: standardization and flexibility.[61] Together with local and state agencies, NIMS establishes doctrine,

Pandemic
An epidemic of an infectious disease that involves a large area, usually crossing international boundaries and involving multiple continents.

National Incident Management System (NIMS)
The comprehensive, nationwide systematic approach to incident management adopted by FEMA to manage and standardize responses to critical incidents and/or disasters.

What NIMS Is:	What NIMS Is Not:
• A comprehensive, nationwide, systematic approach to incident management, including the Incident Command System, Multiagency Coordination Systems, and Public Information	• A response plan
	• Only used during large-scale incidents
	• A communications plan
• A set of preparedness concepts and principles for all hazards	• Only applicable to certain emergency management/incident response personnel
• Essential principles for a common operating picture and interoperability of communications and information management	• Only the Incident Command System or an organization chart
• Standardized resource management procedures that enable coordination among different jurisdictions or organizations	• A static system
• Scalable, so it may be used for all incidents (from day-to-day to large-scale)	
• A dynamic system that promotes ongoing management and maintenance	

FIGURE 13–11
What NIMS Is and Isn't[62]
Source: National Incident Management System (Washington, D.C.: Department of Homeland Security, December 2008), p. 6, www.fema.gov/pdf/emergency/nims/NIMS_core.pdf.

concepts, principles, terminology, and organizational processes that are standard in emergency management.[63] Further, all federal departments and agencies are required to adopt NIMS standards. For local, state, and tribal governments to receive funds through the National Preparedness Grant Program (NPGP) they must also use NIMS.[64]

It is common knowledge that incidents can range from small to catastrophic. Although disaster incidents are often deadly they usually are not large scale. They begin locally and are often managed to a relatively quick conclusion at that level,[65] such as an active shooter in a high school. However, if there was an explosion at a nuclear power plant, a large hurricane hitting the entire Gulf Coast, or the eruption of a volcano, successful incident management operations will depend on the involvement of multiple jurisdictions, all levels of government, and private-sector experts.[66] Regardless of the size or severity of an incident, the NIMS template provides a systematic approach to integrating the best processes and methods into a unified national framework.[67] NIMS is valuable because it provides a set of nationally standardized organizational structures and procedures that emergency responders understand. It can be applied to any incident (large or small), allowing different jurisdictions that also use it to quickly work together in a predictable, coordinated manner.[68] Figure 13–11 summarizes the characteristics of NIMS.

The NIMS template consists of five components that work together to create a systematic, all-hazards approach to any event or incident:

Preparedness

Effective emergency and incident response activities begin with preparedness activities conducted on an ongoing basis well in advance of any incident.[69] From local government to the federal level preparedness must include all partners. Preparedness essentially means being ready to respond effectively to incidents. Illustrations of preparedness activities include threat assessments, planning, developing procedures and protocols, providing training, conducting exercises, and ensuring personnel and equipment have the appropriate certification/licenses for their roles.[70]

An important aspect of preparedness is realistically determining what levels of capabilities and resources can be provided before, during, and after an incident. Preparedness is not simply a planning exercise; the capabilities must actually be established, sustained, and improved (see Figure 13–12).

Communications and Information Management (CIM)

Establishing and maintaining a common operating picture and communication interoperability are the principal goals of this NIMS component.[71] Information sharing on a timely

FIGURE 13–12
The NIMS Preparedness Cycle, which can be applied to other emergency preparedness activities as well.
(Courtesy Federal Emergency Management Agency)

Quick Facts
The U.S. Coast Guard National Strike Force

The U.S. Coast Guard National Strike Force responds to any hazard, any place, at any time involving an oil or dangerous substance that threatens to pollute the marine environment. The team consists of over 200 active-duty civilian, reserve, and auxiliary personnel and includes the National Strike Force Coordination Center. The team has responded during every major hurricane and such high-profile events as the Exxon Valdez spill in Prince William Sound Alaska (1989), the 9/11 terrorist attacks (2001), the Space Shuttle Columbia recovery (2003), and the Deep Water Horizon explosion and oil spill (2010).

basis is essential to making good decisions about coordination and operations,[72] keeping responders informed and safe, and other matters. Therefore, communications and information management is a critical function. Communication and information exchanges allow first responders, emergency managers, and follow-on personnel to understand the operational environment. To facilitate this understanding CIM ideally must be able to transmit voice, data, and video in real time.[73] Many emergency management operations have mobile communications vehicles to deploy for communication and information management purposes. Elsewhere, CIM may be provided out of tents, abandoned buildings, or other locations.

Some local, regional, state, and federal agencies, including Missouri, Washington, Indiana, Kansas, Connecticut, Kentucky, and North Dakota, use WebEOC, which is a secure, real-time, Internet-based communication system. In 2006, the federal Emergency Communications Preparedness Center (ECPC) was created to help fill the significant gaps emergency responders had in communicating across platforms, functions, and jurisdictions. ECPC consist of 14 agencies working to improve emergency communication interoperability in five areas: policy, regulations, operations, grants, and technical assistance."[74] The basic goal in ECPC is to provide a communication and information management system that affords interoperability and standardization for all jurisdictions and entities responding to an emergency or catastrophic event, thereby enhancing coordination of effort and the effective use of all resources.

Information Link
Learn more about the National Interagency Fire Center at www.nifc.gov/.

Resource Management

The right types of resources (e.g., personnel, equipment, and supplies) are needed at the right time, at the right place, in the right quantities. Communications provides fluidity to managing resources so that they can be directed or redirected to rapidly changing incidents. As an illustration, two or three smaller wildfires may quickly merge to form a single large-scale fire when winds gust and change directions. Addressing a disaster or events during a rapidly changing weather environment is particularly challenging, and is often encountered during fire and flood emergencies. Incident commanders must quickly get their new requirements to the resource manager, who must be nimble in responding. For this reason, large stockpiles of equipment are pre-positioned near urban areas throughout the United States. In addition, private-public agreements are often pre-developed to be used during an emergency. For instance, the U.S. Coast Guard has existing relationships and agreements with private-sector manufactures of spill boom (devices placed in water to contain an oil spill) and other oil-absorbent materials. These items can be quickly located through the private sector and delivered to an open water emergency in a matter of hours almost anywhere within the continental United States. Additionally, the U.S. Forest Service has similar agreements with private-sector helicopter and air flight services to provide water and fire retardant quickly to burning areas, as well as their own resources (see Figure 13–13).

FIGURE 13–13
A Forest Service air tanker dropping fire retardant. Having the right equipment available in a timely manner at the location of an emergency is often a critical factor in effectively managing the event. The Federal Interagency Fire Center coordinates wildfire fighting assistance from a number of agencies, including the U.S. Forest Service.
(Courtesy © Keith Crowley/Alamy)

Command and Management

The command and management component is responsible for providing effective and efficient incident management and coordination and has three separate components:

1) The Incident Command System (ICS),[75] which was developed by America's fire service over a period of 30 years.[76] In 2004, its applicability to natural disasters, terrorist attacks, and other types of incidents resulted in it being incorporated into NIMS. The ICS is covered in detail in the next section.

2) If multiple jurisdictions are responding to an incident, a Multi-Agency Coordination (MAC) group may be activated. MAC membership consists of the department heads of units that are supporting or are heavily committed to the ICS. A MAC group doesn't need to be in the **Emergency Operations Center (EOC)** and can work virtually if the capabilities for it exist. A MAC exercises no direct control over the ICS or EOC, but helps acquire resources and prioritize the delivery of staff and equipment requested by the Incident Commander (IC).

3) Public Information consists of the processes, procedures, and systems to communicate timely, accurate, and accessible information about the incident's cause, size, and current situation to the public, responders, and additional stakeholders (both directly and indirectly affected). Well-developed public information strategies help to ensure that lifesaving measures, evacuation routes, threat and alert systems, and other public safety information are coordinated and communicated to numerous audiences in a timely, consistent manner.[77]

Emergency Operations Center (EOC)
Mandated by the National Incident Management System, the EOC's primary role is to provide support, coordination, resource allocation, and information analysis and dissemination during an incident or event.

When Malaysian Airlines Flight 370 disappeared in 2014, both the carrier and the Malaysian government were slow to release information and were soundly criticized by experts and the families of those on the plane. The chief criticisms were that holding back information served no legitimate purpose and doing so placed additional stress on the families. In emergency management, the public information component may literally save lives. Individuals may also be able to get severe weather or other warnings[78] on their mobile devices from Wireless Emergency Alerts (WEAs). WEAs don't require an automated application (app) and originate with an authorized governmental authority. MyWarn is similar, but requires downloading a free app.

Ongoing Management and Maintenance

Within this component are two elements, both within FEMA's National Integration Center (NIC):

1. NIC provides strategic direction, oversight, and coordination of NIMS and supports routine maintenance and the continuous refinement of NIMS.

2. Supporting Technologies: As NIMS and other systems evolve, they will be increasingly reliant on technology.[79] Consequentially, NIC also oversees and coordinates the ongoing development of incident management-related technology in partnership with the Department of Homeland Security's Science and Technology Directorate. An example of the application of technology to incidents is seen in the Orange County, California, Emergency Operations Center (EOC). It can function as a virtual EOC so that persons who need to be involved, but can't be there, may be included by real time face-to-face communication.

The Incident Command System (ICS)

The Incident Command System (ICS) is a vital part of NIMS and represents a standardized, on-scene, all-hazards incident management approach that allows for the integration of facilities, equipment, personnel, procedures, and communications operating within a common organizational structure.[80] ICS also enables a coordinated response among various jurisdictions, both public and private, as well as establishes a common process for planning and managing diverse resources from multiple venues.

The ICS includes the use of a temporary organizational structure in the field that is established as close as safety permits to the scene of an incident—the Incident Command Center (ICC). That structure is "retired" after each incident. Beyond actual incidents, the Incident Command Center is also activated during readiness exercises. The staffing of the structure will vary depending on the complexity of the incident. The Incident Command System is used by all levels of government, as well as many non-governmental organizations and the private sector. For instance, almost every hospital utilizes ICS during an emergency in order to create a triage system and provide specialty expertise, equipment, and resources to various trauma centers throughout a specific region during a crisis. This type of information sharing, coordination of services, and use of valuable resources is vastly enhanced through ICS. The Incident Command System can be used with any type or size of event. By using it in smaller incidents, valuable experience can be gained, which will be useful in dealing with larger incidents later.[81]

More specifically, ICS is a standardized, on-scene, all-hazards management structure and process that:[82]

1) Allows for integration of facilities, equipment, personnel, procedures operating within a single organizational structure (see Figure 13–14) and using a common terminology.

2) Enables a coordinated response among the various responders to incidents.

3) Establishes common processes for planning and managing resources. For example, most incident communication is not based on dispatch codes; everything is communicated in plain English. However, an encryption system is also needed for incidents such as an ongoing terrorist attack or active shooter situation.

4) Communicates and coordinates with its Emergency Operations Center (EOC), which is normally activated if the ICS commander requests additional support and resources. State statutes may provide other ways a local EOC can be activated, such as by the sheriff, the county judge, the emergency center director, or some other arrangement. City/County EOCs have a policy/executive board comprised of key local officials, such as the sheriff, mayors, and chairs of county commissions, who may be present in the EOC during an incident.

The first arriving emergency responder to an incident automatically becomes the **Incident commander** and remains in that role until (1) a more senior person arrives and takes command; (2) he/she needs rest or is injured and the EOC director appoints a replacement; or (3) he/she is replaced for cause or other reason and the EOC director designates a new incident commander. One of the most important elements of the Incident Command System is the development of a **unified command**. The unified command is a structure that combines all incident commanders from all major organizations or responding agencies involved in an incident under one umbrella. The idea is to link all organizations together and provide a forum for all agencies to coordinate a specific response

---

Information Link
For more information on NIMS and ICS, visit the "Updated National Incident Management System Training Program" at www.training.fema.gov/EMIWeb/IS/ICSResource/assets/IncidentTypes.pdf.

Incident commander
The most senior commander first arriving at the scene of an incident from a specific first responder agency, such as from police, fire, or emergency services.

Unified command
The primary command organization for the Incident Command System in the field; incident commanders from different agencies combine to form a single unified command structure.

FIGURE 13–14
The ICS Command and General Staff Structure
Depending on the type and severity of an incident the General Staff structure may be less or more specialized (e.g., air support, decontamination centers, and the presence of NGOs such as the American Red Cross).
Source: National Incident Management System (Washington, D.C.: Department of Homeland Security, December 2008), p. 53.

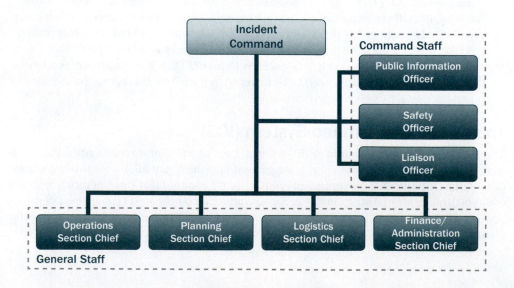

to an incident based on the combined expertise of the agencies responding. Under the unified command, decisions are made by consensus of those leaders that are actually on the scene so that an integrated and efficient response can occur (see Figure 13–15).

The Emergency Operation Center (EOC)[83]

An Emergency Operation Center (EOC) is a concept used by many jurisdictions and is mandated by NIMS. When activated, its primary purpose is to provide support to the incident commander. An EOC has levels of activation, such as:

1) A stand-by/warning alert to the EOC staff that activation may occur (for instance, due to a hurricane that is 72 hours from making landfall in the area),

2) Partial activation (for instance, the interstate that runs through the city/county is blocked by tornado debris and there are some medical emergencies, requiring a limited level of EOC services), and

3) Full activation (for instance, a violent lightning storm with winds gusting to 65 miles an hour with softball-sized hail causes a series of ongoing fires; signs and some roofs are torn off in the business district, along with broken windows which led to looting in that area; and a school bus has been overturned with an unknown number of injuries to middle school students).

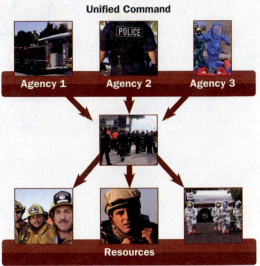

Unified Command

Agency 1 Agency 2 Agency 3

Resources

FIGURE 13–15
The unified command organization consists of incident commanders from various agencies working together to form a single command structure in the field.

(Left to Right (top): Courtesy Mike Brake/Shutterstock, bikeriderlondon/Shutterstock, TFoxFoto/Shutterstock; Center: © Christopher Penler/Alamy; Left to Right (bottom): bikeriderlondon/Shutterstock, © MC Images/Alamy, Ben Carlson/Shutterstock)

Some states require all EOC activations to be reported to their regional and federal coordinators. Other states have a list that identifies the mandatory incident reporting to the state. In Indiana, that list includes incidents involving weapons of mass destruction, sniper activity, severe flooding, suspected or actual acts of terrorism, catastrophic failure of buildings, and injury or death to members of the legislature, the executive branch, and judiciary. A number of EOCs have an alternate or back-up location in case the primary site is damaged or destroyed. For instance, the Emergency Operations Center for the City of Dallas (Texas) is located in the basement of city hall, while the back-up EOC is the existing fusion center within the Dallas Police Department, located several miles away. Personnel within the EOC often work 12-hour shifts during an emergency and stay on-site versus going home. The need to have personnel working on an extended basis often requires the EOC to have lodging capabilities, food services, and showers and restroom accommodations in the likely event that staff coming and going will not be feasible during an incident.

The EOC's broader role is to provide support such as incident coordination, resource allocation, and information collection, analysis, and dissemination. Most states have an EOC, as do many local jurisdictions, and some states require cities of a certain size to have one or to join a multi-jurisdictional emergency operational center. EOCs are usually housed in a permanent location and may be "hardened" to protect them from severe weather or other threats. They are not routinely staffed unless their anticipated workload justifies it or a major incident occurs. An EOC is staffed from emergency "disciplines," such as the police, fire, health, and public works departments, and geographic information support (GIS) and mutual aid personnel. Key elected officials in the EOC do not have authority over the incident commander, who is on the scene and responsible for all tactical decisions, although key officials are empowered to issue disaster declarations. The types of emergency management disciplines represented at an EOC may change as the incident passes to a different phase, that is, from response to recovery, and produces new needs that must be met.

The National Preparedness System

In 2011, President Barak Obama distributed Presidential Protective Directive-8 (PPD-8). It required a series of actions, including disaster planning as a whole community, a National Preparedness Goal, a National Preparedness System, and an annual National Preparedness Report. Another purpose of PPD-8 was to meet many of the requirements required by the Post-Katrina Emergency Management Reform Act of 2006.[84] PPD-8 also identified five key missions for FEMA—Prevention, Protection, Mitigation, Response, and Recovery—that are central to today's emergency management doctrine.

The National Preparedness Goal

National Preparedness Goal
Released in September 2011, the National Preparedness Goal defines national preparedness as: *"A secure and resilient nation with the capabilities required across the whole community to prevent, protect against, mitigate, respond to, and recover from the threats and hazards that pose the greatest risk."*

The **National Preparedness Goal** provides a consistent common structure and language for emergency management and is scalable, meaning that it can be applied to small towns and counties or large cities and metropolitan areas. National preparedness is based on the all-hazards approach, as discussed in various places in this book.[85] This approach uses a capabilities-based preparedness to prevent, protect against, respond to, and recover from terrorist attacks, major disasters, and other emergencies.[86] The National Preparedness Goal requires the "whole community" to be prepared for all types of disasters and emergencies (natural, technological, or terrorist/human caused). More specifically, the National Preparedness Goal is:

> A secure and resilient nation with the capabilities required across the *"whole community"* to prevent, protect against, mitigate, respond to, and recover from *"the threats and hazards that pose the greatest risk.*[87]

"Whole community"
A concept within the National Preparedness Goal referring to all of the federal, state, and local government agencies, as well as the non-governmental organizations, private sector, schools, families, and individuals focused on national preparedness.

"Whole community" includes not only FEMA and its partners at the federal level, but also local, tribal, state, and territorial partners; non-governmental organizations like faith-based and non-profit groups; the private sector; schools and academia; media outlets; individuals; and families.[88] Both the composition of the community and the individual needs of community members, regardless of race, color, religion, nationality, gender, age, language, or disability, must be accounted for when planning and implementing disaster strategies.[89] For instance, among populations that require special assistance are those who are medically fragile, wheelchair bound, diabetic, deaf, cognitively or intellectually impaired, and those who need an interpreter or someone proficient in American Sign Language (ASL).[90] *"The threats and hazards that pose the greatest risk"* include natural disasters, disease pandemics, chemical spills and other manmade hazards, as well as terrorist and cyber-attacks.[91]

Figure 13–16 summarizes the relationship of missions and core capabilities. Note that the core capabilities are distributed across five missions. Three capabilities apply to all

FIGURE 13–16
The relationship between emergency management's 5 missions and 31 core capabilities.

(Courtesy Federal Emergency Management Agency)

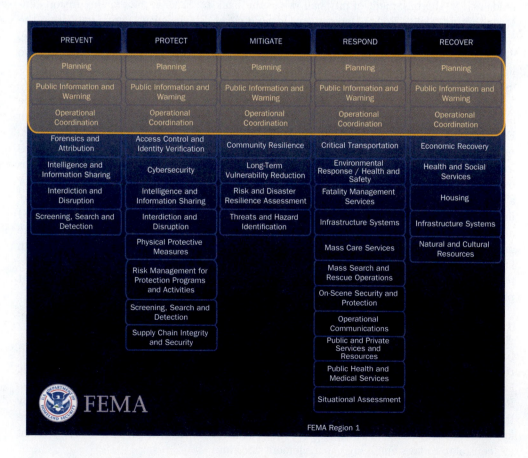

five missions and several others to more than one. The missions and the core capabilities in Figure 13–16 support the achievement of the National Preparedness Goal by:

- Preventing, avoiding, or stopping a threatened or actual act of terrorism;

- Protecting our citizens, residents, visitors, and assets against the greatest threats and hazards in a manner that allows our interests, aspirations, and ways of life to thrive;

- Mitigating the loss of life and property by lessening the impact of future disasters;

- Responding quickly to save lives, protect property and the environment, and meet basic human needs in the aftermath of a catastrophic incident; and

- Recovering through a focus on the timely restoration, strengthening, and revitalization of infrastructure, housing, and a sustainable economy, as well as the heath, social, cultural, historic, and environmental fabric of communities affected by a catastrophic incident.[92]

Core capabilities are critical elements that contribute to achieving the NPG. Each core capability has a target level of performance. Metrics or measurements are used to determine the degree to which the target level of performance is attained. A 2012 report using FEMA metrics assessed the capacity of states and territories to deliver the core capabilities.[93] Cyber security rated lowest, reaching only 19 percent of capability, while on-scene security and protection was highest at 61 percent.[94] These figures improved over an earlier study, but there is still much to be done.

The integrated emergency management system works well with small- to moderate-scale disasters, but the real challenge is preparedness for an unprecedented catastrophic event.[95] The first 72 hours following such an event are critical.[96] FEMA is now developing core capabilities for stabilization and restoration (see Figure 13–17) from such an event. As a preliminary target, basic community services would be restored in 60 days, but as much as five to ten years might be needed to recover from the long-term effects of an unprecedented catastrophe like the 9/11 attack on the World Trade Center and the Pentagon.[97]

The National Preparedness System

The **National Preparedness System (NPS)** is the instrument emergency management relies on to build, sustain, and deliver capabilities to achieve the goal of a *"secure and resilient Nation."*[98] Capabilities are the means to accomplish a mission, function, or objective based on the performance of related tasks, under specified conditions, to reach target levels of performance.[99] The most essential of these is the core capabilities. The NPS builds on and refines existing capabilities. When needed, it produces new tools and processes.[100] As shown in Figure 13–18, the NPS is a six-step process that is continually changing and evolving to address current and future needs.

The National Preparedness Report

The last step of the National Preparedness model presented by President Obama in Presidential Policy Directive #8 is the National Preparedness Report (NPR). The NPR is an annual assessment of national progress toward delivering the core capabilities outlined in the National Preparedness Goal (NPG). The report focuses on the progress made by the whole community partners—including all levels of government, private and non-profit sectors, faith-based organizations, communities and individuals—in the previous year. The report identifies strengths and progress, as well as weaknesses and gaps that still remain.

Enable Response:
- Situational Assessment
- Public Messaging
- Command, Control, and Coordination
- Critical Communications
- Environmental Health and Safety Critical Transportation

Survivor Needs:
- On-Scene Security and Protection
- Mass Search and Rescue Operations
- Health and Medical Treatment
- Mass Care Services
- Public and Private Services and Resources
- Stabilize and Repair Essential Infrastructure
- Fatality Management Services

Restoration:
- Essential Service Facilities
- Utilities
- Transportation Routes
- Schools
- Neighborhood Retail Businesses
- Offices and Other Workplaces

FIGURE 13–17
Targeted Core Capabilities for the Stabilization and Restoration Mission of FEMA

(Courtesy Federal Emergency Management Agency)

National Preparedness System (NPS)
An organized process for the "whole community" within the United States to move forward with preparedness actives in an effort to achieve the National Preparedness Goal.

FIGURE 13–18
Mission Components of the National Preparedness System

(Courtesy Federal Emergency Management Agency)

Findings from the 2013 Report[101] identified areas of national strength in the following core capabilities as well as areas for improvement:

- *Planning:* The integrated, all-hazards approach to planning and responding to routine emergencies as well as catastrophic events continues to integrate the "whole community" perspective on a positive framework.
- *Operational Coordination:* The National Incident Management System (NIMS) continues to provide a common doctrine for incident management, enhancing the "whole community" ability to share language and standardize operations.
- *Intelligence and Information Sharing:* The national network of fusion centers and Joint Terrorism Task Forces (JTTFs)—refer back to Chapter 9—continues to mature and enhance interagency cooperation and structure.
- *Operational Communications:* States and U.S. territories continue to develop State Emergency Communication Plans that facilitate interoperability between agencies and governmental units as well as a move toward a nationwide public safety broadband system.
- *Cybersecurity:* Although some improvement was noted in the report, significant challenges remain in this area.
- *Infrastructure Protection:* Two new national areas for improvement were identified in this core capability: enhancing the resilience of infrastructure systems and maturing the role of public-private partnerships.

The 2013 National Preparedness Report was only the second time that the nation reflected on the progress of its national preparedness in the wake of serious terrorist threats and catastrophic natural disasters. Reviewing the core capabilities identified in the National Preparedness Goal (Figure 13–16), the report provides a national perspective on critical preparedness and represents a systematic methodology for measuring improvement and identifying weaknesses in our efforts to be a *secure and resilient Nation!*

Chapter Summary

SUMMARY BY LEARNING OBJECTIVE

1. Describe and give examples of the three major categories of threats or hazards.

The three major categories of threat or hazards are: (1) natural, which include weather conditions as well as animal and human diseases. Examples include tornadoes, hurricanes, Mad Cow disease, and Ebola; (2) technological and accidental, examples of which are dam failures and accidental/unintended release of hazardous materials into the environment; and (3) terrorist and human-caused, events are intentional and intended to disrupt systems, destroy property, and/or kill people. The attack may be made using chemical, cyber, radiological, or other means. In late 2014, a lone wolf terrorist, a recent convert to Islam, shot his way into Canada's Parliament before he was killed.

2. Summarize the severity continuum.

The severity continuum is a guide to categorizing events so that important distinctions can be made between them. It is composed of four points: (1) An "*emergency*" marked by actual danger to the lives of persons and/or the safety of property that requires a response (emergencies ordinarily are handled locally). (2) A "*disaster*" is more severe than an emergency because it causes a serious disruption of the functioning of an entity, such as a community, and produces widespread human, material, economic, and/or environmental losses that exceed the ability of a community to cope with it using just its own resources. (3) A "*catastrophe*" is an incident that directly or indirectly affects large portions or all of an entire country and requires national and sometimes international responses. (4) An "*extinction event*" is the final event in human history, resulting in the loss of all human life on the planet. The probability of a human extinction event is presently very slight.

3. **Explain how the New Deal Programs of the 1930s altered the federal government's long-standing position that relief assistance was a local government issue.**

The New Deal Programs were developed by President Franklin D. Roosevelt and the Congress as a direct response to the stock market crash of 1929 and the prolonged depression which lasted well into the 1930s. The programs focused on unemployment and ushered in two federally sponsored work programs, The Civilian Conservation Corps (CCC) and the Work Progress Administration (WPA), that concentrated on building the infrastructure of the country. The New Deal Programs reflected a policy shift away from the federal government's long-standing attachment to the self-reliant philosophy … some problems were just too big for communities and states to address alone." Indeed, some of these issues were national in scope and involved the entire country, hence the federal government had to provide aid to people in these circumstances. The New Deal programs established a major precedent for the federal government to provide assistance to people in distress.

4. **Discuss the impact of World War II and the development of the Federal Civil Defense Administration on emergency management.**

During World War II (1941–1945) the nation was gripped with fear of attacks on the mainland. In 1941, the newly created Office of Civilian Defense (OCD) coordinated federal, state, and local defense programs for the protection of civilians during air raids and other emergencies, as well as facilitating civilian participation in war programs. In other words, the emphasis of emergency management was much more focused on civilian defense and protection from enemy forces during the war. To no small degree, emergency management took a "backseat" to matters involving the war effort. At the end of the war, the threat of nuclear war seemed possible, ushering in the Cold War between the United States and Russia. Again, the focus was not on disaster planning, prevention, and response, but on civil defense from a possible nuclear war.

5. **Explain the rise and role of FEMA.**

Building on the federal National Flood Insurance Act of 1968 that recognized taking steps in advance to reduce the impact of a disaster, Congress passed the Disaster Relief Act of 1970, setting forth the first major attempt by the federal government to emphasize hazard mitigation as a priority to reduce the impact of future disasters. By 1975, nearly 100 federal agencies had some aspect of disaster assistance. Frustrated with governmental fragmentation, the National Governors Association (NGA) pushed for a single agency to have jurisdiction over natural and environmental disasters. In 1978, President Jimmy Carter responded by issuing Executive Order 12127 creating the Federal Emergency Management Agency (FEMA). The bombing of Oklahoma City's Alfred P. Murrah Federal Building in 1995 by Timothy McVeigh and his co-conspirators elevated America's awareness about terrorism. The Antiterrorism and Effective Death Penalty Act of 1996 required the Department of Justice (DOJ) and FEMA to train metropolitan firefighters in responding to events caused by weapons of mass destruction. Three years later, the Defense Against Weapons of Mass Destruction Act required training state and local first responders on handling threats and actual weapons of mass destruction incidents. In 2001, FEMA supported Pennsylvania, Virginia, and New York in responding to the 9/11 attacks with thousands of staff and mobile communications gear. In 2003, FEMA was officially moved to the Department of Homeland Security, where it remains today, as the primary agency over disaster relief and mitigation. Further, FEMA's top official is the president's principal advisor on emergencies and disasters regardless of causation, natural or man-made.

6. **Describe the acronyms WMD, CBRNE, and CDC.**

WMD is an acronym to mean "weapons of mass destruction." The term is used to mean any and all weapons that are designed to cause mass casualties. In May 2011, the White House initiated the National Strategy for CBRNE to address and been define attacks that were WMD in nature. The acronym CBRNE is a standard within emergency management doctrine to mean Chemical, Biological, Radiological, Nuclear, and Explosive in reference to types of WMD attacks. CDC is an acronym for the Centers for Disease Control and Prevention located in Atlanta, Georgia. The CDC not only responds directly to CBRNE attacks, but also prepares first responders and community leaders for these potential hazards. The CDC provides assistance in the design and development of protective gear for first responders as well as information relating to mitigation after an incident, such as cleanup protocols and best practices.

7. **Describe and briefly explain the National Incident Management System (NIMS) and the Incident Command System (ICS).**

The National Incident Management System is the federal government's template of best all-hazards incident management practices for local, state, tribal, and federal governments, non-governmental organizations, volunteer organizations, and the private sector. The approach is standardized using NIMS doctrine, concepts, principles, terminology, and organizational processes, and flexible for all types, sizes, and severity of emergencies and/or disasters. NIMS can be applied to any incident (large or small), allowing different jurisdictions that also use it to quickly work together in a predictable, efficient, and coordinated manner. The NIMS template consists of five components that work together to create a systematic, all-hazards approach to any event or incident: (1) Preparedness, (2) Communications and Information Management, (3) Resource Management, (4) Command and Management, and (5) On-Going Management and Maintenance.

The Incident Command System (ICS) is a vital part of NIMS and represents a standardized, on-scene, all-hazards incident management approach that allows for the integration of facilities, equipment, personnel, procedures, and communications operating within a common organizational structure. ICS also enables a coordinated response among various jurisdictions, both public and private, as well as establishes a common process for planning and managing diverse resources from multiple venues. The ICS includes the use of a temporary organizational structure in the field that is established as close as safety permits to the scene of an incident—the Incident Command Center (ICC). The Incident Command System can be used with any type or size of event. More specifically, ICS is a standardized, on-scene, all-hazards management structure and process that (1) allows for integration of facilities, equipment, personnel, and operational procedures within a single organizational structure and sharing a common terminology; (2) enables a coordinated response among the various responders to incidents; (3) establishes common processes for planning and managing resources; and (4) communicates and coordinates with all agencies responding to the incident via an incident commander and an Emergency Operations Center.

8. **State the National Preparedness Goal and define the concept of "whole community."**

The National Preparedness Goal is:

> A secure and resilient nation with the capabilities required across the "*whole community*" to prevent, protect against, mitigate, respond to, and recover from the threats and hazards that pose the greatest risk.

"*Whole community*" includes not only FEMA and its partners at the federal level, but also local, tribal, state, and territorial partners; non-governmental organizations like faith-based and non-profit groups; the private sector; schools and academia; media outlets; individuals; and families. Both the composition of the community and the individual needs of community members, regardless of race, color, religion, nationality, gender, age, language, or disability, must be accounted for when planning and implementing disaster strategies. "Whole community" means every individual in the United States.

9. **Explain the National Preparedness Report and identify the areas of national strength and weakness noted in the 2013 NPR.**

The National Preparedness Report is an annual assessment of national progress toward delivering the core capabilities outlined in the National Preparedness Goal (NPG) under each mission. The report focuses on the progress made by the whole community partners—including all levels of government, private and nonprofit sectors, faith-based organizations, communities, and individuals—in making progress in the previous year. The report identifies strengths and progress, as well as weaknesses and gaps that still remain. Findings from the 2013 Report identified areas of national strength in the following core capabilities as well as areas for improvement:

- *Planning:* The integrated, all-hazards approach to planning and responding to routine emergencies as well as catastrophic events continues to integrate the "whole community" perspective on a positive framework.

- *Operational Coordination:* The National Incident Management System (NIMS) continues to provide a common doctrine for incident management, enhancing the "whole community" ability to share language and standardize operations.

- *Intelligence and Information Sharing:* The national network of fusion centers and Joint Terrorism Task Forces (JTTFs) continues to mature and enhance interagency cooperation and structure.

- *Operational Communications:* States and U.S. territories continue to develop Emergency Communication Plans that facilitate interoperability between agencies and governmental units as well as a move toward a nationwide public safety broadband system.

- *Cybersecurity:* Although some improvement was noted in the report, significant challenges remain in this area.

- *Infrastructure Protection:* Two new national areas for improvement were identified in this core capability: enhancing the resilience of infrastructure systems and maturing the role of public-private partnerships.

REVIEW QUESTIONS

1. What are the major issues that have retarded the development of emergency management historically?
2. What are the goals of emergency management?
3. What are mutual aid agreements and how important are they in planning for emergencies or disasters?
4. Explain the major philosophical changes in the development of emergency management historically. What agency is at the forefront of emergency management today, and when was it developed?
5. What is a WMD, and what does CBRNE have to do with WMD?
6. What is a pandemic and what is the role of the Centers for Disease Control and Prevention during such an incident?
7. What are the primary purposes of an Emergency Operations Center?
8. Describe the concept of the "whole community" as it relates to the National Preparedness Goal.

CRITICAL THINKING EXERCISES

1. Compare the population density of California with Alaska and then do the same for the largest city in each of those states. What does population density suggest about the consequences of natural disasters and preparedness?
2. Visit and explore the website of the CDC at www.cdc.gov/. Under the tab labelled "Emergency Preparedness," explore the recent "outbreaks and incidents" that have recently occurred around the world. What has been the role of the CDC during these incidents? Discuss the importance of this agency in responding to a terrorist strike using CBRNE agents.
3. Discuss the possibility of a disaster in your community. What is the most likely type of disaster—natural, technological, man-made—and what do you think is the probability that an act will occur in the next two years? Five years? Ten years? How severe do you think this event will be, what agencies will respond, and what plans are already in place to address such an event? Ask an appropriate local official to discuss emergency management in your area.

NOTES

1. *Principles of Emergency Management Supplement*, September 11, 2007, p. 1, www.ndsu.edu/fileadmin/principlesofemergencymanagement.pdf.
2. *Fundamentals of Emergency Management* (Washington, D.C.: Federal Emergency Management Agency, January 14, 2010), p. 217.
3. Loc. cit.

4. "Bellevue Hospital Staffers Reportedly Take Sick Days Than Treat New York's First Ebola Patient," *Fox News*, October 25, 2014, www.foxnews.com/health/2014/10/25/hospital-staffers-reportedly-take-sick-day-rather-than-treat-new-yorks-first.

5. *How Flood Smart Are You?* (Washington, D.C.: Federal Emergency Management Agency, undated) p. 1, www.floodsmart.gov/floodsmart/pages/media_resources/fact_floodfacts.jsp.

6. This information is taken in part from "Saddam's Iraq, Chemical Warfare 1983–1988," *BBC News*, undated, http://news.bbc.co.uk/2/shared/spl/hi/middle_east/02/iraq_events/html/chemical_warfare.stm; and "Chemical Agents," *Centers for Disease Control and Prevention*, April 18, 2013, http://emergency.cdc.gov/agent/agentlistchem-category.asp.

7. Holly Fletcher, "Aum Shinrikyo," Council on Foreign Relations, June 19, 2012, pp. 1–3, www.cfr.org/japan/aum-shinrikyo/p9238.

8. FEMA Administrator Craig Fugate came up with the idea of a Waffle House Index. See Ewen MacAskill, "FEMA Uses 'Waffle House Index' to Take Stock of Oklahoma Tornado Disaster," *The Guardian*, May 21, 2013, p. 1, www.theguardian.com/world/2013/may/21/fema-waffle-house-index-oklahoma.

9. Ibid., p. 5.

10. "Grain Elevator Explosion Chart," *Occupational Safety and Health Administration*, www.osha.gov/sltc/grainhandling/explosion%20chart.html.

11. B. Wayne Blanchard, "Guide to Emergency Management and Related Terms, Definitions, Concepts, Acronyms, Organizations, Programs, Guidance, Executive Orders, and Legislation," October 22, 2008, pp. 284–285, www.training.fema.gov/emiweb/docs/terms%20and%20definitions.pdf.

12. In 1952, President Truman issued Executive Order 10427, which emphasized this point.

13. The information in this Quick Facts box is drawn from *Preparedness* (Washington, D.C.: Federal Emergency Management Agency, July 24, 2014), p. 1.

14. Loc. cit.

15. Nationally Adopted Interstate Mutual Aid Agreement, April 10, 2014, p. 1, www.emacweb.org.

16. "Haiti Earthquake," January 13, 2014, Thomson Reuters Foundation, www.trust.org/spotlight/Haiti-earthquake-2010.

17. Loc. cit.

18. Richard Sylves, *Disaster Policy and Politics* (Washington, D.C.: CQ Press, 2008), p. 3.

19. Some of the structure on self-reliance is drawn from Claire B. Rubin, "Local Emergency Management," pp. 26–17 in William L. Waugh, Jr. and Kathleen Tierney, *Emergency Management* (Washington, D.C.: International City/County Management Association, 2007).

20. Ralph Waldo Emerson, "Self Reliance," in *Essays*, originally published in 1841. See www.emersoncentral.com/selfreliance.htm.

21. Thomas Sowell, *Ethnic America* (New York: Basic Books, 1983), p. 117.

22. Richard Sylves, *Disaster Policy and Politics* (Los Angeles: Sage, 2008), p. 3.

23. Rubin, "Local Emergency Management," p. 27.

24. *Civil Defense and Homeland Security: A Short History of National Preparedness Efforts* (Washington, D.C.: Federal Emergency Management Agency, September 2006), p. 5.

25. Loc. cit.

26. Jennifer D. Keene, *World War I* (Westport, Connecticut, Greenwood Publishing Group, January 1, 2006), p. 114.

27. Sylves, *Disaster Policy and Politics*, p. 5.

28. Loc. cit.

29. Loc. cit.

30. "The New Deal," The Roosevelt Institute, undated, p. 1, http://rooseveltinstitute.org/policy-and-ideasroosevelt-historyfdr/new-deal.

31. "The Great Depression," The George Washington University Eleanor Roosevelt Papers Project, undated, p. 1, www.gwu.edu/~erpapers/teachinger/glossary/great-depression.cfm.

32. Gene Smiley, "Great Depression," *Library of Economic and Liberty*, undated, p. 1, http://www.econlib.org/library/Enc/GreatDepression.html.

33. Records of the Office of Civilian Defense, National Archives, Record Group 171, 171.1, Administrative History, undated, p. 1, www.archives.gov/research/guide-fed-records/groups/171.html#171.1.

34. For more information on this program see *A Handbook for Air Raid Wardens* (Washington, D.C.: Office of Civilian Defense, April 1942).

35. Library of Congress Prints and Photography Online Catalog, from 1943 photograph caption, www.loc.gov/pictures/item/oem2002008497/pp.

36. "Introduction: The Civilian Conservation Corps," *PBS*, undated, p. 1, www.pbs.org/wgbh/americanexperience/features/introduction/ccc-introduction.

37. Loc. cit.

38. Loc. cit.

39. Thomas J. Kerr, *Civil Defense in the U.S.* (Boulder, Colorado: Westview Press, 1983), pp. 27–28.

40. Andrew D. Grossman, *Neither Dead Nor Red* (New York: Routledge Press, 2001), pp. 41–42.

41. No author, Annual Report for 1952, Federal Civil Defense Administration (Washington, D.C.: Federal Civil Defense Administration, 1952), pp. 1–2.

42. *Duck and Cover* (York, Nebraska: Wessels, undated), p. 1, www.livinghistoryfarm.org/farminginthe1950s/life_04.html.

43. *Annual Report of the Office of Civil and Defense Mobilization for Fiscal Year 1959* (Washington, D.C.: Government Printing Office, 1960), p. 1, http://training.fema.gov/EMIWeb/edu/docs/HistoricalInterest/Office%20of%20Civil%20and%20Defense%20Mobilization%20-%201959%20-%20Annual%20Rep.pdf.

44. Loc. cit.

45. "For Preppers, Every Day Could Be Doomsday," *USAToday*, November 13, 2012, p. 1, www.usatoday.com/story/news/nation/2012/11/12/for-preppers-every-day-could-be-doomsday/1701151.

46. "Beecher 50th Anniversary Commemoration," *National Oceanic and Atmospheric Administration*, undated, p. 1, www.crh.noaa.gov/dtx/1953beecher/facts.php.

47. See Joseph A. Pratt, *The Challenge of Remaining Innovative in the Twentieth Century* (Redwood, CA: Stanford University Press, 2009), p. 10.

48. Loc. cit.

49. "Origins of U.S. Emergency Management," Anna Maria College, undated, p. 1, http://online.annamaria.edu/emergencymanagementhistory.asp.

50. Ibid., p. 7.

51. Among other agencies, FEMA absorbed the Federal Insurance Administration, the National Fire Prevention and Control Administration, the National Weather Service Community Preparedness Program, the Federal Preparedness Agency of the General Services Administration, the Federal Disaster Assistance Administration activities from HUD, and Civil Defense responsibilities from the Defense Department's Defense Civil Preparedness Agency.

52. Blaine Harden, "Explosive Lessons of 25 Years Ago," *The Washington Post*, May 18, 2005. p. A3.

53. The Federal Emergency Management Agency, "About the Agency," August 14, 2014, www.fema.gov/about-agency.

54. Ibid., pp. 9–10.

55. Ibid., p. 10.

56. Ibid., p. 12.

57. White House Memorandum, President Clinton to 14 Key Administrative Officials, U.S. Policy on Counterterrorism, June 21, 1995, Unclassified January 24, 1997 (or possibly 1999, handwriting is difficult to read) with redactions.

58. See www.whitehouse.gov/sites/default/files/microsites/ostp/chns_cbrne_standards_final_24_aug_11.pdf.

59. Al Mauroni, "Homeland Insecurity: Thinking About CBRN Terrorism," *Homeland Security Affairs Journal*, Volume VI, No. 3, September 2000, www.hsaj.org/?fullarticle=6.3.3

60. Homeland Security Presidential Directive/HSPD-5.

61. *National Incident Management System* (Washington, D.C.: Department of Homeland Security, December 2008), pp. 6–7.

62. Loc. cit.

63. Ibid., p. 3.

64. Loc. cit.

65. Ibid., p. 5.

66. Loc. cit.

67. Loc. cit.

68. Ibid., p. 6.

69. Ibid., p. 7.

70. Loc. cit.

71. Ibid., p. 23.

72. Ibid., p. 23.

73. Loc. cit.

74. *Emergency Communications Preparedness Center* (Washington, D.C.: Federal Emergency Management Center, Undated), p. 1, www.dhs.gov/emergency-communications-preparedness-center.

75. Technically, the fire service developed the Incident Management System (IMS) and FEMA made some terminology and other changes to it, and re-badged it as the Incident Command System (ICS).

76. *NIMS and the Incident Command System* (Washington, D.C.: Federal Emergency Management Agency, November 23, 2004), p. 1.

77. The information in this paragraph is taken, with minor restatement, from Public *Information Overview* (Washington, D.C.: Federal Emergency Management Agency, May 8, 2013), p. 1, http://www.fema.gov/public-information.

78. The Amber Alert broadcasts details about specific child abduction cases, making each recipient an extra set of eyes looking for that child. The system operates as a collaboration between local law enforcement and the National Center for Missing and Exploited Children (NCMEC) and is broadcast to mobile devices, Facebook, and other outlets.

79. This conclusion is embedded in a number of FEMA documents. For example, see Federal Emergency Management Agency, "Technological Development and Dependency," May 2011, pp. 1–5, www.fema.gov/pdf/about/programs/oppa/technology_dev_%20paper.pdf.

80. See www.fema.gov/incident-command-system.

81. *Incident Command System (ICS) Overview* (Washington, D.C.: Federal Emergency Management Agency, April 22, 2014), www.fema.gov/incident-management-system.

82. Ibid., p. 3.

83. The information in this box was influenced by reading a number of EOC plans and procedures. For example, see *Support Staff Procedures for EOC/Command Post Operation* (San Joaquin County, California: Department of Emergency Operation, February 2009), www.sjgov.org/oes/getplan/EOC-Staff%20procedures.pdf; and *Emergency Operations Center (EOC) Operations Guide* (Lewis and Clark County, Montana, Disaster and Emergency Services, May 11, 2011), www.lccountymt.gov/disaster-and-emergency-services.html.

84. Jared T. Brown, *Presidential Policy Directive 8 and the National Preparedness System: Background and Issues for Congress* (Washington, D.C.: Congressional Research Service, October 21, 2011), from Summary.

85. *National Preparedness Guidelines* (Washington, D.C.: Federal Emergency Management Agency, September 2007), p. 3, www.fema.gov/pdf/emergency/nrf/National_Preparedness_Guidelines.pdf.

86. Loc. cit.

87. *National Preparedness Goal* (Washington, D.C.: Federal Emergency Management Agency, September 2011, updated May 1, 2014).

88. "Whole Community," *FEMA*, May 8, 2013, p. 1, www.fema.gov/national-preparedness/whole-community.

89. *No Discrimination on FEMA Disaster Assistance* (Washington, D.C.: Federal Emergency Management, January 18, 2013), p. 1, www.fema.gov/news-release/2013/01/18/no-discrimination-fema-disaster-assistance.

90. *Special Needs Information* (Honolulu, Hawaii: Hawaii State Civil Defense, undated), p. 1, www.scd.hawaii.gov/contact.html.

91. *National Preparedness Goal*, pp. 4–5.

92. *PPD-8 Overview Presentation* (Washington, D.C.: Federal Emergency Management Agency, January 16, 2013), p. 8.

93. *National Preparedness Report* (Washington, D.C.: Federal Emergency Management Agency, March 30, 2013), p. 8.

94. Loc. cit.

95. FEMA Strategic Plan Fiscal Years 2011–2014 (Washington, D.C.: Federal Emergency Management Agency, February 2011), p. 11.

96. Loc. cit.

97. Ibid., p. 12.

98. *National Preparedness System* (Washington, D.C.: Federal Emergency Management Agency, November 11, 2011), p. 1.

99. Loc. cit.

100. Loc. cit.

101. The following national strengths were developed in the 2013 National Preparedness Report. Refer to the following website for additional information: www.fema.gov/national-preparedness-report.

Combatting Terrorism

Learning Objectives

After completing this chapter, you should be able to:

1. Distinguish between anti-terrorism and counterterrorism efforts.

2. Identify and explain the role of NORTHCOM during an emergency, disaster, or terrorist attack.

3. Summarize the work of the Foreign Terrorist Tracking Task Force.

4. Compare and contrast the national security policy shift in the United States from one based on mutually assured destruction (MAD) versus preemptive military action.

5. Identify the five subcommands of USSOCOM.

6. Name the five types of military action associated with counterterrorism.

7. Identify the the U.S. Military counterterrorism units discussed in this chapter.

8. Profile SAS, GSG9, and Mistavarim.

U.S. Navy SEALs discovered a vast al-Qaeda network of caves and tunnels in Eastern Afghanistan and destroyed munitions, arms, and other goods
(Courtesy U.S. Navy www.navy.mil)

Introduction

Over the past two decades, the United States has improved its capabilities to address domestic and transnational terrorism, including protecting U.S. interests abroad.[1] Two short definitions of important elements of fighting terrorism are: (1) **anti-terrorism**, which is defensive in nature, and 2) **counterterrorism**, which is offensive in nature, "taking the fight to the enemy" (see Figure 14–1).

Many, but not all, anti-terrorism activities are carried out by units of local and state governments, as well non-military organizations of the federal government and private contractors. Local and state governments often have units with "counterterrorism" in their titles, but they usually perform anti-terrorism duties. This may happen for two reasons: (1) precise definitions sometimes don't survive their encounter with reality and 2) local and state law enforcement leaders know the difference between anti- and counterterrorism, but they may reason that their citizens may feel safer with a more aggressive sounding "counterterrorism" unit, and therefore it may be easier to get appropriations for a unit titled "counterterrorism."

The military, and to a much smaller degree, the Central Intelligence Agency, execute the majority of all counterterrorism efforts, but they may also have some anti-terrorism responsibilities. Housed within the U.S. Department of Defense, the **U.S. Special Operations Command**[2] (USSOCOM or SOCOM) is the organization responsible for many counterterrorism actions by the military. America's allies, such as Great Britain and Australia, also participate in the global war on terrorism. In 2014, other allies, such as Pakistan, became more active in counterterrorism. Allies in combating terrorism participate in the ways that reflect their capabilities and their political choices. One nation may not commit combat troops, but it shares intelligence or provides critical geographical space for bases and/or listening posts.

Some information about the U.S. Department of Defense's anti-terrorism and counterterrorism programs is available, but details are often sparse for security reasons. To illustrate, the **Joint Special Operations Command (JSOC)** at Fort Bragg, North Carolina, is a joint services headquarters responsible for studying operational requirements and techniques, ensuring the interoperability and standardization of equipment, planning and conducting special operations exercises and training, and developing joint special operations tactics.[3] Information about these responsibilities and operations is closely held. The existence of JSOC illustrates another important feature of anti-terrorism and counterterrorism: It is often a cooperative, interdependent undertaking supported by multiple partners from different branches of the armed forces, which is why "Joint" is part of JSOC's designation.

Overview of Anti-Terrorism

A complete definition of anti-terrorism is the defensive actions taken to reduce the vulnerability of people and property to terrorist acts, to include rapid containment by local military and civilian forces.[4] Note that anti-terrorism programs have a proactive component of engaging in activities that are intended to prevent an attack or reduce the losses caused by one and a reactive component of managing the aftermath of an attack (see Figure 14–2).[5] Many countries have anti-terrorism programs; South Korea and Israel have particularly robust anti-terrorism programs, largely because they both have borders with countries opposed to their existence. Referring back to Chapter 13 many actions taken as part of emergency preparedness, for example "hardening" of emergency operations centers and the National Infrastructure Protection Plan, are anti-terrorism measures.

America's anti-terrorism program has been characterized as being geographically limited to the United States. However, this is not always the case. The U.S Department of State's Anti-Terrorism Assistance Program trains personnel in friendly foreign countries in such topics as protecting critical infrastructures, cyber security, dignitary protection, terrorist interdiction, countering violent extremism, and handling improvised explosive devices (IEDs). In any typical year, the Anti-Terrorism Assistance Program (ATAP) provides over

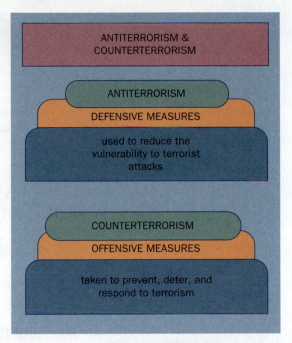

FIGURE 14–1
A basic version of the anti-terrorism and counterterrorism concepts.

Anti-terrorism
Defensive actions taken to reduce the vulnerability of people and property to terrorist acts, including rapid containment by local military and civilian forces.

Counterterrorism
Offensive actions (usually military or paramilitary) taken to prevent, deter, or respond to terrorist threats or attacks.

U.S. Special Operations Command
(USSOCOM or SOCOM) The organization responsible for many counterterrorism actions by the military.

Joint Special Operations Command (JSOC)
In addition to the responsibilities already mentioned, JSOC IS one of the five components reporting to SOCOM. As a joint command, JSOC has a number or units under its "umbrella," such as Seal Team 6, Delta Force, 24th Special Tactics Squadron, and the Intelligence Support Activity.

500 courses in over 50 countries (see Figure 14–3).[6] Some of the countries served include the Philippines, Columbia, Kenya, Bahrain, Mexico, Peru, and countries in the Caribbean.

Anti-Terrorism Organizations and Activities

This section provides a discussion of American anti-terrorism organizations and what they do. For each agency identified, one or more examples of its anti-terrorism activities are covered. The agencies selected are intended to convey a sense of the broadness of anti-terrorism efforts. Coverage of all American anti-terrorism efforts is beyond the scope of this chapter.

U.S. Northern Command (NORTHCOM)

The **U.S. Northern Command** (**NORTHCOM**) has much wider responsibilities than anti-terrorism, such as directing the entire North American Aerospace Defense Command, but those other important responsibilities are not relevant here. Established in 2002, NORTHCOM's area of responsibility[7] for securing the United States includes land, air, and sea approaches to all 48 continental states, Alaska, Hawaii, Canada, and Mexico.[8]

U.S. Northern Command (NORTHCOM)

Directs the U.S. Department of Defense's homeland security efforts and the planning, organizing, and execution of military support to civil authorities during emergencies, disasters, and/or terrorist attacks.

FIGURE 14–2
The proactive and reactive portions of anti-terrorism programs are depicted.
(Courtesy Joint Tactics, Techniques, and Procedures for Anti-Terrorism, Joint Chiefs of Staff)

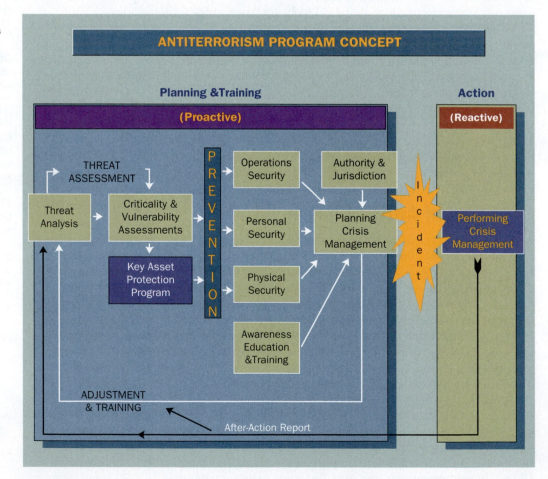

NORTHCOM directs the U.S. Department of Defense's homeland security efforts and the planning, organizing, and execution of military support to civil authorities[9] (see Box 14–1). An easy way of thinking about the relationship between NORTHCOM and civilian authorities is that NORTHCOM is responsible for accurately identifying and quickly deploying to civilian agencies the right mix of Department of Defense assets to address natural and manmade disasters. Such assistance does not violate the federal Posse Comitatus Act because NORTHCOM is not directly involved in law enforcement activities.

NORTHCOM established Joint Task Force North in 2004 to assist local, state, and federal law enforcement agencies protecting the border between Mexico and the United States,[10] reasoning that reducing the number of illegal border crossers diminishes the opportunity for terrorists and weapons of mass destruction to enter the country. In 2010, NORTHCOM worked closely with the Canadian government to protect athletes and visitors to the 2010 Vancouver Winter Olympics, which was beneficial to the protection of both countries from terrorist attacks. In the last several years NORTHCOM has made progress with Mexican authorities on matters of mutual interest, including drug smuggling. NORTHCOM, like some other federal agencies, focuses on the relationship between terrorist groups and sophisticated criminal organizations.[11]

NORTHCOM sets the level (Alpha, Bravo, Charlie, and the highest, Delta) of force protection at Department of Defense installations, facilities, and units within its area of responsibility. Force protection is an anti-terrorism effort defined as the preventative measures taken to mitigate hostile actions against Department of Defense personnel and family members, resources, facilities, and critical information.[12] In turn, military commanders are responsible for ensuring those standards are met or exceeded. NORTHCOM, as do other federal agencies, focuses on dealing with the consequences of cyber, chemical, biological, radiological, and nuclear attacks.

FIGURE 14–3
In addition to ATAP a number of other U.S. entities provide training to foreign governments. Here Special Forces "Green Berets" work with Mali troops, training them in counter ambush tactics.
(Courtesy Alfred de Montesquiou/ AP Images)

U.S. Department of Treasury

The U.S. Department of Treasury's Office for Terrorism and Financial Intelligence is led by an Under Secretary. This unit is responsible for the Department's twin goals of safeguarding the financial system against illicit use and combating rogue nations, terrorist facilitators, weapons of mass destruction (WMD) proliferators, money launderers, drug kingpins, and other national security threats.[13] The intelligence and enforcement functions are executed by several units, including the Financial Crimes Enforcement Network (FinCen) and the Executive Office for Asset Forfeiture.

An example of the Department of Treasury's anti-terrorism work is the investigations conducted into potential criminal cases involving charitable giving. Between 2001 and 2011, seven "charities" with Muslim affiliations were shut down.[14] These "charities" revealed a practice of diverting contributions to al-Qaeda and Hamas[15] or otherwise supporting terrorism. As a result, new guidelines were put in place and monitoring of other potential sources of funding to terrorist organization increased.

Federal Bureau of Investigation

The FBI is the lead agency for the Foreign Terrorist Tracking Task Force, which was created by Homeland Security Presidential Directive-2 in 2001. It directed federal agencies to cooperate in an effort to (1) deny entry of aliens into the United States associated with,

Box 14–1
NORTHCOM Civil Support Following Hurricane Katrina

Although these NORTHCOM responses are not anti-terrorism efforts, they do serve as an indicator that it has the capability to respond quickly to a major terrorist attack, or even if several of them occur simultaneously.

In response to Hurricane Katrina in 2005, NORTHCOM forces deployed more than 22,000 personnel from every branch of military service.[16] NORTHCOM personnel in the New Orleans area provided a wide range of essential services, including search and rescue; evacuation; recovery of deceased persons; health and medical support; debris removal; restoration of infrastructure; logistics, including distribution of food, water, and ice; temporary shelter; housing

of FEMA officials and relief workers; and provision of geospatial products and evaluations, including monitoring changing conditions and providing a high level of situational awareness.

Other illustrations of NORTHCOM civil support include responding in 2007 to wildfires in Western states, spring flooding in the central United States in 2008, and to Haiti's devastating earthquake in 2010.

How well do you think NORTHCOM will be able to respond to a major terrorist incident? What if there were three simultaneous major attacks with 200,000 total casualties?

---

suspected of being engaged in, or supporting terrorist activity; and (2) locate, detain, prosecute, and deport any such aliens already present in the United States (see Figure 14–4).[17]

The Department of Justice's Office of the Inspector General conducted an audit of the Foreign Terrorist Tracking Task Force (FTTTF), which was released in 2013 and concluded that it was of "significant value."[18]

Information Link
For more information on the Inspector General's audit of the FBI's Foreign Terrorist Tracking Task Force, visit www.justice.gov/oig/reports/2013/a1318r.pdf.

Immigration and Customs Enforcement

In the Department of Homeland Security, the Immigration and Customs Enforcement has a Terrorist Tracking and Pursuit Group that identifies non-immigrants who have overstayed the terms of their admission and who may pose a potential risk or threat to national security.[19] "The "terms of their admission" is defined as admissions to the United States for business or pleasure, academic or vocational study, temporary employment, or to act as a representative of a foreign government or international organization.[20]

State and Local Law Enforcement

American state and local law enforcement agencies have an important role to play in anti-terrorism. Local law enforcement has been cast as the "eyes and ears" on the front lines of anti-terrorism and counterterrorism efforts. States and large cities are ordinarily members of Joint Terrorism Task Forces, but also have their own "counterterrorism" units, which actually perform more defensive anti-terrorism tasks as opposed to executing offensive operations.

FIGURE 14–4
This flow chart depicts what happens after the FTTTF identifies a person considered a national security threat.[21]

(Courtesy The Federal Bureau of Investigation's Foreign Terrorist Tracking Task Force, Department of Justice, Office of the Inspector General, March 2013, p. 5).

New York, several times a target of terrorist attacks, has made the largest American municipal commitment to combating terrorism with more than 1,000 officers assigned to various specialized "counterterrorism" units, some of whom are assigned abroad. The New York Police Department's counterterrorism program is sophisticated. Its Transit Order Maintenance Sweep illustrates a defensive tactic, with many New York Police Department officers randomly appearing at different commuter train cars and going through all suspicious packages and checking all suspicious people. The NYPD's Intelligence Division & Counter-Terrorism Bureau is resource intensive, but far less expensive than the consequences of a major terrorist attack. Despite the Bureau's vigilance, a terrorist attack or attempt is still made. For instance, in 2010, a Pakistani-born, naturalized American citizen, Faisal Shahzad, parked a bomb-filled car in Times Square.[22] The ignition system failed and immediately attracted police. Shahzad, who received training from the Taliban, subsequently pleaded guilty to bombing-related charges and was sentenced to life in prison.

U.S. Marine Corps

Among the U.S. Marine Corps' anti-terrorism units is the Chemical, Biological, Immediate Response Force (CBIRF), a battalion-sized unit (usually over 500 soldiers) that can be deployed to a terrorist incident anywhere in the world within 24 hours. The unit is stationed at the Naval Support Facility, Indian Head, Maryland.[23] CBIRF consist of Marines and Navy sailors representing over 40 different specialties. CBIRF will assist local, state, and federal agencies and military commanders when there is a credible threat of or an actual incident involving chemical, biological, radiological, nuclear, or high-yield explosives (CBRNE). CBIRF's capabilities include agent detection and identification, casualty search and rescue, personnel decontamination, emergency medical care, stabilization of contaminated personnel, and consequent management. Depending on the fact situation of an incident, CBIRF could come under the command of NORTHCOM.

U.S. Attorney's Office

Across the country, every United States Attorney's Office has substantial responsibility for combating domestic and international terrorism. One way that responsibility gets expressed is through an Anti-Terrorism Advisory Council, each headed by a U.S. Attorney and with wide-ranging membership, including the National Guard and state, local, and federal law enforcement agencies. The Anti-Terrorist Advisory Councils seek to deter, detect, and prevent future attacks within the United States by creating partnerships that (1) coordinate anti-terrorism initiatives, (2) initiate and support anti-terror training programs, and (3) facilitate information sharing across all levels of government.

Transportation Security Administration

As part of the U.S. Department of Homeland Security, the Transportation Security Administration is responsible for security of America's transportation systems and freedom of movement for people and commerce. Testifying before the House of Representatives in 2013, TSA Administrator John Pistole stated that the Transportation Security Agency was making "steady progress" in transforming itself into a high-performing anti-terrorism and counterterrorism agency.[24] The Transportation Security Agency's enforcement arm is the federal air marshals, responsible for primarily securing aviation transportation assets (e.g., commercial airliners) domestically and internationally. The exact number of air marshals is not public information for security purposes.

The transportation sector is comprised of all modes of transportation (aviation, maritime, mass transit, highway, freight rail, and pipeline). As described in Chapter 12, it is a vast, open, interdependent networked system that daily moves millions of passengers and millions of tons of goods to their destinations.[25] Mass transit and passenger rails account for nearly 30 million trips daily.[26] America's transportation network connects cities, manufacturers, and retailers, moving people and goods through a complex network of approximately 4 million miles of roadways, more than 140,000 miles of active rail, 600,000 bridges and tunnels, some 350 maritime ports, hundreds of thousands of pipeline miles, and about 450 U.S. commercial airports.[27]

U.S. Department of Energy

Under the Atomic Energy Act, the Federal Bureau of Investigation is responsible for investigating illegal activities involving the use of nuclear materials within the United States, including terrorist threats concerning the use of nuclear materials. A series of executive orders authorizes the Department of Energy's National Nuclear Security Administration to provide technical assistance to the FBI. The National Nuclear Security Administration has a number of assets related to a potential nuclear incident. In a terrorist situation, Nuclear Emergency Support Teams (NESTs) can search for and identify nuclear materials, assess potential nuclear devices, render such devices safe, and package them for transportation to a place of final disposition. NESTS consist of five to several dozen specialists depending on the situation. Terrorism involving a nuclear device is both a public concern and a focus of the federal government.

U.S. Special Operations Command (USSOCOM)

The Special Operations Command (USSOCOM or simply SOCOM) was formed in 1987 and is headquartered at MacDill Air Force Base in Tampa, Florida. Its mission is to provide fully capable Special Operations Forces to defend the United States and its interests and to synchronize global military operations against terrorist networks.[28] Essentially, SOCOM is the "parent" organization for the special operations community. It is composed of special warfare elements from various branches of the military (see Figure 14–5). It is important to remember that the Joint Special Operations Command (JSOC) is a subordinate command of SOCOM.

Operation Eagle Claw
Failed U.S. military attempt to rescue hostages held by Iran in 1980.

Before the establishment of SOCOM in 1980, the United States executed **Operation Eagle Claw** to rescue 66 hostages seized in late 1979 at the American Embassy in Tehran, Iran, by

FIGURE 14–5
Organizational Chart for SOCOM (USSOCOM)

Box 14-2
Operation Eagle Claw: Anatomy of a Disaster

Reducing the plan to bare bones, Operation Eagle Claw's elements included: (1) the infiltration of U.S. agents into Tehran to gather intelligence; (2) the rendezvous of three EC-130 refueling planes and eight helicopters at a secret location (Desert 1) in the Iranian desert; (3) Delta's seizure of the American Embassy and freeing the hostages; (4) Delta escorting the hostages to a soccer stadium; (5) Army Rangers controlling a nearby airfield; (6) helicopters transferring Delta and hostages to the seized airport; (7) a C-14 landing and flying the hostages to safety; and (8) other mission forces egressing from Iran.[29]

A post-mission analysis revealed problems: (1) the plan was too complex; (2) intelligence was limited and collected more slowly than anticipated; (3) weather intelligence did not predict the severe dust storms ("Haboobs") that caused the helicopter flight separation and eliminated one of the needed helicopters; (4) a weather reconnaissance C-130 should have been incorporated into the plan; (5) although there were more qualified Air Force helicopters pilots, Marine Corp pilots were used; (6) the Marine pilots did not train on the actual type of helicopters that were used; (7) unanticipated traffic passing Desert 1 resulted in 44 bus riders being taken prisoner and a fuel tanker stopped with an anti-tank weapon, creating a fireball that could be seen for miles in the night; (8) in flight, one helicopter had an automated warning of an impending rotor blade failure, landed and checked it out, and had to abandon the aircraft; (9) a third helicopter had damaged hydraulics and couldn't be used; (10) the loss of three helicopters reduced the number available to five, one less than the mission required; (11) there should have been more helicopters; (12) the mission was scrubbed and a maneuvering helicopter hit one of the fuel EC-130s, killing eight servicemen and destroying both aircraft; and 13) for operational security, all of the different services involved in the mission trained separately and there were no thoroughly integrated mission rehearsals.[30]

Mission planning tried to limit the aircraft at Desert 1 to avoid detection, but the post-mission analysis called for more of them. More helicopters may also have required a fourth EC-130 fueling plane, further increasing the possibility of being detected. Change the fact situation just a little and one post-mission problem identified would be that the footprint was too large, leading to detection, and the mission being scrubbed.

Planning for a second rescue attempt was cancelled when intelligence learned that the hostages had been dispersed to different locations, realistically eliminating any further rescue attempts.

The hostages were taken on November 4, 1979, and released on January 20, 1981. President Carter's inability to rescue or otherwise affect the release of the hostages made him an ineffective figure. On the same day Ronald Reagan made his inaugural address the hostages were released after 444 days of captivity.

What should have America learned from this incident as it looked to the future?

---

radical Muslims.[31] The success of the final plan depended on a near perfect execution of all of its phases during the mission's 40-hour timetable. Instead, a confluence of mistakes resulted in a badly failed mission (see Box 14–2).[32]

Albeit at a terrible price, positive things ultimately resulted from Operation Eagle Claw's failure. It stimulated interest in the U.S. Department of Defense to reform the entire special operations community.[33] By 1983, there was also a small but growing sense in Congress for the need for military reform.[34] Adding impetus to these developments were two events that happened during that same year: (1) the terrorist bombing of the U.S. Marine Barracks in Lebanon, and (2) the continuing failure of command and coordination special operations revealed during the invasion of Grenada by the United States and its allies in order to re-establish order and protect the lives of American students in that island nation. Legislative hearings were held during 1986 on bills to create a special operations command.[35] By most accounts, retired army Major General Richard A. Scholtes gave the most compelling reason for creating such a command: Leaders of conventional forces did not understand how to use special operations personnel or to take advantage of their unique abilities, which led to avoidable casualties during the Grenada Invasion.[36] Arguably, special operations needed its own major command structure to protect it from commanders of conventional forces.

Overview of Counterterrorism

Counterterrorism includes a constellation of strategies, such as denying the rationale for terrorism and promoting other more attractive ideas, such as reducing the flow of recruits by providing them with alternative futures, strengthening the economies of failing nations to eliminate terrorists sanctuaries, interdicting materials (supplies and weapons) intended for use by terrorists, impounding funds in transit to terrorists, implementing civil action programs, and direct military action (see Figure 14–6). While many of these activities have been discussed in earlier chapters, this chapter focuses on combatting terrorism through the use of specially-trained military and law enforcement counterterrorism units, many of which are under the umbrella of the Joint Special Operations Command within SOCOM.

FIGURE 14–6
The counterterrorism
model depicts a variety
of actions, including
eroding support for violent
extremist organizations,
disrupting their plans,
and countering support
for them.

*(Courtesy Counterterrorism,
Joint Publication 3-26, Joint
Chiefs of Staff)*

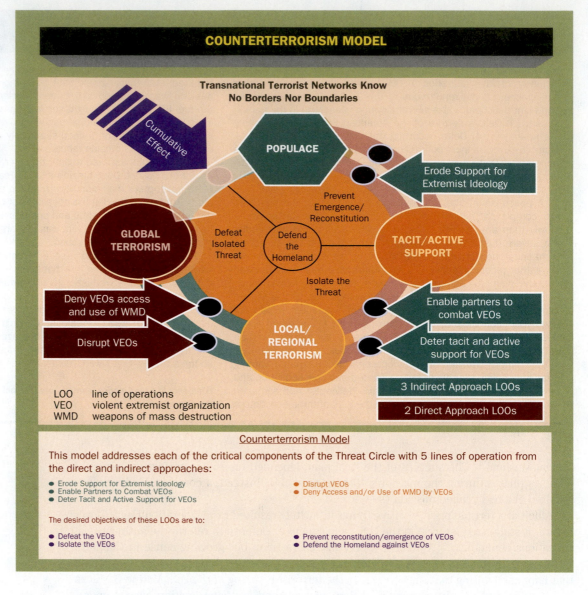

Counterterrorism and Forms of Military Action

In contrast to anti-terrorism, a counterterrorism program is characterized by direct actions (usually military) that prevent, deter, and respond to terrorists.[37] A key component of counterterrorism is identifying, locating, and taking action against high-value human targets. This action disrupts terrorists' intentions, capabilities, and operations. Counterterrorism military operations are frequently, but not exclusively, carried out by units within the Joint Special Operations Command (JSOC) under SOCOM. Counterterrorism includes the use of military force, in any of several forms:

Open Warfare

Examples of open warfare include the actions of the United States and its allies in Iraq during the First Gulf War (1991), triggered by Iraq's invasion of Kuwait. As a preemptive action, discussed more fully below, the United States and its allies returned to Iraq (2003–2011) to conduct open warfare, although special operations units were also active (e.g., searching for the deposed dictator Saddam Hussein). After gaining control of the country, the United States spent billions of dollars training and equipping the Iraqi police and military to foster a stable government. Fostering a stable government is often a difficult and time-consuming task. In 2014, the terrorist group Islamic State exploited long-standing conflicts between the Sunni and Shia populations in Iraq and began military operations against the government of Iraq,[38] raising questions whether America and its allies left Iraq too soon.

Raids

Raids may be executed to take prisoners, gather intelligence, and for other purposes. Raids may also be punitive in reaction to terrorist acts for which there is no peaceful redress (e.g., the United States bombed Tripoli and Benghazi, Libya, in 1986 because of that nation's role in the bombing of a nightclub in Berlin that was frequented by American soldiers). Similarly, in 1998, President Bill Clinton ordered missile strikes on terrorist sites in the Sudan and Afghanistan in reaction to the bombings of American Embassies in Kenya and Tanzania.[39]

Preemptive Strikes

In 1950, President Harry Truman declared, "We do not believe in preemptive war. Such a war is the weapon of dictators, not of free democratic countries like the United States."[40] The 16th century Italian scholar Alberico Gentili held a different opinion, "No one ought to wait to be struck unless he is a fool."[41] These contrasting views fundamentally undergird the debate about preemptive strikes and wars, which is often tied to the moral question "Is preemptive military action moral?" **Preemptive military action** is defined as striking a target in advance of a reasonably anticipated attack to circumvent its occurrence and to avoid suffering its effects.

During the Cold War Era, roughly 1947–1991, the Russians and Americans did not fight a "hot war," but they were ideologically opposed, which played itself out in situations like the Soviet's isolation of East Berlin and their support of regimes opposed to the United States and its allies. Because both Russia and the United States had numerous nuclear missiles, warfare did not erupt because **mutually assured destruction (MAD)** would be the result. Transnational terrorism has no equivalent to mutually assured destruction: Terrorists have no nation or citizens to defend.[42] As a result, President George W. Bush announced a major shift in American foreign policy—the right to take preemptive military action to protect the United States, its citizens, and interests.

In 2001, preemption was used to justify the American attack on Afghanistan, which had been harboring al-Qaeda terrorists and Usama bin Laden before and after 9/11. The ultra-conservative Islamic Taliban had seized control of most of the country by 1996, and in the wake of the 9/11 attacks refused to deliver bin Laden to the United States. Anticipating further attacks on the homeland, the United States and its allies softened Afghanistan's defenses with missile and air strikes before executing a ground invasion. The Second Gulf War (2003–2011) was also a preemptive action in the mistaken belief, that Iraq's Saddam Hussein had weapons of mass destruction and would use them against the United States or arm terrorists with them for such an attack.

Preemptive military action
Striking a target in advance of a reasonably anticipated attack to circumvent its occurrence and to avoid suffering its effects.

Mutually assured destruction (MAD)
A military doctrine prevalent during the Cold War between the United States and the former Soviet Union, postulating that an all-out nuclear war would effectively destroy both entities (the attacker and the defender).

Direct Action

The United States has used direct action to eliminate leaders of terrorist organizations in order to disrupt their plans and operations. Two examples from 2011 illustrate this point: (1) A drone attacked a convoy in Yemen and killed American-born Anwar al-Awlaki, an important al-Qaeda figure. Coincidentally, Samir Khan, a naturalized American citizen who operated the *Jihadi Internet Magazine*, was also killed; and (2) Usama bin Laden was killed at his compound in Abbottabad, Pakistan, by Navy SEALs. It is not publically known if his death was a tactical necessity. Arguably, if captured he may have divulged significant intelligence, but if put on trial, bin Laden would have had a commanding venue from which to justify al-Qaeda's actions.

Hostage Rescue

Historically, there are a number of incidences where highly trained military units attempted to or did rescue hostages. The rescue of Captain Richard Phillips from Somali

FIGURE 14–7
The USS *Bainbridge* (L) tows the orange lifeboat in which Captain Phillips was held to the USS *Boxer* (C) where it was processed for evidence.

(U.S. Navy photograph by Megan E. Sindelar)

pirates is a recent example. In 2009, Somali pirates hijacked the cargo ship *Maersk Alabama* in the Indian Ocean.[43] The pirates held an American, Captain Richard Phillips, hostage in a covered lifeboat and threatened to kill him unless they were given $2 million dollars. The FBI Crisis Negotiation Unit maintained communication with the pirates to reduce volatility. A Navy SEAL team parachuted into the ocean "over the horizon" and moved to a Navy ship without the pirates noticing. The Captain as well as three pirates were in an 18-foot, hard-covered lifeboat, in the open sea, bobbing up and down. When it seemed that Captain Phillips was in imminent danger of being killed, the SEAL Team snipers were give the "green light" to shoot. All three pirates in the lifeboat were killed and Captain Phillips was rescued unharmed (see Figure 14–7). A fourth pirate, Abduwali Muse, was being treated for injuries and negotiating for Captain Phillips' release aboard the USS *Bainbridge* when the SEALs fired. He later pleaded guilty to piracy charges and received a sentence of 33 years. Two private security contractors were found dead on the Maersk Alabama. The 2013 movie, *Captain Phillips* tells the story of this incident.

Counterterrorism Organizations and Activities

Much of the war on terrorism is fought by special military operational units, as opposed to conventional forces. When they were first formed in the early 1950s, soon after World War II, the conventional army at that time, and for some years thereafter, was suspicious and somewhat resentful of specialized tactical units. There was a concern that a tour of duty in such a unit might make a soldier unsuitable for service in the conventional military.. Some conventional commanders thought just the existence of special military units deprived them of outstanding soldiers. Presently, service in a special operational command is where many career-minded soldiers in the armed forces want to be.

The actions taken by special operations forces are newsworthy, if known about, and action movies featuring them are popular. The reality is that such units are only the "tip of the spear." Behind them are small armies of data collection experts, analysts using **metrics**, experience, and their best judgment, communications arrays, and a variety of transportation systems to deliver and recover specially trained operators from the field.

This section is a sampler of American counter terrorism units including The U.S. Army Special Forces (Green Berets), U.S. Army Delta Force, U.S. Navy SEAL Teams, and the U.S. Army 75th Ranger Regiment. The two civilian entities are the CIA Special Activities Division and the FBI Hostage Rescue Team (HRT). Federal law dictates which units have a primary counterterrorism mission. All of the above units have such a mission, except the 75th Ranger Regiment. While the Regiment does not have such a formal mission, it often conducts such operations or augments units that do have that primary mission. For this reason the 75th Ranger Regiment was included in this discussion.

Metrics
Standard measures taken periodically to determine the level of performance in a given field. For instance, a metric used during the Vietnam War was enemy body count. Terrorism metrics can be an indication of how we are doing in the global war on terrorism if carefully selected, defined, and measured.

U.S. Army Special Forces—Green Berets

At the end of World War II in 1945, Colonels Aaron Banks and Russel Volckmann returned to the Army from the soon to be disbanded Office of Strategic Services (OSS). They believed the world was changing and that a new type of military force would be needed for unconventional warfare.[46] As a result of their efforts, U.S. Army Special Forces was created in 1952 at Fort Bragg, North Carolina. Colonel Banks became its first commander, and he is regarded as the father of Special Forces. Some 2,300 positions[47] were allocated to the incipient unit; they came from the deactivation of Ranger companies deemed no longer needed after the war.[48] These slots were also filled with former OSS members and experienced soldiers from the war. Although the unit was poorly funded and not well supported within the traditional military establishment, it had a unique and vital role to play in the Cold War. In the event of a Russian invasion of Europe, Special Forces were to stay behind enemy lines, recruit and arm partisans, and wage war against the Russians,[49] severing supply lines and eliminating communications centers. To some degree, Special Forces assumed the mission of World War II commandos.

The initial volunteers were fluent in two languages, held the rank of Sergeant or higher, and were well-trained in airborne and infantry skills.[50] The federal Lodge Act (1950) allowed for 2,500 alien males to gain citizenship in return for five years service in the U.S. Army.[51] Many of those taking advantage of the Lodge Act came from Eastern European countries, were staunchly anti-communist, and had significant military and combat experience. These immigrants tended to gravitate to Special Forces, which used those experiences in the burgeoning Cold War with Russia.[52]

OSS personnel who joined Special Forces often wore berets of the foreign military units with which they operated,[53] and Europeans joining Special Forces came from a culture where many men wore berets. Consequentially, it was not surprising that Special Forces began wearing a green beret informally. In 1954, the Special Forces command authorized wearing of the green beret, although the U.S. Department of the Army did not recognize it as official headwear. In 1957, the Fort Bragg, North Carolina Post Commander banned it, although Special Forces soldiers continued wearing it in the field. In 1961, President John F. Kennedy visited Fort Bragg and was impressed with the Special Forces training and activities. By no coincidence, several months later the U.S. Department of Army suddenly reversed itself and authorized the beret. President Kennedy called the Green Beret "a symbol of excellence, a badge of courage, a mark of distinction in the fight for freedom."[54] Since that time, Special Forces members have been known as "Green Berets." When President Kennedy was assassinated in 1963, Special Forces sent a 48-man delegation to Washington, D.C., and they placed their "mark of distinction" on the President's grave. On each anniversary of President Kennedy's death they send a delegation to honor him (see Figure 14–8).

In 1967, the communist revolutionary Che Guevara was captured by Bolivian soldiers who had been trained and equipped by Special Forces and other U.S. special operations personnel.[55] American Special Forces were with the Bolivians when Guevara was

FIGURE 14–8
Every year Special Forces commemorate President Kennedy's death by having a delegation go to his gravesite in Arlington National Cemetery. They honor him as the man who gave them their namesake Green Berets.

(Courtesy Photographer Sgt. 1st Class Jeremy D. Crisp, United States Army)

FIGURE 14–9
Members of the 3rd Special Forces Group (Airborne) recon Afghanistan's remote Shok Valley. Previously, accompanied by Afghan troops, they had fought a six-hour battle with terrorists in a village in that valley.

(Courtesy David N. Gunn/United States Army)

Delta Force
"Delta Force" has used a variety of names, including 1st Special Forces Operational Detachment-D (1st SFOD-D), Combat Applications Group (CAG) and Army Compartmentalized Elements (ACE). It is believed there are five active duty Special Forces Groups and two National Guard Groups. The strength of each Group is in its four battalions. The number of people in a SF battalion is classified. Each SF Group has limited counterterrorism mission and capability.

wounded and captured. He was executed by the Bolivians in the field shortly after his capture. During the 1960s, Special Forces were heavily involved in the Vietnam War, often building "camps" astride routes used by the North Vietnamese Army (NVA) to infiltrate troops and supplies into South Vietnam. The camps provided vital intelligence for air and missile strikes, and soon became major targets for the NVA. Defended by paramilitary indigenous troops recruited and trained by Green Berets, the camps were often defended successfully. More recently, during the Persian Gulf War (1991), Iraq's Saddam Hussein shot missiles into Israel, Saudi Arabia, and Bahrain, as well as launched an all-out attack on Kuwait. Special Forces and other special operations units were deployed into the desert to gather intelligence on Hussein's army, and to find and destroy military targets. Special Forces were among the earliest American units on the ground in Iraq, and continued their counterterrorism activities in Afghanistan as well (see Figure 14–9).

U.S. Army—Delta Force

Lieutenant Charles Beckwith saw combat during the Korean War (1952–1953).[56] Upon returning to the United States, he completed Ranger training and joined Special Forces. In 1960, then-Captain Beckwith and other Special Forces "Green Berets" were sent to Laos to train local forces in special warfare.[57] During 1961–1962 he served with the elite British Air Service (SAS) and fought communist insurgents in Malaya. The "SAS way" left him confused because there was little emphasis on rank, things seemingly were done casually, and yet its accomplishments could not be denied.[58] Beckwith lamented, "I couldn't make heads or tails of it … everything I'd been taught about soldiering, been trained to believe, was turned upside down."[59]

Upon his return, he submitted several concept papers to senior commanders to form an SAS-type unit, but the papers were brushed aside. Intermittently over the next 14 years he made addition attempts, to no avail. As terrorism became more prominent during the 1970s, the Army concluded it needed a counterterrorism unit. In 1977, Lieutenant Colonel Beckwith was given two years to create and make the new "**Delta Force**" mission-ready. Most of the personnel for this new unit came from Special Forces.[60] In 1980, Delta participated in Operation Eagle Claw. In the wake of its failure, now-Colonel Beckwith saw the need for more special operations training.

The secrecy surround Delta[61] is such that the U.S. government routinely denies its existence.[62] Still, a limited number of missions assigned to Delta by the U.S. Special Operations Command have become public. One such incident involves activities in Somalia in 1993.

Although the Battle of Mogadishu, Somalia, did not involve terrorism, Delta operators participated in it to assist in capturing Warlord Mohamed Farrah Aidid. Somalian dictator and strongman Siad Barre seized power in Somalia during 1969.[63] Barre showed increasing ferocity to those who opposed him, and ultimately the Somalian army and the people turned against him. He fled the country in 1991 and the country quickly descended into clan warfare in the absence of a functional national government. Drought and famine brought starvation that private and voluntary relief could not control because warlords hijacked the food to sell for weapons or to feed their clan to ensure loyalty. United Nation humanitarian efforts fared no better and ultimately an international coalition sent military forces to quell the fighting and ensure the distribution of food. Warlord Mohamed Farrah Aidid opposed this move and his irregular militia began using improvised explosive devices (IEDs) to kill American servicemen.

Aidid was a major obstacle to restoring Somalia's national government, and thus had to be removed. As part of that process, a raid was planned to seize two of Aidid's lieutenants. That raid by American forces was supposed to last an hour, but actually ended more

Quick Facts
Ghillie Suits

Ghillie suits are often used by Special Forces and other snipers. They are made by weaving local fresh foliage into a net that is worn as camouflage. The suits originated with Scottish gamekeepers during the 18th century who were hired by landowners to protect stock and game animals from predators and poachers. The ghillie allowed a gamekeeper to "hide in plain sight," making them more efficient. During World War I ghillies were used by a British sniper unit and soon picked up by other military units.

▲ Snipers practicing their stalking and marksmanship skills.
(Courtesy United States Army)

than a day later. During the operation two American helicopters were shot down and a long battle ensued between Aidid's irregulars and a force of Army Rangers and Special Forces and Delta operators. Two Delta members, Master Sergeant Gary Gordon and Sergeant First Class Randy Shughart, were inserted into the heart of the firefights to protect the downed aircraft crews. Help failed to reach them in time and eventually both were killed. Both received the Medal of Honor for their actions. The 2001 movie *Blackhawk Down* covers the raid and subsequent battle.

U.S. Navy—SEAL Teams

Navy SEALs evolved out of four separate World War II organizations. Like other elite special operations units, members volunteer and then pass one of the most rigorous selection courses in the armed forces of the world. Those in the selection course for the 75th Ranger Regiment say "On a slab or with the tab;" meaning that they will either die trying or earn the slender gold and black ranger tab. For aspiring SEALs, it's "The only easy day was yesterday!"

The four World War II legacy units comprising today's Navy SEALs were (1) The Amphibious Scouts and Raiders, which conducted amphibious reconnaissance and raids in Europe and the South Pacific; (2) The Naval Combat Demolition Units, which trained exclusively for clearing beach obstacles on D-Day, June 6, 1944; (3) The Underwater Demolition Teams (UDT), which conducted hydrographic reconnaissance and obstacle demolitions for beach landings in the Pacific; and (4) The Office of Strategic Service (OSS) maritime operators.[64] OSS used the maritime operators for covert operations from the sea, including infiltrating agents, supplying resistance groups, engaging in maritime sabotage, and developing special equipment for their needs.[65]

The end of World War II meant that millions of men and women in the armed forces were released to restart their lives as civilians. It also meant the end of many units essential to the war effort, but not to a peacetime military. The rapid demobilization eliminated thousands of servicemen from the legacy units. From these units, only two Underwater Demolition Teams (UDTs) survived, each with 7 officers and 45 enlisted men. One UDT unit was stationed on the East Coast and the other on the West coast.[66]

The sudden attack by the North Korean army on South Korea in June 1950 rapidly propelled allied forces into the shrinking and defensive "Pusan Pocket" in Southern Korea. South Korea's army was not well equipped to resist the invasion and stationed U.S. forces were not well-honed combat troops. Instead, they were fundamentally peacetime garrison troops. However, U.S. General Douglas MacArthur conceived a surprise amphibious landing at Inchon, South Korea, that completely changed the tactical situation of the war, and the North Korean aggressors were steadily driven back from that point.

Prior to the amphibious landing at the port city of Inchon, UDT units provided detailed information for the operation (e.g., information about defenses, tides, channels, and the like) and cleared mines from the bay, essentially preparing the way for landing craft to reach the beachhead.[67] During the balance of the Korean War (1950–1953), the UDT units were used throughout the Korean peninsula because of their familiarity with the use of explosives.[68] They were assigned to blow up tunnels, bridges, and other targets.[69] This enlargement of the use of the UDT units onto land was a crucial part of their evolution into today's SEAL teams.

As President John F. Kennedy assumed office in 1961, Russian Premier Nikita Khrushchev gave a speech "establishing the legitimacy" of "wars of national liberation."[70] This resulted in Russia supporting movements, with training and arms, that were often anti-American and an indirect challenge to the United States. President Kennedy envisioned a new type of military capability—one that was required to fight guerilla and unconventional wars in foreign lands. He championed that agenda in the military as well as in Congress for additional funding.

The Army's Special Forces ("Green Berets") had been established in 1952; however, the unit was given few resources with which to build and expand. President Kennedy rebadged the UDT teams as U.S. Navy SEALs (**SE** – **A**ir – **L**and) in 1962 and gave them a much wider mandate than underwater demolition. The Vietnam War resulted in plentiful resources flowing to Special Forces and SEALs because they had important roles. Today, the most visible SEAL contributions have been in Iraq and more recently Afghanistan,[71] as well as in isolated incidents involving hostages such as the Captain Phillips rescue previously mentioned. SEAL Team 6 represents the apex of a counterterrorism unit. It received considerable, but unwanted, attention for the 2011 raid on Abbottabad, Pakistan, that resulted in the death of Usama bin Laden. Most Americans associate SEAL Team 6 with all SEAL teams. In reality, SEAL Team 6 is a specific team, often referred to as the U.S. Naval Special Warfare Development Group (DEVGRU). DEVGRU is SEAL Team 6, whose primary mission is counterterrorism. Most information regarding DEVGRU is classified and details regarding its existence and mission are difficult to obtain. DEVGRU (SEAL Team 6) and their Army counterpart, Delta Force, are the U.S. military's primary direct action counterterrorism units.

FIGURE 14–10

Although SEALs can infiltrate by sea, air, or land, they must also be able to do so under extreme conditions. SEALs performed Advance Cold Weather training in Kodiak, Alaska, to experience the physical stress of the environment as well as test how their equipment would operate and perform under such conditions.

(Courtesy Eric S. Logsdon/U.S. Navy www.navy.mil)

There are approximately 2,200 members of SEAL Teams (divided into nine active-duty teams, including SEAL Team 6) and perhaps 600 in the Special Boat Squadrons that transport each team.[72] All SEAL teams are required to be ready to deploy within 18 hours after notification. Their assigned missions include (1) direct warfare action, (2) special reconnaissance, (3) unconventional warfare (i.e., training, leading, and equipping guerilla forces behind enemy lines), (4) foreign defense strengthening (i.e., training and advising military, paramilitary, and law enforcement personnel of allied nations, normally in a non-combat environment), and (5) counterterrorism operations.[73] As with all special military operators, training is constant within the SEAL teams when not deployed in order to learn new skills (see Figure 14–10).

U.S. Army—75th Ranger Regiment

Rangers have a long and distinguished military history. In New England during 1675–1678, Captain Church led a company of rangers to fight against Native Americans led by "King Phillip," as he was called by the colonists.[74] During the French and Indian War (1754–1763), Major Rogers's rangers scouted ahead to find routes for regular British troops, conducted reconnaissance missions, and attacked distance targets. Major Rogers wrote a set of rules for his rangers that are still used by Rangers today. A Corps of Rangers, led by Francis Marion (1732–1795, the "Swamp Fox"), fought for colonists in the Revolutionary War. Marion is considered the American father of military guerilla tactics. During America's Civil War (1861–1865), Union troops were baffled by the Confederate's John Mosby (1833–1916), the "Grey Ghost") who led lightening quick cavalry raids and would then disappear.

FIGURE 14–11
Some of the members of the 6th Ranger Battalion who freed American and Filipino prisoners of war (POWs) held at Cabanatuan. Many of the POWs were captured in 1942.

(© Bettmann/Corbis)

Rangers reappeared during World War II, referred to as Darby's Rangers after their leader, Colonel William Darby. On D-Day on the Normandy Beach of France Rangers received their motto, "Rangers lead the way." In the Philippines, the 6th Ranger Battalion was the force that liberated and evacuated 500 allied prisoners held by the Japanese at Cabanatuan in 1945 (see Figure 14–11). Another popular movie, *The Great Raid* (2005), depicted this event.

The Korean War (1950–1953) again signaled the need again for Rangers. Fifteen Ranger Companies were formed to do reconnoitering work: scouting, patrolling, raids, ambushes, and spearheading assaults. Small units in the Army, for example, Long Range Reconnaissance Patrols ("LURPS"), were highly effective during the Vietnam War in providing operational and strategic intelligence. The 75th Ranger Regiment was reorganized in 1969 (at the height of the Vietnam conflict) to consolidate many of these units. However, it was deactivated in 1973 as combat commands returned to the United States.

In 1974, ranger battalions were again created and the 75th Ranger Regiment with three battalions was designated in 1986. Elements of the 1st Ranger Battalion participated in Operation Eagle Claw in 1980, and in Operation Urgent Fury Rangers parachuted from low altitudes to seize Grenada's Salines Airfield and rescue students at the medical school. Rangers have played key roles in action in Panama, Kosovo, Somalia, Afghanistan, and Iraq. The 75th Ranger Regiment has taken part in every major combat operation since their initial development during the Vietnam War.[75]

Today's 75th Ranger Regiment consists of the 1st Battalion (Hunter Army Air Field, Georgia), 2nd Battalion (Fort Lewis, Washington), and the 3rd Battalion and the Regimental Special Troops Battalion (Fort Benning, Georgia).[76] The 1st, 2nd, and 3rd Battalions each have approximately 600 rangers. The Regimental Special Troops Battalion (RSTB) provides the Ranger Regiment and Special Operations Forces with increased operational capabilities to sustain combat operations. The RSTB conducts command and control communications, computers, intelligence, surveillance, and reconnaissance functions in support of the Regiment and other special operations task forces.

The 75th Ranger Regiment has six primary missions: (1) direct action, seize, destroy, or capture enemy facilities and materials; (2) airport seizure for use by follow-on forces; (3) special reconnaissance, locate hostile forces for future operations; (4) personnel recovery, including evacuation or rescue of civilians and POWS in enemy territory or hostile terrain; (5) clandestine insertion to surprise the opponent, seize the initiative, and instill confusion in hostile forces; and (6) sensitive site exploitation, collect and analyze information gained on missions to conduct rapid follow-on operations.

It is fair to say that Rangers lack a primary counterterrorism mission. Rangers may be called on to perform counterterrorism operations on their own or augment the premier direct action counterterrorism units, Delta Force and SEAL Team 6. Nonetheless, the Rangers' counterterrorism operations are important contributions to the global war on terrorism.

More than 70 percent of current Rangers have multiple deployments in support of America's war against terrorists.[77] That experience is valuable in the special operations community.

Rangers, all of whom are volunteers, are highly trained, and a battalion can be deployed anywhere in the world within 18 hours, infiltrating by land, sea, or air. Because of this flexibility and their capabilities, the 75th Ranger Regiment is often formally used to augment other units in joint counterterrorism operations.

Central Intelligence Agency—Special Activities Division

The Central Intelligence Agency (CIA) was established by the National Security Act of 1947.[78] Fundamentally, the Act directed the CIA to collect, analyze, and disseminate intelligence.[79] Although conducting covert operations was not specifically authorized, the language of the Act was sufficiently elastic that the CIA soon began such operations. America's Office of Strategic Service (OSS) had been quickly disbanded following the end of World War II. However, the federal government substantially preserved OSS's Secret Intelligence and Counter Espionage branches, which later joined the newly minted CIA, giving the agency a wealth of **covert activity** experience from its very inception.[80]

The Special Activities Division (SAD) is a group of paramilitary officers within the Central Intelligence Agency. Their exact number is not publically known. Many of them were recruited from highly experienced military units. They conduct clandestine military operations in foreign countries, including counterterrorism and capture or kill missions. During 1967, in one of SAD's best-known actions, they collaborated with U.S. and Bolivian Special Forces in the capture of Che Guevera, who was executed by the Bolivians in the field.

Following the 1979 invasion of Afghanistan by the USSR, SAD aided the Muslim Mujahedeen in fighting the Soviets with training and weapons.[81] When the Soviets left the country in 1989, Afghanistan factions fought for control and the Taliban seized power. Under its protection, al-Qaeda trained, operated, and prepared for its attacks on America.[82] Following the 9/11 attacks, the Taliban refused to surrender Usama bin Laden to the United States. President George W. Bush told the Taliban to "…act immediately … or share their (al-Qaeda's) fate."[83] The Taliban made a counterproposal, to try bin Laden before an Islamic court. The U.S. response to this unsatisfactory proposal was to quickly deploy cutting-edge military technology and precision weapons, making it possible to use a smaller sized ground force[84] against the Taliban and al-Qaeda.

Within two weeks SAD personnel, later augmented by approximately 300 special operations personnel (Delta and SEALs), had infiltrated into Afghanistan and were working with Taliban opposition forces, many of them from the so-called indigenous Northern Alliance.[85] The ensuing barrage of missile, drone, and precision air strikes, guided by ground forces, drove the Taliban out of their cities and al-Qaeda into Pakistan.[86] In 2014, only a small coalition of military forces, led by the United States, remains in Afghanistan. CIA operators there and elsewhere continue their secret and largely unheralded fight against terrorism.

Federal Bureau of Investigation—Hostage Rescue Team

As discussed in Chapter 9, the FBI is the lead agency in more than 103 Joint Terrorism Task Forces spread across the country. Their membership consists of federal agencies, such as Customs and Border Protection and Immigration and Customs Enforcement from the Department of Homeland Security, as well as state and local law enforcement agencies. The mission of Joint Terrorism Task Forces is to investigate, detect, interdict, prosecute, and remove terrorists and dismantle their organizations.[87] Less well known is the FBI's involvement in military counterterrorism raids in foreign countries.

In 2014, Ahmed Abu Khatallah was arrested in Libya by a combined unit consisting of Delta operators and FBI agents on outstanding felony warrants for his role in the 2012 attack on the American Consulate compound in Benghazi, Libya.[88] It is alleged he was the mastermind of the attack.[89] If convicted in federal court, Abu Khatallah could receive the death penalty. Libya claimed their sovereignty was violated by the United States, which maintains it was a preemptive action because of intelligence information revealing that Abu Khatallah was planning further attacks against America.[90] Abu Khatallah was transported to the United States on a U.S. Navy vessel, and interrogated by civilian law enforcement

Covert activity
An action of the U.S. government intended to influence politics, economic, or military conditions abroad, where it is intended that the role of the government will not be apparent or acknowledged publically.

(FBI) personnel. As the alleged mastermind of the attack, he will be tried in civilian federal court as a criminal. The FBI was embedded in Delta because of the law enforcement knowledge required to potentially convict Abu Khatallah in federal court. These include expertise in evidence identification, collection, and preservation, skills and knowledge not normally the concern of special operations units.

The FBI and the Joint Special Operations Command (JSOC) have an alliance that benefits both parties and has moved the FBI deeper into counterterrorism operations in Iraq, Afghanistan, and other countries.[91] FBI agents have participated in hundreds of such operations.[92] JSOC enjoys access to FBI expertise in civilian law enforcement, such as criminal investigation techniques, analyzing digital material and codes, interrogation, and safeguarding the chain of evidence for prosecution;[93] that expertise helps to identify insurgents and terrorists; to detect terrorist plots, including those against the United States; and most importantly, to convict those individuals in civilian courts of law.[94]

Foreign Counterterrorism Organizations

Across the world the challenge of confronting terrorism has resulted in many governments creating special units. Military action against terrorists is referred to as **low intensity conflict** because it is somewhere between the diplomatic or economic tensions that flare up between countries and open/conventional warfare between them. However, there is nothing "low intensity" for people who are killed by terrorists or have to risk their lives fighting against them.

This section covers foreign counterterrorist organizations from three Allied nations: (1) The British Special Air Service (SAS) is included because it became a model for so many other countries, including the U.S. "Delta" counterterrorism unit; (2) the rationale for covering Germany's GSG9 is that the necessity for it arose out of one of history's most heinous terrorist attacks—the murder of members of Israel's delegation to the 1972 Olympics in Munich; and (3) Israel's Sayeret Matkal, Shayetet-13, and Mistaravim are included in this discussion because in the modern world, Israel may have more experience dealing with terrorism than any other nation. Other foreign counterterrorism units with substantial capabilities include France's National Gendarmerie Intervention Group (GIGN), Austria's Einsatzkommando Cobra (EKO Cobra), Turkey's unique motorcycle teams called the Yunaslar (or Dolphins), Mexico's Force Marines (FEAM), and the Russian Alpha Group.[95]

Great Britain—22nd Special Air Service (SAS) Regiment

The British SAS is responsible for counterterrorism, intelligence gathering, forward air control, behind enemy lines sabotage, close protection (in America often called dignitary protection), and training foreign militaries. SAS was originally formed as "L Detachment" Special Air Service Brigade and initially conducted raids on airfields behind German lines in Africa during 1941–1942.[96] Beginning in 1943, SAS's missions became more varied, striking behind enemy lines to rescue prisoners of war, gathering intelligence, disrupting enemy forces, arming and training partisan groups, and severing rail and communications lines.[97] On D-Day, June 6, 1944, Allied forces landed on the coast of France. To prevent German supplies and reinforcements being quickly brought to the front, SAS cut rail lines in Southern France.[98] For the rest of the war, SAS specialized in intelligence collection and unconventional warfare against the Germans. Thought to be unnecessary after the war, the British government disbanded SAS, only to reconstitute it two years later.[99] The selection course for SAS is very demanding (see Figure 14–12).

During the years that followed, SAS successfully fought insurgents in Malaya during the 1950s and 1960s, and in Oman in the 1970s. In 1980, desperate to create their own

Low intensity conflict
A level of military action that falls short of a full-scale conventional war; includes peacekeeping, anti-terrorism programs, assistance to foreign militaries and police organizations, fulfillment of international treaty obligations, as well as subversive and counterterrorism actions.

Information Link
For more information on the Special Air Service (SAS) Selection Process, visit the website at www.eliteukforces.info/special-air-service/sas-selection/.

FIGURE 14–12
The SAS selection course is the most demanding test in the British Armed Forces, with a pass rate of only 10 percent. It is a test of endurance, strength, and resolve. The endurance phase culminates with a 40-mile "walk" over mountain terrain that must be completed in 24 hours while carrying a 55-pound Bergen (Rucksack).

(© Andrew Chittock/Alamy)

homeland, six Iranians seized their country's Embassy in London. When their demands for a new homeland and the release of prisoners were rebuffed, the incident turned into a siege. After a daring raid, the SAS successfully freed 24 of 25 hostages and killed five of six terrorists, without loss of a single soldier. During the First Gulf War (1990–1991), the SAS ran deep reconnaissance behind Iraqi lines. The SAS has made a concerted effort to learn about terrorist threats from events in other countries. For instance, in 1993, at least one SAS officer was observed at the Branch Davidian Compound siege in Waco, Texas. It is also believed that one or more SAS representatives were also present in the 1996/1997 hostage-taking incident at the Japanese Ambassador's residence in Lima, Peru, by the Marxist Tupac Amaru Revolutionary Movement. This type of activity represents a forward-thinking perspective of gathering intelligence information on tactics used by terrorists from a global perspective. Today, informal arrangements between friendly-country intelligence and counterterrorism forces allow "observers" at protracted conflict or terrorist events.

In Iraq during 2005–2008, SAS reportedly joined forces with operators from the U.S. Army's 1st Special Forces Operational Detachment-Delta (1st SFOD-D, "Delta").

FIGURE 14–13
GSG9 members practicing a fast-rope insertion. Two snipers are on the roof and an officer in a ghillie suit is in front of the door. On the near side of the road note the operator has a bipod on his weapon. It may be an automatic weapon, although it seems small for that purpose, suggesting he has a sniper rifle.

(© Guido Ohlenbostel/Zuma Press/ Newscom)

The low-profile unit had several different names, including "Task Force Black" (TFB). Over a period of 18 months, the unit took 3,500 insurgents "off the street," most of which were captured.[100] The primary targets were persons involved with suicide bombings in Baghdad, which substantially declined due to "Task Force Black's" development of a network of spies and informers to identify potential targets.[101] "Task Force Black" also killed between 350 and 400 people, most of whom were senior Islamic militants with ties directly to al-Qaeda.[102] American General David Petraeus, then-commander of American forces in Iraq, had high praise for SAS: "They have exceptional initiative, exceptional skill, exceptional courage and savvy. I can't say enough about how impressive they are in thinking on their feet."[103] In Afghanistan during 2009–2010, SAS operations were credited with "completely destroying the Taliban's middle management."[104] British SAS has been the model for a number of other nations who formed special units of the same name, including Australia, Canada, New Zealand, and Rhodesia.

Germany—GSG9 (Grenzschutzgruppe 9)

At the 1972 Olympics in Munich Germany, members of the Palestinian terrorist group Black September entered the Olympic compound. As they tried to enter the Israeli quarters, Yossef Gutfreund, a wrestling referee, held the door against them. Although he was killed, he gave others time to escape. At various points Moshe Weinberg and Yossef Romano also fought their captors and although killed, their valor allowed one more Jewish hostage to escape. The terrorists demanded the release of Palestinian prisoners held by Israel, helicopters to fly them and eight Israeli hostages to an airbase, and a jet airline to eventually fly them all on to Egypt. As the helicopters were being boarded a rescue attempt failed badly and the hostages and terrorists all died.[105]

Recognizing that existing German military units were not trained for hostage rescue and counterterrorism, GSG9 was formed six months later. Like other leading counterterrorism units, its training is demanding and 80 percent of GSG9 candidates cannot meet standards.[106] If attempting to join GSG9 from a military unit, candidates must give up their rank and enter training as a private. GSG9 has become one of the elite counterterrorism forces in the world (see Figure 14–13). It specializes in hostage rescue, particularly in regards to aviation terrorism.[107] In an early operation in 1977, GSG9 was active in combating the Red Army Faction. The unit freed German hostages held on a plane in Somalia by Palestinian terrorists by entering the plane at multiple points, and killing or capturing all the terrorists.[108] None of the hostages nor any of the GSG9 group were killed. In another incident, during 2011–2012, GSG9 arrested four members of a terrorist cell planning to conduct attacks on German transit systems.[109]

Israel—Sayeret Matkal, Shayeter-13, and Mistavarim

Sayeret Matkal may be Israel's most respected counterterrorism unit and its most secretive.[110] Since the founding of Israel as a modern nation in 1948, Sayeret Matkal has participated in practically every major Israeli counterterrorism operation,[111] including the rescue of hostages held by terrorists at Entebbe, Uganda. It was founded in 1957 and patterned after the British SAS. Sayetet Matkal also has responsibility for hostage rescue within the country, and during war, deep reconnaissance behind enemy lines to develop strategic intelligence.[112] Sayeret Matkal is comparable to America's Delta Force.

Since the terrorist attack in 2000 on the USS *Cole* while docked in a Yemeni port, "maritime security" has become a much greater concern.[113] Although maritime terrorism has only accounted for 2 percent of all terrorist incidents since 1969, maritime security continues to be a major concern.[114] Israel was forward thinking about maritime security, creating a special unit within the Israeli Defense Forces in 1948 called Shayeter-13. Although its existence was not made public until 1960,[115] it has been very active in combating maritime terrorism and is comparable to the U.S. Navy SEALs.

Israel has a coastline on the Mediterranean Sea that is approximately 170 miles long, and traditional terrorist enemies such as the Palestinian Liberation Front, Hamas, Palestinian Islamic Jihad, and Lebanese Hezbollah all have maritime capabilities.[116] Israel has suffered 80 maritime attacks over the past decades, most of which were foiled.[117] Maritime terrorism in Israel may present itself as a single point attack or simultaneous attacks at multiple points from a "mother ship."[118] Maritime terrorists have raided beachfront hotels for hostages, planted mines on coastal roads, and filled speedboats and fishing vessels with explosives for suicide drivers. Both al-Qaeda and Hezbollah have launched rockets toward ships in Israeli ports.

Mistavarim is a secretive undercover counterterrorism unit attached to the Israeli Border Guard (Magav).[119] However, it reports to the Israel Security Agency, better known as Shin Bet, which is responsible for internal security and counterterrorism. Members of Mistavarim are substantially drawn from minority Arabs, such as the Druze, who have become more assimilated to Israel than other Arab people living there. Mistavarim operators work undercover in disguise to locate and take direct action against suicide bombers, and capture or kill wanted terrorists. Mistavarim operates with a great deal of secrecy. In addition to other requirements, recruits must speak Arabic fluently and be able to pass as an Arab in an undercover operation. The extensive training course spends months teaching recruits the smallest details of Arab life, Islam, and the Arabic language. Members of the Mistavarim are also required to live and pass as an Arab to gather intelligence and discover plots against Israel.

Chapter Summary

SUMMARY BY LEARNING OBJECTIVE

1. **Distinguish between anti-terrorism and counterterrorism efforts.**

   Fundamentally, anti-terrorism efforts are defensive in nature. Anti-terrorism efforts are defensive actions taken to reduce the vulnerability of people and property to terrorist acts, including rapid containment by local military and civilian forces. On the other hand, counterterrorism efforts are offensive in nature, and usually involve military or paramilitary actions taken to prevent, deter, or respond to terrorist threats or attacks.

2. **Identify and explain the role of NORTHCOM during an emergency, disaster, or terrorist attack.**

   The U.S. Northern Command (NORTHCOM) has a wide role in protecting the national security of the United States. It is responsible for directing the entire North American Aerospace

Defense Command—securing land, air, and sea approaches to all 48 continental United States, Alaska, Hawaii, Canada, and Mexico. In addition, NORTHCOM directs the U.S. Department of Defense's homeland security efforts and the planning, organizing, and execution of military support to civil authorities. During an emergency, disaster, or terrorist attack, NORTHCOM is responsible for accurately identifying and quickly deploying to civilian agencies the right mix of Department of Defense assets to address the specific incident, whether natural or manmade. Because these activities do not involved law enforcement duties, such assistance does not violate the Posse Comitatus Act.

3. **Summarize the work of the Foreign Terrorist Tracking Task Force.**

The FBI is the lead agency for the Foreign Terrorist Tracking Task Force, which was created by Homeland Security Presidential Directive-2 in 2001. Its purpose is to (1) deny entry of aliens into the United States associated with, suspected of being engaged in, or supporting terrorist activity; and 2) locating, detaining, prosecuting, and deporting any such aliens already present in the United States.

4. **Compare and contrast the national security policy shift in the United States from one based on mutually assured destruction (MAD) versus preemptive military action.**

During the Cold War, both the Soviet Union and the United States had numerous capabilities to deliver and detonate nuclear missiles against their enemy. Warfare did not erupt because the resulting end would be an all-out nuclear war, which would effectively destroy both entities (the attacker and the defender) preemptive strike was not viewed as a viable choice because such action would ensure destruction of both countries. In contrast, today's threats are much more from transnational terrorists versus individual recognized countries that have standing armies and a nuclear arsenal. There is no equivalent to mutually assured destruction (MAD); terrorists have no nation or citizens to defend. As a result, President George W. Bush shifted the emphasis in national security policy toward one that includes the inherent right to take preemptive military action, defined as striking a target in advance of a reasonably anticipated attack to protect the national security of the United States, its citizens, and interests.

5. **Identify the five subcommands of USSOCOM.**

The U.S. Special Operations Command (USSOCOM or simply SOCOM) was formed in 1987 and is headquartered at MacDill Air Force Base in Tampa, Florida. Its mission is to provide fully capable Special Operations Forces to defend the United States and its interests and to synchronize global military operations against terrorist networks. USSOCOM is the "parent" organization for the special operations community, and is composed of the five major special operations or special warfare commands from each military branch. They are U.S. Army Special Operations Command, Naval Special Warfare Command, Air Force Special Operations Command, U.S. Marine Corps Special Operations Command, and Joint Special Operations Command. The last command, Joint Special Operations Command (JSOC), commands the special military operational units like Army Delta, Army Special Forces, and Navy SEAL Teams that are often used for counterterrorism missions.

6. **Name the five types of military action associated with counterterrorism.**

The five types of military action associated with counterterrorism are (1) open warfare, (2) raids, (3) preemptive strikes, (4) direct action, and (5) hostage rescue.

7. **Identify the the U.S. Military counterterrorism units discussed in this chapter.**

These units are Special Forces (Green Berets), "Delta Force," All SEAL Groups have a limited counterterrorism mission and capability, SEAL Team 6, and the 75th Ranger Regiment. Although the Rangers do not have a primary counterterrorism mission they are called to perform them and occasionally augment the two premier direct action counterterrorism units: Delta Force and Seal Team 6.

8. **Profile SAS, GSG9, and Mistavarim.**

Forerunners of Great Britain's Special Air Service (SAS) were operational during World War II and by war's end were running intelligence collection and unconventional warfare operations. Disbanded at the end of that war, SAS was reconstituted two years later and fought communists in Malaysia and Omen in the 1960s and 1970s.

SAS ran deep reconnaissance during the first Gulf War in Iraq and during 2005 worked with Delta to eliminate people associated with suicide bombers and to eliminate terrorists associated with al-Qaeda. SAS and Delta also developed a network of informers and spies. Delta was developed using SAS as a model, as were similar units in Canada, New Zealand, Rhodesia, and Australia.

Germany's GSG9 is also one of the elite counterterrorism groups in the world. It was created following Germany's poor performance in trying to rescue the Israeli hostages taken by Black September at the 1972 Olympics in Munich. Recognizing its need for an anti-terrorist and hostage rescue force, Germany formed GSG9, which is particularly skilled in aviation hostage rescue operations. Soldiers who want to become a GSG9 member must give up all of their military rank to become a candidate.

Mustavarim is an Israeli secret undercover unit whose members work in disguise and must speak Arab fluently. Their job is to work against suicide bombers and capture or kill wanted terrorists.

REVIEW QUESTIONS

1. Counterterrorism is often thought of as just being military actions, although it is a constellation of activities. Can you name some counterterrorism activities other than military?
2. Why is it important for South Korea and Israel to have robust anti-terrorism programs?
3. "Force Protection" is an anti-terrorism program. What is it?
4. Assume Usama bin Laden was captured instead of killed. What drawbacks could arise from his capture?
5. After Operation Eagle Claw failed in 1980, there were no more attempts to rescue the American hostages. Why?
6. What are the most compelling reasons for creating a special operations command?

CRITICAL THINKING EXERCISES

1. In 2011, U.S. Army Ranger Sergeant Kristoffer B. Domeij (75th Ranger Regiment) was killed in Afghanistan on his 14th combat deployment—after four tours in Iraq and ten in Afghanistan. He and two other soldiers were killed by an IED (improvised explosive devise) in Kandahar province. Sgt. Domeij was 29 years old. Should there be a policy on limiting combat tours? If so, what should it be? Would America and Sgt. Domeij's family (wife and two children) have been better served by taking his vast experience and assigning him to another task, such as training and preparing others for combat, intelligence analysis, or the like? Is it possible Sgt. Domeji is a "natural warrior" and would have left the military if assigned to a state-side job?
2. Read the report by Seth G. Jones, "Counterterrorism and the Role of the Special Operations Forces" (Santa Monica, CA: RAND Corporation, April 2014) stemming from testimony before the Committee on Foreign Affairs, Subcommittee on Terrorism, Non-Proliferation, and Trade, U.S. House of Representatives, at www.rand.org/content/dam/rand/pubs/testimonies/CT400/CT408/RAND_CT408.pdf.

   What groups and countries continue to pose major threats to U.S. national security? According to the report, what are the key roles that special operation forces should conduct in the future? Thinking critically, what are the problems with these types of intermittent reports given to Congress? How timely are these reports? How accurate are these reports? How important do you think these reports are relating to the funding of counterterrorism units?
3. Visit the official website of the U.S. Navy SEALs at www.navy.com/careers/special-operations/seals/?campaign=search_Reprise/google/SEAL+Navy/%2Bnavy%20seals/mkwid/seveGdP0B|dc/pcrid/5239775796/pmt/b

   What is BUD/S? Explore the training schedule. Could you complete the training? What is the "easiest day?"

NOTES

1. A. Hunsicker, *Understanding International Counter Terrorism* (Boca Raton, Florida: Universal Publishers, 2006), p. 58. Hunsicker's statement was the "last decade." To account for a publication date of 2006 and our own knowledge of what has happened since, the authors changed the statement to "Over the past two decades."

2. The Department of Defense defines special operations as operations conducted in hostile, denied, or politically sensitive environments to achieve military, diplomatic, informational, and/or political objectives employment military capabilities for which there is no broad conventional force requirement.

3. Joint Special Operations Command, undated, www.socom.mil/pages/jointspecialoperation-scommand.aspx, p. 1.

4. *Counterterrorism*, Joint Publication 3-26, p. GL-4.

5. Loc. cit.

6. *Annual Report on Assistance Related to International Terrorism* (Washington, D.C.: U.S. Department of State, Office for the Coordination for Counter Terrorism, February 11, 2014), p. 1, www.state.gov/j/ct/rls/other/rpt/221544.htm.

7. NORTHCOM Anti-Terrorism Operations Order (U) 05-01, July 9, 2009, contains a more extensive description of its area of responsibility (AOR).

8. Loc. cit.

9. Loc. cit.

10. William Knight, *Homeland Security Roles and Missions for United States Northern Command* (Washington, D.C.: Congressional Research Service, June 3, 2008), p. CRS-4.

11. Cheryl Pellerin, "NORTCOM Prioritizes Homeland Defense, Cyber Partners," March 13, 2012, DoD Armed Forces Press Service, www.defense.gov/news/newsarticle.aspx?id=67535.

12. *Protection*, ADRP 3-37 (Washington, D.C.: Headquarters, Department of the Army, August 2012), p. v.

13. *Terrorism and Financial Intelligence* (Washington, D.C.: Department of the Treasury, June 28, 2013), p. 1, www.treasury.gov/about/organizational-structure/offices/Pages/Office-of-Terrorism-and-Financial-Intelligence.aspx.

14. Nathaniel J. Turner, *U.S. Muslim Charities and the War on Terror* (Washington, D.C.: Charity and Security Network, December 2011), p. 3.

15. *Anti-Terrorist Financing Guidelines* (Washington, D.C.: Department of the Treasury, undated), p. 1, www.treasury.gov/resource-center/terrorist-illicit-finance/Pages/protecting-charities-intro.aspx.

16. *A Short History of The United States Northern Command* (Peterson Air Force Base, Colorado: Northern Command, December 31, 2012), p. 7.

17. *Homeland Security Presidential Directive-2* (Washington, D.C.: Office of the President, October 29, 2001), p. 1, http://georgewbush-whitehouse.archives.gov/news/releases/2001/10/20011030-2.html.

18. *The Federal Bureau of Investigation's Foreign Terrorist Tracking Task Force* (Washington, D.C.: U.S. Department of Justice, Office of the Inspector General, March 2013), p. i.

19. *Counterterrorism and Criminal Exploitation Unit* (Washington, D.C.: Immigrational and Customs Enforcement, undated, but the likely date is 2012 because it is reporting 2011 program data), p. 1, www.ice.gov/counterterrorism-criminal-exploitation/.

20. Randall Monger, *Nonimmigrant Admission to the United States* (Washington, D.C.: Immigration and Customs Enforcement, undated), p. 1, www.dhs.gov/xlibrary/assets/statistics/publications/ni_fr_2011.pdf.

21. Ibid., p. 5.

22. This account is drawn with restatement from Aaron Katersky and Richard Esposito, "Faisal Shahzad: "War With Muslims Has Just Begun," *ABC News*, October 5, 2010, pp. 1–3, http://abcnews.go.com/Blotter/times-square-bomber-faisal-shahzad-sentenced-life/story?id=11802740.

23. The description of CBIRF is taken from *Marine Expeditionary Force: Chemical, Biological Incident Response Force*, undated, p. 1, www.cbirf.marines.mil/About/History.aspx.

24. John S. Pistole, Transportation Security Administration, Department of Homeland Security before the U.S. House of Representatives Committee on Appropriations, Subcommittee on Homeland Security, February 27, 2013, www.tsa.gov/sites/default/files/publications/pdf/testimony/022713_jsp_appropriations_subcommittee.pdf.

25. *Intermodal Transportation Systems* (Washington, D.C.: Transportation Security Administration, September 24, 2013), p. 1, www.tsa.gov/stakeholders/intermodal-transportation-systems.

26. Loc. cit.

27. Loc. cit.

28. *Mission of U.S. Special Operations Command*, undated, p. 1, www.socom.mil/Pages/Mission.aspx.

29. Dr. Christine Coker, "Planning in Hostage Rescue Missions, U.S. Operation Eagle Claw and U.K. Operation Barras," *Military Technology*, Vol. 30, Issue 9, 2006, details taken and restated from p. 66.

30. Ibid., with restated facts from pp. 66 and 67; Statement of Admiral J. L. Holloway (Retired) "Iran Hostage Rescue Mission Report," *Report of the Special Operations Review Group to the Joint Chiefs of Staff,, Admiral Holloway Chair, August 1980*, pp. 20, 23, 29, 33, and 40, www.history.navy.mil/library/online/hollowayrpt.htm; and Otto Kreisher, "Desert One," *Air Force Magazine*, Vol. 82, No. 1, January 1999, p. 1, www.airforcemag.com/MagazineArchive/Pages/1999/January%201999/0199desertone.aspx.

31. Forrest L. Marion, "Air Force Combat Controllers at Desert One: April 24-25, 1980," *Air Power History*, Vol. 56, Issue 1, Spring 2009, p. 48.

32. Loc. cit.

33. *United States Special Operations Command History, 1987–2007* (MacDill Air Force Base, Tampa Florida: United States Special Operations Command, 2008), p. 5.

34. Loc. cit.

35. Ibid., p. 6.

36. Loc. cit.

37. *Dictionary of Military and Associated Terms*, Department of Defense, August 15, 2014, p. 130, www.dtic.mil/doctrine/dod_dictionary.

38. Terrence McCoy, "ISIS, Beheadings and the Success of Horrifying Violence," *The Washington Post*, June 13, 2014.

39. The account of this incident is taken with restatement from James Bennet, "U.S. Cruise Missiles Strike Sudan and Afghanistan, Targets Tied to Terrorist Network," *The New York Times* (International Edition), August 21, 1998.

40. Henry Shue and David Rodin, *Preemption: Military War and Moral Justification* (Oxford, New York: Oxford University Press, 2007), p. 1.

41. Loc. cit.

42. Brigitte L. Nacos, *Terrorism and Counterterrorism* (Glenview, Illinois: Pearson, 4th Edition, 2012), p. 181.

43. The description of this incident is taken with restatement from Robert D. McFadden, "In Rescue of Captain, Navy Kills 3 Pirates," *The New York Times*, April 12, 2009.

44. Jeff Thompson, "Crisis of Hostage Negotiation? The Distinction Between Two Important Terms," *FBI Law Enforcement Bulletin*, March 2014, no page number, http://leb.fbi.gov/2014/march/crisis-or-hostage-negotiation-the-distinction-between-two-important-terms.

45. See U.S. Army Intelligence Support Activity at www.oafnation.com/united-states-army/.

46. Fred J. Pushies et al., *U.S. Counter Terrorist Forces* (St. Paul, Minnesota: MBI Publishing Company, 2002), p. 22.

47. At the end of 1952, SF had filled 1,700 of those positions, 10th SFG (A) History, U.S. Special Operations Command, undated, p. 1, www.soc.mil/USASFC/Groups/10th/history.html.

48. John M. Glenn, "Father of the Green Berets," *Military History*, Vol. 13, Issue 6, February 1998, 7 pp., unnumbered manuscript.

49. 10th SFG (A) History, U.S. Special Operations Command, p. 1.

50. Pushies et al., *U.S. Counter Terrorist Forces*, pp. 23–24.

51. Public Law 597 (1950).

52. Charles K. Dalgleish, "A New Lodge Act for the U.S. Army-A Strategic Tool for the Global War on Terrorism," *National War College*, undated, p. 1.

53. "History of the Green Beret," *Military.com*, 2014, p. 1, www.military.com/special-operations/army-special-forces-missions-and-history.html.

54. "Green Berets," John F. Kennedy Presidential Library and Museum, 2014, p. 1, www.jfklibrary.org/JFK/JFK-in-History/Green-Berets.aspx.

55. Peter Kornbluh, "The Death of Che Guevara: Declassified," *National Security Archive Electronic Briefing Book 5*, 2011, p. 1, www2.gwu.edu/~nsarchiv/NSAEBB/NSAEBB5/#chron.

56. "Charging Charlie" Beckwith attended the University of Georgia where he enrolled in the ROTC program and played left guard on the University's football team. He turned down an offer to play for the Green Bay Packers to accept an Army commission as a Second Lieutenant. Beckwith retired as a Colonel and a much-decorated combat veteran.

57. David Morrison, Lewis Grizzard, and Jim Stewart, "Charging Charlie Beckwith—The Green Berets One-Man Gang," *Lakeland (Florida) Ledger*, May 25, 1980 (Obituary), http://news.google.com/newspapers?nid=1346&dat=19800525&id=buhMAAAAIBAJ&sjid=IfsDAAAAIBAJ&pg=7142,3955873.

58. Tony Geraghty, *Black Ops: The Rise of Special Forces in the C.I.A., the S.A.S. and Mossad* (New York, Pegasus Books, 2010), p. Xlii.

59. Loc. cit.

60. John C. Fredriksen, *Fighting Elites: A History of U.S. Special Forces* (Santa Barbara, California: ABC-CLIO, 2011), p. 154.

61. Delta has had a number of names, including Special Forces Operational Detachment D (SOFD-Delta), Combat Applications Group (CAG), and Army Compartmented Element (ACE). Given its secrecy, we don't know what it is called and will therefore continue to use "Delta" as a convenience.

62. Jack Kelley, "Commando Force Poised to Track and Kill Saddam," *USAToday*, March 18, 2003.

63. Many of the details in this account of the Battle of Mogadishu are drawn with restatement from *United States Forces, Somalia After Action Report and Historical Overview, 1992–1994* (Washington, D.C.: Center for Military History, 2003).

64. Tom Hawkins, "U.S. Navy SEAL Teams: Origins and Evolution 1942–1962," *Defense Media Network*, December 26, 2013, p. 2, www.defensemedianetwork.com/stories/origins-and-evolution-of-u-s-navy-seal-teams-1942-1962/, with restatement.

65. Ibid., p. 7.

66. "Navy SEALs: Background and Brief History," undated, p. 1, www.military.com/special-operations/about-the-navy-seals.html.

67. Hans Halberstadt, *U.S. Navy SEALs* (Minneapolis, Minnesota: Zenith Press, 2011), p. 27.

68. Loc. cit.

69. Loc. cit.

70. J. Paul de B. Taillon, *The Evolution of Special Forces in Counter Terrorism* (Westport, CT: Praeger Publishers, 2001), p. 72.

71. Ronald O'Rourke, *Navy Irregular Warfare and Counter Terrorism Operations: Background and Issues for Congress* (Washington, D.C.: Congressional Research Service, October 18, 2012), p. 2.

72. Halberstadt, *U.S. Navy SEALs*, pp. 7 and 11.

73. Ibid., pp. 15–16.

74. The Ranger history is taken from "75th Ranger Regiment History," May 6, 2014, pp. 1–2, www.benning.army.mil/tenant/75thRanger/history.htm; and "75th Ranger Regiment History," undated, pp. 1–2, www.soc.mil/Rangers/history.html, with restatement and reorganization.

75. "75th Ranger Regiment," p. 1, 2012, www.baseops.net/militarybooks/Armyranger.html.

76. "Army Rangers: The 75th Ranger Regiment," p. 1, 2014, www.military.com/special-operations/army-rangers-75th-regiment.html.

77. Loc. cit.

78. Richard A. Best Jr and Andrew Feickert, *Special Operations Forces (SOF) and Paramilitary Operations: Issues for Congress* (Washington, D.C.: Congressional Research Service, August 3, 2009), p. 1.

79. Loc. cit.

80. *An End and a Beginning* (Washington, D.C.: Central Intelligence Service, March 15, 2007), p. 2, www.cia.gov/library/center-for-the-study-of-intelligence/csi-publications/books-and-monographs/oss/art10.htm.

81. Steve Bowman and Catherine Dale, *War in Afghanistan: Strategy, Military Operations, and Issues for Congress* (Washington, D.C.: Congressional Research Service, December 3, 2009), p. 6.

82. Ibid., p. 7.

83. Loc. cit.

84. Ibid., p. 8.

85. Loc. cit.

86. Loc. cit.

87. *Joint Terrorism Task Forces* (Washington, D.C. Immigration and Customs Enforcement, undated, but containing dates through 2010), p. 1, www.ice.gov/jttf/.

88. Michael Martinez, Evan Perez, and Barbra Starr, "Sources: Benghazi 'Mastermind' Captured without a Single Shot Fired," *CNN World News*, June 17, 2014, pp. 1–2, www.google.com/webhp?sourceid=chrome-instant&ion=1&espv=2&ie=UTF-8#q=martinez%2C%20benghazi%20mastermind%20captured.

89. Michael Zennie and James Nye, "Libyan Government Demands U.S. Return Benghazi Mastermind and Calls Delta Force Raid That Captured Him an Attack on Our Sovereignty," June 18, 2014, p. 1, www.google.com/webhp?sourceid=chrome-instant&ion=1&espv=2&ie=UTF-,8#q=michael+zennie,+Libyan+Government+DEmands+U.S.+Returns&tbm=nws.

90. Ibid., pp. 1, 4.

91. Adam Goldman and Julie Tate, "Inside the FBI's Secret Relationship with the Military's Special Operations," *The Washington Post*, April 10, 2014, p. 2, www.google.com/webhp?sourceid=chrome-instant&ion=1&espv=2&ie=UTF-8#q=fbi+works+with+delta+force&start=0.

92. Loc. cit.

93. Loc. cit.

94. Loc. cit.

95. Henry Plater-Zyberk, *Russia's Special Forces* (Shrivenham, England: Conflict Studies Research Centre, September 2005), p. 3.

96. "Chronology of Major SAS Operations," 2002, p. 1, www.sasspecialairservice.com/sas-history-timeline-operations-list.html.

97. For information about special operations units during World War II, see Chris Burton, "The Eureka-Rebecca Compromises: Another Look at Special Operations Security During World War II," *Air Power History*, Vol. 52, Issue 4, Winter 2005, pp. 23–37.

98. Ibid., p. 2.

99. "SAS Regiment," History of the SAS Regiment, 2012, p. 1, www.sasregiment.org.uk.

100. Sean Rayment, "SAS Kills Hundreds of Terrorists in Secret War Against Al-Qaeda in Iraq," *The Telegraph* (England), August 30, 2008, p. 1.

101. Loc. cit.

102. Jason Burke, "Task Force Black by Mark Urban," *The Guardian* (England), February 27, 2010, p. 1.

103. Rayment, "SAS Kills Hundreds of Terrorists in Secret War Against Al-Qaeda in Iraq," p. 2.

104. Ben Endley, "If the SAS Leave Afghanistan the Taliban Will Take Over Say Top U.S. Generals," *The Daily Mirror* (England), April 26, 2014.

105. This account is drawn from Terry Martin, "Munich Massacre Remembered," *Europe*, October 1, 2001, p. 43; and "Munich Olympic Massacre: Background and Overview," *Jewish Virtual Library*, undated, but the most recent source cited in this article was 2012, www.jewishvirtuallibrary.org/jsource/Terrorism/munich.html.

106. Cindy C. Combs and Martin Slann, "Grenzschutsgruppe 9 (GSG9)," *Encyclopedia of Terrorism*, 2007, New York, Facts on File Inc., p. 2, www.fofweb.com/History/MainPrintPage.asp?iPin=TER0126&DataType=WorldHistory&WinType=Free.

107. *GSG9 (Grenzschutzgruppe 9)* (St. Andrews, Scotland: University of St. Andrews, undated), p. 1, www.terroism.com/gsg9.

108. Loc. cit.

109. Loc. cit.

110. David B. Green, "The Different Faces of Ehud Barak," *New Leader*, Vol. 82, Issue 8, July 12, 199, p. 5,

111. "Israel Defense Forces: Commando and Special Forces," *Jewish Virtual Library*,2014, p. 3, www.jewishvirtuallibrary.org/jsource/society_and_culture/forcestoc.html.

112. Loc. cit.

113. Akiva Lorenz, *The Threat of Maritime Terrorism to Israel* (Herzliya, Israel: International Center for Counter-Terrorism, September 24, 2009), p. 1,

114. Loc. cit.

115. No author, "Israel's Special Forces—Shayetet 13," *Armed Forces History Museum*, undated, p. 1, http://armedforcesmuseum.com/israels-special-forces-shayetet-13.

116. Loc. cit.

117. Loc. cit.

118. Ibid., p. 12.

119. Mathieu Deflem, "Yehida Mishtaritit Mistaaravim (YAMAS) (Israel)," in Frank G. Shanty, editor, *Counter Terrorism: From the Cold War to the War on Terror*, Volume 2 (Santa Barbara, CA: Praeger/ABC-CLIO, 2012), pp. 71–72.

Terrorism, Intelligence and Homeland Security: The Future

Learning Objectives

After completing this chapter, you should be able to:

1. Describe broad trends in terrorism, including general statistics about frequency, location, and targets of attacks.

2. Elaborate on the rise of homegrown and lone wolf terrorists and their weapons usage.

3. Discuss how al-Qaeda has been splintered and what the effects of that phenomenon might be.

4. Identify targets currently favored by terrorists, as well as future means of attack.

5. Discuss the role of modern media in terrorism.

6. Describe policies and strategies that might be implemented in counterterrorism in the future.

Many terrorist groups ensure their future by grooming children to accept their same intolerant beliefs. In Nashville, Tennessee children are seen with familiar symbols of hate.

(© Zuma Press/Newscom)

Introduction

At this point in any text on modern terrorism, some variation of the phrase "after the events of September 11, 2001" has been used countless times throughout the pages. Nearly 15 years later, that terrible day still figures so strongly in this country that it continues to inform foreign relations, domestic policy, law enforcement, and everyday life—including travel, Internet privacy, and more. It's led to wars that continue, to suspicions that linger, and even to petty personal annoyances that persist (such as airport security checkpoints). And it's something that happened in the past—yet still manages to shape perceptions about what the future of terrorism looks like. Many citizens of this country—and many policy makers, as well—continue to see terrorism as something that may be best prevented by increased security measures and traditional methodologies, such as 'target hardening' of specific locations, use of new technology to bolster airport security, targeting radical Muslims both home and abroad for surveillance, and focusing intelligence on the same networks of informants, couriers, and organizations that have been major players in the past decade and a half.

However, just as policy and intelligence related to terrorism have evolved, so too have the terrorists themselves. Today, known al-Qaeda sympathizers use YouTube and Twitter as a means of recruitment and communication—establishing an audience that reaches far beyond training facilities in remote areas of Afghanistan. Radicalization is increasingly an individual pursuit, cultured in the glow of a computer screen as opposed to in secretive meetings in mosques. The availability and affordability of weapons or elements used to assemble weapons have made them accessible to just about anyone who really wants to obtain them, further widening the pool of potential terrorists. Furthermore, intelligence methods that many consider to have been effective at uncovering terror plots have met with an uproar from human rights and/or privacy advocates in recent years, limiting how information can be obtained—and according to some, the ability to secure our country against certain kinds of attacks. These are just a few examples of how perceptions of terrorism and related intelligence have evolved over the past decade; this chapter will touch on several others, as well.

Trends in Terrorist Activities

In January 2013, a study by the National Consortium for the Study of Terrorism and Responses to Terrorism (START) detailed trends in terrorist activity for the United States. The data they examined indicated that in the span of time between 2001 and 2011, there had been a total of 207 attacks that were classified as terrorist in nature, 21 of which were fatal. From 2001 until 2011, the number of terrorist attacks in this country had declined from a peak of 40 attacks in that first year to 9 in the last. These numbers include serious attacks that were attempted (i.e., bombs that didn't detonate or shootings that didn't meet their target) but ultimately not successful. In 2011 this measure accounted for four out of the nine total reported incidents.[1] The study also included a broad definition of terror attacks, encompassing murders of abortion clinic personnel and a shooting (in 2009) of a guard at the National Holocaust Museum.

The states of New York and California accounted for the only identified "clusters" of multiple attacks in the United States, with New York City, Washington D.C., and Los Angeles being the cities most often targeted (See Figure 15–1). The types of weapons most frequently used in terrorist attacks were incendiary devices, or bombs, which accounted for 53 percent of the total, followed by explosives, which were used 20 percent of the time. Tied for third place at 8 percent were firearms and, somewhat improbable, biological weapons. The data in this last category is highly skewed, as all of the events classified under the biological weapons category were the sole result of a spate of anthrax attacks in October 2001.[2]

Over half of the attacks were aimed solely at damaging property or rendering a system inoperable, and did not involve explosives. These types of attacks were mostly due to arson events perpetrated by extremist animal rights and environmental groups. The major targets of the attacks were businesses (making up a total of 62 attacks), followed closely by

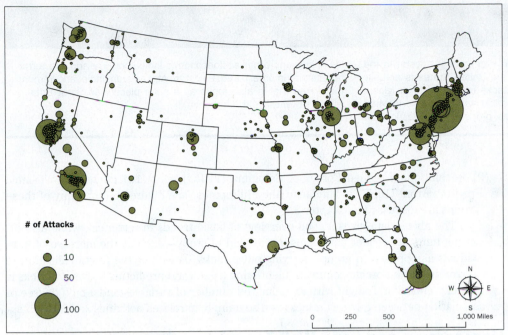

FIGURE 15–1
The Geographic Concentration of Terrorist Attacks in the United States, 1970–2008
This proportional symbol map was created to visually display the concentration of terrorist attacks across the United States. The size of the dots is proportional to the number of attacks. The frequency of attacks mirrors areas with the highest concentration of population in the United States and provides a potential map for future attack if indeed history repeats itself.

Source: Gary Lafree and Bianca Bersani, *Hotspots of Terrorism and Other Crimes in the United States, 1970–2008* (College Park, Maryland: National Consortium for the Study of Terrorism and Responses to Terrorism, University of Maryland, January 31, 2012).

Source: Global Terrorism Database, 1970–2008.
Note: 16 attacks are not shown due to missing geographic information.

private citizens and property (59 attacks), and then government (43 attacks). Twenty-four percent of those attacks were perpetrated by the Earth Liberation Front (ELF), giving that group the distinction of having carried out the most terror attacks on American soil. ELF is followed by another single-issue terrorist associate, the Animal Liberation Front (ALF), which committed 16 percent of the total attacks. Refer to Chapter 7 for more information on ELF and ALF. Al-Qaeda followed—which was responsible for just 2 percent of total attacks, though obviously, that 2 percent included the deadliest of all attacks.[3] Neither ELF nor ALF attacks have claimed any lives, while the al-Qaeda attacks included 98 percent of the fatalities within the study.

What the Data Reveals

Overall, what this data shows is that the frequency of terror attacks in the United States have been trending downward—with the events in 2001 that included the September 11 attacks and the anthrax attacks that killed five people serving as the height of the statistics. However, the number of fatal attacks has increased in the past several years, beginning to climb again in 2008. Another interesting takeaway from this study: The number of attacks perpetrated by individuals has been steadily on the rise, now accounting for somewhere north of 35 percent of the total since the Oklahoma City bombings in 1995.

Finally, the study shows (surprisingly!) that the United States actually ranks near the bottom, internationally, of terror hot spots. In fact, in START data released in 2014 and covering global terror trends in 2013, the United States does not even rank in the report despite the bombings at the Boston Marathon in April of that year. The countries with the highest concentration of terror activity were Iraq, Pakistan, and Afghanistan, where more than half of all attacks occurred. Two-thirds of all fatalities due to terror attacks occurred in these same places, and nearly three-quarters of the injuries resulting from terrorism happened in these areas. Iraq claims the highest number of attacks, fatalities, and injuries by a very wide margin.[4]

Other information on trends in terrorism detailed in the 2013 START report focuses on the terror groups responsible for the attacks. The ten most active groups globally, and in order, include (1) the Taliban in Afghanistan; (2) al-Qaida in Iraq; (3) Boko Haram in Nigeria; (4) Maoists in India; (5) al Shabaab in Somalia; (6) Tehrik-i-Taliban in Pakistan (TTP); (7) New People's Army (NPA) in the Philippines; (8) al-Qaida in the Arabian Peninsula (AQAP)—now morphing into the Islamic State (IS) or the Islamic State in Iraq and Syria (ISIS);

Quick Facts
Terrorism and the United States

Although terrorism is something of an ever-present specter in the American consciousness post-9/11, the United States is actually a relatively safe haven from terror attacks compared to its global counterparts. The United States ranks forty-first in the world when considered on a scale that measures property damage, loss of life, injury, and other socioeconomic indicators. The top five terror targets are (in order): Iraq, Pakistan, Afghanistan, India, and Yemen; the United States also ranks as a safer place than Great Britain, which is twenty-eighth on the list.[5]

Information Link

For more information on the National Consortium for the Study of Terrorism and Responses to Terrorism (START), visit the website at the University of Maryland, www.start.umd.edu/. Browse the site and notice the emphasis placed on research, publication, and education focused on terrorism.

(9) Revolutionary Armed Forces of Colombia (FARC); and (10) Bangsamoro Islamic Freedom Front (BIFF) in Mindanao, the Philippines (see Figure 15–2).[6] Many of these groups are discussed in Chapter 2.

The above data gives a good overview of basic trends in terrorism, while also offering hints at broader paradigms in the field of study—such as the increase of individuals as opposed to groups carrying out attacks, as well as the fractionalization of terror groups in foreign countries. Identifying trends and predicting terrorist attacks is a tricky endeavor, fraught with an unlimited number of variables and a high degree of association between terrorist attacks and seemingly unrelated activities and incidents.

Homegrown and Lone Wolf Terrorists

In the United States, this trend has been relatively easy to spot. The last few major attacks that have occurred in the United States were carried out by so-called homegrown terrorists using lone wolf terrorist tactics. See Chapters 1 and 5 for a more thorough discussion of homegrown and lone wolf terrorism. The term *homegrown terrorist* refers to extremists who are legal U.S. residents or even citizens, and who are linked to or inspired by a specific, often intolerant ideology. This ideology may be motivated by political or religious sources and may be centered in domestic or foreign movements. Indeed, some of them have made connections with well-known, international terror groups, such as al-Qaeda or associated movements.[7] These individuals may receive ideological encouragement, but not financial or material support, making them ancillary to the primary group and very difficult to detect by intelligence and law enforcement services. For instance, Major Nidal Hasan, perpetrator of the 2009 Fort Hood shootings that killed 13 people and wounded more than 30 others, is a prime example of this type of terrorist—a man who was radicalized due to a belief that American wars in Iraq and Afghanistan were wars against the Muslim faith. Hasan had expressed his opposition to these wars, despite his position as a psychiatrist in the United States Army, and carried out his attack about a month before he was to be deployed to Afghanistan. Hasan had been in contact with radical Muslim cleric and suspected al-Qaeda officer Anwar al-Awlaki via a series of emails before his attack.

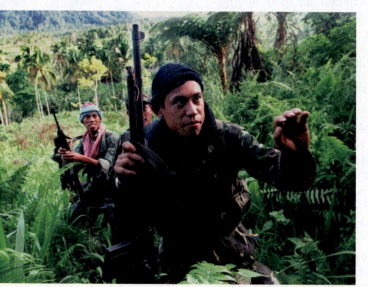

FIGURE 15–2

The Bangsamoro Islamic Freedom Front (BIFF), or Moro Islamic Liberation Front, and the New People's Army threaten the stability of the Philippines. Increased terrorist attacks especially in the rural areas have garnered both groups a place in the top ten most active terrorist groups in the world.

(© Ryan Anson/ZUMA Press/ Newscom)

In other cases, terrorist groups target first-generation foreign nationals living in the United States to join their ranks. The perpetrators of the Boston Marathon bombings in 2013 are good examples of this activity and are considered homegrown terrorists. Tamerlan Tsarnaev, who apparently masterminded the attack with the help of his younger brother Dzhokhar, was another young Muslim who had been radicalized by his anger over perceived injustices against the Muslim faith by the United States. Though no direct connections between the two Chechens and any specific terrorist group have been identified in the year after the bombing, the two did view al-Qaeda training videos on the Internet, and espoused doctrine that is common among al-Qaeda sympathizers.[8]

Why are some Muslim Americans identifying with terror groups? The first reason has already been discussed. They believe that the American presence in Iraq and Afghanistan is an affront to Islam and a direct attack on Muslim nations and people. For instance, a small

Box 15-1
Predicting Terror Attacks

Policies, laws, intelligence, and our fear level are all related to terrorism and can be based on a single attack. However, a specific attack by a specific group or individual is largely unpredictable in nature. While certain clues were overlooked in the months before 9/11, it's still difficult (if not impossible) to say with any certainty that the events of that day could have been predicted. Furthermore, the current trends in terrorism mean smaller-scale attacks perpetrated by individuals that are rarely the subject of previous law enforcement scrutiny, hence there is no historical data on these individuals.

Surprisingly, however, terror attacks may not occur as randomly as we once thought they did. That's the conclusion reached by Aaron Clauset, a 35-year-old data scientist in Denver, Colorado, who examined complex information related to terrorist attacks and identified statistical patterns behind the frequency and severity of terrorist attacks across the globe. What Clauset noticed about terror attacks is that they seemed to mirror earthquakes in some ways, following a power-law distribution. Earthquakes tend to occur in groups of really small quakes, followed by a handful of stronger medium-sized quakes, and then one or two really massive, devastating quakes. Clauset found that terror attacks followed the same pattern; for example, there had been scores of small terror attacks, a couple of medium-intensity attacks (like the Oklahoma City Bombing and the Lockerbie airline explosions), and then the massive 9/11 attack that killed 3,000 people. This is useful for law enforcement, security, and policy makers because the frequency and severity of "small" terrorist attacks may help to determine the likelihood of another "big one"; events like the attacks on Oklahoma City or Lockerbie should have suggested the potential for something much worse in the future.

Despite its seeming applicability to homeland security, Clauset's conclusions have not been utilized by the U.S. government. The methodology is complex, and perhaps beyond the capabilities of many of the agencies that would need to be involved in its use. Interestingly, Clauset points out the following implications for his findings:

> If we believe the power-law is a fundamental property of terrorism— and it appears to be so in a very robust way—it's reasonable to conclude that there may be a really big terrorist attack coming ... involving chemical, biological or radiological attacks. And almost surely, the probability of these kinds of events is much higher than people might expect. If we don't have some people thinking about this in the long term, we are going to be very surprised. We are going to be unprepared.[9]

Source: Excerpt from How Aaron Clauset Discovered a Pattern Behind Terrorist Attacks...And What It Told Him by Joel Warner. Published by Denver Westword, LLC, © 2013.

How effective and accurate do you think these types of prediction models are to police and security agencies?

population of Somali Muslims (mainly teenagers) in Minnesota believe that the U.S, backing of an Ethiopian invasion in their home country was an attack on Islam, resulting in a number of them connecting with **al Shabaab**, an extremist organization affiliated with al-Qaeda in Somalia.[10] (See Figure 15–3.) The second reason is that they have access to such groups via increased connectivity. The Internet and various social media platforms have allowed U.S. residents to reach out to or be recruited by extremists around the globe, gaining access to ideologies, philosophies, propaganda, and even their methods of violence (see Box 15–2). Access to training and operational support, although not as simple as a Google search, can be found online for those seeking it.

In the United States, such homegrown terrorists have largely flown beneath the radar—many have no criminal records, and while their European counterparts tend to be more socially marginalized, it's more likely that American-grown extremists come from a broad variety of educational and socioeconomic statuses. Consider that Major Nidal Hasan had completed medical school; Tamerlan Tsarnaev had gone to college for a time to pursue engineering; and his brother, Dzhokhar, was enrolled in university at the time of the attacks.

The future of homegrown terrorism is one that will see shifts in the composition of participants, as well as in the networking that they engage in with al-Qaeda and other affiliated movements. As the United States continues to see successes in dismantling the major arteries of these terrorist organizations, homegrown terrorists will seek new ways to interact with them. In the past, some had physically attended training camps or, as in the case of Hasan, communicated directly with terror operatives. As surveillance has intensified and travel has become more scrutinized, those who seek out these radically inclined connections will retreat further into the Internet, particularly the "**deep web**," utilizing gaming sites that appear innocuous on the outside but allow encrypted conversations using their platforms, social media

Al Shabaab
A radical Islamic group affiliated with al-Qaeda operating in the country of Somalia.

FIGURE 15–3
There are strong Somali communities in Minneapolis and Cedar Riverside, Minnesota, from which the terrorist group al Shabaab recruits. Since 2006, an estimated 25 to 50 young Somali men have gone to fight with al Shabaab throughout the Middle East and Africa.

(© Johnathan Alpeyrie/Polaris/Newscom)

Box 15-2
Social Media and Jihad

Social media, though fun and entertaining in many ways for many people, is something of a headache for homeland security officials in the Western world. Beyond tracking down high school classmates, following favorite celebrities, and playing Candy Crush, sites such as Facebook and Twitter have a darker side to them—one that allows terrorist organizations to disperse propaganda, maintain networks, operate recruiting, and connect with would-be operatives.

As more terror attacks are perpetrated by lone wolf–style terrorists, who have no direct connection to terrorist groups such as al-Qaeda, social media sites have become an important link to the militant ideologies espoused by terror organizations. Users of the sites who search for and locate other people with similar interests may then be exposed to a virtual rabbit hole of terror networks, with each new contact increasing potential additional contacts exponentially.

Though very few terrorists are openly posting threatening material on these forums, it's the connections that are most valuable—once a 22-year-old student in Michigan makes contacts with jihadists on a social networking site, he or she can then develop online relationships with them; gaining trust, establishing a rapport, and eventually earning credentials to secure chat forums, where explicit information and training materials may be available.

▲ Mohamed Jarmune was arrested by police in Brescia, Northern Italy. He is suspected of planning an attack on Milan's synagogue. The 20-year-old Moroccan man, who has lived in Italy since he was 6, is also suspected of setting up secret Facebook pages providing training on making bombs and using weapons for budding terrorists.

(© Newscom)

This reality has proven difficult for social media conglomerates and policy makers alike to deal with. Twitter, Facebook, and YouTube are reticent to restrict access to their sites by certain users or to turn over information to law enforcement, citing freedom of speech policies. Unless individuals are making outright threats or actively violating generous terms of service policies, they are allowed to utilize the services without disruption—for example, al-Qaeda's public relations arm openly operated a Twitter account for some time in 2013, gaining over 14,000 followers until it was finally suspended for a terms of service violation which has not been disclosed by Twitter.

Even without open and obvious utilization by terror organizations, the sites still pose a threat to homeland security just as a result of the way that they inform and connect homegrown and lone wolf terrorists. Though homeland security officials and policy makers have been and will continue to be stymied by Silicon Valley's privacy guidelines, their best course of action is to keep an open dialogue with these companies in order to identify how their services might be utilized to better track terrorist activity in the future.[11]

Should social media websites restrict access to individuals and groups that express violent or anti-American philosophies? Should law enforcement and intelligence services monitor social media websites?

Deep web
A secret part of the World Wide Web, not accessible through regular Internet browsing or search engines; accessible from dynamic websites requiring the use of an application program called *Tor* that allows encrypted conversations.

Tor network
Synonymous for the deep web; see deep web. Acronym for a previous software program that allows complete anonymity on the web, called, The Onion Router.

sites, and chat rooms to communicate.[12] The deep web is a vast part of the World Wide Web, not accessible through regular Internet browsing or search engines. Most of the information in the deep web is hidden, accessible from dynamic websites requiring the use of an application call *Tor*. The **Tor network** is synonymous for the deep web. This secretive online world remains mostly untraceable and difficult to access for the regular Internet user and even law enforcement and intelligence operatives. This subsequently allows a large criminal domain to thrive and a hidden venue for secret communications between terrorists, particularly astute worldwide terrorists sharing a jihadi Salafist philosophy.[13]

Crude Devises and Non-Sophisticated Weapons

Another result of the effects of splintering terror cells and increased intelligence is that homegrown terrorists are now largely forced to use crude devices or easily obtained weapons (such as firearms) to carry out their attacks. The bombs used in the Boston Marathon attacks were basically pressure cookers, found in any large retailer, filled with nails and ball bearings. They were reportedly made using instructions found online. Major Nidal Hasan used legally obtained firearms. Other terror attacks in the past few years have utilized vehicles as weapons, as well as a litany of homemade explosives. Purchasing materials to make more complex weaponry is made more difficult by policy changes restricting certain hazardous or biologic materials—or, if not restricting them outright, triggering a level of scrutiny that would-be terrorists might avoid.[14]

It's for these reasons that Attorney General Eric Holder stated that these were the types of potential attacks that keep him up at night; he singled out the homegrown, lone wolf terrorist, stating that he was "very concerned about individuals who get radicalized in a variety of ways … sometimes self-radicalized."[15] As we learned in Chapter 5, lone wolves include homegrown terrorists, but the term also encompasses those who identify with ideologies other than radical Islam; lone wolves can be right-wing extremists, anti-abortion

Quick Facts
The Leadership of al-Qaeda

Al-Qaeda, once a highly centralized and well-organized bureaucracy, has suffered many losses within the leadership ranks since the CIA drone campaign began in 2008. Those lost include Abu Laith al-Libi, the third highest-ranking official in the organization; Abu Khabab al-Masri, the group's leading expert on weapons of mass destruction; Abu Jihad al-Masri, al-Qaeda's propaganda chief; and many other lead operatives and high-ranking officials. The deaths of these individuals within al-Qaeda have essentially dismantled the command, control, and communication elements of the group. As of early 2014, only four notable senior members remain: (1) Ayman al-Zawahiri (current head of the organization), (2) Adnan Shukrijumah (head of external relations for the group), (3) Khalid al-Habib (primary leader in Pakistan and Afghanistan), and (4) Saif al-Adel (longtime senior commander within al-Qaeda). It is important to note that each of these individuals is currently being "hunted" by U.S. forces.

Source: National Security Program. "Jihadist Terrorism: A Threat Assessment." Homeland Security Project, Bipartisan Policy Center. September 2013, http://bipartisanpolicy.org/sites/default/files/Jihadist%20Terrorism-A%20Threat%20Assesment_0.pdf.

radicals, and leftist environmentalists. They typically operate the same way that homegrown terrorists do—by networking online, seeking out their own information, and utilizing easily made or easily obtained weaponry for their attacks, though they may have more of a tendency than their radical Muslim counterparts to broadcast their intentions in some way.[16] They generally act on their own accord, in the name of some deeply held ideological belief system. As for their prevalence, a 2012 study by Ramon Spaaij found that lone wolf terror attacks were on the rise—increasing at a rate of about 45 percent between the 1970s and the 2000s.[17] It should be noted, however, that these attacks are still statistically rare—accounting for only 1.28 percent of all attacks between 1968 and 2007 in the United Kingdom, Germany, France, Spain, Italy, Poland, the Netherlands, Denmark, Sweden, Czech Republic, Portugal, Russia, Canada, United States, and Australia.[18]

Al-Qaeda, Fractionalization, and the Rest of the World

Once the "big bad" of global terror, al-Qaeda's threat today is much harder to assess than it was even five years ago. At one point, this enemy was a large organization, headquartered for the most part in one major geographic location and fronted by a figurehead (Usama bin Laden) with undeniable power and reach. Today, this is not the case. The organization has become almost completely unrecognizable, with command and control dismantled through the death of prominent leaders. The centralized and powerful al-Qaeda organization of old is no longer a single entity, but has diffused throughout the Middle East and beyond—maintaining a presence in at least 16 different countries.[19] For example, what was once the core of the organization in Pakistan has been largely decimated as part of the U.S. military involvement in Afghanistan and Iraq. Further, CIA drone strikes in Pakistan, which have killed approximately 33 senior al-Qaeda operatives since 2008, have left only a handful of former leaders in that country.[20] Similar activities in Somalia and Yemen have neutralized al-Qaeda threats in those areas.

Although this was, in theory, the goal of the U.S. military offensive against al-Qaeda, it has had the unintended consequence of allowing the organization to reformulate and still flourish as a decentralized, heavily networked and transnational movement, freed from the bureaucracy of its earlier iterations and able to move about more covertly as a result. The "brand" of al-Qaeda is an enduring one; as discussed previously in relation to homegrown and lone wolf operatives, the message that the United States and other Western powers are waging a war on Islam is one that continues to resonate with an audience throughout the world. This has allowed them to shift their strategy somewhat—encouraging these lone wolf attacks in the United States, and also taking advantage of an extremely unstable situation in the Middle East to launch attacks against Western interests in those areas.

The events of the Arab Spring have also created a new opportunity for al-Qaeda splinter groups to strengthen, allowing groups that were operating in just eight areas of the Middle East (Afghanistan, Indonesia, Iraq, Lebanon, Nigeria, Pakistan, the Philippines, and Somalia) to establish new footholds in just a few short years in Algeria, Libya, Mali, Mauritania, Sudan, Syria, Tunisia, and Lebanon. Large quantities of weapons, used as part of the civil unrest in many of these areas, have made their way into the hands of al-Qaeda spin-offs, and prison breaks due to regional unrest have allowed former al-Qaeda operatives to make their way back into the network.[21]

Boko Haram
A radical Islamic group linked to al-Qaeda in the Islamic Maghreb (AQIM) in North Africa; active in Nigeria.

The al-Qaeda cells that have popped up in the past few years have largely focused on domestic targets—for example, al-Qaeda in Iraq (AQI) has focused on attacking Shia Muslim populations within that country (though al-Qaeda proper has distanced itself from that particular sect), and **Boko Haram**, with ties to al-Qaeda in the Islamic Maghreb in Nigeria, has led a campaign of kidnappings in killings that country.[22] Indeed, in early January 2015, Boko Haram conducted a series of raids on the Nigerian village of Baga, near the border with Chad, resulting in a bloody massacre leaving over 2,000 innocent civilians killed.

There have been some attacks against Western interests perpetrated by those groups—most notably the attacks on the American diplomatic mission and CIA annex in Benghazi, Libya, in September 2012. That particular attack claimed the lives of 3 Americans and injured 10 more. Another group of al-Qaeda-affiliated jihadists from Algeria attacked a British Petroleum facility in January of 2013 in Amenas, Algeria, leaving 37 hostages dead.[23] These remain the exception, rather than the rule, but also illustrate quite clearly the capabilities these groups have to attack Western targets throughout the region.

The continued and current unrest in the Middle East is yet another factor in promoting the successful diffusion of al-Qaeda organizations and philosophy. In late April 2014, al-Qaeda chief Ayman al-Zawahiri (see Figure 15–4) made that clear in an audio recording where he expressed support for the Muslim Brotherhood in the midst of a violent crackdown by the army-backed government in Egypt; he also urged unity among rebels in the fight against Syrian President Bashar al-Assad.[24] He characterized both conflicts as a fight for marginalized Muslims across the globe, stating, "the duty of every Muslim is to deter the aggressor by any means, and especially the oppressed Muslims of the Middle East."[25] Syria in particular has drawn jihadist sympathizers from across the globe to assist in the fight against al-Assad. The fear is that these fighters may become even further radicalized by their experiences and training in Syria, and that al-Qaeda–affiliated jihadists may have access to the large quantities of arms flowing into the country, intended for the rebels.[26] This certainly appears to be the case as the Islamic State became a much more prominent group in 2014. And, on January 7, 2015, terrorist gunmen armed with automatic weapons and having prior military training and experience in Syria and Yemen, attacked the offices of a French satirical newspaper, *Charlie Hebdo* in Paris. The massacre left 12 people dead including the editor and cartoonists associated with the newspaper as well as 11 others injured. The attack was in response to cartoons that radical Muslims believed insulted the Prophet Muhammad published by the magazine over 3 years prior to the attack. The ensuing manhunt for the terrorists, all French citizens of Middle Eastern descent (Cherif Kouachi, Said Kouachi, and Amedy Coulibaly) over the next two days resulted in a series of bloody encounters with the French police, again resulting in numerous deaths of civilians and police officers as well as the terrorists themselves. The bloody attack shocked the world and marked a significant departure in radical Islamic terrorist tactics from random, suicide attacks aimed at inflicting significant human carnage as observed in the past by al-Qaeda and Hamas operatives, to much more sophisticated, militarily-planned attacks with specific targets conducted by trained individuals.

In addition, in the same recording in which he called for jihadist support in Syria and Egypt, al-Zawahiri also introduced a relatively new terrorist tactic in that region, that of kidnapping and extortion, particularly of Americans. Al-Zawahiri stated that this type of activity should be a primary focus of al-Qaeda affiliates, as they may be useful tools in obtaining money to further the jihadi philosophy and the release of jailed al-Qaeda members in the United States: "I ask Allah the Glorious to help us set free Sheik Omar Abdel-Rahman and the rest of the captive Muslims, and I ask Allah to help us capture from among the Americans and the Westerners to enable us to exchange them for our captives."[27] Sheik Abdul Rahman is the blind Egyptian cleric currently serving a life sentence in the United States from charges stemming from the first bombing attack on the World Trade Center in 1993.

This call for increased kidnappings of Westerners certainly signals a new tactical emphasis for the extremists, and should be expected to spur increased activity—kidnappings are a

FIGURE 15–4
The late Usama bin Laden (L), head of al-Qaeda, and his then-deputy Ayman al-Zawahiri meeting at an undisclosed location in Afghanistan on November 8, 2001. Now the leader of al-Qaeda, al-Zawahiri was previously involved with directing the affairs of al-Qaeda for nearly a decade. Recently, he sent video messages aimed at changing the tactical practices of the group.

(© Ausaf Newspapar/EPA/Newscom)

relatively easy task for splinter groups to accomplish, requiring few resources compared to large-scale attacks and generating much publicity. Thus far, however, the United States has expressed an unwillingness to negotiate with terrorist organizations in kidnapping situations. For instance, a 72-year-old contractor kidnapped by al-Qaeda in Pakistan in 2011 was still being held in 2014, as the Obama administration insisted it would not trade prisoners for his release.[28]

Transportation Hubs and Other Terrorist Targets

Since 2001, much of the attention on the potential for terror attacks has focused on transportation hubs. It is not a problem peculiar to America (see Figure 15–5). Aviation travel in particular has been an emphasis for policy and practice related to terror prevention. Toughened security standards around the globe have

FIGURE 15–5
Airport security is not just a domestic concern. Here, a counterterrorism unit practices "taking down" an airplane at the Minsk National Airport in Belarus. The exercise was part of security preparations for the 2014 World Hockey Championship in Minsk.

(© Tatyana Zenkovich/EPA/Newscom)

been largely successful—commercial aviation is a front-loaded access system, and screenings and security checkpoints have been difficult for would-be terrorists to overcome in the past decade and a half. That's not to say that the system is impenetrable, however. In 2014, a California teenager scaled the fences at San Jose International Airport and climbed into the wheel well of an awaiting jet destined for Hawaii. The fact that he was able to access a commercial jetliner fully undetected raises questions about perimeter security of airports, and suggests that physical access from airport perimeters may be a vulnerability that terrorists might attempt to take advantage of in the future. Airport perimeters generally are the jurisdiction of both local and airport police, but the areas are sprawling; even the relatively small San Jose airport contains nearly six miles of perimeter fencing.[29] Nonetheless, aviation targets have been hit relatively few times since 9/11, resulting in around 205 total deaths, a number that is tragic but does emphasize that airline travel remains a mostly safe endeavor.[30]

Ground transportation targeting by terrorists in the same time period, however, remained a point of easy access for terrorists. Buses and trains were struck 1,800 times between 2001 and 2012, killing just under 4,000 people. Such modes of transportation are notoriously difficult to secure—there are far too many access points along bus routes and in train stations. And while closed caption television security has proven to be somewhat effective in deterring certain types of attacks, suicide bombers are inherently unconcerned with having their actions traced on camera. Intelligence and security awareness among the general public seem to be the most important factors in deterring such an event.[31]

Another concern for future terror attacks is that of school shootings. While America has certainly seen far too many of those in the recent past, they are not classified as terrorism, per se, largely because they don't seem to spring from any sort of strongly held political or religious ideology. But an attack in Norway in 2011 showed how devastating such an event could be. In that case, right-wing extremist **Anders Behring Breivik** bombed two buildings in Oslo, killing eight people. He then travelled to an island summer camp for youth affiliated with a Norwegian political party and opened fire on teenagers and staff, killing 69, mainly children and teenagers. Another school attack, this one in Toulose, France, was carried out by an alleged al-Qaeda sympathizer, Mohamed Morah, earlier in 2012. After shooting and killing three French soldiers at close range, he proceeded to a Jewish grade school and killed three children and a rabbi.[32] Both of these attacks illustrate (as does the Newtown school shooting in December 2013) just how easily lone wolf–style attackers can infiltrate schools (or other educational and recreational facilities). Fortunately, these types of **soft targets** have not been utilized extensively by terrorists in the United States. Most of those occurring in the United States have been attributed to individuals with mental and emotional disturbances rather than political or terrorist motivations.

Attacks on random targets also appear to be a new methodology by terrorist individuals and organizations. Though the act of terror itself cannot be considered random, as it is

Anders Behring Breivik
Norwegian ultra-right wing perpetrator of the July 22, 2011, attacks killing 8 people in Oslo, and another 69 more on the island of Utoya, in one of the deadliest mass shootings in history.

Soft target
A military term to describe a non-defended or innocent target—usually refers to innocent civilians; versus a *hard target* that represents armed soldiers, operators, or well-defended locations.

designed to achieve some sort of political or ideological aim, the targets themselves might be unconnected to those ideologies—or might be happened upon by chance. Such is the case with the murder of British soldier Lee Rigby. Rigby was on his way to his barracks after a shift at the Tower of London had ended when he was suddenly hit by a car. The men driving then exited the vehicle and began stabbing and hacking at Rigby in full view of a horrified neighborhood. As cell phone video cameras rolled, Michael Adebolajo and Michael Adebowale attempted to decapitate their victim, then paused to make statements to those with cameras. Adebolajo ranted that the killing was justified as many Muslims had been killed at the hands of British soldiers. The act was extremely violent, mostly captured on video, and the image of Adebolajo standing in front a camera, covered in blood, is particularly unnerving—not only to the public at large, but to police and security agencies. Britain's intelligence service (MI-5) had long feared an attack such as the one on Rigby: an attack on a victim chosen at random, due only to his affiliation with the military, by lone wolf terrorists using easily obtained and relatively crude weapons, and a sympathy toward al-Qaeda minus all the bureaucracy that comes with actually being an affiliate of that organization.[33] Such an attack is extremely difficult if not impossible to predict, much less prevent. Although British soldiers were encouraged shortly afterward to wear their uniforms only while on-duty, it was an impractical suggestion that quickly faded as the months passed. Even in this country, American soldiers are often seen travelling in airports while in uniform, or congregating at a restaurant for lunch or dinner, seemingly unaware of their potential as victims of an attack.

Another random target for a terror attack was the Westgate shopping mall in Kenya, which was the site of a mass shooting in September 2013. Well-organized members of Somalia's al Shabaab entered the shopping center and began shooting randomly at victims, encouraging Muslims to identify themselves and get out of harm's way. Sixty-three victims were claimed in the attack, at a site that wasn't particularly symbolic or strategic, except that it was located in Kenya—a country that had invaded Somalia in 2011. The barbaric killings of small children and families going about their shopping on a Sunday morning speaks even further to the ruthlessness of modern terrorist groups affiliated with al-Qaeda. No longer concerned about answering to a larger organizational structure or centralized command, new jihadi groups are now free to target whomever they choose, including those innocent individuals that enjoy the embodiments of modern social life, like shopping malls, markets, restaurants, schools, and office centers. Clearly, the new modality of terror now targets people for sheer carnage versus the more common political or social statement of the past.

Future Attacks on Critical Infrastructure

As discussed in Chapter 12, America is vulnerable to a variety of attacks, however, none is more concerning than a cyber-attack on our critical infrastructure. Much of our national infrastructure—including water systems, power grids, gas pipelines, nuclear power functions, and financial and communication networks—were built long before the specter of terrorism was a consideration, and contain less-than-desirable defenses against potential attacks by terrorists. There has been much hand-wringing over the possibilities of such assaults, yet relatively few security measures have been taken in regards to these vulnerabilities. In fact, in 2012 the U.S. Department of Homeland Security reported that there had been 198 separate attacks on infrastructure, representing an increase of 52 percent from the previous year.[34] A number of these attacks rose to the level that they could facilitate remote operations—and these are just the attacks that were reported. Many private companies choose not to disclose their attacks in an attempt to limit their vulnerabilities and to maintain their public image.

Many infrastructure companies have been identified with weaknesses such as easy online access to critical operations systems, unsecure or easily guessed passwords (such as 1234) for major controls, and weak credentialing standards. However, experts warn that many industries have become complacent when it comes to the potential for cyber-attacks. Better security protocols and isolated (or offline) control systems should be far more common than they currently are—and many believe that it may take a massive breach into U.S. critical infrastructure to spur action.[35] Rather than focusing on attacks that might stem from weapons of mass destruction (WMD), it might be more prudent to assume that the next terrorist attack may be cyber in nature (see Box 15–3).

Information Link

For more information on predicting the future of terrorism, visit the CNN World website at www.cnn.com/WORLD/. Search the site for articles by correspondent Fareed Zakaria. His GPS podcasts and in-depth analysis of events in the Middle East often provide an excellent analysis of current events and their impact on future terrorist strikes. Read his article entitled, "The Future of the Terrorist Threat to America."

Box 15–3
Has the Potential for Weapons of Mass Destruction Been Exaggerated?

In the dialogue that surrounds our discussion and understanding of the potential for future terrorist attacks, weapons of mass destruction figure prominently. Foreign policy has been preoccupied with access to such types of weaponry, including nuclear, chemical, radiological, or biological agents that could be employed to cause mass chaos, death, and destruction. Funding for homeland security projects has been heavily weighted toward preparation for these types of events. Quite understandably so, even a small devices, like a "dirty bomb" composed of nuclear waste from an X-ray machine attached to an explosive device like a stick of dynamite or a "pressure cooker bomb" like the one used in the Boston Marathon incident could have a massive impact on our society. Even though the initial explosion from such a device may not be very deadly, the impending psychological impact on society would be huge, and the immediate area surrounding the blast may be uninhabitable for years.

A recent report from the Bipartisan Policy Center reveals that since September 11, 2001, no domestic Islamic terror organization or individual has gained access to or used any type of weapon of mass destruction (WMD). Foreign governments, such as the regimes in Syria and Iraq, may have used chemical weaponry against its citizens, but such events have not translated to a transnational or international terror attack. That doesn't mean that preparations for such an attack should be abandoned—just that the main focus of homeland security should not be on such an event. For example, the same report from the Bipartisan Policy Center also noted that smaller terrorist attacks are becoming more deadly. As such, perhaps resources should be funneled more proportionately toward identifying and rooting out small terror cells or lone wolf terrorists increasingly capable of death and destruction with fewer resources than would be required for a WMD attack.

▲ It's a worst-case scenario: A smoke plume rises over a computer-generated image of a city where a dirty bomb explodes.

(National Geographic Channel)

WMD preparations, then, should be focused into two areas: Public health preparedness to deal with the fallout from any one of these types of attacks, and in strengthening the nation's critical infrastructure to both eliminate weaknesses that could be exploited by WMD-style attacks and to increase resiliency in case of a catastrophic terrorist event.[36]

How prepared do you really think the United States is to a major terrorist attack involving a "dirty bomb" that might contain chemical, biological, or radiological elements?

The Role of Modern Media in Terrorism

Terrorism would not exist without the media. In each of the above examples of terrorist attacks and trends, the media transmitted the images from the attacks almost immediately—sending images that were horrific in nature around the globe and frightening audiences the world over. Such is the intent of terrorism—to cause terror on a global scale, and to intimidate or coerce a population. None of these things can be accomplished without the help of the media—populations cannot be intimidated if the news of the event meant to intimidate them does not reach them. As such, modern terrorism is essentially a media phenomenon—both transmitting the news of such events to the public and influencing the behavior of the terrorists themselves. For example, al-Qaeda literally had a media advisor: American-born Adam Gadahn. Gadahn advised the organization on strategies to maximize media exposure, including timing releases of videos strategically after elections and how to exploit the coverage of the ten-year anniversary of September 11 in 2011. He also offered Usama Bin Laden analysis of the various news networks in the United States, criticizing Fox News and mentioning the perceived neutrality of MSNBC.[37]

The news media has also stoked feelings of fear and apprehension after terrorist attacks. On the one hand, it's what audiences demand, to a certain extent; on the other hand, it plays directly into the goals of the terrorist, serving as a mouthpiece for groups looking to instill fear into consumers of media. President Juan Manuel Santos of Colombia said in 2012, "I'm not saying, and be careful not to misinterpret me, that terrorism is the media's fault. No. But terrorism thrives on generating terror."[38] As longtime news anchor and reporter Dan Rather stated, it's not that President Santos expected the media to turn its back on a major story. Rather gave the example of how newspapers in Mexico frequently printed photographs of decapitated and dismembered victims of drug cartels on the front page of its newspapers, effectively turning them into a propaganda tool designed to scare a population into submission.[39] Additionally, the news media can affect individual terrorist behavior, giving them tactical information in ongoing situations. In one case, during an airline hijacking, the BBC reported that they thought the standoff

Dirty bombs
A device or bomb that combines radioactive material with conventional explosives; usually crudely made with the purpose of contaminating a specific area.

was about to be resolved, due to the "slackening will of the terrorists." The hijackers, hearing this, actually killed the pilot of the airline they had overtaken and threw his body onto the tarmac in full view of the cameras to send a message that, indeed, their will was not "slackening."[40]

As a result, Dan Rather recommends that news organizations tread carefully and emphasize the human elements of any terror attack—for instance, focusing less on the gruesome details and more on the small acts that prove resiliency of the population under attack, like the four-year-old in the Westgate Mall attack in Nigeria that stood up to terrorists who injured his mother, or the scores of volunteers at the Boston Marathon in 2013 that rushed to the aid of the injured, saving lives with their quick response.

Rather also cautions that news organizations fill their reporting on terror attacks with context as they make editorial decisions about what images should or should not be shown.[41] For example, in the killing of Lee Rigby, many British media outlets showed unedited video footage of the savage attacks—giving the two perpetrators exactly what they had hoped for: a global audience for their message of jihad. Thousands of viewers and media watchdogs complained: Was it necessary to show a near-beheading of a man live on television? Perhaps the networks could have taken a more intellectual approach to the awful attack; editing their images, asking if everything they showed was a critical part of their reporting, and giving historical perspectives, carefully checking facts, and again—reporting on the information that serves the public, as opposed to unwittingly aiding the terrorists' cause.

The events of the Boston Marathon highlighted not how the media can be manipulated by the terrorists, but rather how the media can mislead the public. In the hours after that attack, many news outlets pulled their information from Twitter, taking information that ordinary citizens tweeted from what they heard on police scanners or from what they thought they saw or heard. The problem with this scenario is that police scanners rely on tips from the general public or investigational leads from law enforcement that are in the middle of an investigation—in other words, bits and pieces of information that are not confirmed and based on unreliable sources and partial facts. Nonetheless, in the fight to be the first to share information about the Boston Marathon bombing, many news agencies ran with unverified information—with some outlets erroneously reporting the capture of a suspect long before that was the case, as well as an additional bombing at a nearby library that never happened, the discovery of five more bombs that didn't exist at the site of the attack, and that cell phone service had been shut down in the immediate area around the bombing site, when, in fact, it had not.[42] These errors prompted President Barak Obama to make a strong statement aimed at the media following the arrest of Dzhokhar Tsarnaev: "In this age of instant reporting and tweets and blogs, there's a temptation to latch on to any bit of information, sometimes to jump to conclusions. But when a tragedy like this happens … it's important that we do this right."[43] This will be a continuing challenge for all media in the future: covering terrorist attacks intelligently and factually, serving the needs of the public as opposed to those of the terrorists, and sifting through social media to uncover facts rather than headlines. (See Figure 15–6.)

FIGURE 15–6
The media's role should be to report the news, accurately and fairly, especially during terrorist events. Recently, however, the media has been criticized for being too sensational during such events. For instance, in their rush to grab headlines during the 2013 Boston Marathon bombing, the media all too often reported on the victims' injuries and the "gore" of the event versus accurately reporting the facts of the case to the public.

(© Charles Krupa/AP Images)

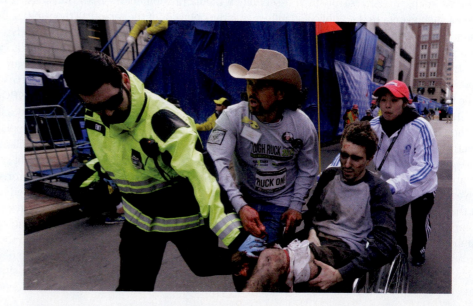

Box 15–4
North Korea's Cyber Attack on Sony Pictures

Cyber terrorist calling themselves the "Guardians of Peace" hacked into Sony Pictures in December 2014 in an effort to stop the showing of a film entitled, *The Interview,* a comedy in which Seth Rogen and James Franco star as television journalists involved in a CIA plot to assassinate President Kim Jon Un, the leader of North Korea. The film was scheduled to premiere in theatres nationwide a week before Christmas 2014. The original cyber hack involved compromising Sony executive passwords to access sensitive information and data on both the corporation as well as past actors and stars. The hackers released data files that included thousands of embarrassing emails, release schedules of future pictures, and financial records for past and future Sony projects.

The cyber attack took an ominous and sudden turn when the group announced that people should stay away from theatres where the film would be shown. Invoking 9/11-type messages, it warned that people should leave their homes if located near theaters where *The Interview* would premiere. Then, the FBI announced that evidence existed directly linking the cyber terrorist group to the country of

Courtesy Eric Charbonneau/ Invision for Sony Pictures/ AP Images.

North Korea. Similar to the Chinese APT-1 group, the "Guardians of Peace" were actually part of a formal North Korean hacking group within the country's General Reconnaissance Bureau known as "Bureau 121." A state actor (North Korea) had successfully attacked America's critical infrastructure—an U.S. entertainment corporation, and threatened people living inside the country. As important, the film premier was cancelled and other corporations began to worry if they would be the next victim to such extortion.

The incident left the United States government with limited options for retaliation and limited means in which to deter not only North Korea, but other countries like China and Russia that have sophisticated cyber attacking capabilities, from conducting such activities in the future. Additionally, it set a dangerous precedent in which corporate America acquiesced to a foreign terrorist threat.

What do you think the United States should do to prevent such acts of cyber hacking and subsequent extortion from either a state actor or a terrorist group?

In December 2014, media involvement in terrorism took on yet another twist. Media giant Sony Pictures fell victim to the largest foreign cyber attack on a U.S. corporation, sparking further debate as to the vulnerability of U.S. infrastructure. See Box 15-4.

Strategy, Policy, and Beyond

Given the history of terrorism, the current paradigm of Middle East unrest, and the always volatile, fluid nature of the issues and players at stake, it stands to reason that there is no one-size-fits-all approach to terrorism prevention. Attacking and destroying the command, control, and communications functions of al-Qaeda has certainly stemmed their capability to implement a large-scale attack, but has splintered the group geographically, allowing for the growth of small ruthless groups and hard-to-detect lone wolf operatives. U.S. counterterrorism policy has largely centered on destroying al-Qaeda, but a more long-term strategy must be employed to address threats posed by future generations of terrorists. Based on our current understanding of the issues surrounding terrorism, the United States has much work to do beyond its current counterterror efforts.

Reevaluate intelligence programs that collect mass amounts of data. Much time and energy is expended by the National Security Agency on the collection of phone records and other types of mass data. However, a report released in early 2014 shows that this type of data analysis "has had no discernible impact on preventing acts of terrorism" and that more traditional law enforcement and investigative methods have been more effective at foiling terror plots.[44]

Ensure that investigations, interrogations, and operations are in line with current human rights practices. Drone strikes that kill innocent bystanders, Guantanamo refugees that have been long cleared for repatriation to their home countries, and allegations of torture during interrogation further stoke the flames of extremist hatred toward the United States. American counterterrorism policy should recognize that drone usage should be overseen carefully, with a centralized program that can be independently evaluated regularly. Guantanamo detainees who are being held indefinitely should be tried in court and handled per the outcome of their cases; to continue to hold suspected terrorists without legal standing is problematic for the United States, a democratic nation that prides itself on the concepts of fundamental fairness, innocent until proven guilty, and justice.

Continue to refine emergency response plans to adapt to smaller-scale incidents. Although the response to the Boston Marathon bombings looked to be well-coordinated, the closure of Boston Logan airport and the downtown areas led to absolute paralysis within the city. The response may have shown future terrorists that even a relatively small—though tragic—attack has a major impact. Emergency plans should consider that inducing complete paralysis in a city is perhaps overreaction, and that a culture of resilience—even during the investigation and apprehension of subjects—should be emphasized.[45]

The Middle East should be carefully and continuously monitored, especially the problematic countries like Iran and Syria. The United States should constantly evaluate the leadership and stability within Middle East nations. In particular, the tenor of leadership within Syria and Iran are of immediate importance. Both countries have historically "meddled" in the politics of their neighbors, causing disruptions and civil wars. Further, the leadership in Iran has been especially aggressive against U.S. interests in the area. Iran's movement toward nuclear power, and hence weapons of mass destruction, poses a serious threat to long-term stability in the region. In Syria, the flow of arms into this volatile country poses additional problems for the future. Many of these weapons could easily fall into the hands of jihadi fighters previously in Iraq and Afghanistan. Care must be taken to identify and track foreign jihadi fighters who have travelled to Syria to assist rebel factions. Historically, the backbone of al-Qaeda emerged in the 1980s as similar warriors who had fought in Afghanistan and Bosnia returned to their home countries in the Middle East.[46] The stage is now set in Syria for the emergence of a similar organization, or the expansion of the existing al-Qaeda remnant groups.

Focus on individuals, as well as known terrorist groups. The United States should focus on the pace and trajectory of the radicalization and recruitment of terrorists who may act as lone wolves, directing intelligence resources and identifying at-risk individuals using law enforcement data and other known risk factors.

Engage the public. Complacency has again become common since the September 11, 2001 attacks. A nation once on high alert has settled into routine, trudging through airport security without much thought about why such measures are necessary. However, the Boston Marathon attack brought to light a number of missed opportunities for friends and family of the perpetrators to report on suspicious behavior and potentially prevent the attacks that left three people dead and injured nearly 300 others. Smartphone applications that make "if you see something, say something" programs easy for users have been developed and should be adopted and promoted in major metropolitan areas.

Evaluate U.S. progress in counterterrorism strategies in the years since September 11, 2001. The United States should hold public congressional hearings that address the following questions:

- Do the various components of U.S. counterterrorism strategy match the shape of the threat today, and are we monitoring threats both domestically and internationally to our nation?

- Are all of these components being implemented? And with what success, or is government bureaucracy and fractionalization between agencies at various governmental levels thwarting coordination of effort?

- Is the nation absorbing the institutional lessons learned since 2001, or are our intelligence failures particularly continuing today?

- Is the government spending money in the right places and getting the most "bang for its buck" in developing an infrastructure that is capable of preventing and responding to terrorism, or are we continuing to throw money at programs that yield very little in terms of effectiveness?

- Are we continually thinking about the future? What is missing from our counterterrorism strategy and can we be flexible and nimble enough to address new threats, new groups, and new types of attacks, particularly those that might be less traditional in nature, like cyber-attacks and the use of "dirty bombs"?[47]

Reflecting on the earlier chapters of this book, we learned that terrorism attacks the very fabric of our society, destroying the mutual trust, respect, and security on which we all rely on to communicate with each other, conduct commerce and business, and most importantly understand and respect cultural, social, and religious differences. Terrorism is emotive as well; it forces each of us to experience our own frailty ... to not only preserve our basic instinct for survival and security, but also to cluster around those that share our own beliefs, culture, and religion. Fear is the most primal and powerful of human emotions. Indeed, the very word "terrorism" evokes fear and the emotional response to protect our own, to fight for our own culture, religion, and personal identity. When we react in such a manner we see things only through our own "rose-colored glasses"; we become **ethnocentric**, believing that our own culture is superior to all others. The most troubling perspective associated with terrorism is not the next attack, but rather how we as a nation and a society react to the next major incident. Will we be more willing to give up those individual liberties and personal safeguards that define our way of life in the folly of additional security? Will our fear be so gripping that we will no longer venture outside the confines of our own homes and cities? Will we be so afraid as to not congregate in mass for fear of another bombing? Or will we be strong enough to embrace those tenets of our nation that have endured the test of time? Remembering that terrorism often targets innocent civilians in an overt attempt to create fear and change governmental policy, it will be the manner in which we cope with the next major attack that will define whether or not terrorism succeeds. Historically, terrorism is a relatively minor "blip" on the litany of incidents that have killed, maimed, and injured mankind across our globe. We stand not on the precipice of crisis and disaster, but rather on the rock of democracy that yields diplomacy and rationality, and most importantly, the enduring hope of freedom, respect, and human dignity for all mankind. We recall the words of President Franklin Delano Roosevelt facing such a dilemma years ago: "The only thing that we have to fear is fear itself—nameless, unreasoning, unjustified terror which paralyzes needed efforts to convert retreat into advance."[48]

Ethnocentric
The belief that one's own culture is superior to all others; often contributes to fear of other people from other cultures.

Chapter Summary

SUMMARY BY LEARNING OBJECTIVE

1. **Describe broad trends in terrorism, including general statistics about frequency, location, and targets of attacks.**

   The number of terrorist attacks in the United States has declined since 2001, though fatal attacks have increased slightly since 2008; explosive devices remained the main types of weapons used, and over half of attacks were aimed at damaging property. Attacks perpetrated by individuals are also on the rise.

2. **Elaborate on the rise of homegrown and lone wolf terrorists and their weapons usage.**

   Homegrown terrorists are American citizens or legal residents who have become radicalized either on their own or through some form of recruitment by al-Qaeda. Increasingly, they act as "lone wolves," allowing them to operate under the radar. Such terrorists are more likely to use crude or easily obtained weaponry, and may communicate with terrorist organizations online or simply view materials of interest that have been posted by terrorist cells.

3. **Discuss how al-Qaeda has been splintered and what the effects of that phenomenon might be.**

   U.S. campaigns against al-Qaeda have been successful in killing much of the leadership; however, this has had the unintended effect of decentralizing the groups and allowing them to operate free of bureaucracy, and in some cases free of any type of rigid operational codes or accountability. This has allowed for militant groups to pop up in areas where conflict is rife, and is also responsible for the expansion of the "lone wolf" phenomenon.

4. **Identify targets currently favored by terrorists, as well as future means of attack.**

   Terrorists still target transportation hubs, including both air and ground travel. Some newer trends, however, include school shootings, seemingly random targeting, and attacks on critical infrastructure.

5. **Discuss the role of modern media in terrorism.**

   The media must tread a thin line between unwittingly assisting the terrorists in their propaganda efforts and informing the public. Careful fact checking plus emphasis on the human element and broad context should outweigh the impulse for media outlets to show graphic images and publish unverified information.

6. **Describe policies and strategies that might be implemented in counterterrorism in the future.**

   Evaluate intelligence programs that collect mass data, line up with globally accepted human rights practices, refine emergency response plans so that they are appropriate for smaller-scale attacks, monitor the situation in Syria carefully, focus on individuals; engage the public in counterterrorism efforts; and evaluate the United States' progress as relevant to counterterrorism.

REVIEW QUESTIONS

1. What do the trends in terrorist activities tell us?
2. What is so dangerous about lone wolf operatives?
3. Describe how fractionalization of al-Qaeda will impact counterterror activities in the future.
4. How has Middle East unrest energized jihadist groups in the past several years?
5. What type of terrorist targets do you think will be most prevalent in the future?
6. Explain the thin line that media organizations must walk when reporting on terrorism.
7. What additional counterterrorism policies or strategies should be adopted to address new issues and paradigms in terrorism?

CRITICAL THINKING EXERCISES

1. **Interactive Terrorism Map.** Visit the website at www.globalincidentmap.com and view the global incident map. Click on one of the flashing items in the Middle East. How many of the incidents represent threats to critical infrastructure (oil and gas wells or pipelines) in the area? How many involve threats from radical Islamic groups? Now click on one of the flashing points in the United States or Europe. Discuss the above questions for the new area. Finally, notice that the entire map is delivered in real-time for subscribers. As a free user, the map is time-delayed 24 to 48 hours. Notice how many of the incidents are "hoaxes," or threats that never materialized. As a class, discuss the value of having real-time access to such a map for response measures, deployment of personnel, identifying trend activity, analytic examination of specific threats, research, and the like.

2. **What is a "Dirty Bomb?"** Visit the BBC News documentary and in-depth report on dirty bombs at http://news.bbc.co.uk/2/shared/spl/hi/in_depth/dirty_bomb/html/1.stm. Review the blast scenarios and discuss the potential of such event occurring within the homeland of the United States. What can be done to predict and prevent such an event from occurring? Discuss the social and economic impact of such an event as well as the long-term effect on the psyche of the American public. Now, visit the National Geographic site on Naked Science: Dirty Bomb Attack at http://channel.nationalgeographic.com/channel/episodes/dirty-bomb-attack/. If a worst-nightmare scenario ever occurred, do you think that the U.S. government and public would continue to support individual freedoms as defined in the Constitution, or would there be calls to abandon the 200-year-old document in favor of one that is more realistic in a nuclear age threatened by radical terrorists? Discuss this question as a class.

NOTES

1. National Consortium for the Study of Terrorism and Responses to Terrorism (START). *Integrated United States Security Database (IUSSD): Data on the Terrorist Attacks in the United States Homeland, 1970 to 2011.* December 2012, www.start.umd.edu/sites/default/files/files/publications/START_IUSSDDataTerroristAttacksUS_1970-2011.pdf.
2. Ibid.

3. Ibid.

4. Erin Miller and Travis Rudd. "START provides 2013 statistical annex for Country Reports on Terrorism." April 30, 2014, www.start.umd.edu/news/start-provides-2013-statistical-annex-country-reports-terrorism.

5. The source for this box item is Jennifer Harper, "As a Target For Terrorists, U.S. Ranks No. 41 in the World," *The Washington Times*, December 4, 2012, www.washingtontimes.com/news/2012/dec/4/as-a-target-for-terrorists-us-ranks-no-41-in-world/.

6. Ibid.

7. Ally Pregulman and Emily Burke, "Homegrown Terrorism," *AQAM Futures Project Case Studies Series,* April 2012, http://csis.org/files/publication/120425_Pregulman_AQAMCaseStudy7_web.pdf.

8. Katherine Q. Seelye, "Bombing Suspect Cites Islamic Extremist Beliefs as Motive," *The New York Times*, April 23, 2013, www.nytimes.com/2013/04/24/us/boston-marathon-bombing-developments.html?hp&pagewanted=all&_r=1&.

9. For more information, refer to the source for this box. See Joel Warner, "How Aaron Clauset Discovered a Pattern Behind Terrorist Attacks … And What It Told Him," *Denver Westword News*, July 4, 2013, www.westword.com/2013-07-04/news/adam-clauset-terrorism-formula/full/.

10. Pregulman and Burke, "Homegrown Terrorism."

11. Refer to the sources for this box item: Janine Zacharia, "Social Media, Terrorism Connect Too Well," *San Francisco Gate*, December 1, 2012, www.sfgate.com/opinion/article/Social-media-terrorism-connect-too-well-4083620.php#page-2; and Agence France Presse. "Al Qaeda Offshoot Joins Twitter, AQIM Threatens to Execute French Hostages," *Huffington Post*, March 28, 2013, www.huffingtonpost.com/2013/03/28/al-qaeda-in-the-islamic-maghreb-joins-twitter_n_2972907.html.

12. Frank Gardner, "How Do Terrorists Communicate?" *British Broadcasting Company*, November 2, 2013, www.bbc.com/news/world-24784756.

13. Robert W. Taylor, Eric J. Fritsch, and John Liederbach, *Digital Crime and Digital Terrorism* (Upper Saddle River, NJ: Pearson, 2014).

14. Pregulman and Burke, "Homegrown Terrorism."

15. Evan Perez and LeeAnn Caldwell, "Holder Fears 'Lone Wolf' Terrorist Attack, Doesn't Want TSA Armed," *CNN*, November 5, 2014, www.cnn.com/2013/11/05/politics/holder-terror-snowden-interview/.

16. Sarah Teich, "Trends and Developments in Lone Wolf Terrorism in the Western World: An Analysis of Terrorist Attacks and Attempted Attacks by Islamic Extremists," *International Institute for Counterterrorism*, October 2013, www.ict.org.il/LinkClick.aspx?fileticket=qAv1zIPJlGE%3D&tabid=66.

17. Ramon Spaaij, *Understanding Lone Wolf Terrorism: Global Patterns, Motivations and Prevention* (Heidelberg, London, New York: Springer, 2012).

18. Ibid.

19. National Security Program, "Jihadist Terrorism: A Threat Assessment," *Homeland Security Project*, Bipartisan Policy Center, September 2013, http://bipartisanpolicy.org/sites/default/files/Jihadist%20Terrorism-A%20Threat%20Assesment_0.pdf.

20. New America Foundation, National Security Studies Program, "Pakistan Strikes: Leaders Killed," July 2, 2013, http://natsec.newamerica.net/drones/pakistan/leaders-killed.

21. National Security Program, "Jihadist Terrorism."

22. Carl Ungerer, "Beyond Bin Laden: Future Trends in Terrorism," *Australian Strategic Policy Institute*, December 2011, www.aspi.org.au/publications/beyond-bin-laden-future-trends-in-terrorism/Beyond_bin_Laden_v2.pdf.

23. Sri Jegarajah, "Experts Had Warned of Attack in Amenas Gas Plant," *CNBC*, January 27, 2013, www.cnbc.com/id/100410586.

24. Reuters, "Al-Qaeda Leader Urges Muslims to Kidnap Westerners," *New York Daily News* April 26, 2014, www.nydailynews.com/news/world/al-qaeda-chief-urges-muslims-kidnap-westerners-americans-article-1.1769947#ixzz30axT084k.

25. Reuters, "Al-Qaeda Chief Ayman Al-Zawahiri Calls For More Kidnappings In Interview Tape," *Huffington Post*, April 25, 2014, www.huffingtonpost.com/2014/04/26/ayman-al-zawahiri-tape_n_5217738.html.

26. National Security Program, "Jihadist Terrorism."

27. Ibid.
28. Ernesto Londono, "Kidnapped American Asks U.S. to Negotiate with al-Qaeda for His Release," *Washington Post*, December 25, 2013, www.washingtonpost.com/world/national-security/kidnapped-american-asks-us-to-negotiate-with-al-qaeda-for-his-release/2013/12/25/8b0f7912-6dcd-11e3-b405-7e360f7e9fd2_story.html.
29. Holly Yann, "Teen Stowaway Raises Questions about Airport Security," *CNN* April 22, 2014,www.cnn.com/2014/04/22/travel/plane-stowaway-security/.
30. K. Jack Riley, "Air Travel Security Since 9/11," RAND Corporation, 2011, www.rand.org/content/dam/rand/pubs/corporate_pubs/2011/RAND_CP635.pdf.
31. Matthew Hardwood, "Trends in Terrorism Targets," *International Centre for Crowd Management and Security Studies*, August 9, 2012, www.iccmss.co.uk/2012/08/surface-transport-vulnerabilities/.
32. Edward Cody, "Mohammed Merah: Face of the New Terrorism," *Washington Post*, March 22, 2013, www.washingtonpost.com/world/europe/mohammed-merah-face-of-the-new-terrorism/2012/03/22/gIQA2kL4TS_story.html.
33. Tom Whitehead, "Woolwich Killing: The Random Attack Has Always Been MI5's Greatest Fear," *The Telegraph* (London) May 22, 2013, www.telegraph.co.uk/news/uknews/terrorism-in-the-uk/10074658/Woolwich-killing-the-random-attack-has-always-been-MI5s-greatest-fear.html.
34. David Goldman, "Hacker Hits on US Power and Nuclear Targets Spiked in 2012,"*CNN Money*, January 9, 2013, http://money.cnn.com/2013/01/09/technology/security/infrastructure-cyberattacks/.
35. Ibid.
36. For more information on this subject, refer to the sources of this box item: National Security Program, "Jihadist Terrorism: A Threat Assessment," *Homeland Security Project, Bipartisan Policy Center*, September 2013, http://bipartisanpolicy.org/sites/default/files/Jihadist%20Terrorism-A%20Threat%20Assesment_0.pdf; and Rachel Oswald, "Expert Report: Talk of WMD Terror Threat to U.S. Has Been 'Overheated,'" *Global Security Newswire*, September 9, 2013, www.nti.org/gsn/article/new-expert-report-says-talk-wmd-terror-threat-us-has-been-overheated/
37. David Ignatius, "How al-Qaeda Tried to Control the Media," *Washington Post*, March 20, 2013, www.washingtonpost.com/opinions/al-qaedas-attempts-to-control-the-media/2012/03/20/gIQAbu0EQS_story.html.
38. Dan Rather, "Media's Balancing Act with Terrorism," *CNN*, September 11, 2012, www.cnn.com/2012/09/11/opinion/rather-media-and-terrorism/index.html.
39. Ibid.
40. Anna North, "How Media Coverage Influences Terrorism," *Buzzfeed,* April 19, 2013, www.buzzfeed.com/annanorth/how-media-coverage-influences-terrorism.
41. Dan Rather, "Media's Balancing Act with Terrorism."
42. Sabrina Siddiqui, "Boston Bombings Reveal Media Full Of Mistakes, False Reports," *Huffington Post*, April 22, 2013, www.huffingtonpost.com/2013/04/22/boston-bombings-media-mistakes_n_3135105.html.
43. Ibid.
44. Ellen Nakashima, "NSA Phone Record Collection Does Little to Prevent Terrorist Attacks, Group Says," *Washington Post,* January 12, 2014, www.washingtonpost.com/world/national-security/nsa-phone-record-collection-does-little-to-prevent-terrorist-attacks-group-says/2014/01/12/8aa860aa-77dd-11e3-8963-b4b654bcc9b2_story.html.
45. National Security Program, "Jihadist Terrorism."
46. Ibid.
47. Ibid.
48. Franklin Delano Roosevelt, *First Inaugural Speech*, Washington, D.C., March 4, 1933.

442nd Regimental Combat Team   A Japanese-American unit that served in the European Theater with great distinction. It consisted of Japanese-American volunteers from Hawaii and the internment camps. The 442nd became the most heavily decorated unit of its size in military history. See Japanese-American internment camps.

Abdulhakim Muhammad   Born in America as Carlos Bledsoe. Bledsoe became a radicalized violent Muslim who murdered a soldier and wounded another in front of a Little Rock, Arkansas, military recruiting station because Americans were killing Muslims in Iraq and Afghanistan.

Abu Bakr   The 1st Caliph or ruler of Arabia and the leader of the Muslim community after the death of the Prophet Muhammad.

Accelerator sanctions   For certain types of crimes, such as hate-based and terrorism, the law provides more severe sentences for persons convicted of them. It is how society demonstrates its revulsion about such crimes.

Active supporters   Participate in fund raising and other activities, such as providing safe houses, medical care, and transportation. They are fully aware of their relationship with the terrorist organization. They may or may not be known to those outside of the terrorist organization.

Ad hoc   A Latin phrase meaning "for this." Ad hoc generally means a process, decision, or solution that applies only to "this" particular situation and does not have a wider/general application.

Agro-terrorism   Malicious acts directed at the agricultural or food supply system in the United States.

Ahmad Shuqayri   The first head of the Palestinian Congress in 1964.

Al-Aqsa Martyrs Brigade   One of the first Palestinian terrorist groups to move from a secular to a radical Islamic ideology.

Alien   A foreign national living in the United States.

Allah   Arabic, literally "The God"; the Islamic God.

Allah u Akbar   Arabic, Allah (God) is great or Allah is the greatest.

All-hazards   National preparedness is based on the all-hazards approach. This approach uses a capabilities-based preparedness to prevent, protect against, respond to, and recover from terrorist attacks, major disasters (natural, technological, or human caused), and all other emergencies.

All-hazards model   The concept that there are similar aspects to planning and responding to a catastrophe or emergency event cause by either natural or man-made origins.

Al-Qaeda   Arabic, "The Base." Foreign terrorist organization (FTO) led by Usama bin Laden until his death in 2011; currently led by Ayman al-Zawahiri.

Al-Shabaab   A radical Islamic group affiliated with al-Qaeda operating in the country of Somalia.

American Civil Liberties Union (ACLU)   A national organization (primarily composed of attorneys and legal scholars) focused on defending and preserving the rights and liberties guaranteed to individuals within the United States Constitution.

American Red Cross   Humanitarian organization originally developed in 1881 by Clara Barton; modeled after the International Red Cross in Europe to provide aid to civilians during emergencies and disasters.

Anarchist   An anarchist believes in the political theory of anarchy. Pure anarchy is characterized by the absence of a central government and strong cooperation between members of a society. Anarchists seek to overthrow rulers and governments. Practical anarchists recognize the impossibility of actually achieving pure anarchy. Consequentially, they are willing to settle for a weak government that is minimally intrusive in the lives of its citizens.

Anders Behring Breivik   Norwegian ultra-right wing perpetrator of the July 22, 2011, attacks killing 8 people in Oslo, and another 69 more on the island of Utoya, in one of the deadliest mass shootings in history.

Andrew MacDonald   See Dr. William L. Pierce.

Anthrax   Spore-forming bacterium that is often "weaponized" or genetically altered to be more deadly.

Anti-terrorism   Defensive actions taken to reduce the vulnerability of people and property to terrorist acts, including rapid containment by local military and civilian forces.

Anwar Al-Awlaki   Born in New Mexico to Yemeni parents. Became radicalized Islamic cleric linked to 19 terrorist operations. Killed in Yemen by drone in 2011.

Arab Spring   Refers to a series of recent revolutions beginning in December 2010 in Tunisia aimed at increasing individual rights and freedoms for the people living in Middle Eastern countries.

Asymmetrical warfare   In warfare it is the attempt to circumvent or undermine an opposing force's superior strengths while exploiting its weaknesses. Asymmetrical warfare often has a major psychological impact, such as shock or fear. Often involves the use of non-traditional strategy, tactics, and weapons. Example: the use of guerilla tactics against a powerful conventional army or flying hijacked planes into buildings.

Aum Shinrikyo   An apocalyptic Christian group in Japan that became the first terrorist organization to use chemical warfare. In 1995, five two-man teams released sarin, a quick-acting nerve agent, in a Tokyo subway system.

Balfour Declaration   A formal letter from British Foreign Secretary Alfred Balfour in 1917 signaling British support for the development of a new, sovereign Jewish state in the Middle East.

Bekaa Valley   Located in Lebanon, it has perhaps the longest continuous history as an operational space for terrorist groups.

Bermuda Triangle of Terrorism   The hundreds of competing definitions of terrorism.

Bill of Rights   The collective name for the first ten amendments of the U.S. Constitution, explicitly enumerating such freedoms of religion, speech, a free press, freedom to assemble, the right to bear arms, freedom from unreasonable searches and seizures, security and privacy of personal effects, freedom from warrantless searches not based on probable cause, guarantee of a speedy trial and judgment by an impartial jury, prohibition of cruel and unusual punishments including torture, prohibition of double jeopardy, and the guarantee to live without unnecessary governmental intrusion.

BitCoin   An online money that can be bought, transferred to someone else, or sold. If sold a check is sent to your bank account. Although it is an interesting system, BitCoin is struggling to find even modest acceptance in the marketplace.

Blackout   The loss of electrical power in a specific area.

Black September   The Palestinian nationalist group that massacred members of the Israeli delegation at the 1972 Summer Olympics in Munich, Germany.

Black Swan Events   Future terrorist attacks that are so different from past experience and what analysts can reasonable foresee that they are unpredictable.

Blind pigs In modern use, unlicensed bars that sell alcohol to patrons after legal bars have closed. Gambling may also be conducted in some blind pigs.

Boko Haram A radical Islamic group linked to al-Qaeda in the Islamic Maghreb (AQIM) in North Africa; active in Nigeria.

Boston Tea Party December 16, 1773, tax protest when colonists, disguised as Indians, threw tea from ships into Boston harbor.

Boundless Informant A real-time global surveillance software tracker used by the NSA that details and maps the metadata it received from computers, phone systems and the Internet.

Bourgeoisie A Marxist term to describe the wealthy upper class, those that were property owners.

Brownout A drop in electrical voltage to a specific area.

Cadre Overall, the dependable nucleus or core group in a terrorist organization. Directs functions such as intelligence, finances, logistics, propaganda, and communication functions. Plans and conducts operations. Mid-level cadre tend to be trainers and technicians, such as surveillance experts. Low-level cadre are direct action specialists, for example, snipers.

Caliph The political leader or head of a caliphate or Muslim state; a successor to the Prophet Muhammad.

Caliphate An Islamic state where the political and religious leader are the same.

Capitalism Economies that focus on competition in a free market enterprise, valuing the ownership of private property to determine wealth.

Carlos Bledsoe See Abdulhakim Muhammad.

Carlos Marighella A Brazilian revolutionary who expressed the concept of guerrilla movements stemming from urban areas. His book, *The Mini-Manual of the Urban Guerrilla*, was very influential in Latin American leftist movements.

Catastrophe A catastrophe is an incident that directly or indirectly affects large portions or all of a country and requires national and sometimes international responses.

Category 4 hurricane Hurricanes are characterized as being one of five categories. Category 1 is the least severe and has winds from 74 to 95 MPH and other descriptors also apply, such as damage to unanchored mobile homes. The most severe hurricane is Category 5, with winds of 156 MPH or greater and descriptors such as complete roof failures of many buildings and massive evacuations may be required.

CBRNE Acronym for **C**hemical, **B**iological, **R**adiological, **N**uclear and **E**xplosive, used to define types of mass destruction attacks.

Cell A cell is multiple terrorists working closely and cooperatively toward the goal of attacking a target, usually unprotected citizens.

Center for Domestic Preparedness (CDP) The primary training facilities in Anniston, Alabama, operated by FEMA to train members of federal, state, and local agencies on all aspects of domestic preparedness; focuses on response training during WMD and CBRNE events.

Center of gravity The primary source of strength, power, and resistance for a nation or organization and that of an adversary.

Chain of command The chain of command, a clear and unbroken line of responsibility from the top to the bottom of the organization, which makes it possible to establish accountability.

Christian Identity movement The CI movement in its most extreme form postulates that the Jews were not God's chosen people, but instead are the spawn of the devil, the mating of Eve and the Serpent in the Garden. Different strands of CI believe it is wrong to mix with other races, interracial marriage is a sin, the Jews are the natural enemies of the Aryan race, racial treason is the greatest crime, and homosexuality should be punished by death. See Counterfeit Christians.

Christian Patriot movement The collection of various right-wing, conservative groups spawning from the Posse Comitatus group; includes white supremacist organizations, sovereign citizens, and Christian Identity churches, the Ku Klux Klan, neo-Nazi groups, and Skinhead groups.

CI/KRs Acronym in reference to <u>C</u>ritical <u>I</u>nfrastructure and <u>K</u>ey <u>R</u>esource(s) identified within the National Infrastructure Protection Plan (NIPP).

Civilian Conservation Corps A federal program during the 1930s that employed young men in a military-style manner to plant trees and build parks, canals, and other recreational sites throughout America's forests and governmental land.

Colonialism A practice of domination, involving political and economic control of a territory.

Command and control cells C2 cells make all of the final decisions about the execution of an attack and other matters pertaining to the activities of a cell.

Communism The ideal utopian state as proposed by Karl Marx, characterized by the total elimination of privately held property and government.

Compartmentalized information Information to which access is restricted to those with a need to know.

Consequence management Developing, coordinating, and managing mitigation after an emergency event.

Constitutional monarchies A form of government commonly observed in the Middle East when a country has a ruling family or kingdom versus a democratically elected republic or dictatorship.

Counterfeit Christians Sometimes used to refer to Christian Identity adherents.

Counterintelligence Activities intended to prevent adversaries from acquiring accurate information about another organization's capabilities.

Counterterrorism Offensive actions (usually military or paramilitary) taken to prevent, deter, or respond to terrorist threats or attacks.

Coup d'état The sudden and quick illegal seizure of a government by a small group of existing governmental people, usually a group from within the existing military.

Covert activity An action of the U.S. government intended to influence politics, economic, or military conditions abroad, where it is intended that the role of the government will not be apparent or acknowledged publically.

Crisis management Developing, coordinating, and managing an effective response to a major emergency event.

Critical infrastructure Those systems and assets, whether physical or virtual, so vital to the United States that the incapacity or destruction of such systems and assets would have a debilitating impact on national security.

Culture the shared beliefs, experiences, and behaviors, such as language, values, customs, history, law, and religion, that causes its members to substantially interpret things in a similar manner and distinguishes then from other cultures.

Cyberterrorism (or Digital terrorism) The premeditated, politically, or ideologically motivated attack against information networks, computer systems, computer programs, and/or data that can result in violence against civilian targets.

Data fusion The exchange of information from different sources, with analysis, that results in meaningful and actionable intelligence.

David Koresh Leader of the Branch Davidians. Died at their compound in Waco, Texas.

Dead drop A dead drop is a secret place where one courier hides documents, often encrypted, for the next courier to pick up.

Deep web A secret part of the World Wide Web, not accessible through regular Internet browsing or search engines; accessible from dynamic websites requiring the use of an application program called *Tor* that allows encrypted conversations.

Detainer An immigration detainer or "hold" is sent to local and state jails to keep a person of interest in custody 48 hours beyond the time they would otherwise be released. This gives ICE time to investigate the subject's immigration status and assume custody if appropriate.

DHS Inspector General (IG) The DHS IG was created by Congress to ensure integrity and efficiency in the DHS. The conducts or supervises studies and research to improve DHS administration and operations.

Diaspora   The scattering or dispersion of people from their native homeland, often to a different, smaller, or less desirable geographic area.

Dirty bombs   A device or bomb that combines radioactive material with conventional explosives; usually crudely made with the purpose of contaminating a specific area.

Disaster   A "disaster" is more severe than an emergency because it causes a serious disruption of the functioning of an entity, such as a community, and produces widespread human, material, economic, and/or environmental losses that exceed the ability of a community to cope with it using just its own resources.

Domestic terrorism   As provided by federal law, domestic terrorism involves violations of federal or state law that appear to intimidate or coerce a civilian population or affect the policy of a government by intimidation or coercion, or affect the conduct of a government by mass destruction, assassination, or kidnapping and occur primarily with the territorial jurisdiction of the United States. See the federal legal definition in Table 1–1.

Drone   Unmanned aircraft flown remotely. Unarmed drones are used for reconnaissance and armed drones can strike against enemy targets.

Drones   Unmanned aircraft that can navigate autonomously.

Dr. William Luther Pierce   As Andrew MacDonald authored *The Turner Diaries*, still considered one of the right wing's most influential publications. He also wrote *Hunter*, which did not receive nearly the acclaim that *The Turner Diaries* did.

Egalitarian democracy   The political concept that all humans are equal in fundamental political, economic, and social worth; hence social economic divisions or classes of people as well as centralized power should be diminished.

Electrical power grid   A system of interconnected electrical processes serving regional areas within the United States.

Emergency   A condition of actual danger to the lives of persons and/or the safety of property that requires a response. Emergencies ordinarily are handled locally.

Emergency Operations Center (EOC)   Mandated by the National Incident Management System, the EOC's primary role is to provide support, coordination, resource allocation, and information analysis and dissemination during an incident or event.

Enemy combatant   A special designation of an individual as engaged in hostilities against the United States or its coalition partners.

English Defence League   The EDL represents a growing phenomenon in Europe right-wing groups that are not simply racist, but profoundly hostile toward Islam and their immigration into Western Europe. The EDL and other anti-jihad movements are united in their belief that Islam and Muslims are a fundamental threat to the resources, identities, and survival of Western nations.

Ernest "Che" Guevara   An iconic, revolutionary figure in Latin America during the 1950s and 60s; he symbolized discontent with capitalism and colonization in the world, and believed that revolution was sparked by those most oppressed in a country—poor farmers living in rural areas.

Eschatology   A part of religion that focuses on the last days, or ultimate destruction, of the world.

Ethnocentric   The belief that one's own culture is superior to all others; often contributes to fear of other people from other cultures.

European Union   The EU is a political and economic union founded in 1993 with 28 member nations that are primarily located in Europe.

Extinction event   An extinction event could result or results in the loss of all human life. In the extreme, there is no effective emergency response to an extinction event.

Extraordinary rendition   The apprehension, detention and extrajudicial transfer of a person from one country to another, outside the confinements and jurisdiction of the United States.

Federal Emergency Management Agency (FEMA)   Originally developed by Presidential Order in 1978 by President Jimmy Carter, FEMA is the primary federal agency responsible for responding to and mitigating a major disaster within the United States.

Force multiplier   A military term that means a capability that when added to, and employed by, a combat unit significantly enhances its combat potential and increases the likelihood of a successful mission.

Foreign Intelligence Surveillance Act of 1978 (FISA)   Passed by Congress in 1978, the law was intended to increase counterintelligence capabilities and established procedures for the judicial authorization of foreign intelligence surveillance and established the Foreign Intelligence Surveillance Court.

Foreign Intelligence Surveillance Court (FISC)   Secret federal court created by the Foreign Intelligence Surveillance Act in 1978. The court authorizes wiretaps and other forms of electronic surveillance and authorizes searches involving suspected terrorists and spies by U.S. intelligence agencies.

Foreign terrorist organization (FTO)   The U.S. Department of State lists an organization as a "foreign terrorist organization" if it engages in terrorist activity or has retained the capacity or intention to do so and it threatens United States nationals of America's national security. See new terrorism.

Frantz Fanon   A black revolutionary writer and medical doctor serving in the French army in Algeria. His writings sparked national liberation movements throughout the Middle East as well as the rest of the world.

Fundamentalism   A strategy in which beleaguered believers attempt to preserve their distinctive identity as a people or group.

Fund-raising cells   FRCs almost exclusively commit illegal acts to raise funds for their terrorist organization or to be used in support of a particular attack. Examples of these illegal activities include kidnapping for ransom, arms and drug smuggling, operating bogus charities, extortion, credit card fraud, and pirating music and videos.

Fusion center   A "clearinghouse" or information "hub" that blends the power of information technology with terrorism prevention and crime fighting.

Gaza Strip   Administered by the Palestinian Authority, 25 miles long and from 3.5 to 7 miles wide. Situated on Eastern Mediterranean, bounded by Egypt to the South and Israel to its East and North.

George Habash   A Christian Marxist physician that led the Popular Front for the Liberation of Palestine (PFLP).

George Lincoln Rockwell   Founder of the American Nazi Party who ran for president in an effort to change the U.S. Constitution and laws to align with the racist perspectives of the Nazi Party.

Geospatial intelligence (GEOINT)   Intelligence information derived from maps, imagery, charts, and/or satellite data.

German-American Bund   In the 1930s, the GAB emerged in this country as a pro-Nazi movement that sang the praises of Hitler and the Third Reich, encouraged Americans to stay out of the war in Europe, and was anti-Semitic. Its members were largely drawn from German Americans. Unlike the wholesale internment of Japanese-Americans, only a small number of the GAB were incarcerated after it was outlawed.

Gilmore Commission   Congressionally sponsored inquiry after 9/11 to assess the domestic response of federal law enforcement and intelligence agencies against terrorism.

Going postal   The phrase "going postal," means becoming uncontrollably mad. It originated at the Edmond, Oklahoma, Post Office. In 1986, a disgruntled postman entered the Post Office and killed 10, wounded 6, and then committed suicide.

Gross domestic product (GDP)   The total value of goods and services produced by a nation during one year.

Hacking   The illegal intrusion into a secure data or computer system.

Hadith   A collection of the words and deeds of the Prophet Muhammad, his closest companions, and the views of luminary Islamic scholars and religious figures within the Islamic faith.

Hamas   Arabic, "zeal," fundamentalist foreign terrorist organization (FTO) that provides extensive social service. It also has a well-armed militia/paramilitary arm. Opposed to the existence of Israel, Hamas has a strong presence in Palestine and Israel.

Hammerskin Nation (HN)   A radical right-wing racist group.

Hang glider   A light-weight, single occupant, unpowered flight apparatus whose "pilot" controls its movement by shifting his/her body, which is suspended under a large delta-shaped wing. The Federal Aviation Administration (FAA) regulates hang gliders.

Hardcore leadership   The hardcore leadership of a terrorist movement may have helped to establish the terrorist organization or come up through its ranks by promotions. It establishes vision, policy, and rules, as well as approves goals and operations. Finally, it ensures that the focus and execution of violence supports ideology and goals.

Hawala   An Asian-based alternative remittance system that is based on trust and which allows users to remain unknown and escape contact with banking and other officials.

Hazardous Materials (HAZMAT)   Substances (solid, liquid or gas) that are dangerous to people, other living organisms, or the environment.

Hezbollah   "The Party of God (Allah)"; the largest Shi'a terrorist group in the world, led by Hassan Nasrallah and headquartered in Lebanon.

Hijab   Dressing modestly within the Islamic religion; it often refers directly to the veil that covers the head and chest of a Muslim female.

Holy or Noble Qur'an   The central book of Islam consisting of 114 chapters developed through the visits of the Archangel Gabriel to the Prophet Muhammad. Simply, the Qur'an or Koran in Western nations.

Homegrown jihadist   A homegrown terrorist who uses Islam as the ideological basis for his or her attacks may be referred to as a "homegrown jihadist."

Homegrown jihadist cell   A group of homegrown jihadists working collectively make up a homegrown jihadist cell. See homegrown jihadist.

Homegrown terrorists   They have no formal connection to, or material support from, a terrorist movement, but may have some psychological affinity with one, or have their own particular cause, such as calling attention to deforestation in Brazil.

Homeland Security Data Network (HSDN)   A classified information network that allows the federal government to move information and intelligence to state and local jurisdictions at the "secret" level.

Homophobia   Describes a range of negative attitudes and feelings toward people who are gay, lesbian, bisexual, or transgender (GLBT).

Hubs   In terrorist network language, "hubs" are "chiefs," from local operational commanders to ideological leaders. The lines between nodes in a cell are called links or edges and represent a communication channel.

Hunter   See Dr. William L. Pierce.

Imam   Local spiritual leader of the Islamic faith, similar to a priest, rabbi, or pastor in other religion.

Incident commander   The most senior commander first arriving at the scene of an incident from a specific first responder agency, such as from police, fire, or emergency services.

Individual perspective   A particular way of thinking about something, reduced to a simple image: on which side of the street do you stand?

Information warfare (IW)   The concept of using information technology to gain tactical or strategic advantage over an opponent.

Insurgency   A type of irregular warfare characterized by subversion, armed conflict, and occasional terrorism to overthrow the legally constituted government of a country.

Intel cells   ICs collect data, make recommendations, may select targets, and provide information about the best routes for ingressing to and egressing from targets.

Intel-driven organization   An organization that combines investigation and intelligence operations to be more predictive and preventative in nature.

Intelligence   An information process and product derived from systematic and thoughtful examination (analysis).

Intelligence community (IC)   Sixteen federal agencies representing various governmental groups reporting to the Office of the Director of National Intelligence.

Intelligence-led policing (ILP)   A new style of policing that integrates intelligence, with an emphasis on predictive analysis derived from the discovery of hard facts, information, patterns, and traditional crime analysis.

International terrorism   As provided for by federal law, international terrorism involves violent acts or acts dangerous to human life that violate federal or state laws if committed within the jurisdiction of the United States or any state, which appear to be intended to intimidate or coerce a civilian population, influence the policy of government by mass destruction, assassination, or kidnapping, and occur primarily outside of the territorial jurisdiction of the United States or transcend national boundaries by the means by which they are accomplished, the persons who appear to intimidate or coerce, or the locale in which the perpetrators operate or seek asylum. See the federal definition in Table 1–1.

Internet Service Providers (ISPs)   An organization or private corporation that provides services for accessing, using, or participating on the Internet (e.g., AOL, NetZero, Comcast, Microsoft Network, EarthLink, Verizon, Google Prodigy, Sprint, and local telephone companies).

Irish Republican Army   Ireland's military arm during the Anglo-Irish War of 1919–1921.

Islam   The religion of Muslims, referred to earlier in history as Moslems, who believe there is no God but Allah and Muhammad is his prophet. It is Allah that founded Islam through Muhammad. Islam's religious book is the Qur'an (Anglicized as the "Koran").

Islamaphobic   An unfounded hostility toward Muslims resulting in a fear or dislike of all or most Muslims. Coined in 1991, the term was developed in the context of Muslims in the United Kingdom in particular and Europe in general.

Islamic Of, or pertaining to Islam.   One who adheres to the beliefs of Islam. See Islam.

Islamic State   A terrorist organization that became an international threat in 2014. Previously known as the Islamic State in Syria (ISIS) and the Islamic State in the Levant (ISIL). Known for its grisly beheadings for Westerners and mass executions of captured Iraqi soldiers.

Israeli Mossad   The intelligence and secret service unit of the country of Israel; responsible for carrying out extensive covert operations throughout the Middle East and the rest of the world.

James Earl Ray   He assassinated civil rights champion Reverend Martin Luther King in Memphis, Tennessee, in 1968.

Japanese-American internment camps   At the outbreak of World War II, Japanese-Americans were place in internment camps for "national security." Some volunteered to serve in the 442nd Regimental Combat Team to demonstrate their loyalty. In 1988, the Congress recognized the "grave injustice" done to those interred and awarded each surviving camp member $20,000; each reparation paid was accompanied by a letter of apology from President Regan.

Jihad   Derived from the Holy Qur'an, the word *jihad* represents an internal struggle to overcome adversity and difficulty in submitting to the will of Allah (God). Perverted historically by Islamic fundamentalists to mean "holy war."

Jihadist Salafism   The ideology of al-Qaeda; a second generation of Islamic Salafism that justifies violence and revolution as the means to an end.

Joint Special Operations Command (JSOC)   One of the five subordinate commands reporting to USSOCOM; commands the special military operational units like Army Delta, Army Special Forces, and Navy SEAL Teams.

Joint Terrorism Task Forces (JTTFs)   A group of highly trained federal, state, and local law enforcement officers and agents focusing on terrorism-related intelligence and investigations.

Kaaba   According to Islam, the alter of Abraham (built by Abraham and his son Ishmael) and the focus of Hajj, or the pilgrimage to Mecca.

Khomeinism   A Shi'a ideology that embraces Islamic worldwide revolution as well as Islamic unity and strict adherence to Sharia; based on the teachings of Ayatollah Ruhollah Khomeini.

Klaverns   Local chapters of the KKK.

Kurdistan Workers Party (PKK)   An ethnic Kurdish terrorist group fighting to create a homeland for ethnic Kurds in northern Iraq and Southeastern Turkey; responsible for significant deaths of Turkish civilians (over 20,000) over the past two decades.

Leaderless resistance cell   This type of cell is characterized by no leaders and equality of members who share the leadership functions.

Left-wing   A political designation that encompasses ideologies more radical in nature, including anarchism and Marxism.

Levant   A geographic and cultural area on the Eastern Mediterranean Sea, composed primarily of modern-day Syria, Lebanon, Jordan, and Israel.

Levees and dams   A dyke, embankment, or wall specifically constructed to regulate water.

Links or edges   In terrorist network language the lines between nodes in a cell are called links or edges and represent a communication channel between nodes and/or hubs.

Logistics cells   LCs provide cells and various types of support to other cells.

Lone wolf attack   A violent attack by a single perpetrator, acting alone, without any direction or assistance from an organization or another person.

Low intensity conflict   A level of military action that falls short of a full-scale conventional war; includes peacekeeping, anti-terrorism programs, assistance to foreign militaries and police organizations, fulfillment of international treaty obligations, as well as subversive and counterterrorism actions.

Mandate system   the system of colonization after World War I dividing areas in Middle East, primarily between Great Britain, France, and Italy.

Manifest Destiny   In 1845, as Americans pushed westward, newspaper editor John O'Sullivan coined the term "manifest destiny," meaning the United States had a divine obligation to push its boundaries ever-forward. At the heart of manifest destiny was the pervasive belief in American cultural and racial superiority.

Marxism   The economic and sociological theories of Karl Marx and Friedrich Engels that encompassed a revolutionary view of social change.

Material support   Defined by the PATRIOT Act as "training," "expert advice or assistance," "service," and "personnel" given to terrorist organizations.

Mecca   The holiest city in the religion of Islam, located in southwest Saudi Arabia near the Red Sea. The birthplace of the Prophet Muhammad and the focus of the Hajj or Pilgrimage to Mecca.

Metadata   Data that describes other data; for example, telephone metadata records the number called, what time the call was made, and how long it lasted.

Metrics   Standard measures taken periodically to determine the level of performance in a given field. For instance, a metric used during the Vietnam War was enemy body count. Terrorism metrics can be an indication of how we are doing in the global war on terrorism if carefully selected, defined, and measured.

Michael Collins   Commander of the Irish Republican Army (IRA) and advocate of selective terrorism.

Military Commissions Act of 2006 (MCA)   An act of Congress signed by President George W. Bush in 2006 to authorize trial by military commission for violations of the law of war and for other purposes. It prohibited detainees who had been classified as enemy combatants or were awaiting hearings on their status from using "Habeas corpus" to petition federal courts in challenges to their detention.

Mitigation   An effort to reduce loss of life and property by lessening the impact of a terrorist attack or natural disaster.

Modernity   An epoch of time, usually referring to post-traditional and post-agrarian (feudal) states toward capitalism, industrialization, secularization, and technological innovation.

Monotheistic   The belief in one God expressed by three major religions in the world: Judaism, Christianity, and Islam,

Mosque   A holy place of worship in Islam.

Muhammad   Born in 570 AD in Mecca, the Prophet Muhammad was believed to be the final messenger of God and the founder of the Islam religion.

Muslim   A derivative of the two words "Muhammad" and "Islam"; westernized to "Moslem or Muslim." One who adheres to the Islamic faith."

Muslim Brotherhood (MB)   An Islamic fundamental movement stemming from the writings of Hassan al-Banna and Sayyid Qubt in 20th century Egypt.

Mutual aid agreement   Mutual aid agreements are agreements between agencies, organizations, and jurisdictions that provide a mechanism to quickly obtain emergency assistance in the form of personnel, equipment, materials, and other associated services. The primary objective is to facilitate rapid, short-term deployment of emergency support prior to, during, and after an incident.

Mutual aid societies   developed in America during the 1800s and were often faith, country of origin, or ethnicity based. They had several purposes, such as preserving cultural heritage and helping immigrants newly arrived in America to adjust.

Mutually assured destruction (MAD)   A military doctrine prevalent during the Cold War between the United States and the former Soviet Union, postulating that an all-out nuclear war would effectively destroy both entities (the attacker and the defender).

National Clandestine Service   The operational wing of the CIA that carries out covert paramilitary operations against terrorist groups and cells outside the United States.

National Criminal Intelligence Sharing Plan (NCISP)   A national effort that combines public partnerships with problem-solving tactics aimed at enhancing police efficiency in preventing terrorist attacks through effective communication and coordination.

National Fusion Center Association (NFCA)   A formal group that represents the interests of state and major urban area fusion centers nationally.

National Incident Management System (NIMS)   The comprehensive, nationwide systematic approach to incident management adopted by FEMA to manage and standardize responses to critical incidents and/or disasters.

National Infrastructure Protection Plan (NIPP)   A formal directive that defines critical infrastructure within the United States and identifies 16 critical infrastructure sectors for protection against man-made (e.g., bombing, terrorist strike, information warfare) as well as natural (e.g., hurricane, flood, tornado, earthquake) disasters.

National Intelligence Program (NIP)   The primary funding budget for the strengthening the nation's intelligence agencies.

National Preparedness Goal   Released in September 2011, the National Preparedness Goal defines national preparedness as: *"A secure and resilient nation with the capabilities required across the whole community to prevent, protect against, mitigate, respond to, and recover from the threats and hazards that pose the greatest risk."*

National Preparedness System (NPS)   An organized process for the "whole community" within the United States to move forward with preparedness actives in an effort to achieve the National Preparedness Goal.

National Security Act of 1947   The Act reorganized the military and foreign policy elements of the federal government, including the creation of the Central Intelligence Agency (CIA). Illustratively, it also combines the War and Navy departments into the Department of Defense.

National Special Security Event (NSSE)   Any national or international meeting deemed by DHS as a potential target for terrorism or other criminal activity.

Nativism   The right wing rests on nativism, the ultra-preference for the traditional culture of a homeland to the exclusion of immigrants and their alien ways, as well as opposition to foreign ideas and influences. Nativism also rejects those in the homeland who champion immigrants, "alien" ways, and non-traditional ways of looking at the world.

Network models   Network models include the chain, hub or star, spoke or wheel, and all channel structures.

New terrorism   Most commonly, a religious belief undergirds the violence. New terrorism is more transnational than the old and unlike the old, it deliberately targets civilians/non-combatants to create fear. Many groups are autonomous or loosely affiliated with another group. Inspires lone wolf attacks. The new terrorism is nimble, quick to learn, technologically savvy, and operationally competent.

Nidal Malik Hasan   Army psychiatrist who killed and wounded American troops at Ft. Hood, Texas. He was convicted by a military court and sentenced to death.

Nisaab   Arabic for "portion," the threshold after which a person is obliged to pay zakat; varies throughout the Middle East.

Nodes   In terrorist network language, "nodes" are more expendable members, such as fighters, whose loss is less critical to the terrorist movement.

Office of the Director of National Intelligence (ODNI)   The national office created to centralize all intelligence information function from all federal, state, and local agencies.

Old terrorism   Generally, it had specific political, social, and economic goals. Because the goals were limited some could ultimately be resolved by negotiation.

Omar Hammami   In 2006, the 27-year-old Hammami left Alabama and went to Somalia where he joined the clan-based Islamic terrorist movement al-Shabaab. Seven years later, after a series of disagreements with al-Shabaab, the movement killed him in an ambush.

Operation Eagle Claw   Failed U.S. military attempt to rescue hostages held by Iran in 1980.

Operational security   A process to deny potential adversaries about capabilities and/or intentions by identifying, controlling, and protecting unclassified information that gives evidence of the planning and execution of sensitive activities, such as future operations (OPSEC).

Operational space   This term means having a sanctuary or safe haven where attacks can be safely planned, trained for, and rehearsed.

Oslo Accords   In 1993, the negotiation of a bilateral peace agreement between the Palestinian Liberation Organization (PLO) represented by Yassir Arafat and Israel represented by Prime Minister Yitzhak Rabin, moderated by President Bill Clinton.

Palestinian Islamic Jihad (PIJ)   One of the early terrorist groups to adopt a radical Islamic ideology that justified violence and suicide bombing as a means to liberate Palestine.

Palestinian Islamic Resistance Movement (Hamas)   The largest and most politically powerful group expressing radical Islamic ideologies to justify the liberation of Palestine and the destruction of Israel.

Palestinians   People of Arab descent tracing their cultural heritage to an area known as Palestine, now occupied by the country of Israel.

Pandemic   An epidemic of an infectious disease that involves a large area, usually crossing international boundaries and involving multiple continents.

Passive supporters   These types of supporters are sympathetic to the goals of terrorist organization, but not committed enough to take an active role. They may assist a front for the terrorist organization and not be fully aware of their relationship to the terrorist organization.

Pen register   Provides law enforcement agency access to the numbers dialed from a subject's phone.

Personal protection equipment (PPE)   Used by first responders to protect them against CBRNE agents.

Pierre-Joseph Proudhon   French philosopher who was the first person to declare himself an anarchist; instrumental in sparking French revolutionary activities in 1848.

Point of entry (POE)   A specific location where one may lawfully enter the United States; typically where passports and visa are inspected (e.g., international airports, seaports).

Political ideology   The set of beliefs about the proper order of society and how that order can be achieved.

Political terrorism   A symbolic act designed to influence political behavior based on extranormal means, entailing the use or threat of violence.

Posse Comitatus   The Latin phrase translates to the "power of the county." It refers to a right-wing movement that opposes the federal government and holds that local authority trumps federal authority. It was founded by William Potter Gale in 1970, but did not gain momentum until he incorporated Christian Identity (CI). The group was substantially defunct by 1990, several years after Gale's death. The term also refers to the Posse Comitatus Act passed in 1878 limiting the power of the federal government in using the military to enforce state (civilian) law.

Post-Traumatic Stress Disorder   Classically, some people involved in a terrifying, life-threatening event develop the anxiety disorder PTSD. They may relive the event frequently, have angry outbursts, dramatic bad dreams and frightening thoughts, be easily startled, or constantly seem "on edge."

Preemptive military action   Striking a target in advance of a reasonably anticipated attack to circumvent its occurrence and to avoid suffering its effects.

"Prepper"   Slang word to describe those individuals who are preparing for major apocalyptic events in the future.

Principle of hierarchy   This principle dictates that each lower organizational unit is under the direct control and supervision of a superior organizational unit. This produces a pyramid shaped form.

Proletariat   A Marxist concept that describes the working class, peasants, or oppressed people.

Propaganda by the deed   An ideology that advocates acts of violence as a principal means of revolution.

Provisional Irish Republican Army (PIRA)   The Provisional Irish Republican Army was the first and primary movement in Ireland to use terrorism as a means to justify its revolt against Great Britain and gain world status as a separate nation (Ireland). The group officially ended its campaign against Great Britain for a unified and separate Ireland in 2005, and now continues in political dialogue for the same goal.

Qur'an   Often referred to as the "Holy Qur'an" or the "Noble Qur'an" is the central religious text of Islam, which Muslims believe to be a revelation from Allah (God)...the Muslim equivalent of the Christian Bible.

Radicalization   the processing of acquiring and holding extremist beliefs. See violent extremism.

Real Irish Republican Army (RIRA)   The Real Irish Republican Army in Northern Ireland uses terrorist tactics to support its ideology of a unified Ireland; RIRA is a successor to the original PIRA.

Red Laces   Worn in the boots of skinheads, they denote the wearer has shed blood for the skinhead movement.

Redundant leader protocol   If the leader of a cell is captured, killed, or otherwise not available, a designated member of the cell will assume the leadership role.

Regional terrorist movements   RTMs may be independent and some of the larger ones are affiliated with al-Qaeda. RTMS are more immediately operationally concerned with specific geographic areas, often to overthrow a government and to establish an Islamic state. They may express transnational attack attitudes, but operations in the West are infrequent or non-existent to date.

Reign of Terror   Particularly violent period during the French Revolution France (1793–1794) when the guillotine was used to behead over 16,000 people including Robespierre. See Robespierre.

Rendition   The "handing over" or transfer of a person from one legal jurisdiction to another. Some apprehended terrorists have immediately been handed over to foreign countries to avoid providing them with the full range of

American legal rights and to be able to use more harsh interrogation methods.

Revolutionary Armed Forces of Columbia People's Army (FARC)   The FARC in Columbia wages an insurgency against its national government, but that insurgency is not nationalistic. FARC grew out of the Columbian Communist Party of the 1960s. It is therefore unsurprising that traditionally FARC's ideology has been based on seizing control of the government in order to institute socialist reforms.

Ricin   An easily made and highly toxic poison refined from castor beans.

Robespierre   A Frenchman and key architect of the reign of terror. He believed terror was the speedy, severe, and inflexible administration of justice from which virtue flowed. Terror and virtue became synonymous to him.

Ruby Ridge (Idaho)   Federal agents went to Randy Weaver's rural home to arrest him on weapons charges. A standoff ensued and eventually gunfire was exchanged, killing Weaver's wife and son. The incident added fuel to the patriot, militia, and right-wing movements.

Sabri al-Banna   A highly entrepreneurial revolutionary and mercenary who headed the Abu Nidal Organization (ANO).

Safe havens   A place or situation that allows illicit actors, including criminals, smugglers, and terrorists, to operate with relative impunity.

Salafism   A broad intellectual movement spawned by the writings of Egyptian scholars such as Muhammad Abdu, Jamal al-Afghani, and Rashid Rida, focusing on the adoption of modernity and technology within Islam; soon became corrupted and blended with Wahhabism.

Sarin   A man-made chemical gas that is extremely poisonous; first used in a terrorist attack by the Aum Shinrikyo group in the subways of Tokyo, Japan, in 1995.

Search Warrant   Legal document that authorizes police to search a specific area for a specific person or item of interest. Must be based on probable cause and signed by a judge.

Secondary bombs   Hidden bombs often set by terrorists targeting first responders to an emergency event.

Secular   Separation of church (religion) and state or government.

Secularism   The separation of church and state; the form of government where persons mandated to represent the state are not members of religious institutions nor are religious dignitaries.

Selective terrorism   Tactic advocated by Michael Collins, Commander of the Irish Republic Army (IRA). Instead of using unfocused, indiscriminate violence that killed many people, Collins used selective violence to focus on the people and institutions that supported continued British subjugation of Ireland. See Michael Collins and Irish Republican Army.

Self-reliant   In colonial America there was already an ingrained belief that people should be self-reliant and responsible for their own lot in life. A corollary of this tradition was that if people were given too much help it would ultimately make them dependent.

Shahid   A Muslim "martyr" who dies in defense of their faith; often inappropriately associated with those that conduct suicide bombings. Originates from the Qur'anic Arabic word for "witness."

Sharia   Islamic law; the moral and religious code of Islam as proscribed by the Prophet Muhammad.

Shi'a or Shiite   One of the two primary Muslim traditions stemming from the "Shi'at Ali" or "The Party of Ali." Followers of the Shi'a tradition believe that Ali was given a divine right of successorship to lead the Muslim community after the death of the Prophet Muhammad.

Skinbyrd   A female skinhead.

Skinhead   A white supremist group originally started in London, England, among working class, white youths in the 1960s; eventually becoming associated with a much larger subculture named for their close-cropped or shaven heads, military-style clothing including Nazi-type "jack boots," and hard rock, punk-style music.

Skyjacking   The diversion of a commercial airline flight away from its scheduled flight plan, usually by violence or threat of violence against passengers and/or crew.

Slave patrols   The first formal racist organization in America.

Sleeper cells   Members of sleeper cells lead normal lives, engaging only in lawful employment and activities that call no attention to themselves. The jobs they select may facilitate future terrorist activities. Illustratively, a taxi driver will learn a great about a city's geography and can identify potential targets and move terrorists around. A sleeper cell may receive a signal that "awakens" it for a specific purpose, such as sabotage or an assassination.

Socialism   A Marxist perspective of a transitory and revolutionary period between capitalism and communism wherein the ruling class is "purged" from the land, all people are equal, and the government owns everything; the period is marked by violence and terrorism.

Soft target   A military term to describe a non-defended or innocent target—usually refers to innocent civilians; versus a *hard target* that represents armed soldiers, operators, or well-defended locations.

Sovereign Citizen movement   Anti-government extremists who believe they are separate or sovereign from the federal government. Referring to themselves as freemen, or free patriots, the people associated with this movement do not pay taxes or recognize any federal or state authority, including the courts, motor vehicle department, or law enforcement agencies.

Speakeasies   Illegal bars operating during the prohibition era gained the name of speakeasies because patrons desiring to enter were allegedly told to knock and softly (speak easy) say the password.

Sunni   The "True Path of Allah" and the largest of the two primary Muslim traditions within Islam.

Sykes-Picot Agreement of 1916   An agreement between Great Britain and France as to the development of colonies resulting from the impending collapse of the Ottoman Empire after World War I.

System disruption   System disruption attacks have been called the "new war." Instead of concentrating on attacks that produce mass casualties, system disruption attacks focus on the systems that are essential to our daily lives, such as mass transit, electrical grids, and water.

Tactical operations cells   TAC-OPS cells execute attacks under the guidance of 2C cells.

Taliban   Pashto, "student." The Taliban largely consists of members of the Pashtun tribes occupying parts of the border between Afghanistan and Pakistan. It is a fundamentalist Islamic movement that insists on strict enforcement of Sharia law. The Taliban came to power in Afghanistan in 1996 and was overthrown by Americans in 2001 for continuing to shelter Usama bin Laden, the leader of the 9/11 attacks.

Taqiyya   Al-Qaeda has adopted the concept of "taqiyya." It absolves Islamic fighters from religious condemnation for shaving off their required beards, not praying five times a day, and adopting a Western life style as part of OPSEC.

Terrorism (General/Working definition)   The deliberate and unlawful use of threats or actual violence to inculcate fear, intended to intimidate or coerce individuals, groups, or governments to change their political, social, or religious basis.

Texas Rangers   In 1823, when Texas was still part of Mexico, Stephen Austin gained permission to employ 10 men to range over the territory and scout for Indian threats. These men were the first of the Texas Rangers.

The Turner Diaries   See Dr. William L. Pierce.

Tor network   Synonymous for the deep web; see deep web.

Trap and trace   Provides law enforcement agency access to incoming numbers on a subject's phone.

Ultralights   Powered ultralights are regulated by the FAA and are single-seat aircraft flown for recreation or sport.

Ummah   The worldwide community of the Islamic faithful.

Unified command   The primary command organization for the Incident Command System in the field; incident commanders from different agencies combine to form a single unified command structure.

Uniform Code of Military Justice (UCMJ) The UCMJ was established by the Congress and is the basis for military law in the United States.

USA PATRIOT Act Act of Congress that was signed into law by President George W. Bush on October 26, 2001. The title stands for Uniting and Strengthening America by Providing Appropriate Tools Required to Intercept and Obstruct Terrorism Act.

Usama bin Laden Saudi Arabian-born American ally who supported Afghanistan mujahedeen's resistance against the Soviets. When the Soviets left, he turned against the Americans and masterminded the 9/11 attacks. Head of al-Qaeda until his death in a 2011 raid on his compound in Pakistan by U.S. troops (Seal Team 6).

U.S. Department of Homeland Security (DHS) The largest civilian federal agency in the United States with over 240,000 employees focused on securing the border and infrastructure of the United States.

U.S. General Accountability Office The U.S. Government Accountability Office (GAO) is an independent, nonpartisan agency that works for Congress. Often called the "Congressional watchdog," the GAO investigates matters of concern to the Congress.

U.S. Northern Command (NORTHCOM) Directs the U.S. Department of Defense's homeland security efforts and the planning, organizing, and execution of military support to civil authorities during emergencies, disasters, and/or terrorist attacks.

USS Cole Successfully attacked in 2000 by al-Qaeda in the Port of Aden, Yemen, by a suicide "bomber" piloting a launch loaded with explosives.

U.S. Special Operations Command (USSOCOM or SOCOM) The organization responsible for many counterterrorism actions by the military.

Vanguard A concept that advocates a method of arousing a level of political consciousness among proletariats in order to foster the belief among them that revolution and any changes it brings are far preferable to the status quo.

Violent extremism Violent action taken on the basis of extremist beliefs.

Virtual terrorist organization A virtual terrorist organization exists in cyberspace. It members are usually dispersed geographically, but work together exploiting information technology to achieve their common goals by sharing their skills and knowledge collaboratively.

Wade Michael Page White supremacist who entered a Wisconsin Sikh Temple and murdered six and wounded three. After being wounded at the scene by police he died from a self-inflicted gunshot wound.

Wadi Haddad A Christian Marxist physician that directed the military and guerrilla actions of the Popular Front for the Liberation of Palestine (PFLP); credited for developing the modern-day hijacking of airliners as a methodology and tactic of terrorism.

Wahhabism A fundamentalist interpretation of Islam stemming from the teachings of Ibn al-Wahhab in the late 1700s; widely adopted throughout the Arabian Peninsula expressing the radicalization of Islam and the alternative meaning of "jihad" as "holy war" against those that do not accept strict adherence to Sharia.

Weapons of mass destruction (WMD) There are at least 50 official definitions of WMDs in the United States and other national governments, as well as international organizations such as the United Nations. A common thread in these definitions approximates: WMDs are nuclear, biological, chemical, radiological, and high explosive weapons capable of producing major destruction, mass casualties, and/or significant infrastructure damage.

"Whole community" A concept within the National Preparedness Goal referring to all

of the federal, state, and local government agencies, as well as the non-governmental organizations, private sector, schools, families, and individuals focused on national preparedness.

Wikileaks A non-profit international organization dedicated to publishing classified documents in the name of transparency.

Wiretaps Surreptitious eavesdropping on a third-party conversation by wire, oral, or electronic communication.

Wolf pack A group of lone wolves that form a cell are sometimes called a "wolf pack."

Works Progress Administration (WPA) An ancillary organization to the Civilian Conservation Corps during the 1930s; employed over 8.5 million people involved in building bridges, public buildings, and airports throughout the country.

Xenophobia An irrational fear, hatred, and hostility toward people who are "different," including not only immigrants but those with different lifestyles or sexual preferences, and "strange" ideas.

Xenophobic A person who manifests xenophobia.

Yassir Arafat The leader of the al-Fatah Palestinian group and later head of the Palestinian Liberation Organization (PLO).

Zakat An annual humanitarian giving by Muslims.

Zionist Occupied Government A right-wing term sometimes used to refer to the U.S. government.

Zionists People sympathetic to the creation of a Jewish state in the Middle Eastern area of Palestine.

Zoot suit A men's fashion that moved from the African-American jazz movement into Chicano style. The exaggerated style was offensive to World War II American servicemen who saw the style wasteful and subversive. The result were some violent clashes between the Chicano "zoot suiters" and servicemen.

Index

Page numbers followed by " f " indicate charts and diagrams or " t " indicate tables. Photos and illustrations have no special designation and are just in regular numbers.